Public choice or rational politics differs from other approaches to the study of political behavior in that it builds [barcode] individuals seek to advance their own int surveys the main ideas and contributions [illegible] [illegible] on *Public Choice: A Handbook* contains twenty-five essays written by thirty scholars, both economists and political scientists, from North America and Europe.

Part I discusses the nature and justification for the existence of government and the various forms it can take, including mixed, private, and public institutions, international organizations, federalisms, and constitutional governments. Part II examines the properties of different voting rules and preference aggregation procedures. Part III explores multiparty systems, interest groups, logrolling and political business cycles. The individual decision maker is the focus of Part IV, with surveys of the experimental literature on individual behavior, on why people vote, and why people vote as they do. The final section applies public choice reasoning to bureaucracy, taxation, and the size of government.

Keech

Perspectives on public choice
A handbook

Perspectives on public choice

A handbook

DENNIS C. MUELLER
University of Vienna

CAMBRIDGE
UNIVERSITY PRESS

PUBLISHED BY THE PRESS SYNDICATE OF THE UNIVERSITY OF CAMBRIDGE
The Pitt Building, Trumpington Street, Cambridge CB2 1RP, United Kingdom

CAMBRIDGE UNIVERSITY PRESS
The Edinburgh Building, Cambridge CB2 2RU, United Kingdom
40 West 20th Street, New York, NY 10011-4211, USA
10 Stamford Road, Oakleigh, Melbourne 3166, Australia

First published 1997

Printed in the United States of America

Typeset in Times

Library of Congress Cataloging-in-Publication Data
Perspectives on public choice : a handbook / edited by Dennis C. Mueller.
p.   cm.
ISBN 0-521-55377-6 (hc). – ISBN 0-521-55654-6 (pbk.)
1. Social choice.   2. Political science – Economic aspects.
I. Mueller, Dennis C.
HB846.8.P47   1996
302'.13 – dc20   95-44023
                                                                CIP

*A catalog record for this book is available from
the British Library*

ISBN   0 521 55377 6 Hardback
ISBN   0 521 55654 6 Paperback

Contents

v

Preface

The original plan for this volume was to publish a handbook in which each essay was twenty-five to thirty typed pages. This length is substantially under that of, say, a *Journal of Economic Literature* survey, and so the intent was not to be as comprehensive in referencing the literature as this more standard survey, but for the author to describe and discuss an area highlighting the main ideas and contributions in it. Many of the authors stuck to this early game plan, but some did not owing to the nature of the subject matter surveyed, or to personal style. In addition, the last of the manuscripts to be completed received less intensive editorial cutting, because I, mistakenly as it turned out, did not think I had the time to do it. Thus, the articles vary somewhat in length and in the length of their reference lists.

For a variety of reasons including my move from College Park, Maryland to Vienna, the "development time" of this volume has been lengthier than most. The earliest of the essays were completed in 1992, and even the latest in 1994. Thus, some recent articles or books that the reader would expect to see referenced may be missing, *not* because of the author's negligence, but because the essay was finished before the work appeared. (A single set of references for the entire manuscript is at the end of the book.)

Preparation of the manuscript in College Park, including much retyping of references, editing of files, and so on was done by my long-time coworker there Becky Flick. Once again I offer her my hearty thanks. Because some files could not be read by our computers in Vienna, and some papers were completed after I left College Park, my new coworker Heidi Wurm had to do and redo a lot of work on the manuscript. To her I also offer my sincere gratitude. Finally, let me thank the contributors to the volume for their cooperation, patience, and understanding during the long, and rather unusual history of this book.

Contributors

JOHN ALDRICH is professor and chair of the Department of Political Science at Duke University. He is a scholar of American politics and the author of *Before the Convention,* the election series *Change and Continuity in Elections,* and, most recently, *Why Parties?*

DAVID AUSTEN-SMITH is professor of political science at the University of Rochester. He has contributed articles to a variety of journals in both economics and political science and is currently completing a manuscript, *Positive Political Theory* (with Jeffery S. Banks) for the University of Michigan Press. His work focuses on social choice theory and positive political theory.

THOMAS E. BORCHERDING is professor of economics and politics at the Claremont Graduate School. Besides the growth of government, he has written on bureaucracy and public enterprise, the demand for public spending, intergenerational equity and natural resources, the private supply of public goods, and public schooling and segregation. He is currently researching social capital formation and the uncoordinated supply of joint consumption goods. He has been the editor of *Economic Inquiry* and now serves as senior editorial advisor.

JAMES M. ENELOW is professor of government at the University of Texas at Austin. He is the coauthor of *The Spatial Theory of Voting: An Introduction* and coeditor of *Advances in Spatial Theory of Voting.* He has served on the editorial board of the *American Journal of Political Science* and is currently a member of the editorial board of *Public Choice.*

MORRIS P. FIORINA is a professor of government at Harvard University. He has written widely on American national government and politics, with special emphasis on elections and electoral influences on Congress. His books include *Representatives, Roll Calls, and Constituencies, Congress–Keystone of the Washington Establishment, Retrospective Voting in American National Elections, The Personal Vote: Constituency Service and Electoral Independence* (with Bruce Cain and John Ferejohn), and most recently, *Divided Government.* From 1986 to 1990 Fiorina served as chair of the Board of Overseers of the National Election Studies.

BRUNO S. FREY is professor of economics at the University of Zurich, Switzerland. He is the author of *Economics as a Science of Human Behavior, Muses and Markets, International Political Economics,* and *Democratic Economic Policy,* as well as over 250 articles. His research interests cover political economy, the connections of economics and psychology and applications of economics to fields such as the environment, the family, history and art.

WALTER HETTICH is professor of economics at California State University in Fullerton. His work has appeared in the *American Economic Review, Journal of Public Economics, National Tax Journal, Canadian Journal of Economics, Public Choice,* and other professional journals. The main focus of his research is on the application of microeconomic analysis and collective choice to taxation and public expenditures.

CHERYL M. HOLSEY is visiting assistant professor of economics and politics at the Claremont Graduate School. Her research focuses on explaining state and local government constraints and behavior, with a current emphasis on services that can be differentially allocated across members of the constituency, and the extent to which changing socioeconomic environments have affected the demand and supply of public sector services.

ELIZABETH HOFFMAN is professor of economics and dean of the College of Liberal Arts and Sciences at Iowa State University, Ames. She is the coauthor of numerous articles in experimental economics on cooperation, fairness, and the effects of property rights in two-person and multiperson bargaining. In 1986, she and her coauthor Matthew L. Spitzer won the Coase Prize for Excellence in the Study of Law and Economics for their experimental work on the Coase theorem.

ROBERT P. INMAN is a professor of finance and economics at the University of Pennsylvania, and research fellow at the National Bureau of Economic Research. He has been a visiting professor at the University of London, the University of California, Berkeley, and Stanford University, and a visiting research fellow at Harvard University, Australian National University, and the Center for Advanced Study in the Behavioral Sciences at Stanford University. He is the editor of *The Economics of Public Services* and *Managing the Service Economy.* His published research includes articles on urban public finance, health care finance, tax policy, and political economy. He is completing a book on federalism with Daniel L. Rubinfeld.

STEPHEN P. MAGEE holds the Bayless/Enstar Chair and is a professor of finance and economics at the University of Texas at Austin. He is the coauthor (with William A. Brock and Leslie Young) of *Black Hole Tariffs and Endogenous Policy Theory.* His book *A Plague of Lawyers* (forthcoming with Frances T. Magee) reports data from fifty-four countries over twenty-five years that reveal an optimum lawyer curve.

TERRY M. MOE is professor of political science at Stanford University and senior fellow at the Hoover Institution. He is the author of *The Organization of Interests, Politics, Markets, and America's Schools* (with John E. Chubb), and numerous articles. His work centers on American political institutions, organization theory, and rational choice.

DENNIS C. MUELLER is professor of economics at the University of Vienna. His main research interests are in public choice and industrial economics. He is the author of *Public Choice II, Profits in the Long Run,* and *Constitutional Democracy,* as well as many articles. Dennis Mueller is a past president of the Public Choice Society, the Southern Economic Association, the Industrial Organization Society, and EARIE.

PETER C. ORDESHOOK is professor of political science at the California Institute of Technology. He is the author or coauthor of *An Introduction to Positive Political Theory* (with W. H. Riker), *Game Theory and Political Theory, A Political Theory Primer, Lessons for Citizens of a New Democracy,* and *The Balance of Power* (with E. M. S. Niou and G. Rose), as well as nearly a hundred articles published in professional journals and edited volumes. A member of the American Academy of Arts and Sciences, he has also held appointments at the University of Texas, The University of Rochester, and Carnegie Mellon University.

ELINOR OSTROM is codirector of the Workshop in Political Theory and Political Analysis and the Arthur F. Bentley Professor of Political Science at Indiana University, Bloomington. She is the author of *Governing the Commons, Crafting Institutions for Self-Governing Irrigation Systems, Institutional Incentives and Sustainable Development* (with Larry Schroeder and Susan Wynne), and *Rules, Games, and Common-Pool Resources* (with Roy Gardner and James Walker).

MARTIN PALDAM is professor of economics at Aarhus University, Denmark. He has published numerous articles in international economic and political science journals and edited books on political economy, macroeconomics and economic development. He is presently working on the microeconomics of vote and popularity functions, the economic development of Greenland and Danish Development Assistance. He has been and is a consultant at the World Bank, the Interamerican

Development Bank, the OECD and the Rockwool Foundation, and has lived in Nigeria, Chile, and the United States.

PRASANTA K. PATTANAIK is professor of economics at the University of California, Riverside, and a fellow of the Econometric Society. He has worked on welfare economics and the theory of social choice, trade theory and decision theory including the theory of fuzzy preferences and choice, and is the author of many papers and books in these areas.

DOUGLAS W. RAE is the Ely Professor of Public Management at the Yale School of Management. He is the author of *The Political Consequences of Electoral Laws, Equalities* and many articles on topics related to public choice. He is presently at work on issues of urban blight and violence in the United States.

DANIEL L. RUBINFELD is Robert L. Bridges Professor of Law and professor of economics at the University of California, Berkeley. He is coeditor of the *International Review of Law and Economics,* and the author of *Microeconomics* (with Robert S. Pindyck) and *Econometric Models and Economic Forecasts* (with Robert S. Pindyck), and is completing a book on federalism with Robert P. Inman.

ERIC SCHICKLER is a doctoral candidate in the Department of Political Science at Yale University. He has published articles on partisanship in the United States and on the implications of new information technologies for democratic theory and practice. His dissertation focuses on formal models of the legislative process.

NORMAN SCHOFIELD is the William Taussig Professor and director of the Center of Political Economy at Washington University in St. Louis. He is the author of *Social Choice and Democracy,* of *Multiparty Government* (with Michael Laver) and coeditor of two volumes in political economy and social choice. His other published work is in formal political economy, cooperative game theory, and mathematical economics.

THOMAS STRATMANN is associate professor of economics at Montana State University, Bozeman. He has published articles in the *American Economic Review, Journal of Political Economy,* and *Review of Economics and Statistics.* His work in public choice focuses on analyzing legislator and interest group behavior.

T. NICOLAUS TIDEMAN is professor of economics at Virginia Polytechnic Institute and State University. He is the author (with Gordon Tullock) of "A New and Superior Process for Making Social Choices" (*Journal of Political Economy,* 1976) and various other articles on issues of efficiency and fairness in taxation and in collective decision mechanisms.

ROBERT D. TOLLISON is Duncan Black Professor of Economics and general director of the Center for Study of Public Choice at George Mason University in Fairfax, Virginia. He is the author of numerous papers and books in the area of public choice, and he is presently serving as president of the Public Choice Society.

JAMES WALKER is professor of economics and associate director of the Workshop in Political Theory and Policy Analysis at Indiana University, Bloomington. His principal research focus is the use of experimental methods in the investigation of individual and group behavior related to the voluntary provision of public goods and the use of common-pool resources. Recent publications include "Rent Dissipation and Probabilistic Destruction of Common-Pool Resource Environments: Experimental Evidence" (with Roy Gardner, *Economic Journal,* 1992); "Group Size and the Voluntary Provision of Public Goods: Experimental Evidence Utilizing Large Groups" (with Mark Isaac and Arlington Williams, *Journal of Public Economics,* 1994); and *Rules, Games, and Common-Pool Resources* (with Elinor Ostrom and Roy Gardner).

STANLEY L. WINER is professor of economics and public policy in the School of Public Administration at Carleton University, Ottawa. His work has appeared in the *Journal of Political Economy,* the *American Economic Review, Journal of Public Economics, Kyklos,* the *Canadian Journal of Economics,* and other professional journals. The main focus of his research is on the development of models that help to explain the structure of taxation and public expenditures.

RONALD WINTROBE is professor of economics at the University of Western Ontario. He is the author of many articles in political economy, and coauthor (with Albert Breton) of the *Logic of Bureaucratic Conduct* (Cambridge, 1982). Recently, he has been working on dictatorship and has written a number of articles on that subject, including "The Tinpot and the Totalitarian: An Economic Theory of Dictatorship" (*American Political Science Review,* September 1990). He has just completed a new book, *The Political Economy of Dictatorship.*

H. PEYTON YOUNG is professor of economics at The Johns Hopkins University and a visiting fellow at the Brookings Institution in Washington, D.C. He has written on game theory, public finance, social choice, bargaining theory, and distributive problems in the public sector. His books include *Fair Representation* (with M. L. Balinski), *Cost Allocation, Negotiation Analysis,* and *Equity in Theory and Practice.*

CHAPTER 1

Public choice in perspective

DENNIS C. MUELLER

1. Forerunners

Public choice applies the methodology of economics to the study of politics. As such it is inherently interdisciplinary and has been so more or less from its inception.

This inception might be said to have occurred over two hundred years ago in the investigations of the properties of voting rules undertaken by two french mathematicians, Jean-Charles de Borda (1781) and the Marquis de Condorcet (1785). Subsequent analytic investigations of voting rules over the next century were also largely carried out by mathematicians.[1]

One of these, the Reverend Charles L. Dodgson, a lecturer in mathematics at Cambridge, is better known for his fictional works under the pseudonym Lewis Carroll. His pamphlets on voting procedures were published over a span of twelve years beginning in 1873 (Black 1958, chap. 20). Mention should also be made of the book by Dodgson's countryman, John Stuart Mill, published in 1861. Although Mill's *Considerations on Representative Government* contains no mathematical demonstrations of the kind found in Dodgson's pamphlets and should be regarded as a (classic) contribution to political science, it also can be viewed as the first investigation of political institutions by an economist.

Before leaving the nineteenth century the important contribution in 1896 of the Swedish economist Knut Wicksell must be noted. Although a "classic in public finance," it also had a significant and direct influence on the development of public choice through the work of James Buchanan. A chance reading of Wicksell's treatise in 1948 had a "dramatic" effect on the young Buchanan and helped shape the contractarian perspective he has brought to public choice throughout his career.[2]

---

1. For an account of the early history of the study of voting rules, see Duncan Black (1958, part 2). See also Peyton Young's essay in this volume.
2. For Buchanan's own account of his discovery of Wicksell's essay and its impact upon him, see Buchanan (1992, 5–6).

Although Wicksell's essay had an important influence on the development of public choice, this influence was not felt until half a century after it was written. Other "continental" scholars were also making original contributions with relevance to public choice at the beginning of the twentieth century, but their work remained largely unknown to the English reading community until the public choice field was well launched.[3] It therefore cannot be said to have contributed to the field's development. Nor did the earlier work of the continental and english mathematicians. Both Dodgson and Mill wrote about the newly invented methods of proportional representation, and the academic debate over systems of representation that flourished in the nineteenth century did undoubtedly contribute to the adoption of proportional representation in virtually every European country *except* the England of Dodgson and Mill. But the mathematical methods that Condorcet, Dodgson, and their contemporaries employed to study voting procedures were not taken up by those studying politics during the first half of this century. Duncan Black, who brought much of this work to the modern profession's attention, discovered it *after* he had worked out his own theories (Black 1958, xi).

Three additional contributions, all by economists, should be mentioned before turning to the modern literature. Harold Hotelling (1929) used a two–candidate election to illustrate the characteristics of spatial competition, and Hotelling's modeling was adopted by Anthony Downs in his 1957 classic. Downs (1957, 27, n11) credits Schumpeter's *Capitalism, Socialism, and Democracy,* first published in 1942, as being "the inspiration and foundation for [his] whole thesis." Schumpeter's link to Downs's book, and more broadly to public choice, seems almost exclusively through his emphasis upon the pursuit of self-interest by politicians and the role competition plays in politics. In general, Schumpeter's *Capitalism, Socialism, and Democracy* appears to have had much more influence on political scientists than economists.[4] The third contribution by Howard Bowen in 1943 was pioneering both in its discussion of voting and treatment of public goods.

2. The modern literature

Although Bowen's article has all of the properties we think of as characterizing public choice, it did not launch the field. The emergence of public choice as an identifiable discipline did not occur until after

---

3. For discussions of this work, see Buchanan (1985, chap. 3) and Peacock (1992).
4. For a discussion of the nature and importance of Schumpeter's ideas, see Mitchell (1984a, 1984b).

World War II with the appearance of papers by three economists – Duncan Black (1948a, 1948b), James Buchanan (1949), and Kenneth Arrow (1950).

The Arrow essay and subsequent book (1951) immediately spawned a torrent of articles and books written mostly by economists but also by a few mathematicians. The publication of Anthony Downs's *Economic Theory of Democracy* in 1957, James Buchanan and Gordon Tullock's *Calculus of Consent* in 1962, and Mancur Olson's *Logic of Collective Action* in 1965 made it clear that the "economic approach" to the study of politics had something important to contribute to our understanding of how political institutions work. Since the authors of these now classic works were all economists, one might well have guessed, as the 1960s were drawing to a close, that public choice was destined to be not only the "economic approach" to the study of politics but also an approach to the study of politics that only economists pursued.

But even then there were signs that this was not to be so. William Riker had published a paper in the *American Political Science Review* as early as 1961 surveying the literature on the Arrow theorem. His *The Theory of Political Coalitions* was published a year later. Although clearly a contribution to political science, it employed the kind of analytic rigor one would come to associate with the field of public choice.

In 1966 the sociologist, James Coleman, would employ the public choice methodology in two articles about politics – one published in the *American Journal of Sociology,* the other in the *American Economic Review.* These early contributions by future presidents of the Public Choice Society indicate that public choice was, even at this early stage in its modern history, an interdisciplinary field and foreshadowed its further development in these directions.

The interdisciplinary nature of pubic choice is well reflected in the essays in this book. Roughly half of them are by people who are not members of economics departments. It is further reflected in the many references to articles published in noneconomics journals.

3. Main themes

3.1 The first generation

The methodology of economics is often described as resting on the postulate of *methodological individualism.* The individual agent is taken as the fundamental building block for all economic analysis. Agents are assumed to have certain objectives or preferences and to interact in particular institutional settings (e.g., markets). Aggregate outcomes are discovered and characterized by examining the consequences of the assumed behavior of individual agents and the institutional constraints on that behavior. The most famous of the aggregation results of economics is, of course, the invisible hand theorem demonstrating that under certain conditions the institution of competitive markets leads to an allocation of aggregate resources that is Pareto optimal.

Given the prominence of methodological individualism in economic analysis, and the attraction of the invisible hand theorem, it was natural that when economists turned their attention to the examination of the consequences of political institutions they would adopt the same methodological building block and try to establish a similar aggregate result. These methodological links to economics had the further consequence that much of public choice at the beginning was inherently normative.

The normative emphasis of the early public choice literature is perhaps most clearly revealed in the characterization of the subject matter itself. Public choices were assumed to be made by *democratic* governments, and often democracies of a fairly ideal type. Thus, James Buchanan and Gordon Tullock in *The Calculus of Consent* (1962) investigate the properties of governmental institutions that are designed by the citizens to advance their common interests. Their contractarian approach to government leads them to inquire as to the Pareto optimality of democratic choices, just as Pareto optimality is used as the normative benchmark in much of economics.

Kenneth Arrow (1951) also included Pareto optimality as one of the axioms his ideal set of institutions would satisfy, along with the absence of dictatorship. His treatise is the most markedly normative of the early classics. His famous theorem that *no* set of institutions can produce outcomes that are Pareto optimal and nondictatorial, and satisfy a few other seemingly weak axioms both posed and answered an essentially normative question.

Duncan Black's (1948a, 1948b) pioneering studies of majority rule can also be viewed as a largely normative quest to define the conditions under which the majority rule aggregates preferences to produce an equilibrium outcome. Even Anthony Downs's investigation of representative democracy, a work that launched much future positive analysis, was intended to see whether competition between parties could not produce the same kind of normatively attractive political outcomes as competition among firms produced in the market place (1957, 17–19).

William Riker's *The Theory of Political Coalitions* (1962) and Mancur Olson's *The Logic of Collective Action* (1965), studies of coalition and interest group formation, are, among the early classics, the only truly positive studies of political behavior.

Each of the early classics helped launch a stream of research that has continued to the present day. Among economists, Arrow's theorem had the most immediate impact. One theorem followed upon another show-ing the inconsistency of all aggregation procedures with small sets of axioms. When possibility proofs appeared, they rested on such improba-ble conditions that they underlined only the negative implications of Arrow's theorem. The first wave of research in this area tended to focus upon the dichotomy between dictatorship and stability. Instability, or cycling, appeared to be a ubiquitious property of all preference aggrega-tion procedures. Later work showed that the same sorts of axioms im-plied that all nondictatorial procedures were vulnerable to the strategic misrepresentation of preferences by individuals. Even minimal notions of liberalism were inconsistent with certain weak axioms of aggregation. This axiomatic literature is reviewed by Prasanta Pattanaik. Peyton Young reviews the axiomatic properties of various aggregation rules but concentrates on the early contributions of Borda and Concorcet. It is striking how much more positive (optimistic) the eighteenth-century mathematicians were about the possibility of preference aggregation than are their twentieth-century counterparts who are economists.

Although Arrow and many of his followers studied the properties of all preference aggregation procedures, an important subset of that group concentrated on a particular voting rule, namely the simple majority rule. Here, there are two streams of research: One seeks to establish the conditions under which majority rule produces equilibrium outcomes; the other sidesteps the cycling problem by focusing on binary choices and describes the normative properties of majority rule in this context. The literature defining conditions under which the simple majority rule yields equilibrium outcomes can be traced back to Duncan Black's work on committees and is reviewed here by James Enelow and by Douglas Rae and Eric Schickler. The study of majority rule's properties in binary choices goes back to Condorcet, and in the modern literature to Ken-neth May (1952). This literature is taken up by Peyton Young and by Rae and Schickler.

In contrast to the Arrow literature, much of the work focusing on the simple majority rule paints a prettier picture. Majority rule can produce an equilibrium, under certain assumptions. It can help a modestly well-informed population choose the *best* of two possible outcomes. It has the properties of being egalitarian and fair often associated with democracy.

These results are important, and the works that derive them have appropriately received much attention. But the conditions under which majority rule produces an equilibrium with three or more possible out-comes, or the restriction that there be only two possible outcomes, seem so restrictive that many public choice scholars have not concluded that all problems of preference aggregation can be solved by relying on the simple majority rule to make collective decisions. For all its attractive properties, the majority rule does not throw off the shadow cast by Arrow's theorem.

Arrow's book had its greatest impact on more mathematically inclined economists, but Anthony Downs's book was perhaps the most influential among political scientists. Certainly, it had the biggest immediate impact on political scientists of any of the early classics in public choice written by an economist. Indeed, it had two sets of impact, one methodological, the other substantive. Writing in the late 1950s, Downs presented his ideas diagramatically, a pedagogic style often adopted by economists at that time. But the depiction of voter preferences and candidate choices geometrically was sufficiently novel in political science that it was given a name, "the spatial theory of voting."

Downs's main results, like those of Black, seemed to sound a happier note than the Arrow literature. Competition for votes in a two-party system would produce an equilibrium outcome. But, like Black's theorem, this finding was soon judged to be "an artifact" of the assumption of a single-dimensional issue space.[5] Candidates who competed for votes over multidimensional issue spaces would be just as prone to cycles as committees. The literatures on electoral politics that Downs launched is reviewed by Peter Ordeshook.

Although Downs's influence is perhaps most conspicuous in the spatial voting literature on electoral politics, another line of research he started has arguably had even more profound, and more negative, implications regarding the outcomes of democratic processes. Building on some observations of Schumpeter, Downs, in the latter portion of his book, took up the behavior of rational voters. Given the infinitismal probability that an individual's vote affects an election, the rational individual does not bother to become informed about possible electoral outcomes and, if he is only interested in affecting these outcomes, does not bother to vote. The literature spawned by Schumpeter and Downs on why and how people vote is reviewed by John Aldrich and Morris Fiorina.

Downs devoted a chapter to multiparty systems, but it has had little impact on the subject. Much more influential has been William Riker's account of why grand coalitions tend to devolve into minimum winning coalitions. Multiparty parliaments often produce coalition governments, and Riker's concept of a minimum winning coalition has proven extremely valuable in the analysis of these systems. Norman Schofield reviews the literature on multiparty systems and coalition governments.

A particular stream of research cannot be related to Mancur Olson's

---

5. The term "artifact" is borrowed from Hinich (1977), but the potential for cycling in two-candidate elections was recognized much earlier.

(1965) book in the same way that Anthony Downs's book can be to the literature on spatial models of electoral politics. Interest groups are major actors in politics, however, and Olson's work is the pioneering application of public choice analysis to the study of interest groups. These figure prominently in the essays by David Austen-Smith, Thomas Stratmann, and Cheryl Holsey and Thomas Borcherding.

Although its 1971 publication date is perhaps too late for William Niskanen's book to qualify as an *early* classic, it resembles the other works discussed in this section in that it is a direct and original application of public choice reasoning and modeling to a topic usually thought to lie in the domain of political science (or, alternatively, sociology). And, like the early classics, it launched a stream of the public choice literature, the one concerned with bureaucracies. The public choice work on bureaucracies is reviewed by Ronald Wintrobe and Terry Moe.

As even this brief overview will make clear (and if not, certainly, the cited essays will), many of the most important results of the early public choice literature conveyed a rather negative message about the potential of democracy and about its effects. No procedure for aggregating individual preferences was consistent with minimal sets of normative constraints. Equilibria did not exist. Small groups with narrow interests exercised a disproportionate influence on democratic outcomes. Government bureaucracies grew too big and inefficient. Voters remained rationally ignorant of the issues.

Among the early classics Buchanan and Tullock's *Calculus of Consent* (1962) is almost alone in presenting the positive potential of democracy. Adopting Wicksell's (1896) voluntary exchange approach to government, they emphasize the potential government has to advance the interests of *all* citizens and demonstrate the essential link between the existence of market failures (or other latent Pareto moves) and the creation of government. The literature on why governments and other forms of organizations for making collective decisions exist as well as their different characteristics is reviewed by Russel Hardin, Elinor Ostrom and James Walker, and Bruno Frey.

Central to the constitutional approach to government developed in *The Calculus of Consent* is the distinction between the selection of rules at the constitutional stage and later decisions made within the rules. The implications of this constitutional approach and the literature that has evolved from it are discussed in my subsequent essay.

The Calculus reproduces Tullock's (1959) earlier demonstration that the simple majority rule can lead to excessive government spending and waste, and in general Buchanan and Tullock have little good to say about the simple majority rule. But even here a more optimistic massage is offered with the suggestion that majority rule when combined with vote trading (logrolling) might actually lead to better social outcomes since it takes into account the preference intensities of voters. The public choice literature on logrolling is reviewed by Thomas Stratmann.

3.2 The second generation

The imprint of the early classics in public choice can be seen in several of the main streams of research in the field, and in a number of chapters in this volume. But not all the major developments in public were touched upon or anticipated in the early classics.

As I have already stressed, the message of the early public choice literature about the potential of democratic institutions seemed to be largely negative. This negative theme dominates my first survey of the field, which was published in 1976. But around the time I was writing this survey, a literature began to emerge that carried quite a different message. Edward Clarke (1971, 1972) and Theodore Groves (1973) published papers describing "the demand revelation process," and soon article after article showing that it was possible to induce people to reveal their preferences and aggregate them in a normatively appealing way appeared. Nicholas Tideman surveys this literature.

All of the early classics in public choice discussed above were theoretical contributions, thus, my 1976 survey even at that late date makes scant reference to an almost nonexistent empirical literature. The second generation of public choice, however, has seen a blossoming of empirical testing of models and hypotheses. No single essay in this volume is devoted to the empirical literature in public choice per se. But empirical contributions are discussed in Morris Fiorina's chapter on how people vote, Stratmann's essay on logrolling, Martin Paldam's review of political business cycles, Robert Tollison's review of rent seeking, Stephen Magee's essay on protectionism, and Cheryl Holsey and Thomas Borcherding's review of the growth of government literature.

The normative properties of many voting procedures and other sorts of democratic questions rest on what are essentially empirical questions. Will individuals behave strategically? How quickly does an iterative procedure converge? Answers to such questions are perhaps best obtained in the experimental laboratory. It is not surprising, therefore, that pioneers in the development of experimental research in economics like Vernon Smith and Charles Plott are also major contributors to the public choice literature. Parts of the experimental literature as it pertains to public choice are reviewed by Elizabeth Hoffman and by Elinor Ostrom and James Walker.

Its 1967 publication date might qualify Tullock's seminal article on rent seeking as an *early* classic in the public choice field. But the significance of the rent-seeking idea and its importance to public choice did not become apparent until the next decade, when it was rediscovered by several authors. Since the 1970s the rent-seeking literature has exploded. Robert Tollison overviews this vast literature, Stephen Magee discusses the special case of rent seeking as protectionism, and Holsey and Borcherding mention it as one of the possible explanations for the growth of government.

Some of the early important contributors to public choice like James Buchanan and Mancur Olson were trained in public finance and taught and wrote in this field as well as in public choice. Consequently, from the field's beginnings there has been a close relationship between public finance and public choice. The emphasis on the normative side of government in the early literature, and on explaining why governments ought to exist, led to a close connection between the *expenditure* side of public finance and public choice. This connection is apparent in many of the essays in this volume, from Russell Hardin's and Elinor Ostrom and James Walker's essays on why governments exist and the forms they take, through my own review of constitutional public choice and Holsey and Borcherding's analysis of the question of government size. Although there has always been a close link between the expenditure side of public finance and public choice, the taxation side was neglected for a long time by public choice scholars. Walter Hettich and Stanley Winer were among the first to begin remedying this deficiency, and their essay reviews the recent but rapidly growing public choice literature on taxation.

The economics literature on fiscal federalism, like the literature on public goods, is one that has traditionally been treated as part of public finance. Charles Tiebout's (1956) influential article on "voting with the feet" might be regarded as one of the early classics in *public choice,* as well as a seminal contribution to public finance. But, like taxation, the literature on fiscal federalism has to a considerable extent evolved as part of public finance, and so I have not included Tiebout as one of the pioneers of public choice. The ties between the literature on fiscal federalism and public choice are the subject matter of Robert Inman and Daniel Rubinfeld's essay.

4. Accomplishments, failures, potential

In my 1976 survey of public choice I observed that "much remains to be done" in answering the many difficult questions raised by the early literature concerning both the normative and positive properties of democratic institutions. In closing I stated that "one can remain optimistic about the field's future growth and development," and thus its ability to answer these difficult questions, because "public choice attracts so many fine scholars." A generation has elapsed since those words were written and, as the public choice field is roughly half a century old now, one might well take stock of the field today and inquire how successful it has been in answering these and other important questions about politics and political institutions. Such stock taking seems all the more needed in light of the highly critical evaluation of the field's accomplishments in the recent book by Donald Green and Ian Shapiro (1994).

To a considerable degree *this volume* constitutes such a stock taking, for it reviews and evaluates most of the major areas in the public choice literature. Each reader can decide for herself after reading the book whether the findings in a particular area, as well as of the entire field, have added anything useful to our knowledge of how individuals behave and how political institutions do or could affect that behavior. But no single paper looks at the entire field and tries to evaluate its accomplishments and failings. Although space constraints preclude a thorough examination of these questions, some discussion of them, however brief, does seem warranted, if only to convince the reader that she should continue reading this volume.

4.1 Accomplishments, normative

The salient characteristic of the public choice approach to politics, which distinguishes it from other approaches, is the prominent role played by the behavioral assumption that individuals seek rationally to advance their self-interest. Both casual observation and systematic experimental evidence indicate that individuals do not behave in the sophisticated, super-rational ways some public choice models presume, that individuals are not driven only by the very narrow definitions of self-interest many models assume. Rationally, self-interested individuals will not bother to vote to influence election outcomes, yet millions of seemingly normal and rational individuals vote in every election.

Empirical anomolies such as these are disturbing and imply that rational actor models must be modified to explain certain kinds of behavior. One must recognize, however, that regardless of how devastating one deems some empirical observations for rational actor models as predicitive devices, these observations *in no way* detract from the validity and importance of the *normative* literature of public choice.

The Arrow theorem states that we cannot in general construct an ordering of the possible social outcomes from the preference orderings of the individuals in the society without violating nondictatorship or one of the other axioms. This result seems rather disturbing. And is made no less disturbing by the knowledge that individuals sometimes cannot construct an ordering over their own private choices and perhaps do not even know how they rank various outcomes. If we cannot construct a social ordering from the preferences of rational individuals, is it likely that we can do so if individuals are not rational? What kind of political institutions should one select for a society whose citizens are presumed to behave irrationally?

Buchanan and Tullock (1962) sought to analyse the kinds of political institutions rational individuals might choose to advance their individual and collective interests. Is the constitution their analysis describes not a reasonable normative benchmark? Should we try and discover the characteristics of a constitution that irrational people would choose? Given the choice, would not even irrational people prefer a constitution designed by and for rational people?

Once we broaden the definition of self-interest to allow individuals to have altruistic preferences and the like, I cannot see how one would go about constructing a normative theory of democracy that did not presume that individuals were rational, in the sense that this term is employed in public choice, and sought to advance their interests broadly defined. Since all the normative theories in public choice are consistent with this interpretation of rational self-interest, all remain valid no matter how poorly some models based on a particular definition of rational self-interest fit certain data.

One of the implications of the Arrow-type theorems is that, in the absence of dictators, cycles are possible and, with certain sets of preferences, almost inevitable. Another conspicuous contradiction of rational actor models would appear to be the relative stability of political outcomes in many democratic societies.

Two observations are in order. First, stability is a relative concept and lies partly in the eye of the beholder. A senior citizen of Italy, having experienced (as of February 1995) fifty-four governments in less than fifty years, might regard cycling as one of the most strongly supported predictions of the public choice literature. Second, the theorems do not state that cycling is inevitable. Stability can always be induced by violating one of the other axioms. Dictatorship is one obvious way to end cycles. Coin flips are a fairer, although somewhat arbitrary way. The absence of cycles does not prove the irrelevance of the cycling theorems but rather leads to the question of which of the other axioms is violated and the normative implications of this violation.

4.2 Accomplishments, positive

Much of the more recent public choice literature emphasizes its positive side, the capacity of public choice models to help us understand what governments actually do. If the models do not help us understand the work of government better, then public choice has failed in one of, for many its only, important objective. Can public choice help us understand and explain what governments do? Has it in fact done so? In addressing these questions, I shall consider two strands of the public choice literature.

The idea that individuals would sell or trade their votes seems repugnant to most citizens in a democracy. Yet, the belief that congressmen trade votes has been around a long time (Bentley 1907; Schattschneider 1935). Indeed, the expression used to describe this trading, "logrolling," is peculiarly American. But do congressmen really trade votes? Do they trade votes on all issues or only on some? If only on some, which ones? What are the normative implications of this trading?

Barter and trade are *the* central focus of economic analysis. The analysis of vote trading was thus an obvious topic for public choice to take up. Buchanan and Tullock discuss it at length in *The Calculus of Consent,* and it has been a recurring topic of interest in the public choice literature ever since.

To make progress in science one has to know precisely what it is one is studying. One of the simplest yet most important contributions of public choice to our understanding of logrolling was a precise definition of what it is: A logrolling situation exists when issues X and Y both are defeated when individuals sincerely state their preferences on these issues and pass when some individuals trade votes.[6] Armed with a good definition, we can begin to prove theorems. Among the most important of these was the proof that the set of preferences that result in a logrolling situation, also would induce a cycle under sincere voting. Logrolling and cycling are ineluctably intertwined. All of the normative questions that arise when cycling occurs carry over to logrolling.

A precise definition of logrolling also allows us to test for its presence. Trading should only occur on issues where the vote is close *and* the votes of the traders are crucial to the victory of the winning issues. Tests for the presence of logrolling confirm these predictions and reveal that logrolling occurs on some, but not all, issues (see Stratmann's chapter).

Consider next the question of government size. One of the most conspicuous differences in the outcomes of democratic processes is simply the disparity in size of the public sectors one observes. The Swedes allocate over 60 percent of their GNP through the government, the Swiss about half as much. Federal expenditures accounted for 3 percent

---

6. More precise definitions exist, but this one suffices for our purposes here. See Thomas Stratmann's essay in this volume and the references therein.

of GNP in the United States in 1929, eight times as much today. Why does such a large difference in government size exist between these two small European countries with similar levels of national income? Why does such a large difference in the size of the federal sector exist in the United States over time? Certainly any good theory of government should be able to account for such differences.

One possible explanation in a democracy, of course, is that citizens want different amounts of government services in different countries or in the same country over time. But how does one model what the citizens want and how these wants are effectuated? One approach in public choice has been to employ the median voter theorem and to estimate the *demand* for government services by the median voter. Other models rely on probabilistic assumptions about voter behavior and weigh the preferences of all voters and groups.[7] Such approaches allow one to specify rather precisely the characteristics of voters that should explain government expenditure differences.

Probably no citizen or student of government believes that government outcomes reflect only the preferences of voters. The preferences of those in government also count. Here again direct application of public choice reasoning – those in government have particular goals they seek to advance – leads directly to testable implications. As Holsey and Borcherding's review makes clear, no single hypothesis explains all the differences in government size, and, as is often the case in empirical work, many tests have been mixed successes. Nevertheless, we know more about what does and does not account for differences in government size than we did before.

Indeed, perhaps the strongest endorsement for the public choice approach comes when one engages in Frank Capra's *Gedankenexperiment* from "Its a Wonderful Life." Imagine that public choice had never been invented, the literature reviewed in this book did not exist. How would one then proceed to explain differences in government size? Would one try to model voter preferences, the preferences of government officials? If one did, one would be on the way to developing a model that would look like the public choice models extant today. If one eschewed such models, what would one substitute in their place? How would one test one's hypotheses against someone else's? In explaining sizes of governments, as in testing for the presence of logrolling, it is difficult to see how one would develop and test hypotheses rigorously, without first positing some objectives for the relevant actors and then deriving the implications of the pursuit of these objectives in the form of some sort of model.

7. This approach is also discussed by Peter Ordeshook and David Austen-Smith.

4.3 Failures

Economic modeling at its best provides insight as to the consequences of certain actions and institutions based on a modest number of assumptions about the motivations behind that behavior and the constraints upon it. Modeling behavior in a rigorous way often exposes the logic of the underlying relationships better, thus allowing one to check the logic and even to reject the model on the basis of this test. Another advantage of rigorous modeling is that it can lead to implications that can then be tested empirically. As I have already stressed, the most important "failures" of public choice must lie in the positive area (i.e., failures to explain observed behavior), since the assumption of rational self-interest seems reasonable as a basis for normative analysis and the logic of the normative literature's major theorems has by now been thoroughly scrutinized.

The failure of a particular model to explain certain facts or data must be traced to an erroneous assumption about either the behavior of individuals or the nature of the constraints on that behavior. Public choice models, like their economic counterparts, often are built upon a few, simple behavioral assumptions. The bureaucrat maximizes the size of his or her bureau, an interest group the wealth of its members. Often such simply defined objectives do seem to capture the essential characteristics of a subject's behavior, just as the wealth maximization assumption does for some interest groups. When simple behavioral assumptions suffice they are obviously to be preferred, since they allow the modeler to describe his or her subject matter with minimum complexity.

But sometimes simple behavioral assumptions do not suffice or the researcher chooses the wrong objective entirely. Today an individual who wishes to maximize his or her personal wealth probably will not marry and certainly will not have children. The fact that people do marry and have children demonstrates that this simple behavioral assumption does not suffice, or may be of no use at all, in explaining these sorts of choices. It does not imply that the wealth maximization goal is inadequate for modeling other sorts of choices. One certainly could not use the failure of this particular application of a rational behavior assumption to reject all applications of rational actor models.

The prediction that people will not vote and the observation that they do is probably the most discussed and best known of the empirical failures of the public choice literature. As John Aldrich observes in Chapter 17, this particular failure of rational actor modeling comes about, if one assumes that individuals view voting instrumentally (i.e., as a way of affecting the outcome of an election). Aldrich suggests that voting can be easily accommodated in a rational actor model if it is viewed as an *expressive act* rather than as an instrumental one.

Public choice scholars have sometimes been too quick to adopt simple (naive) behavioral assumptions and too slow to abandon them when confronted with contradictory evidence, tendencies that carry over from economics. Like economists, public choice scholars may become mesmerized by the beauty of their models and construct ever more complex versions one upon the other without concern for whether the models do explain the behavior that they purport to describe.[8] But these are failings of the modelers themselves, not of their models per se or of the methodology that underlies them.

4.4 Potential

A decade ago I used "failures" of public choice models, such as the prediction that no one will vote, to chastise my colleagues in public choice for assuming too strong a form of rational behavior in some of their modeling (Mueller 1986). Public choice, like the game theoretic models it often employed, typically assumed that individuals were entirely forward looking, rational creatures. They calculated the future payoffs from each possible action and chose the optimal one. I argued that many decisions individuals make are influenced by their past experiences. People are conditioned to behave in certain ways in certain situations. A particular stimulus produces a particular reaction. Such a view of human behavior is fully consistent with the egoistic portion of the rational egoism postulate. Hedonistic man is conditioned by his past rewards and punishments. Such a view of human behavior leads to quite a different interpretation of rationality from that usually found in economic and public choice models. People behave *as if* they were maximizing a particular objective function. What goes into their objective functions, however, depends on how they have been rewarded and punished in the past.

This way of describing "preference formation" can easily accommodate acts of altruism, expressions of preferences through voting, and other actions that seem difficult to explain under strong-form rational, narrow self-interest assumptions. One is brought up to be a "good citizen," and good citizens express their preferences by voting. Most importantly, it leads us to formulate models to explain voting by looking at the histories of individuals. Which members of the community are most likely to have grown up in environments in which good citizenship is rewarded?

8. See the discussion at the end of Peter Ordeshook's essay.

One of the hottest topics in game theory today is evolutionary game theory. Individuals are assumed to select actions in each game situation based on their *past payoffs* from such actions. The environment rewards and punishes such actions and equilibria emerge over time. Evolutionary game theory describes how norms and conventions might evolve, the kinds of institutions that sometimes create trouble for strong-form, rational actor models. I discuss the relevance for public choice of some of these results in my essay below.

In the last fifteen years or so psychologists have published several articles in economics and political science journals with experimental evidence contradicting the strong-form rationality assumptions economists and public choice theorists often use. A consequence has been a modification of the behavioral assumptions that some of the latter use. Terms like "cognitive dissonance" and "conditioned behavior" now appear in economics and public choice writings. Richer, more realistic behavioral assumptions are made more often now.

Much of the experimental literature in economics and public choice may be viewed as testing the reasonableness of the behavioral assumptions made in various models, that is, attempting to determine what behavioral assumptions are most reasonable. Portions of this literature most relevant for public choice are reviewed by Hoffman and by Ostrom and Walker.

The importance of the kind of behavioral assumption one makes is brought out in the political business cycle literature reviewed by Martin Paldam. Some models assume sophisticated voters with rational expectations, others assume more myopic, adaptive behavior. The different assumptions lead to quite different model specifications and produce different degrees of fit to the data. Although a consensus has yet to emerge in this literature, it does promise us a better understanding not only of the behavior of parties and governments but also of the individual voters (see also the essays by Aldrich and Fiorina).

Psychology, sociology, political science, and economics are all concerned with different aspects of human behavior. Each seeks in its own way to describe different aspects of individual and social behavior. Until recently, the most conspicuous difference between economics and the other social sciences has been the reliance of economics on formal modeling and a single methodological paradigm that informs that modeling.

There is a kind of Gresham's law at work in academia that leads theory to drive out nontheory, formal theory to drive out informal theory. This has happened in economics, is happening in political science, and is beginning to happen in psychology and sociology. As modeling techniques spread across the social sciences, the possibility arises that the specialized knowledge of human behavior and institutions in each branch will be integrated into a set of theories joined by a common methodology, that is, a common perspective toward human action. In its mixing of economics and political science, public choice gives a preview of what such an integrated set of theories might look like. Although the field is not without its failures, I hope that after reading the following essays the reader will conclude that the field's accomplishments to date warrant further efforts to develop the potential for a methodologically integrated social science.

PART I

The need for and forms of cooperation

CHAPTER 2

Economic theories of the state

RUSSELL HARDIN

In rough outline, political economists have contributed to three categories of explanatory theories of the state based on arguments from, respectively, public goods, coordination, and evolutionary stability. The best known of these and the most extensively articulated are theories that build on public goods, in part perhaps because the theory of public goods has long been relatively well understood in a crude form, and in part perhaps because the public goods theory seems to yield not only an explanation for but also a justification of the state. In any case, the long tradition that grounds the state in the demand for public goods and in the state's capacity to deliver such goods has been both normative and explanatory. The other two traditions are primarily explanatory and not normative.

In its most literal variants, the public goods tradition supposes that people deliberately create the state in order to provide themselves with goods they could not individually provide for themselves, as, for example, by literally contracting to establish government. This bootstrapping move is circular if it is supposed that the state is itself a public good. In frustration at failing to provide ourselves some public good, we merely provide ourselves another that then provides us the one we failed to provide. Although it has not fully withered away and may occasionally betray signs of spontaneous regeneration, this branch of the tradition was finally cut off by Mancur Olson's argument of the logic of collective action (Olson 1965). According to this logic, I rationally contribute to the provision of a collective good only if I get more value from the bit of the collective good that my contribution buys than that contribution costs me. Commonly, in the contexts of large scale collective action, my contribution returns vanishingly small benefits to me, so that it costs me more than it is worth to me. Hence, although all of us might receive a large net benefit *if we all contribute*, none of us may have any interest in contributing.

In its credible variants, however, the tradition that associates the state with public goods is largely about what difference it makes that some goods are more successfully or efficiently provided collectively through the state than individually through the market. The public goods theory of the state seems to involve one or both of two claims. The first claim is that certain characteristics of public goods require that they be provided by a central agency acting on behalf of the larger group of beneficiaries. The second is that collective provision merely has advantages over individual provision. This claim is surely true in some cases, but it should be weighed against the disadvantages of a state empowered to provide bads as well as goods. The claim is consistent with the possibility of totalitarian and exploitative states as well as liberal states; totalitarian and exploitative states seem either contrary to or outside the first claim. The sanguine view of David Hume and Adam Smith that the state can perform miracles of dredging harbors and raising armies beyond the capacities of individuals spontaneously acting together – which is often taken as a statement of the public goods theory – is consistent with both the first and second claims. Just because we are coordinated in support of the state, the state can exercise great power. But this could be a by-product of coordination for mere order.

From even a casual survey, it should be clear that there are two classes of strategic interactions that produce what might sensibly be called collective goods or collective provisions of benefits. One of the these has the traditional form of the prisoner's dilemma and fits Olson's logic of collective action. At least some of the goods that can be provided through interactions of this form have central characteristics of Paul Samuelson's public goods. Many others do not; for example, collectively negotiated wage increases take the simple form of money in individual pockets, not the form of radio signals or national defense.

The second class of strategic interactions that lead to collective benefits comprises coordinations on mutually preferred outcomes. In a prisoner's dilemma interaction, I prefer the outcome in which everyone else contributes to the provision of our good while I do not contribute but free ride; every other member of our group prefers a different but analogous outcome. Hence, our choice is not one of simple coordination. But in the regime of driving either on the left or on the right, we all share the identical interest of driving on the side that virtually all others choose. If we successfully coordinate on one side or the other, we all benefit. The language of prisoner's dilemma, collective action, and public goods has come in recent decades to dominate the image of what it is we collectively want to do. But much of what we want is much less conflictual than the free-rider problem. For example, for most of us, there is no incentive to free ride on various coordinations. Indeed, there is no coherent meaning for "free riding" in the driving and other conventions, except for thrill seekers for whom risking accidents is a source of pleasure.

Much of what makes the state plausibly valuable is not its provision of genuine public goods, many of which can successfully be provided by market devices. For example, radio signals are among the best examples of public goods, but they are often provided by the market. The state's chief role in providing them in some cases is merely to regulate band-widths and interference between stations. That is to say, the state mainly helps in the coordination of the multiple provision. That is the value of the state.

In an economic theory of the state, these two classes of strategic interactions might play substantially different roles. In particular, the class of coordinations may be very important in the explanation of the rise of the state, as in the theories of Hume and Smith, or in the explana-tion of the maintenance of order, as in the theory of Hobbes, whereas the class of prisoner's dilemma interactions may be especially important in the justification of the state, as in many contractarian theories. There are, however, no clear lines that separate these two classes into different realms. Both yield both explanations and justifications. In explanations of the rise of the state, however, coordination interactions have a concep-tually prior status. Without substantial coordination to produce order there is likely to be little exchange, hence little successful collective action. This is essentially Hobbes's theory of the state: The state pro-duces order that allows individuals to benefit from relations with one another by first protecting them from one another. We first get to a state by coordinating on it out of a possibly large array of potential states (Hobbes 1651, chaps. 13–15, 20; Hardin 1991). This is a view shared by many of the American constitutionalists in 1787–8 when they argued for the creation of a strong government but against the concern to make it exactly right or nearly perfect (Hardin 1989).

1. A brief history

To simplify somewhat, Hobbes presented essentially a coordination theory of the state, the chief benefits of which were order among indi-viduals and the possibility of property and exchange. Coordination on a government could come by contract or it could come from a past history of conquest or revolution.

Hume and Smith presented philosophical (that is, speculative) theo-ries of the rise of the state. They combined a coordination theory with a nascent public goods theory. Hume (1739–40, 541) supposed the earliest governments were a response to fear of external attack. They were monarchical because their central concern was capacity to respond to sudden events; hence, capacity to coordinate in the face of attack even dictated the form of government. Once a leader arose, all others had an interest in following him. The engaging part of their theories is their focus on explaining the growth of centralized power in its relation to mutual interest and then, eventually, the amassment of resources. But the literature they spawned generally drifted into a relatively uninteresting debate on whether their sequences of development from primitive societies through pastoral to large agrarian states were historically correct or functionally determinate.

Hume and Smith also contributed to the growth of the public goods theory of the state. In this theory, it is supposed that the state arises in order to supply collective benefits that would not be provided by spontaneous collective action. Hume comments that government can perform minor miracles in doing such things as dredging harbors and defending the nation. He seems to have recognized the difficulty of doing these things through voluntary collective action (Hume [1739–40] 1978, book 3, part 2, sec. 7, 538–9). The public goods theory is often not simply an explanatory theory but a normative theory. In its normative variant, it is state provision of public goods that justifies the existence of the state and the use of its coercive devices. If the theory is strictly explanatory, it is subject to the bootstrapping complaint above – we resolve the problem of failure to supply public goods by supplying a super-public good, the state, so that it can supply lesser public goods.

A more plausible way to fit the public goods theory to explanation is to suppose that the capacity to provide public goods gives a state survival value. Hence, those states that can supply public goods tend to prevail over those societies that cannot supply them. In Smith's vision of the market economy, the state that provides public facilities of some kinds enhances the prospects for productivity and prosperity – Smith's wealth of nations. Such wealth then may feed back into empowering the state for further actions.

Much of contemporary writing has dropped the coordination theory to focus exclusively on the public goods theory. Part of the reason for the latter development may be the sophisticated articulation of the public goods theory, especially in the work of William Baumol (1952) and Olson, that goes well beyond the understanding of Smith, Mill, and others among the classical political economists. Olson built his argument from Samuelson's elegant theory of public goods (Samuelson 1954). Despite clear articulation of general coordination theory (Schelling 1960; Lewis 1969), it has not been as widely developed.

John Stuart Mill frequently made arguments that some provisions cannot be rationally motivated at the level of the individual acting spontaneously but must be accomplished through centralized state intervention. For example, he argued that it is conceivable that workers could not secure themselves a nine-hour workday merely by individually refusing to work longer, but that they might require a law against a longer day. This would be true if the following incentives applied. All workers would rather work nine hours than ten if they could make nearly the same pay for the shorter day. But if some voluntarily worked only nine hours, others would then prefer to work ten hours for the hour's bonus pay. Finally, all would be forced to work ten hours and to take less pay than ten times the hourly rate of a nine-hour day. Under these conditions, the workers face the logic of collective action and they would benefit from legal enforcement of the nine-hour day. The nine-hour day might therefore be a benefit that virtually requires coercive state provision (Mill 1965, book 5, chap. 11, sec. 12, 958).

Economic theories of the state are now commonly stated in terms of Samuelsonian public goods, the prisoner's dilemma, and coordination games, all of which have been well articulated only in the past half century. These seem consistent with elements of theories of the state and government from the earliest days of western political philosophy. The prisoner's dilemma and public goods analyses are closely related. The prisoner's dilemma is more general than the public goods analysis in that it depends only on the relationships of net payoffs independently of whether these are technically subject to the conditions defining public goods. It is less general in that it does not include cases of public goods whose costs of provision are less than their benefits to single players (as for Olson's "privileged" groups). Coordination theory is distinctively different from the prisoner's dilemma and public goods theories.

2. Coordination

In many contexts we all benefit if only we all coordinate on doing the same thing. We all drive right, speak the same language, or use the same measuring system. There need be nothing inherently right about the choice we de facto make. All driving left would be as good as all driving right. But if all have coordinated on driving right, then driving left would be wrong because harmful to some and not beneficial to anyone. Our coordination is not itself a good; rather it is a means, it enables us to do other things more successfully.

The greatest of coordinations is that which maintains social order or which selects one out of an array of possible governments or forms of government. Consider the maintenance of social order. We create or find ourselves in a state. Even with very limited power that state can maintain order by sanctioning the occasional miscreant. Faced with our government, most of us have no expectation of gain from various crimes. Our effective acquiesence in the state's ordering of the society is what enables the state to marshal its limited resources against the few who do not acquiesce. When this works well, then, ex ante, none of us can free ride on the order created by others. We virtually all face a net expectation of personal loss from going against that order.

At any given moment I might wish to cheat and break the law. But I cannot free ride in the sense of free riding on the general coordination that establishes order. If, along with others, I coordinate on the creation or maintenance of order through the creation or maintenance of a government and its laws, I am then subject to whatever coercions are available to that government to make me be orderly. Moreover, in most moments, I am inclined in favor of imposing order on others who might violate it. Therefore, the regime of order continues to be a preferred coordination outcome. Indeed, since few people have ever participated in the creation of their society's order, the only coordination of which they are actually part is that of continuing support for order. The order that we have is largely archeological; we could probe down through many layers of history and not ever find anything that could pass for the creation of order.

Hobbes supposed that we would want to coordinate on the creation or maintenance of state order because this would get us out of the violence and uncertainty of anarchy. Hume assumed, on the contrary, that primitive anarchy is attractive. "Nothing but an increase of riches and possessions could oblige men to quit [the state of society without government]" (Hume [1739–40], 541). Self interest is sufficient to create order in a small society, such as that of primitive anarchy; government and law are required for a large society. If the large society can achieve greater productivity than the small society, then we may actively prefer the large society with government to the idyllic life of the small society without government. In the views of both Hobbes and Hume, government in relevant circumstances benefits everyone; hence, we are in harmony in opting for it or in wanting it well maintained.

Oddly, it may be in each individual's interest to support an extant order that is generally defective. For example, most Germans during the Third Reich may have had a perverse interest in coordinating on the stability of the Nazi regime even when they thought it might bring them disaster in the longer run. Most Soviet citizens may have had a similar interest in supporting the stability of the Soviet regime, even in its harshest days. And those who are in a subjugated class, such as the American slaves before the Civil War, may have an interest in supporting the order that subjugates them (Ullmann-Margalit 1977, 162–4, 173–6). Hence, it may be that, although the class of all citizens or that of all those who are subjugated would benefit from a change in regime, no individual would benefit enough to take the costly action necessary to change it. In general, the logic of collective action can be devastating for any hope that we can collectively provide ourselves with collective benefits. An odd analog of that logic applies just as forcefully to the burden of switching from a defective to a more beneficial coordination. But if a Gorbachev comes along to take the lead in moving us from a defective to an alternative coordination, we may find it remarkably easy to switch for some matters.

Smith's explanation of the rise of larger from smaller pastoral states addresses the issue of coordination in selecting a government. Smith supposes that pastoral societies travel virtually as whole societies and enter into battle in conditions in which the losing side may be absorbed by the larger side. It is clearly in the interest of the individual pastoral family, once their society has been defeated and perhaps ravaged, to join with the more successful society. Hence, a victorious pastoral society may grow to be relatively invincible (Smith 1978).

3. Public goods

In Samuelson's account, public goods have two characteristics (Samuelson 1954). First, they are joint or nonrival in supply. That is to say, my enjoyment of such a good does not subtract from the possibility that others enjoy it. I turn on my radio and hear music broadcast over the air and everyone else with a radio in the relevant geographic area can still enjoy the same broadcast. Second, the goods are subject to nonexclusion. That is to say, I cannot be blocked from enjoying the good once it is provided for anyone else. Ordinary consumption goods sold in the market and such collective provisions as toll roads are subject to exclusion. When I buy a dinner, I can exclude others from consuming it. Any driver without the funds for the toll can be excluded from a toll road.

The peculiarity of the ideal type of a good that is nonrival in supply is that, once it has been provided for the enjoyment of one person, it is providable at no further cost to all other persons within the range of the good. For example, a radio signal, once provided at all, may be freely used by all. Productive efficiency generally requires that goods be sold at their marginal prices. The marginal price of a good that is nonrival is zero. Hence, if it is to be efficiently provided, the good should be given away. Provision by the state therefore might be more efficient than provision by the market.

Technically speaking, there may be no good of any political or economic significance that is inherently subject to nonexclusion. Indeed, the technology of exclusion is a growth industry with frequent innovation. At worst, we may use the law to penalize those who enjoy goods that are virtually joint in supply and thereby to exclude people from their enjoyment. But if exclusion is costly, paying for provision of a good with general revenues and making its use free to the user might be far more efficient than individual provision only to those who pay.

An extreme coordination theory might hold that a desirable state need provide few public goods. It could merely enable individuals to provide such goods. This is analogous to the state's role in dyadic exchange. The state does not provide the gains from dyadic exchange – it merely enables us to enter exchanges with confidence by blocking unilateral appropriations and providing contract enforcement. So, too, it may provide merely the regulatory backing for independent entrepreneurs to provide actual public goods, such as radio signals, ideas, computer software, and so forth. Mandeville and Smith supposed that the pursuit of private profit could lead to great public benefit, although it would be odd to say that the pursuit of private profit is a public good itself.

For many writers, the defining public good that requires and justifies the state is defense. Many writers follow Hume in supposing that defense was the initial reason for government. Maintaining order may require little more than coordination in which no one bears an expected cost in return for the expected benefits. Defense, however, seems necessarily to require individual risks or outlays of costs that the individual might be able to dodge while still benefiting from the risks and outlays of others. For a very small society, such as Smith's hunting society, the incentives that come from reciprocal interaction can induce the cooperation of all. For a large society, such incentives may not suffice and the state may require legal sanctions. In Olson's theory, the small society would be an intermediate group and the large society would be a latent group.

4. Prisoner's dilemma

Prisoner's dilemma is the game theoretic model of dyadic exchange interactions when there are potential gains from trade. Suppose we both prefer to be in the state in which I have your property or labor in return for mine, although either of us would prefer to have both. To make exchange work, we need incentives to keep either of us from merely taking what the other has with nothing given in return. In Hobbes's theory, the first purpose of government is to prevent such unilateral appropriation. Once the outcomes of unilateral appropriation are blocked, exchange reduces to a matter of coordination in which we both move to become better off as compared to our condition in the status quo before exchange.

In an iterated interaction in which two people repeatedly face a similar prisoner's dilemma structure of choice, we can commonly expect that they will cooperate for mutual benefit even without regulation by the state. If I refuse to cooperate and, instead, defect continuously, you will soon also defect in order to reduce your losses. When we both defect in standard exchange contexts, we maintain our status quo positions and lose opportunity for mutual gain. By cooperating repeatedly, we gain repeatedly from the implicit exchange of our prisoner's dilemma (Taylor 1976; Hardin 1982; Axelrod 1984).

Some scholars suppose that even in iterated prisoner's dilemma cooperation is irrational. By backwards induction they argue that, in a fixed run of n iterations, on the nth play rational players must defect in what is, after all, now a single-play prisoner's dilemma. But since this choice is now fixed in advance, it follows that the immediately previous play is de facto the last on which a choice can be made. If it is de facto last, it follows that rational players must defect on it as though it were a single play. And so on back to the first play (Luce and Raiffa 1957, 98–9). Against this deterministic argument, note that a chooser facing the first play in an iterated prisoner's dilemma can give the other player a contrary signal by cooperating rather than defecting. This wrecks the backwards induction, thus making it rational for the second player to consider cooperation. If the players are able to cooperate for even a few plays in many iterated prisoner's dilemmas, they stand to have a larger payoff than if they defect in all plays. Hence, it may be rational for each player to wreck the backwards induction argument by playing against it. The backwards induction argument is therefore self-contradictory, because it recommends deliberately cooperating in order to wreck its assumptions – if the induction is correct, it is therefore rational to violate it. Hence, in iterated prisoner's dilemma, mutual cooperation can be rational (Hardin 1982, chap. 10). The prospect of such cooperation gives some support to anarchist and extreme libertarian views that we can do without the state beyond, perhaps, very minimal functions, including the function of preventing theft (Nozick 1974). (There are other arguments against the backward induction conclusion. Many of these depend on bits of clever reasoning that seem to be more nearly the invention of theorists than a characterization of the choices of any actual choosers. The most widely cited of these is perhaps that of Kreps et al. [1982].)

Unfortunately, however, this conclusion does not generalize to n-prisoner's dilemma. If n is very small, we might expect some cooperation, but if it is very large, a group of cooperating players typically cannot be made better off by defecting in response to a single defecting player. In 2-person iterated prisoner's dilemma, my defection in response to your defection is directly in my interest. It need not be motivated by an urge to sanction you or even by a long-run hope of getting you to cooperate. In iterated *n*-prisoner's dilemma, successful cooperators lose the benefits of their subgroup cooperation when they defect against a defector. Hence, it is not in their immediate collective interest per se to defect. They might nevertheless do so in order normatively to punish the defector or in order rationally to induce that player to cooperate in the future. But the latter hope may be very dim. In *n*-prisoner's dilemma, it can be possible continuously to take a free ride on the cooperative efforts of others over many iterations. In 2-person prisoner's dilemma, this is typically not possible.

Two-person prisoner's dilemma is resolvable with cooperation when iterated, but *n*-prisoner's dilemma for large *n* is not resolvable. Smith supposed the maintenance of order is a simple matter in a primitive hunting society – not least because there is little property to provoke theft – and that it can be sustained by democratic decision and action. His account, though brief, is essentially that of later anarchists. It could be filled out with claims that there are reciprocal, iterated interactions among all the members of such a society, so that they can successfully sanction one another to act appropriately. In a pastoral society, the scale is greater and there may be need for specific leadership and authority to sanction miscreants. In more advanced societies, there is finally need for law and its regular application. Somewhere between a small pastoral society and the more advanced society, the anarchist's model can no longer work because we cannot be engaged in reciprocal, iterated interactions with more than a small percentage of our fellows. There is no free riding in the small hunting society because there are not enough people to let anyone free ride. Everyone is face-to-face with everyone else.

5. Composition from individual to collective

Among the oldest problems of social theory is the fallacy of composition. In the social variant of this fallacy, it is supposed that many individuals, all of whom have some property or characteristic, such as rationality, can be composed into a collective of some kind that has that same property or characteristic. One might generally suppose it is such an assumption that lies behind the standard move in international relations to treat states as rational actors. By his own account, Kenneth Arrow once thought it obvious that citizens' preferences on international policies could be composed into a coherent state policy (1983, 3–4). Challenged to show this, he showed instead that it was false in general. With more than four decades in which to ponder Arrow's result (ibid, 4–29), we now suppose it obvious that a state's policies are not merely an aggregation of its citizens' preferences. A striking implication of the public goods theory of the state is that it fits contexts in which there might be uniform preferences, so that the state could merely aggregate individual preferences. That this is an implausible assumption for a state in any complex society with diverse preferences suggests the irrelevance of the public goods theory for any but a few basic matters, such as defense against outside forces.

To skirt the problems of Arrow's result (and perhaps its implications for the public goods theory), some writers suppose we could reach harmonious agreement on a form of government that would then handle the issues on which we have little hope of achieving harmonious agreement directly. Hobbes's theory essentially fits this view (Hardin 1991), which is also the view of the contemporary Virginia school (Buchanan and Tullock 1962; Brennan and Buchanan 1985). If the condition of anarchy is sufficiently chaotic and destructive of productivity and wealth, as Hobbes assumes it must be and as recent experience in Lebanon, El Salvador, Somalia, and many other societies suggests it often is, then the critical move of the public goods theory is the initial creation and maintenance of a viable state. But this must be the result of social evolution and coordination, not of bootstrapping.

In his theory of democratic voting, Anthony Downs (1957) avoids Arrow's problem by assuming that the issues for collective decision can be arrayed on a single dimension, such as from left to right. Then, although we typically would not achieve harmonious agreement, we could achieve majority agreement. Adding further dimensions to the choice brings back the possibility of cyclic collective preferences and even of chaos that could lead us collectively to select almost any point in the choice space.

6. The contractarian tradition

We cannot give a straightforwardly intentionalist account of the creation of the state as a direct response to demands for collective provision. This move fails in Thomas Hobbes's account, as he himself seemed to recognize. He noted that mere agreement to select an all-powerful sovereign could not endow the sovereign with power (Hardin 1991, 170–1). The nearest such event was perhaps in Philadelphia and then in U.S. state conventions in 1787–8. However, even this event was made possible by the existence of a prior state under the Articles of Confederation. The creation and adoption of the Constitution was essentially a reform of the prior form of government. That constitution coordinated the thirteen states and their citizens on a new form of government with substantially more power at the federal level (Hardin 1989).

What we can often give, instead of an intentionalist account, is a social-evolutionary account. If a state happens to take on the task of some collective provision that gives the state greater survival value in the competition with other states and with potential anarchy, then the relevant collective provision tends to support that state. For example, state provisions that lead to greater productivity increase the scope for taxation to enhance the resources of the state. These resources might be used to block external competition or to control internal opposition. Hence, the capacity of the state to provide collective goods may be critical for its survival even if not for its origins. Provision of goods such as roads and of coordinations such as order makes life enormously better, partly by stabilizing expectations and partly by elevating general welfare.

Pufendorf (Book 2, chap. 2, sec. 2) says that "the complaint of the masses about the burdens and drawbacks of civil states could be met in no better way than by picturing to their eyes the drawbacks of a state of nature." This claim fits the quasi-evolutionary account of the rise of states through their successes in survival as well as it fits the intentionalist contractarian creation of a state out of anarchy. Much of the force of contractarian argument often is in such statements, which do not in fact have a necessary connection to contractarian procedural justification but only to substantive, welfarist justification.

One might still think that ordinary people much of the time do follow quasi-contractarian norms in their interactions with each other even without iteration. Moral and political theorists typically want to go further and say something to the effect that the tacit agreement between a citizen and her government *obligates* the citizen to be obedient. That is, agreement is right making or right defining. This normative contractarian argument seems clearly wrong (Hardin 1990). Hume ([1748]) long ago demolished the descriptive supposition that government is in fact based on agreement. All that might be left is the Rousseauist, Kantian view that we are rationally bound to obey that which we would rationally (somehow defined) agree to. Call this view rationalist contractarianism. To make the view compelling, Rousseau, Kant, John Rawls (1971), and others virtually assume that anyone would agree to what it is a priori rational to agree to. This is a universal claim, and Rawls therefore need put only a single representative person behind the veil to choose the principles of justice (some contract). In rationalist contractarianism, therefore, the terms "contract" and "agreement" are otiose. All we really need to do is *discover* what is the universally right institution, principle, or whatever for government. We do not agree as we would in an exchange or an actual contract; rather, we agree more nearly as logicians or mathematicians would when they comprehend a demonstration. Much of the relevant theory must therefore be a definition of rightness.

The rationalist contractarian view is not related to common-sense cases of actual but tacit contracting. For example, a tipper on the highway far from home may treat the particular interaction as tacitly one of contractual agreement. This is not a rationalist or ideal claim, but a particular and actual claim. Some tippers might just be contractarian about the relevant interactions. Because they must commonly let social conventions determine the fair content of the contractual exchanges in which they tip, it would be wrong to say that their contractarian conclusions were rationalist or universal or a priori. Contractarianism in political theory cannot easily get started if it must first have a similarly strong social determination of its content.

7. Normative and explanatory theory

It is difficult to read much of contractarian theory without the impression that it is largely a normative, justificatory theory. Much of public goods theory similarly has a normative ring. A defining characteristic of the state is that it acts as a collective. Perhaps it tends to do many things that are collective, as resolving prisoner's dilemmas and supplying public goods typically are. But it might also do collectively what could be done much better individually. Worse still, it might do collectively what brings harm to virtually all its subjects. The economic theory is primarily a theory of capacities. Yet, economic theorizing about the state often runs normative and explanatory arguments together. We can derive some limited normative conclusions from the economic theories. The state makes the achievement of many collective provisions possible. It therefore makes the achievement of good possible, so that the state is an empirically necessary instrument for achieving much that is good. It is also an empirically necessary instrument for achieving some horrendous harms.

Note that Hobbes's theory is simultaneously explanatory and justificatory. States just happen by coordination. And they are good because they make us all potentially better off as compared to a state of anarchy (Cambodian experience under Pol Pot might make anarchy seem preferable, at least sometimes). To get this joint result, however, Hobbes had to make a normative commitment to welfare, perhaps crudely defined. Xenophon justified Cyrus's despotic rule with the claim that Cyrus's interests were identical with those of his subjects (Xenophon, 4th century B.C., VIII.1.4). Xenophon's argument is somewhat trivialized by his claim that what makes their interests common is that they have common enemies, whom they wish to defeat. Evidently, Cyrus's rule would immediately have ceased to be just had he lived to see victory over those enemies. Despots have commonly held Xenophon's view of themselves, with a slight twist – that the people's interests are identical with the despot's. James Madison supposed that the best way to achieve good government was to design institutions to make it the case that the governors' interest is to do what is in the interest of the people. If this condition is genuinely met, we have a strong Hobbesian, welfarist justification for the state even though the particular state and governors we have may be merely one choice from among many possible choices that might be equally good.

CHAPTER 3

Neither markets nor states: Linking transformation processes in collective action arenas

ELINOR OSTROM AND JAMES WALKER

1. Collective action problems

Since the foundational work of Mancur Olson (1965), the concept of collective action has gained prominence in all of the social sciences. Given the structure of an initial situation, collective action problems occur when individuals, as part of a group, select strategies generating outcomes that are suboptimal from the perspective of the group. In the most commonly examined case, individuals are involved in a collective action game where the unique Nash equilibrium for a single iteration of the game yields less than an optimal outcome for all involved. If such a game is finitely repeated and individuals share complete information about the structure of the situation, the predicted outcome for each iteration is the Nash equilibrium of the constituent game. If uncertainty exists about the number of iterations, or if iterations are infinite, possible equilibria explode in number. Among the predicted equilibria are strategies yielding the deficient Nash equilibria, optimal outcomes, and virtually everything in between. The *problem* of collective action is finding a way to avoid deficient outcomes and to move closer to optimal outcomes. Those who find a way to coordinate strategies receive a "cooperation dividend" equal to the difference between the payoffs at a deficient outcome and the more efficient outcome.

Public choice theorists have focused primarily on those collective action problems related to public goods, common-pool resources, and club goods. All three of these types of goods potentially involve deficient equilibria in provision or consumption activities. Pure public goods have been considered the paradigm case for the necessity of the state. The state is viewed as the vehicle necessary to select and provide the "proper" outcome as opposed to that which would occur without the state. On the other hand, the problems of providing public goods, re-

The authors are appreciative of the support they have received from the National Science Foundation (Grant nos. SBR-9319835 and SES-8820897) and the useful comments received from Vincent Ostrom and Audun Sandberg.

gardless of scope, are not so obviously solved by a state (McGinnis and Ostrom 1996). If the purpose of an analysis is to demonstrate how market institutions fail to provide optimal levels for a wide variety of goods and services, demonstrating market weakness or failure is relatively easy. Demonstrating the failure of one type of institution is not, however, equivalent to establishing the superiority of a second type of institution.[1] An institutional arrangement with a monopoly on the legitimate use of force – the state – has itself been shown to suffer substantial failures and weaknesses as a provider of public goods in many countries of the world (see Bates 1981; V. Ostrom 1984, 1991, 1993; Wunsch and Olowu 1990; Sawyer 1992).

The choice that citizens face is not between an imperfect market, on the one hand, and an all-powerful, all-knowing, and public-interest-seeking institution on the other. The choice is, rather, from among an array of institutions – all of which are subject to weaknesses and failures. Various forms of associations and networks of relationships are successfully used to solve aspects of collective action problems. These include families and clans, neighborhood associations, communal organizations, trade associations, buyers and producers' cooperatives, local voluntary associations and clubs, special districts, international regimes, public-service industries, arbitration and mediation associations, and charitable organizations. Some institutional arrangements, such as gangs, criminal associations, and cartels, solve collective action problems for some participants by harming others. Predatory states may solve some collective action problems for those who are in power but do so by diminishing productivity and benefits for others.[2]

No doubt exists about the importance of governments – at supranational, national, and subnational levels – in coping with aspects of collective action. Given recent events in Russia and Eastern Europe, however, it is particularly important in the post–1989 era to explore how a wide diversity of institutions, that are neither markets nor states, operate to enhance the joint benefits that individuals achieve in collective action situations. Many of these institutions are constituted by participants in a self-governing process rather than imposed by external authorities. The creation of these institutions is itself a collective action problem. Understanding how individuals solve different types of collective action problems is of substantial analytical and normative importance.

---

1. This is especially true when the model of the second kind of institution – the state – is based on a set of assumptions about the behavior of officials who are "economic eunuchs," to use James Buchanan's description of Pigovian policymakers (Buchanan 1973).
2. See Sandler (1992) and Schmidtz (1991) for recent work on related issues.

To understand how institutions that are neither markets nor states evolve and cope with collective action problems, we need to unpack larger and more complex problems into a series of transformations that occur between the provision of *any* good and its consumption. For each transformation process, we need to understand the kind of behavior that individuals adopt. Research conducted in the field and in experimental settings provides substantial evidence about the capacity of those affected to develop institutions that are neither markets nor states. After discussing key theoretical concepts, we provide an overview from the field and from laboratory experiments of how individuals cope with diverse collective action problems.

1.1 Transformation processes

Many processes transform inputs into outputs that jointly affect some set of individuals. Drawing on Plott and Meyer (1975) and our own previous research (E. Ostrom, Schroeder, and Wynne 1993; E. Ostrom, Gardner, and Walker 1994), we define and discuss the following eight transformation processes: provision, production, distribution, appropriation, use, organization, monitoring, and sanctioning.[3]

The linkage among these processes may be accomplished within diverse institutional arrangements, including: (1) strictly private market or governmental enterprises, (2) independent actors engaged in *quid pro quo* transactions or more loosely defined reciprocal relations, (3) independent actors who lack communication or contracting capabilities, or (4) some combination of the above. The particular attributes of a collective action problem depend upon the transformation functions involved and the institutional rules that define available strategies. Considerable confusion has been generated by conflating these processes and/or ignoring the importance of alternative institutional arrangements. Treating the provision, production, and consumption of a public good, for example, as if these were a single process or independent of institutional rules is often misleading.

We emphasize that each of these transformation processes is involved

---

3. We do not present these eight as the exhaustive list of transformation processes of relevance to understanding public economies but rather as a core set that has been useful in organizing our own work. Each process can be further unpacked. Also, we do not focus here on the epistemic orders that are closely related to the economic and political orders we do discuss (see V. Ostrom forthcoming).

in all efforts to produce and consume goods, regardless of the attributes of the good to be produced or the institutional context. In our discussion, however, we highlight each process in its relation to market and/or nonmarket processes. Our goal is to emphasize how each is naturally linked to the diverse attributes of particular goods and/or the institutional setting in which those goods are produced.

Transformations normally associated with a market context. First consider four of the processes that are normally associated with markets:

> *Production:* Combining private and/or public inputs to yield one or more outputs.
>
> *Distribution:* Making outputs available.
>
> *Appropriation:* Taking, harvesting, or receiving one or more outputs.
>
> *Use:* Transforming one or more outputs into final consumption and waste (or through another production process into other outputs).

When institutional conditions allow production and distribution to be handled by one entity – the supplier – and appropriation and use to be handled by another – the appropriator – the key linking transaction occurs at the point of appropriation. When *quid pro quo* market exchanges link suppliers and appropriators (who are buyers in this context), anyone who appropriates a unit of a good is liable under an institutional constraint to pay for it or be penalized if caught stealing (Plott and Meyer 1975).

Transformations associated with a nonmarket context. If appropriators are not liable to pay for goods and services they receive, then suppliers cannot exclude potential beneficiaries. Thus, the dimension of exclusion and nonexclusion relates to the type of liability an individual faces who appropriates goods that are made available by a supplier (or nature) (Plott and Meyer 1975). When exclusion is complete, a potential consumer is fully liable for any goods or services appropriated (whether or not the individual exercised choice in appropriating benefits). When exclusion is entirely incomplete, a supplier does not have the physical or legal means to withhold goods from individuals who receive a positive or negative benefit from their receipt. Clearly, goods and services vary substantially in the difficulty of excluding potential beneficiaries once the good is made available. This variation results both from the particular attributes of the good involved and the legal structure in which the transformation processes occur.

1.2 Public goods

In the case of *pure public goods*, there exists a shared outcome of production and distribution (whose value may be either positive, zero, or negative to recipients). Exclusion does not occur and consumption is nonsubtractable. When *all* individuals are affected by the provision of a public good – without crowding or subtracting from its availability – the public good is global. The availability of knowledge and gravity are examples of global public goods. Most public goods, however, have a scale of effects that is less than global. Local public goods include a subset of individuals, often as small as a household (sharing the lighting and heating in the household) or a neighborhood (sharing the security provided by the surveillance efforts of neighbors and a local police department).

Turning once again to transformation processes, the difficulties of exclusion lead to a fundamental problem to be solved in relation to public goods – that of provision (V. Ostrom, Tiebout, and Warren 1961).

> *Provision:* The articulation of demand, the arranging for production, and the supplying of funding/inputs necessary for production.

In *quid pro quo* market exchanges, all aspects of provision are accomplished as a by-product of a series of transactions. Buyers articulate their demands by selecting and purchasing those items they prefer. When beneficiaries are not excluded from appropriating, however, potential appropriators are not motivated to pay for the positive value they receive from the goods provided. If the value of the public good is negative, individual appropriators are not motivated to pay for the collective action required to reduce the negative public good. Underprovision (overprovision) occurs, implying an inefficient allocation of resources. This behavior, often referred to as free riding, leads to a fundamental proposition concerning the provision of public goods:

P1 *Without some form of coordination or organization to enable individuals to agree upon, monitor, and sanction the contributions of individuals to the provision of a public good with positive (negative) value, the good will be* underprovided *(overprovided).*

When the institutional setting is extremely sparse and yields equilibria that imply suboptimal outcomes, there is no theoretical challenge to this proposition. And we know of no evidence that contradicts it.[4] There is,

---

4. The experimental evidence presented later in this chapter suggests that even in some sparse settings the degree of suboptimality that is theoretically predicted may be overly "pessimistic."

however, considerable debate in the literature on two issues: the extent of suboptimality that results and the form of coordination or institutional setting that can overcome the suboptimal provision of public goods.

1.3 Common-pool resources

Common-pool resources (CPRs) are goods for which subtractability in units appropriated from and restricting access to the resource or facility is a nontrivial institutional problem. For CPRs, either appropriation or consumption (or both) occurs *within* a resource or facility. If the resource is a fishing grounds, one must fish in the grounds even though the tons of fish captured can then be bought and sold as private goods. If the CPR is a commonly provided and maintained irrigation system, water appropriated becomes a private good, but the facility itself must be provided and maintained. Further, allocation mechanisms for appropriating water must be crafted by those who govern the use of this facility.

Confusion often exists about the meaning of nonexclusion and subtractability as it applies to CPRs. One difficulty is that theorists are not always clear about what "the" good that was being accessed or appropriated is. Clarity is introduced by recognizing that jointly accessed or appropriated goods involve both a facility and a flow of services (or use units) from that facility (Blomquist and Ostrom 1985; E. Ostrom, Gardner, and Walker 1994). The facility, the flow of services to one individual, and the flow of services to other individuals may all potentially affect an individual's benefit stream.[5]

In the case of a market-produced private good, attention is generally focused on the attribute of the good that creates a benefit stream, that is, the flow of goods or services that one individual appropriates and uses. Appropriating and consuming these goods is not generally undertaken in a shared manner. The decoupling of production, appropriation and use, and the liability function that links appropriation eventually to production are basic reasons that private goods are not plagued with the panoply of collective action problems discussed in this chapter.

Finding the right mix of incentive-compatible institutional arrange-

---

5. Eitan Berglas (1981, 390) stresses that to understand the equilibrium conditions of the private provision of some club goods, "one has to distinguish between the manufacture of swimming pools and the services that swimming pools provide" (see also Berglas 1976). One might even wonder why these are not strictly private goods in the first place since exclusion is easy and consumption is rival. The collective aspect is the joint facility that must be utilized with others; deciding upon the appropriate size of membership and the rules of allocation is, however, a collective choice problem.

ments to provide the optimal facility and an acceptable rule system for defining appropriation rights is a difficult problem of collective action. Further, creating institutions to facilitate exclusion can range from the relatively simple to the impossible. The problem of exclusion must be solved by those who wish to utilize a large array of CPRs efficiently over the long run (E. Ostrom, Gardner, and Walker 1994). Such resources range from the global commons – generating joint benefits with reference to the stratosphere and biodiversity – to moderately sized fisheries, grazing lands, forests, irrigation systems, oil pools, and groundwater basins. At the other extreme, the users of many jointly used facilities, such as theaters, golf clubs, and toll roads, solve problems of exclusion at relatively low cost given the existence of particular legal rights and appropriate technologies. These goods have been called *club goods* (Buchanan 1965a; Cornes and Sandler 1986).

The *initial provision* of natural resources that have the incentive structure of a CPR may be nonproblematic. For example, nature has already provided fisheries, lakes, oceans, groundwater basins, and oil pools. The key problems for such collective action situations are the maintenance of the resource and the *appropriation* of the benefits. Frequently, individual users acting independently face temptations to overharvest from a CPR leading to the well-known "tragedy of the commons" (G. Hardin 1968). In other cases, individual users acting independently generate technological externalities for others or fight over the best sites located within a CPR. If no agreement exists about how to regulate the production technology or the quantity, timing, and location of harvesting a CPR, little incentive exists for individuals to take into account their adverse effects on each other or the resource. The problems associated with diverse externalities of appropriation lead to a second fundamental proposition concerning the independent appropriation of CPRs:

P2 *Without some form of coordination or organization to enable individuals to agree upon, monitor, and sanction the patterns of appropriation by individuals from a CPR, the resource will be* overused.

As with the first proposition, we know of no contradictory theoretical or empirical challenge. There are many open questions, however, about how coordination or organization can evolve and about whether one should impose market or state institutions on those who use CPRs.

1.4 Crafting institutions

To minimize the degree of suboptimal provision and appropriation, appropriators of collective goods may find recourse to the final three transformation processes – organization, monitoring, and sanctioning. These processes, which are related to rule orderings, are defined as:

> *Organization:* Devising rules and agreements about member-ship, distribution of obligations, and benefits, and about how future collective choice decisions will be made.
> *Monitoring:* Measuring inputs, outputs, and conformance to rules and agreements.
> *Sanctioning:* Allocating inducements or punishments related to conformance or lack thereof to agreements.

Farmers who jointly use an irrigation system, for example, must orga-nize a variety of provision activities primarily related to maintenance or watch their system deteriorate toward uselessness (Hilton 1992). Orga-nizing the provision side of an irrigation CPR involves deciding upon how many days a year should be devoted to routine maintenance, how work will be allocated to individual farmers, how emergency repairs should be handled, who is responsible for repairing broken embank-ments caused by grazing animals, and how new control gates and regula-tory devices are to be installed and paid for. Appropriation activities are closely linked to these provision activities. How much water is available for distribution is dependent upon whether a system is kept in good repair. The level of conflict over water distribution is apt to be higher on a poorly maintained system than on a well-maintained system. Organiz-ing the appropriation side of an irrigation CPR involves deciding upon the method of water allocation and the formulae for allocating water during the different seasons of the year (E. Ostrom 1992).

When individuals craft their own institutions, some arrangements are recorded on paper. Many however, are left unrecorded as problem-solving individuals try to do a better job in the future than was done in the past. In a democratic society, problem-solving individuals craft their own institutions all the time. Individuals also participate in less fluid decision-making arrangements (elections to select representatives, for example). Elected representatives may then engage in open, good-faith attempts to solve a wide diversity of problems brought to them by their constituents. It is also possible in a formal governance system where individuals are elected for patterns to emerge that are not strictly prob-lem solving. Incentives exist to create mechanisms whereby one set of individuals dominates others. Attempts to dominate and avoid being dominated increase the complexity of the processes by which new institu-tions are crafted.

Many activities of self-organization do not occur in formal decision-making arenas. Consequently, external public officials frequently presume that individuals in local settings cannot coordinate activities and thus face the suboptimalities predicted by the first and second fundamental propositions. The working rules that individuals develop are invisible to outsiders unless substantial time and effort is devoted to ascertaining their presence and structure.[6]

In legal systems where individuals have considerable autonomy to self-organize, they may develop rules of their own. These might be called customary rules, contracts, communal organizations, or associations. They are often referred to as "informal" by those who perceive governments as the source of all rules. Many of these locally devised rules would, however, be considered as binding if challenged in a court of law. Thus, calling them informal confuses these self-organized but legal rules with other self-organized but illegal rules. What is important for the analysis of collective action problems, however, is to recognize that individuals can consciously decide to adopt their own rules that either replace or complement the rules governing an initial collective action situation.

Once one recognizes that those involved in collective action may shift out of a current "game" to a deeper-level game, the necessity of using multiple levels of analysis becomes apparent. All rules are nested in another set of rules that if enforced defines how the first set of rules can be changed. Changes in the rules used to order action at one level occur within a currently "fixed" set of rules at a deeper level. Changes in deeper-level rules usually are more difficult and more costly to accomplish, thus increasing the stability of mutual expectations among individuals interacting according to a set of rules.

It is useful to distinguish three levels of rules that cumulatively affect the actions taken and the outcomes obtained in any setting (Kiser and Ostrom 1982):

1. *operational rules* directly affecting day-to-day decisions made by the participants in any setting,
2. *collective choice rules* affecting operational activities and out-

6. It is not always the case, however, that participants explain their actions to outsiders in the same way they explain them to fellow participants. Consequently, learning about the working rules used in a particular CPR may be very difficult. Further, rule following or conforming actions are not as predictable as biological or physical behavior explained by physical laws. Rules are formulated in human language. As such, rules share the problems of lack of clarity, misunderstanding, and change that typifies any language-based phenomenon. Words are "symbols that name, and thus, stand for classes of things and relationships" (V. Ostrom 1980, 312). Words are always simplifications of the phenomenon to which they refer (V. Ostrom 1991).

comes through their effects in determining who is eligible and the specific rules to be used in changing operational rules, and

3. *constitutional choice rules* affecting operational activities and their outcomes in determining who is eligible and the rules to be used in crafting the set of collective choice rules that in turn affect the set of operational rules.

At each level of analysis there may be one or more arenas in which decisions are made. Policymaking regarding the rules that will be used to regulate operational-level actions is usually carried out in one or more collective choice arenas and enforced at an operational level as well. Dilemmas are not limited to an operational level of analysis. They frequently occur at the collective choice and constitutional levels.

The art of crafting institutions can be viewed as one of creating coordinated strategies for players in multilevel games. Two types of coordinated strategies enable participants to extricate themselves from collective action dilemmas: one exists when individuals agree upon a joint strategy within a set of preexisting rules; another when an effort is made to change the rules themselves by moving to a collective choice or constitutional choice arena. The possibility of switching arenas is frequently ignored in current analyses of collective action problems.

There are two reasons why the possibility of changing the rules of a game have been ignored. The first is a methodological position that eliminates analysis of structural change while examining the effects of one structure on outcomes, in other words, the existing conditions that one uses to specify a problem for analysis are not to be changed in the process of analysis. It is easy to overcome this limit by overtly taking a long-term perspective. It is with a long-term perspective that the given constraints of a particular physical facility are changed into variables that can be changed and thus analyzed. A similar approach can be taken with rules. The second is the assumption that rules are a public good. Agreement on better rules affects all individuals in the group whether they participate in the reform effort or not. The temptation to free ride in the effort to craft new rules may be offset by the strong interest that most individuals have in ensuring that their own interests are taken into account in any set of new rules. Further, the group might be "privileged" in the sense that one or a very small group of individuals might expect such a high return from provision that they pay the full cost themselves (Olson 1965).

It is generally assumed that the higher the order of a collective action dilemma, the more difficult it is to solve. An even higher-order dilemma than a rule change is the dilemma involving monitoring and sanctioning to enforce a set of rules (Bendor and Mookherjee 1987; Bianco and Bates 1990). Even the best rules are rarely self-enforcing. It is usually the case that once most appropriators follow these rules, there are strong temptations for some appropriators to break them. If most farmers take only the legal amount of water from an irrigation system so that the system operates predictably, each farmer will be tempted from time to time to take more than a legal amount of water because his or her crops need water. Once some farmers take more than their allotment of water, others are tempted to do the same, and the agreed-upon rules rapidly crumble. Monitoring each other's activities and imposing sanctions are costly activities. Unless the rewards received by the individual who monitors and sanctions someone else are high enough, each potential monitor faces a situation in which not monitoring and not sanctioning may be the individually preferred strategy even though everyone would be better off if that strategy were not chosen (Weissing and Ostrom 1991, 1993). Designing monitoring and sanctioning arrangements that sustain themselves over time is a difficult task involved in transforming a collective action dilemma.

2. Evidence from field settings

Most of the emphasis in the public choice tradition has been on predicting behavior *within* the structure of a game, rather than on the processes of organizing new games and on self-monitoring and sanctioning activities.[7] Consequently, the literature from field settings concerned with organizing, monitoring, and sanctioning activities has been largely written by scholars in the fields of anthropology, sociology, history, and specialists who focus on one sector or one region. During the mid-1980s, an interdisciplinary panel was established by the National Academy of Sciences to examine common-property institutions and their performance in managing smaller-scale natural resources. Since the publication of the Panel's report (National Research Council 1986), a flurry of book-length publications has documented the extraordinary diversity of self-organized institutions operating at constitutional, collective choice, and operational levels, as well as situations in which the participants undertake most of their own organization, monitoring, and sanctioning activities.[8]

7. With the obvious exception of the work of James Buchanan and many colleagues who have been associated with Buchanan throughout the years. See in particular Buchanan and Tullock (1962) and Brennan and Buchanan (1985), as well as literature reviewed by Mueller in this volume.
8. See McCay and Acheson (1987); Fortmann and Bruce (1988); Wade (1988); Berkes (1989); Pinkerton (1989); Sengupta (1991); Blomquist (1992); Bromley et al. (1992); Dasgupta and Mäler (1992); Tang (1992); Thomson (1992); Netting (1993); and V. Ostrom, Feeny, and Picht (1993). See also the influential article by Feeny et al. (1990) and recent important works on property rights (Libecap 1989; Eggertsson 1990; Bromley 1991) that examine common-property institutions.

The most important findings regarding the emergence and consequences of self-organized institutional arrangements in field settings include the following:

1. Overuse, conflict, and potential destruction of *valuable* natural resources is likely to occur when users act independently due to lack of meaningful collective action or the inability to make credible commitments (Christy and Scott 1965; Anderson 1977; Libecap and Wiggins 1984).
2. Conditional on existing collective choice rules, overuse, conflict, and destruction can be substantially reduced through the crafting, implementation, and sustainment of alternative norms, rules, and property-rights systems (Schlager 1990; Tang 1992; Schlager and Ostrom 1993).
3. Locally selected systems of norms, rules, and property rights that are not recognized by external authorities may collapse if their legitimacy is challenged or if large exogenous economic or physical shocks undermine their foundations (Alexander 1982; Davis 1984; Cordell and McKean 1992).
4. Regulation by state authorities is effective in some settings, but is frequently less effective than regulation by local users – especially in relation to smaller-scale systems where user groups are stable and interact frequently in regard to the use of resources (Thomson 1977; Feeny 1988b; Gadgil and Iyer 1989; Lam, Lee, and Ostrom forthcoming).
5. Efforts to establish marketable property rights to natural resource systems have substantially increased efficiency in some cases (e.g., Jessup and Peluso, 1986; Blomquist, 1992) and encountered difficulties of implementation in others (e.g., Wilson 1982; Copes 1986; Townsend 1986; Townsend and Wilson 1987).

2.1 Design principles and robust institutions

In addition to knowing that various institutions can reduce the externalities involved in collective action arenas, we are also beginning to understand the design principles of robust institutions. *Robust institutions* are found in systems that have survived for long periods of time. Such institutions survive when operational rules are adapted in relation to a set of collective choice and constitutional choice rules (Shepsle 1989). There appear to be several key design principles found in robust institutions (these are summarized in Table 1). Evidence from the field suggests that *fragile institutions* tend to be characterized by only some of these design principles, though *failed institutions* are characterized by

Table 1. *Design principles illustrated by long-enduring CPR institutions*

1. Clearly defined boundaries
   Individuals or households with rights to withdraw resource units from the CPR and the boundaries of the CPR itself are clearly defined.
2. Congruence between appropriation and provision rules and local conditions
   Appropriation rules restricting time, place, technology, and/or quantity of resource units are related to local conditions and to provision rules requiring labor, materials, and/or money.
3. Collective choice arrangements
   Most individuals affected by operational rules can participate in modifying operational rules.
4. Monitoring
   Monitors, who actively audit CPR conditions and appropriator behavior, are accountable to the appropriators and/or are the appropriators themselves.
5. Graduated sanctions
   Appropriators who violate operational rules are likely to receive graduated sanctions (depending on the seriousness and context of the offense) from other appropriators, from officials accountable to these appropriators, or from both.
6. Conflict resolution mechanisms
   Appropriators and their officials have rapid access to low-cost, local arenas to resolve conflict among appropriators or between appropriators and officials.
7. Minimal recognition of rights to organize
   The rights of appropriators to devise their own institutions are not challenged by external governmental authorities.

For CPRs that are part of larger systems:

8. Nested enterprises
   Appropriation, provision, monitoring, enforcement, conflict resolution, and governance activities are organized in multiple layers of nested enterprises.

Source: E. Ostrom (1990, 90).

only a few (if any) of these principles. In addition, initial analysis from irrigation systems governed by farmers suggests that systems characterized by most of these principles are associated with higher agricultural yields and crop intensities – provided the physical characteristics of the systems are controlled for (Lam, Lee, and Ostrom forthcoming).[9]

9. For a theoretical discussion of why these design principles work in practice see Coward (1979); Siy (1982); Ruddle (1988); E. Ostrom (1990); E. Ostrom and Gardner (1993); and E. Ostrom, Gardner, and Walker (1994).

2.2 Factors affecting institutional change

Not only is there substantial variety in the institutions crafted to facilitate efficient use of resources across types of resources but it seems that neighboring systems that appear to face similar situations frequently adopt different institutional solutions. The variety of rules selected by individuals facing similar circumstances raises the question of whether institutional change is an evolutionary process in which more efficient institutions are selected over time.[10] If such an argument is correct, then to explain institutional change, one would have to analyze the specific relationships between variables characterizing the resource, the community of individuals involved, and the rules for making and changing rules.

The existing theoretical and empirical research on CPR situations enables one to specify several important variables that appear to be conducive to the development of institutions that increase efficiency:[11]

1. Accurate information – regarding the condition of the resource, provision costs, and consequences of appropriation – is technologically and economically feasible to obtain.
2. Users are relatively homogeneous in regard to asset structure, information, and preferences.
3. Users share a common understanding about the potential benefits and risks associated with the continuance of the status quo as opposed to alternative (feasible) options.
4. Users share generalized norms of reciprocity and trust that can be used as initial social capital.
5. The user group sharing the resource is relatively stable.
6. Users' discounting of future resource use is sufficiently low.
7. Users have the autonomy to craft operational rules that are supported by, and potentially enforced by, external authorities.
8. Users use collective choice rules that fall between the extremes of unanimity and control by a few, avoiding high transaction or high deprivation costs.
9. Users can develop relatively accurate and low-cost monitoring and sanctioning arrangements.

Many of these variables are in turn affected by the larger regime in which users are embedded. If the larger regime facilitates local self-organization by providing accurate information about natural resource systems, provides arenas in which participants can engage in discovery

---

10. See Gardner, Ostrom, and Walker (1993) for further discussion of this topic.
11. See E. Ostrom (1990); McKean (1992); and Schlager, Blomquist, and Tang (1994) for further discussion.

and conflict-resolution processes, and provides mechanisms that back up local monitoring and sanctioning efforts, the probability of participants adapting more effective norms and rules over time is higher than in regimes that either ignore resource problems entirely or, at the other extreme, presume that all decisions about governance and management must be made by central authorities.

The extensive evidence from field settings poses an initial challenge to our current theoretical understanding of the role of either states or markets in solving collective action problems. Many of the institutions that are designed by those directly involved in appropriating from a CPR use elements frequently associated with markets (such as auctions or transferable rights to the use units generated by a CPR). But on close examination, these institutions are not fully market institutions since entry and exit into the "market" is strictly controlled and a group of individuals jointly owns or manages the resource or facility itself. Furthermore, many of these self-organized institutions use elements frequently associated with states (such as the election of officials who prepare budgets, make rules), monitor conformance to rules, and sanction those who break these rules. But, they are not fully state institutions either, since they exist in a polycentric system involving many public organizations all with varying levels of autonomy and organized in a nested manner at many scales. In some instances, the self-organized institutions are not even recognized by state officials. In others, these self-organized institutions may come close to being outlaw organizations, since their activities are contrary to what is written in formal legislation or administrative regulations.

3. Public goods and CPRs: Experimental evidence

Turning from the field to the laboratory allows a closer look at the strategic nature and behavior in collective action situations. While research in field settings is essential for understanding the effect of institutions in diverse physical, social, and economic settings, it is exactly the diversity of these settings that makes it difficult to understand which of many variables account for differences in observed behavior. Laboratory experiments are particularly useful for testing well-specified models of behavior where one variable at a time can be changed and control is therefore enhanced. In parameterizing experiments, the experimenter controls: (1) the number of participants, (2) the positions they may hold, (3) the specific actions they can take, (4) the outcomes they can effect, (5) how actions are linked to outcomes, (6) the information they obtain, and (7) the potential payoffs. That is, the experimenter creates the institutions that structure the decision situation facing the subjects.

A key step in linking a theoretical model to laboratory conditions is inducing incentives. That is, the laboratory situation must lead the subjects to perceive and act on payoffs that have the same properties as the payoffs in the linked theoretical model. Value over alternative outcomes is most commonly induced using a cash reward structure. As discussed by Smith (1982), the following conditions constitute a set of sufficient conditions for inducing values:

> *Nonsatiation:* Subjects' utility must be monotone-increasing in payoffs. This guarantees that given alternatives that are identical except in payoff space, a subject will always choose the alternative with the greater reward.
>
> *Saliency:* For rewards to be motivationally relevant, or *salient,* their level must be directly tied to participants' decisions.
>
> *Dominance:* An important element of the economic environment is the subjects' utility functions, which contain many arguments in addition to the rewards associated with payoffs. To induce value successfully, the cash reward structure must dominate the subjective benefits and costs of an action derived from these other utility function arguments.
>
> *Privacy:* Subjects may not be autonomous own-reward maximizers. To the extent allowed by the underlying theoretical model under investigation, subjects' payoffs should be made private.

While a laboratory situation can be designed to match a theoretical model closely, it cannot be expected to parallel far more complex naturally occurring settings to which the theoretical model may also be applied. Nevertheless, to the extent that a logically consistent model is put forward as a useful explanation of naturally occurring phenomena, laboratory experimental methods offer the advantage of control, observation, and measurement.

3.1 Decision settings: Stark institutions

Our discussion of laboratory studies applied to public goods and CPR decision situations begins with two "stark" institutional settings referred to as the "Voluntary Contributions Mechanism" in the case of public goods and the "CPR Appropriation Game" in the case of CPRs. The term "stark" is used to emphasize that the institutional settings of these decision situations are null in regard to subjects' ability to coordinate decisions overtly or create an alternative institutional situation. This discussion draws substantially on the work found in Isaac, Walker, and Williams ([1994], hereafter IWW) and E. Ostrom, Gardner, and Walker ([1994], hereafter OGW).[12]

The voluntary contributions mechanism (VCM). In the VCM decision setting, N subjects participate in a series of decision rounds. Each participant is endowed with z tokens that are to be divided between a "private account" and a "group account." Tokens cannot be carried across rounds. The subject is informed that for each token she places in the private account she earns p cents with certainty. The subject is also informed that earnings from the group account are dependent upon the decisions of all group members. For a given round, let X represent the sum of tokens placed in the group account by all individuals in the group. Earnings from the group account are dependent upon the preassigned earnings function $G(X)$. Each individual receives earnings from the group account regardless of whether she allocates tokens to that account – thus the publicness of the group account. For simplicity, each individual is symmetric with respect to her earnings from the group account. Each earns an equal amount from the group account of $[G(X)]/N$ cents. Figure 1 illustrates the type of information subjects receive for a given parameterization of the game. Prior to the start of each decision round, each individual knows the number of remaining rounds and the groups' aggregate token endowment for prior rounds. The decisions for each round are binding and rewards are based on the sum of earnings from all rounds. During each round, subjects can view their personal token allocations, earnings, and total tokens placed in the group account for all previous rounds.

The CPR appropriation game. Contrast the VCM public goods provision game with the CPR appropriation game. In the appropriation game, subjects are instructed that in each decision round they are endowed with a given number of tokens that they can invest in two markets. Market 1 is described as an investment opportunity in which each token yields a fixed (constant) rate of output and each unit of output yields a fixed (constant) return. Market 2 (the CPR) is described as a market that yields a rate of output per token dependent upon the total number of tokens invested by the entire group. Subjects receive a level of output from market 2 that is equivalent to the percentage of total group tokens

---

12. For other related studies, see for example Marwell and Ames (1979, 1980, 1981); Isaac, Walker, and Thomas (1984); Kim and Walker (1984); Isaac, McCue, and Plott (1985); Isaac and Walker (1988b, 1993); Andreoni (1989, 1993); Brookshire, Coursey, and Redington (1989); Dorsey (1992); Asch, Gigliotti, and Polito (1993); Chan et al. (1993); Fisher et al. (1993); Palfrey and Prisby (1993); Sefton and Steinberg (1993); Ledyard (1995a); and Laury, Walker, and Williams (1995).

Round 1 currently in progress

Your endowment of tokens in each round: 50 ; Group size: 10
Total group endowment of tokens in each round: 500
Each token retained in your Private account earns: $ 0.01

Examples of possible earnings from the Group Account

Tokens in Group Account (from the entire group)	Total Group Earnings	Your 10% Share of Group Earnings
0	$ 0.000	$ 0.000
31	$ 0.930	$ 0.093
63	$ 1.890	$ 0.189
94	$ 2.820	$ 0.282
125	$ 3.750	$ 0.375
156	$ 4.680	$ 0.468
188	$ 5.640	$ 0.564
219	$ 6.570	$ 0.657
250	$ 7.500	$ 0.750
281	$ 8.430	$ 0.843
313	$ 9.390	$ 0.939
344	$ 10.320	$ 1.032
375	$ 11.250	$ 1.125
406	$ 12.180	$ 1.218
438	$ 13.140	$ 1.314
469	$ 14.070	$ 1.407
500	$ 15.000	$ 1.500

-HELP→ review instructions.
-LAB→ view the earnings from the Group Account for any possible value of "Tokens in Group Account."
How many tokens do you wish to place in the Group Account?≫

Figure 1. Illustration of VCM decision problem.

they invest. Subjects furthermore know that each unit of output from market 2 yields a fixed (constant) rate of return. Figure 2 illustrates the type of information subjects see in a given parameterization of the game. Subjects know the total number of decision makers in the group, total group tokens, and that endowments are identical.

3.2 Behavior in stark settings

The discussion below focuses on several regularities from an extensive program of experimental investigations related to VCM and the CPR appropriation game. Results are reported as summary observations with emphasis placed on the relationship between behavior and game theoretic predictions for noncooperative games of complete information.

Units produced and cash return from investments in market 2 commodity 2
value per unit = $ 0.01

Tokens invested by group	Units of commodity 2 produced	Total group return	Average return per token	Additional return per token
8	168	$ 1.68	$ 0.21	$ 0.21
16	304	$ 3.04	$ 0.19	$ 0.17
24	408	$ 4.08	$ 0.17	$ 0.13
32	480	$ 4.80	$ 0.15	$ 0.09
40	520	$ 5.20	$ 0.13	$ 0.05
48	528	$ 5.28	$ 0.11	$ 0.01
56	504	$ 5.04	$ 0.09	$−0.03
64	448	$ 4.48	$ 0.07	$−0.07
72	360	$ 3.60	$ 0.05	$−0.11
80	240	$ 2.40	$ 0.03	$−0.15

The table shown above displays information on investments in market 2 at
various levels of group investment. Your return from market 2 depends on
what percentage of the total group investment is made by you. Market 1 returns you one unit of commodity 1 for each token you invest in market 1. Each
unit of commodity 1 pays you $ 0.05.

Figure 2. Illustration of CPR decision problem.

Theory and behavior in VCM. The strategic nature of the VCM decision
problem is straightforward. Each participant's decision to allocate a
marginal token to the group account costs that individual p cents. For
appropriate initializations, however, allocations to the group account
yield a positive gain in group surplus of $[G'(\cdot) - p]$. In the VCM mechanism, the marginal per capita return from the group account (MPCR) is
defined as the ratio of "$" benefits to costs for moving a single token
from the individual to the group account, or $[G'(\cdot)/N]/p$. In the experiments that we focus upon here, $p = \$.01$ and G' is a constant greater
than $.01$ so that the Pareto optimum (defined simply as the outcome
that maximizes group earnings) is for each individual to place all tokens
in the group account. On the other hand, the single-period dominant
strategy is for each individual to place zero tokens in the group account.
The "social dilemma" follows strategically because p and $G(\cdot)$ are
chosen so that the MPCR < 1. For finitely repeated play, the outcome of
zero allocations to the group account is also the unique, backward induction, complete information Nash equilibrium. In summary, for all parameterizations in which MPCR < 1, complete information noncooperative game theory yields the same prediction – zero allocations to the

group account. In actuality, behavior is affected by the specific parameterizations of the setting.

Figure 3 portrays the type of behavior that is "typical" for VCM experiments with group size of $N = 10$ and MPCR $= .30$. Shown are allocations to the group account as a percentage of optimum across decision rounds. In the upper panel, average decisions are shown for a series of experiments in which subjects received (did not receive) additional information on the consequences of alternative individual and group decisions. In summary, the additional information explained to subjects how an individual and how the group could maximize and/or minimize their experimental earnings. Note the lack of any strong effect of this treatment condition. In the lower panels, results are shown from several experiments using highly experienced VCM subjects and a larger number of decision rounds.

For groups of size 4, 10, 40, and 100, experiments reported by IWW yield the following conclusions:

1. Depending upon specific parameterizations, replicable behavior is observed where allocations are very near the predicted outcome of zero allocations to the group account or are significantly above zero allocations to the group account.
2. Allocations to the group account are either unaffected by MPCR or are inversely related to MPCR.
3. Holding MPCR constant, allocations to the group account are either unaffected by group size or are *positively* related to group size.
4. Increasing group size in conjunction with a *sufficient* decrease in MPCR leads to lower allocations to the group account.
5. There tends to be some decay (but generally incomplete) to the predicted outcome of zero allocations to the group account.
6. Even with a richer information set regarding the implications of alternative allocation decisions, highly experienced subject groups continue to follow a pattern of behavior generally inconsistent with the predictions of the complete information Nash model.
7. Inconsistent with models of learning, the rate of decay of allocations to the group account is inversely related to the number of decision rounds.

Theory and behavior in the CPR. In the experimental investigations reported by OGW, the CPR is operationalized with eight appropriators ($n = 8$) and quadratic production functions $F(\Sigma x_i)$ for market 2, where

$$F(\Sigma x_i) = a\Sigma x_i - b(\Sigma x_i)^2$$

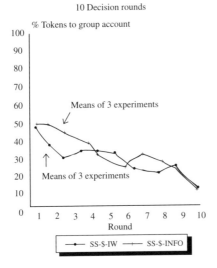

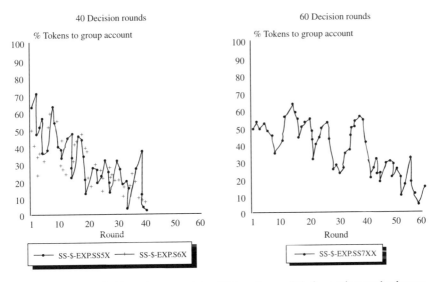

Figure 3. Experiments with additional payoff information and a larger number of decision rounds. *Source:* Isaac, Walker, and Williams (1994).

Table 2. *Experimental design baseline: Parameters for a given decision period*

Experiment type:	Low endowment	High endowment
Number of subjects	8	8
Individual token endowment	10	25
Production function: Mkt.2[a]	$23(\Sigma x_i) - .25(\Sigma x_i)^2$	$23(\Sigma x_i) - .25(\Sigma x_i)^2$
Market 2 return/unit of output	$.01	$.01
Market 1 return/unit of output	$.05	$.05
Earnings/subject at group max.[b]	$.91	$.83
Earnings/subject at Nash equil.	$.66	$.70
Earnings/subject at zero rent	$.50	$.63

[a] Σx_i = the total number of tokens invested by the group in market 2. The production function shows the number of units of output produced in market 2 for each level of tokens invested in market 2.
[b] In the high-endowment design, subjects were paid in cash one-half of their "computer" earnings. Amounts shown are potential cash payoffs.

with $F'(0) = a > w$ and $F'(ne) = a - 2bne < 0$, where w is the per token return from market 1, n is the number of subjects, and e is individual token endowments. Their analysis uses the parameter specifications summarized in Table 2. Subjects are endowed each round with either 10 or 25 tokens depending upon design conditions. With these payoff parameters, a group investment of 36 tokens yields the optimal level of investment. The complete information noncooperative Nash equilibrium is for each subject to invest 8 tokens in market 2 (regardless of the endowment condition) – for a total group investment in market 2 of 64 tokens.[13]

Much of the discussion of experimental results for the CPR game focuses on what is termed "Maximum Net Yield" from the CPR. This measure captures the degree of optimal yield earned from the CPR. Specifically, net yield is the return from market 2 minus the opportunity costs of tokens invested in market 2 divided by the optimal return from market 2 minus the opportunity costs of tokens invested in market 2 at the optimum. For the CPR game, opportunity costs equal the potential return that could have been earned by investing the tokens in market 1. Dissipation of yield from the CPR is known in the resource literature as "rent" dissipation. Note, as with the symmetric Nash equilibrium, optimal net yield is invariant to the level of subjects' endowments across the

---

13. See E. Ostrom, Gardner, and Walker (1994) for details of the derivation of this game equilibrium.

two designs OGW examine. Thus, even though the range for subject investment decisions is increased with an increase in subjects' endowments, the equilibrium and optimal levels of investment are not altered. At the Nash equilibrium, subjects earn 39 percent of maximum net yield from the CPR.

Figure 4 presents data from a series of CPR experiments in which individual token endowments were either 10 or 25. Displayed is average net yield from the CPR as a percentage of optimum across decision rounds. The data in these panels are typical of the "baseline" experiments reported by OGW, leading to the following summary observations:

1. Subjects make investment allocations to market 2 (the CPR) well above optimum leading to significant "rent" dissipation.
2. Investments in market 2 are characterized by a "pulsing" pattern in which investments are increased leading to a reduction in yield, at which time investors tend to reduce their investments in market 2 and yields increase. This pattern reoccurs across decision rounds within an experiment, with a tendency for the variation across rounds to diminish as the experiment continues.
3. Investment behavior is affected by token endowments. Yields as a percentage of optimum are less in 25-token experiments than in 10-token experiments.
4. The Nash equilibrium is the best predictor of *aggregate* outcomes for low-endowment experiments. In the high-endowment setting, aggregate behavior is far from Nash in early rounds but approaches Nash in later rounds. However, at the individual decision level, there is virtually no evidence that behavior converges to the Nash equilibrium.

In an alternative design, Walker and Gardner (1992, hereafter WG) alter the CPR decision setting to add "probabilistic destruction" as one consequence of overinvestment in the CPR. In one of their designs, destruction implies the experiment ends – there is no further opportunity for earning money. A safe appropriation zone is created by allowing for a minimal level of appropriation for which the probability of destruction is zero. For market 2 investments above the minimum "threshold" level, the probability of destruction increases monotonically. In the design investigated by WG, the threshold appropriation level is set at a point that generates near optimum investments – 100 percent net yield. This threshold becomes one equilibrium for the game. There is, however, another subgame perfect equilibrium in which overinvestment occurs, yielding an expected return of less than 25 percent of optimum. Interestingly, in their stark institutional setting with no overt possibilities for coordination, WG find that subjects do not tend to coordinate on the

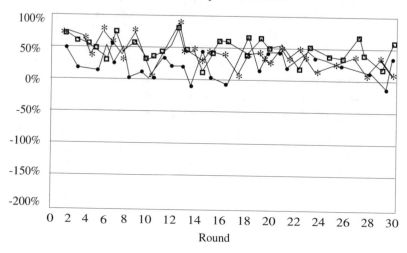

Average net yield as a percentage of maximum
10 - Token parameterization

25 - Token parameterization

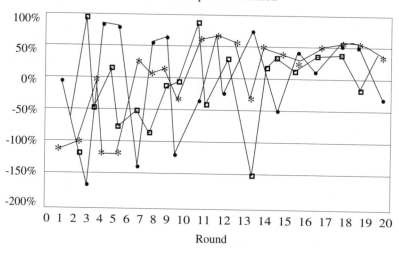

Figure 4. Individual baseline experiments. *Source:* E. Ostrom, Gardner, and Walker (1994).

best equilibrium. In every experimental session the CPR is destroyed and, in most cases, rather quickly. The consequence of this destruction is a significant loss in yield from the resource.

VCM and CPR behavior: Puzzles. The results summarized above offer several puzzles from the perspective of noncooperative game theory. In the VCM environment, especially for some parameterizations that are inconsequential from the perspective of the theory, there is just "too much" cooperative play. What aspects of the VCM game are fostering the degree of cooperation exhibited and what explains the interaction between the level of cooperation, MPCR, and group size? In the CPR environment, game theory does a pretty good job of explaining aggregate behavior (especially with repetition of the game). On the other hand, game theory predicts no endowment effect, but the data clearly show one. Finally, the subjects used in both of these decision settings are drawn from the same sampling population. What might explain the tendency for what appears to be greater cooperative play in the VCM game in comparison to the CPR game?

In their efforts to explain discrepancies between the theory and the data, IWW consider learning and/or the failure of backward induction. Their experiments with richer information sets and longer game horizons suggest, however, that there is more going on than just learning the consequences of alternative strategies. Complementing this research, Laury, Walker, and Williams (1995) investigate the VCM decision setting in an operationalization in which (1) group members' identity is anonymous and (2) subjects' decisions and earnings are anonymous to other group members and the experimenters. Their results, however, parallel those reported by IWW. Anonymity (or the lack of) does not appear to be a significant variable that can be used to explain behavior in the VCM decision setting.

It is interesting to consider the "knife edged" prediction of the theory for the VCM game. If the MPCR > 1, a 100 percent allocation of all tokens to the group good is the single period dominant strategy. If the MPCR < 1, zero allocations of tokens to the group good is the single-period dominant strategy. On the other hand, in experimental payoff space, if the MPCR is near 1, the payoff consequences of different strategies are minimal from an individual's perspective but can be great from that of the group's perspective. The greater the MPCR, the greater the gains from some form of group (subgroup) cooperation. Further, holding MPCR constant, in any public goods setting, increasing group size increases the gains from the group achieving some form of tacit cooperation.

In an attempt to model MPCR and group size overtly as an artifact of the game that may affect behavior, several modeling approaches have been suggested. Ledyard (1995a) proposes an equilibrium model in which individuals "get some satisfaction (a warm glow) from participating in a group that implicitly and successfully cooperates." In modeling a "warm glow," Ledyard's assumption is related to the work of Andreoni (1989). Individuals are distinguished by types, based upon the strength of their "warm glow" preferences.[14] Under certain assumptions on the population distribution of preferences, Ledyard finds that (1) there can be deviations from complete free riding even in a single-shot game and (2) individuals will be more likely to deviate from complete free riding in large groups.

Miller and Andreoni (1991) present a model based on the adaptive behavior of replicator dynamics. Their approach is consistent with the findings of IWW that the percentage of tokens allocated to the group account appears to be directly related to both group size and MPCR. On the other hand, while the replicator dynamic approach also predicts decay toward complete free riding, it does not explain behavior in which the rate of decay is inversely related to the number of replications of the decision setting.

IWW propose a "forward" looking model of behavior in which players allocate tokens toward the group good in an effort to solicit cooperation. The approach is composed of three principle components: (1) the assumption that individual i believes her decisions have signaling content to others, (2) a benchmark earnings level for measuring the success of signaling, and (3) the formulation of a subjective probability function for evaluating the likelihood of success. In this model, ceteris paribus, the likelihood that a signal (allocations to the group account) succeeds increases with both group size and MPCR and rate of decay in group allocations is inversely related to number of replications of the game.

One explanation for the discrepancy between theory and data in both VCM and CPR games may be that the theory accounts for the behavior of many individuals, but not *all*. The play of these "nontheoretical" players prevents convergence to a theoretical equilibrium, and the impact of such players can be decision setting and institution specific. Contrast, for example, the low-endowment CPR game with the high-endowment game. Assume that in the CPR game, some players are trying implicitly to reach a cooperative solution to the game. Noncooperative players reap (at least short-term) benefits from taking advantage

---

14. Also see Palfrey and Rosenthal (1988) where they model "uncontrolled preferences" that derive from "acts of social cooperation or contribution, the utility of altruism, or social duty."

of such players by investing more heavily in the CPR. In the low-endowment game, however, there are clear constraints on an *individual's* ability to unilaterally defeat (take advantage of) such an attempt. In the high-endowment parameterization, an individual's strategic "leverage" is increased. One or two players can invest sufficiently in the CPR to take full advantage of attempts at cooperation, yielding an aggregate result that is near the deficient game equilibrium. Now consider the VCM game. Especially for large groups and/or high MPCR parameterizations, an individual has very limited strategic leverage to take advantage of cooperative attempts. It is the strategic decision space of the VCM game that differs fundamentally from that of the CPR game. For example, if in the VCM game, players could either contribute toward provision or appropriate tokens that have been contributed by others, the strategy space of the game would be altered in such a way that a noncooperative player could more readily offset attempts at cooperation by others.

Understanding the linkages and discrepancies between the data and theory for these stark institutional settings remains an important goal for future research in collective action decision settings. But results from field settings suggest that equally important is behavior in settings that are institutionally richer than the stark settings discussed above. Considerable experimental research has been undertaken using more complex institutions. We summarize part of this research to give the reader an idea of the types of institutional settings that may significantly alter individual decisions in collective action arenas.

3.3 Behavior in richer institutional settings

Face-to-face communication. The effect of communication in collective action situations is open to considerable debate. Words alone are viewed by many as frail constraints when individuals make private, repetitive decisions between short-term, profit-maximizing strategies and strategies negotiated by a verbal agreement.[15] The inability to make enforceable agreements is at the core of the distinction between cooperative and noncooperative theories for:

> the decisive question is whether the players can make enforceable agreements, and it makes little difference whether they are allowed to talk to each other. Even if they are free to talk and to negotiate an agreement, this fact will be of no real help if the agreement has little chance of being kept. An ability to negotiate agreements is useful only

---

15. See E. Ostrom, Walker, and Gardner (1992) for further discussion of this topic.

if the rules of the game make such agreements binding and enforceable. (Harsanyi and Selten 1988, 3)[16]

Thus, much of contemporary, noncooperative game theory treats the ability to communicate as inessential and unlikely to change results unless the individuals involved can call on external agents to enforce agreements.[17]

Studies of repetitive collective action situations in field settings, however, show that individuals in many settings adopt cooperative strategies that enhance their joint payoffs without the presence of external enforcers. Many situational factors appear to affect the capacity to arrive at and maintain agreed-upon play. The ability to communicate appears to be a necessary but not a sufficient condition. Experimental research on face-to-face communication has shown this mechanism to be a powerful tool for enhancing efficiency. As Dawes states, "The salutary effects of communication on cooperation are ubiquitous" (1980, 185).[18] Hypotheses forwarded to explain why communication increases the selection of cooperative strategies identify a process that communication is posited to facilitate: (1) offering and extracting promises, (2) changing the expectations of others' behavior, (3) changing the payoff structure, (4) reenforcing of prior normative orientations, and (5) developing of a group identity. Experimental examination of communication has demonstrated

16. Harsanyi and Selten (1988, 3) add that in real life, "agreements may be enforced externally by courts of law, government agencies, or pressure from public opinion; they may be enforced internally by the fact that the players are simply unwilling to violate agreements on moral grounds and know that this is the case." To model self-commitment using noncooperative game theory, the ability to break the commitment is removed by trimming the branches that emanate from a self-commitment move to remove any alternative contrary to that which has been committed. In a lab setting, this would mean changing the structure of the alternatives made available to subjects after an agreement (which was not done).

17. Self-commitment is also possible, but whether the agreement is backed by external agents or self-commitment, the essential condition is that all branches of the game tree are removed that correspond to moves violating the agreement that has been made (Harsanyi and Selten 1988, 4). In the lab, this would mean that the experimenters would reprogram the experiment so that no more than the agreed upon number of tokens could be invested in the CPR. This condition was never imposed in the laboratory experiments. In the field, this would mean that some action was taken to remove the feasibility of certain types of activities – an almost impossible task.

18. Among the studies showing a positive effect of the capacity to communicate are Jerdee and Rosen (1974); Caldwell (1976); Dawes, McTavish, and Shaklee (1977); Edney and Harper (1978); Braver and Wilson (1984, 1986); Dawes, Orbell, and van de Kragt (1984); Kramer and Brewer (1986); van de Kragt et al. (1986); Bornstein and Rapoport (1988); Isaac and Walker (1988a, 1991); Bornstein et al. (1989); Orbell, Dawes, and van de Kragt (1990); Orbell, van de Kragt, and Dawes (1991); E. Ostrom and Walker (1991); and Hackett, Schlager, and Walker (1994).

the independent effect of all five of these processes, but they also appear to reenforce one another in an interactive manner.[19] Prior research that relied on signals exchanged via computer terminals rather than face-to-face communication has not had the same impact on behavior. Sell and Wilson (1991, 1992), whose experimental design allowed participants in a public good experiment to signal a promise to cooperate via their terminals, found much less sustained cooperation than reported for face-to-face communication.

A deeper examination of the role of communication in facilitating the selection and retention of efficient strategies is thus of considerable theoretical (as well as policy) interest.[20] The summary below focuses primarily on the findings from a series of experiments in which face-to-face communication was operationalized (without the presence of external enforcement) in the CPR appropriation environment of OGW.[21] The role of communication and its success in fostering outcomes more in line with social optimality is investigated in settings in which (1) the communication mechanism is provided as a costless one-shot opportunity, (2) the communication mechanism is provided as a costless opportunity on a repeated basis, and (3) the subjects face a dilemma of having to provide the communication mechanism in a voluntary contribution decision environment.

The procedure for operationalizing costless face-to-face communication in the laboratory generally follows a protocol similar to the following announcement used by OGW for a one-shot opportunity to communicate:

> Some participants in experiments like this have found it useful to have the opportunity to discuss the decision problem you face. You will be given ten minutes to hold such a discussion. You may discuss anything you wish during your ten-minute discussion period, with the following restrictions. (1) You are not allowed to discuss side payments. (2) You are not allowed to make physical threats. (3) You are not allowed to see the private information on anyone's monitor.

If the experimental design calls for repeated opportunities to communicate, the subjects are told that after each decision round they will return

---

19. Orbell, van de Kragt, and Dawes (1988) summarize the findings from ten years of research on one-shot public good experiments by stressing both the independent and interdependent nature of the posited factors explaining why communication has such a powerful effect on rates of cooperation.
20. See Banks and Calvert (1992a, 1992b) for an important discussion of the theoretical significance of communication in incomplete information games.
21. See E. Ostrom and Walker (1991) and Isaac and Walker (1991) for a more detailed discussion of the role of communication and the experimental evidence summarized here.

to a common area and have further opportunities to discuss the decision problem.

The results of face-to-face communication reported by OGW can be summarized as follows:

1. Subjects in repeated, high-endowment CPR games, with one and only one opportunity to communicate, obtain an average percentage of net yield above that obtained in baseline experiments in the same decision rounds without communication (55 percent compared to 21 percent).
2. Subjects in repeated, high-endowment CPR games, with *repeated opportunities* to communicate, obtain an average percentage of net yield that is substantially above that obtained in baseline experiments without communication (73 percent compared to 21 percent). In low-endowment games, the average net yield is 99 percent as compared to 34 percent.
3. Repeated communication opportunities in high-endowment games lead to higher joint outcomes (73 percent) than one-shot communication (55 percent), as well as lower defection rates (13 percent compared to 25 percent).
4. In no experiment where one or more subjects deviated from an agreed-upon joint strategy, did the other subjects then follow a grim trigger strategy of substantially increasing their investments in the CPR.

The OGW experiments summarized above focused on situations in which individuals were homogeneous in decision attributes. It is possible that the strong efficiency-enhancing properties of face-to-face communication are dependent upon homogeneities in decision attributes. In fact, the literature provides several arguments that point to heterogeneity as a serious deterrent to cooperation (R. Hardin 1982; Johnson and Libecap 1982; Libecap and Wiggins 1984; Wiggins and Libecap 1985, 1987; Isaac and Walker 1988a; E. Ostrom 1990; Kanbur 1992; Hackett 1992). For example, Kanbur argues, "theory and evidence would seem to suggest that cooperative agreements are more likely to come about in groups that are homogeneous in the relevant economic dimension, and they are more likely to break down as heterogeneity along this dimension increases" (1992, 21–2).

The task of agreeing to and sustaining agreements is more difficult for heterogeneous individuals because of the distributional conflict associated with alternative sharing rules. In heterogeneous settings, different sharing rules generally produce different distributions of earnings across individuals. While all individuals may be made better off by cooperating, some benefit more than others, depending upon the sharing rule chosen. Consequently, individuals may fail to cooperate on the adoption of a sharing rule because they cannot agree upon what would constitute a fair distribution of benefits produced by cooperating.[22]

Hackett, Schlager, and Walker (1994, hereafter HSW), building on the experimental research of OGW, examine the CPR decision setting with heterogeneous players. Heterogeneity is introduced by varying the input endowments of the subjects. Heterogeneities in endowments imply that alternative rules adopted to reduce overappropriation from the CPR will have differential effects on earnings across subjects. HSW find that, even with heterogeneity, face-to-face communication remains a very effective institution for increasing efficiency. Investigating two designs, one in which heterogeneities in endowments were assigned randomly and one in which they were assigned through an auction mechanism, both treatment conditions led to significant increases in net yield over baseline (no-communication) conditions. With noncommunication, HSW report a level of net yield relatively close to that predicted by the Nash equilibrium for their designs (48.9 percent). With communication, overall yield increases to over 94 percent on average in both designs.

The opportunity to communicate in a CPR dilemma situation can be viewed as enabling individuals to coordinate strategies to solve the first order CPR dilemma. In the field, providing such an institution for communication would require costly investments on the part of group members. E. Ostrom and Walker (1991) report results from a set of experiments in which the opportunity to communicate became a costly public good that subjects had to first provide through voluntary (anonymous) contributions. The provision mechanism imposed on the right to communicate placed subjects in a second order public good dilemma (with a provision point). Second order dilemma games exist whenever individuals must expend resources to provide a mechanism that may alter the strategic nature of a first order dilemma game (Oliver 1980; Taylor 1987).[23] The results reported in E. Ostrom and Walker (1991) can be summarized as follows:

> The provision problem players faced in the costly communication experiments was not trivial and did in fact create a barrier. In all experiments with costly communication, the problem of providing the institution for communication diminished the success of either: (a) having the ability to develop a coordinated strategy and/or (b) dealing with players who

22. Hackett (1992) suggests that heterogeneous resource endowments can lead to disagreement over the supply and implementation of rules that allocate access to CPRs.
23. Yamagishi (1986, 1988) examines the imposition of sanctioning to change the structure of a simple public good dilemma situation.

cheated on a previous agreement. On the other hand, all groups succeeded to some degree in providing the communication mechanism and in dealing with the CPR dilemma. On average, efficiency in these groups increased from approximately 42 percent to 80 percent.

In general, these results are consistent with research on public goods reported by Isaac and Walker (1988a, 1991). They found face-to-face communication as a very effective mechanism in facilitating increased efficiency in the VCM decision setting. Further, increasing the complexity of the environment by making communication a costly second order public good reduced the success of face-to-face communication, but even with this reduction, the institution remained a successful mechanism for improving allocative efficiency.

Sanctioning. As we have found in both field and laboratory settings, nonbinding, face-to-face communication can be a very effective institution for facilitating cooperation. In some instances, such as those in which the high endowments of players lead to very strong temptations to defect on a verbal agreement, the nonbinding character of the institution can be problematic. Further, no well-specified theoretical model explains the diverse types of sanctioning behavior observed in field settings. In many instances, theory predicts that individuals will not self-monitor or impose sanctions on others that are costly on the sanctioner. Understanding internally imposed monitoring and sanctioning behavior more thoroughly provides a key to understanding endogenous solutions to collective action dilemmas. OGW report the results from several experiments in which a sanctioning institution was exogenously imposed on decision makers and several face-to-face communication experiments in which the opportunity to use a sanctioning institution was an endogenous decision for the group of decision makers.

The sanctioning mechanism investigated by OGW required that each subject incur a cost (a fee) to sanction another. OGW found in experiments with an imposed sanctioning institution and no communication:

1. Significantly more sanctioning occurs than predicted by subgame perfection, and the frequency is inversely related to cost.
2. Sanctioning is primarily focused on heavy market 2 (CPR) investors. However, there is a nontrivial amount of sanctioning that can be classified as error, lagged punishment, or "blind" revenge.
3. Average net yield increases from 21 percent with no sanctioning to 37 percent with sanctioning. When the costs of fees and fines are subtracted from average net yield, however, net yield drops to 9 percent.

Thus, subjects overused the sanctioning mechanism, and sanctioning without communication reduced net yield. In experiments where communication and sanctioning was combined, on the other hand, the results are quite positive. OGW report that:

1. With an imposed sanctioning mechanism and a single opportunity to communicate, subjects achieve an average net yield of 85 percent. When the costs of fees and fines are subtracted, average net yield is still 67 percent. These represent substantial gains over baseline where net yield averaged 21 percent.
2. With the right to choose a sanctioning mechanism and a single opportunity to communicate, subjects who adopt a sanctioning mechanism achieve an average net yield of 93 percent. When the costs of fees and fines are subtracted, average net yield is still 90 percent. In addition, the defection rate from agreements is only 4 percent.
3. With the right to choose a sanctioning mechanism and a single opportunity to communicate, subjects who do not adopt a sanctioning mechanism achieve an average net yield of only 56 percent. In addition, the defection rate from agreements is 42 percent.

Thus, subjects who use the opportunity to communicate and agree upon a joint strategy and choose their own sanctioning mechanism achieve close to optimal results based entirely on the promises they make, their own efforts to monitor, and their own investments in sanctioning. This is especially impressive in the high-endowment environment, where defection by a few subjects is very disruptive.

Public good settings with provision points. One useful method for organizing collective action experiments is to partition experiments along two conditions: (1) settings with a unique Nash equilibrium yielding suboptimal provision and (2) settings based on more complex parameterizations or with contribution-facilitating mechanisms that yield multiple equilibria.

One direct way of changing the public goods decision setting is to investigate provision where the public goods are discrete (provision point or step function public goods). Such experimental situations have naturally occurring counterparts in decision settings in which a minimum level of provision support is necessary for productive services (a bridge, for example). For illustration, consider the VCM setting with an MPCR $= .30$ and $N = 4$. Isaac, Schmidtz, and Walker (1989, hereafter ISW) examined this setting, but with the following change. If allocations to the group account did not meet a specified minimum threshold, there was no provision of the public good and all allocations were lost (that is, had a zero value). ISW examined several designs in which they varied the minimum threshold. This type of decision situation creates an "assurance problem." Zero contributions to the group good is no longer a dominant strategy or the unique Nash strategy. Players have an incentive to contribute to the public good if they have some expectation (assurance) that others will contribute. On the other hand, if others will provide the public good, the individual has an incentive to free ride on their contributions. ISW found that:

1. In designs with provision points that require relatively low levels of contributions, numerous experimental groups were able, in early decision rounds, to overcome the assurance problem and provide the public good.
2. In experiments with higher provision points and in later decision rounds of most experiments, free-riding behavior tended to increase with resulting low levels of efficiency.

These results are similar to results from a closely related provision point setting discussed by van de Kragt, Orbell, and Dawes (1983). In this study (where subjects made a binary decision to contribute or not to contribute to a group good), groups met the provision point in less than 35 percent of the decision trials. In an interesting modification to the standard decision setting, Dorsey (1992) examines the VCM decision setting with provision point settings and "real time" revision of individual decisions. More specifically, Dorsey allows subjects a continuous information update of "others" contributions' and the opportunity to revise one's own contribution. In provision point designs with revisions that can *only increase,* allocations to the group good significantly increase.

In anticipation that the specific rules of the contribution mechanism might significantly affect decision behavior, several studies have examined the provision point decision setting using an alternative contribution mechanism. For example, Dawes, Orbell, and van de Kragt (1984), Isaac, Schmidtz, and Walker (1989), and Bagnoli and McKee (1991) investigate several versions of what is commonly referred to as the "payback" mechanism.[24] Contributions are made toward the provision of the public good. If they do not meet the specified minimum, all are returned to the players making the contributions. As one might expect, this simple change can significantly affect decision incentives, equilibria,

---

24. Palfrey and Rosenthal (1984) discuss strategic equilibria in provision point games with and without the payback mechanism; see Bagnoli, Shaul, and McKee (1992) for further results.

and observed behavior. Certainly the risks involved in making contributions are reduced. On the other hand, there is still an incentive to free ride if others will provide the public good.

The variation in findings of the three studies cited above is quite interesting. In one-shot decisions (with no value for contributions above the provision point and binary decisions to contribute or not to contribute), Dawes, Orbell, and van de Kragt found no significant effects on levels of contributions when comparing provision point experiments with and without the payback mechanism. On the other hand (in a decision setting in which contributions above the provision point have a positive value and subjects make nonbinary choices), ISW found that using the payback mechanism substantially increased efficiency in settings with higher provision points and to a lesser extent in the low provision point setting. ISW still observed significant problems in low and medium provision point settings (especially later decision periods) due to what they refer to as "cheap" riding. Significant numbers of subjects strategically attempted to provide a smaller share of the public good than their counterparts, in some cases leading to a failure to meet the provision point. Finally (in a decision setting in which contributions above the provision point have no value and subjects make nonbinary decisions), Bagnoli and McKee found very strong support for the cooperative facilitating features of the payback institution. In their experiments, the public good was provided in 85 of 98 possible cases, and there was very little loss in efficiency due to overinvestments.

4. Summary comments and conclusions

Collective action problems offer a unique and challenging setting for social scientists interested in the linkages between theory, institutions, and behavior. Evidence from field and experimental studies provides support for the following two fundamental propositions:

P1 *Without some form of coordination or organization to enable individuals to agree upon, monitor, and sanction contributions to the provision of a public good, the good is* underprovided.

P2 *Without some form of coordination or organization to enable individuals to agree upon, monitor, and sanction the patterns of appropriation from a CPR, the resource is* overused.

Evidence from field and experimental studies, on the other hand, challenge many currently accepted theoretical understandings of the likelihood of those directly involved in smaller-scale public good or CPR settings to develop their own forms of coordination or organization.

Field studies have generated a wealth of examples of individuals organizing themselves and changing the structure of their own settings to reduce the incentives to underprovide public goods or CPRs and to overappropriate from CPRs. Many of these endogenously designed institutions do not easily fit with prior conceptions of the state or the market. But it is also obvious from field studies that self-organization is not universal and frequently fails. Consequently, evidence from laboratory experiments that more precisely identify the specific variables that are associated with particular behavioral tendencies is crucial for further theoretical development. Below we provide a brief summary of what we have learned in the lab about provision, appropriation, organization, and sanctioning.

4.1 Findings related to provision

1. In stark institutional settings where subjects cannot communicate, the theoretical prediction of suboptimal provision is supported.
   a. In repeated decision rounds, initial efficiencies were greater than predicted, generally with some decay over time.
   b. In repeated decision rounds, the path of decline toward the Nash equilibrium often showed a distinct pulsing pattern.
2. Ceteris paribus, when the marginal value of contributing to a public good was higher, efficiencies were higher.
3. Increasing the number of individuals – holding marginal return from the public good constant – generally had no impact or *increased* efficiency.
4. Face-to-face communication increased efficiency – even under circumstances where individuals were not symmetric in regard to asset endowments.
5. Establishing a pay-back mechanism (whereby those who contributed to a good when a sufficient number of others did not contribute were assured a rebate of their contribution) led to an increase in efficiency.
6. A provision point (or, lumpy production function) was often more conducive to the efficient provision of public goods than a smooth production function.

4.2 Findings related to appropriation

1. In stark institutional settings where subjects could communicate, the theoretical prediction of overappropriation (or, where relevant, destruction) was supported.
   a. In repeated decision rounds, initial inefficiencies were often

greater than predicted by the Nash equilibrium for a one-shot game.

   b. In repeated decision rounds, the path of movement toward the Nash equilibrium showed a distinct pulsing pattern.

2. Increasing asset endowments used for appropriation reduced efficiencies, even when the predicted Nash equilibrium was unchanged.

3. Face-to-face communication increased efficiencies.

4.3 Findings related to organization, monitoring, and sanctioning

1. When given an opportunity, subjects spent time and effort designing agreements to share the costs and benefits of providing and appropriating under mutually developed constraints.

2. When the only sanctioning mechanisms available for punishing those who did not follow agreements were verbal chastisement or switching to deficient outcomes:

   a. small deviations by a few subjects were usually met by small deviations by other subjects and a return to behavior consistent with the agreement, but

   b. large deviations by a few subjects tended to lead to the unraveling of agreements.

3. When given an opportunity, subjects overutilized a costly exogenous sanctioning system.

4. When given an opportunity, subjects who chose to impose a sanctioning system upon themselves were able to earn higher efficiencies in repeated decision rounds.

Findings from experimental settings complement those from field settings and help to identify relevant variables associated with the endogenous development of efficiency-enhancing institutions. While the two fundamental propositions concerning suboptimal provision and over-appropriation in stark institutional settings are supported in both field and experimental studies, many other commonly accepted propositions about the helplessness of individuals to change the structure of their own situations are not.

When turning to policy prescriptions, the importance of the complex mixture of variables that exist in distinct settings is substantial. The particular features of a natural setting that might effectively be used by participants in selecting rules cannot be included in general models. The likelihood is small that any set of uniform rules for all natural settings within a large territory, such as developing marketable rights or imposing state regulations, will produce optimal results. This is unfortunately the case, whether or not the particular rules can be shown to generate optimal rules in sparse theoretical or experimental settings. Theoretical and empirical research though can be used to help inform those who are close to particular natural resource systems as well as those in larger, overarching agencies, about the principles that may be used to improve performance. It is important to keep these differences in mind when making policy prescriptions. Slogans such as "privatization" or "regulation" may mask important underlying principles rather than provide useful guides for reform.

The findings summarized above are also important because they challenge the propensity to use an extremely limited set of simple models to characterize behavior in highly complex settings. All theory involves necessary simplification. One of the important lessons from game theory, however, is that a very small difference in the structure of a game can make an immense difference in the predicted behavior and outcomes. Empirical research conducted in experimental laboratories reinforces this lesson, as does systematic field research conducted in multiple sites. Presuming that the institutional world of relevance to the study of public choice is limited to either the market or the state brackets together an immense variety of rich institutional arrangements that should not be lumped together. Our conceptual language loses considerable analytical bite when highly disparate phenomena are viewed as if they were essentially equivalent in oversimplified models of the world.

CHAPTER 4

The political economy of federalism

ROBERT P. INMAN AND DANIEL L. RUBINFELD

Recent changes in the institutions of government economic policymaking in western and eastern Europe, efforts to write new constitutions for Russia and South Africa, and the less dramatic, but no less important, pressures to redefine policy responsibilities between levels of government in such contrasting economies as the United States and China suggest that now is a good time to revisit a long-standing topic of traditional political economy: the design of federalist political institutions. The framing in 1787 of the United States Constitution marked the beginning of the contemporary debate, pitting Montesquieu's ideal of a decentralized "confederate" republic composed of sovereign member city-states against the vision of Madison and the other Federalists of a "compound" republic with an overarching central government responsible to the union's common citizenry. The tension between the confederate model of independent city-states each with an effective veto over central government actions and the compound model of a central government capable of acting against local interests remains at the center of today's debates over the design of federalist constitutions. Can contemporary political economy help us to understand better the important trade-offs implicit within the choice between a confederate and a compound republican constitution? This survey seeks to provide one answer.[1]

The authors would like to thank the Smith Richardson Foundation and the National Science Foundation (SES-9022192) for financial support and the Center for Advanced Study in the Behavioral Sciences for a congenial environment in which to pursue our joint work on federalism. The comments on an earlier version of this paper by William Fletcher, Michael Fitts, David Lieberman, Dennis Mueller, and seminar participants at Washington University of St. Louis and the Center for Advanced Study (Stanford) are gratefully acknowledged.

1. The focus of this survey will be on the "political" theory of federalism – a theory of federalist institutions that maps the multiplicity of citizen interests onto policy decisions. The political theory of federalism is grounded in social choice theory and the new political economy.

   There is a parallel literature in economics and public administration seeking to develop an "administrative" theory of federalism – that is, a theory of institutions that

Section 1 reviews the political and economic arguments for the confederate republic, while Section 2 reviews the economic theory behind the compound republic. Two federalist dimensions of any republic's constitution are identified: representation (R) of the local city-states to the central government and the assignment (A) of governmental tasks to the city-states or the central government. We suggest one approach for choosing the efficient compound republic as a preferred combination of R and A.

The analysis in Sections 1 and 2 will reveal a central tension between economic efficiency and democratic rights and virtues. Choosing values of R and A ultimately requires a balancing of these potentially competing economic and political objectives. The decentralized federalist structure of the confederate republic favors the goals of democracy; the more centralized compound republic places a greater weight on economic efficiency.

Section 3 explores the stability of federalist constitutions: When might an individual city-state secede from a confederate or a compound republic? Economic conditions and political institutions required to hold a federalist republic together are identified.

Section 4 offers a concluding comment on directions for new research.

1. City-states and political union: The confederate republic

1.1 The Political case for the city-state: Protecting democratic rights and promoting civic virtue

From Plato and Aristotle through Rousseau and Montesquieu to contemporary federalist legal scholars,[2] one hears continuing praise for the political virtues of small government. Small governments are seen by many to protect the rights of the individual against the tyranny of the majority. Small governments are also seen to encourage political participation, the mutual accommodation of all views, political compromise, and the value of community.

Controlling the ability of the majority to overrule the rights of the

---

turns policy decisions into allocative outcomes. The latter draws its theoretical structure from the principal-agent and transactions cost literatures; see Holmström and Tirole (1989) generally, Tirole (1994) for an application of these literatures to government, and Bender and Mookherjee (1987) and Klibanoff and Morduch (1993) for an application to the design of federalist institutions. The large empirical literature on the effects of incentive grants on local government allocations will provide a useful basis for the application of the new administrative theory of federalism. See Inman (1979) and more recently Wildasin (1986) for surveys of that literature.

2. See, for example, Frug (1980, 1987, 1993), Rapaczynski (1986), and Amar (1987).

individual is a fundamental challenge for democratic societies. For several reasons, small democratic city-states are often proposed as a solution. First, small city-states are argued to be more fluid politically; that is, open to the vagaries of the voting cycles. With no stable majority, the distinction between the ruler and the ruled is blurred. Tyranny is less attractive if there is a significant risk of being tyrannized in return (Frug 1980, 1069). Second, exit from a repressive state to a less repressive state is possible. Mobile individuals can join that city-state having their most preferred set of rights and responsibilities (McConnell 1987, 1503). Third, no small city-state is likely to be able to defeat and oppress another city-state without high military cost.

In addition to protecting individual rights, small governments also are seen as the wellspring of the virtuous public life. To the Greeks, to Rousseau and Montesquieu, to de Tocqueville and Dewey, political participation is the source of public values.[3] Through political participation citizens become educated and come to know fully, and to respect, the points of view of others. For classical and contemporary communitarians, only small governments are likely to encourage the required level of participation and thus foster the valued public virtues.

1.2 The economic case for a political union

Though small governments may protect individual rights and foster public virtue, it has long been appreciated that small governments are vulnerable in modern commercial economies. Larger nations can overrun a small city-state militarily, unless it is protected geographically by impassable mountains or narrow harbors. Even without a military threat, small states might be disadvantaged in trade and commerce through their imposition of self-defeating competitive tariffs or their failure to control the overutilization of their shared natural resources. Missing was a theory of government that balanced the political advantages of the small city-state with the necessity of providing for their common economic interests. Montesquieu's vision of a confederate republic sought to meet this need.

To Montesquieu "if a republic be small it is destroyed by a foreign force; if it be large, it is ruined by an internal imperfection [of a] thousand private views" (quoted in Beer 1993, 219, 220). Montesquieu sought a solution to this dilemma through a "confederate republic" com-

---

3. Frug (1980, 1067–73) provides a useful overview of the importance of participation for political life in the writings of Aristotle, Rousseau, de Tocqueville, and Arendt. For more detail, see Dahl and Tufte (1973, chap. 1) and Pateman (1976). Frug (1980, 1987) provides a contemporary application of these theories to U.S. urban policy.

posed of small city-states acting in unison when their common interests are at risk. The United Netherlands and the Swiss cantons were his models. Montesquieu's ideal confederate republic is a mutual agreement between city-states to pursue joint economic objectives, each state having the right to exit the union when it feels its private interests are harmed by the action of the republic. While secession is a right, decision making is by bargaining.[4] How well the confederacy performs its tasks depends upon how well the union meets the conditions for efficient bargains. From a contemporary perspective, Montesquieu's ideal confederate republic can be seen as a bargain among independent city-states. The theory can be understood and evaluated on these terms.

In a powerful challenge to the need for strong central governments in modern economies, Ronald Coase (1960) suggests that market failures created by economic spillovers or the inefficient provision of public goods can be resolved by successful bargaining between the affected parties to the extent that the property rights of the parties are well specified and the costs of bargaining are low (see Cooter 1987a). Coase's theory has direct application to Montesquieu's confederate republic as a bargain between city-states. The assumptions underlying the Coasian framework are

(C1) There are no resource costs associated with reaching agreement.

(C2) Preferences over bargaining outcomes and the resources of participants are common knowledge.

(C3) Bargaining agents perfectly represent the economic interests of their constituents.

(C4) All bargaining agreements are costlessly enforceable.

(C5) The parties will agree to a division of the economic surplus from bargaining.

Assumptions (C1) through (C5) ensure that economic efficiency will be achieved in a fully decentralized confederation of city-states. Assumption (C1) ensures that bargainers can get together and reach agreements costlessly – there are no decision costs. Assumptions (C2) and (C3) guarantee that all parties are fully informed – there are no costs of revelation. Assumption (C4) establishes that all agreements are valid and enforceable – there are no monitoring or enforcement costs. Finally,

---

4. Montesquieu discusses alternative models for organizing confederate republics, some of which allow a majority of member states to discipline a corrupt member. His ideal, however, remains decision making by unanimity. See Beer (1993, chap. 7) for a summary of Montesquieu's theory of federalism.

assumption (C5) ensures that bargains do not unravel over the question of how to share the economic surplus from agreement.

In Montesquieu's confederate republic the task of the central government is to provide property rights so as to protect the integrity of participating city-states and facilitate and enforce all city-state agreements for the control of interstate spillovers (e.g., barriers to free trade) and the provision of public goods (e.g., a common defense). Coasian bargains in the halls of government ensure that economic efficiency obtains. The tasks of the small city-states are to protect individual freedom and to encourage political participation. Political debate and open discussion fosters a spirit of community and respect for the views of others. In the end, the confederate republic is hypothesized to be both free and efficient.

1.3 Are confederate republics free and efficient?

How valid is the theory of the confederate republic, resting as it does on a belief in the virtues of community and the efficiency of Coasian bargains? There are a number of reasons to be skeptical.

The evidence relating small governments to the protection of individual rights and to good government is mixed at best. History is replete with counterexamples wherein small governments repress the rights of minorities and larger, more encompassing, governments protect those rights. But there are valid examples that make the opposite point.[5] And there is no compelling evidence that countries that explicitly protect small governments through confederate constitutions have better human rights records (see Riker 1964, 14–16).

Studies that have sought to draw the relationship between the size of the state and political participation also have given mixed results. For example, there appears to be no systematic evidence that voter turnout varies with the size of the electorate (Dahl and Tufte 1973, 45; Verba, Nie, and Kim 1978, chap. 13). Surveys do show that citizens are more likely to seek to influence their local governments than national governments through nonelectoral channels and that these informal activities are more likely in stable rural communities than in large, urban centers (Verba, Nie, and Kim 1978, chap. 13). Further, these local efforts are likely to have a greater effect of policy (Dahl and Tufte 1973, 58–9). Still, no more than 28 percent of those surveyed in the United States have ever tried to influence their local governments, and of those only a

---

5. U.S. southern states' support of slavery and recent Serbian efforts at ethnic cleansing are examples where small states suppressed rights, while the larger state – United States and Yugoslavia – protected rights. Conversely, Germany and the Holocaust, and the United States's historical treatment of Native Americans, suggest the opposite.

bit more than half felt it was likely they would have a significant effect on policy; the percentages were substantially lower in the other countries surveyed.[6]

Against this evidence, it is difficult to see the small city-state as the necessary protector of individual rights and promoter of democratic values. Certainly, small government can contribute to these political goals, but today these institutions are far removed from the Greek ideal. If we are to make a decisive case for the small city-state in a theory of federalism, additional arguments must be advanced.

The dependence on efficient and costless bargaining of the confederate republic theory is also problematic. One can be critical of each of the five Coasian assumptions for efficient bargains. Contrary to (C1), representatives must communicate positions and consider alternatives, which is often a time-consuming, costly task. Rarely is there full information about the parties' preferences and endowments as required by (C2). Parties may fail to find the best allocations because they do not know the full range of possible trades. If the parties make poor estimates of each other's threat points when bargaining, they may underestimate the potential surplus to be gained and consequently take a hard line in the bargaining process. To the extent that parties succumb to such strategic behavior, Coasian bargains may not occur (see Mailath and Postlewaite 1990). Preferences and economic endowments of the bargainers can be revealed, but only at a cost (see Laffont 1987). Again, not all intergovernmental bargains will be efficient.

Assumption (C3) assumes perfect agency on the part of city-state representatives to the confederate republic, but this too seems unlikely. Representatives might have an agenda independent of the citizens of the city-state they represent. These imperfect agents must be identified and replaced – at a cost. How will the agents be chosen and whom will they represent? If the citizens within each city-state have distinct preferences for the outcomes of the republic's bargains, then, as Bowen (1943) first showed, there is no guarantee that the median's representatives under majority rule voting will approve fully efficient resource allocation for all the citizens of each city-state.

Without enforceability – assumption (C4) – city-states will have the incentive to break agreements as conditions or interests change over

6. See Dahl and Tufte (1973, 58–9). A more recent survey by the Advisory Commission on Intergovernmental Relations of citizen participation found that most local participation occurs through selected advisory committees (60 percent) rather than through general citizen discussion (16 percent) as envisaged by the advocates of political participation; ACIR (1979, 223). Only 3 percent of the surveyed officials said citizen participation resulted in a "substantial" change in the budget; 66 percent said "very little change"; see ACIR (224).

time; consequently, members of the confederation may have little incentive to reach agreements in the first place.[7] Control of cheating can be restored, but only at a cost of monitoring the agreement and such costs can be substantial (see Williamson 1985).

Without assumptions (C1–C4) there will be potentially important revelation, decision, monitoring, and enforcement costs when reaching agreements in Montesquieu's confederate republic. Some bargains that were originally efficient under assumptions of costless communication and full information may no longer be efficient when transactions costs are positive. More importantly, when transactions costs are significant, the efficient federalist structure may no longer be a confederate republic of many city-states (see Section 2.3).

Finally, if assumption (C5) no longer holds (even if transaction costs are zero), the parties may not be able to divide the economic surplus. Every Coasian bargain does two things: it establishes an efficient exchange creating economic surplus *and* it distributes that surplus among the bargaining parties. Proponents of Coase emphasize the first but have largely ignored the implications of the second (see Cooter 1982). Yet it is well known that the division of any economic pie is a bargaining problem that may have no solution. Only in the special case of two players with a pre-established order to their offers is an efficient allocation likely (see Rubinstein 1982). When the number of participants is greater than two, a shared sense of fairness – called a "focal point" – may be required (see Schelling 1960 and Haller 1986). Assumption (C5) is meant to guarantee such a focal point. Without it, however, confederate republics may fail to achieve full economic efficiency.

In summary, while the theoretical case for the confederate republic can be made, available evidence is far from decisive that such confederations will achieve their goals. Modern city-states do not appear to be unique protectors of democratic rights and civic virtues. Efficient bargains that underlie the economic case for the confederation's central government are unlikely to be achieved in practice.[8] Against these facts,

---

7. A point appreciated by Madison when criticizing the Articles of Confederation; see Beer (1993, 248–9).
8. One telling example is the failure of the Continental Congress during the period 1777 to 1785 adequately to provide for the financing of the U.S. War of Independence and to effectively manage foreign affairs following the war. The Congress had been established by the Articles of Confederation as a vehicle for "Coasian agreements" between the colonies. These failures led to the calling of the Constitutional Convention in 1787 and, ultimately, to the formation of Madison's compound republic; see Rakove (1989, 5–6).
   Sandler and Murdoch (1990) offer a more contemporary example of the failure of Coasian bargains to efficiently provide public goods. In their study of NATO allocations, they conclude that for the period 1956 to 1987, NATO members behaved inefficiently, free riding on other nations's contributions to the collective defense of western Europe.

confederate republics may just as easily be unjust and inefficient. Alternatives must be considered.[9]

2. The political economy of the compound republic

While the classical and contemporary communitarians championed the city-state for its potential to promote democratic rights and civic virtues, James Madison valued the small city-state for its ability to satisfy the economic needs arising from local circumstances. A relatively strong central government, in sharp contrast to the fragile alliance of a confederate republic, is the core of Madison's compound republic. The central government receives its legitimacy not from the unanimous consent of all city-states but from the majority approval of all its individual citizens. The preferences of citizens are expressed through the local election of representatives to a national legislature and through the national election of a single executive. The executive implements the laws approved by the legislature. While Montesquieu might have asked "Why have a Union?" Madison would have asked "Why have states?" In contrast to Montesquieu, Madison's case for city-states was economic not political; they better serve the "local and particular."[10] Public finance economists know this argument today as the Tiebout (1956) theory of local government.

2.1 The economic case for the city-state: Efficiency

In the Tiebout model of intergovernmental competition, small cities competing for mobile residents ensure the efficient supply of local public goods.[11] Five conditions define the Tiebout economy:

9. Were the theory of a confederate republic to rest only upon the efficiency advantages of Coasian bargains between small city-states it would not be a theory of federalism. Logically, if the Coase assumptions hold, both a single central government or a loose confederation of states could achieve the fully efficient outcome (the former through bargains among representatives to the national legislature, the latter through bargaining among city-states). Montesquieu rightly finds his reasons for local governments in their hypothesized contribution to the democratic good of civic virtue and citizen devotion to the public welfare.
10. Madison feared that local economic interests would be lost within the national legislature unless separate states were established to provide those interests with "superintending care"; again, see Beer (1993, 293–4) for a full review of Madison's economic argument.

    In contrast to Montesquieu and the Anti-federalists Madison was skeptical of the political arguments for small governments. He saw the central government as the individual's best protection against tyranny; see McConnell (1987, 1500–7).
11. We only sketch the argument here, simply to place Tiebout's argument within the broader literature on federalist political institutions. Rubinfeld (1987) and Wildasin (1986) provide detailed surveys of this literature.

(T1) Publicly provided goods and services are produced with a congestible technology.

(T2) There is a perfectly elastic supply of jurisdictions, each capable of replicating all attractive economic features of its competitors.

(T3) Mobility of households among jurisdictions is costless.

(T4) Households are fully informed about the fiscal attributes of each jurisdiction.

(T5) There are no interjurisdictional externalities.

A Tiebout equilibrium arises when each household resides in the jurisdiction of its choice, and where no household can improve its economic welfare by moving elsewhere.[12]

With a congestible technology (T1), publicly provided goods are rival public goods, and the per-household cost of providing each level of a public good first decreases and then increases as more households move into the jurisdiction. For each level of output, there is a technically efficient population size that minimizes the average cost per household of providing that service. Ensuring that these efficient alternatives exist in the Tiebout economy is the task of public sector entrepreneurs. Implicit in assumption (T2) is the fact that these entrepreneurs are fully capable of providing all public goods and private amenities (including jobs or job access) in each jurisdiction.

Assumptions (T3) and (T4) ensure that there are informed and mobile citizens to discipline the public sector entrepreneurs. When inefficiencies arise, households move to otherwise similar jurisdictions with efficient production. The no spillover assumption (T5) ensures that all public goods can be provided within these efficient jurisdictions and that no citizens can consume the public service without paying their full marginal cost of consumption.

Current empirical evidence suggests that most public services satisfying (T1) and (T5) can be efficiently provided at minimum cost in communities with populations of five to ten thousand residents (see Rubinfeld 1987, for a summary of that literature). Further, such communities are allocatively efficient, providing all citizens with their preferred levels of the public goods at each good's minimum production costs.

What happens to the argument if one or more of the Tiebout assumptions is lost? Relaxing assumption (T1) does not fundamentally alter the

---

12. The Tiebout argument focuses on static efficiency. Not considered are issues of dynamic efficiency. Weingast (1993), however, has made the argument that Tiebout fiscal competition will limit the taxation of mobile capital enhancing investment and economic development. Tiebout competition is also seen by many as source of innovation in public goods technologies and management, though Rose-Ackerman (1980) is skeptical.

efficiency advantages of a fully decentralized Tiebout economy, *if* assumptions (T3) and (T5) still hold. Thus, even if the production of government services has a public component, efficiency remains, provided citizens can costlessly relocate to consume the service (T3) and exclusion (T5) is still possible. Entrepreneurs can sell their excess capacity to other jurisdictions at competitive prices. In effect, one local jurisdiction can become the public supplier for the other jurisdictions. Governments will vary in size depending on the technology of the services supplied (Olson 1969).

Assumptions (T2–T5) are more fundamental. With the loss of Tiebout assumption (T2) – the elastic supply of jurisdictions – three potentially adverse consequences for economic efficiency are likely to arise. First, because their number is limited, each jurisdiction is composed of citizens with different demands for local public goods. Local politics now becomes important. If local decisions are made by majority rule, for example, the median voter's choice need no longer be economically efficient – a point first emphasized by Bowen (1943). Second, when the public goods economy can no longer replicate attractive local jurisdictions, economic rents can be earned. The presence of these publicly created rents in turn introduces an additional layer of economic bargaining – between the fiscal entrepreneur and the owners of the scarce factor. The presence of rents requires lump-sum taxes and transfers for their efficient distribution. Without such policy, bargaining may lead to inefficiencies in the public goods economy (see Epple and Zelenitz 1981 and Wildasin 1986). Third, once the supply of jurisdictions is fixed, the analogy of the decentralized model of federalism to free market competition is no longer valid. Each local government may now see itself as a Cournot competitor, aware of the potential effect of its action on other jurisdictions, while assuming no direct competitive response. In this framework, the actions of each local jurisdiction, even if small, can have a substantial effect on the welfare of the rest of the decentralized world. Essentially, a self-interested decision by those in power in one jurisdiction can result in a series of distortions arising throughout the affected network of other jurisdictions.[13]

When mobility becomes costly and assumption (T3) no longer applies, the perfect Tiebout economy cannot guarantee overall (market plus public sector) efficiency. When the production of the public good is site-specific *and* when the relocation of the household is costly on the *margin* (i.e., the relocation affects private resource allocations), household relo-

---

13. For example, states might be encouraged to relax their environmental controls to encourage business migration, or to forestall the loss of business to other states with relaxed environmental regulations; see Oates and Schwab (1988).

cations to achieve a more efficient public sector will create real externalities for the private economy. The usual example is labor leaving one jurisdiction for less productive employment in another fiscally more attractive jurisdiction; the consequence is a less efficient private economy (see Buchanan and Goetz [1972] for the initial presentation of this argument and the summaries in Boadway and Flatters [1982] and Wildasin [1986]).

When assumption (T4) no longer holds, that is, when there is incomplete information about the costs and levels of public goods production, there are additional difficulties for the Tiebout economy. Households have two options: go it alone and risk being exploited by better informed fiscal entrepreneurs and local factors of production *or* hire an agent (called a "city manager" or "mayor" for households in place, and a "real estate agent" for relocating households) to protect household interests. To the extent that the market for "agents" works perfectly – all inefficient or exploitive providers are exposed, and only truthful agents survive – the final public goods outcome will still be efficient, but some households' fiscal surpluses will be allocated to the agents as payment for services performed.

Complications arise, however, when information about agent performance is costly and some deceitful agents survive, or when the expertise provided by agents to households cannot itself be kept private. In both instances externalities in the market for agents will cause an inefficient amount of information to be provided about the fiscal performance of the Tiebout communities.[14] Inefficient information leads to inefficient public sector allocations.

Assumption (T5) – no spillovers – ensures that all communities can exclude consumers who free ride by not contributing to the costs of providing their public goods. With free riding there will typically be an underprovision of public services by competitive city-states (see Pauly 1970).

What is the evidence that competitive city-states do enhance the economic performance of the public goods economy? First, with competitive governments, production costs for any level of output should be minimized, as should rent transfers from one group to another. Thus,

---

14. With costless information, agent efforts can be monitored (avoiding moral hazard) and agent abilities will be known (avoiding adverse selection). When information about agents is costly, however, there is no guarantee that the agent market will be efficient; see Holmström (1985). Similarly, when the information provided by the agents to households cannot be kept private, the information market will be inefficient; see Allen (1990).

were decentralized and centralized public goods economies providing the same levels of public good outputs to be compared, the decentralized public economy composed of many city-states would have lower spending and taxes than the centralized single-state economy, all else equal.

Testing this efficiency prediction has recently become known as the search for Leviathan. (The presence of a powerful central rent-seeking authority, Leviathan, would be evidence of inefficiency.) Oates's (1985) pioneering efficiency study regresses total state and local government spending per capita in a state on the aggregate number of local governments per capita in the state and finds no significant negative effect on spending. Using the Oates's approach and data, Nelson (1987) and Zax (1989) find that more governments per square mile and more general purpose governments per capita reduce government spending per capita, while states with many special district governments and more governments per capita – typically rural states – have higher spending per capita, all else equal. Finally, Forbes and Zampelli (1989) seek to explain county government spending by the number of counties in the SMSA and find no effect.

There is a pattern in these conflicting results. Very small governments (special districts in rural states) are too small to take advantage of economies of scale. A few large governments (counties) are not sufficiently competitive to ensure efficiency. Between these extremes – namely, general purpose governments in urbanized states – competition does appear to affect spending.

Although the Leviathan efficiency results are suggestive, they are not decisive. One cannot infer cost and demand performance from aggregate expenditure studies without very strong identifying restrictions.[15] A preferred approach is to test directly for the effects of competitive governments on public sector costs. Inman (1982) and Zax (1988) provide two tests of the effects of a competitive suburban fringe on center city labor costs, confirming the expected negative effect of competition on costs.[16]

15. If a decentralized governmental structure determines the cost of public goods and the demand for public goods depends on a vector of demand variables and costs, then the expenditure equation to be estimated will involve unspecified interactions of cost and demand variables.

16. Zax (1988) finds that more suburban governments reduce aggregate labor expenditures in their adjoining central city. Inman (1982) refines the test by allowing for income differences between city and suburban residents, noting that when city incomes are significantly greater (a rich city with a rural fringe) or significantly less (a poor city with a rich fringe) than suburban incomes, then suburbs do not offer an effective competitive alternative for current city residents. A U-shaped relationship between the ratio of city to suburban income and wage and benefits is predicted and confirmed.

Even if costs are minimized, however, there is no guarantee that small city-states provide residents with their preferred levels of publicly provided goods. Specifically, there is no certainty that the Samuelson condition for allocative efficiency within city-states (the sum of the individual residents' marginal benefits being equal to the marginal cost of production) will be satisfied. Again, there are indirect and direct tests of this proposition.

In a series of papers Brueckner (1979, 1982, 1983) shows that, under certain restrictive conditions, communities that provide public goods so as to maximize the value of residential property will satisfy the Samuelson condition.[17] Brueckner (1979, 1982) finds that education is overprovided in New Jersey communities, while other services are efficiently provided. The latter conclusion also applies to Massachusetts.

Barlow (1970) was the first to offer a direct test of allocative efficiency within small city-states. He used estimated citizen demand curves for education obtained from a median voter model and aggregate community data to infer marginal benefit schedules for community residents. Knowing the distribution of demand characteristics within each community, Barlow then calculated the sum of residents' marginal benefits for education at the community's current level of school spending. Finally, comparing the sum of marginal benefits to the marginal cost of producing education, Barlow concluded that education was overprovided (from the perspective of community residents).

Using sophisticated microeconometric techniques to estimate family demands from survey data, Bergstrom et al. (1988) repeated the Barlow test for intrajurisdictional allocative efficiency using a sample of Michigan school districts. Importantly, they were able to identify a potential source of overprovision in some communities – the U.S. federal government's provision of federal tax subsidies for school spending. They concluded, however, that government provision of education was locally efficient within the majority of communities, given the rate of federal subsidy.

Though not fully decisive on the point, the current empirical evidence suggests competitive local governments can provide an efficient level of congestible (local) public goods. In such economies, production costs are minimized and citizens often do vote for the efficient level of the local public good. These are encouraging results.

17. Brueckner (1983) qualifies his efficiency result by noting that the property value maximization test assumes each household is a "community taker," where the allocation of households across communities is given. The value maximization condition is therefore a local efficiency condition. However, reallocation of households across communities may improve the welfare of all households. Eberts and Gronberg (1981) provide one effort to test this global efficiency condition, concluding that families collect in communities by their demands for public goods.

What is not assured is the efficient allocation of public goods with significant spillovers. In this case, a subsidy is needed to internalize the externalities. But any such policy to control interjurisdictional spillovers would require the agreement of the competitive city-states. For such agreements we must look to more encompassing political institutions. In Madison's compound republic this is the representative central government.[18]

2.2 The political economy of representative government

The focal institution of Madison's compound republic is the central government legislature composed of representatives elected from subsets of the city-states. Henceforth, we call these groups of city-states "states." Within the central legislature representatives from the states are free to fashion coalitions and set policies, subject only to the constraint that policies receive the approval of a majority of the legislators. Though numerous specifications of this legislative game are possible, two are prominent in the political economy literature – the minimum-winning-coalition legislature (MWC) and the universalistic (U) legislature. We explore implications of each for the design of federalist constitutions.

The minimum-winning-coalition legislature. Policies chosen in the MWC legislature reflect the preferences of the winning 51 percent majority. When policies are one dimensional (e.g., spending on a single, national public good) the outcome will be that preferred by the median representative in the legislature. When policies are multidimensional (e.g., spending on projects with local benefits such as income redistribution or local public goods) then additional legislative structure will be necessary to ensure stable, majority rule outcomes. MWC legislatures find this additional structure in agenda rules.

In legislatures run by open-rule agendas – the agenda setter's proposal can be amended by a 51 percent majority of the legislature – power is diffuse, residing in all members of the legislature who are allowed to offer proposals.[19] Baron and Ferejohn (1989) offer a theory

18. A point made explicitly by James Wilson to the Pennsylvania ratifying convention for the new U.S. Constitution: "[w]hatever the object of government extends, in its operation, *beyond the boundaries* of a particular state, should be considered belonging to the government of the United States" (italics in the original; quoted in McConnell 1987, 1495).

19. In contrast, in legislatures run by closed-rule agendas, the agenda setter's proposal cannot be amended on the floor of the legislature. Here power rests with the select few who are given control over the agenda, for example, legislative committees (Shepsle

of legislative choice over government economic policies in open-rule legislatures. Only two rules apply: (1) amendments must be germane to the economic policy issue under consideration and (2) all members of the legislature have an equal probability of being recognized to offer a new, amended proposal. Baron (1993a) has characterized the equilibrium allocations for the provision of pure (national) public goods and for particularistic (local) goods by this central legislature run by open-rule agendas. Figures 1a and 1b illustrate the allocations and their likely consequences for economic efficiency.

In the case of a single pure public good (G), the chosen policy is the one that satisfies the legislature's decisive median representative and his constituents. Figure 1a shows the resulting allocation at the point G^{mwc}, where the marginal benefit curve for the median representative's constituents – say, the median voter's marginal benefit of $mb_m(G)$ – equals that representative's constituents' (e.g., median voter's) share (ϕ_m) of the social cost of producing the national public good: $mb_m(G^{mwc}) = \phi_m C(G^{mwc})$. The socially efficient allocation is at point G^e, where the social marginal benefit of the public good equals the good's social marginal cost: $MB(G^e) = C(G^e)$. Whether the national public good is overprovided, underprovided (as shown in Figure 1a), or set at the efficient level $(G^{mwc} = G^e)$ will depend on the distribution of citizen demands for the national public good and the distribution of tax burdens.[20]

Central government legislatures are not limited to providing national public goods, however. Nothing prevents these legislators from using central government taxation to provide local, or "particularistic," public goods (g) that benefit the residents of only one state or small group of city-states. Local public goods financed nationally are necessarily redistributive, as a national tax finances a good that benefits only a few residents.

1979) or the leadership of organized political parties (Cox and McCubbins 1993). What remains unexplained in these closed-rule models is the source of the agenda setter's monopoly power over policymaking, though recent efforts by Krehbiel (1992) and Cox and McCubbins (1993) are promising. We do not explore the federalist implications of their work here, though this is a promising avenue of future research.

20. This point was made originally by Bowen (1943). Define the relationship between the social marginal benefit and the decisive constituent's marginal benefit by the proportional relationship: $\Psi_m MB(G) \equiv mb_m(G)$. Note that $\Psi_m MB(G) \equiv mb_m(G)$ by construction, and $mb_m(G) = \phi_m C(G)$ by the political process. Thus, $\Psi_m MB(G) \equiv mb_m(G) = \phi_m C(G)$ or $(\Psi_m/\phi_m)MB(G) = C(G)$. The demand share parameter for the decisive constituent (Ψ_m) is defined by the distribution of citizens' demands for the national public good, while the cost share parameter for the decisive constituent (ϕ_m) is defined by national tax rates and the distribution of tax base. Public goods are overprovided $(MB(G) < C(G))$, efficiently provided $(MB(G) = C(G))$, or underprovided $(MB(G) > C(G))$ as $(\Psi_m/\phi_m) > 1, = 1$, or < 1 – that is, as the decisive constituent's share (Ψ_m) of national benefits exceeds, equals, or is less than his share (ϕ_m) of national costs.

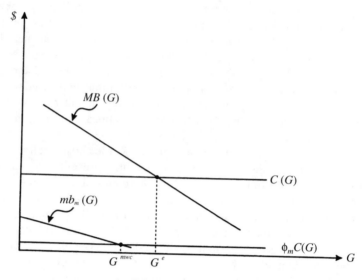

1a. "National" public goods.

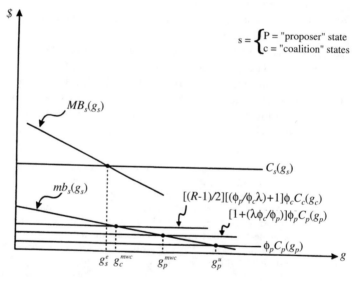

1b. "Local" public goods.

Figure 1. Economic policy in open-agenda MWC legislatures.

Redistributive public policies are susceptible to voting cycles. How will an open-rule MWC legislature allocate these goods? If chosen to propose a public policy, each legislator's first choice is to spend nothing on the particularistic goods of other states and only to spend on his own state's preferred project (g_p). The first choice is g_p^u in Figure 1b, where the proposer's (p's) constituents' marginal benefit from the local public good equals his constituents' marginal cost: $mb_p(g_p^u) = \phi_p C_p(g_p^u)$.

If offered, however, such a proposal is sure to lose. To carry the necessary 51 percent majority, a proposer must offer some benefit to legislators from one half of the other states. Baron (1993) shows that these benefits come as a smaller project for the proposer's own state at level g_p^{mwc} and as modestly sized projects for each of one-half of the other states in the proposer's coalition (c) at levels g_c^{mwc}.[21] Those states not included in the proposer's coalition receive no local project from the central government.

Either inefficient oversupply or inefficient undersupply may result from the central government's provision of state particularistic public goods. As an example, assume that all states have identical marginal benefit and cost curves from the provision of g. Then, in Figure 1b, g_s^e is the efficient level of output of the local public good to state s, defined

---

21. The need to build a minimal winning coalition imposes an additional "shadow cost" on a proposer above the direct tax costs of $\phi_p C_p(g_p)$ in Figure 1b. Since each dollar spent on the proposer's own project imposes a tax burden on others in the minimal winning coalition, they must be compensated through increased spending on their projects. This compensation to coalition members makes the proposer's own spending more costly, as his project's marginal costs now equal his project's direct costs of $\phi_p C_p(g_p)$ plus the required coalition compensation at a rate λ. Thus, the full marginal costs of another unit of g_p are $[1 + (\lambda\phi_c/\phi_p)]\phi_p C_p(g_p)$ shown in Figure 1b.

In a legislature of size R a support coalition of $(R - 1)/2$ legislators is needed to pass the proposer's budget. To win this support the proposer must supply particularistic goods (g_c) in the $(R - 1)/2$ coalition states at a cost to the proposer of $[(R - 1)/2]\phi_p C_c(g_c)$ in direct tax costs. (For simplicity Figure 1b assumes project costs $C_s(g_s)$, where $s = c$ or p, are identical in all states.) This spending also imposes an added tax burden on a typical decisive citizen in each coalition state, but that burden is offset by the benefits received by that decisive citizen from the increase in g_c: $[R - 1)/2]\phi_c C_c(g_c) - mb_c(g_c)$. (For simplicity Figure 1b assumes project benefits $MB_s(g_s)$ and $mb_s(g_s)$, where $s = c$ or p, are identical in all states.) Again the proposer must offer compensation at rate λ for this added net burden on citizens in the coalition. A small increase in g_c costs the proposer the sum of these direct costs plus compensation:

$$[(R - 1)/2]\phi_p C_c(g_c) + \lambda\{[(R - 1/2]\phi_c C_c(g_c) - mb_c(g_c)\}$$

or

$$\{[(R - 1)/2][(\phi_p/\phi_c\lambda) + 1]\phi_c C_c(g_c) - mb_c(g_c)\}.$$

Aggregate costs of coalition building to the proposer are minimized when this marginal cost of coalition building is equal to zero, or when:

$$mb_c(g_c) = [(R - 1)/2][(\phi_p/\phi_c\lambda) + 1]\phi_c C_c(g_c).$$

This is shown as project size g_c^{mwc} in Figure 1b.

where the marginal benefit of the good to residents of the state equals the good's marginal production cost: $MB(g_s^e) = C(g_s^e)$. As shown, the proposer and all states in the winning coalition receive more than the efficient amount: $g_s^e < g_c^{mwc} < g_p^{mwc}$.[22] The states excluded from the 51 percent majority receive no spending on their local public goods from the central government. This latter inefficiency is reduced, however, if local supplementation to central government provision is allowed. With supplementation, the decisive voter in each excluded state now buys the local public good using local tax revenues. Thus, the states in the 49 percent minority receive their median voter allocations (which may or may not be efficient).

The universalistic legislature. While MWC legislatures overcome the difficulty of the voting cycle through agenda rules, universalistic legislatures control the cycle through the adherence to an informal norm of deference. Under the norm each legislator defers to the choices of all the other legislators. If any legislator or group of legislators fails to defer, the norm requires that all legislators penalize the defectors by denying their first choices. This norm of deference – "You scratch my back, I'll scratch yours" – results in legislative proposals that are approved unanimously.[23] For this reason such legislatures are often called "universalistic" (U) legislatures. Empirical evidence suggests that policy allocations in U legislatures typically favor the high demander on each well-defined policy dimension (see Weingast and Marshall 1988, and Hall and Grofman 1990).

Figure 2a illustrates a universalistic legislature's allocation of a national public good (G). The downward sloping $mb_h(G)$ schedule measures the marginal benefit from a national public good of size G to the decisive (e.g., median) voter in the high demand state. Similarly, the $MB(G)$ schedule measures the aggregate social marginal benefit from the provision of the public good. The horizontal curve $C(G)$ measures the marginal social cost of providing the project of size G, while the lower curve $\phi_h C(G)$ measures the share (ϕ_h) of the cost born by the median voter in the decisive high demand state. Social efficiency is again defined by point G^e where $MB(G^e) = C(G^e)$. The predicted allocation for the universalistic legislature is at the high demander's personally

22. Baron (1993a) shows this pattern of inefficiencies result for the case of constant marginal benefit curves and rising social marginal costs.
23. Weingast (1979) and Niou and Ordeshook (1985) have shown that legislative allocations under this norm of deference will be preferred by legislators to those expected from a MWC legislature with open agendas. Chari and Cole (1993) derive the legislative equilibrium under a norm of deference. Weingast and Marshall (1988) provide institutional details for how the norm of deference might be enforced.

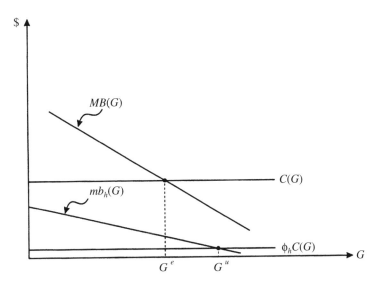

2a. "National" public goods.

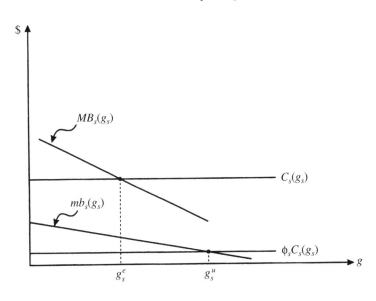

2b. "Local" public goods.

Figure 2. Economic policy in U legislatures.

preferred allocation, where $mb_h(G) = \phi_h C(G)$ – point G^u in Figure 2a. Whether national public goods are overprovided (as shown in Figure 2a), underprovided, or efficiently provided depends upon the distribution of citizen demands for the national public good and the distribution of tax burdens, and the identity of the decisive representative.[24]

The allocation of particularistic public goods (g) to individual states in a U legislature is shown in Figure 2b. The aggregate marginal benefit to all residents in state s is shown as $MB_s(g_s)$, while the benefit to the state's decisive (e.g., median) voter is given by $mb_s(g_s)$. The social marginal cost of the particularistic public good is $C_s(g_s)$, and the decisive voter's share of that cost when financed by national taxation is $\phi_s C_s(g_s)$. Social efficiency requires $MB_s(g_s^e) = C_s(g_s^e)$, given by the allocation g_s^e. The U legislature operating under a norm of deference will provide g_s^u in each state, where $mb_s(g_s^u) = \phi_s C_s(g_s^u)$.

Again, the efficiency of these allocations depends upon the distribution of citizen demands relative to the distribution of tax burdens. Since the median voter's share of state benefits from g_s is likely to be much larger than his or her share of the national cost of g_s, an overprovision of statewide public goods seems the most likely outcome – that is, $g_s^u > g_s^e$ as shown in Figure 1b.[25] Inman (1988) and Inman and Fitts (1990) present evidence in support of this prediction.

Federalism and representative legislatures. The constitutional relationship between city-states and the central government in federalist republics can have significant consequences for the economic and political performance of the representative central legislature. Two dimensions of the constitution have been emphasized in the federalism literature as

24. National public goods are overprovided ($MB(G) < G(G)$), efficiently provided ($MB(G) = C(G)$), or underprovided ($MB(G) > C(G)$) as (Ψ_h/ϕ_h) > 1, $= 1$, or < 1 – that is, as the high demander's share (Ψ_h) of national benefits exceeds, equals, or is less than the high demander's share (ϕ_h) or national costs.

25. The efficiency analysis parallels that for national public goods. Local public goods are overprovided ($MB_s(g) < C_s(g)$), efficiently provided ($MB_s(g) = C_s(g)$), or underprovided ($MB_s(g) > C_s(g)$) by the national legislature as (Ψ_s/ϕ_s) > 1, $= 1$, or < 1 – that is, as the state's median voter's share (Ψ_s) of *state* benefits exceeds, equals, or is less than that median voter's share (ϕ_s) of *national* tax costs.

When drafting the U.S. Constitution the Anti-federalists noted this potential inefficiency when the "Impartial Examiner" argued that each state would prefer national to local taxation so as "to raise revenue by such means, as may appear least injurious to its own interest." Alexander Hamilton, in response, stressed that national taxation must be allocated for services that are "General not local; its operation extending in fact, or by possibility, throughout the Union, and not being confined to a particular spot" (Quoted by McConnell 1987, 1496–7).

particularly influential: the extent of *representation* of the city-states to the central legislature and the *assignment* of policy responsibility between the state-local and central levels of government (Rose-Ackerman 1981).

The representative structure (R) of the central government may vary from a "town-meeting" format in which each of N city-states sends one representative to the central legislature ($R = N$) to a "presidential" format in which all city-states vote in a single central election for one central representative ($R = 1$). More typically, representative legislatures group city-states into subsets of legislative districts called "states" – say, n cities to one state – and then each of R ($= N/n$) legislative states sends one representative to the central legislature.

As the federalist constitution creates more legislative states, *representation* (R) increases. The effects of changes in R on resource allocations in the central legislature depend on technology (a national or particularistic public good) and on how the legislature chooses to do business (U or MWC).

In U legislatures, an increase in R is likely to increase the level of aggregate spending by the central legislature on national and particularistic public goods. Spending on the national public good rises if an increase in R means a "finer" partition of representation of citizen demands for G, giving direct representation to a new, even higher, high demand coalition – $mb_h(G)$ shifts upward in Figure 2a. Particularistic spending rises with R since more city-states now have direct representation in the legislature and each new state gets to choose a level of $g_s = g_s^u$. The hypothesized bias in U legislatures towards inefficiently high government spending (Figures 2a and 2b) is likely to increase as R increases.

In open-agenda MWC legislatures, increased representation has an uncertain effect on national and local public goods. Spending on national public goods changes only to the extent that increases in R alter the location of the decisive representative in the legislature. If the increase in R adds representatives equally to the low and high ends of the distribution of demand for G, then G^{mwc} will remain unchanged. Adding more (less) representation to the low end of the distribution will decrease (increase) the provision of the national public good by a MWC legislature.

For particularistic public goods, increasing R means each proposer must build a larger supporting coalition (($R - 1)/2$) to reach his majority; this increases aggregate spending on g_s. However, building such a coalition is more costly to the proposer, since his own taxes must rise to pay for increased spending. This reduces g_s for each state in the proposer's coalition. On balance, therefore, aggregate spending and economic efficiency may rise or fall as R increases in open-agenda MWC legislatures.[26] We conjecture, however, that if the demand for local public goods is price inelastic – as the evidence seems to indicate (Inman 1979) – then the positive effect of larger coalitions on aggregate spending offsets the negative effect of higher costs of coalition building, and spending on local goods in MWC legislatures rises with R.

If representative central legislatures overspend on particularistic public goods, and if this overspending rises with increased representation of local interests in the legislature, then a compound federalist republic faces a trade-off between economic efficiency and the democratic advantages – enhanced participation, protection of rights, and developed civic virtues – that have been hypothesized by political theorists (Section 1) to follow from more extensive political representation. How might this trade-off be resolved? One answer is to look for additional federalist institutions that retain a level of representativeness while controlling economic inefficiencies. The constitutional *assignment* of economic tasks to the central or local levels of government is one such institution.

Specifying the assignment of central and local government responsibility for economic policy has been the primary concern of previous economic theories of federalism (see Oates's classic text, *Fiscal Federalism* 1972). When economic spillovers are significant and goods are national, small city-states are likely to provide those services inefficiently. If economic spillovers are absent and goods are local, then provision by large central legislatures is likely to be inefficient.[27] For economic efficiency, the assignment principle becomes: constitutionally assign national public goods to the central legislature and local public goods to city-states. Application of the principle requires us to define the extent of spillovers from government activities.

New evidence on spillovers, coupled with a growing appreciation for the inefficiencies of central legislatures, is raising important questions about how best to assign government activities within the federalist hierarchy. Old conclusions may no longer hold. Monetary, deficit, and

---

26. Adding to the uncertainty is the fact that changes in representation also may alter the location of the decisive voter in each state.

27. We have offered two theories – one each for the U and MWC legislatures – explaining why the central government will inefficiently provide local public goods. Oates (1972, 54–63) using the work of Tullock (1969) offers a different approach that assumes that the central government must provide the same level of a local public good to everyone in the nation. One needs a compelling reason to impose this equal provision constraint, however. Since the constraint is not technological – local goods can be provided at different levels in different areas – the constraint must be found in a behavioral model of legislatures.

redistribution policies, once considered the sole domain of the central government, are now seen as potentially valid local government activities (see Gramlich 1987 and Pauly 1973). Conversely, education policy, once seen as a task for only local governments, arguably now can be added to the national agenda as human capital externalities are identified (see Bénabou 1993). If the reach of a given activity's spillover becomes open to dispute, then application of the assignment principle becomes political.[28] If the central legislature assumes responsibility for deciding assignment, then assignment no longer stands as a feasible control to limit legislative inefficiencies. If assignment ceases to work as an independent federalist institution, then we must look for other institutions to "soften" the trade-off between the economic efficiency and the democratic advantages of representation.

In his study of federalism, Riker (1964, 101–3) argues for a strong executive to protect the nation's interest in economic efficiency. Through constitutional powers giving the nationally elected executive the right to veto and to execute legislative policies, the national interest in efficient policies can be protected against excessive local spending on particularistic public goods. Fitts and Inman (1992) model executive influence over universalistic legislatures and provide econometric evidence (Inman and Fitts 1990) that U.S. presidents who have used their executive powers effectively have controlled particularistic spending by congress.

The risk, of course, is that strong executive leadership dominates the central legislature in national policymaking. Rather than easing the trade-off between efficiency and democratic outcomes allowing us to achieve more of both, the strong, nationally elected executive may achieve its efficiency gains by sacrificing democratic rights and civic virtue. Only one (e.g., the national median) voice ($R = 1$) is heard on any issue.

Riker's (1964, 91–101) solution is to add a second political institution to balance executive influence and to express local interests. Locally run political parties can be organized into effective majorities in the central legislature. Through their control of the legislature these parties can "block" policies of the powerful executive, unless at least a majority of those local interests are respected.

Sunstein (1988) offers yet another approach. His analysis seeks to strengthen the hand of local interests in executive actions directly by

---

28. The framers of the U.S. Constitution intended the Supreme Court to be the enforcer of the Constitution's assignment principle. The Court has found this an impossible task, however, and has essentially conceded the job to the political arena. See *Garcia v. San Antonio Metropolitan Transit Authority*, 469 US 528 (1985) and the discussion in Rapaczynski (1986).

opening the executive's administration of existing laws and the executive's deliberations on new laws to public hearings. More efficient public policies with increased representation – and all attending democratic virtues – might then result.

2.3 Choosing a federalist constitution for a compound republic

Two dimensions of constitutional design are uniquely federalist: (1) The creation of hierarchical levels of government – for example, central and state, state and local, or central, state, and local – each with separately *assigned* spheres of policy responsibility, and (2) the specification of *representation* for local interests within the central government, typically through a representative central legislature.

The assignment dimension allocates policy to the higher, central ($A = 1$) or the lower, state or local levels ($A = 0$), where the responsible level of government has the right to finance and execute a policy without fear of a unilateral "veto" by the other level of government. Representation (R) is defined (for example) most simply by equally sized subsets of city-states forming states or provinces, where each state sends a single representative to the central legislature; thus, $R = N/n$, where the N city-states in the union are divided into R states of n communities each with $1 \le R \le N$. In the simplest case, the R states both provide assigned government services and send one representative to the central legislature to set central government policies. The federalist constitution defines A for each government activity and specifies a (usually, single) value of R.[29]

To specify a federalist constitution that is economically efficient, a careful detailing of the costs and benefits of alternative specifications of A and R is required. Breton and Scott (1978) were the first to systematically pursue the design of federalist constitutions from this strictly economic perspective. Their unique contribution was to add the transactions cost of government to the discussion of federalist constitutions. They identified four transactions costs that must be borne in any federalist structure: (1) the costs of revealing positions and selecting a representative for the central legislature (*revelation costs* $= \alpha(R,A)$); (2) the costs of reaching agreements in the state and central legislatures (*decision costs* $= \delta(R,A)$); (3) the costs of monitoring executive or bureaucratic implementation of

---

29. Typically, the assignment dimension lists those activities that are uniquely the responsibility of the central government (e.g., defense policy, commercial policy, trade, and foreign policy) and then specifies a residual rule such as the U.S. Constitution's Tenth Amendment. The representation dimension can be defined for a unicameral or bicameral legislatures. We assume a unicameral legislature for simplicity.

the legislature's decisions (*monitoring costs* = $\sigma(R,A)$); and (4) the costs to citizens of moving from one state (or city) to another to achieve preferred policy outcomes (*moving costs* = $\mu(R,A)$).

The total transactions cost of government is simply $T(R,A) = \alpha(R,A) + \delta(R,A) + \sigma(R,A) + \mu(R,A)$. While Breton and Scott focus on the effects on costs of variations in A, both A and R are likely to be important in a fully specified model of governmental transaction costs. Inman and Rubinfeld (1994) provide empirical evidence that each of Breton and Scott's separate transaction costs and therefore total costs, $T(A,R)$, are all likely to be U-shaped in R and, for each value of R, rising in A. Figures 3a–3d shows plausible specifications for $T(R,A = 1)$ and $T(R,A = 0)$, respectively.

The economic benefit from a particular federalist structure is also shown in Figures 3a–3d, assuming an exogenous policy set of public goods and legislative institutions (L). Benefits are measured by the aggregate consumer surplus (S) generated from the provision of the public activity. Both representation (R) to the central legislature and the assignment of responsibility for the elements of the policy set (A) can affect the allocative performance of federalist governments. Thus, $S = S(R,A; L)$.[30] Consumer surplus will be maximized when the federalist structure provides the efficient level of national (G^e) and particularistic (g_s^e) public goods.

Figure 3a illustrates two plausible patterns of allocative efficiency for national public goods for the MWC and L legislatures when the central government has assignment responsibility for these goods ($A = 1$). In the case of the $L = MWC$ legislature, if increased representation leaves the national median in the legislature unaffected – new members equally represent positions from the left and the right of the median – then as R increases, allocations are fixed and allocative efficiency, $S(\cdot)$, is unaffected. In the case of the $L = U$ legislature, increased representation brings in additional high demanders and spending on the national public good is likely to increase beyond G^e; thus $S(\cdot)$ declines as R rises.

Figure 3b illustrates $S(R,A = 1; L = MWC$ or $U)$ for particularistic public goods. As noted above (2.2.3), $S(\cdot)$ is likely to decline for both the minimum winning coalition ($L = MWC$) and universalism ($L = U$) legislatures; we conjecture that the decline in efficiency as R increases is larger for the universalistic legislature.

---

30. The policy set and legislative institutions can be set by the constitution or they can be left undefined. If left undefined, they become endogenous and functions of R and A. For one model of how the policy set might be determined, see Becker (1983). There is a vast literature on endogenous legislative institutions, beginning with Riker (1982a); the best recent survey is Krehbiel (1992).

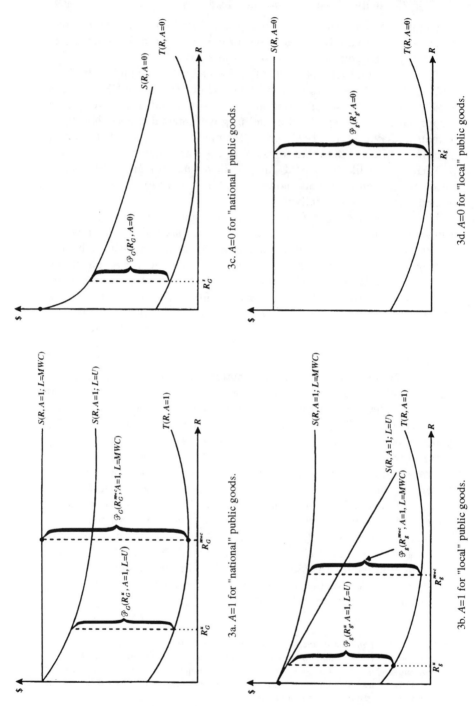

3a. A=1 for "national" public goods.

3c. A=0 for "national" public goods.

3b. A=1 for "local" public goods.

3d. A=0 for "local" public goods.

Figure 3. Representation and assignment.

Figures 3c and 3d show how economic efficiency might change when both national and particularistic public goods are assigned to the states only ($A = 0$).[31] For national public goods, allocative efficiency is likely to decline when only states provide those goods, since free-rider problems discourage efficient interstate bargaining. This is shown in Figure 3c by the steep downward decline in $S(R,A = 0)$ as more states (R) encourage free-riding behavior (see Olson 1965).[32] State-only provision of particularistic public goods is likely to enhance economic efficiency, however (see Figure 3d). When states pay for their own state public goods, they balance the full marginal cost against state benefits; allocations closer to g_s^e are likely to result. Here increasing the number of states (R) will have no effect on S if the benefits of the state good are fully internal to state residents; thus, $S(R,A = 0)$ is horizontal in Figure 3d.

Overall economic efficiency in the compound republic is maximized when the gains from allocative efficiency $S(R,A)$ less the transactions costs of running the government $T(R,A)$, $\mathcal{P}(R,A) = S(R,A) - T(R,A)$, is maximized. In Figures 3a and 3b, $\mathcal{P}(R,A = 1)$ is maximized at the levels of representation R_G^{mwc} and R_G^u and R_g^{mwc} and R_g^u respectively. In Figures 3c and 3d, $\mathcal{P}(R,A = 0)$ is maximized at the levels R_G^s and R_g^s respectively.

When the central government provides public goods ($A = 1$), the MWC legislature is more efficient. Importantly, the ability of MWC legislatures to control excessive government spending allows the public sector to be more representative ($R_G^{mwc} > R_G^u$; see Figure 3a). When only the states provide national and particularistic public goods ($A = 0$), R_G^s is likely to be small for national public goods to internalize spillovers. A comparison of Figures 3a and 3c for national public goods, shows that central provision is likely to be preferred to state provision, despite the potential allocative imperfections of central legislatures:

$$\mathcal{P}_G(R_G^{mwc}, A = 1; L = MWC) > \mathcal{P}_G(R_G^u, A = 1; L = U)$$
$$> \mathcal{P}_G(R_G^s, A = 0).$$

31. Since the central legislature does not allocate the public goods, economic efficiency in this case will be independent of central government legislative institutions – that is, $S = S(R,A)$.

32. Bell (1989) presents a model of state provision of a national public good in which $S(R, A = 0)$ has an inverted U shape. In Bell's model state governments are Leviathans capable of capturing all consumer surplus through lump-sum taxation. When R is small, individual states can exploit citizens. As R rises, state fiscal competition increases and this makes citizens better off. However, the increase in R means more states provide the national public good, which is inefficient. Bell shows that for plausible consumer preferences and spillover technologies a finite value of R greater than 1 is second-best efficient.

Thus, for national public goods, $A = 1$ is the efficient assignment in this case.[33] A similar comparison of Figures 3b and 3d for particularistic public goods favors state provision:

$$\mathcal{P}_g(R_g^s, A = 0) > \mathcal{P}_g(R_g^{mwc}, A = 1; L = MWC)$$
$$> \mathcal{P}_g(R_g^u, A = 1; L = U).$$

Thus, for particularistic public goods, $A = 0$ is the efficient assignment.

With the possibility of efficient assignment, an efficient level of representation can be specified for each public goods technology. Ideally, we would select R_g^s *from Figure 3d and, say,* R_G^{mwc} from Figure 3a, allowing for a separate partitioning of the national population based on the goods to be allocated.[34] If only one partition is allowed so that each state must both provide state goods and select central legislators, then a single value of R must be chosen. This will be that value of R that maximizes $\mathcal{P}_g(R, A = 0) + \mathcal{P}_G(R, A = 1; L = MWC$ or $U)$. Finally, if restricting the domain of the central government through assignment is constitutionally difficult – as the U.S. Supreme Court has discovered (see Rapaczynski 1986) – then $A = 1$ for both particularistic and national public goods and R has meaning only as it determines the number of central government legislators. In this case, the second-best efficient R is that which maximizes $\mathcal{P}_g(R, A = 1; L = MWC$ or $U) + \mathcal{P}_G(R, A = 1; L = MWC$ or $U)$.

While the analysis here clarifies how assignment and representation affect resource allocations in a federalist public economy, the particular conclusions from Figures 3c–3d are, of course, only illustrative. More detailed information about the determinants of the transactions costs of government and additional studies of how central and state legislatures allocate public sector resources are required before confident specifications of the efficient A and R are possible.

Even this information offers only a beginning to setting the federalist constitution. Legal scholars and new communitarians have stressed that important democratic values of protecting rights, encouraging participa-

---

33. This is not the only possible efficiency ordering of federalist institutions, however. For example:

$$\mathcal{P}_G(R_G^{mwc}, A = 1; L = MWC) > \mathcal{P}_G(R_G^s, A = 0) > \mathcal{P}_G(R_G^u, A = 1; L = U),$$

could well result. In this case, we should only centralize the provision of the national public good if we are confident the relatively more efficient MWC regime holds for the central legislature. Otherwise, we should decentralize the provision of the national public good and set $A = 0$.

34. Here the recommendation of separate governments for separate technologies is only partly due to the extent of spillovers. The ability of legislatures to efficiently allocate goods and services given the technologies also matters. This analysis extends the usual spillover-only model (Olson 1969) to accommodate the efficiency effects of political decision making.

tion, and developing civic virtues may be affected by the choice of representation and assignment. Economic equity may weigh in the balance too. Important trade-offs between these values and economic efficiency may emerge as representation and assignment impact jointly on all valued outcomes. If so, hard choices must be made (see Cooter 1987b or Hausman and McPherson 1993). Finally, as economic and political circumstances change over time the preferred federalist structure may change as well. A federalist constitution must be a flexible document capable of responding to new economic and social orders (Mueller 1973).

3. Stability of the federalist constitution

Having chosen a federalist constitution by specifying values of R and A, the question remains: Will that constitution survive the pressures of domestic politics, or will one or more city-states opt to secede from the federalist union? Stability is an issue for both the confederate republic of Montesquieu and for the compound republic of Madison.

3.1 Stability of the confederate republic

Why should a confederate republic that requires unanimity of all participating city-states for any central government action be concerned with secession? One answer is the frustration individual city-states might feel with the process of Coasian bargaining, the cornerstone of public decision making in the compound republic. For reasons noted in Section 2.3, unanimous agreements between city-states, particularly when N is large, may be impossible. Yet even when there is collective agreement as to how to improve the collective welfare of the member city-states, disagreements are sure to arise over the distribution of the resulting economic surplus. City-states that consistently get the smallest share of the benefits from collective action because of high taxes or low services may consider the option of leaving the union. Exit will occur and the confederate republic will be unstable, when the benefits of exit to one or more members are greater than the costs.

Formal models of exit from federal confederate republics have been developed by Buchanan and Faith (1987), Wei (1991), Austin (1994a), and Berkowitz (1994). The models clarify the likely sources of instability. Exit occurs when (1) the long-term fiscal exploitation of a city-state by the union is substantial; (2) the city-state offers few nonfiscal benefits to others in the union; (3) the city-state itself receives few nonfiscal benefits from the union; and, (4) the city-state has a comparative advantage in defending its territory against military or economic (trade war) attack.[35]

Wei (1991) uses his model of exit to explain the decline of the Soviet Republic in which the richer states (Russia, Ukraine, Belorussia, Lithuania, Latvia, and Estonia) have the strongest incentive to exit from a union. Austin (1994b) studied the voting behavior by republics in the All-Union Referendum of March 1991 and found that republics enjoying the greatest net economic benefits from the Union were the most likely to support the Union. Litvack (1994) shows that the same difficulties remain within the new Russian Republic, since the regions rich in natural resources (Bashortostan, Tatarstan, and Yakutia) have withheld taxes, ignored export regulations, and threatened independence.

Wei (1991) notes that the fiscal pressures for secession present in the old Soviet Union also exist within China today. In China, however, the central government has acted by reducing fiscal transfers from the wealthy south to the poorer regions of the north and west. Africa, too, experimented with the confederate republic model of federalism when Tanganyika, Kenya, and Uganda joined together in the 1960s to form the East Africa Federation. Coasian bargains proved difficult, however, when the parties could not agree on the division of the surplus from

---

35. Buchanan and Faith (1987), Wei (1991), and Berkowitz (1994) consider the case of just two players, the potential seceder and the remainder of the polity. The candidate for exit balances the benefits to residents if the city-state exits the union (the saving in fiscal exploitation [F] less any nonfiscal benefits such as access to inexpensive natural resources [T]) against the cost of exit.

Costs are incurred to withstand an "attack" by the rest of the polity seeking to hold the city-state within the union. The remainder of the polity will spend up to A dollars to attack, where $A \leq$ the value to the polity of holding the potential seceder within the union. That value equals the noneconomic benefits of having the seceder in the union (V) plus the net fiscal surplus earned from the seceder (F). Thus, $A \leq V + F$. These A dollars can buy α units of attack, where $\alpha = A/p_a$ and p_a is the cost of the attack. To be successful, the potential exiter must buy at least δ ($\geq \alpha$) units of defense. Defense δ can be bought by spending $D = p_\delta \delta$ dollars. Thus, the successful exiter must spend at least $D = (p_\delta/p_a)(V + F)$ dollars to leave the union.

Finally, exit will occur if benefits are equal to or greater than costs, or if $B = F - T \geq (p_\delta/p_a)(V + F) = D$ or when

$$F[1 - (p_\delta/p_a)] \geq (p_\delta/p_a)V + T.$$

Exit occurs when fiscal exploitation (F) is large, the seceder offers few nonfiscal benefits to others in the union (V low), gets little in return (T low), and has a comparative advantage in defending its territory (p_δ/p_a is small).

These two-player models reveal the central forces which lead to instability, but they are inadequate for predicting whether a confederate republic will actually unravel. More complicated models of coalition formation and stability with $N \geq 3$ city-states will be needed; see Austin (1994a) for a start.

shared facilities – sugar production plants (Leys and Robson 1965). The union dissolved over this and other distribution issues.[36]

3.2 Stability in the compound republic

The compound republic overcomes the difficulties of reaching unanimous agreements in confederacies by requiring simple majorities of representatives from the city-states – not unanimity – for its decisions. Although decision making by majority rule helps ease central government inaction, it increases the likelihood of fiscal exploitation of minorities by majorities. The economic pressures to exit noted above should be even stronger here than in the confederate union run by unanimity because each city-state losses the protection of its legal veto over redistributions. Perhaps the most telling example of attempted exit from a compound republic is the U.S. Civil War.

There is another, more subtle threat, to the federalist constitution in the compound republic, however. Riker (1964) has called it the "overawing" of the states by the central government. Effective federalism must give some responsibilities to the R ($\leq N$) states and protect that agenda through the assignment dimension of the constitution (recall that $A = 0$ for those activities assigned to the states). Riker (1964, chap. 4) examines forces within the republic which act to undo this assignment. Inman (1988) has documented the strong drift toward central government financing and regulation of state and local government activities in the United States over the last fifty years. One major cause has been the shift at the central government level from a MWC legislature to a U legislature. The temptation of locally elected legislators to use central government financing to share the costs of state and local services is present in a compound republic, and under universalistic legislative structures those legislators are not sufficiently constrained. Although the constitution says $A = 0$, political realities give $A = 1$ for many goods and services.

What can be done to protect the integrity of assignment? Riker (1964, 102–3) is skeptical that the judicial branch can effectively enforce assignments. The recent experiences of the U.S. courts provides ample evidence for his concern (see Rapaczynski 1986 and Merritt 1988). For Riker (1964, chap. 4) the national political process itself is the only effective check.

36. There is an extensive historical and political science literature on secession and the formation of nations of which the federalism literature is only a part; see Bookman (1992) and Hobsbawm (1990) for an introduction to these literatures.

To protect assignments, three conditions must hold. First, the desired assignments to the states must be clearly understood and supported in the populace as a whole. Here the federalist constitution, and perhaps the judiciary, plays a crucial role. Second, information about violations of assignment and their consequences must be available to citizens. Here economic analyses of the efficient use of local, state, and federal governments are important (Rivlin 1992). Finally, political institutions that are capable of restoring the assignment balance must be established outside the centralizing forces of government.

Studying the explosion of U.S. central government activity following the 1930s depression, Riker (1964, 91–101) focused on executive branch politics as the cause of central government influence over the states. He looked to strong political parties rooted in local politics to protect state assignment against executive interventions.[37] In contrast, using data from a second period of central government growth in the 1960s and 1970s, Inman (1988) and Fitts and Inman (1992) found the centralizing forces to lie within a locally dominated national legislature, and they advocate nationally elected executives to internalize the inefficiencies of universalism.

Weingast (1993) has brought a broader historical perspective to the question. Weingast finds, contrary to recent U.S. experience, that an independent judiciary establishing local political authority was the key to protecting seventeenth-century England's federalist structure. His analysis of nineteenth-century U.S. federalism stresses, like Riker's analysis of contemporary politics, the importance of strong national political parties grounded in a commitment to limited federal government.

This brief historical record makes clear there is no unique political institution certain to protect assignment in the compound republic. Yet in each of these examples when a political institution did rise to the defense of the federalist constitution – whether it was the executive, the judiciary, or a legislative political party – a single truth prevailed: the vast majority of the citizens in that society believed the federalist constitution to be worth protecting (Elazar 1993).

4. Conclusion

Originally the central issue in the writing of the United States Constitution in 1787, the design of federalist political institutions has once again emerged as crucial for many of the world's economies. The emerging

---

37. A view currently shared by the U.S. Supreme Court in their decision to place the protection of state activities within the legislatures of the central government; see Rapaczynski (1986) and Merritt (1988).

economies in the Russian Republic, Eastern Europe, and South Africa are each struggling to define an appropriate federalist constitution to guide their public choices. The established and stable economies of China, the United States, and Western Europe are searching for new federalist structures for their existing public sectors.

This survey reveals two important dimensions for any federalist constitution: local representation to the central government (R) and assignment (A) of responsibility. Two objectives of any federalist constitution are also identified: protecting rights/promoting civic virtue and achieving economic efficiency. Unfortunately, choices of R and A may not permit the ideal on each objective. Our review of the Coasian bargaining and political economy literatures suggests high values of R and $A = 0$ thought to enhance democratic rights and civic virtues may discourage public sector efficiency. Conversely, low values of R and values of $A = 1$ may enhance efficiency but might diminish citizen representation in government choices. Federalist constitutions must make hard choices and be responsive to the potentially changing economic and political conditions that lay behind those choices.

We reviewed the arguments for two federalist constitutions that come down on opposite sides of the trade-off between democratic rights and virtues, and economic efficiency. Montesquieu strongly favors the goal of citizen representation and thus his confederate constitution is strongly decentralized, setting $R = N$ and $A = 0$. Madison, on the other hand, sought a balance between efficiency and representation. His more centralized compound republic sets $R < N$ and $A = 1$ for many important public activities.

Which of these federalist constitutions is best? We cannot resolve this issue here. We hope, however, that our survey has identified the important questions to be answered before this choice is made. First, how do representation and assignment affect the important political values of participation, protection of individual rights, and the development of civic virtues? Second, how do representation and assignment affect the allocation of goods and services, and thus economic efficiency? Third, knowing how representation and assignment affect rights and efficiency, what combination of these important values do we desire? Fourth, having chosen a constitution, what safeguards can be created to ensure it survives the pressures of daily politics?

Finding answers to these questions will require careful analyses from a full range of scholarly talents – political science, economics, history, philosophy, and law. Each discipline has already made important contributions. We hope this review encourages new research and facilitates a dialogue among scholars working on the federalist question.

CHAPTER 5

The public choice of international organizations

BRUNO S. FREY

International organizations are of great and increasing importance today. There exist at least 350 intergovernmental international organizations with far more than 100,000 employees. A more extensive definition, based on the *Yearbook of International Organizations* lists more than 1,000 intergovernmental units. They constitute a rather new phenomenon: an overwhelming share of international organizations was created after 1939, and the rate of their establishment has accelerated. Some of the international organizations have established themselves as independent forces, existing next to the strongest world powers; most prominent among them is the United Nations. In Europe, the European Union has assumed an important economic and political role. Consequently, the inputs going into, and the activities undertaken by particular international organizations, have greatly expanded. In the European Union, for example, the number of full-time employees has grown from 5,200 (1970) to 12,900 (1990), the number of meetings held by the Council of Ministers has risen from 41 (1970) to 92 (1990), the budget has reached 47 billion ecus (an ecu is approximately equivalent to 2 deutschmarks and 1.20 U.S. dollars), and more than 6,200 legislative acts (regulations, decisions, directives, etc.) have been issued (1990).

There are widely divergent views on international organizations: some consider them to be a necessity in an increasingly interdependent world, characterized by dramatic external effects and economies of scale, and thus a logical development of political and administrative units beyond the historical nation states. Indeed, more than half of the existing organizations have an economic task. Accordingly, international organizations are positively evaluated, and questions of efficiency are considered unimportant. Others, however, take international organizations to be an extreme example of waste and lack of democracy and their activity to be useless if not noxious. Accordingly, international organizations are evalu-

The author is grateful to Iris Bohnet, Isabelle Busenhart, Reiner Eichenberger, and Angel Serna for helpful criticism.

ated negatively and it is often suggested that there exist much better alternatives for the resources used.

On the whole, orthodox neoclassical economists (those assuming social welfare maximizing governments) tend to share the first view, while public choice economists are inclined to subscribe to the second view. This basic orientation is reflected in the general attitude toward international organizations, as well as in the specific topics treated within public choice.

International organizations have been rather neglected by public choice scholars. A major contribution is the fourteen papers collected in Vaubel and Willett (1991), which cover a broad range of topics on international organizations. There are a few journal articles devoted to a *general* public choice theory of international organizations (in particular Fratianni and Pattison 1982; Vaubel 1986, 1992; Frey and Gygi 1990, 1991). In other areas of public choice, international organizations play at best a minor role. Even in international political economy (see e.g., Bernholz 1985, 1992b; Magee, Brock, and Young 1989; Weck-Hanneman 1992) international organizations are referred to only in passing and are not analyzed (exceptions are Frey and Schneider 1984 and Frey 1986, chap. 8). International organizations have, of course, been extensively treated in political science, particularly in international relations. Normally the public choice contributions are either overlooked or neglected on purpose but, again, there are noteworthy exceptions (e.g., Crane and Amawi 1991). In any case, the public choice view of international organizations has so far not had any major impact on other research in this area.

Although there has been little public choice work on international organizations in general, *specific* institutions have attracted much more attention. It should be noted here that public choice scholars use the term "international organization" also for supranational organizations into which individual nations merge (such as the European Union). Nongovernmental international organizations (NGOs), on the other hand, are generally excluded. An abundance of literature exists on their "embryonic" state, namely, on macroeconomic policy coordination and cooperation (see, e.g., Feldstein 1988a, 1988b; Guerrieri and Padoan 1988), but it is often analyzed under the assumption that governments maximize social welfare (for a public choice analysis, see Gygi 1991). Although such coordination may come about as the result of contracts between nations, in most cases some form of centralized institutionalization arises. Important examples are the United Nations Law of the Seas Conference (UNCLOS), the International Energy Program, the GATT and OECD, which have been subjected to public choice analyses (see Tollison and Willett 1976, Eckert 1991; Smith 1991; Moser 1990, Finger 1991; Fratianni and Pattison 1976, respectively). Among the international institutions with a well-established bureaucratic structure, NATO (Olson and

Zeckhauser 1966; Sandler 1977) and the United Nations have received particular attention. Public Choice inspired studies have especially focused on UN financial institutions. The International Monetary Fund has been analyzed by Dreyer and Schotter (1980) and Vaubel (1983, 1991a), the World Bank by Frey (1984), and Frey and Schneider (1986). Not surprisingly, the formation and functioning of the European Union has led to a number of public choice studies (e.g., Faber and Breyer 1980; Forte 1985; Faiña and Puy-Fraga 1988; Josling and Moyer 1991; Pierce 1991a, 1991b; Vaubel 1991b, 1992, 1994; and Schuknecht 1992).

The public choice analyses of international organizations use the generally accepted methodology (see Mueller 1989 for public choice in general and Dillon, Ilgen, and Willett 1991 for specific areas), that is, they are based on individuals who are rational and essentially selfish, distinguish clearly between preferences and constraints, attribute changes in behavior to changes in constraints (rather than to unobserved differences in preferences), and consider equilibrium situations (Becker 1976; Kirchgässner 1991; Frey 1992). Compared to other areas in public choice, the studies of international organizations tend to be less formal and more problem oriented and use more empirical data, though, with few exceptions (Vaubel 1992; Frey and Schneider 1986), no econometric estimates have been performed. These studies try to explain what is observed in reality (though there is, as already indicated, a certain normative overtone); policy conclusions are more an incidental result than a main purpose of the analysis.

The basic constitutional issues including the different voting rules employed in international organizations set the stage in the survey (Section 1). The question of how far the behavior of international institutions responds to the preferences of individuals is dealt with in Section 2. This leads to analysis of bureaucracy and efficiency in international organizations (Section 3). A final section evaluates the strengths and weakness of the public choice of international organizations and discusses future research needs and possibilities. The purpose of this survey is not to provide a comprehensive account of all contributions in the area but rather to give the reader an idea of the state of existing research. As will become apparent, in some of the areas dealt with, a substantial amount of research has been undertaken, while other (equally important) areas have so far scarcely been touched.

1. Constitutional issues

1.1 Externalities and free riding

The international community presents an ideal case (in the sense of Max Weber) for a constitutional or social contract: the underlying units are sovereign (there is no preexisting world government) but their behavior results in a clearly Pareto-inferior situation. Although the constitutional contract is normally applied to individuals (Buchanan and Tullock 1962; Brennan and Buchanan 1980; Mueller 1996), it can also be applied to nations as actors (e.g., Forte 1985).[1] Indeed, the Hobbesian jungle of *bellum omnium contra omnes* seems to be even more relevant for the interaction among nations. Military and trade wars (protectionism) with their destructive outcomes for all participants are all too common events; international public goods (e.g., those relating to the global environment) are underproduced and international common property resources (e.g., the fish in the seas) are overexploited (see, e.g., Olson 1971). There is no world government in sight that would be able to control effectively the behavior of nations pursuing their own selfish interests. A Pareto-superior outcome can only come about by voluntary consent among the nations. Countries that do not find the expected cost–benefit ratio of common action to be worthwhile for themselves do not join. Only a consensus among participants constitutes a social contract of practical consequence. Hence, the question is not whether the set of all actors reaches a consensus but rather over what set of issues some actors are able to agree (Frey 1983). This point can be illustrated with the example of the United Nations: while *almost* all nations on earth are members (an exception is Switzerland), this organization does not really constrain its members to any significant degree and is therefore of limited productivity. Other international organizations cover only a limited share of all potential and relevant members, but the voluntary agreement reached is more productive because it more effectively restrains those actions of its members that reduce Pareto-optimality (an example is a free trade agreement such as those reached within the European Community [EC] and the European Free Trade Association [EFTA]). Obviously, not all international agreements start *ex nihilo;* often the countries joining in are bound by preexisting contracts – in the case of the EU, for instance, the member countries were members of treaties such as NATO, GATT, and IMF, and many were connected by close bilateral agreements.

The formation of international agreements can be usefully analyzed with the help of club theory which stresses the voluntary nature of membership and the exclusion of nonmembers who may not benefit from the goods jointly provided (Buchanan 1965; Sandler and Tschirhart 1980; Cornes and Sandler 1986; and Ostrom and Walker in this volume apply club theory to international issues).

A central concept behind all this theorizing is free riding in the

---

1. Such an approach risks to loose the relationship to the fulfillment of individual preferences. This aspect will be taken up in Section 2.

presence of public goods as originally developed by Olson (1965). Indeed, one of the earliest empirical applications has been to burden sharing within NATO. The small member states are able to exploit the large ones because they can free ride on the public good defense provided. It has been shown that the large countries, especially the United States, pay a more than proportional share of the defense effort (Olson and Zeckhauser 1966). The same has been suggested for the European Union. The three largest member countries (Germany, the United Kingdom, and France) pay more taxes than they receive in benefits (transfer fees), while a very small country like Luxembourg receives the largest net receipts per capita (1985–9; see Vaubel 1992, 31).

International public goods need not be provided by international organizations. A once-and-for-all assignment of property rights may give nations incentives (see Tollison and Willett 1976 for transnational externalities). Cooperation and a satisfactory provision of such goods may also come through a network of bilateral contracts (Coase 1960), provided the transaction costs are not excessive. Most international agreements lead to the establishment of at least a secretary's office charged with putting into effect and supervising the agreements, thus forming the nucleus of an international organization. A more developed international body has a certain amount of decision-making power within the rules laid out in its constitution. The agreement reached among the member states relates only to the general rules not to particular actions. A consensus on these "rules of the game" can only be arrived at behind the veil of uncertainty, that is, no country knows for certain how it will be affected in particular but expects to benefit from their existence over a sequence of yet unknown future events. One of the most basic ground rules relates to the way the decisions are to be taken (i.e., the voting rules).

1.2 Voting rules

There are a great many options in the way decisions are to be taken in an international organization (Facts are given in Zamora 1980). Three aspects are primordial.

First, what *kind* of decision rule has to be applied for what kind of issue. In public choice theory, a large number of different procedures has been suggested (see Mueller 1989). They range from the well-known majority rule over rank and point voting to new decision rules such as the demand-revealing process (see Tideman and Tullock 1976), approval voting (Brams and Fishburn 1978) or veto voting (Mueller 1978). It is interesting to note that the voting rules in international organizations tend to be very conservative, and none of the new alternatives to the majority rules seem to have been applied.

Second, within the majority rule the *size* of the majority has to be determined (Buchanan and Tullock 1962; Rae 1969). In this respect, the situation in a national polity or committee and an international organization differ considerably. In the former, the citizens can exit only with considerable cost and are thus vulnerable to exploitation by the rest of the community through the political process, that is, Buchanan and Tullock's "external costs" of decision making are large. In an international organization, on the other hand, the autonomous member states can exit fairly easily. This difference forces the collective decision process to focus more on public good-type issues and to adopt higher qualified majorities in their voting rules. Indeed, the extreme of 100 percent majority or unanimity is important in many international organizations (e.g., the UN Security Council), a major reason being that nations forced against their will either do not observe the decision or may even leave the organization. Other forms of qualified majority and of blocking minorities, or veto power, are common in international organizations, in particular in order to secure the rights of some special class of members.

Third, the voting rules have to specify the *number* of votes attributed to a member nation. The attribution of one vote per country applies only to some institutions (e.g., to the General Assembly of the UN). Often, more populous countries get more votes (as in the EU Council of Ministers), and in the case of the UN financial institutions the countries get a vote weight corresponding to their financial contribution to the budget. A quota change thus affects a country's influence measured by the ex ante Shapley–Shubik or Bhanzaf power index (for the International Monetary Fund, see Dreyer and Schotter 1980).

The allocation of vote weights has a rather straightforward effect on the expenditure behavior of the members of an international organization (Frey and Gygi 1991). Consider the one-country, one-vote rule obtaining in the UN General Assembly. A very small number of countries carry the overwhelming share of the organization's finance: the United States (in 1991 roughly 25 percent of the total), Japan (approximately 11 percent), Germany (approximately 8 percent), France (approximately 6 percent), and the United Kingdom (approximately 5 percent) contribute more than half the budget while 150 countries contribute the remaining; most pay far less than 1 percent of the total. These latter countries have, of course, a strong incentive to vote for any increase in the budget (and even more so against a decrease) because they are not financially affected but may participate in the benefits of such extensions. Hence, not surprisingly, this constitutional vote assignment leads to chronic financial problems. Only the few large payers have the incentive to keep the budget under control (see Section 4). The situation is quite different for UN financial institutions. In the International Monetary Fund the countries that mainly finance the budget have a corresponding vote weight. Thus, the United States has roughly 19 percent of the vote share, and the UK, Germany, France, and Japan between 5 and 7 percent. As a consequence, those members that have the largest stake in these organizations also have the possibility to affect their policy by using the votes attributed to them by the charta.

The effect of voting rules on formal (ex ante) vote power and on outcomes has been intensively studied for the European Union (Faber and Breyer 1980; Brams and Affuso 1985). The major decision-making body is the EU Council of Ministers, which since the mid-1980s has employed qualified majority voting in a vast range of areas and will increasingly do so provided integration does not suddenly stop.[2] The voting weights of the member states in the Council of Ministers mainly depend on population size, but the smaller states (especially Luxembourg with two votes) get a disproportionately high weight.

An ex ante voting power index has been used to show the influence of new members to the organization (Hösli 1993). The change in the Bhanzaf power index has been calculated from the foundation of the European Community of six nations in 1958 to a possible enlargement to nineteen nations, including the EFTA member states. Each of the large countries (France, Germany, and Italy) would experience a drop in voting power from 24 percent to less than 10 percent in an extended EU of nineteen nations. The same power decrease would be experienced by the middle-sized countries with five and three votes each. Luxembourg, on the other hand, would *gain* in power due to the addition of new members, a phenomenon that has been termed "paradox of new members" (Brams and Affuso 1985). Though from 1858 to 1973 this smallest country with two votes could never turn a losing into a winning coalition (i.e., the Bhanzaf power index was zero), the addition of the United Kingdom, Spain, Greece, Portugal, Denmark, and Ireland increased its voting power to 1.8 percent, and the possible addition of the seven EFTA states would further *raise* it to 2.2 percent.

The strengths and weaknesses of the ex ante power indexes, including the differences between the Bhanzaf and Shapley–Shubik indexes have been extensively discussed in the public choice literature (e.g., Brams

---

2. Nevertheless, the fear of member states of being outvoted led to the Luxembourg compromise in 1966, according to which issues legally subject to majority voting would still be decided by unanimity in the EC Council of Ministers if a member state feels "crucial national interests" threatened. Although it never attained a legal status, this agreement perpetuated consensual decision making in practice until the mid-1980s (see Hösli 1993).

1992). Though capable of capturing only a fraction of what is generally considered to be "power," such an index is well suited to the study of constitutional issues of voting. It assumes that the choice between voting rules and voting weights has to be taken behind the veil of uncertainty insofar as the issues forthcoming, and the possible interests and coalitions between the member states, are unknown, so that all possible cases have to be considered and, absent further knowledge, weighted equally.

2. Representation and responsiveness

2.1 Nations and delegates

Most studies analyzing the behavior of international organizations (including the public choice approaches discussed in the last section) assume nations to be the relevant actors (e.g., Bernholz 1985; Forte 1985). Such a view is useful for some types of analyses, but it is inconsistent with the basic tenet of economics. Only individuals act in accordance with their preferences and constraints. Nations do not have preferences nor do they respond to incentives in a way comparable to individuals (for instance, they are not necessarily subject to the "law of demand").

Within international organizations, not nations but country representatives or delegates are the actors (Frey and Gygi 1990). While they often claim to pursue solely the "national interest," the public choice approach holds that they pursue their *own* interests. "National interest" as perceived by the delegates is just one determinant of their behavior. There are marked conflicts between the constitutional rules desired by the delegates and the rules desired by the national voters. Also, within the given rules (i.e., in the post-constitutional context) the behavior of delegates may systematically and significantly deviate from the wishes of the national voters.

In representative and direct democracies the national representatives are not directly elected by the voters but are usually appointed by the government or by the heads of the national public administrations, in a few cases by the national parliaments. The delegates may be politicians or members of the national bureaucracies (diplomats). These individuals do not necessarily have common interests and are not subject to the same constraints, but they are in many aspects similar and so can be treated as a group.

According to the economic model, behavior is determined by preferences and constraints. A delegate's preference function contains income, prestige, and a peaceful (conflict-free) life. These are all positively connected with the existence and growth of the international organization to which they are delegated. (This corresponds to Niskanen's [1971] assumption). This positive association is strengthened by a self-selection process, because those politicians and bureaucrats with a favorable view of an international organization are more inclined to apply to, and accept, such an assignment. For those representatives who are appointed "contre coeur," cognitive dissonance tends to lead to a positive identification with the particular international organization. It is also rational (in the narrow economic sense) because the other members of the international organization oppose and block the actions of delegates who are considered to be a threat. To have any influence, delegates are well advised to support strongly the organization to which they are attached. Politicians and bureaucrats who are the delegating decision makers tend to identify the performance of the international organization with the performance of the respective delegates. Moreover, the national delegates may see the international organization as a possible future job provider. Not rarely, national delegates participate in the foundation and development of an international organization, to be thereafter offered high level jobs in it.

Delegates are subject to a number of constraints. First of all, each delegate has to take into account the actions of other national representatives as well as those of the international organization's administration. Secondly, national bureaucrats see to it that the international organizations do not interfere too much with their own functions and in particular oppose actions of the delegates that tend to make them superfluous. The national ministry of finance is interested in controlling the funds going to the international organizations to maintain its influence. The delegates are thus subject to financial constraints. Finally, the national politicians in need of reelection make an effort to force the delegates to act in a way the politicians conceive to be popular with the voters. The delegates must respect this demand to act in the so-defined national interest because they depend in turn on the politicians to remain in their function.

As a result of this constellation of preferences and constraints, national delegates tend to be favorably disposed toward the international organization to which they are attached, but they must make sure that the national sovereignty is not restricted too much and that the national interest as perceived by the delegating politicians is adequately served.

The national delegates support rules and actions that further the growth and importance of, and increase their influence in, the respective international organization. In particular they are in favor of establishing the following rules:

1. The delegates must have extensive possibilities to act within the particular international organization and to exert influence, or

at least to have their views known. Assemblies, meetings, sessions, and working groups serve this purpose, allowing the delegates to project themselves favorably to the public and to their own governments. These forms of get-togethers are considered to be output both by the delegates and by the administrators of international organizations.

2. Each nation's share of employees in the international organization's administration must be secured, mitigating the conflict between national delegates and contributing to a peaceful life. At the same time such rules make it clear that the delegates fight for their respective national interest.

3. An international organization must as far as possible be given a monopolistic position in a particular field. Due to the positive association with the development of the organization, the delegates personally benefit thereby.

4. Rules are demanded that make it difficult for a nation to leave the international organization. For a national delegate this has the obvious advantage that she can further enjoy the rents produced by her position. Furthermore, the international organization is better able to expand its activities at the national taxpayers' cost, which has positive spin-offs for the national representatives. In the same vein, the delegates support rules that make exit an all-or-nothing decision. As is known from Niskanen's (1971) model of bureaucracy, such a situation enables the suppliers of the services (i.e., the international organizations) to "exploit" the demanders for the services, in this case the national finance ministries and indirectly the taxpayers.

5. Rules serving to enlarge the financial autonomy of an international organization are welcomed by delegates; most favored are the admissibility of budget deficits and fixed contributions attached to a growing tax base. The best system for the delegates is to have the national contributions fixed once and for all as a percentage of the international organization's budget (i.e., of expenditures). Once established, the respective financial contributions are not normally questioned by the national parliament and government but are taken as sacrosanct. As most international organization's administrations are to some extent able to determine the budget, the spenders at the same time determine the receipts, once the financing rule is set. National contributions as a fixed percentage of the budget is indeed the common financing rule in the UN system (except for financial suborganizations such as the IMF and the World Bank).

2.2 National politicians

Why are national politicians prepared to transfer competencies to an international organization? Prima facie, they therewith restrict their discretion and reduce their power; hence, this question is pertinent. Several explanations have been offered (see Vaubel 1993).

First, by joining an international organization, the national politicians can protect or raise their power vis-à-vis the governments of nonmember nations. This applies, for instance, to trade negotiations and parts of foreign policy. Politicians also increase their influence as they see to it that their nationals employed in the international organization are assigned responsibilities which are particularly important to their country (for the assignments in the European Union see Kuhn 1993). Second, joining an international organization can serve to reduce criticism and opposition. The common action of an international organization makes it impossible for the voters to compare alternative policies, in particular with respect to taxation, regulation, and monetary policy. Budgetary policies (say an extension of transfers) may serve as a pretext to develop similar domestic activities (Breton and Wintrobe 1982), and an agreement on minimum tax rates (as, for example, in the European Union with respect to the value-added tax) may make it less unpopular to increase domestic taxes. This is the "political dustbin" theory whereby an international organization serves as an alibi and scapegoat for local politicians undertaking measures undesired by the local voters and interest groups (Vaubel 1986, 1992; Peirce 1991a, 1991b). Third, as a consequence of the homogenization of policy achieved and information provided via an international organization,[3] the voters have less scope to protest (to raise their voice) or to exit (Hirschman 1970), which serves to bolster the domestic politicians' position or, more drastically, the cartel of national politicians against the national voters. Fourth, joining an international organization tends to blur the division of responsibilities between it and the national government, which enables domestic politicians to at least partially shirk their responsibilities (see Scharpf 1988 for the case of Germany and the European Community). Fifth, the national politicians who (in a representative democracy) decide to enter an international organization and who maintain the contact with it use this to weaken the power of competing domestic lower-level governments and independent public institutions such as the courts, the central bank, and regulatory agencies. Finally, national politicians are prepared

---

3. Fratianni and Pattison (1982) show, for example, that forecasts and policy evaluations provided by international organizations are biased in favor of their member governments.

to transfer competencies to an international organization because of the job prospects that open up.

2.3 Individuals

In representative and direct democracies international organizations are only one of many issues on which elections are decided, but the individuals may to a limited degree exert some influence, in particular via the press and public opinion surveys (see, e.g., Kay 1977 for the views of American citizens concerning the United Nations or the continuous EUROBAROMETER reporting on European citizens' attitudes toward the European Union).

The citizens are interested in rules that induce the international organizations to take their preferences into account. The first way of achieving this is to induce the national delegates to fight for their interests. This can be done by having the delegates elected directly by the citizens, or at least by parliament in a public session. Another possibility is to introduce the national constitutional rule that the entry into, and the exit from, international organizations are to be subjected to popular referendum. Yet another would be to regulate the career pattern of national representatives by rewarding them for pursuing the citizens' interests and punishing them for not doing so. Such a compensation scheme is, however, extremely difficult to devise.

The second way to induce international organizations to act according to individual preferences is via rules that constrain their behavior in an appropriate way and that in particular reduce the discretionary room available to the national delegates and the managers of the international organizations. Various constitutional rules serve this purpose. First, competition between international organizations can be allowed, and possibly created, so that they are forced to serve individuals' interests. Competition may come also from alternative institutional arrangements for providing the international public good. Such competitive institutions rarely seem to exist, but there are in fact many instances in which there is some competitive pressure. Examples are the Red Cross and Amnesty International (a nongovernmental international organization), which are both active in the care and release of political prisoners; the United Nations General Assembly and the Summit Meetings, where the heads of governments of industrial nations meet for consultations; or ad hoc banking consortia, which, together with the UN's financial institutions, are active in international public debt negotiations. The national voters are interested in strengthening competition and, above all, preventing a monopolistic position for any one international organization. Second, exit can be facilitated (see Buchanan 1990; Bernholz 1992a for the case of the European Union). Such rules weaken the possibility of the international organization's administration disregarding the interests of the citizens of any member state. Third, output can be partitionable. Such a rule allows the international organization to support those of its undertakings that benefit national individuals and resist others that are harmful. "Exit in steps" is herewith made possible, as has, for instance, been done by the United States and France in the United Nations (see e.g., Brinkmann 1978). And, fourth, the "government" or "board of managers" of international organizations can be elected by popular vote, either directly (this could, for example, be envisaged for the commissioners of the European Union) or by some indirect procedure. Such a voting rule would give the leaders of an international organization an incentive to pay more attention to the preferences of the citizens of the member nations. It would also help to resist the demands of particular producer interest groups whose influence compared to consumer and tax payer interests tends to be even stronger on the international than on the national level (Olson 1965; European Community lobbying is discussed, for example, by Andersen and Eliassen 1991).

The analysis reveals striking differences as to what rules governing international organizations are desired by delegates and politicians as compared to individual citizens. Indeed, their interests are antagonistic particularly with respect to whether an international organization should have a monopoly or be subjected to competition and whether exit should be facilitated or prevented. The sharp differences in the interests concerning these rules do not normally become apparent. The conflicts are not easily seen by the individual voters, particularly because the delegates and politicians use the rhetoric of the "general national interest" to help construct rules that are "reasonable" from their point of view.

An occasion in which the conflict about the rules becomes visible is when the voters are allowed to make their views known by a referendum. Such a case occurred in Switzerland. On 16 March 1986 the voters were asked whether Switzerland should join the United Nations as a full member. In the preceding campaign the whole political establishment – the members of the federal executive and parliament, the top bureaucrats of the federal administration, and the media – were unanimous in urging entry. Visible opposition was raised only by some marginal groups. All the more surprising was the result of the vote: 75 percent of the Swiss voters rejected the proposition and not one single canton could muster a majority for it. The Swiss press criticized the rejection of entry into the UN heavily. The citizens were accused of being uninformed and incompetent. Public choice theory suggests quite a different interpretation. In contrast to the politicians, the overwhelming majority of Swiss citizens did not expect any benefit from joining the UN, given the rules that presently apply within the United Nations.

3. Bureaucracy and efficiency

3.1 Ill-defined output

Public choice looks at international organizations as a public bureaucracy – but one in which its characteristics are more pronounced than in the national setting. International bureaucracies and bureaucrats have greater room for discretionary behavior because the national bureaucrats, politicians, and voters have little incentive and possibility (see Section 2) to control them effectively. No political actors would gain by tightly monitoring and overseeing an international organization. They find it more advantageous to let things go and intervene only if they feel their own nationals employed in the organization are unfairly treated or that their interests are directly threatened by the organization's activity. This also happens when major scandals connected with international organizations become known, because domestic voters may hold the national politicians responsible. Otherwise, the international bureaucrat's discretionary room remains unaffected.

The large leeway granted international organizations for their current activities is also due to the immeasurableness of their output and therewith efficiency (e.g., Leff 1988; Frey and Gygi 1991). Outside public choice, many studies have sought to determine the "efficiency" with which international organizations act. Thus, for example, the Joint Inspection Unit looks at administration within the UN system. But its members may not attack the larger question, in particular whether a "useful output" is produced. This is a political issue that they may not discuss and evaluate. Even if they were allowed to do so (an effort for a scientific analysis is made, for example, by Scoble and Wiseberg 1976), it is impossible to find an objective standard of what an international organization's output is. Such an organization undertakes many activities, say the pursuit of world peace, the promotion of economic development, and the achievement of justice (more equal world income distribution). If the member states (who for the moment are taken to be a behavioral unit) have different preferences, it is in general impossible to consistently define what aggregate output is. If the members decide by majority rule, they cannot agree on the relative weights attributed to the three activities, which is a case for the Condorcet paradox producing cycles. The same happens when other aggregation mechanisms are used, provided some rationality conditions apply (Arrow's 1951 impossibility theorem). Output can, of course, be defined unilaterally by a state but this judgment is not relevant for the other (sovereign) member states of an international organization. There may be some international organizations whose activities can be reduced to one dimension, in which case their output can be consistently defined provided the member states' preferences are sufficiently similar (Black's 1958 single-peakedness requirement). As a rule, however, the activities of international bodies are complex and multidimensional, so that a decision of what constitutes aggregate output is possible only if the preferences of the members were practically identical (see Plott 1967), a condition that does not apply in reality in view of the intercountry differences with respect to goals and resources. It follows that to define and to measure an international organization's output and efficiency is inherently elusive. The managers and bureaucrats in international organizations are well aware of this fact and use it for their own benefit. By manipulating the agenda at the general assemblies (see the literature on agenda setting, starting with McKelvey 1976) but also vis-à-vis the media, they are able to expand their discretionary room.

3.2 The use of discretion

The public choice literature is rather mute on the question of how the employees in an international organization use the leeway accorded to them. A partial exception is Vaubel's (1993) study of the European Union. The EU Commission is even further removed from the control of voters because it is not elected by them. As, according to "Popitz's (1927) law" politicians are attracted to the largest budget and the correspondingly large discretionary room, a position within the EU Commission is particularly attractive to politicians of member countries whose central government budget is small compared to the EU budget. An economic analysis reveals indeed that ceteris paribus a commissioner's political status (according to a formal criterion) is higher if she comes from a small country with a small central government budget.

The discretionary room is partly used by increasing the number of employees; since 1960 it has been raised almost ten times and has more than quadrupled relative to the Community's population. Even more pertinent are the high net salaries paid in the EU administration: EU bureaucrats earn between 70 and 100 percent more than a bureaucrat in the German Federal government for a comparable activity (Frey 1985, table 8.3). Promotion has little to do with ability or effort; employees get on mainly because of nationality or political affiliation. That there exists a substantial rent is also suggested by the fact that (even under favorable general employment conditions) there were on average fifty times more job applications than vacancies within the EU administration.

Similar observations have been made for other international organizations. The staff of the International Monetary Fund has grown more quickly than that of the American Federal Reserve (between 1950 and 1986, 3.8 percent compared to 2.8 percent per annum), and the ratio of salary cost per man year has increased from 1.2 in 1950 to 1.6 in 1986 in favor of IMF employees (Vaubel 1991, tables 3 and 5). The chiefs' income at the World Bank and IMF (which are equal) is almost three times the salary of the chairman of the Federal Reserve (if taxes are taken into account). The net salary, for example, of economists is also much higher than in national bureaucracies (*The Economist,* 24 April 1993, 75–6). The substantial perks in terms of luxurious offices, receptions, and travel frequently commented on in the popular press also supports the public choice notion that ill-controlled bureaucracies exploit the slack for selfish purposes, and not least for direct monetary benefits. The use of the discretion available to managers of international organizations is also reflected in economic indicators. The selfish international bureaucrats pursue those policies that give them the most prestige and influence within the reference groups with which they are connected. In the case of the World Bank, for instance, this is the international financial community. Hence, the top World Bank bureaucrats gain utility by giving credits to countries according to the principles of fiscal conservatism and a friendly attitude toward (direct) foreign investment. Developing countries with low rates of inflation, small budget deficits, and a climate conducive to capitalism, are ceteris paribus treated more friendly. At the same time, the top bureaucrats do well to yield to the demands of the major donors (traditionally the United States, the United Kingdom, and France) because they are the only ones who would interfere to the bureaucrat's disadvantage. As a consequence, it may be expected that the LDCs connected with these donors (i.e., their former colonies and dominions) ceteris paribus get more credits. This model of World Bank behavior has been econometrically tested for the period 1972–81 in a comparative perspective (Frey and Schneider 1986). The competing models are based on "need" (credits given on the basis of LDCs that are in the worst situation and require the credits most), "desert" (to LDCs that exhibit the strongest potential for development and gain the most from the credits), and "benevolence" (to LDCs that best fulfill the World Bank's officially declared goals, that is, where the top bureaucrats act as if they were only concerned with the Bank's objectives). The results (including ex-post forecasts) suggest that the politicoeconomic model is best able to account for the differences in

World Bank credits received by thirty-two developing countries. In particular, the former states of a recipient country as a colony or dominion helps to receive credits, an aspect that would be difficult to explain in a behavioral model based on "need," "desert," or "benevolence."

4. Evaluation

The major strength of the public choice of international organizations is its issue orientation, coupled with a sound and imaginative use of the concepts of (modern) political economy. In contrast to other areas of economics and also public choice (e.g., social choice theory or the modeling of perfect political competition), the analysis has not become increasingly self-contained and academically oriented but has looked at real world issues from the particular point of view of public choice. Therewith it has brought in a completely new element into the research object, in particular, the emphasis on selfish individual behavior and the incentives faced under varying circumstances (different constraints) as well as on the choice of rules in a constitutional setting. The approach constitutes a significant departure from the organic view of international organization common in international relations theory and (traditional) political science. To a considerable extent, the public choice scholars active in the field could draw on a ready-made theory, an example being the whole area of voting theory, ranging from the general impossibility theorem over agenda setting to the properties of particular voting rules, including the theory of pivotal groups on which the game theoretic power indexes (discussed in Section 2) are based. On the whole, however, these models have (so far) not proved to be useful because they were constructed for national policies. Thus, the well-known models of bureaucracy by Niskanen (1971) rely on special institutional assumptions (the U.S. political system) that are not relevant to the same extent for the setting in which international organizations act. More general models of bureaucracy (e.g., Breton and Wintrobe 1982) seem more applicable.

The public choice theory of international organizations is only at its *beginnings.* Many parts of public choice have not yet been applied, or at least not adequately exploited. Examples that immediately come to mind are international organizations as clubs; the role of exit and voice in a comparative perspective; a fuller use of rent-seeking models; the whole supply process of international organizations (including its particular production technology features); the determinants of the size and growth of the bureaucracies; the competition between international organizations and their relationship to bilateral and multilateral contracts and agreements, and so forth. The public choice approach in this area has only made first attempts to use econometric methods to test the theoretical propositions; there is scope for much more, especially as the databases for such work can be borrowed to some extent from quantitative international relations theory.

With respect to *policy,* public choice has contributed the crucial insight that there is little prospect of changing an international organization's behavior in the current politicoeconomic process (e.g., by substituting its top bureaucrats). Rather, the "rules of the game," which affect the incentives and the behavior of the member countries and employees in the organization, need to be changed. This has, for instance, been exemplified in the deviation between the vote share and the financial contributions share on an international organization's budget.

Several concrete constitutional reforms have been suggested that, behind the veil of uncertainty, may serve to better fulfill the preferences of citizens as consumers and taxpayers: competition between various international organizations; facilitation of exit of member countries and a partitioning of the activities or the possibility of a partial exit; fiscal equivalence; and a strengthening of the direct participation of the citizens via election of top decision makers in the international organizations and via popular initiatives and referenda (see Schneider 1992 for the European Union). Such constitutional proposals should also be analyzed for, and adapted to, extensions of international organizations (such as the United Nations or the European union). So far little thought has been given to the possibility of at least partly privatizing (governmental) international organizations. The willingness to pay for some of the services offered by them might be exploited, say the use of international waterways (provided a respective international organization keeps them open and secures them); the development of natural resources especially on the seabed or in Antarctica; the use of outer space (where the service may consist of allocating scarce goods such as frequencies or satellite orbits); or the preservation of cultural goods (where, for example, UNESCO may receive a share of entry fees). More speculative is a monetary compensation for the preservation of peace (which is at best implicitly done today), the peace-keeping operations of the United Nations, for example. One would even think of an "insurance system for peace" (Frey 1974) wherein an international organization offers to maintain the physical integrity of a country against an appropriate premium. The task of public choice economists is to go beyond mere proposals to carefully analyze the incentives created by the rules of international organizations, as well as the effects of these incentives on the behavior of international bureaucrats. If economists take up this challenge, they could make the public choice of international organizations even more relevant and important. This could transform the area from a rather neglected one into one central to public choice.

CHAPTER 6

Constitutional public choice

DENNIS C. MUELLER

Political history is largely an accounting of past events and people. Almost every rendering of the political history of this country gives the impression that specific individuals played important, and often decisive, roles in determining past events: George Washington launched the American democracy; Thomas Jefferson purchased the Louisiana Territory, which defined the geographic dimensions of the United States; Abraham Lincoln preserved the union; and Franklin Roosevelt inaugurated the era of big government during the depression.

The perspective of public choice is, however, directly at odds with this interpretation of political history, for it assumes all men and women seek to advance their own interests and that the political, economic, and social institutions that surround them shape the choices they make in pursuit of that goal. If institutions do not "make the man," they do, in combination with his goals, determine his actions. Political events are in turn the aggregate consequences of these actions. From the perspective of public choice, political history is an accounting of events and institutions not of specific people and personalities.

Almost all public choice treats political institutions as given constraints on the self-interested actions of individuals. This emphasis on positive analysis also characterizes the contributions to this volume. In this essay, I wish to take up the question of where these institutions come from.

There are two ways to approach this question, one is essentially normative: What political institutions ought a society to choose to advance the individual interests of its citizens? The other is positive: Why does country A have one set of political institutions and country B another? Given the heavy emphasis placed on the positive analysis of political behavior in public choice, it is perhaps surprising that most of the literature that has examined the selection of political institutions falls into the former category (i.e., it is implicitly if not overtly normative). We shall accordingly begin with and concentrate on the question of the optimal set of political institutions from the point of view of a group (society) of self-interested individuals and, toward the end of the essay, turn to more positive questions concerning the actual origins of political institutions.

1. The creation of government

The methodological cornerstone of public choice is what Joseph Schumpeter (1908) termed "methodological individualism."[1] The focal point of analysis is the individual. His goals and actions are modeled, and from these one aggregates up to the level of society. The first question public choice asks is why rational, self-interested individuals would create the institutions of government. The answer usually given is that there exist situations (often depicted with the help of a prisoners' dilemma matrix)[2] in which the independent, self-interested actions of each individual lead to outcomes that are Pareto inferior to what could be achieved through cooperative agreement. For example, Crusoe and Friday may be able to survive quite well gathering food independently of one another, but if stealing food is easier than gathering it, both may devote some of their time to this activity, and since stealing diverts Crusoe and Robinson from food gathering, it reduces the total amount of food gathered; both may therefore benefit from an agreement to prohibit stealing. Two individuals stranded on an island can be expected to reach informal agreements to prevent stealing. But, when numbers are large the transaction costs of making an enforcing informal agreement can make government the least cost institution for achieving cooperation. Thus, government (viewed as an institution created by rational, self-interested individuals) is a set of institutions for resolving prisoners' dilemmas – providing public goods, eliminating externalities, and achieving other mutual gains from cooperation in the lowest cost manner (Wicksell 1896; Buchanan 1965; Hardin 1982; Inman 1987).

Although any voluntary agreement among rational, self-interested individuals must make them all better off, they need not be all equally well off following the agreement. How well off each is, will depend on their positions when bargaining begins, their relative bargaining abilities, and perhaps chance. Let the "natural distribution" of goods in anarchy lead to utility levels for Crusoe and Friday as represented at point S in Figure 1 (Bush 1972). Friday is much better at gathering (or stealing) and thus achieves a much higher utility level in anarchy. PP' is

---

1. Swedberg (1991, 43) credits Schumpeter with inventing this term.
2. The prisoners' dilemma is but one of several social dilemmas that can make cooperation mutually beneficial. On the game of chicken, see Schelling (1966, chap. 2), Taylor and Ward (1982), and Ward (1987).

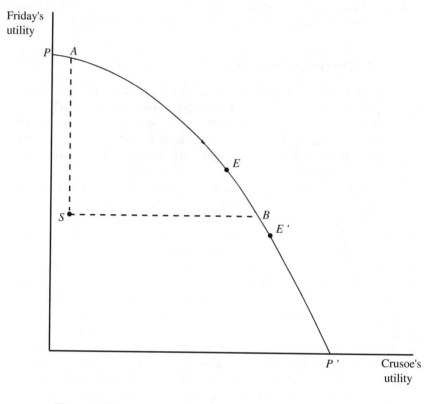

Figure 1. The move from anarchy.

the locus of utility levels Crusoe and Robinson can attain if they agree not to steal from one another. Any voluntary agreement must lead to a point (such as E) on the segment AB since both must be better off than at S. Crusoe gains relatively more from the move from S to E, but Friday is still better off than Crusoe even after the agreement.[3]

Once government forms, changes in the environment, technology, tastes, and other chance events can shift both S and PP' and lead to shifts in E relative to S. Should these produce an outcome like E' where one individual is worse off than he would be in the state of anarchy, the stability of the cooperative agreement is jeopardized. Revolutions and other social upheavals can be expected to arise when one or more groups find their positions under the existing political institutions to be far out

3. I assume here that the axes measure cardinal, interpersonally comparable utilities.

of line with what they could achieve if society returned to anarchy and created these institutions anew (Buchanan 1975, 77–86).

If a modern, developed, urbanized society were to plunge suddenly into anarchy, most of its members could barely survive. From any point on the utility possibility frontier, the anarchic status quo is so distant that it can barely be distinguished from the origin. The institutions of government (including those that create and protect markets) determine both the location of the utility possibility frontier and the position of each individual on it.

The normative nature of much of constitutional public choice is well illustrated by this depiction of "the origins" of government. The actual origin of political institutions in many societies might better be depicted as Crusoe's enslavement of Friday, by guile or force, with the gains from "cooperation" going entirely to Crusoe.[4] But constitutional public choice begins with the premise that government is or could be formed by a voluntary contractual agreement of all citizens and proceeds from this premise to investigate the nature of the institutions that best advance the interests of a society's citizens.

2. The choice of voting rule

2.1 Public goods provision

Thinking of government as formed by a voluntary agreement among all citizens (a constitutional contract) focuses attention on the set of governmental activities that make all citizens better off, such as the provision of pure public goods. This view of government is the one Knut Wicksell (1896) adopted a century ago, and it led him to advocate the unanimity rule for governmental decisions. With a community of two, the unanimity rule would work fine; but with larger communities and heterogeneous preferences for public goods, considerable time might be required to reach a collective decision. Some fraction of the community falling short of full unanimity is likely to be optimal, and constitutional decision is required to decide what fraction this should be.

Buchanan and Tullock (1962, 63–91) were the first to analyze this

---

4. Both the voluntary cooperation and involuntary exploitation accounts of the origins of "the state" can be found in the political anthropology literature. For an interesting survey with references to the major works, see Haas (1982). Iceland during the thirteenth century appears to have passed from a society in which voluntary participation in the provision of public goods gave way to rent-seeking redistributional activities by its chiefs and the church (Solvasson 1993).

problem. They did so under the assumption that individuals at the constitutional stage were uncertain whether they would be on the winning or losing side of a future issue. To see what is involved, let s be the gain (subsidy) an individual expects if an issue that she favors passes and t the loss (tax) if she is opposed. Furthermore, let $p(m)$ be the probability that an individual benefits from a government action, with m the majority required to reach a collective decision. With a pure public good, p could be 1.0 and will be higher, the higher m is, since raising m forces the community to search longer for a combination of quantity and tax shares that can achieve the required majority $[p' > 0, p'' < 0, p(1.0) = 1.0]$.

The higher the required majority, the more time a community must spend to reach a collective decision. Decision-making costs (d) increase with m $[d'(m) > 0, d''(m) > 0]$. An individual at the constitutional stage who is uncertain of whether she will gain or lose by future collective actions maximizes her expected gain by choosing m to maximize

$$E(G) = p(m)s - [1 - p(m)]t - d(m). \tag{1}$$

This m must satisfy

$$p'(s + t) = d'. \tag{2}$$

Each individual at the constitutional stage must balance the expected marginal gain from increasing the required majority and thereby increasing the probability that she gains from collective action (g [the left hand side of (2)] against the marginal decision-making costs of increasing m, d'. Depending on the values of s and t and the shapes of p and d, different majorities can be expected to be optimal for different categories of decisions. Some possibilities are depicted in Figure 2. The d' curve is not drawn to the left of $m = 0.5$, since with $m < 0.5$ mutually inconsistent proposals (an increase in expenditures *and* a decrease) can *both* pass, and the rule does not yield a determinate outcome. For a wide class of relatively unimportant issues, that is, issues with small expected s and t, the marginal gains from collective action will be such as to pass under the d' curve (curves g_1 and g_2). For these, if collective action is required at all, the simple majority rule will be optimal since it is the smallest required majority that can be chosen and still avoid the problem of mutually inconsistent issues passing.[5] With higher gains or losses from collective action or lower marginal decision-making costs, qualified majorities above the simple

5. That the marginal gains from increasing m are less than marginal decision costs does not imply that no collective action should be taken. To answer that question one must compare total gains and costs. Curves like g_1 and g_2 imply that, were it not for the problem of mutually inconsistent issues, passing the marginal gains and costs from increasing m are such that an $m < 0.5$ would be optimal.

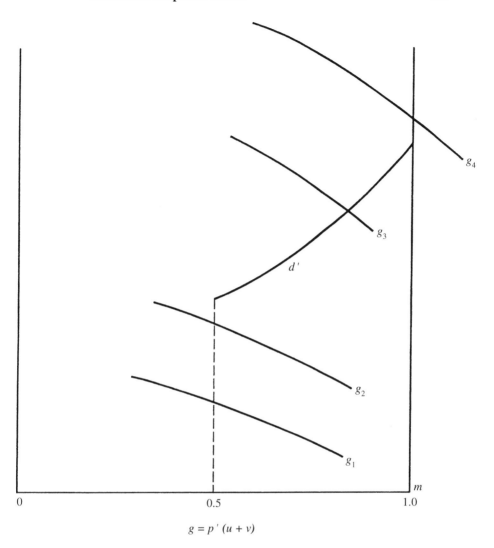

Figure 2. The optional majority.

majority become optimal (g_3). With marginal gains relative to marginal costs like g_4, the unanimity rule is again optimal.[6]

When all collective decisions involve public goods, the key determi-

6. Spindler (1990) argues that the expected losses from rent seeking are highest when the simple majority rule is used. The addition of rent-seeking costs would increase the likelihood of a supramajority rule's selection.

nants of the choice of voting rule, from the family of qualified majority rules, are the marginal expected gain from increasing the fraction of the community that benefits from the collective action and the marginal decision-making costs from doing so. Since these gains and losses are likely to differ from community to community and across different categories of public goods, one does not expect one voting rule to be optimal for all communities and all types of decisions. Given the simple majority rule's ubiquity, one searches for an alternative explanation.

2.2 Property rights and redistribution

Douglas Rae (1969) conceptualized the choice of voting rule in much the same way as Buchanan and Tullock did. Members of the constitutional convention assumed the community over time would be confronted by a series of binary choices (x or y), and that each individual, uncertain whether to favor x or y, would be assumed to have an equal probability of favoring either since each would receive the same utility gain whether issue x or y won. These assumptions suggest that the issues the community must decide are not (or at least not exclusively) pure public goods issues. If y were the status quo, then for a pure public good there would be many x's (i.e., many combinations of public good quantities and tax share combinations that might be proposed as alternatives). If x were a pure public good (e.g., a police force), the probability that one would favor its provision over the status quo of no provision would not be 0.5. Nor would the anticipated gain to someone favoring the provision of a public good be expected to equal the loss to someone opposing it.

The assumptions Rae makes in his analysis of the optimal voting rule seem better suited to redistribution and property rights issues. In a zero-sum transfer from one group to another of equal size, the tax paid (t) if one is on the losing side would equal the subsidy received (s) if one is on the winning side. The gain to those who win (who favor an increase in the maximum speed allowed on interstate highways, for instance) might reasonably be expected to equal the loss to those who oppose (if the speed limit is raised).

In terms of the above example, Rae's assumptions imply that $s = t$ and that the probability a given individual favors x is the fraction of the community that votes for x (let us call this k). Then, assuming that decision-making costs are zero, the expected gain to an individual at the constitutional stage from choosing a voting rule that will select x is

$$E_G = ks - (1 - k)s = (2k - 1)s. \tag{3}$$

The expected gain from having x win is positive for any $k > 1/2$. The simple majority rule under these assumptions is the only rule that selects *all* outcomes promising positive net gains.[7]

2.3 Discussion

Buchanan and Tullock (1962) and Rae (1969) conceptualize the constitutional choice of voting rule in similar ways: the citizen at the constitutional stage assumes the position of any future citizen. Buchanan and Tullock assume, however, that future collective decisions will involve the provision of public goods and other Pareto improvements. Their (amended) analysis implies that the simple majority rule will be used for decisions with small expected gains or losses relative to decision costs, but that some supramajority rule becomes optimal when the public good decision can provide large gains and/or losses relative to decision-making costs. No single voting rule is likely to be optimal for all groups and all decisions. Rae (1969) demonstrates the optimality of the simple majority rule for all distributional and rights issues for which the expected gains and losses are the same. Together these works illustrate the fundamental importance of the distinction between allocative efficiency improvements and distributional changes, *and* the possible desirability of both separating them procedurally and employing different voting rules for each.

---

7. See Taylor's (1969) proof.

   May (1952) proved equivalence between the following four axioms and the simple majority rule for binary choices, where each member of the committee, i, registers a vote, D_i, equal to $+1$ if i favors x, -1 if i favors y, and 0 if she is indifferent between the two alternatives:

> *Decisiveness:* the group decision function, D, is defined and single valued for any given set of preference orderings.
>
> *Anonymity:* D is determined only by the values of D_i, and is independent of how they are assigned. Any permutation of these ballots leaves D unchanged.
>
> *Neutrality:* If x defeats (ties) y for one set of individual preferences, and all individuals have the same *ordinal* rankings for z and w as for x and y (i.e., $xR_iy <-> zR_iw$, etc.), then z defeats (ties) w.
>
> *Positive responsiveness:* If D equals 0 or 1, and one individual changes his vote from -1 to 0 or, or from 0 to 1, and all other votes remain unchanged, then $D = 1$.

Anonymity and neutrality are attractive properties, if the equal intensity assumption Rae makes holds. Thus, as a normative case for majority rule May's theorem resembles Rae's.

2.4 Empirical tests

Most constitutions are not drafted at conventions in which all citizens, or even a representative subsample, meet and deliberate. The predictions of Buchanan and Tullock, Rae, and similar works therefore cannot be "tested" by examining actual constitutions in different countries. Voting procedures are used to make many sorts of group decisions, however, and in some contexts their selection may resemble the constitutional setting assumed in much of the public choice literature. Condominium associations are one possible example. They are typically formed by the developer of the complex, who has an incentive to adopt rules that maximize the value of the property. Such rules would in turn maximize equation (1), where s and t are the expected gains and losses from collective decisions of a representative member of the association. Barzel and Sass (1990) and Sass (1992) have studied the "constitutions" of condominium associations and found them to be broadly consistent with the Buchanan–Tullock theory. Developers tend to choose modes of representation and voting rules that minimize decision-making costs. The greater the heterogeneity of the membership (and thus the larger the relative sizes of s and t), the more inclusive the voting rule tends to be. Although this line of research is still in its infancy, it does suggests that constitutional public choice has both positive and normative implications.

3. The choice of rights

An implication of the rationality assumption is that individuals know best the actions they should take to advance their interests. Rational individuals would write a constitution that allowed themselves the freedom to pursue their own interests, as long as this pursuit did not impose disproportionate harm on others. Many actions (e.g., driving rapidly in congested areas) do have the potential of imposing significant costs on others. Therefore, rational individuals when writing a constitution will not guarantee themselves unlimited freedom to act. They will grant themselves and their dependents the authority to impose constraints on individual actions in situations in which these actions entail significant externalities.

A collective decision curtailing the freedom to choose the speed at which to drive might, as suggested above, involve equal expected gains and losses to those on either side of the issue. The simple majority rule may well be deemed the optimal rule for resolving this type of issue. In other cases, however, great asymmetries in expected gains and losses may exist. The strictures of a religion may require that its members not shave or wear unconventional attire. These practices may irritate some (many) members of the community; however, the individual losses might well be expected to be small relative to the cost imposed on the member unable to follow the dictates of the religion. When significant differences in the relative sizes of gains and losses are expected, the simple majority rule may not be optimal.

To see what is involved, let the relative magnitudes of t and s be expressed as $t = bs$, $b \geq 0$. Different categories of decisions are expected to have different b's. If m^* is the optimal majority as defined by equation (2), then it can be shown that $\partial m^*/\partial b > 0$. As the expected loss to those on the losing side increases relative to the gain to those on the winning side of a proposal to restrict an individual's freedom, the g' curve in Figure 2 shifts to the right. The higher t becomes relative to s, the higher the optimal majority becomes. With a high enough b, the optimal voting rule becomes the unanimity rule.

Now even under the unanimity rule, a proposal to restrict certain actions of a group might pass. Those harmed by the action may convince those carrying it out that their losses in this instance are severe, and the group consents to the restriction. Those harmed may offer a sufficiently large bribe to win the group's consent. But if the constitution framers correctly anticipate the direction and extent of asymmetries in future costs and benefits from restrictions on religious practices, they can anticipate that religious groups in the future are likely to cast the veto provided to them by the unanimity rule and defeat proposals to constrain their religious freedoms. Knowing this, the constitution framers can achieve the same likely outcomes as under the unanimity rule, but at lower decision-making costs, by granting future members of all religious groups the unconditional right to follow the strictures of their religion. Since individuals are not required to exercise their rights, those offended by the actions of a religious group may still be able to convince or bribe the group to refrain from a particular practice. But in general this is unlikely to occur, and the same result that one expects from the unanimity rule will arise without incurring the costs of a formal vote. Rights, from the perspective of constitutional public choice, are a substitute for the unanimity rule with lower decision costs (Mueller 1991).

To the extent that actual constitutions define institutions that advance the interests of all citizens, this analysis of rights has positive implications. For example, the choice of rights at the constitutional stage hinges crucially on the existence of uncertainty among the framers of the constitution about which side of a particular externality they might eventually be on. Given the variety of religious backgrounds in the United States at the end of the eighteenth century and the importance of religious freedom to many immigrants, true uncertainty over which religion might someday be the target of the state or of other religions might have existed, and so a constitutional guarantee of religious freedom is predicted.

Slavery also involves the kind of severe asymmetries between gains and losses that would lead self-interested individuals to define a constitutional right to political and economic freedom. But those gathered in Philadelphia during the summer of 1787 were not uncertain over who might or might not be a slave in the United States in the future, and thus no provisions regarding slavery – other than those that protected the slaveowners – were included in the Constitution or the subsequent Bill of Rights.

4. The choice of representative system

Following Buchanan and Tullock's pioneering exposition, several scholars have explored the issue of the choice of voting rule. No one has approached the question of the choice of system of representation from the constitutional choice perspective, however. Perhaps because public choice has been dominated by authors from English-speaking countries, the bulk of the literature assumes that the number of parties is given and equal to two. But the number of parties a country has is a function of its electoral rules, and these generally are elements of constitutional choice. Thus, the existing literature on the consequences of electoral rules is central to the issue of constitutional choice.

One can distinguish two fundamentally different modes of selecting representatives. In plurality and majority systems one representative is chosen from each electoral district. Under the plurality system the candidate getting the most votes on the first ballot is elected. Under the majority system, the candidate is elected only if she receives a majority of the votes. If no one receives a majority on the first ballot, a run-off is held after the candidates receiving the fewest votes are eliminated. Under the plurality and majority systems the country is divided into as many geographic districts as there are seats in the parliament. Under multimember-proportional representation (PR), the country is divided into fewer geographic districts than the number of seats, and several representatives are chosen from each district in rough proportion to the number of votes their parties receive. In the polar case of a PR system, the entire country is defined as a single electoral district, and parties are awarded seats in the parliament in proportion to the votes they receive across the country. The Netherlands and Israel have this system; Germany's complex rules essentially produce the same result.

The hypothesis that the number of parties represented in the parliament is determined by its method for electing representatives is usually attributed to Duverger (1946, 1954). Douglas Rae (1971) was the first to examine this issue empirically. His work has been recently updated and corrected by Lijphart (1990). Lijphart's central findings are summarized in Table 1. Each entry is the percentage by which those parties that are overrepresented are overrepresented. Perfectly proportional matching of seats to votes would produce an entry of 0.0. The degree to which the largest parties are overrepresented is strongly related to the mode of representation. Plurality and majority systems overrepresent the largest parties by more than four times the degree of the most proportional PR systems. This overrepresentation in turn tends to produce fewer effective numbers of parties in the parliaments of plurality and majority systems (Lijphart 1984, 160). More generally, the degree of proportionality of representation is greater, the larger the number of representatives elected from each district.

A third regularity is evidenced in the table. Hare's original formula and its equivalent derived by Sainte-Lagué give the most proportionate distributions of seats of all of the formulae used to convert votes into seats.[8] If one wished to have parties represented in the parliament in direct proportion to the votes they receive in the election, one would define the entire nation as a single electoral district and use Hare's largest remainders formula to convert party votes into seats.

But should a member of a constitutional convention want to adopt electoral rules that allocate seats in the parliament in close approximation to the votes parties receive? On this question political scientists have had much to say, public choice scholars almost nothing. But there is much in the public choice literature that is relevant to this question. I shall merely mention some of the most important considerations.

The properties of two-party systems have been exhaustively explored. Hotelling's (1929) and Downs's (1957) pioneering analyses demonstrated that equilibria existed in a one-dimensional issue space with both candidates (parties) adopting the position favored by the median voter. Subsequent analyses of multidimensional issue spaces suggested that equilibria were unlikely (Plott 1967; Kramer 1973; Schofield 1978), but, again, under the assumptions of the probabilistic voting literature, it seems reasonable to assume that electoral equilibria

---

8. To allocate seats by Hare's method, one first computes the Hare quotient for each district, $q = v/s$, where v is the total number of votes cast in the district, s the number of seats filled by the district. The number of votes each party received is then divided by q, $v_p/q = I + f$, $0 \leq f < 1$. Each party is first awarded its integer number of seats won, I. These integers are then added, and if they sum to less than the number of seats the district can fill, the remaining seats are awarded to the parties having the highest fractional remainders, f.

   The various formulae are illustrated and compared by Carstairs (1980, chaps. 2, 3) and Lijphart (1986). For a more formal analysis, see Balinski and Young (1982).

Table 1. *Disproportionality of different electoral systems classified by district size 1945–85 (percentages by which overrepresented parties are overrepresented)*

Adjusted district magnitude	LR-Hare and pure Sainte-Laguë	LR-droop, LR-imperiali, modified Sainte-Laguë, and STV-droop	d'Hondt	Plurality and majority	All
1–1.1	—	—	—	12.93 (6)	12.93 (6)
1.1–5	—	4.60 (1)	8.51 (3)	—	7.53 (4)
5–10	—	5.18 (3)	5.83 (6)	—	5.61 (9)
10–25	2.81 (2)	—	4.28 (3)	—	3.69 (5)
100–150	2.46 (3)	3.53 (2)	4.39 (2)	—	3.32 (7)
All[a]	2.60 (5)	4.53 (6)	5.87 (14)	12.93 (6)	6.45 (31)

Note: The number of cases on which each average is based are in parentheses.

[a] Except France 1951–6.

Source: Lijphart (1990, 485).

exist.[9] Moreover, under some variants of these models the winning platform maximizes a Nash or Benthamite social welfare function (Coughlin and Nitzan 1981; Ledyard 1984). Constitution framers who sought to maximize their future utilities through the choice of a system of representation would have reasonable justification for instituting a two-party system. Competition for votes between the two parties would maximize the welfare of society defined as a product or sum of the utilities of its members.

Under electoral rules that produce multiparty parliaments, no party is likely to have a majority of the seats in the parliament. Majority rule voting on issues will often produce cycles. Cycling on the issue of the identity of the cabinet will manifest itself as the collapse of the government. Governmental instability is the primary disadvantage of PR systems most of its critics raise.

Although cabinet lives are shorter under multiparty than under two-party systems (Schofield, in this volume), many countries with multiparty systems (Austria, the Netherlands, Germany, and Norway) do not seem to have suffered much from this, at least over the last half century. Moreover, the instability that has arisen under PR systems has not been the consequence solely of multiparty representation but rather of this mode of representation *combined* with the use of majority rule *and* the requirement that the cabinet's – the government's – stability rest on the stability of a majority coalition. One of the most important contributions public choice has made to our understanding of how political systems work has been to demonstrate the serious shortcomings of the simple majority rule. Cycling and the propensity for zero-sum redistribution under majority rule can be reduced or eliminated simply by requiring a higher majority to pass an issue than 50 percent plus one (Caplin and Nalebuff 1988). Other voting rules exist that avoid cycling and have additional attractive properties (e.g., the demand revelation process [Clarke 1971; Groves and Ledyard 1977], voting by veto [Mueller 1978], point voting [Hylland and Zeckhauser 1979], see Tideman, in this volume). A PR system when combined with an appropriate voting rule could conceivably produce outcomes as good as, or better than, those described above for two-party systems.[10] The understanding of the properties of voting rules obtained from public choice would be valuable to any constitution framer considering establishing a PR system of representation for his country.

9. See Ordeshook's contribution to this volume.
10. Cabinet instability can be totally eliminated by separating the cabinet from the parliament. For further discussion and comparison of two- and multiparty forms of government, see Mueller (1996).

5. Bicameralism

Another important feature of representative democracies is the number of legislative assemblies established. Buchanan and Tullock analyzed bicameralism from a public choice perspective in 1962 (chap. 16); surprisingly little has been done on the question since.

As Buchanan and Tullock demonstrate, requiring that legislation pass in a second chamber can increase the effective majority required to pass an issue. To see why this may be so, let us assume that a country is mx kilometers wide and nx long. Its population is uniformly distributed over the rectangle. One chamber of the parliament is formed by dividing the country into m districts x kilometers wide, each running the length of the country. If this chamber is filled by electing one representative from each district, then the simple majority rule requires that the representatives of at least half of the population support an issue for it to pass.[11] Now let a second chamber be constituted by electing one representative from each of n districts with boundaries perpendicular to the first chamber's districts and x kilometers apart. If the second chamber also employs the simple majority rule, then an issue will pass in both houses only if the representatives of at least 75 percent of the population support it (e.g., the representatives from the $m/2 + 1$ eastern most districts in the first chamber, and from the $n/2 + 1$ northern most in the second). Constituting a second chamber with boundaries orthogonal to the first increases the effective majority by 50 percent.

Although bicameralism may potentially increase the effective required majority, it is not clear why this is a superior alternative to simply requiring a higher majority than the simple majority in a unicameral parliament, thereby saving the costs of the second chamber.

A second argument in favor of bicameral systems is that they may reduce or eliminate the likelihood of a cycle (Hammond and Miller 1987; Brennan and Hamlin 1992). Assume, for example, a two-dimensional issue space such as the one in Figure 3. Voter indifference curves are concentric circles around their ideal points. Line pp' divides the set of

---

11. Of course, this does not imply that at least half of the population supports each winning issue, even if all citizens voting for a representative, who votes for an issue, also favor the issue. If district boundaries run north to south, an issue can pass with all of the votes of the $m/2 + 1$ eastern most districts (m is even). If each of the representatives of these districts had won her election by one vote, the coalition's victory would guarantee that at least one-fourth of the population supported the winning issue. If all of the representatives in the losing coalition had run unopposed, an issue could receive a majority of the votes in the parliament with only slightly more than one-fourth of the voters favoring it. If more than two candidates run in some races, the winning coalition could account for even less than a quarter of the population.

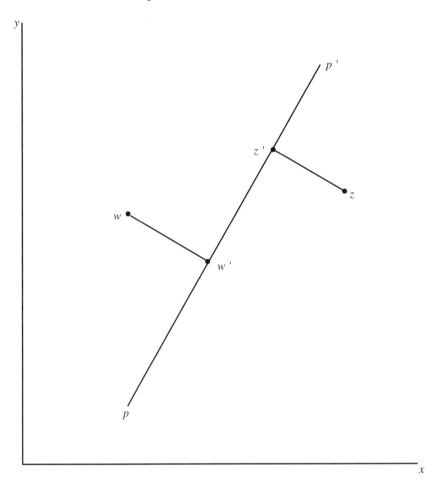

Figure 3. The Pareto set for a bicameral legislature.

ideal points with m to the left of pp' and n to the right. For every point like z to the right of pp' there is a point z' at the intersection of pp' and the perpendicular from z that all m voters on the left prefer to z (Enelow and Hinich 1984, chap. 3). Similarly, points like w to the left of pp' are dominated in the eyes of the n voters on the right by points like w' on it. If separate legislatures are formed with voters to the left of pp' represented in one and those to the right in the other, pp' becomes a Pareto set for the two disjoint groups, and some point along it can be expected to be agreed upon by both houses. Although bicameralism could in principle avert cycles in this manner, it is not obvious that it is in practice feasible to divide the electorate into the disjoint preference groups required.[12]

6. The constitution as constraints

As described by constitutional public choice, constitutional democracy is a principal-agent problem on a colossal scale. The citizens create the institutions of government (parliament, the executive, courts) in a rare, almost heroic act of civic responsibility. They then retire to their private pursuits, leaving those in government to advance the future collective interests of the citizenry. But those in government have interests of their own. Thus, the original constitutional contract must build in incentives and constraints to induce governmental agents to act for the citizens they supposedly serve (Elster 1988). Bicameralism, rights, voting rules, and so forth can be viewed under this interpretation as possible checks on the discretion of governmental agents.

Nowhere is this principal-agent problem more starkly drawn than in Brennan and Buchanan's (1980) Leviathan model. Here government is a sort of Prometheus who if unbound exploits the citizenry for his own advantage. Writing the constitution is the only opportunity the citizens have to bind Prometheus. Brennan and Buchanan are led to suggest a variety of constraints that go well beyond voting rules and rights, for example, balanced budget requirements, independent monetary authorities and money supply rules, and constraints on the kinds of taxes that can be levied. In many cases their proposals run directly counter to ones that have been made in orthodox public economics, where it is assumed that Prometheus is bent on maximizing a social welfare function that aggregates the individual utilities of the citizens (see Hettich and Winer, in this volume). This contrast highlights the most fundamental problem the constitution framers face: how to design institutions that grant governmental agents the authority to do efficiently that which is in the interests of the citizens and yet deny those agents the discretion to pursue their own interests at the expense of the citizens.

7. Positive constitutional analysis

In the normative public choice literature a constitution is an actual document (contract) written by the citizens. To the extent that the political

---

12. If preferences for government services varied systematically with income, then the division of Parliament along class lines as originally occurred in Great Britain might have resulted in such disjointness. Such a solution to the cycling problem would seem to run the risk of polarizing society and encouraging "class conflict," however. Against this alternative cycling seems like the lesser of two evils.

institutions of a country have been consciously chosen by its citizens, the normative analysis becomes positive. But the political institutions of most countries appear to have evolved in ways that are not well characterized as the intended outcomes of rational actors. The positive analysis of political institutions must take into account the role played by chance and its unpredicted and unintended consequences.

7.1 The emergence of norms

In the public choice literature, rational individuals, suspended in an institutional vacuum, choose political (and social and economic) institutions to maximize their expected welfare. But no human groups exist that do not have some social institutions. The customs, traditions, and mores of the primitive society are institutions that accomplish much the same ends as do the more formal political institutions of developed societies. As a society develops, its customs and traditions may shape its choice of political institutions. An understanding of how and why primitive societies "choose" their social institutions may help us understand the choices advanced societies make.

Two strands of this literature can be traced. The one identifies individual actions that are seemingly irrational in the short run but optimal in the long run. Cooperation as a repeated prisoners' dilemma is a frequent example (Axelrod 1984; Taylor 1987). The rational individual adheres to norms and other social institutions that deter short-run opportunistic behavior that would lead to Pareto-inferior long-run outcomes (Elster 1979; Brennan and Buchanan 1985).

A second strand emphasizes the adaptive nature of human behavior. Here both chance and human intelligence can play a role in the selection of institutions. A primary objective of this literature has been to explain the choice of a particular Nash equilibrium of the many that often exist in repeated game contexts. Social conventions are an apt example of this. Consider, for example, the two-person coordination game with the following payoff matrix.

		Column			
		a		b	
	a	1	1	0	0
Row	b	0	0	2	2

At the beginning all players are ignorant of the payoffs in the matrix and hence choose either an a or b strategy at random. After several periods, each generation of players begins to make its choices based on the experiences of the players in previous games. With large enough samples, players will observe that the highest payoffs are obtained when both players choose the b strategy and will coordinate on the (b, b) outcome (Young 1993).

It would be nice, of course, if evolutionary forces would always choose the Pareto-dominant equilibrium when one exists. Under some assumptions of course it will (Binmore 1990), but alas not always. If the samplings of previous payoffs at an early stage of the game happened to contain no (b, b) pairings, the society in our example might converge on the Pareto dominated, Nash equilibrium (a, a). In real world contexts, shifting from one convention to another can involve substantial transaction costs (Waerneryd 1990). For example, a society that has adopted an alphabet that is inefficient (in the sense that it requires more symbols to represent ideas and thus more time to learn and use) might not abandon it because no generation would be willing to undertake the costs of learning a simpler alphabet. A society that happened upon an (a, a) equilibrium might remain at it, even after discovering that a (b, b) convention would be superior in the long run, if the transaction costs from shifting from (a, a) to (b, b) were high enough.

When one player can benefit at another's expense by opportunistic behavior, as in a prisoners' dilemma, for Pareto-superior equilibria to survive they must be able to withstand attacks from "mutants" who deviate from the mores that produce the socially superior outcomes. Several authors have analyzed the conditions for evolutionary stability in the presence of mutants (Schotter 1981; Maynard Smith 1982; Sugden 1986; Witt 1986; Binmore 1990; Waerneryd 1990).

As yet the gap between the results obtained from evolutionary game theory and our understanding of real world social and political institutions is large, but the field holds much promise.

7.2 From norms to constitutions

Several studies have investigated the relationship between the institutions of primitive societies and the satisfaction of their collective wants. Of primary interest among economists has been the institution of property rights, which often appear to be efficiently defined even where formal legal institutions are lacking (Demsetz 1967; Posner 1980; and Bailey 1992). For example, individual property rights tend to be protected in societies that rely heavily on agriculture, while communal rights are more common in hunting and gathering societies. In the latter, communal property rights have advantages, because they both encourage cooperation where teamwork is important and help spread risks.

The importance of continual care and monitoring in agricultural activities favors individuals property rights, on the other hand, when plants are an important source of food.

Political institutions appear to play an important role in determining the economic performance of American Indian tribes. Cornell and Kalt (1990, 1991) find that tribes with strong executive or legislative authority are better able to curb the rent-seeking activities of their members and thereby achieve superior economic performance.

Bates (1989) also sees political institutions as important determinants of the degree of success African nations have in achieving economic development. More generally, Douglass North (1981, 1990) has placed great weight on institutional factors (including those of government) in explaining the growth and decay of Western societies. Although North does not see history as necessarily producing ever more efficient institutional structures, Yoram Barzel (1993) has argued, for the case of England, that the gradual shift from monarchy to democracy over the current millennium was a Pareto move, given the property rights of the Crown and the aristocracy. Following the Norman Conquest three-quarters of the land of England was owned by the king and his barons. Sharing political authority with these barons and later with other groups was, according to Barzel, the optimal way for the king to induce the kind of teamwork activities and tax contributions needed to protect his land from foreign invaders.

At a more macro level, Vorhies and Glahe (1988) and Scully (1992) have found that countries with more liberal and democratic institutions have more rapid rates of economic growth, higher productivity, and more equal distributions of income.

7.3 Constitutions and rent seeking

While the literature of the previous section might be termed "the effects of constitutions," the literature discussed in this section deals with "the determinants." It attempts a positive analysis of the *choice* of constitutional structures in the United States.

The first contribution to public choice by an American might well be regarded as Charles Beard's (1913) analysis of the U.S. Constitution. James Buchanan has called public choice "politics without romance," and Beard's book certainly was that. Beard viewed the Constitution writers as wealth maximizers whose wealth was largely in the form of land and slaves. Under Beard's analysis the Constitution defines a set of institutions to protect the wealth of an aristocracy of land- and slave-owners from the masses without property.

Landes and Posner (1975, 892) see the Constitution not as a means of protecting a particular group's wealth but as a means of protecting or transferring wealth to any group powerful enough to shape or amend it, and as a means of defining the political rules by which subsequent rent seeking takes place. They view all government activity as essentially rent seeking, with Congress selling legislation to the highest bidders. Given cycling and turnover in Congress, no present Congress can guarantee that its actions today will not be overturned tomorrow. This potential impermanence lowers the value of any legislation sold today. An independent judiciary adds permanence to legislation through its authority to sustain the bargains made by past legislatures and exists in the United States to increase the revenue Congress can earn by selling legislation to competing interest groups. Consistent with the Landes and Posner thesis, Anderson et al. (1990) find that at the state level interest groups concentrate relatively more on obtaining legislative action in states with independent judiciaries and relatively more on constitutional amendments where the judiciary is not independent.

7.4 The Constitutional Convention

Beard saw the Constitutional Convention as dominated by representatives of the landowning aristocracy. Landes and Posner see interest groups both writing and amending it (e.g., the First Amendment by "publishers, journalists, pamphleteers, and others who derive pecuniary and nonpecuniary income from publication and advocacy of various sorts" [893]). But they do not undertake an analysis of the convention itself and the interests represented there. (For example, much of their discussion would seem to imply that the Constitution was written by Congress, since under their analysis it has the most to gain from an independent judiciary.)[13]

McGuire and Ohsfeldt (1986) and McGuire (1988) have analyzed the voting patterns at the Philadelphia convention and concluded that the delegates each state sent voted to advance a combination of their own and their constituents' interests. Eavey and Miller (1989) have found that both self- and constituent interests were important in the ratification of the Pennsylvania and Maryland constitutions. These findings accord with the assumptions underlying the public choice literature and

---

13. Indeed, the United Kingdom would appear to be a better example for their hypothesis since the British Parliament is totally unconstrained in its actions and can, effectively, rewrite the "British Constitution" whenever it chooses. It has, presumably, the same interest in selling legislation as the U.S. Congress has and could create an independent judiciary with authority to overrule it if it so chose. But so far it has not done so (Landes and Posner 1975, 887).

are further buttressed by an examination of constitutional conventions and revisions in other countries.

Quite often new constitutions are written by elected parliaments or subcommittees thereof. In these cases the electoral rules chosen typically reflect the interests of the parties in the parliament drafting the constitution (Elster 1991; Mueller 1996, chap. 21). In Latin America, for example, institutional transformations tend to occur only when the current set of institutions is out of line with the current distribution of political power (Geddes 1990). A presidential system is replaced by a parliamentary system only when the dominant party(ies) in the parliament does not control the presidency. The most blatant example of this self-serving behavior occurs in France, where the parliament is empowered to choose the electoral system to be used in each election. Thus, France shifts back and forth between a majority and a PR system, depending on which system the current majority party of the coalition thinks it will fare better under (Knapp 1987). Other transparent displays of self-serving political interest in constitution drafting occur when dictators take a hand in drafting them (Mueller 1996, chap. 21). The study of the processes by which constitutions are drafted is a fertile ground for positive analysis with important normative implications. To achieve a constitution that advances the interests of all citizens as assumed in the normative literature, some way of effectively representing all citizens when the constitution is drafted and/or ratified must be employed.

8. Conclusions

Much of public choice can be thought of as contributing to our knowledge of the properties of different constitutional provisions (e.g., studies of the relationship between the use of referenda and direct democracy and the size of government [Pommerehne 1978; Santerre 1986, 1989]). This literature confirms the fundamental premise of public choice: institutions do matter. Whether citizens can directly express their preferences in town meetings or in referenda does affect the nature of political outcomes. Economic and political liberties are positively correlated with economic performance. Almost every contribution to this volume describes the effects of different forms of political institutions on social outcomes.

Although virtually all public choice deals indirectly with constitutional issues, surprisingly little focuses directly on them. Buchanan and Tullock's (1962) classic contribution, unlike say those of Downs (1957) or Arrow (1951), has produced a fairly modest set of contributions that examine the properties of political institutions that rational individuals ought to (will) agree on to advance their interests. An equally modest, and very recent, literature investigates the causes and consequences of different constitutional structures.

But interest in constitutional issues, fueled by events in Eastern Europe and Asia since 1989, is growing. Public choice scholars are regular contributors to the *East European Constitutional Review*. A journal has appeared (*Constitutional Political Economy*) devoted entirely to the study of constitutional issues from a public choice perspective. These developments suggest that some day in the not too distant future, public choice will be able to claim important "policy implications" related to constitutional questions.

PART II

Voting rules and preference aggregation

CHAPTER 7

Cycling and majority rule

JAMES M. ENELOW

Cycling and majority rule is one of the most heavily researched areas of public choice. The literature on this subject dates back to Condorcet (1785), who discovered the famous three-voter, three-alternative example of cyclical majorities so well known to public choice theorists, in which one majority prefers an alternative A to an alternative B, another majority prefers B to alternative C, and a third majority prefers C to A. Dodgson (1876) rediscovered this paradox in the nineteenth century, but serious investigation of this area begins with Black (1958) and Arrow (1951). In the last half of the twentieth century, the literature on cycling and majority rule has become quite extensive. Cycles are considered a defect in majority rule and the question most frequently asked is how they can be avoided. More precisely, scholars have sought conditions sufficient and/or necessary for the existence of an alternative that cannot be defeated by any other alternative in a majority contest. Such an alternative is known as an undominated point. Though an undominated point does not preclude the existence of a cycle among other alternatives, the type of cycle that concerns most theorists is what Schwartz (1986) calls a "top cycle," one that leaves no alternative unbeatable.

Of course, the full transitivity of the majority preference relation means that an undominated point exists, but this requirement is stricter than necessary for the existence of an undominated point. Thus, beginning in the 1960s, theorists switched their focus from the transitivity of the majority preference relation to the existence of an undominated point, since the latter is all that is required for society to possess a "best" alternative.

The properties of majority rule have been investigated both in the finite and infinite alternative settings. The second setting is most frequently associated with the spatial model of voting developed by Black (1958) and Downs (1957) and generalized by Davis and Hinich (1966). In the spatial model, the alternatives are a subset of Euclidean space, and the voter judges alternatives by their closeness to his ideal point in this space. In a famous paper, Plott (1967) first showed that an undominated point is unlikely to exist in the spatial model under simple majority rule when the alternatives are evaluated on two or more dimensions. Though his conditions were sufficient and not necessary, later generalizations proved that Plott was right – an undominated point in the spatial model under simple majority rule is a rare event. At the same time, Tullock (1967) argued that the nonexistence of an undominated point is no great cause for alarm since majority rule cycles would be likely contained in a small subset of the alternative space. This conjecture would later be shown to be incorrect by McKelvey (1976), Schofield (1978) and others, who proved that when an undominated point does not exist, a cycle can be constructed that includes every alternative.

Succeeding theorists have been largely concerned with how to escape these gloomy results. Several points of attack have been used, each of which involves some modification of the standard multidimensional spatial model. In the following sections, we will survey the conditions that guarantee the existence of an undominated point. We break these conditions into three types: (1) *preference restrictions*, which limit either the preference orders individuals can hold or the distribution of preference types among voters; (2) *domain restrictions*, which limit the dimensionality of the alternative space or restrict which alternatives can be paired against each other in a majority vote; and, lastly, (3) *different majority sizes*, which involves varying the minimum majority size from a simple majority up to unanimity. We will describe the most important relationships between each of these three types of conditions and the existence of an undominated point. Frequently, a combination of different types of conditions is required for an undominated point to exist. We will also discuss the related issues of the likelihood of cyclical majorities and the relationship between the existence of majority rule cycles and opportunities for strategic voting.

1. Defining the majority decision problem

Two basic models have been used to express the majority rule decision problem: the Arrowian conception and the spatial model. The basic distinction between these two models is that in the former individual preferences are required to satisfy fairly weak conditions usually over a finite set of alternatives (see Pattanaik in this volume for a fuller discussion of Arrow's model). In the latter, individual preferences are described by some form of Euclidean distance and the alternatives are normally an infinite subset of a Euclidean space. It is also typical for individuals in the Arrowian model to comprise a finite set, while in the spatial model the set of individuals is often described by a continuous density.

Going back and forth between the two models may produce some confusion. To minimize this problem, we will start with the Arrowian framework (which is the older of the two and in some ways more general) and build the spatial model on top of it as the need arises. In Arrow's model, society consists of the set $N = \{1, \ldots, n\}$ of individuals ($n > 2$) and the set X of alternatives, where $x \in X$ is an alternative. Individual preferences are defined over X. For individual $i \in N$, and alternatives $x, y \in X$, i prefers y to X is written $y \, P_i \, x$. Individual preferences are binary relations. Furthermore, they normally satisfy certain consistency requirements, such as reflexivity, transitivity, and completeness (an "ordering"), but these requirements vary from one version of the model to another.

The fraction of the society for whom $y P_i x$ is $m(x,y)$. Under d-majority rule, society is said to prefer y to x if $m(x,y) > d$, written $y P_d x$. If $m(x,y) \leq d$ and $m(y,x) \leq d$, then society is said to be indifferent between y and x, written $y I_d x$. If $d = 50$ percent then society's preferences are determined by simple majority rule. A d-majority winner (or an undominated point under d-majority rule) is an alternative that cannot be defeated under d-majority rule. In other words, x is a d-majority winner if no y exists such that $m(x,y) > d$. A P-cycle under d-majority rule consists of a set of alternatives $x_1, \ldots, x_k \in X$ such that $x_1 \, P_d \, x_2 \ldots x_{k-1} P_d \, x_k \, P_d \, x_1$. If no P-cycles exist under d-majority rule then a d-majority winner exists for any subset of alternatives, but the converse is false since a P-cycle can exist among three or more alternatives and yet an alternative may exist that is undefeated by any of the alternatives in the P-cycle.

As mentioned in the introduction, the cycling and majority rule literature originally focused on the question of how to avoid cycles under 50 percent-majority rule. This concern grew out of Arrow's theorem, which showed the impossibility of a social welfare function (SWF) given a few other reasonable requirements. A SWF assigns to any set of individual orderings a social ordering, and, as Condorcet showed 50 percent-majority rule is not a SWF. Sen (1970a), among others, shifted attention to a social decision function (SDF), which satisfies the weaker requirement of always yielding an undominated point (or "best element"). The question then becomes conditions that are necessary and/or sufficient for the existence of an undominated point, or a d-majority winner.

2. The existence of a 50 percent-majority winner

Simple or 50 percent-majority rule has received the earliest and the greatest amount of attention by voting theorists. In a nutshell, the history of work on this subject can be described as follows: Black (1958) proved his famous median voter theorem in the 1940s, which established sufficient conditions for the existence of a 50 percent-majority winner. Arrow (1951) then showed at a much higher level of generality that median voter-type results are a special case. Black framed his result in the context of the spatial model of voting, while Arrow used the leaner framework of social choice described above. It remained for Plott (1967) to ask the question of how likely 50 percent-majority winners are in the spatial model. The answer he gave was, highly unlikely.

To appreciate Plott's results, we must add a few ingredients to the Arrowian model to give it a spatial cast. First, the set of alternatives X is now defined to be a subset (normally nonempty, compact, and convex) of w-dimensional Euclidean space ($w > 1$), $X \subset R^w$. An alternative $x \in X$ is now a w-dimensional vector, with x_t the t-th coordinate $1 \le t \le w$. Individual preferences are now defined over R^w. Typically, individual preferences are assumed to be Euclidean, which means that for individual i, yP_ix if and only if $\|y\text{-}x^i\| < \|x\text{-}x^i\|$, where x^i is i's most preferred alternative, or ideal point, in R^w and $\|.\|$ is the Euclidean norm. As Davis, DeGroot, and Hinich (1972) show, a 50 percent-majority winner in the spatial model is equivalent to the existence of an alternative that is a "median in all directions." Such a point possesses the property that any hyperplane passing through it is a median hyperplane.

Plott's (1967) conditions, generalized by Slutsky (1979) and McKelvey and Schofield (1987), require a symmetric distribution of ideal points in R^w for a 50 percent-majority winner to exist. For an even number of voters, a 50 percent-majority winner can exist at no voter's ideal point if and only if the ideal points of the voters can be divided into pairs such that for each voter in one direction from the 50 percent-majority winner, there exists another voter in the opposite direction. For an odd number of voters and one ideal point at the 50 percent-majority winner, the same condition is required. Obviously, these conditions are quite severe and unlikely to be found in any real society. The conclusion clearly appears to be that 50 percent-majority cycles are almost inescapable.

Reinforcing Plott's conclusion are the findings of Niemi and Weisberg (1968), who asked, in the context of the Arrowian model, what the probability is that no alternative will have a simple majority against every other alternative. Assuming that all individual strict preference orders are equally likely, they showed that the probability of nonexistence is fairly insensitive to the number of individuals in the society but quite sensitive to the number of alternatives. For a large number of individuals, as the number of alternatives increases, the probability of 50 percent-majority cycles rapidly approaches 1.

Rubinstein (1979) later showed, relative to a certain topology, that the set of societies for which a 50 percent-majority winner exists is of measure zero, pounding one of the last nails into the coffin of simple majority rule. However, while 50 percent-majority cycles may be unavoidable, Tullock (1967) pointed out that this may be of small importance. Looking at a uniform density of voter ideal points over a rectangle, Tullock argued that 50 percent-majority cycles would be confined to a small space around the middle of the rectangle. McKelvey (1976), however, showed that 50 percent-majority cycles are not, in general, well-behaved. To be precise, when a 50 percent-majority winner does not exist in the multidimensional spatial model, a cycle can be constructed that includes every alternative in the alternative space. Schofield (1978) and McKelvey (1979) extended this result.

3. Cyclical majorities and strategic voting

It was stated at the beginning of this essay that cycles, or more precisely, the nonexistence of a d-majority winner, is considered a defect of majority rule. There are several reasons for holding this opinion. First, the nonexistence of a d-majority winner leaves society without a best alternative, making the quality of the majority decision open to doubt. A related criticism of majority rule in the absence of a d-majority winner is that the majority decision is an artifact of the *agenda* used by the society. An agenda is a set of rules that determines which alternatives face each other in a contest, with the possibility of multiple contests. In the three alternative examples of Condorcet, one agenda is to have a majority contest between A and B, with the winner facing C and the winner of the second contest being declared the final choice.

Now, if a d-majority winner exists (assuming there are no ties), any binary agenda using d-majority rule will produce the d-majority winner as the final choice as long as this alternative gets voted on. However, if a d-majority winner fails to exist, or if it is never voted on, the agenda can determine which alternative is the final choice. Thus, in Condorcet's example and the above agenda, the final choice is C. However, if the first contest is between B and C, the final choice is A; though if the first contest is between A and C, the final choice is B. Clearly, picking the agenda is no small matter to the voters.

Implicit in these examples is the assumption that in any contest between two alternatives, the individual votes for the alternative she prefers. Known as "sincere" voting, this assumption may be questionable when there is more than one vote contest. If the agenda and the majority preferences of the society are known, individuals may use backward induction on the agenda tree (if it is finite) to determine their optimal votes. This strategic behavior is better known as "sophisticated" voting (so named by Farquharson 1969) and, if applied to the above three agendas, yields B as the final choice for the first agenda, C for the second agenda, and A for the third. The final choice is still an artifact of the agenda.

General results about final choices under binary agendas for sincere and sophisticated voting can be found in Ordeshook and Schwartz (1987). The point of these examples is that the absence of a d-majority winner is associated with opportunities for strategic behavior and makes majority decision making a game among the individuals of the society. In keeping with game theory, the rules of the game and the information individuals possess about each other need to be specified, since they affect how the game is played.

The consequences of majority cycles go even further. Since cycles give rise to strategic opportunities, individuals may wish to "contrive" cycles for personal gain. In other words, an individual may misrepresent his preferences in order to create a majority cycle. Suppose the preferences of three individuals 1, 2, and 3 over three alternatives A, B, and C are $A\ P_1\ B\ P_1\ C$, $C\ P_2\ A\ P_2\ B$, and $B\ P_3\ A\ P_3\ C$. A is a 50 percent-majority winner and under any of the three agendas described above, A will be the final choice. However, suppose individual 3 reveals the preference order $B\ P_3\ C\ P_3 A$. If the first agenda is used and voting is sophisticated, 3 will get his or her first choice, B. The general impossibility of devising a reasonable social choice mechanism that is immune from this type of "cheating" is shown by Gibbard (1973) and Satterthwaite (1975).

4. Conditions for the existence of a d-majority winner

The picture we have painted so far is fairly bleak. Majority cycles appear inescapable and the consequences for majority decisions are serious. In fact, Riker (1980, 443) reacted to the global cycling results of McKelvey and Schofield by attempting to bring down the curtain on this field of research, concluding that politics is "*the* dismal science" and that "in the absence of such equilibria we cannot know much about the future at all. . . ." Most others, however, had a different reaction, best exemplified by Tullock (1981), who stated that these "chaos" theorems do not square with reality. In the real world, we do not observe alternatives endlessly being overturned by one majority after another (or do we?). Something must be wrong with the model.

In the sections that follow, we will summarize the conditions that *do* guarantee the existence of d-majority winners. We divide these conditions into three types: (1) preference restrictions, (2) domain restrictions, and (3) different majority sizes. We will try not only to describe which combinations of conditions give rise to d-majority winners but also to motivate these conditions so that the reader can appreciate the arguments in favor of invoking these conditions in the context of the standard model of d-majority rule.

4.1 Preference restrictions

The best known preference restriction is Black's *single-peakedness*. This condition can be expressed naturally in terms of the spatial model, but it can also be defined in terms of the Arrowian model. Single-peakedness in the spatial model requires that each triple of alternatives in X can be ordered along a single dimension such that for each voter, his preferences over the alternatives can be described by a single-peaked curve. This means that for each voter, one or more alternatives are most preferred, constituting a preference peak or plateau. On each side of this peak or plateau, alternatives are less preferred the further away they are. In Arrowian terms, preferences are single-peaked if for any triple of alternatives, voters agree that one alternative is not worst.

Single-peakedness is a preference restriction because voters are not allowed to hold certain preference orders. Thus, if $x,y,z \in X$ are ordered from left to right in alphabetical order along one dimension, the preference order xP_izP_iy is not single-peaked. Black (1958) showed that if all individual preferences are single-peaked with respect to each triple of alternatives, a 50 percent-majority winner always exists. Furthermore, this winner will be the median most preferred alternative (which may be a closed interval of median points if the number of voters is even). If the number of voters is odd, the simple majority preference relation is fully transitive.

Sen (1970a) generalized this result to show that if voters agree that for each triple of alternatives one alternative is not best *or* all agree that one is not medium *or* all agree that one is not worst, then a 50 percent-majority winner will always exist. This condition is *value restriction* (VR) and includes single-peakedness as one of its forms. Sen (1970a) lists two other forms of preference restriction, *limited agreement* (LA) and *extremal restriction* (ER). LA requires that in each triple, everyone agrees that some alternative is at least as good as some other alternative. ER requires that in each triple if someone prefers x to y and y to z, then someone regards z as uniquely best if and only if he regards x as uniquely worst. VR, LA, and ER are all independent of each other; and Sen (1970a) shows that if X is finite, then satisfaction of at least one of these three conditions guarantees the existence of a 50 percent-majority winner.

Any optimism associated with preference restriction theorems was dealt a heavy blow by Kramer (1973). While it was understood that single-peakedness was a highly restrictive assumption in the spatial model, the spatial meaning of other forms of VR as well as LA and ER was not understood. Combining these three conditions under one heading, the *generalized exclusion* (GE) restriction, Kramer showed that in the multidimensional spatial model, if voter preferences were even modestly heterogeneous, not only was GE violated but so were several other exclusion conditions. Thus, like Plott's symmetry conditions, Kramer concludes that exclusion principles are unlikely to be satisfied in real societies. Thus, he states "Cyclical majorities, or the absence of stable outcomes under majority rule, are thus very likely the rule rather than the exception in problems involving voting over multi-dimensional choice spaces" (296).

Euclidean preferences over a multidimensional space are restricted in the sense that certain preference orders are excluded and preferences are constrained to be symmetric (Caplin and Nalebuff 1988), but these restrictions are much weaker than any of the preference restrictions discussed above. All of the instability theorems described above hold under Euclidean preferences (and usually under preferences of a more general type), so this restriction buys nothing in stability terms when the alternatives are multidimensional.

A different type of preference restriction concerns the distribution of voter preference types. In spatial terms, where most of this work is done, this restriction is placed on the density of voter ideal points $f(x^i)$. In Caplin and Nalebuff (1988), f is assumed to be concave over a convex subset of R^w with positive but finite volume. In Tovey (1992b), voter ideal points are sampled independently from a centered distribution (a distribution is centered around a point if all hyperplanes through the point cut the distribution in half). Much earlier work by Davis and Hinich (1968) assumes that the distribution of voter ideal points is multinormal. Davis and Hinich combine this assumption with Euclidean preferences to prove the existence of a 50 percent-majority winner at the mean of the voter distribution. Tovey (1992b) combines his preference restriction with other restrictions not yet introduced, while Caplin and Nalebuff (1988) show the existence of a d-majority winner for $d > 50$ percent. For these reasons, we will defer discussion of the major results of these two articles.

Preference restrictions, of both the qualitative and quantitative type, represent a degree of social consensus. As Caplin and Nalebuff (1988) point out, majority cycles are most likely to occur in "divide-the-pie" problems, where each individual wants the largest possible piece. These are instances of the war of "all against all." It should not be surprising that in these latter cases, majority decision making is unstable. Unfortunately, Kramer's result shows that it takes very little dissension for these breakdowns to occur.

4.2 Domain restrictions

There are two types of domain restriction we will discuss. The first concerns w, the dimensionality of the alternative space. The second concerns limits on which alternatives can be paired in a majority vote. The second type of restriction goes under the name "institutions" and originates with Shepsle (1979), although much earlier work on this subject was done by Black and Newing (1951).

Since 50 percent-majority winners are rare when $w > 1$, perhaps d-majority winners are more likely if $d > 50$ percent. Greenberg (1979) addresses this question in the context of a spatial model that allows for a more general class of individual preference than the Euclidean type. If the set of alternatives is a convex, compact subset of R^w, he shows that a d-majority winner is guaranteed if and only if $d = w/(w+1)$. If $w = 1$, $d = 50$ percent and we have Black's median voter result. If $w = 2$, then a 67 percent-majority winner is guaranteed, and so on. As w increases d approaches 100 percent, so in general only the rule of unanimity guarantees the existence of an undominated point. If X is finite with cardinality T and individual preferences are orderings, Greenberg (1979) shows that a d-majority winner is guaranteed if and only if $d = (T-1)/T$. Again, only the rule of unanimity generally guarantees a d-majority winner. Sen (1970a) has an interesting analogue to these two results, since he shows that if X is finite, an SDF exists that satisfies all of Arrow's other conditions. This SDF is the Pareto rule, which is a form of the rule of unanimity.

Schofield (1985) has a more general result than Greenberg for a weighted majority game $(d; r_1, \ldots, r_n)$, where r_i is the number of i's votes and decisions are made under d-majority rule. The *Nakamura number A* is the minimum number of minimal winning coalitions with an empty intersection, where a minimal winning coalition (MWC) is a subset of N with the property that if any individual is subtracted from the coalition, the remaining votes are d or less of the total. Schofield (1985) shows that if $A \geq w+2$, a d-majority winner exists. For the weighted majority game (50 percent; 4,3,2,1,1) the MWC's are (1,2), (1,3), (1,4,5), (2,3,4), and (2,3,5). The Nakamura number is 3, since no two MWC's have a nonempty intersection, but (1,2), (1,3), and (2,3,4) fail to have an individual in common. This means that a 50 percent-majority winner is guaranteed only if $w = 1$. For the simple majority, three-voter game (50 percent; 1,1,1), $A = 3$ and again a 50 percent-majority winner is guaranteed only if $w = 1$. From Greenberg, we get the same result since $d = w/(w+1)$ only if $w = 1$.

Greenberg and Schofield's results are only slightly more encouraging than Plott's regarding the likelihood that d-majority winners exist. Furthermore, they are open to a game theoretic interpretation. Since the likelihood of instability increases as the dimensionality of the alternative space increases, it may be advantageous for some individual to increase the dimensionality of the space. This point is made by Riker (1986). A 50 percent-majority winner in one dimension may be destroyed if a second dimension is added by introducing a new issue. As we have seen, creating a majority cycle can be a profitable exercise.

A more optimistic literature is associated with Shepsle (1979), who, like Tullock, felt that more stability exists in the real world than the above results would indicate. Of course, the jump from the theoretical world described above to the real world is considerable, and it is unwarranted to conclude that the real world is in chaos just because the model world is. As a theoretical description of pure majority rule, the above results are beyond reproach. The difficulty arises when these results are used to make predictions about majority rule decision making in the real world.

In this latter spirit, Shepsle (1979) began an examination of real world institutions that constrain majority decision making in ways not described above. In this regard, Shepsle contrasted preference-induced with structure-induced equilibrium. The former is the type we have considered thus far, a d-majority winner. However, if a d-majority winner does not exist, perhaps a structure-induced (SI)-majority winner exists, based on the assumption that certain alternatives are prohibited from competing against each other under the "rules of the game." To take the most researched example, suppose that in a multidimensional decision problem, voting takes place one dimension at a time, so that each contest is one dimensional. By deciding each dimension separately, two alternatives that differ on more than one dimension are not allowed to compete. Shepsle's justification for this restriction is based on a stylized form of the congressional committee system, which assigns each dimension to a separate committee.

A new complexity created by dimension-at-a-time voting is that a formerly one-stage voting problem is now a multistage problem, similar to the agendas described earlier. Voter predictions about the decisions reached on succeeding dimensions may influence their votes on the present dimension. In other words, voters may be sophisticated, contrary to Euclidean-based voting which is sincere. Ordeshook (1986) summarizes the problems and results of the dimension-at-a-time voting literature. If preferences are Euclidean, regardless of whether voters are sophisticated or sincere, a SI-majority winner exists at the vector of dimensional medians. If voter preferences are determined by *weighted* Euclidean distance (which induces ellipsoidal rather than circular indifference contours), then a SI-majority winner may not exist if voters are sophisticated.

Enelow and Hinich (1990) offer a different approach to this multistage problem by assuming that due to uncertainty about voter preferences, each voter uses least-squares assumptions to statistically forecast decisions on future dimensions. They obtain a multidimensional median result based on each voter's preference and forecast parameters.

A great advantage of the pure majority decision models as compared with the structure-imposed majority models is that the former are much more general and do not depend on institutional details that may be hard to characterize or subject to change. Structure-based models, on the other hand, recognize that it's probably hopeless to build models that have real world predictive power without including the kind of institutional detail that characterizes real world decison making. The problem appears to boil down to deciding how many rules a model should have, with generality being traded off against predictive power.

On the other hand, if game theoretic behavior is endemic to majority rule decision making, the pure majority rule models described above are probably underspecified. What is called for, instead, is a full description of the game that the society is playing. This raises a list of complexities. Just for starters, in models of committee voting, the players are the individual members of the committee, while in mass elections, the players are normally assumed to be the candidates running for office. All kinds of rules (some fixed, some not) govern the behavior of these players and it is important to specify what the players know about each other. We are now in the world of game theory, which is outside the scope of this essay.

On the subject of fluctuating rules, McKelvey and Ordeshook (1984) show through a series of experiments that if individuals are allowed to hold prevote discussions, institutional restrictions, such as dimension-at-a-time voting may be bypassed. Majority coalitions may select a multidimensional alternative other than the vector of dimensional medians. This same point was made by Riker (1980), who observed that the rules themselves may be unstable.

Returning to our discussion of domain restrictions, Tovey (1992b) combines the centeredness assumption described above with each of several "real world" restrictions and shows that the probability of a 50 percent-majority winner is 1 as the voter population increases. Some of these restrictions are voter limitations rather than domain restrictions, but the domain restrictions capture the essence of his model. One of his domain restrictions is a minimal distance assumption, which requires that a threshold value $\epsilon > 0$ exists such that two alternatives may not compete unless they differ by at least ϵ. The assumption of minimal distance corresponds to an unwillingness on the part of voters to consider a new alternative that is only barely different from the status quo.

Another domain restriction is that the set of alternatives comprise a discrete set. As Tovey points out, congressional debates over taxes or spending are over discrete dollar amounts. From a practical standpoint, the alternatives under consideration in real decision bodies do not take an infinite set of values.

Either the mimimal distance or the discrete values assumption combined with the assumption that the voters are independently sampled from a centered distribution is sufficient for the existence of a 50 percent-majority winner. For the minimal distance assumption, ϵ can be any positive number.

While Tovey's results are, like Shepsle's, motivated by a desire to square the predictions of voting theory with majority decision making in the real world, the question of whether real world majority decision making is stable or not has not been given a rigorous answer. Whether d-majority winners exist in reality has only been addressed in very limited settings other than experiments (e.g., Chamberlin, Cohen, and Coombs 1984). The existence of majority rule cycles in Congress has received some attention (e.g., Riker 1986). Basically, the empirical literature testing the theory we have described consists of a small set of examples.

The scientific problem with the nonexistence of d-majority winners is that it leaves us without a prediction, and without a prediction, work in this area is open to the charge of being purely philosophical. Of course, Romer and Rosenthal (1978) argue that even when a d-majority winner exists, real decision makers may pick something else. This is another brand of the institutional literature known as "take-it-or-leave-it" voting. In its simplest form, the Romer–Rosenthal model assumes that a budget-maximizing agenda setter forces voters to choose between a high dollar alternative and a low dollar reversion level. The high dollar alternative is picked so that the median voter barely prefers it to the low dollar alternative, which causes the high dollar alternative to be selected. Rosenthal (1990) reviews this model. Whether agendas are openly arrived at or not, most voting theorists feel it is incumbent on them to construct models that do make vote predictions, and a d-majority winner is important for this reason.

4.3 Different majority sizes

The last type of condition we will survey is that of supramajorities (i.e., examining $d > 50$ percent). It has long been recognized that increasing d increases the likelihood of d-majority winners. As d approaches 100 percent, d-majority winners are obviously guaranteed. What has not been known until recently is the precise relationship between d and several other parameters, such as the dimensionality of the alternative space, and the existence of d-majority winners. The result of Greenberg (1979) described above is the first major one of this type.

Caplin and Nalebuff (1988) have another important result. As mentioned above, they assume that the density of voter ideal points $f(x^i)$ is concave over its support, which both contains X and is also a convex subset of R^w with positive and finite volume. This preference restriction is paired with Euclidean preferences to derive the result that a d-majority winner always exists if $d = 1 - [n/(n+1)]^n$. In the limit, this number approaches $1 - 1/e \approx .632$, so, regardless of the dimensionality of the alternative space, if $d = 64$ percent, a d-majority winner is guaranteed. Among the d-majority winners is the min-max set identified by Simpson (1969) and Kramer (1977). This is the set of alternatives x^* such that the maximal fraction against x^* is least among the alternatives in X.

5. A "best bet"

Bartholdi, Narasimhan, and Tovey (1990) make use of complexity theory to address a question not previously asked: "if an undominated point exists, how do we know?" Their answer is surprising. While recognizing a dominated point is a straightforward matter of finding another point that defeats it, except for the special case where a possible undominated point is no one's ideal, determining whether a point is undominated is "computationally infeasible for all but small or specially structured instances" (19).

The upshot of this finding is that it may be very difficult to know whether a d-majority winner exists. Bartholdi, Narasimhan, and Tovey (1990) show that if an undominated point exists, it is what they call a "best bet." If the ideal points of four voters are at the corners of a square, the best bet is the point of intersection of the two diagonals. The general algorithm for finding the best bet is described in their paper and in two dimensions is the intersection of the two unique "transverse tangents." Because, in general, it is computationally difficult to show that the best bet is *not* an undominated point, for all practical purposes, it is! This is an unusual way of looking at the problem of existence for d-majority winners.

6. Conclusion

Our main concern has been conditions that guarantee the existence of d-majority winners. As we have seen, 50 percent-majority winners are rare unless individual preferences are strongly restricted. A structure-induced winner may exist, but if the structure itself is unstable, then so is the winner. d-majority winners become more likely as d increases and less likely as the dimensionality of the space increases. Still, it is, in general, computationally difficult to find an alternative that defeats a "best bet," so even if a d-majority winner does not exist, it may be hard to know.

The existence of majority cycles opens the door to strategic voting. In fact, d-majority winners can be destroyed simply to create strategic opportunities. While these possibilities loom large theoretically, we still do not know the general frequency of cyclical decision making in the real world or, when cycling exists, the general size of the alternative space over which cycling occurs. In the end, we may not be able to answer these questions.

CHAPTER 8

Majority rule

DOUGLAS W. RAE AND ERIC SCHICKLER

Majority rule is at once the simplest of institutions and one of human-kind's most remarkable inventions. Asking that the few give way to the many is, after all, a simple idea. The remarkable invention is the use of majority voting as the central mechanism in the formation of self-transforming institutions – systems of rules capable of turning them-selves into new systems over time, in light of changing conditions and changing beliefs. Following the convenient terminology of H. L. A. Hart (1961) we may call the ordinary rules by which institutions regulate human conduct *primary,* and the rules by which these primary rules themselves are regulated *secondary.* It is the integration of primary and secondary rules that institutionalizes self-transformation and, in turn, opens up the high ideals of democracy and freedom. Majority rule is the simplest and most celebrated of secondary rules and this chapter ex-plores the grounds for its celebrity.

Let us distinguish two broad levels of analysis. First, the level of abstract binary choice. Given two abstract options (x,y), choose $xPy,$ $yPx,$ or xIy as the collective decision from the pair.[1] This is the level at which majority rule's elegance is most visible, and the level at which axiomatic justification flourishes. A second level of analysis concerns the general choice problem of forming a collective judgment among m objects, such as (x,y,z). Here, the object is to begin with n individual preferences in the form $xR_iyR_iz,$ where R denotes preference P or indif-ference I over the m objects. This is notoriously the level at which majority rule becomes an outlaw with respect to logical standards such as transitivity. This is the level of analysis that underlies Arrow's (1951) general possibility theorem, and it is the level contemplated two centu-ries earlier by Condorcet in the formulation of his famous voting para-dox (1785). It is perhaps fair to say that the bulk of public choice work on majority rule has been conducted at this level over the past forty

---

1. At this level, it is logically appropriate to acknowledge the possibility of indifference between the two options. At some other levels, having greater political significance, indifference is not a feasible outcome.

years. The best of this work embeds majority rule in the more specific context of secondary rules governing institutions bearing on the circumstances of groups and individuals in a community. Here we have an ensemble of secondary rules, including an agenda rule, a participation rule, and an information system, all of which condition the operation of majority rule itself. Majority rule is a specific species of decision rule, belonging to a specific genus within that class, the genus being anonymity-respecting or unweighted voting rules. It will be combined with some string of selections from the other headings and will function in accepting or rejecting a series of primary rule changes (PRCs.) In this context, much of what matters lies in the relationship between majority rule and *other secondary rules* as they function in generating PRC's and in opening opportunities for participation. The repeated question is "How, if at all, are the desirable features of abstract majority rule to be realized given a certain potential hazard?" The hazards include such features as clogged agendas, large numbers, unevenly distributed information, and simultaneous decision processes apt to distort outcomes.

We take up the two levels of analysis in turn.

1. Majority rule for abstract binary choices

At this high level of abstraction, there are two major lines of argument in justification of majority rule. The first begins by positing equity of power and control as a test and then goes on to show how majority decision fulfills these criteria. Kenneth May's (1952) theorem showing the uniqueness of majority decision is by far the most elegant and powerful of these demonstrations. A second family of arguments at this high level of abstraction begins by positing criteria for efficient matching of preferences to outcomes and goes on to show majority rule's special suitability to such matching tasks.

In reviewing these two lines of justification, let us confine attention to what might be termed *minimally efficient decision rules.* This class is neatly carved out by the conjunction of May's axioms for decisiveness and positive responsiveness. Consider first the idea that Pareto-superiority might be made a necessary condition for any collective preference.[2] This would order neatly enough the sorts of transactions that occur in markets and would accommodate decisions on rule changes that advantaged (or disadvantaged) everyone. It would not, however, decide

---

2. Pareto superiority as a decision rule can be defined as follows: given two alternatives, x and y, xPy iff for each individual i, xR_iy and for at least one individual, xP_iy, yPx iff for each individual i, yR_ix, and for at least one individual, yP_ix.

any case entailing conflicting judgments. Along with many other possible decision rules, it is ruled out by May's decisiveness axiom:

> *Decisiveness:* For any possible combination of individual preferences over any pair of options (x,y) a rule must generate a single outcome $(xPy, yPx, or xIy)$.[3]

Notice at once that this is a far from innocent requirement if political equality is our subject matter. In thinking about political equality, one is always confronted by something like a paradox. The standard problem for political equality is to strike a balance between conflicting views. If *no* deliberate discrimination is built into the decision process, then either no choice can be effected or such choices as are achieved must be deeply arbitrary. Thus, to pick an absurd case, we might set down a process something like this: Given two options (x,y), choose xPy, yPx, or xIy as the collective decision from the pair. We are given n persons with preferences over (x,y) and set out a decision rule *requiring that every individual's ordinary preference be matched by the decision*. This is, if nothing else, evenhanded. Yet it is obviously untenable since we would generate self-contradictory results given any two individuals with differing preferences, since xP_iy » xPy and at the same time yP_jx » yPx. Any workable decision rule violates this absurd requirement and in so doing bestows favor on those who have one preference and disfavor on their antagonists. In this primordial sense, any workable decision rule embodies some seed of inequality. Decision itself is otherwise impossible, and the test of decisiveness commits us to this fact.

Next, think about such mechanisms as the reading of tea leaves, numerical lotteries, and voting systems that invert preferences that is, by saying that the votes of persons i and j for x (x,y) are counted instead as votes for y (x,y). These mechanisms are wildly inefficient in the specific sense captured by May's requirement of positive responsiveness:

> *Positive responsiveness:* Suppose that for a given set of individual preferences over (x,y), the collective choice is xRy. Then suppose that some individual, j, shifts her vote so that it is more favorable to x than in the initial case (from yP_jx to yI_jx or xP_jy, or from yI_jx, to xP_jy), then it must be the case that xPy for the collectivity.

This rules out inverted voting in an obvious way, and it rules out arbitrary or random procedures (tea leaves, say) since an x-ward shift in i's preference could be paired with a y-ward shift in the procedure's out-

---

3. In reference to the example just given, notice that Pareto undecidable outcomes are not instances of collective indifference.

come. In ruling out all lotteries and sortitions, it takes away probabilistic methods for giving voice to small minorities.[4] Bringing these two criteria together, we have the class that interests us:

> *Minimal efficiency:* The class of minimally efficient decision procedures consist of those procedures that meet the tests of decisiveness and positive responsiveness.

Notice that this is a rather strong restriction and that it portends a certain vulnerability for those who find themselves committed to unpopular values and opinions. Nevertheless, in what follows, we confine attention to the very large class of decision procedures that fall within this class.

1.1 Political equality as a basis for majority rule

Begin with the simple intuition that a good decision procedure would have us share control over the decisions ". . . so that the preferences of no one citizen are weighted more heavily than the preferences of any other citizen."[5] This extremely broad idea spans two distinct forms of equality: (1) between persons, and (2) between the outcome types they may choose to support and oppose. The first is captured by May's idea of anonymity; the second is captured by his test of neutrality.

> *Anonymity:* Suppose we exchange the preferences of any two equal-sized subsets of voters. Members of the one subset give

---

4. Probabilistic voting mechanisms, though they violate the requirement of positive responsiveness, may have some desirable theoretical properties (see Mueller 1984).
5. Dahl and Lindblom (1953, 41). In this paper we do not take up all the many institutional nuances of political equality. An interesting and acute introduction is offered by Still (1981), who analyzes six distinct criteria for political equality: universal equal suffrage, equal shares, equal probabilities, anonymity, majority rule, and proportional representation. Still argues that authors discussing equality rarely distinguish among these criteria and therefore are unable to provide guidance for determining whether a given change in procedure promotes or undermines political equality. The six criteria advanced by Still appear, in many cases, to be nested alternatives: for example, satisfying the fourth criterion in general implies satisfying the first three. Although Still argues that there are only rare, insignificant exceptions to this lexical ordering, Grofman (1981) points out ways in which the criteria are likely to be in systematic conflict. For example, if one abandons the assumption that voters are homogenous (that is, have equal propensities to support any given alternative), it is easy to demonstrate that in any single-member system, equal shares and equal probabilities conflict (Grofman 1981). Grofman also argues that other criteria need to be added to Still's list: these include political competition and absence of partisan or racial bias in the seats-to-votes ratio. In any case, Still and Grofman's work make it clear that what equity means as a criterion for assessing a decision rule is in general far from obvious.

up their previous preferences in favor of those held by the
other subset and vice versa. If the decision rule meets the test
of anonymity, then no such switching can alter the collective
outcome.

Put another way, the decision rule must never need to know the names
of voters, once they are deemed qualified to participate at all. This
obviously rules out weighted voting rules and schemes that give special
consideration to identified classes, genders, races, and so on. This identity masking is extended to the outcomes themselves by May's neutrality
axiom:

> *Neutrality:* Suppose that all individual ordinal preferences over
> (x,y) are the same as they are over (w,z), then the collective
> outcomes over the two pairs of options must be the same.

Thus, if each individual makes the same judgment between x and y as
she makes between w and z, then x must fare as does w, and y must fare
as does z. This ensures blindness to outcomes and their labels. The
intuition is again simple: Neutrality rules out a wired-in preference for
one option or option-class over another option or option-class. Requiring, for instance, more than a majority to impose change or to depart
from market practice would violate neutrality. Taken together, these two
criteria define a very important construction of political equality:

> *Strict formal political equality:* Decision procedures meeting
> both anonymity and neutrality instantiate strict formal politi-
> cal equality.

The arms-length tone of this definition is intended. Following Mueller
(1989, 98), imagine two questions: (1) Should John Doe's property be
confiscated and distributed to the rest of the community? (2) Should the
lights on the Christmas tree in the town square be red or blue? It might
well be asked whether anonymity between Doe and the rest of us should
prevail on the first question, and whether neutrality should compel us to
treat the two questions in the same way. These reservations notwithstanding, we arrive at May's theorem:

May's theorem: *One and only one minimally efficient decision procedure
meets the test of strict political equality, and that decision procedure is majority rule.*

This is an extremely powerful result. If we really believed that the conditions of minimal efficiency and strict formal equality had to be embodied
in any legitimate decision procedure, then we could afford to demand no
further properties whatever. Since majority rule is the unique result,

requiring anything *else* drives us to axiomatic bankruptcy and an impossibility theorem. Requiring these things plus, say, transitivity or path-independence or anything else that majority rule is capable of violating yields an impossibility – and each will be child's play to prove, given May's theorem as a starting point.[6]

Even though May's theorem is in this sense exhaustive – since it yields a unique result – it is in some basic way misleading. It sets rather weak tests for efficiency (decisiveness and positive responsiveness) that fail to capture the variable efficiency of decision procedures in matching preferences with outcomes. It is therefore useful to look at another basic line of analysis that inverts May's emphasis by presuming a thin version of equality and then asking what rule most efficiently matches outcomes to preferences.

1.2 Political efficiency as a basis for majority rule

Suppose we think about an anonymous individual in a community whose agenda she is unable to forecast. As formulated by Rae (1969):

> . . . suppose that the individual with whom we are concerned has some personal schedule of values. We know nothing about the specific content of his value schedule – its selfishness or altruism, its sophistication or naiveté, its generality or specificity – since this individual, whom we may call "Ego," is a purely generic figure. We must, however, suppose that his schedule is complete enough that it leads Ego to like or dislike each proposal which comes before the committee. Accordingly, our major assertion is that Ego would like to optimize the correspondence between his preferences and the policies which are imposed by the committee:[7] he wants to have his way by defeating proposals which his values lead him to dislike and by imposing those which they lead him to like.

Notice that this formulation is implicitly egalitarian in that it weighs all individuals equally and implies a sort of social contract among individuals harboring unknown but presumably different schedules of values. Neither special persons nor special values are singled out for attention. But its main focus is on efficient matching between individual preferences and collective outcomes. What Rae shows is that where the individual is as likely to favor as oppose an unspecified proposal and is equally concerned about imposing changes she likes and blocking ones she dis-

---

6. On the proof of May, see May (1952) or Mueller (1989).
7. This assumption is less innocuous than it may appear: complete indifference is not improbable even among the very active (viz., committee members).

likes, she is compelled to select majority rule over all other decision rules. This result is later generalized by Taylor (1969) and by several others. Curtis (1972) shows that the result holds if individual probabilities of favoring and opposing proposals can vary from one-half and vary independently of one another. Schofield (1972) carefully examines the impact of electorate size on the result and shows that for some important distributions of outcomes, the optimality of majority rule is robust across communities of all sizes.

Another way of looking at majoritarian preference efficiency is to consider any array of community disputes and then find the rule that is least-bad in the worst case. The answer is again majority rule in as much as majoritarianism *minimizes the size of the largest group whose preferences are ever violated by a binary decision.* The reasoning is simple: If system X's maximum losing coalition is one short of a majority, then X is majority rule. In every other case, X is inferior to majority rule since a larger coalition may be compelled to accept an unwanted outcome.

It should be clear that the efficiency of majority rule in preference matching implies nothing about its efficiency in a Paretian sense. Indeed, as Mueller (1989) observes, majority decision may well get in the way of conflict settlements that would take account of preference intensities. Where a Coasian improvement is possible, there is no particular reason to suppose that majority rule will achieve it; it may, indeed, allow people to inflict outcomes that are suboptimal in a Paretian sense.

1.3 Two logical problems

By way of transition to the more complex case, note two well-known oddities. First, suppose that we apply majority rule reflexively – to *itself.* This creates a logical possibility (and an historical one too) that majority rule will *reject itself.* If we favor majority rule and extend that to a willingness to honor its outcomes, then we cannot possibly arrive at a consistent stance in evaluating the antimajoritarian uses of majority rule.

This self-canceling possibility is a real one and is in many respects consistent with the classic works of political sociology. In a world of technical elites, uneven powers of exit, and widespread economic marginalization, it is not farfetched to suppose that advantaged groups may in effect withdraw from hazardous polities, leaving behind resource-poor populations unable to back their collective decisions with appropriate resources. This is not quite the logically pure case of antimajoritarian majoritarianism, but it is importantly connected to it if majorities adopt a passive attitude toward the withdrawal of advantaged groups – as commonly occurs in American cities.

If we combine this process of selective withdrawal with a Black (1958) median voter model of majority voting, we may generate a decidedly perverse sequence in which the majority equilibrium shifts away from the exit-prone section of an electorate, provoking further exit. In simplest form we might begin with:

0 00 000 000 0 0   0Q0   0 0 0 0 0 0 0 0 0 0 0

where each "0" is a voter's optimum and "Q" is the majority equilibrium. If voters to the right are exit-prone, this array may be replaced by:

0 00 000 000   0Q0   00 0 0 0 0 0 0 0

which might in turn yield another round of exit on the right with yet another leftward shift in the majority equilibrium. In this way, majority rule with uneven exit may produce a quite antimajoritarian dynamic (see Hirschman 1970 for a more general consideration of this dynamic in voluntary associations).

A second difficulty is of course the cyclic majority, as in the standard example. We have voters A, B, and C who rank alternatives x, y, and z as follows:

A	B	C
X	Z	Y
Y	X	Z
Z	Y	X

As can be seen immediately, X beats Y and Y beats Z. But, in violation of transitivity, Z beats X. Paper wraps rock, rock breaks scissors, scissors cut paper. This problem is important less from a logical point of view than from a practical one. If it allows agenda setters to work unmajoritarian results via majority rule, it tends to undermine the normative case for such systems. The actualities are more complex, as we will see in Section 2.

2. Complex majoritarian decision

In all but the last paragraph of Section 1, we have focused on abstract choice between two alternatives. Under majority rule, the outcome resulting would simply be the alternative preferred by more voters. This alternative, which we will call Q, would be a dominant point in the sense that no potentially decisive coalition would have an incentive to replace Q with the other feasible alternative. When one extends the range of feasible alternatives to include more than two alternatives, the definition of an equilibrium remains unchanged: Q is a dominant point if there is no proposal that can beat Q in a majority contest (see Enelow and Hinich 1984, 25).

In an important paper, Plott (1967) demonstrates that a point is an equilibrium under majority rule, given an odd number of voters, if that point is a "maximum for one (and only one) individual, and the remaining even number of individuals can be divided into pairs whose interests are diametrically opposed; that is, whenever a proposal is altered so as to benefit a given individual A, a given individual B must be made worse off" (as cited in Mueller 1989, 67–8).[8] This condition is known as "pairwise symmetry." When the feasible alternatives differ solely along a single dimension, Plott's result simplifies to the well-known median voter theorem (see Downs 1957; Black 1958), which is reviewed in this volume in the essay by Enelow.[9]

To illustrate the implications of Plott's result, let us begin with an electorate of five voters, who must select a budget for the local parks department. The feasible range of budgets is given in the line segment in Figure 1, along with each voter's ideal point. A voter's preferences are single-peaked if for any two points on the same side of the voter's ideal point, the voter prefers the point closer to her ideal point (for example, in Figure 1, committee member B prefers that the policy be the ideal point of member D as opposed to the ideal point of member E. If voter preferences are single-peaked, we know from the median voter theorem that the ideal point of member C is the unique majority rule equilibrium. It is majority preferred to each alternative in the space. In Plott's terms, it is the ideal point of exactly one voter, and the remaining four voters can be divided into pairs such that any move from C makes one member of each pair better off, and one member worse off. A notable feature of this result is that if voter C's ideal point shifts in either direction, his new ideal point is the equilibrium, as long as he remains to the right of voter

8. When there is an even number of voters, a point Q will be a majority rule equilibrium if there is no voter with a maximum at Q, and the voters can be divided into pairs such that a move from Q in any direction will make one member of each pair worse off and one member of each pair better off. Enelow and Hinich (1983a) point out that Plott's condition is sufficient for the existence of a majority rule equilibrium, but not necessary. However, the necessary conditions for the existence of an equilibrium addressed by Enelow and Hinich do not appear to be significantly more likely to be realized in committees or electorates with more than three to five voters.

9. See the Enelow essay in this volume for a more complete, technical discussion of the Plott result.

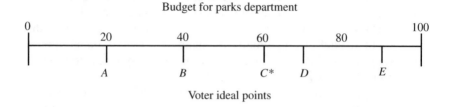

Figure 1. Illustration of the median voter result. *Denotes majority rule equilibrium (the median).

B and to the left of voter *D*.[10] This implies that majority rule is robust in situations resembling that shown in Figure 1: a shift in the median voter's ideal point changes the *location* of the equilibrium, but does not threaten the *existence* of a dominant point. From an efficiency standpoint, this dominant point minimizes the maximum number of voters who would prefer some other alternative in the space.

Now, imagine that the five voters must select a budget for the Parks department and a budget for schools. This introduces a second dimension of judgment to the choice problem depicted in Figure 1. However, Plott's theorem tells us that this new situation also has a majority rule equilibrium if there is a voter, in this case again *C*, who has an ideal point that is located such that the remaining voters can be divided into pairs, where a move away from *C* that makes one member of a pair better off must make the other member of the same pair worse off. Figure 2 illustrates such a situation. Under majority rule, point *C* again beats any alternative in the space and therefore is a dominant point.

The difficulty is that once there are two or more dimensions of judgment, the likelihood of satisfying Plott's pairwise symmetry condition appears to be remote. For example, if one shifts the location of voter *C* even slightly to the point *C'* (as in Figure 3), there no longer is a majority rule equilibrium. Therefore, equilibrium under majority rule is extremely fragile in the multidimensional case, in contrast to its robustness in the presence of a single dimension of judgment.[11]

Plott's result which built on the earlier, famous Arrow (1951) impossibil-

---

10. The reader should be able to prove for herself that if *C* moves further to the right than voter *D*, then the ideal point of voter *D* is the new equilibrium under majority rule (a parallel conclusion of course holds if *C* shifts to the left of voter *B*).

11. Enelow's essay in this volume reviews possible restrictions that might be placed on voter preferences or on the dimensionality of the issue space to reduce the likelihood of disequilibrium.

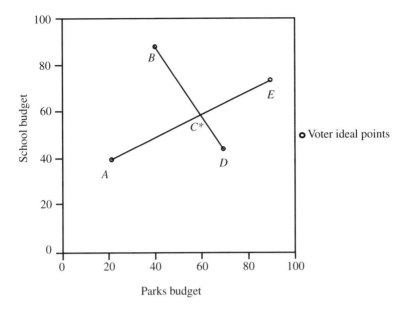

Figure 2. Illustration of equilibrium in two dimensions. *Denotes majority rule equilibrium. *Note:* each voter is assumed to have Euclidean preferences.

ity theorem, generated considerable work on the likely effects of the absence of a dominant point under majority rule. The absence of an equilibrium implies the presence of "instability," or cycling – for any point Q in the space of alternatives, one can find some alternative R that beats Q. Furthermore, this alternative R can be defeated by some other alternative in the space, S. This would not seem so discomforting if one knew that R and S were at least likely to be located in some specific, small region of the alternative space (in which case, one could roughly predict the outcome). McKelvey (1976) proves, however, that in the absence of a majority rule equilibrium, an agenda setter controlling the sequence of pairwise votes can lead a committee to any point in the space that she chooses, as long as each member always votes for the alternative she prefers among the offered pair (in other words, if each member votes sincerely).[12]

12. For extensions of this result, see McKelvey (1979) and Schofield (1983). See Cox (1987) for a discussion of the uncovered set, arguably the most popular solution concept in multidimensional majority rule games. The uncovered set may be small and centrally located for certain issues, but is likely to take up a much larger portion of the space when redistributive issues are considered (Green and Shapiro 1994, 134).

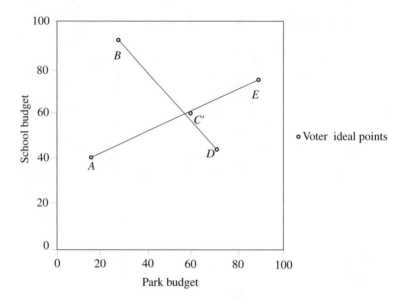

Figure 3. Majority rule disequilibrium in two dimensions.

The theoretical possibility of majority rule instability has spawned two related literatures. The first attempts to explore the normative implications of cycling for our understanding of the operation of majority rule (see, for example, Riker 1982; Miller 1983; Riker and Weingast 1988). With the exception of Miller (1983), most authors in this literature argue that the presence of cycles at the least offers a serious challenge to the justification of decisions reached by majority processes. The second literature begins with the observation that the endless cycling that one would expect from the McKelvey result does not appear to characterize most politics and hence seeks to construct explanations for the observed stability (Shepsle 1979; Shepsle and Weingast 1981, 1987; Tullock 1981; Enelow and Hinich 1984, 1989, 1990; Coughlin 1986, 1992).

The divergent empirical premises motivating the two literatures (cycling is ubiquitous; cycling is rare) has led Green and Shapiro (1994) to question whether the literature on majority rule equilibrium has offered any contributions to our understanding of politics. Green and Shapiro argue that in spite of the path-breaking theoretical work of Arrow, Plott, McKelvey, Schofield, and others, authors working in this literature have yet to generate testable hypotheses with the potential to illuminate the importance of the presence or absence of a majority rule equilibrium in real world politics. If Plott's theorem holds – and it does – then we must assume the latent possibility of majoritarian disequilibrium in most relatively complex decisions. Teasing out its phenomenological or empirical importance is another matter, largely neglected in the literature.

We will first explore the conditions under which cycling is particularly likely to be important and will then address the implications of cycles for the normative evaluation of majority rule processes.

2.1 Majority rule instability: Empirical complications

Endless cycling is particularly likely when policies involve redistribution (cf., Aranson and Ordeshook 1981; Mueller 1982; Caplin and Nalebuff 1988). Since issues involving redistribution involve as many dimensions as there are voters (minus one), Mueller (1982, 155) concludes that "political instability seems likely, therefore, when issues or platforms are constrained to distributional issues." Mueller presents evidence that the stability of governing coalitions in Europe and the American states has tended to decline during periods when issues involving redistribution dominate politics. This is a quite indirect test in that Mueller's primary indicator that distributive issues are dominant is slow economic growth. Ordeshook (1986) argues that politicians tend to avoid the consideration of tax legislation in election years because the inherently redistributive nature of tax policy lends it to cycles that would advantage challengers against less mobile incumbents. This again is an indirect test open to other interpretations, for example, that voters are willing to credit candidates with inconsistent accomplishments (low taxes, high spending) if not reminded of tax hikes just before elections.

Whatever the case may be on these specifics, it is easy to see that the potentiality of distributive disequilibrium will be common under majority rule wherever: (1) resources are transferable and finely divisible, (2) information is widely held (cf. Congleton and Sweetser 1992), (3) agendas are open, and (4) voters are self-interested. Let any individual (or organization or constituency) hold some share of resources at stage j in the decision process. Let someone propose to distribute that share of resources among a majority of other players. They, by hypothesis, vote for it. Since the description is extremely general, the potentiality is likewise quite general. Often, some mechanism inhibits the actual acting out of such a process – but its potentiality is there anyway.[13]

Recent theoretical developments nevertheless challenge the view that

13. Institutional rules might make it difficult to change the status quo, but these rules are themselves subject to change. There may be higher transaction costs and uncertainty involved in rules changes, but this does not eliminate the potential for determined and skilled politicians to change or bypass the rules.

the politics of distribution is inherently unstable. Baron and Ferejohn (1989) present a model of an n-person legislature that has the task of dividing a dollar among its members by majority rule. The Baron and Ferejohn model assumes that every member has a known probability of being recognized to propose a division of the dollar and that legislators care only about their own share of the dollar. The amendment rule specifies whether this proposed division is voted on immediately or is subject to amendment. In the case of an open rule, when a proposal is made, a second legislator is recognized who may either move the previous question or propose an amendment. The game ends when a proposal passes. If the proposed division does not pass, the legislators move to the next session, but the value of the dollar is reduced by a discount factor δ that represents the legislators' time preference.

Baron and Ferejohn demonstrate that under a closed rule, the benefits are distributed to a minimal majority and the legislator recognized receives a greater share of the benefits than the other members; moreover, this proposed distribution always passes in the first session.[14] For example, if each member has an equal probability of being recognized,[15] the member recognized proposes to receive $1-\delta(n-1)/2n$ of the dollar and offers $(n-1)/2$ of the remaining members δn of the dollar. This proposal passes because the expected value of continuing the game is only δ/n,[16] and therefore the $(n-1)/2$ members receiving δ/n join the proposer in voting for the proposal.

Under an open rule, the distribution is more equal – a more than minimal majority is likely to receive some share. Furthermore, the game may last more than a single session (if a legislator who is excluded from the proposed benefits is recognized to offer an amendment). The gains to the proposer are less pronounced under an open rule and are reduced further as the discount factor approaches 1.

The proposer's share is larger in the case of the closed rule because she knows that her proposal will pass as long as she offers a bare majority of members a share that is as large as each member's expected value

14. This result corresponds to the unique subgame-perfect Nash equilibrium for finitely lived legislatures. For infinitely lived legislatures, this corresponds to the unique stationary subgame-perfect Nash equilibrium.

15. Baron and Ferejohn's results do not require the probability of being recognized to be identical across members. Indeed, Baron and Ferejohn (1989, 1189) find that members with a higher probability of being recognized may be less likely to be included in the winning coalition because they have a higher continuation value of the game and thus will demand a greater share of the benefits in exchange for voting for a proposal.

16. Members are assumed to be risk neutral. The continuation value of the game is determined by each member's probability of being recognized, the amendment rule, the size of the legislature, and by the discount factor.

of continuing the game (δ/n). In the case of the open rule, the proposer has an incentive to offer more members a share in the dollar to reduce the likelihood that the next person recognized proposes an amendment instead of moving the previous question.[17]

Baron and Ferejohn argue that their noncooperative model of legislative bargaining is superior to cooperative approaches, which do not model the sequential aspects of legislative choice. In other words, cooperative models yield instability and disequilibrium because they do not explicitly take into account the ways in which the sequencing of proposals induces an equilibrium. Against this we would note the limitless ingenuity of legislators in adding dimensions to a choice space and in finding nuanced differences among proposals (cf. Riker 1986).

A very general distinction is required between *the mere fact of stability and the condition of equilibrium.* Given that most issues must be ignored most of the time in a society facing real transaction costs, policies rest unmoved in vast numbers. This fact does not imply either equilibrium or induced equilibrium. It merely means that there is not time in the day or the year to tinker with everything all the time. This is suggestive of the common view that democracy can sure eat into a person's weekend, and of the sound observation that policies change at most incrementally most of the time (Lindblom 1959).

2.2 From empirical to normative considerations

From a normative standpoint, the latent possibility of majority rule disequilibrium does pose important challenges to our faith in the equity and efficiency of majority rule processes. From an equity standpoint, McKelvey's (1976) result indicates that a monopoly agenda setter may be able to manipulate the order of consideration of alternatives in order to lead to her own preferred outcome, even if that outcome is far from the ideal points of the vast majority of voters. The most extreme forms of manipulation are less likely to succeed if voters can vote strategically (that is, insincerely); however, Banks (1984) shows that agenda control can still distort outcomes significantly when legislators vote strategically.

Furthermore, the distorted outcomes introduced by majority rule disequilibrium may benefit those actors free to engage in sophisticated voting at the expense of legislators who for electoral or other reasons are forced to vote sincerely (see Denzau, Riker, and Shepsle 1985). A co-

---

17. The specific proposals offered in the case of the open rule are fairly complex and depend on each member's probability of being recognized, the size of the legislature, and the discount factor. See Baron and Ferejohn (1989, 1196–7) for the precise results.

ordinated minority with the skills and electoral security to engage in sophisticated voting and agenda manipulation may be able to capitalize on cycles to scuttle proposals that have strong support and pass programs that only a minority supports.[18]

The existence of majority rule disequilibrium also poses a challenge to the efficiency argument for majority rule. If the outcome reached by a majority process depends heavily on the order in which the alternatives are arranged on an agenda, there is no a priori reason to believe that this outcome will match preferences better than will some other alternative. In any situation involving multiple evaluative dimensions, there are numerous possible majority rule outcomes, each corresponding to one or more feasible agendas for voting. Comparing the efficiency of majority rule with other voting rules in such a situation requires that one balance several possible criteria for efficiency: these would include the maximum number of dissatisfied voters, susceptibility to cycling, and the time costs of reaching a decision.

The decision-costs criterion points to the possibility that the ease of changing policies under majority rule will lead to "endless" cycling in which politicians constantly overturn past decisions in order to gain a greater share of the benefits. Glazer and McMillan (1992) offer an innovative model of legislative choice demonstrating that legislators might have incentives to propose universalistic policies that reduce the likelihood of observable instability. Their model assumes that finding solutions to new problems and proposing amendments to old policies each have opportunity costs: the effort involved in devising and proposing an alternative distribution of existing benefits could be spent attempting to find solutions to problems that have arisen in the interim. Legislators face the choice of focusing their energies on the zero-sum game of redistributing existing benefits or attempting to find positive-sum solutions to new problems. Glazer and McMillan prove the existence of a subgame-perfect Nash equilibrium (in either finitely lived or infinitely lived legislatures) in which legislators propose and pass universalistic solutions to problems to induce their fellow legislators to spend future periods finding solutions to new problems rather than revisiting the old distribution. By providing a universalistic distribution in implementing the solution to a given problem, there are smaller incentives to attempt to amend this solution in the future, and legislators instead invest their time in finding solutions to new problems.

The Glazer and McMillan model presents the intriguing possibility

---

18. Krehbiel and Rivers (1990) and Green and Shapiro (1994) suggest that there is a dearth of systematic empirical evidence to support the claim that this possibility is actually realized in American politics with any frequency.

that the opportunity costs of foregone legislation may provide an incentive for each legislator to avoid proposing policies that would encourage endless cycling. The common interest in addressing new problems can reduce the tendency for the sorts of proposals that encourage the constant revisiting of old policies. Nonetheless, empirical evidence on the size of distributive coalitions is mixed (Collie 1988), leaving one uncertain to what extent universalistic coalitions explain the observed stability of many policies.

We conclude, therefore, that it is disingenuous to assume away the latent possibility of majority rule disequilibrium when one is evaluating majority rule. However, social decisions must be made, and there is no decision rule that satisfies all of the equity and efficiency criteria that one might consider important (cf. Arrow 1951). Riker and Weingast (1988), Caplin and Nalebuff (1988), and others argue that the susceptibility of majority rule to cycling justifies placing limits on what a majority can accomplish, either through designating certain "rights" that cannot be violated by a majority vote (as in Riker 1982a; Riker and Weingast 1988) or by requiring a supermajority to pass legislation (Caplin and Nalebuff 1988). These solutions each face difficulties. Shapiro (1990) points out that the choice of protected "rights" requires a social decision, which may be subject to the same cycles present at later stages. The allowed scope of public action is itself a political decision. Supermajority requirements increase the likelihood that there will be a dominant point, but they also place a disproportionate burden on those who would change the status quo. If one views democracy as a movement historically opposing entrenched constellations of power (cf. Shapiro 1990, 1994), supermajority requirements emerge as bulwarks protecting those privileged by the status quo from democratic challenges.

3. Conclusions

The normative case for majority rule is, as we have seen, easiest to explicate for the instance of simple binary choice. In such choice, certainly, the argument from political equality and the argument from political efficiency have considerable elegance and credibility. In the more unwieldy world of complex majority decision explored in Section 2, the twists and turns are innumerable, and the opportunity for undermining both political equality and political efficiency are frequently visible. These factors are made more important by what we know about the ethnography of elites, with their networks of cooperation and exclusivity, and by the uneven rates of political participation with which they are associated.

It is, moreover, important to recognize the institutional complexity of all real systems, mixing as they do market and nonmarket mechanisms, transcripts of communication that are open to some and not others (Scott 1990), and bases of identity that are not readily set forth in a relatively brief formal analysis.

All that being said, it is worth remembering that the very idea of political decision implies the prospect that we have to set priorities and make choices in ways more favorable to some than to others. When we are able to foresee the shapes of these choices, or imagine ourselves able to do so, then agreement on majority rule or any other decision mechanism is called into question. Looking at the political world emerging at the end of the twentieth century – filled with ethnic and racial strife in places as different as Soweto and Sarajevo, the West Bank and West Los Angeles – it is clear that institutional designs far more complex than those considered here are required. And research combining abstract analysis with history and sociology is a high priority.

CHAPTER 9

Group choice and individual judgments

H. PEYTON YOUNG

1. Optimal group decisions

Methods of voting have been used since ancient times. The systematic study of voting rules, however, and the search for a "best" rule originated in eighteenth-century France. The stimulus for much of the thinking in this period is the following famous passage from Rousseau's *The Social Contract:*

> When a law is proposed in the people's assembly, what is asked of them is not precisely whether they approve of the proposition or reject it, but whether it is in conformity with the general will . . . each by giving his vote gives his opinion on this question, and the counting of the votes yields a declaration of the general will. When, therefore, the opinion contrary to my own prevails, this proves only that I have made a mistake, and that what I believed to be the general will was not so. (153)

This idea was given a more precise formulation some twenty years later by the mathematician and political philosopher Marie Jean Antoine Nicolas Caritat, Marquis de Condorcet. Like Rousseau, Condorcet began with the premise that the object of voting is to discover what decision or choice is in the best interest of society. Unlike Rousseau, he provided a logically coherent framework within which to analyze this issue (Grofman and Feld 1988; Young 1988). Suppose that a group of n individuals must make a decision between two alternatives a and b, one of which is in fact better than the other. (Whether this is a meaningful assumption will be considered below.) Each individual makes a judgment and votes accordingly. Sometimes, of course, they judge incorrectly. But let us assume – perhaps too optimistically – that each voter is *more likely* to make the right choice than the wrong choice. Condorcet showed that, if they make their choices independently, then the laws of probability imply that the choice with the most votes is the one that is most likely to be correct. In other words, majority rule is an *optimal* method of group decision making.

Consider the following example. There are one hundred voters choosing between two alternatives a and b. Let the outcome be 55 votes for a and 45 votes for b. Assume that each of these individuals is right 60 percent of the time. If a is the best choice, the probability of the observed voting pattern (55 for a, 45 for b) is $\alpha = (100! / 55! 45!).6^{55} .4^{45}$. If, on the other hand, b is the best choice, the probability of the observed voting outcome is $\beta = (100! / 45! 55!) .6^{45} .4^{55}$. As the former is about 58 times more probable than the latter, we conclude that a is more likely to be correct than b. This style of reasoning is known in statistics as maximum likelihood estimation. It is similar to Bayesian inference with uniform priors, though formally it does not rely on the notion of priors at all.[1]

The reader may balk at the idea that there really is such a thing as a "best" or "correct" decision for the group, yet in fact such situations are quite common. Consider any decision in which everyone agrees about the objective, but there is disagreement about the best means to achieve this objective. The board members of a central bank, for example, may all want to maximize the long-run rate of economic growth. But at any given moment they may be uncertain whether lowering or raising interest rates is the best way to achieve this end. Similarly, the directors of a corporation may agree that their objective is to maximize the firm's long-run profitability, but they may have different views about which candidate for chief executive is most likely to realize this goal. In these situations Condorcet's argument makes perfect sense.

A particularly telling application is to jury trials, a case that Condorcet himself examined in considerable detail. Suppose that a twelve-member jury must vote whether to convict a defendant. Let a be the proposition that he is guilty, b that he is innocent. If all twelve members of the jury vote for conviction, and if the probability that each is correct is 0.6, then the probability that the defendant is in fact innocent is less than one in fifty thousand (assuming equal prior probability of guilt or innocence).

This "unanimity rule" is called for if a false conviction is deemed much worse than letting a guilty party go free. But if the objective is simply to reach the *correct* decision with highest probability, then clearly this is not the best one can do. The probability of making the correct choice under unanimity rule is only slightly greater than one-half (about .501). But under simple majority rule the probability of making a correct choice is

---

1. A Bayesian analysis would proceed as follows. Assume a and b are equally likely to be correct a priori. A posteriori the probability that a is correct is $(\alpha/2)/(\alpha/2 + \beta/2) = .983$, while the probability that b is correct is $(\beta/2)/(\alpha/2 + \beta/2) = .017$. Thus, we would choose a rather than b.

about .665. Moreover, the probability that majority rule yields the correct answer increases the more voters there are.

Theorem 1 (Condorcet 1785): *Let* n *voters (n odd) choose between two alternatives that have equal likelihood of being correct a priori. Assume that voters make their judgments independently and that each has the same probability* p *of being correct* $(1/2 < p < 1)$. *Then the probability that the group makes the correct judgment using simple majority rule is*

$$P_n = \sum_{h = (n+1)/2}^{n} [n! \, / \, h! \, (n - h)!] \, p^h \, (1 - p)^{n-h},$$

which approaches one as n *becomes large.*[2]

This is a fundamental justification for democratic rule, since it shows that the more voters there are, the more likely it is that the majority verdict will be correct. Is it possible, however, that some other rule would do even better? The answer is contained in the following result.

Theorem 2 (Nitzan and Paroush 1982; Shapley and Grofman 1984): *Let* n *voters (n odd) choose between two alternatives that have equal likelihood of being correct a priori. Assuming that voters make their judgments independently and are equally competent in their judgments, simple majority rule maximizes the probability that the group judgment is correct.*[3]

2. Optimal binary decision rules with different levels of competence

Let us now suppose that some voters have better judgment than others (as evidenced by their previous votes, for example). Should we still give their votes equal weight, or should we perhaps ignore all voters *except* those whose judgment has proven to be best in the past? In fact neither answer is correct. To see why, consider a situation in which five members of a central bank are voting whether to raise interest rates. Assume that each member votes yes if and only if she believes that not increasing rates will cause inflation to exceed the target set by the bank. Assume further that the track record of each member of the committee – how often she has

---

2. For variations on this result see Poisson (1837), Grofman, Owen, and Feld (1983), and Urken and Traflet (1984).
3. The case where voters do not make independent judgments is considered by Shapley and Grofman (1984).

been right about the effect of interest rates on inflation – is known from previous experience. Perhaps A and B have been right 90 percent of the time, while C, D, and E have been right only 60 percent of the time. If we give all votes equal weight, we ignore the fact that A's and B's opinions convey more accurate information than the others. But if we set aside all opinions except those of A and B, we are losing information from the others that is accurate on the whole. This suggests that the votes of A and B should be given more weight than the others, but not all the weight. It turns out that *the optimal decision rule is to use a weighted majority, where the weight on each member's vote is log [p_i/(1 $-$ p_i)] and p_i is the probability that individual i makes correct judgments* (Nitzan and Paroush 1982; Shapley and Grofman 1984).

3. The case of more than two alternatives: Voting cycles

When we try to extend this reasoning to three or more alternatives, however, matters become more complicated. For, as Condorcet was the first to show, there *is* no direct analog of simple majority rule in this case. The difficulty is that there are situations in which *no* alternative obtains a simple majority over every other. Consider the following example involving three alternatives and sixty voters. To make the example concrete, let us suppose that a stands for the policy "hire more police," b stands for the policy "increase prison sentences," and c for the policy "offer training programs for ex-convicts." Each of these policies aims at reducing crime, and we shall suppose that the voters are trying to judge which will be the most effective, that is, which will reduce the crime rate most per dollar spent. In other words, there really is a correct ranking of the policies, but there are differences of opinion about what that ranking might be.

23	17	2	10	8
a	b	b	c	c
b	c	a	a	b
c	a	c	b	a

Example 1

Unfortunately, majority rule comes up empty-handed because it leads to a voting cycle: a beats b by 33 to 27, b beats c by 42 to 18, and c beats a by 35 to 25. The problem that Condorcet set himself was to determine the voting rule that is optimal under these circumstances.

Assume that, given any two of the policies to compare, each voter has

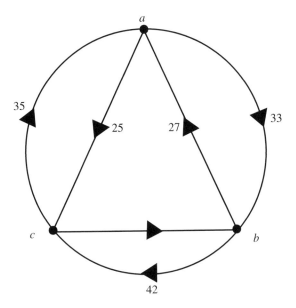

Figure 1.

a fixed probability p, $1/2 < p < 1$, of choosing the right one (i.e., the most effective one). Assume further that each voter's judgment about any pair is independent of the other voters' judgments, and that his judgment about a given pair is independent of his judgment about the other pairs. (One can quibble with the realism of these assumptions but they merely serve to simplify the calculations.)

For each possible ranking of the alternatives, we want to compute the conditional probability that the above voting pattern would occur given that the ranking is correct. Suppose, for instance, that the correct ranking is $a\ b\ c$. Then the probability of the above vote is the product of three terms: the probability that a gets 33 votes over b, the probability that b gets 42 votes over c, and the probability that a gets 25 votes over c. Hence, it is proportional to $p^{33}(1 - p)^{27}\ p^{42}(1 - p)^{18}\ p^{25}(1 - p)^{35} = p^{100}(1 - p)^{80}$. In general, the larger the exponent of p, the higher the likelihood that this is the correct ranking, because by assumption p is greater than one-half. Thus, we will have solved the problem once we compute the exponent of p for each of the six possible rankings.

A convenient way to visualize the problem to is draw a *vote graph* like that shown in Figure 1.

There is one vertex for each alternative, and between every pair of vertices there are two edges, one in each direction. The *weight* on an edge is the number of votes that the alternative at its base gets over the alternative at its tip. To evaluate the probability of a ranking such as *a b c,* consider the three pairwise propositions: *a* is above *b, b* is above *c,* and *a* is above *c.* These correspond to the three directed edges $a \rightarrow b$, $b \rightarrow c$, and $a \rightarrow c$, which have weights 33, 42, and 25 respectively. We define the total *support* for the ranking *a b c* to be 33 + 42 + 25 = 100. This is the same as the exponent on *p* and hence is a measure of the ranking's likelihood. The support for the other rankings is found in like fashion. Namely, each ranking corresponds to a set of three directed edges that do not form a cycle, and the corresponding exponent on *p* equals the total weight on these edges. The results are given below, and they show that *b c a* is most likely to be correct in this case.

a b c	100	*b c a*	104
a c b	76	*c a b*	86
b a c	94	*c b a*	80

In general, whenever there is a voting cycle among three alternatives, the maximum likelihood ranking is obtained by breaking the cycle at its weakest link, that is, by deleting the edge in the cycle that has the smallest majority. (In the above example the cycle $a \rightarrow b \rightarrow c \rightarrow a$ would be broken at the link $a \rightarrow b$.) When there is no voting cycle, the maximum likelihood ranking is the one that accords with simple majority rule on all pairs of alternatives. This rule identifies the maximum likelihood ranking when there are exactly three alternatives and is known as *Condorcet's rule of three.*

Unfortunately, when there are more than three alternatives, Condorcet seems to have become confused; at any rate he did not get the correct answer.[4] Nevertheless, the solution can be found by a straightforward extension of the previous argument. Given a voting outcome and a ranking *R* of the alternatives, the conditional probability of observing the vote, given that the true ranking is *R*, is proportional to $p^{s(R)}(1-p)^{M-s(R)}$ where $M = nm(m-1)/2$ and *s(R) is the total number of pairwise votes that higher alternatives get over lower alternatives in R.* We call *s(R)* the *support* for the ranking *R.* The maximum likelihood rankings are precisely the ones with maximum support. To compute them, it suffices to find *the maximum weight set of edges in the vote graph that does not contain a cycle.* This *maximum likelihood ranking (MLR)* rule is the solution to Condorcet's problem.[5]

---

4. For a discussion of Condorcet's somewhat obscure argument in this case, see Young (1988) and Crepel (1990).

5. Young (1986, 1988). It should be noted that this can be formulated as an integer programming problem. Define a variable x_{ab} for each directed edge $a \rightarrow b$ in the vote graph, that is, one variable for each ordered pair of distinct alternatives. Let v_{ab} be the

4. Borda's rule

At this point we need to pick up a second strand in our story that actually begins somewhat earlier. In 1770, some fifteen years before Condorcet published his work on voting theory, his colleague Jean-Charles de Borda read a paper on the design of voting procedures to the French Academy of Sciences. Like Condorcet, Borda was a prominent figure in scientific circles with interests that spanned a wide variety of subjects. Unlike Condorcet, he had a strong practical bent. In addition to doing important research in mechanics, hydraulics, and optics, he was one of the leading lights in developing the metric system. This put him in the applied faction of the Academy, which was often at loggerheads with the purists like Condorcet. This rivalry seems to have spilled over into their work on voting theory, as we shall see later on.

Borda began by observing that, when there are three or more alternatives, the one that achieves the most first-place votes is not necessarily the one that has the most overall support. As an example, consider the following situation. There are three alternatives and twenty-one voters who rank them as follows:

7	7	6	1
b	a	c	a
c	c	b	b
a	b	a	c

Example 2

Under the conventional *plurality method,* a gets 8 votes, b 7, and c 6. But this fails to take into account that all but one of the people who prefer a like c better than b, and everyone who prefers b likes c better than a. One could therefore argue that c is the most natural compromise candidate even though it receives the *fewest* first-place votes. To assess the true strength of the various candidates, said Borda, one must look at their overall standing in the individual rankings. This led him to propose the following rule. Let each voter strictly rank-order the candidates. (For simplicity of exposition we assume no indifference.) In each voter's list, assign a score of 0 to the alternative ranked last, a score of 1 to the alternative ranked next-to-last, a score of 2 to the alternative next above

weight on the edge $a \rightarrow b$, that is, the number of votes for alternative a over alternative b. The maximum likelihood ranking corresponds to the solution x that maximizes $\Sigma v_{ab} x_{ab}$ subject to $x_{ab} + x_{ba} = 1$, $x_{ab} + x_{bc} + x_{ca} \leq 2$, and all $x_{ab} = 0$ or 1. If the voters have different competences, individual i's vote is weighed by $\log (p_i/(1-p_i))$, where p_i is the probability that i is correct and $1/2 < p_i < 1$.

that, and so forth. The *Borda score* of an alternative is its total score summed over all voter lists, and *Borda's rule* is to rank the alternatives from highest to lowest Borda score. In the above example the scores are 26 for *c*, 21 for *b*, and 16 for *a*. Thus, according to Borda's rule, the proper ordering of the alternatives – *c b a* – is *exactly the opposite* of the one implied by the number of first-place votes.

Although it may not be obvious at first, Borda's rule (like Condorcet's) actually depends only on the *pairwise votes* between the various alternatives. The simplest way to see this is to observe that the Borda score of an alternative within a particular voter's list is just the number of alternatives ranked below it. It follows that the total Borda score of an alternative *x* is the total number of times that *x* beats other alternatives, summed over all of the voter lists. In terms of the vote graph, it is the sum of the weights on all edges directed away from the vertex corresponding to *x*.

Another easy way to compute the Borda solution is to construct a matrix indicating the pairwise votes. For each ordered pair of alternatives *a, b*, let v_{ab} denote the total number of times that *a* is ranked above *b* in the voter lists. In other words, v_{ab} is the number of votes that *a* would get over *b* in a pairwise contest between the two. (This is the weight on the edge directed from *a* to *b* in the vote graph.) The $m \times m$ matrix $V = (v_{ab})$ is called the *vote matrix*. It follows from the above discussion that the Borda score of each alternative *x* is just the sum of the entries in *x*'s row. The vote matrix for example 2 is shown below, together with the row sums.

	a	*b*	*c*	Row sum
a	–	8	8	16
b	13	–	8	21
c	13	13	–	26

5. Borda's rule as a maximum likelihood method

It turns out that Borda's rule can also be justified as an optimal method for group decision making, though Borda himself does not seem to have realized this fact. Consider the following situation with sixty voters and three candidates (Condorcet 1785, lxiii):

13	10	13	6	18
a	*a*	*b*	*b*	*c*
c	*b*	*c*	*a*	*b*
b	*c*	*a*	*c*	*a*

Example 3

The vote matrix in this case is

	a	*b*	*c*	Row sum
a	–	23	29	52
b	37	–	29	66
c	31	31	–	62

Thus, *c* has a simple majority over both *a* and *b*, while *b* has a majority over a, so there are no cycles. Condorcet's rule of three therefore yields the ordering *c b a,* which is also the maximum likelihood ranking. However, the Borda scores for *a, b* and *c* are 52, 66, and 62 respectively, so the Borda ranking is *b c a.* In particular, the majority alternative (*c*) is not top-ranked. In Condorcet's view this proved that Borda's method is fundamentally flawed.

On closer examination, however, it turns out that a case can be made for Borda's method by extending Condorcet's own argument to a full-fledged Bayesian analysis. Recall that Condorcet's objective was to find the *ranking* that is most likely to be correct given the voting outcome. In Bayesian terms this is equivalent to choosing the ranking with the greatest posterior probability of being correct, assuming that all are equally likely to be correct *a priori.* But suppose that the objective is to choose the *single alternative* that is most likely to be best. This is not the same thing as choosing the top-ranked alternative in the most likely ranking, because there are several rankings in which a given alternative is top-ranked. Instead, we must look at the sum of the (posterior) probabilities of *all* rankings in which a given alternative places first.

Let us illustrate with example 3. The posterior probabilities of the six rankings, assuming equal a priori odds, are as follows (we omit the multiplicative constant):

$$abc \quad p^{81} (1 - p)^{99}$$
$$acb \quad p^{83} (1 - p)^{97}$$
$$bac \quad p^{95} (1 - p)^{85}$$
$$bca \quad p^{97} (1 - p)^{83}$$
$$cab \quad p^{85} (1 - p)^{95}$$
$$cba \quad p^{99} (1 - p)^{81}$$

Therefore the posterior probabilities of the *alternatives* are as shown below.

Relative posterior probabilities

$$
\begin{array}{ll}
a & p^{81}\,(1-p)^{99} + p^{83}\,(1-p)^{97} \\
b & p^{95}\,(1-p)^{85} + p^{97}\,(1-p)^{83} \\
c & p^{85}\,(1-p)^{95} + p^{99}\,(1-p)^{81}
\end{array}
$$

This does not give as neat a result as the maximum likelihood ranking rule, because the most probable alternative *a posteriori* depends on p. Nevertheless, we can make some estimates. When p is close to unity, $1 - p$ is close to zero and the smallest exponent of $(1 - p)$ is decisive. In other words, the overwhelmingly largest term is the one with the largest exponent of p and the smallest exponent on $1 - p$. This means that the most probable alternative *a posteriori* is the one that is top-ranked according to the maximum likelihood ranking rule.

Now consider the case in which p is slightly larger than one-half, say $p = .5 + \varepsilon$. Substituting into the above expression we obtain the following:

$$
\begin{array}{ll}
a & (.5 + \varepsilon)^{81}\,(.5 - \varepsilon)^{99} + (.5 + \varepsilon)^{83}\,(.5 - \varepsilon)^{97} = 2(.5^{\,180} - 16\,\varepsilon + O(\varepsilon^2) \\
b & (.5 + \varepsilon)^{95}\,(.5 - \varepsilon)^{85} + (.5 + \varepsilon)^{97}\,(.5 - \varepsilon)^{83} = 2(.5^{\,180} + 12\,\varepsilon + O(\varepsilon^2) \\
c & (.5 + \varepsilon)^{85}\,(.5 - \varepsilon)^{95} + (.5 + \varepsilon)^{99}\,(.5 - \varepsilon)^{81} = 2(.5^{\,180} + 4\,\varepsilon + O(\varepsilon^2).
\end{array}
$$

It follows that, when ε is sufficiently small, the optimal choice is b. More generally, *when p is close to one-half, the alternative most likely to be best is the one with the highest Borda score* (Young 1988).[6] Thus, the methods of both Condorcet and Borda can both be viewed as optimal decision rules, where the former estimates the most likely ranking and the latter estimates the most likely choice.[7]

6. Condorcet's critique of Borda: Independence of irrelevant alternatives

Condorcet may or may not have been aware of the maximum likelihood interpretation of Borda's rule. In any event, he argued strongly against Borda's method, adding a certain amount of personal venom to

---

6. Let V be the vote matrix. When $p = .5 + \varepsilon$, the posterior probability of an arbitrary alternative a is proportional to $.5^{nm(m-1)/2} + (\Sigma v_{ab} - \Sigma v_{ba})\varepsilon + O(\varepsilon^2)$. This probability is maximized when $\Sigma_b v_{ab}$ is a maximum, that is, for those alternative(s) that have maximum Borda score.

7. When the voters have different competence levels p_i, $1/2 < p_i < 1$, Borda's rule generalizes as follows. Define the *weighted vote matrix* W such that w_{ab} is the sum of all votes for a over b, where each of i's votes is weighted by the value log $(p_i/(1 - p_i))$. The *generalized Borda scores* are the row sums of W. The alternatives with maximum generalized Borda score are the ones that are most likely to be correct when all p_i are close to one-half (Young 1986).

the attack. (Throughout the *Essay* Condorcet refers sarcastically to the "method of a famous mathematician" but fails to mention him by name.)[8]

A particularly telling argument against Borda is the following. Suppose, said Condorcet, that there are three candidates named Peter, Paul, and Jack, and eighty-one voters with the following preferences:

30	1	29	10	10	1
Peter	Peter	Paul	Paul	Jack	Jack
Paul	Jack	Peter	Jack	Peter	Paul
Jack	Paul	Jack	Peter	Paul	Peter

Example 4

According to Borda's rule, the proper ordering is Paul, Peter, Jack. But this is absurd, Condorcet argued, because Peter obtains a simple majority over *both* Paul *and* Jack. Surely, this means that Peter is stronger than Paul. More generally, Condorcet formulated the following "majority principle": *if there exists an alternative that obtains a simple majority over every other alternative, then it should be ranked first.* Such an alternative is known as a *Condorcet alternative* or a *majority alternative.* Condorcet went on to examine why Borda's rule gives the "wrong" result in this case.

> [H]ow is it that Paul is not the clear winner when the only difference between himself and Peter is that Peter got 31 first places and 39 second, while Paul got 39 first and 31 second? Well, out of the 39 voters who put Peter second, 10 preferred him to Paul, whereas only one of the 31 voters who put Paul second preferred him to Peter. The points method [of Borda] confuses votes comparing Peter and Paul with those comparing either Peter or Paul to Jack and uses them to judge the relative merits of Peter and Paul. *As long as it relies on irrelevant factors to form its judgments, it is bound to lead to error,* and that is the real reason why this method is defective for a great many

8. Condorcet's contemptuous view of Borda is borne out in his private correspondence. For example, in a letter to Turgot he wrote: "[M. Malesherbes] makes a great case for Borda, not because of his memoirs, some of which suggest talent (although nothing will ever come of them, and no one has ever spoken of them or ever will), but because he is what one calls a good academician, that is to say, because he speaks in meetings of the Academy and asks for nothing better than to waste his time doing prospectuses, examining machines, etc., and above all because, feeling eclipsed by other mathematicians, he, like d'Arcy, has abandoned mathematics for petty physics" (Henry 1883).

voting patterns, regardless of the particular values assigned to each place. The conventional method [plurality] is flawed because it ig-nores elements which should be taken into account and the new one [Borda's] because it takes into account elements which should be ignored. (italics added)[9]

In other words, Condorcet is saying that the comparison between Peter and Paul should depend only on the relative ordering of these two candi-dates in the voters' lists not on their relation to other candidates. Here is a clear forerunner of Arrow's principle of the independence of irrelevant alternatives!

Condorcet noted the remarkable fact that *any* scoring system leads to the same outcome as Borda's rule in this example and is therefore subject to the same criticism. In general, a *monotone scoring method* is defined by a sequence of real numbers $s_1 > s_2 > \ldots > s_m$, one for each alternative. Given an individual's ranking of the alternatives, assign a score of s_1 to the alternative that occupies first position, a score of s_2 to the alternative in second position, and so forth. The total score of each alternative is the sum of its scores over all voter lists, and the alternatives are ordered according to their total scores. Borda's rule corresponds to the scoring system $s_i = m - i$; in fact, it is equivalent to any scoring system in which the successive differences $s_i - s_{i+1}$ are equal and positive.

Consider now any monotone scoring system for three alternatives with scores $s_1 > s_2 > s_3$. In example 3, the score for Peter is $31s_1 + 39s_2 + 11s_3$ whereas the score for Paul is $39s_1 + 31s_2 + 11s_3$. Therefore, Paul obtains a higher score than Peter, even though Peter is the majority candidate. From this we conclude that *any* scoring system violates the majority principle. Moreover, it shows that any scoring system yields outcomes that are based on "irrelevant factors."

7. Local independence of irrelevant alternatives

Condorcet's broadside against Borda is fine as far as it goes. But exactly how far does it go? We know from Arrow's theorem that independence of irrelevant alternatives is violated by *every* reasonable decision rule when there are more than two alternatives. Why should we believe

---

9. This is from a later paper of Condorcet's entitled "On the Constitution and the Func-tions of Provincial Assemblies" (Condorcet 1788). The translation is by Sommerlad and McLean (1989), who were the first to call attention to the importance of this passage and its connection with independence of irrelevant alternatives.

that Condorcet's approach is any better than Borda's? In this section we shall argue that it is, in fact, considerably better.

To motivate the discussion, let us first consider why a condition like independence of irrelevant alternatives is worth having. Essentially it says that the way a given group of alternatives is ordered should depend only on opinions about those alternatives.[10] There are at least two reasons why this is desirable from a practical standpoint. First, if it does not hold, then it is possible to manipulate the outcome by introducing extraneous alternatives (Gibbard 1973; Satterthwaite 1975). Second, independence allows the electorate to make sensible decisions within a restricted range of choices without worrying about the universe of all possible choices. It is desirable to know, for example, that the relative ranking of candidates for political office would not be changed if purely hypothetical candidates were included on the ballot.

While Arrow's theorem shows that independence cannot be fully realized by any democratic rule, we shall show that it can be realized to a significant extent. Consider example 3 again. The real contest is between Peter and Paul; Jack is a distinctly weaker alternative. We could argue that Jack ought to be "irrelevant" to the choice between Peter and Paul because Jack is inferior to both. Moreover, under Condorcet's rule, this is actually the case.

The key point is that Peter and Paul occur *together* in the consensus ranking; they are not separated by other alternatives. More generally, define an *interval* of an ordering to be any subset of alternatives that occurs in succession in that ordering. Suppose we insist that, whenever a set of alternatives forms an interval of the consensus preference ordering, then independence of irrelevant alternatives applies – that is, the ordering within the interval remains fixed when alternatives outside the interval are ignored. In particular, the ordering of alternatives toward the top of the list is unaffected by the removal of those at the bottom. Similarly, the ranking of the alternatives toward the bottom of the list is unaffected by the removal of those at the top, and so forth. We shall say that such a ranking rule (MLR) satisfies *local independence of irrelevant alternatives* (LIIA). It is a remarkable fact that the maximum likelihood ranking rule satisfies LIIA.[11] Moreover, as we shall argue in a later section, it is the only reasonable ranking rule that does so.

To further illustrate this idea, consider the following vote matrix involving six alternatives and one hundred voters.

---

10. I neglect various distinctions in the way that one formulates the independence condition.
11. See Young (1988), where LIIA condition was called *local stability*.

	a	b	c	d	e	f	Sum
a	–	51	54	58	60	62	285
b	49	–	68	56	52	58	283
c	46	32	–	70	66	75	289
d	42	44	30	–	41	64	221
e	40	48	34	59	–	34	215
f	38	42	25	36	66	–	207

Example 5

Here we may think of a, b, and c as being the real choices under discussion, while d, e, and f are red herrings that have been dragged in by political strategists to attempt to manipulate the outcome. (Note that each of a, b, c has a solid majority over each of d, e, f, so the latter three could be considered weaker than the former.) Moreover, this attempt will succeed if Borda's rule is used. The row sums determine the Borda ordering $c\ a\ b\ d\ e\ f$. Now suppose that the three red herrings had not been introduced into the debate. Then, the vote matrix would be the one enclosed by the dashed lines. The Borda scores for this three-alternative situation are 105 for a, 117 for b, and 78 for c. Hence, in the absence of d, e, f, the top three alternatives would be ordered $b\ a\ c$. But this is exactly the *reverse* of how they are ordered when all six alternatives are considered together. This example shows why Borda's rule is highly susceptible to manipulative practices, just as Condorcet claimed.

Now consider the MLR solution to this problem. We begin by observing an important property of this rule: *if some alternative has a simple majority over every other, then the MLR rule must rank it first.* The reason is simple. Suppose that the majority alternative, say x, were not ranked first. Then it must be ranked immediately below some other alternative y. By assumption, x defeats y by a simple majority. Therefore, if we switch the positions of x and y, we obtain a new ranking that is supported by more pairwise votes. But then the new ranking is more likely than the original ranking, which is a contradiction.

This simple fact can be used to deduce the MLR solution to the above problem almost immediately. Since a is the majority alternative, it must be ranked first. Among the remaining alternatives, b obtains a simple majority over c, d, e, and f. Hence a similar argument shows that b comes next. Then comes c by the same argument. As for d, e, and f, they will be ordered relative to one another *as if they were the only three alternatives*. (Since they form an interval of the consensus ranking, LIIA applies). It is easy to see that the MLR solution for these three alternatives is $d\ f\ e$ (use Condorcet's rule of three and break the cycle at its weakest link). Putting all of this together, we conclude that the MLR solution to the whole problem is $a\ b\ c\ d\ f\ e$.

Notice the important point that the top three alternatives are ranked as they would be in the absence of d, e, and f. Similarly, the bottom three are ranked as they would be in the absence of a, b, and c. Likewise, any interval of alternatives is ranked as it would be in the absence of the others. The reason is this: if it were not, then one could shuffle the alternatives *within the interval* and obtain an ordering that is supported by a larger number of pairwise votes, hence an ordering that has greater likelihood. This contradiction shows why the maximum likelihood rule satisfies local independence of irrelevant alternatives. In particular, it cannot be *manipulated from below* by introducing inferior alternatives, nor can it be *manipulated from above* by introducing utopian (i.e., attractive but infeasible) alternatives.

8. Voting as a form of compromise

So far we have proceeded on the premise that there really is a best ordering to be estimated. Moreover, we have argued that this is often the right way to think about group choice problems. But it is not always the right way to think about them. There are many situations in which differences of opinion do not arise from erroneous judgments, but from differences in values. In this case it seems better to adopt the view that group choice is an exercise in defining consensus, that is, in finding a compromise between conflicting opinions. Arrow's axiomatic approach is one way of analyzing this issue, and we shall pick up this scent again in the next section. First, however, I want to draw attention to another interesting approach along these lines that was pioneered by John Kemeny (1959).

Kemeny argued that we should think of the voters' reported opinions as *data* and ask what ordering best represents or averages these data. For the notion of "average" to make sense, of course, we must have some way of measuring how far apart one ranking is from another. That is, we need a metric defined on the set of rankings. Kemeny proposed the following natural metric: *the distance between two rankings R and R' is the number of pairs of alternatives on which they differ.* Thus, if R' is obtained from R by interchanging two adjacent alternatives, then $d(R, R') = 1$. If R' is obtained from R by reversing the order of all alternatives, then $d(R, R') = m(m - 1)/2$, and so forth.

Suppose now that each member of a group of n voters submits a ranking of the alternatives. Given these n data points, what is the best definition of a compromise ordering? A statistician would say there are two obvious answers: the mean and the median. The *mean* is the ranking (or rankings) that minimize the sum of the squares of distances from the n given rankings. The *median* is the ranking (or rankings) that minimizes the sum of the distances from the n given rankings. It is not difficult to show that the median is equivalent to the maximum likelihood method, whereas the mean yields a very different scheme.[12]

Kemeny left open the question of whether the mean or the median is to be preferred. There can be little doubt, however, that the median is the better choice under the circumstances. To see why, consider the following example with forty-one voters and three alternatives.

21	5	11	4
a	b	c	c
b	c	b	a
c	a	a	b

Example 6

Alternative a has an absolute majority of first-place votes, so *a fortiori* it is the majority alternative. The ranking $a\ b\ c$ is the median ranking, that is, it has maximum likelihood. (Note that Borda's rule yields the same result.) A simple calculation shows, however, that the *mean* ranking is $b\ a\ c$. This seems to be a less credible conception of consensus than does $a\ b\ c$. The problem with the mean is that it places a lot of weight on extreme observations. In the present case, the voters who announce the ordering $c\ b\ a$ shift the outcome in favor of b, not because they are especially attached to b, but because their top candidate is c, which is at odds with the views of most of the other voters. In other words, their opinion about b versus a is heavily weighted because their opinion about something else (namely c) differs from most of the others. This does not seem very sensible. We conclude that if the object is to find a *compromise* between the various rankings

---

12. For every ranking R of the alternatives, and for every ordered pair of alternatives a, b, let $\delta_{ab}(R) = 1$ if a precedes b in R and let $\delta_{ab}(R) = 0$ if a follows b in R. Given a set of rankings $R_1, \ldots, R_n$, one for each voter, the Kemeny distance between R and the R_i is:

$$\Sigma_i d(R, R_i) = \sum_{1 \le i \le n} [m(m-1) - \sum_{a \ne b} \delta_{ab}(R)\delta_{ab}(R_i)].$$

Let V be the associated vote matrix. Then the above expression is equivalent to $\Sigma_i d(R, R_i) = nm(m-1) - \Sigma_{a \ne b} V_{ab}\delta_{ab}(R)$. Thus, the median ranking R maximizes $\Sigma_{a \ne b} V_{ab}\delta_{ab}(R)$, which is the same as the MLR rule.

reported by the voters, then the median is, in a statistical sense, the most appropriate solution. This reinforces the argument for the maximum likelihood ranking rule, but from a completely different (and more modern) perspective.

9. Ranking rules from first principles

Pursuing this point of view a bit further, one might wonder whether the MLR rule can be justified from a purely axiomatic perspective. We shall show that it can. Indeed, it is the unique ranking rule that satisfies three standard axioms in the social choice literature plus local independence of irrelevant alternatives.

Define a *ranking rule* to be a function F that associates one or more consensus rankings with every set of rankings reported by a group of individuals on a finite set of alternatives. The rule is *anonymous* if it treats all voters alike. It is *neutral* if it treats all alternatives alike.[13] It is *Pareto* if, whenever everyone ranks one alternative above another, then so does every consensus ranking.

A ranking rule F *satisfies reinforcement* if, whenever two distinct groups of voters reach the same consensus ordering under separate votes, this ordering is also the consensus for the two groups merged together. For example, if the House of Representatives orders three choices *a b c,* and the Senate also orders these choices *a b c* (using the same voting rule), then *a b c* is the outcome when their votes are pooled.[14] (In practice almost all rules have this property.)

Finally, F *satisfies local independence of irrelevant alternatives* if the ordering of every interval of $R \in F(\mathbf{R})$ depends only on the opinions of the voters about the alternatives in that interval.[15]

---

13. Given any set of rankings $\mathbf{R} = (R_i)_{i \in G}$ reported by the members of a finite group G, let $F(\mathbf{R})$ be the consensus rankings associated with the profile $\mathbf{R}$. Every permutation π of the voter set G induces a permutation of $\mathbf{R}$ that we shall denote by $\pi\mathbf{R}$. The rule F is *anonymous* if $F(\mathbf{R}) = F(\pi\mathbf{R})$ for all π and all $\mathbf{R}$. Any permutation σ of the set of alternatives induces a corresponding permutation of the rankings that we shall also denote by σ. For any profile of rankings $\mathbf{R} = (R_i)$, let $\sigma\mathbf{R} = (\sigma(R_i))$. The rule F is *neutral* if $F(\sigma\mathbf{R}) = \sigma F(\mathbf{R})$, that is, $\sigma R \in F(\sigma\mathbf{R})$ if and only if $R \in F(\mathbf{R})$.
14. Formally, for any profiles R and R' on disjoint groups G and G',
    $F(R) \cap F(R') \neq \varnothing$ implies $F(R \cup R') = F(R) \cap F(R')$.
    This idea was introduced by Young and Levenglick (1978). A variation of the concept characterizes scoring methods (Smith 1973; Young 1974, 1975).
15. Formally, *local independence of irrelevant alternatives* states that, for every $R \in F(\mathbf{R})$ and every interval B of R, $R|_B \in F(\mathbf{R}|_B)$; moreover, if $S \in F(\mathbf{R}|_B)$ then $R' \in F(\mathbf{R})$ where R' is the unique ranking that agrees with S for all pairs in $B \times B$ and agrees with R for all other pairs.

Theorem 3 (Young 1988): *The maximum likelihood rule is the unique ranking rule that is anonymous, neutral, Pareto, satisfies reinforcement and local independence of irrelevant alternatives.*[16]

10. Choice rules from first principles

In Section 5 we showed why finding the most likely ranking of alternatives is quite different from choosing the alternative that is most likely to be best when there is some objective idea of better and best in the background. Here, we shall argue that this dichotomy between ranking and choice is quite fundamental by showing that the same axioms give decidedly different results when applied to choice rules instead of ranking rules.

A *choice rule* is a function *f* that associates one or more alternatives to every profile of rankings **R**. In other words, $f(\mathbf{R})$ is a nonempty subset of *A* for every profile **R** defined on a finite set of alternatives *A*. Most of the principles that we have been considering for ranking rules have natural analogs for choice rules as well. For example, a choice rule is *anonymous* if it treats voters symmetrically, and it is *neutral* if it treats alternatives symmetrically. It *satisfies reinforcement* if, whenever two disjoint groups of voters make the same choice under separate votes, they still make this choice when their votes are pooled.[17]

Viewed as a choice rule, it is clear that Borda's rule satisfies all three of these principles. In particular, reinforcement holds because the Borda score of any alternative with respect to the combined group $G \cup G'$ is just its Borda score in *G* plus its Borda score in *G'*. Of course, this last remark applies equally well for any scoring rule, that is, any rule that associates a fixed point value with each position in a voter's ranking. (Here we do not need to assume that the scores are descending in value.) Hence, every scoring rule, viewed as a choice rule, is anonymous, neutral, and reinforcing. We say that a choice rule *f'* is a *refinement* of a choice rule *f* if $f'(R) \subseteq f(R)$ for every profile *R*.

Theorem 4 (Young 1975): *Every scoring rule is anonymous, neutral, and reinforcing; moreover, every choice rule with these properties is a scoring rule or the refinement of one.*

It is important to observe that scoring rules have quite different characteristics than the ranking rules discussed in the previous section. The simplest way to see this is recall that, in example 3, any scoring rule

---

16. This consequence of Young and Levenglick (1978), theorem 3. See Young (1988).
17. Formally, *f satisfies reinforcement* if, whenever *R* and *R'* are profiles on disjoint groups *G* and *G'*, $f(\mathbf{R}) \cap f(\mathbf{R}') \neq \emptyset$ implies $f(\mathbf{R} \cup \mathbf{R}') = f(\mathbf{R}) \cap f(\mathbf{R}')$.

(with strictly descending scores) necessarily chooses Paul rather than Peter. Yet Peter has a simple majority over Paul, and both have a majority over Jack. Hence, the maximum likelihood ranking rule puts Peter first, then Paul, then Jack. Thus, we see that very similar axioms can lead to quite different methods depending on whether we wish to make a singe choice or rank the alternatives.

In fact, we had already noticed this seeming paradox in our discussion of the maximum likelihood approach, where the maximum likelihood ranking rule usually differs from the maximum likelihood choice rule. When the judgmental competence is close to one-half, we know that the best choice is given by Borda's rule. Borda's rule can also be justified from first principles. Let us say that a choice rule satisfies the *pairwise comparisons principle* if the outcome depends only on the vote matrix (not on the voter lists themselves). It is *unanimous* if it uniquely selects the alternative that everyone ranks first in cases where there is such an alternative. The following result shows that Borda's rule is, from a purely axiomatic standpoint, the analog of the MLR in the domain of choice rules (compare theorem 3).

Theorem 5   (Young 1974): *Borda's rule is the unique choice rule that is anonymous, neutral, unanimous, and satisfies the pairwise comparisons principle.*

11. Conclusion

We began this survey by looking at voting as the philosophers of the French Enlightenment did, namely, as a collective quest for truth. For them the question was how to design voting rules that yield good outcomes. Although at first this idea seemed somewhat dubious, we have seen that it is actually a reasonable description of many forms of decision making. Indeed, it makes sense whenever individuals agree about the objective but are uncertain what means are most likely to achieve that objective – what bill is most likely to reduce crime, what foreign policy will minimize the prospect of war, and so forth. The solution depends on whether we want to rank all of the alternatives or merely select one. In the first case the maximum likelihood ranking (MLR) rule is most appropriate, whereas in the second Borda's rule has a strong claim on our attention.

On the other hand, there are situations where it is more natural to think of voting as a compromise between conflicting values than as an estimate of the best course of action. Here the MLR rule emerges as a statistical definition of a compromise proposal – the median opinion.

Another objective in designing a voting rule is to make it resistant to strategic manipulation. As we know from the Gibbard–Satterthwaite theorem, almost no method has this property, which is intimately connected with independence of irrelevant alternatives. It is possible, however, to design ranking rules that are immune to manipulation from above by utopian alternatives and from below by inferior alternatives. The MLR rule is the only method that satisfies this local independence of irrelevant alternatives property plus other standard conditions in the literature.

The remaining question is whether these approaches are really practical. Borda's rule has already proved itself – it is frequently used in committees to rank candidates for positions, and there is no reason it could not be used in legislative situations too. The MLR rule, by contrast, is not very well known. One of the problems is that, compared with traditional voting methods – like majority voting with sequential elimination – the MLR rule is more complicated to calculate. The truth is, however, that given modern computing capability the issue is largely moot. To compute the maximum likelihood solution for six or fewer alternatives – the largest number of options that can be considered at one time in a congressional vote for example – is a near triviality. Even for much larger numbers of alternatives, the method can be implemented in about the same amount of time that it takes people to cast their votes. The more important issue is whether the method is intuitively easy to grasp and whether it improves on methods currently in use. On both of these counts I think that the answer is affirmative. It is particularly desirable because it is relatively immune to manipulation. I predict that the time will come when it – like Borda's rule – will be considered a standard tool for legislative and committee decision making.

CHAPTER 10

Some paradoxes of preference aggregation

PRASANTA K. PATTANAIK

1. Introduction

The purpose of this paper is to provide a brief review of some of the major paradoxes or impossibility theorems in social choice theory and the important issues highlighted by these theorems. The first and most famous of these theorems is, of course, Arrow's (1950, 1951, 1967), but, over the four decades or so since Arrow proved his impossibility result, numerous other impossibility theorems have been proved in social choice theory, giving a very distinctive flavour to this particular area where economics, politics, and ethics overlap in a significant fashion. These results, which often differ much in their formal structures, have one basic similarity. Essentially, a paradox or an impossibility theorem in social choice theory shows that there does not exist a social decision procedure satisfying certain plausible properties: the more plausible or appealing these properties, the more dramatic is the impossibility result under consideration.

At first sight, the impossibility results in the literature on social choice may seem to be purely intellectual exercises without much practical interest. If the objective of studying the theory of social choice is to provide a solution to the normative problem of how the society should choose one of the possibly many different options available to it (or, alternatively, how the society should rank these different options), then why should anyone be interested in a proposition that shows that certain appealing properties of a social decision procedure are logically incompatible in the sense that no social decision procedure can simultaneously satisfy all these properties? This rhetorical question does have a point. Impossibility theorems, by themselves, do not provide a solution to the perennial problem of how the society should choose an option from the set of available options. However, it is possible to exaggerate the point. While impossibility theorems, by themselves, do not provide a solution to the basic ethical problem of social choice, they do generate valuable insights and sharpen our ethical intuition in several ways. By showing that the social decision procedure cannot simultaneously satisfy certain

201

desirable properties, an impossibility result forces us to reexamine the intuitive content of these apparently appealing properties and to face the problem of trade-offs that one may have to make between the different values embodied by these different properties. The result is often a much sharper perception of what is really implied by these properties – a perception that might not have been attained without the impossibility result under consideration.

The impossibility theorems in social choice theory can be classified into two broad groups. First, we have the results dealing with the ethical problems involved in deciding what social state(s) the society should choose (or, alternatively, what the society's ranking of the alternative social states should be). Though the framework in which these impossibility results are proved assumes that social choice or evaluation should be based on individual preferences over social alternatives, the difficulties of ascertaining the individual preferences are ignored. The individuals' true preferences are assumed to be known somehow, and the focus is on the ethical problem of aggregating these preferences so as to arrive at a social decision or evaluation. This is the classic Arrow problem explored in a large part of the literature on social choice theory. In contrast, we have another class of impossibility results that deal with the difficulties in ascertaining the true preferences of individuals. For strategic reasons, individuals may choose to reveal a distorted version of their preferences. The well-known impossibility results of Gibbard (1973) and Satterthwaite (1975) focused on this issue. In this paper, I deal only with the first category of impossibility results, namely, those that relate to the problem of aggregation of individual preferences. However, there are numerous paradoxes or impossibility results within this category and even a minimally comprehensive survey of these results would need a full-length book. In this paper, my purpose is much more modest: I have sought to outline only a few major ideas and landmarks in the literature.

The plan of the paper is as follows. I start by introducing the basic definitions and notation in Section 2. Section 3 outlines the seminal theorem of Arrow. Section 4 discusses some impossibility results that arise even when one relaxes Arrow's original condition of collective rationality. These sections deal with impossibility results for procedures for ranking social alternatives. However, most of these results have their counterparts in a framework where social choice rather than the social ranking constitutes the primitive notion. Section 5 outlines how impossibility results proved for social evaluation or ranking procedures can be reformulated in terms of social choice. In Section 6, I discuss Sen's (1970a, 1970b) paradox of the Paretian liberal that brought fundamentally new concerns, namely, concerns about individual rights, into the literature on social choice theory. Section 7 deals with a number of issues such as stochastic social choice, social decision rules with restricted domains and interpersonal comparisons of utility. I conclude in Section 8.

2. The basic notation and some definitions

In this section, I introduce some very basic notation and definitions that I shall need throughout this paper. Let $N = \{1,3, \ldots ,n\}$ denote the set of individuals constituting the society. I assume that $2 \leq n < \infty$. Let X denote the set of all conceivable social states or social alternatives. A social state can be interpreted in many different ways, but I shall interpret it as a complete description of the state of affairs prevailing in the society, except for a specification of the decision-making mechanism. Of course, at any given point of time, not all conceivable social states may be feasible. Let $\mathscr{X}$ be the set of all nonempty subsets of X. At a given point of time, the feasible set of social states will be an element A of $\mathscr{X}$. The elements of $\mathscr{X}$ will be called *issues*.

In the theory of social choice, one can choose to have as one's primitive concept, the notion of social preference over social states, reflecting the society's relative evaluation of the different social states. In that case, social choice of social states is to be visualized as being generated by the society's preferences over social states. Alternatively, one can have, as one's primitive concept, the notion of social choice itself. If one follows this option, then one can think of social preferences as being "revealed" through social choice. The distinction between these two alternative frameworks is clearly analogous to the distinction between the theory of individual preferences and individual choice based on these preferences and the theory of "revealed preference" of individuals (see Samuelson 1947, 1948).

Irrespective of whether one chooses to formulate one's analysis in terms of social evaluation and preferences or in terms of social choice, the question arises as to what constitutes the basis of such social evaluation or social choice. The usual, though not universal, assumption made in social choice theory is that social evaluation or choice of social states must be grounded on individual preferences. Here again one has the choice of taking either cardinal individual utility functions or ordinal individual preferences as the basis of social evaluation/choice. I start with ordinal individual preferences, though later on I shall briefly comment on results that are proved in the framework of cardinal individual utility functions.

Let $\mathscr{R}$ be the set of all reflexive and connected binary relations defined over X. The elements of $\mathscr{R}$ will be denoted by R, R', R_i, and so on. Let

$\mathcal{R}$ be the set of all $R \in \mathcal{R}$ such that R is transitive. $\mathcal{R}$ is then the set of all orderings. The elements R, R', R'_i . . . of $\mathcal{R}$ are all to be interpreted as weak preference relations ("at least as good as"). Thus, for all $x,y \in X$, xRy will denote that x is at least as good as y under the weak preference relation R. For all $R \in \mathcal{R}$ and all $x,y \in X$, [xPy iff xRy and not yRx] and [xIy iff xRy and yRx]. Clearly, P is the strict preference relation corresponding to R, and I is the indifference relation corresponding to R.

Definition 2.1:   *A Social evaluation rule (SER) is a function* f : T $\rightarrow$ $\mathcal{R}$ *where* T *is a nonempty subset of* $\underline{\mathcal{R}}^n$.

Definition 2.2:   *A social decision rule (SDR) is a function* g : $\underline{X} \times$ T $\rightarrow$ X *such that* $\underline{X}$ *is a nonempty subset of* X; T *is a nonempty subset of* $\underline{\mathcal{R}}^n$; *and, for every* A $\in$ $\underline{X}$ *and every* (R_1, . . . , R_n) $\in$ T, g(A,R_1, . . . ,R_n) $\subseteq$ A.

"(R_1, . . . ,R_n)" figuring in definitions 2.1 and 2.2 is to be interpreted as an n-tuple or a profile of individual preference orderings, with R_i denoting the preference ordering of individual i ($i = 1$, . . . ,n). $\mathcal{R}$ in definition 2.1 is to be interpreted as the set of all social weak preference relations over X and $g(A,R_1$, . . . ,$R_n)$ in definition 2.2 is to be interpreted as the set of chosen social states when the feasible set of alternatives is A and (R_1, . . . ,R_n) is the profile of individual orderings. An SER gives us a social evaluation (in the form of a social weak preference relation R) of the alternatives in X, for every profile of individual orderings belonging to some specified nonempty subset T of $\underline{\mathcal{R}}^n$. In contrast, a social decision rule specifies the set of socially chosen elements in A for every issue A belonging to some specified nonempty subset $\underline{X}$ of X and for every (R_1, . . . ,R_n) belonging to some specified nonempty subset T of $\underline{\mathcal{R}}^n$.

When the domain T of an SER f coincides with $\underline{\mathcal{R}}^n$, we say that f has an unrestricted domain. An SDR g : $\underline{X} \times$ T $\rightarrow$ X is said to have an unrestricted domain if and only if $\underline{X} = X$ and $T = \underline{\mathcal{R}}^n$.

Should one use the notion of an SER or the notion of an SDR? To some extent, it depends on one's "aesthetic sense" about such formal structures. The notion of social evaluation as reflected in a social weak preference relation and the notion of socially chosen alternatives both have sufficient intuitive content to serve as the basis of social choice theory, and, formally, one can translate results formulated in terms of social preference to results formulated in terms of social choice, and vice versa, without much difficulty. However, historically, the theory was first formulated in terms of social preferences, and, therefore, that is the framework with which I start in the next section.

3. The impossibility theorem of Arrow

Arrow's (1950,1951,1967) impossibility theorem is the most celebrated impossibility theorem in the literature on social choice theory. Arrow postulated four different restrictions for an SER. They are as follows:

> *Condition 3.1 (Unrestricted domain and collective rationality):* The SER should have an unrestricted domain and the range of the SER should be a set of orderings (so that, for every profile of individual orderings, the SER should specify a social ordering).
>
> *Condition 3.2 (Weak Pareto criterion):* For every profile of individual orderings in the domain of the SER and, for all $x, y \in X$, if all individuals strictly prefer x to y, then the society must strictly prefer x to y.
>
> *Condition 3.3 (Independence of irrelevant alternatives):* Consider any two profiles of individual orderings in the domain of the SER and any $x, y \in X$. If the ranking of x and y is the same for every individual as between the two profiles of individual orderings, then the social ranking of x and y must be the same in both cases.
>
> *Condition 3.4 (Nondictatorship):* There does not exist any individual i such that, for every profile of individual orderings in the domain of the SER and for all distinct $x, y \in X$, if i strictly prefers x to y, then the society must also strictly prefer x to y.

The impossibility theorem of Arrow shows that, if X has at least three distinct alternatives, then no SER can simultaneously satisfy the conditions of unrestricted domain and collective rationality, weak Pareto criterion, independence of irrelevant alternative, and nondictatorship. Thus, if $|x| \geq 3$, then every SER satisfying the first three conditions will be characterized by the undesirable feature of dictatorship, that is, the existence of an individual whose strict preference over every pair of distinct alternatives gets automatically translated into social strict preference over that pair of alternatives, irrespective of the preferences that the other individuals in the society may have. A slightly different way of looking at the theorem is to interpret it as follows: what the theorem tells us is that the class of SERs that satisfies conditions 3.1, 3.2, and 3.3, is a trivial class with an extremely nonrich structure.

To appreciate the content of Arrow's theorem, it is useful to view it in its historical context. Much of normative economics that preceded Arrow was based on the narrow foundation of the Pareto criterion. While the basic ethical implication of Paretianism – that the society should not choose a Pareto inoptimal social state – seemed appealing as far as it went, it did not go very far: it did not provide any basis for comparing Pareto optimal social states. Not only the attempt of "new welfare economics" to go beyond the Pareto principle through the Kaldor–Hicks compensation criterion (see Kaldor 1939 and Hicks 1939) involved unacceptable distributional ethics, but it also got enmeshed in problems of internal consistency. Finally, while the Bergson–Samuelson concept of a social welfare function emphasized the crucial importance of value judgments for normative economics, the analysis of Bergson (1938) and Samuelson (1947) did not explore any specific value judgement that could supplement the appealing but tenuous Pareto principle. In this context, Arrow's theorem can be viewed as an exploration of what may happen when one seeks to overcome the inadequacy of the simple Pareto principle by introducing other specific value judgments. The traditional Pareto principle is, of couse, retained by Arrow (see condition 3.2). However, when, to the Pareto principle, one adds the requirements that the social weak preference relation must be an ordering for every profile of individual orderings (condition 3.1) and must satisfy independence of irrelevant alternatives, the resultant class of SERs becomes extremely trivial insofar as it includes only dictatorial SERs. The only diversity that this class of SERs admits is in the choice of who should be the "dictator" and what should happen when the dictator is indifferent between two distinct alternatives. Thus, if the problem with the weak Pareto criterion (condition 3.2) was that it imposed too little restriction on an SER (so that the class of SERs satisfying the weak Pareto criterion was bewilderingly large), the problem with supplementing the weak Pareto criterion by the addition of conditions 3.1 and 3.3 is that the new set of conditions is too restrictive (so that the class of SERs satisfying the three conditions is a trivial class containing only dictatorial SERs).

An impossibility theorem such as Arrow's naturally raises questions about the plausibility of the restrictions postulated for SERs in the theorem. Indeed, the value of the theorem lies precisely in the fact that it raises such questions, compelling us to reexamine our own normative standards regarding SERs. Since condition 3.4 (nondictatorsip) is unexceptionable and since condition 3.2 (weak Pareto criterion) is widely accepted by economists (see, however, the discussion of Sen's paradox of the Paretian liberal below), it is natural that the remaining two conditions of Arrow – unrestricted domain and collective rationality, and independence of irrelevant alternatives – should have been the subject of scrutiny.

Condition 3.1 (unrestricted domain and collective rationality) has two distinct components. First, it requires that the range of the SER should be a social ordering. Secondly, it also requires that every profile of individual orderings should be in the domain of the SER. Attempts have been made to relax each of these two restrictions implied by condition 3.1. In particular, a number of writers have successively weakened the requirement of a social ordering. However, as it has turned out, impossibility results persist even with the most pared-down versions of the requirement of collective rationality. In Section 4, I discuss some of these impossibility results with weaker conditions of collective rationality.

4. Impossibility results with weaker versions of collective rationality

4.1 The justification for the condition of collective rationality

Arrow's requirement that the social weak preference relation should be an ordering is the exact counterpart of the condition of "rationality" that economists typically postulate for individuals. The requirement of a social ordering comprises three distinct properties of the social weak preference relation: reflexivity, connectedness, and transitivity. Of these, reflexivity ("every social state is at least as good as itself") is an obviously reasonable property. Though less obviously plausible than reflexivity, connectedness ("for all distinct $x,y \in X$, either x is socially at least as good as y or y is socially at least as good as x") is also an attractive property, since, in the absence of connectedness, there will be distinct $x,y \in X$ such that the society will not be able to compare x and y and will, therefore, be unable to choose between x and y.

Transitivity is a far more complex property the justification for which is not obvious. One possible justification for the transitivity of social preferences is that it is an integral part of social "rationality" and is an end in itself. From this point of view, to say that x is socially at least as good as y and y is socially at least as good as z, but x is not socially at least as good as z is bizarre simply because it violates our deep-rooted intuition about rationality. Arrow himself did not follow this line of defense. Instead, he offered justifications for the transitivity of social preferences as a means for achieving certain ends. First, he argued that, in the absence of such transitivity, the society may find itself unable to make a choice. Given a social weak preference relation R, let the social choice set (i.e., the set of socially chosen elements) generated by R be defined to be

$$C(A,R) = \{x \in A \mid \text{for all } y \in A, \, xRy\} \tag{4.1}$$

(thus, the choice set for A, given R, is the set of all elements x in A such that x is at least as good as every element in A). Then $C(A,R)$ may be empty if R is nontransitive. For example, if we have (xPy and yPz and zPx), then $C(\{x,y,z\},R)$ is empty. In this case, it is not clear what the society should choose, since, for every alternative in $\{x,y,z\}$, there exists a socially better alternative in $\{x,y,z\}$. Such a situation cannot arise when R is transitive, assuming that the feasible set of alternatives is finite: it can be shown that, if R is reflexive, connected and transitive, then $C(A,R)$ is nonempty for every finite A in X. Therefore, one possible defense of transitivity of R is that transitivity of R, together with reflexivity and connectedness of R, ensures the existence of a nonempty social choice set for every finite feasible set of alternatives. Arrow also had a second justification for the transitivity of R, based on the notion of path independence to be formalized later by Plott (1973). As Plott (1973) observes,

> the process of choosing, from a dynamic point of view, frequently proceeds in a type of "divide and conquer" manner. The alternatives are "split up" into smaller sets, a choice is made over these smaller sets, the chosen elements are collected, and then a choice is made from them. Path independence, in this case, would mean that the final result would be independent of the way the alternatives were initially divided up for consideration. (1973, 1079–80)

If the set of socially chosen elements is given by $C(A,R)$ (see [4.1]), where A is the feasible set of alternatives and R is the social weak preference relation, path independence of social choice requires that

$$C(B_1 \cup B_2, R) = C(C(B_1,R) \cup C(B_2,R)) \text{ for all } B_1,B_2 \in \mathcal{X}.$$

It is easy to check that, if R is an ordering and $C(A,R)$ is nonempty for all $A \in X$, then (4.2) must hold. However, if R is reflexive and connected, but not necessarily transitive, then (4.2) may not hold even when $C(A,R)$ is nonempty for all $A \in \mathcal{X}$. Suppose $X = \{x,y,z\}$ and suppose [xPy and yPz and xIz and for all $a \in X$, aIa]. Then $C(A,R)$ is nonempty for all $A \in \mathcal{X}$. However, when X is split into $\{x,y\}$ and $\{z\}$, we have $C(C(\{x,y\},R) \cup C(\{z\},R)) = \{x,z\} \neq C(X,R)$, though when X is split into $\{y,z\}$ and $\{x\}$, we have $C(C(\{y,z\},R) \cup C(\{x\},R)) = \{x\} = C(X,R)$.

While reflexivity, connectedness, and transitivity of R, together, are sufficient for the existence of a nonempty social choice set, $C(A,R)$, for every finite $A \in \mathcal{X}$ (see Sen 1970a), transitivity of R is not a necessary condition for $C(A,R)$ to be nonempty for all finite $A \in \mathcal{X}$. In fact, a necessary and sufficient condition for $C(A,R)$ to be nonempty for every finite $A \in \mathcal{X}$ is that R should be reflexive and connected and P should be acyclic over X (P is said to be acyclic over X if and only if there do not exist $x_1, \ldots, x_m \in X$ such that $x_1 P x_2$ and $x_2 P x_3$ and ... and $x_{m-1} P x_m$ and $x_m P x_1$), and acyclicity of P is a much weaker condition than transitivity of R (see Sen 1970a). Similarly, a sufficient condition for $[C(B_1 \cup B_2, R) = C(C(B_1, R) \cup C(B_2, R))$, for all finite $B_1, B_2 \in X]$ is that R should be reflexive, connected, and quasi-transitive (R is said to be quasi-transitive if and only if P is transitive); and quasi-transitivity of R, though stronger than acyclicity of P, is a weaker condition than transitivity of R. Thus, if a nonempty set of socially chosen alternatives for every finite issue and path independence of social choice are the only reasons for requiring R to be transitive, then one could as well weaken one's demand to quasi-transitive of R. How much mileage would one get if one replaces transitivity of R by quasi-transitivity of R? This is an issue that was first investigated by Gibbard (1969) (see also Guha 1972 and Mas-Colell and Sonnenschein 1972).

4.2 Quasi-transitivity of the social weak preference relation and oligarchies

Consider the following condition, which is obviously weaker than condition 3.1 insofar as it relaxes transitivity of R to quasi-transitivity of R.

> *Condition 4.1:* The SER should have an unrestricted domain and the range of the SER should be a set of reflexive, connected, and quasi-transitive weak preference relations.

Though the relaxation of condition 3.1 to condition 4.1 does provide some relief from Arrow's problem, it does not really go very far. Gibbard's (1969) theorem shows that, if $|x| \geq 3$ and if an SER satisfies conditions 4.1, 3.2 (weak Pareto criterion), and 3.3 (independence of irrelevant alternatives), then there must exist an oligarchy, that is, there must exist a unique nonempty subset L of the society N such that, for every profile $(R_1, \ldots, R_n)$ of individual orderings and for all distinct $x, y \in X$,

$$\text{if } (x P_i y \text{ for all } i \in L), \text{ then } x P y \qquad (4.2)$$

and

$$\text{if } (x P_i y \text{ for some } i \in L), \text{ then } x R_i y. \qquad (4.3)$$

With conditions 4.1, 3.2, and 3.3, we do not necessarily have a dictator. Indeed, it can be checked that the following SER satisfies conditions 4.1, 3.2, and 3.3 in addition to satisfying Arrow's condition of nondictatorship (the example is due to Sen 1970a):

The Pareto extension rule: *For all* x,y $\in$ X, xRy *if and only if not* [yP$_i$x *for all* i $\in$ N].

However, given conditions 4.1, 3.2, and 3.3, we must have a unique coalition satisfying two conditions. First, unanimous strict preference of all individuals in the coalition over any pair of distinct alternatives automatically gets translated into social strict preference over that pair. Secondly, every individual in the coalition has a weak veto over every pair of distinct alternatives in the sense that if an individual in the coalition strictly prefers an alternative x to another alternative y, then the society cannot strictly prefer y to x. Note that the existence of a unique coalition satisfying (4.2) and (4.3) for every profile $(R_1, \ldots ,R_n)$ and for all distinct $x,y \in X$ does not necessarily imply any concentration of power in the hands of a small number of individuals. For example, the coalition could be the entire society itself (this is the case under the Pareto extension rule cited above). In that case, the unanimous strict preference of all individuals in the society results in corresponding social strict preference, and, if any two individuals have strictly opposing preferences over any two alternatives, then we have social indifference over those two alternatives. However, if this is the case, then, in general, the society is likely to be widely indecisive, with social indifference over many pairs of alternatives. If the size of the unique coalition figuring in the Gibbard theorem is small, then we have less of social indecisiveness but more concentration of power. At an extreme, if the unique coalition has only one member, then we have dictatorship. Thus, conditions 4.1, 3.2, and 3.3 together pose a dilemma: one is forced to choose between social indecisiveness and a greater degree of concentration of power.

Since relaxing transitivity of social preferences to quasi-transitivity of social preferences does not help much, it is natural to consider further relaxation of the notion of collective rationality. In particular, since acyclicity of P together with reflexivity and connectedness of R guarantees the existence of a nonempty $C(A,R)$ for every finite issue $A \in X$, the question naturally arises as to whether relaxation of quasi-transitivity of R to acyclicity of P may help us escape paradoxes. A number of writers have explored this issue and we consider only a sample of the relevant theorems.

4.3 Acyclicity of social strict preference relations

The basic message that emerges from various explorations of the property of acyclicity of social strict preference relations and its implications is that replacing transitivity or quasi-transitivity of R by acyclicity of P does not necessarily provide a solution to the basic Arrow problem. However, this should not be a complete surprise to any one familiar with the classical voting paradox. For a society with at least three individuals, if we have at least three social alternatives, x, y and z, and if the preference profile $(R_1, \ldots, R_n)$ is such that $xP_1y\ P_1z$, $yP_2z\ P_2x$, zP_3xP_3y and for all $i \in N - \{1,2,3\}$, xI_iyI_iz, then the simple majority-decision rule yields the social ranking (xPy and yPz and zPx) and, thus, violates P-acyclicity (note that, under the simple majority decision rule, for every preference profile $(R_1, \ldots, R_n) \in \mathscr{R}^n$ and for all $a,b \in X$, aRb if and only if $|\{i \in N|xP_iy\}| \geq |\{i \in N|yP_ix\}|$). The violation of P-acyclicity by the simple majority decision rule is disturbing since the simple majority decision rule has a number of attractive properties. From an important theorem of May (1952a), we know that the simple majority decision rule is the only SER that satisfies, in addition to condition 3.3 (independence of irrelevant alternatives), the appealing conditions of decisiveness, neutrality, anonymity, and positive responsiveness, defined below.

> *Condition 4.2 (Decisiveness):* The domain of the SER is $\underline{\mathscr{R}}^n$ and every R in its range is reflexive and connected.
>
> *Condition 4.3 (Neutrality):* For every permutation σ of the alternatives in X and for all preference profiles $(R_1, \ldots, R_n)$ and $(R'_1, \ldots, R'_n)$ in the domain of the SER, if [for all $i \in N$ and all $a,b \in X$, aR_ib if and only if $\sigma(a)R'_i\sigma(b)$] then [for all $a,b \in X$, aRb iff $\sigma(a)R'\sigma(b)$] (where R and R' are the social weak preference relations corresponding to the profiles $(R_1, \ldots, R_n)$ and $(R'_1, \ldots, R'_n)$, respectively).
>
> *Condition 4.4 (Anonymity):* For every permutation σ^* of the individuals in N and for all preference profiles $(R_1, \ldots, R_n)$ and $(R'_1, \ldots, R'_n)$ in the domain of the SER, if [for all $i \in N$, $R_i = R_{\sigma^*(i)}$], then $R = R'$.
>
> *Condition 4.5 (Positive responsiveness):* Let $(R_1, \ldots, R_n)$ and $(R'_1, \ldots, R'_n)$ be any two preference profiles in the domain of the SER. Let $x,y \in X$ be such that
>
> > for all $i \in N$ and all $a,b \in X - \{x\}$, $[(aR_ib$ if and only if $aR'_ib)$ and $(bR_ia$ if and only if $bR'_ia)]$;　(4.4)
> >
> > for all $i \in N$ and all $a \in X - \{x\}$, $[(xP_ia$ implies $xP'_ia)$ and $(xI_ia$ implies $xR'_ia)]$;　(4.5)
>
> and
>
> > for some $i \in N$, $[(yP_ix$ and $xR'_iy)$ or $(xI_iy$ and $xP'_iy)]$.　(4.6)
>
> Then $(xPy$ implies $xP'y)$ and $(xIy$ implies $xP'y)$.

Since the simple majority decision rule is the only SER that satisfies decisiveness, neutrality, anonymity, positive responsiveness, and independence of irrelevant alternatives, and since the simple majority decision rule violates acyclicity of P when there are at least three distinct individuals and at least three distinct alternatives, it follows that, given three or more distinct individuals and three or more distinct alternatives, no SER can simultaneously satisfy decisiveness, neutrality, anonymity, positive responsiveness, and independence of irrelevant alternatives (see, Kelly 1978).

The violation of P-acyclicity is a problem that affects a large class of SERs, of which the simple majority decision rule is only one conspicuous member. Consider the class Ω of all SERs that satisfy independence of irrelevant alternatives, decisiveness, neutrality, and nonnegative responsiveness defined as follows.

> *Condition 4.6 (Nonnegative responsiveness).* Let $(R_1, \ldots, R_n)$ and $(R'_1, \ldots, R'_n)$ be any two preference profiles in the domain of the SER. Let $x \in X$ be such that (4.4) and (4.5) hold. Then, for all $a \in X - \{x\}$, $[(xPa$ implies $xP'a)$ and $(xIa$ implies $xR'a)]$.

Blau and Deb (1977) show that, if $|x| \geq n \geq 3$, then, for every SER f belonging to Ω, either f must violate P-acyclicity or f must permit the existence of an individual who has a "weak veto" for every alternative against every other alternative (we say that individual i has a weak veto for x against y if and only if $x \neq y$ and, for all $(R_1, \ldots, R_n)$ in the domain of the SER, xP_iy implies xRy).

Note that Ω is a large class of SERs that includes most "democratic" SERs that one can think of. The Blau–Deb theorem shows that, if the number of alternatives is sufficiently large, then every SER in this class that rules out the existence of an individual with a weak veto for every alternative against every other alternative in X violates P-acyclicity. To see how this important theorem works, consider the special case where $n = 4$ and $|x| \geq 4$. Suppose $f \in \Omega$ does not give to any individual a weak veto for every alternative against every other alternative in X. Take distinct alternatives $x_1, x_2, x_3, x_4 \in X$ and orderings R_1, R_2, R_3, and R_4 such that

$$x_1P_1x_2P_2x_3P_1x_4$$
$$x_2P_2x_3P_2x_4P_2x_1$$
$$x_3P_3x_4P_3x_1P_3x_2$$
$$x_4P_4x_1P_4x_2P_4x_3.$$

Note that only 2 strictly prefers x_2 to x_1 and everyone else strictly prefers x_1 to x_2. Therefore, if we have x_2Rx_1, then, given that f satisfies independence of irrelevant alternatives and nonnegative responsiveness, it is easy to see that 2 will have a weak veto for x_2 against x_1. In that case, by neutrality, 2 will have a weak veto for every alternative against every other alternative in X. Since this is ruled out by our assumption, we cannot have x_2Rx_1. Therefore, by decisiveness, we must have x_1Px_2. Similarly, it can be shown that (x_2Px_3 and x_3Px_4 and x_4Px_1). Thus, f violates P-acyclicity.

There are numerous other impossibility theorems that use the weak rationality property of P-acyclicity rather than transitivity or quasi-transitivity of R (see Fishburn 1973 and Kelly 1978 for an account of many of these theorems). One of the most important of these is Sen's (1970a, 1970b) theorem on the impossibility of Paretian libertarianism. However, the focus of Sen's result is not the weakening of Arrow's collective rationality condition as such but the notion of individual rights. Sen's theorem will be discussed in Section 6. Meanwhile, in the following section, I consider some impossibility results for social decision rules.

5. Impossibility results for social decision rules

So far, I have discussed impossibility results in the framework of social evaluation rules. However, one can also prove the counterparts of many of these results in the context of social decision rules. Recall that, unlike social evaluation rules, social decision rules take social choice rather than social preference as the primitive notion (see definitions 2.1 and 2.2), but one can establish a formal link between the two notions. Suppose we start with a social decision rule $g: \underline{X} \times T \rightarrow X$. Then, for all $(R_1, \ldots, R_n) \in T$, define a binary relation $R[g]$ over X such that for all

$$x, y \in X, \ xR[g]y \text{ iff } \{x, y\} \in \underline{X} \text{ and } x \in g(\{x, y\},$$
$$(R_1, \ldots, R_n) \tag{5.1}$$

We can now use g to "induce" an SER $f_g: T \rightarrow \mathfrak{R}$ such that

$$\text{for all } (R_1, \ldots, R_n) \in T, f_g(R_1, \ldots, R_n) = R[g] \tag{5.2}$$

Suppose we require g to satisfy the following conditions:

Condition 5.1: For all $x, y \in X$, $\{x, y\} \in \underline{X}$; $T = \mathfrak{R}^n$; and, for all $(R_1, \ldots, R_n) \in T$, $R[g]$ is transitive.

Condition 5.2: For all $x, y \in X$ and all $(R_1, \ldots, R_n) \in T$, if $\{x, y\} \in \underline{X}$ and, for all $i \in N$, xP_iy, then $g(\{x, y\}, R_1, \ldots, R_n) = \{x\}$.

Condition 5.3: For all $x, y \in X$ and all $(R_1, \ldots, R_n)$, $(R'_1, \ldots, R'_n) \in T$, if $\{x, y\} \in \underline{X}$, and, for all $i \in N$, $[(xR_iy \text{ iff } xR'_iy)$ and $(yR_ix \text{ iff } yR'_ix)]$, then $g(\{x, y\}, R_1, \ldots, R_n) = g(\{x, y\}, R'_1, \ldots, R'_n)$.

Condition 5.4: There does not exist any $i \in N$ such that, for all $(R_1, \ldots, R_n) \in T$ and for all $x,y \in X$, if $\{x,y\} \in \underline{X}$ and xP_iy, then $g(\{x,y\},R_1, \ldots, R_n) = \{x\}$.

It is easy to see that if the SDR g satisfies conditions 5.1, 5.2, 5.3, and 5.4, then the SER f_g induced by g will satisfy conditions 3.1, 3.2, 3.3, and 3.4, which is impossible by Arrow's impossibility theorem. Therefore, if follows that an SDR cannot possibly satisfy conditions 5.1, 5.2, 5.3, and 5.4 simultaneously.

This is one of many possible translations of Arrow's impossibility theorem in terms of SDRs. As Blair, Bordes, Kelly and Suzumura (1976) have shown, by suitably weakening condition 5.1 to condition 5.5 below and strengthening condition 5.4 to condition 5.6 below we can also reformulate Gibbard's theorem on oligarchies in the framework of SDRs.

Condition 5.5: For all $x,y \in X$, $\{x,y\} \in \underline{X}$; $T = \underline{\mathscr{R}}^n$; and, for all $(R_1, \ldots, R_n) \in T$, $R[g]$ is quasi-transitive.

Condition 5.6: There does not exist a unique nonempty subset L of the society N such that, for all $(R_1, \ldots, R_n) \in T$ and for all distinct $x,y \in X$,

if xP_iy for all $i \in L$, then $g(\{x,y\},R_1, \ldots, R_n) = \{x\}$

and

if xP_iy for some $i \in L$, then $x \in g(\{x,y\},R_1, \ldots, R_n)$.

It can be easily checked that, if g satisfies conditions 5.5, 5.2, 5.3, and 5.6, then the induced SER f_g will satisfy conditions 3.1, 3.2, and 3.3, and, further, f_g will rule out the possibility of any oligarchy in the sense of Gibbard (1969). Since, by Gibbard's theorem, there does not exist any such SER, it follows that g cannot satisfy conditions 5.5, 5.2, 5.3, and 5.6 simultaneously.

The two examples given above illustrate one possible way of reformulating, in terms of SDRs, impossibility results proved for SERs. In each of them, the reformulated conditions impose restrictions involving only social choices from two-element issues. As a consequence, the type of dictatorship (resp. oligarchy) that arises from conditions 5.1, 5.2, and 5.3 (resp. conditions 5.5, 5.2, and 5.3) is a rather weak form of dictatorship (resp. oligarchy). Consider what happens when a GDR satisfies conditions 5.1, 5.2, and 5.3 and, therefore, ends up by violating condition 5.4. Violation of condition 5.4 implies the existence of an individual i such that his strict preferences are always respected by social choices from two-element issues, but it does not necessarily imply any concentration of power in i's hands so far as social choices from issues with more than two elements are concerned. However, one can prove dictatorship of a stronger variety by strengthening condition 5.1 into condition 5.7.

> *Condition 5.7:* The SDR g has an unrestricted domain; for all $(R_1, \ldots, R_n) \in T$, $R[g]$ is transitive; and the following condition holds for all $(R_1, \ldots, R_n) \in \mathfrak{R}_n$:
>
> for all $A, B \in X$, if $A \subseteq B$, then $[A - g(A, R_1, \ldots, R_n)]$
> $\subseteq [B - g(B, R_{1:}, \ldots, R_n)]$. \hfill (5.3)

Condition 5.7 is stronger than condition 5.1 in two respects. First, condition 5.7 requires a completely unrestricted domain while condition 5.1 only requires that $T = \mathfrak{R}^n$ and every two-element issue should belong to $\underline{X}$. Secondly, and this is crucial, condition 5.7 imposes conditional restrictions on social choices from issues with more than two elements by requiring that, given a preference profile, if an alternative is not socially chosen from a certain issue, then that alternative cannot get chosen when the issue is expanded by adding further alternatives (this last requirement is well known in the literature as condition α). It can be easily shown that if an SDR g satisfies conditions 5.7, 5.2, and 5.3, then it must violate the following condition (condition 5.8).

> *Condition 5.8.* There does not exist any i such that, for all $(R_1, \ldots, R_n) \in T$, for all $A \in \underline{X}$ and for all distinct $x, y \in A$, if xP_iy, then $y \notin g(A, R_1, \ldots, R_n)$.

Violation of condition 5.8, of course, means that some individual i will have the power that, if he prefers x to y, then y will never be chosen from any issue that contains x.

Thus, we have another version of Arrow's theorem in the framework of SDRs.

Virtually every impossibility theorem proved for SERs has its counterpart for SDRs, and sometimes one can think of several counterparts. The cases discussed above should give the reader an idea about the close logical link that exists between the two alternative formal structures because of which the results proved in one framework can often be reformulated and proved in the other.

6. Individual rights and the Pareto principles

In this section, I consider Sen's (1970a, 1970b) well-known paradox of the Paretian liberal. The paradox is remarkable in many ways. It does not make use of Arrow's condition of independence of irrelevant alternatives, which figures in so many impossibility results. It was one of the earliest theorems to weaken the requirement of transitivity or quasi-transitivity of the social weak preference relation to P-acyclicity. Above all, it introduced the notion of individual rights for the first time in the formal theory of social choice and welfare economics.

The notion of individual rights and the result showing the conflict between individual rights and the Pareto principle were originally formulated by Sen (1970a, 1970b) in terms of SERs. However, subsequently, he restated them in terms of social choice (see Sen 1983). The discussion in the rest of this section will be in terms of social choice and SDRs.

Sen imposes three conditions on SDRs. The first condition stipulates that the SDR $g: \underline{X} \times T \rightarrow X$ should have an unrestricted domain. The other two conditions, Weak Pareto optimality and minimal libertarianism, are as follows:

> *Condition 6.1 (Weak Pareto optimality):* For all $(A, R_1, \ldots R_n)$ in the domain of the SDR, and, for all $x, y \in A$, if $x P_i y$ for all $i \in N$, then $y \notin g(A, R_1, \ldots, R_n)$.

Condition 6.1 just requires that social choices should always be weakly Pareto optimal.

> *Condition 6.2 (Minimal libertarianism):* There exist distinct $i, j \in N$ and $x, y, z, w \in X$ such that $(x \neq y$ and $z \neq w)$ and, for all $(R_1, \ldots, R_n) \in T$ and all $A \in \underline{X}$, [if $x P_i y$ and $x \in A$, then $y \neq g(A, R_1, \ldots, R_n)$]; [if $y P_i x$ and $y \in A$, then $x \notin g(A, R_1, \ldots, R_n)$]; [if $z P_j w$ and $z \in A$, then $w \notin g(A, R_1, \ldots, R_n)$]; and [if $w P_j z$ and $w \in A$, then $z \notin g(A, R_1, \ldots, R_n)$].

Sen (1970a, 1970b) interpreted minimal libertarianism in terms of individual rights. x and y figuring in condition 6.2 are interpreted as two social alternatives that are identical in all respects except for some aspect that relates to the personal life of individual i. Similarly z and w are intended to be identical in all respects except for some aspect relating to the personal life of j. For example, x and y may be identical in all respects except that, in x, the bedroom wall of i is painted blue, and, in y, it is painted white. If condition 6.2 is satisfied, then there exist at least two individuals, i and j, who enjoy the following type of power: for at least one pair of distinct alternatives, x and y, which differ only with respect to some aspect of i's personal life, if i strictly prefers x to y then y cannot be socially chosen from an issue that contains x, and similarly for individual j. Thus, the view of individual rights that is implicit in condition 6.2 is that the following is a necessary condition for individual i to enjoy rights, at least with respect to his private life:

there must exist distinct $x, y \in X$ such that for all $A \in \underline{X}$ and all
$(R_1, \ldots, R_n) \in T$, [if xP_iy and $x \in A$, then $y \notin g(A, R_1, \ldots, R_n)$]
and [if yP_ix and $y \in A$, then $x \notin g(A, R_1, \ldots, R_n)$]   (6.1)

Sen (1970a, 1970b) shows that no SDR with an unrestricted domain can possibly satisfy conditions 6.1 and 6.2 simultaneously. Though relatively simple in its technical structure, the result is almost as dramatic in its impact as the impossibility theorem of Arrow. For, it shows that, if we subscribe to the view that (6.1) is a necessary condition for an individual to have a right over his private life, then the respect for such rights of at least two individuals clashes with the condition of weak Pareto optimality – a condition that has been so widely accepted in much of welfare economics. In fact, since the requirement of weak Pareto optimality for social choices can be considered to be an essential feature of welfarism, that is, the view that social choices should be based only on information about individual preferences, Sen's theorem has been interpreted as demonstrating the tension that exists between individual rights and even the very weak versions of welfarism represented by the condition of weak Pareto optimality.

While Sen's theorem was intended to highlight the clash between individual rights and the Pareto principle, Gibbard (1974) proved an important result that has been interpreted as showing the possible conflict between the rights of different individuals. Gibbard assumed X to be a Cartesian product $X_0 \times X_1 \times \ldots \times X_n$, where X_0 denotes the set of alternative options with respect to those aspects of the social state that lie in the "public" domain and, for all $i \in N$, X_i denotes the set of alternative options with respect to those aspects of the social state that relate to i's private life. Thus, an option in X_0 may refer to the educational system in the society, the rate of income tax, and so forth, while an option in X_i may refer to the religion of individual i, his dietary habits, and so forth. When X can be written as a Cartesian product $X_0 \times X_1 \times \ldots \times X_n$ in this way, we say that X is decomposable. Given that X is decomposable, $x, y \in X$ are said to be i-variants ($i \in N$) iff $x_i \neq y_i$ and for all $j \in \{0, 1, \ldots, i-1, i+1, \ldots, n\}$, $x_j = y_j$. Gibbard (1974) postulated the following restriction for an SDR $g: \underline{X} \times T \rightarrow X$.

> *Condition 6.3 (Gibbard's libertarianism):* Let X be decomposable. Then, for all $i \in N$, all $A \in \underline{X}$, all i-variant $x, y \in A$ and all $(R_1, \ldots, R_n) \in T$, [if xP_iy then $y \notin g(A, R_1, \ldots, R_n)$].

Note that, under condition 6.3, if individual i strictly prefers x to y, where x and y are i-variants, y can never be socially chosen from an issue that contains x. Gibbard showed that, if, for at least two distinct individuals, i and j, $|X_i| \geq 2$ and $|X_j| \geq 2$, then no SDR with an unrestricted domain can satisfy condition 6.3. An example may be helpful in clarifying the intuition underlying Gibbard's theorem. Suppose we have a two-individual society, $\{1,2\}$. Suppose the public aspects of the social state have already been fixed so that we can ignore X_0. For $i = 1,2$, let $X_i = \{w,b\}$ where w stands for a white shirt for i and b stands for a blue shirt for i. Then $X = X_1 \times X_2 = \{(w,w),(b,b),(w,b),(b,w)\}$, where (b,w) denotes a social state where 1 wears a blue shirt and 2 wears a white shirt, and similarly for (w,w), (b,b) and (w,b). Suppose the preference profile is

$$(w,w)P_1(b,b)P_1(b,w)P_1(w,b)$$

and

$$(w,b)P_2(b,w)P_2(b,b)P_2(w,w).$$

Since (w,w) and (b,w) are 1-variants; (b,b) and (w,b) are 1-variants; and $[(w,w)P_1(b,w)$ and $(b,b)P_1(w,b)]$, by condition 6.3, the society must not choose either (b,w) or (w,b). Similarly, by considering 2-variant social alternatives and 2's preferences, it can be shown that, given condition 6.3, the society must not choose either (w,w) or (b,b). Thus, condition 6.3 implies that the society should not choose any of the alternatives in X, which is a contradiction, since $g(X,R_1,R_2)$ must be nonempty.

Following the contributions of Sen (1970a, 1970b) and Gibbard (1974), a large literature sprung up in which different writers made various suggestion for resolving the paradoxes of Sen and Gibbard by modifying the relevant condition of libertarianism or the weak Pareto principle (for a very lucid presentation of many of these proposals, the reader may consult Suzumura 1983 and Wriglesworth 1985). It may be worth considering here two interesting proposals for resolving Sen's paradox of Paretian libertarianism. One of these comes from Sen himself. Sen (1976) distinguishes between the actual preferences of an individual and the preferences that the individual would like to be counted for the purpose of social choice. Let x and y be two distinct alternatives that differ only with respect to some aspect of i's private life (say, his religion) and with respect to which i enjoys a right in the sense of (6.1). Let i strictly prefer x to y, but let another individual, say j, strictly prefer y to x. Then j may not want his own preference for y over x to count for social choice on the grounds that x and y differ only with respect to i's private life and i prefers x to y. Thus, for the purpose of social choice, j may not want some parts of his own ordering to count, even though he does have a complete ordering over X. Let R_j^* be a subrelation of j's actual preference ordering R_j, the interpretation of R_j^* being that R_j^* represents those parts of j's actual preference ordering that j himself would like to be the basis of social choice. Then given an actual preference profile $(R_1, \ldots , R_n)$, we can consider subrelations R_k^* of R_k $(k = 1, \ldots , n)$, each R_k^* being interpreted in this fashion. Now suppose there exists an individual i who always respects other people's rights in the following sense: for all $(R_1, \ldots , R_n) \in \underline{\mathscr{R}}^n$, there exists an ordering J over X such that R_i^*, as well as the preference of every individual j over every pair of alternatives, x and y, with respect to which j has a right in the sense of (6.3), is a subrelation of J. Sen (1976) shows that, if such a "rights-respecting" individual exists, then there exists an SDR with an unrestricted domain that satisfies his minimal libertarianism and a modified version of the requirement of weak Pareto optimality where the modification consists of defining weak Pareto optimality in terms of $(R_1^*, \ldots , R_n^*)$ rather than $(R_1, \ldots , R_n)$. Of course, the crucial point is whether such a "rights-respecting" individual is there: if all individuals always want their actual orderings to count for social choice so that $R_k^* = R_k$ for all $k \in N$ and all $(R_1, \ldots , R_n) \in \underline{\mathscr{R}}^n$, then the impossibility result of Sen would reassert itself.

Several writers (see Barry 1986 and Hardin 1988, among others) have suggested another route for resolving Sen's paradox. Essentially, the argument is that, if the individuals are permitted to enter into voluntary contracts with each other, under which they can give up their rights, if they want to, then, ultimately, they will reach a Pareto optimal social state through such contracts. The main problem with the proposal is that, in the absence of a mechanism to enforce such contracts, the individuals will often have an incentive to violate the contracts. Thus, suppose social alternatives x and y differ with respect to i's religion and i enjoys a right, in the sense of (6.3), with respect to x and y. Further, suppose i enters into a contract with others under which, in exchange for a payment, he agrees to stay at x, adopting the religion specified for him in x. However, in the absence of a mechansim to enforce this contract, what can prevent i from taking the payment and then switching to y by practicing the religion specified for him in y? At the same time, to bring in a mechanism for enforcing the contract, which would prevent i from switching from x to y, would seem to be against the spirit of libertarianism itself, since x and y differ only with respect to i's religion, which is assumed to be a matter of i's private life.

A number of writers (see, for example, Nozick 1974; Gärdenfors 1981; Sugden 1985; and Gaertner, Pattanaik, and Suzumura 1992) have raised an important conceptual issue regarding the intuition of Sen's condition of minimal libertariansim itself. They claim that, even when viewed as a necessary rather than sufficient condition for the existence of a right, (6.1) is intuitively misleading. An individual's right, according to this view, is a matter of what actions (or strategies) are permissible for the individual concerned and also for other agents, and what outcome results from each of the n-tuples of permissible actions (one action for each agent involved). Rights, under this conception, have very little to do with individual preferences over social alternatives as they are traditionally conceived in the theory of social choice. To see how this view of rights leads to conclusions radically different from those that follow from Sen's approach, consider again the shirt example of Gibbard discussed above. Suppose each individual enjoys the right to wear any one of the two shirts (white or blue) that he owns (presumably, this right also implies that neither of the two individuals can be harassed or penalized in any way for choosing a particular shirt). In Sen's approach, which views (6.1) as a necessary condition for the existence of a right, if 1 enjoys this right, then there must exist a pair of distinct social alternatives x and y such that x and y differ only with respect to i's shirt color, and, for every $(R_1,R_2) \in \mathcal{R}^2$ and for every issue A, if xP_1y and x is available, then y must not be socially chosen, and, if yP_1x and y is avaliable, then x must not be socially chosen. Without loss of generality assume that (w,w) and (b,w) are two such alternatives. Then assume R_1 and R_2 to be:

$$(w,w)P_1(b,b)P_1(b,w)P_1(w,b)$$

and

$$(b,w)P_2(w,b)P_2(w,w)P_2,(b,b).$$

Now, suppose that, though each individual is completely free to choose whichever of the two shirts he likes, each of the two individuals has to make his or her choice without knowing what the other individual is going to choose and without having any information about the other individual's preferences. Further, suppose that each individual is extremely pessimistic so that each will choose a "maximin" strategy or action. Then it can be easily checked that 1 will choose b, 2 will choose w, and, as a consequence, (b,w) will emerge as the social outcome. However, since $(w,w)P_1(b,w)$ and since 1 is assumed to have a right, in the sense of (6.1), over the pair of alternatives $((w,w),(b,w))$, the social choice of (b,w) will compel us to say that i's right is violated. Yet, since the two individuals are assumed to be completely free to choose their respective shirts and since neither individual can be penalized for his or her shirt choice, intuitively, there does not seem to be any violation of any one's choice despite the emergence of (b,w) as the social outcome. Thus, assuming that 1 enjoys a right over $((w,w),(b,w))$ in the sense of (6.1) leads us to a counterintuitive position. An exactly similar counterintuitive conclusion can be derived if we assume that 1 enjoys a right over $((w,b),(b,b)$, in the sense of (6.1). Therefore, it has been claimed (see, for example, Gaertner, Pattanaik, and Suzumura 1992) that Sen's formulation of rights in terms of (6.1) is intuitively problematic and that one should explore alternative formulations of individual rights.

One approach to individual rights that has been suggested as an alternative to Sen's formulation is in terms of game forms. In this approach, the right of an individual is formally formulated by: (1) specifying the permissible actions of the individual under consideration and also the permissible actions of other agents in the society and (2) specifying the social outcome for each possible configuration of permissible actions of all the agents. This approach which originated in Nozick (1974) has been discussed by Gärdenfors (1981), Sugden (1985) and Gaertner, Pattanaik and Suzumura (1992) among others. The debate about the relative merits of the game-form formulation of individual rights and the traditional formulation in terms of (6.1) is still continuing (see, for example, Sen 1992). However, it is clear that the game-form formulation of individual rights, by itself, does not provide a solution to Sen's problem of a conflict between the Pareto principle and individual rights. To see this, one only needs to reinterpret the well-known game of prisoner's dilemma so that the two strategies of each of the two players in the game are assumed to be the only permissible strategies of that player. Then the exercise by the two individuals of their respective rights to choose one of the permissible strategies leads to a Pareto-inoptimal outcome in the game; this shows that Sen's insight regarding the tension between the Pareto principle and individual rights remains intact even when one chooses to replace his formulation of individual rights by the game-form formulation.

7. Stochastic social choice, restricted domains, and interpersonal comparison of utility

7.1 Stochastic social choice

A social decision rule $g: \underline{X} \times T \rightarrow X$, as defined earlier, specifies a set of socially chosen alternatives for every issue in $\underline{X}$ and every preference profile $(R_1, \ldots, R_n) \in T$. If there are several socially "chosen" alternatives, then the intended interpretation is that the society can choose any one of them: which one of them is "finally" chosen is supposed to be of no consequence since they are all considered to be "equally good" for the society. One can think of an alternative framework where, given an issue A and a preference profile $(R_1, \ldots, R_n)$, a social decision procedure specifies a lottery over A rather than a set of socially chosen alternatives. For example, in a society of three individuals, if the issue is $\{x,y\}$ and the preference orderings are such that xP_1y, xP_2y, and yP_3x, then the social decision procedure could specify a lottery that assigned, say, probability 2/3 to x and probability 1/3 to y. This would mean that, given the issue $\{x,y\}$ and the orderings as specified, the society would use a random mechanism to choose between x and y – a random mechanism that would assign choice probability 2/3 to x and choice probability 1/3 to y. This intuitive idea has some appeal since random mechanisms are often thought to be fair. After all, if there are two mutually exclusive options and there are two individuals with exactly opposite preferences over these options, then flipping a coin often seems to be a perfectly fair way of deciding the issue.

Models where social choice can be stochastic have been explored by several writers (including Intriligator 1973; Fishburn and Gehrlein 1977; Barberá and Sonnenschein 1978; and Pattanaik and Peleg 1986). To give the reader a flavor of models of stochastic social choice, I present here an outline of the result of Barberá and Sonnenschein.

Given any set of objects K, a lottery over K is defined to be a function p_K which, for every $x \in K$, specifies exactly one real number $p_K(x)$ such that, for all $x \in K$, $0 \le p_K(x) \le 1$ and $\Sigma_{x \in K} p_K(x) = 1$. Thus, a lottery over K just assigns probability numbers to the elements of K. A stochastic social decision rule is defined to be a function h that, for every A belonging to some nonempty subset $\underline{X}$ of X and for every $(R_1, \ldots , R_n)$ belonging to some nonempty subset T of $\underline{\mathfrak{R}}^n$, specifies exactly one lottery over A.

Now consider a stochastic social decision rule h. Barberá and Sonnenschein propose the following properties for h (the analysis of Barberá and Sonnenschein is really in terms of stochastic social preferences, but I am stating it here in terms of stochastic social choice). First, the domain of h is assumed to be $X \times Q^n$ where Q is the set of linear or strict orderings over X (thus, intuitively, it is assumed that individual preferences never show indifference between distinct alternatives). Secondly, Barberá and Sonnenschein require that, for all $A = \{x,y\} \in X$ and for all $(R_1, \ldots , R_n) \in Q^n$, if xP_iy for all $i \in N$, then $p_A(x) = 1$ and $p_A(y) = 0$ where p_A is the lottery over $A = \{x,y\}$, given $(R_1, \ldots , R_n)$. This is, of course, just the weak Pareto criterion restated with reference to h. Thirdly, Barberá and Sonnenschein introduce the stochastic counterpart of Arrow's independence of irrelevant alternatives, which stipulates that, if all individual rankings over $\{x,y\}$ remain the same, then the probabilities of the society's choosing x and y, respectively, remain the same. Lastly, it is required that, for every $(R_1, \ldots , R_n) \in Q^n$, the set of lotteries $p_A(A \in X)$ is "rationalizable" in terms of a lottery over Q – The set of lotteries p_A $(A \in X)$ is said to be rationalizable in terms of a lottery p_Q over Q if and only if, for all $A \in X$ and all $x \in A$, $p_A(x)$ is the sum of all $p_Q(R)$ such that $R \in Q$ and x is the R-greatest element in A. Barberá and Sonnenschein show that if the stochastic social decision rule satisfies these four conditions, then, for each coalition L, there exists a real number $w_L(0 \le w_L \le 1)$ such that for all distinct $x,y \in X$ and all $(R_1, \ldots R_n) \in Q^n$, if everybody in L strictly prefers x to y and all other individuals strictly prefer y to x, then the probability of the society's choosing x from $\{x,y\}$ is given by w_L. Further, these numbers w_L, which, intuitively, reflect the powers of different coalitions with respect to two-element issues, satisfy the following properties: $w_\emptyset = 0$ (the power of the empty coalition is nil); $w_N = 1$ (the society as a whole is all powerful); and, for all coalitions L and L', $w_L + w_{L'} \geq w_{(L \cup L')}$. When individual orderings are assumed to be linear orderings, Barberá and Sonnenschein's result can be shown to imply Arrow's theorem as a special case.

The result of Barberá and Sonnenschein deals with the structure of coalitional power over two-element issues under stochastic social decision rules satisfying their four conditions. With a set of conditions similar to but in some respects somewhat stronger than the conditions of Barberá and Sonnenschein, Pattanaik and Peleg (1986) show that, over every issue that constitutes a proper subset of X, the power structure takes the form of random dictatorship. That is, for all $i \in N$, there exists a "weight" w_i ($0 \leq w_i \leq 1$ and $\sum_{i \in N} w_i = 1$) such that, for every issue A that is a proper subset of X, for every $(R_1, \ldots, R_n) \in Q^n$ and for every $x \in A$, the probability that the society will choose x from A, given $(R_1, \ldots, R_n)$, is $\sum_{i \in \underline{N}} w_i$, where $\underline{N}$ is the set of all individuals j who consider x to be best in A.

7.2 Restricted domains

Consider the social choice (as distinct from social preference) framework that we discussed in Section 5. Recall that one social *choice* version of Arrow's theorem, which we discussed in Section 5 and which dealt with the structure of power in general (rather than the structure of power over only two-element issues), involved the assumption that the domain of the SDR is unrestricted. What happens if the SDR $g: \underline{X} \times T \rightarrow X$ has a "restricted" domain so that $\underline{X} \neq X$ or $T \neq \mathfrak{R}^n$? The question is of considerable interest in economics since economic theory often postulates specific properties for individual preference orderings and also for feasible sets of alternatives. For example, it may be postulated that the individual preferences are convex and continuous so that preference orderings not satisfying one of these properties may not be admissible at all. Similarly, it may be postulated that the feasible set of social alternatives is a compact subset of $\mathbb{R}_+^k$ where k is some positive integer.

The possible consequences of relaxing the assumption that $[\underline{X} = X$ and $T = \mathfrak{R}^n]$ so as to permit the SDR to have an "economic domain" has been explored by a number of writers (see, for example, Kalai, Muller and Satterthwaite [1979], Border [1983], Bordes and Le Breton [1989],

Campbell [1992], Redekop [1991, 1993] and Le Breton and Weymark [1996]). In general, the existing results in the literature indicate that Arrow's paradox tends to persist when we relax the assumption $[T = \mathcal{R}^n]$ while retaining the assumption $[\underline{X} = X]$, and also when we relax the assumption $[\underline{X} = X]$ while retaining the assumption $[T = \mathcal{R}^n]$. However, the simultaneous relaxation of both parts of the unrestricted domain assumption seems to be somewhat more promising in providing relief from the paradox of Arrow (see Le Breton [1994]).

7.3 Interpersonal comparisons of utilities

Arrow (1951) started with the position that "interpersonal comparison of utilities has no meaning" (9), but, in the second edition of his book, Arrow considered the possiblity of interpersonal comparisons through what he called "extended sympathy." Since then, a large number of writers have explored various issues relating to interpersonal comparisons of utilities (see, among others, Arrow 1977; Blackorby and Donaldson 1982; Blackorby, Donaldson, and Weymark 1984; d'Aspremont and Gevers 1977; Gevers 1979; Hammond 1991b; Roberts 1980a, 1980b; Sen 1970a, 1977a, 1979; and Suzumura 1983). One major line of exploration has been through the notion of extended sympathy. Suppose each individual i has an "extended" preference ordering $\hat{R}_i$ defined over $X \times N$. For all (x,t), $(x',t') \in X \times N$, $(x,t)\hat{R}_i(x',t')$ is to be interpreted as "individual i considers being in the position of individual t in social state x to be at least as good as being in the position of individual t' in social state x'." It should be noted that being in the position of, say, individual t in social state x involves acquiring t's subjective characteristics besides acquiring t's objective circumstances in social state x. While this type of comparison may seem somewhat unusual at first sight, statements such as "I would rather be myself in my humble position than be individual i with his affluence" are often made in real life and do seem to make sense.

There do not seem to be compelling reasons why the extended preference orderings of two individuals will be necessarily identical. However, suppose the extended preference orderings of all individuals happen to be always identical. Even then, as the results of Gevers (1979) and Roberts (1980a) show, there do not exist very appealing procedures for constructing a social ordering over the social states on the basis of the single extended preference ordering. Of course, if the extended preference orderings are allowed to be different for different individuals, then we are faced with the problem of aggregating these possibly diverse extended preference orderings so as to arrive at a social ordering over the social states. Here again, we have negative theorems (see, for example, Roberts

1980a) that show that there do not exist aggregation procedures for this purpose (i.e., that satisfy certain plausible conditions).

The notion of an extended preference ordering involves ordinal interpersonal comparisons. However, one can expand the informational structure further by bringing in interpersonally comparable cardinal individual utilities. The prospect of finding "reasonable" rules for social welfare evaluation seems to improve somewhat with such enriched informational basis (see Blackorby, Donaldson, and Weymark 1984; and d'Aspremont 1985).

8. Concluding remarks

At the end of any review of the paradoxes of preference aggregation in social choice theory, the question naturally arises as to what exactly has been achieved by this very large and diverse class of negative results. It is true that we still do not have any "solution" to the problem of how social welfare evaluations should be made or of how the society should make its choices (it will be surprising if we ever find such a solution). However, the impossibility results in social choice theory have contributed to our understanding of various aspects of this complex problem. They have also made us aware of many different pitfalls in our search for satisfactory criteria for social welfare evaluation. That, in itself, would seem to be a significant gain.

CHAPTER 11

Voting and the revelation of preferences for public activities

T. NICOLAUS TIDEMAN

1. Introduction

Making collective decisions about public activities through voting is justified by the idea that individuals reveal their preferences through voting, and that knowledge of individual preferences permits determinations of which potential public activities are worthwhile. This raises the question of how voting should be structured to provide the most useful information about individual preferences. This chapter addresses that question.

One might suppose that if accurate individual preferences are needed to make good collective decisions, the natural thing to do would be just to ask people for their preferences. Indeed, a tradition has developed that regards the value of public activities as something that can be determined through public opinion surveys. The name that is given to a valuation obtained in this way is a "contingent valuation." The idea behind this phrase is that respondents are asked how much value they would place on a contingency, such as a new road that provided improved access to a recreation area. When contingent valuation is used, there is generally no determinate relationship between the results of a survey and levels of spending on public activities. Thus, it is not clear that contingent valuation should be regarded as a form of voting. One can imagine, however, that if the results of contingent valuation surveys were regarded as credible, then a determinate relationship between survey results and public spending might be prescribed: all public activities revealed by contingent valuation to be worthwhile shall be provided. In such an event, contingent valuation might be regarded as a form of voting.

Among economists, the idea that it is possible to obtain credible estimates of the value of public activities through surveys of such a sort is highly controversial (Diamond and Hausman 1994; Hanneman 1994; Portney 1994). To economists, the concept of value is intimately connected to individual willingness to make a sacrifice. A "valuation" that is not connected to an individual commitment to sacrifice some opportu-

226

nity simply does not count as a valuation in the standard paradigm of economists. This attitude is summarized in the words of Samuelson.

> One could imagine every person in the community being indoctrinated to behave like a "parametric decentralized bureaucrat" who *reveals* his preferences by signalling in response to price parameters or Lagrangian multipliers, to questionnaires, or to other devices. But there is still this fundamental technical difference going to the heart of the whole problem of *social* economy: by departing from his indoctrinated rules, any one person can hope to snatch some selfish benefit in a way not possible under the self-policing competitive pricing of private goods; . . . (1954, 389)

Economists are interested in procedures that generate attractive outcomes even when voters are assumed to behave selfishly and strategically.

Ideally, outcomes should be Pareto improvements. They should make some people better off and no one worse off. It may be impossible to achieve this ideal in practice, but the goal can still serve as a useful guide, just as the ideal of a frictionless machine provides a useful but unattainable guide for engineers.

The goal of having collective decisions be Pareto improvements involves two important implicit assumptions: (1) That it is possible to specify what the status quo is, so that the component of what happens that constitutes a change can be identified. In principle, to evaluate the consequences of a decision, one would need to know what would have happened into the indefinite future in the absence of a decision. In practice, analysts tend to limit their analyses to comparative statics or else assume that, in the absence of a decision, existing patterns would be replicated in every future time period. (2) That the status quo is just. One cannot reasonably insist that no one be made worse off by changes if the status quo is not just. Economists get around this difficulty by separating distribution and allocation. If the status quo is unjust, this fault should be addressed by a system of distributive justice. In focusing on allocative decisions, economists presume that there is another process that ensures that the distribution prior to allocative decisions is just.

Presuming then that the *status quo ante* is adequately specified and is just, a mechanism for making collective decisions can be judged by its ability to achieve Pareto improvements or approximations thereto. All potential decisions that would raise total income should be made, and with a minimum of decision-making cost. All costs should be taken into account and allocated among beneficiaries of public activities in such a way that no one is worse off. These are the standards by which mechanisms for making collective decisions are judged in the sections that follow.

The ideas that are discussed are divided into four categories. Section 2 discusses ideas that are based on bargaining; the ideas of Wicksell and Lindahl and the bargaining system of Ferejohn, Forsythe, and Noll are discussed in this section. Section 3 discusses ideas based on the purchase of insurance by voters against changed that would harm them; ideas developed by Thompson, Drèze and de la Vallée Poussin, Malinvaud, and myself are discussed in this section. Section 4 discusses an idea of Hylland and Zeckhauser regarding voting based on the allocation of influence points. Section 5 discusses a concept of voting based on marginal-cost pricing, namely the "demand-revealing process" that was first proposed by Clarke; a related idea developed by Groves and Ledyard is also discussed. In Section 6, the concluding section, these four approaches to the revelation of preferences are compared.

2. Valuing public activities through bargaining

Even before Pareto developed the idea of a Pareto improvement, Knut Wicksell ([1896] 1958) had the insight that ordinary democratic processes based on majority rule could not be relied upon to discriminate between productive and unproductive public activities. The fact that a proposed activity is favored by a majority does not establish that its benefits exceed its costs, because the average intensity of the concern of the opposing minority can exceed the average intensity of the concern of the majority.

Anticipating the ideas of Pareto, Wicksell realized that for every worthwhile public activity, there is a distribution of costs of the activity that makes everyone better off. He suggested that the quality of public decisions could be improved by raising the proportion of legislators that would have to approve a spending decision. To implement their proposals, politicians would then need to find ways of allocating costs that came close to matching the patterns of benefits. Ideally, one would insist upon unanimous consent, but for the problem of individuals holding out for more favorable treatment and thus blocking almost all action. So Wicksell was content to recommend a criterion of "near-unanimity," without specifying precisely what that meant.

Wicksell's suggestion could be expected to improve both the efficiency and the fairness of public taxing and spending decisions. Efficiency would be improved by the elimination of activities that could not secure nearly unanimous approval, no matter how they were financed, because they were not worthwhile. Fairness would be improved by the closer correspondence between benefits and costs to individuals. The disadvantages of Wicksell's suggestion are that there would be an increase in bargaining costs from the effort to find an allocation of program costs that secured nearly unanimous approval, and that the need to achieve near-unanimity would lead to some efficient activities not being undertaken because, even though there was an allocation of costs that could secure nearly unanimous approval, it would not be possible to discover that allocation with the effort that people were willing to expend. An appropriate specification of the level of approval that was needed to pass a spending decision would equalize these benefits and costs of the rule at the margin.

Wicksell's proposal can be considered a primitive form of revelation of preferences because, in approving a particular combination of spending and taxes, a legislator reveals that he regards the benefits of that program to his constituents to be greater than its costs. As negotiations about the allocation of costs proceed, every increase in cost allocation that a legislator approves reveals further information about the distribution of benefits for that legislator's constituents. A disapproval, on the other hand, could be strategic and is therefore not as informative.

Lindahl ([1919] 1958) contributed the idea that if the representatives of groups with different interests succeed in bargaining to a result that provides for the production of the efficient level of a public activity, then, at least at the margin, cost shares can be expected to follow marginal benefit shares. This insight, however, does not lead to a workable process for achieving agreement. Indeed, if there are more than a few persons who must all agree, the chances of reaching agreement are quite small.

A workable scheme for achieving agreement on certain types of public activity was developed by Ferejohn, Forsythe, and Noll (1979), who cut through the problem of achieving agreement by dealing with excludable, discrete public activities and relaxing the requirement of unanimous consent. The activity dealt with in developing their idea was the production of programs for public television. Programs could only be produced if stations were willing to pay enough for them to cover their costs. But the cost to any one station depended on how much money other stations were willing to offer.

In the scheme developed by Ferejohn et al., the bargaining problem is simplified by providing that the relative cost to any station will be a function of the size of its market. Bargaining over programs proceeds iteratively. In the first iteration, each station manager is shown an estimate of the cost of a program to his station, based on an estimate of the number of stations that will be willing to share in its costs. Based on these estimated costs, each manager specifies the programs that he or she is prepared to support. The set of stations supporting a program and the cost of developing the program determine the prices in the second iteration. Facing these prices, station managers once again specify the programs they are willing to support. The process continues in this way until there are no changes from one iteration to the next.

This process does achieve agreement, but it is not completely efficient. The fixedness of the relative prices that different stations must pay greatly simplifies what would otherwise be an intractable bargaining problem. But because of this simplification, opportunities to achieve agreement through revision of cost shares can be missed. Furthermore, to maintain the incentive for participation, stations must be denied the chance to broadcast programs they have not helped to finance, even though the marginal cost of providing programs to additional stations is zero.

3. Valuing public activities through uncertainty in the direction of movement

Mechanisms that rely on uncertainty in the direction of movement permit 100 percent participation and offer every participant an opportunity to specify a personal value of the activity under consideration. Earl Thompson (1966) proposed the first of these schemes. His idea can be illustrated as follows: Suppose that there were a public project that, by common agreement, had a 20 percent probability of being adopted. Suppose further that those who opposed the project were given the opportunity to buy insurance against its being adopted at a price of 20 percent of the losses they wished to insure against, while those who favored it could buy insurance against its *not* being adopted for a price of 80 percent of the prospective gains that they wished to protect. Only by buying insurance that exactly reflected one's projected gain or loss could a person ensure that, whichever way the decision went, his or her wealth would be unaffected. The wealth of a person who bought such insurance would be at a level 20 percent of the way from its initial level to the level that it would have if the project was adopted and no insurance had been bought.

After such insurance had been bought, it would be possible to determine whether the project was worthwhile by comparing the gains of those who acknowledged that they would gain with the losses of those who said they would lose. If the gains were greater, then there would be more than enough money from the premiums paid by the gainers to pay the part of the losses not covered by 20 percent premiums paid by the losers. If the losses were greater, then the premiums paid by those who would lose would be more than enough to pay for the part of the potential gains not covered by the 80 percent premiums paid by the potential gainers. Whichever course of action was more efficient, there would be enough money to pay all the claimed costs of taking that action.

While Thompson's idea is logically consistent, the institution it describes would not be practical. The chief difficulty is that consensus on a probability of adoption is crucial and unlikely. If someone believes that the probability of adoption is 30 percent rather than 20 percent and is personally unaffected by the project, then that person has an incentive to claim high losses from the project. Every dollar of such claimed losses has an expected return of 10 percent (the difference between 30 percent and 20 percent). Only risk aversion limits such claims. Since the procedure does not generate reliable preferences, it cannot reasonably be used to identify efficient activities.

A second difficulty with Thompson's idea is that if people are so risk averse that they respond completely truthfully, whatever probability is announced, then the process by which a probability of adoption is announced becomes a process of ethically questionable redistribution. If an idea that I oppose is decreed to have a 25 percent chance of adoption, then the announcement of the 25 percent probability induces me to part with money equal to 25 percent of the losses that I would incur from uncompensated adoption. It is problematic to vest such redistributive power in the agency responsible for announcing the probability of adoption. It would be possible to develop a market process that yielded the probability of adoption as an equilibrium price of insurance, but those who participated in that market would have incentives not to reveal their true preferences for the activity. It does not seem to be possible to use Thompson's idea to yield both a market valuation of a proposed project and a market probability of its adoption.

Drèze and de la Vallée Poussin (1971) developed the idea that, when a public decision is to be made about the level of a continuous variable (the amount of spending on libraries or the speed limit, for example), then it should be possible to determine whether efficiency requires an increase or a decrease in the variable by asking each voter to name an amount of money that he or she would be willing to pay, per unit of movement, for movement in the preferred direction – an amount the voter would also accept as adequate compensation for movement in the opposite direction. This idea relies on the notion that a demand schedule ought to be continuous, so that, for small changes of the same magnitude, a change in quantity in one or the other direction has the same value. Malinvaud (1971) developed a similar idea.

The principal limitation of this idea is that a self-interested person is motivated to respond honestly only if he or she believes that the probability of an increase in the parameter under consideration is equal to the probability of a decrease. Otherwise, it is possible to make an expected profit either by claiming to be harmed by movement in the more likely direction or by not acknowledging all of the personal benefits that will be received from that movement. The combination of many such responses would make movements haphazard and drastically slow the rate of movement toward the efficient level of output.

I have offered a variation on the idea of a uniform price for incremental movements in both directions (Tideman 1972). In this scheme, the movement would not be continuous but rather a sequence of discrete jumps, each intended to hit the efficient equilibrium, based on an assumption of a uniform elasticity of demand among participants. This was intended to make it more difficult for participants to guess the direction of movement and profit by slowing the rate of convergence. However, this scheme is susceptible to being slowed by speculation if individuals do not regard the current position of the parameter being controlled to be an unbiased estimate of the position to which it will move in its next jump.

4. Valuing public activities by comparison with other public activities

Hylland and Zeckhauser (1979) developed a scheme in which public activities are valued by having voters allocate influence points among activities. Many of the systems of point voting that have been proposed have had a serious defect. A self-interested voter would have an incentive to allocate all of his or her points to the one issue where influence was likely to be most effective (Mueller 1973). Hylland and Zeckhauser proposed, as others had, that each voter be given a budget of "influence points" to be allocated on different public activities, with the crucial difference that a voter's impact on the level of spending on a public activity would be proportional to the square root of the number of points that the voter allocated to it. Equilibrium would be attained when the sum of the square roots of the points allocated to increasing expenditure on each activity was equal to the sum of the square roots of the points allocated to decreasing expenditure on that activity. Hylland and Zeckhauser showed that, under reasonable assumptions, this system motivates voters to report accurately their relative valuations of changes in levels of spending on different public activities, and that it is reasonable to believe that the system would converge.

A physical analogue of the Hylland and Zeckhauser scheme for two activities is a system in which the levels of two public activities are represented by positions in a two-dimensional coordinate system. Every voter is given a rope, the ropes are tied together in a single knot, and every voter is allowed to pull on his or her rope with a specified force (the square root of the total number of influence points), in whatever direction he or she chooses. The square of the total force that a voter applies is the sum of the squares of the force vectors that the voter applies in individual dimensions. The force applied in each individual dimension is thus the square root of the number influence points allocated to that dimension, and the point where the knot comes to rest is the voting equilibrium.

The Hylland and Zeckhauser scheme motivates voters to reveal the value that they place on changes in continuous parameters of public activities relative to the value that they place on other continuous parameters of public activities. It does not provide a way of comparing the value of discrete changes with the value of changes in continuous parameters. It works most coherently when all the parameters under consideration are measured in the same units, since a change in the units in which one dimension is measured (e.g., from dollars to pennies), leaving the other dimensions unchanged, will generally change the voting equilibrium.

If all the dimensions of public activity were continuous commensurate parameters and if it were agreed that every voter ought to have the same total influence (as measured by the sum of the squares of his or her influence in all dimensions), then the Hylland and Zeckhauser scheme would solve the problem of choosing a pattern of public activities. Similarly, if the dimensions of public activity were continuous commensurate parameters and if it were agreed that people ought to have different amounts of total influence, with consensus on the proper distribution of total influence (e.g., more influence for those near the center of a city, less for those at the periphery), then again the Hylland and Zeckhauser scheme would solve the problem of choosing the levels of continuous parameters of public activity. An important goal that the Hylland and Zeckhauser scheme does not achieve is a measure of the value of public activities to voters compared to the value of their money or any other private good. This idea discussed in the next section.

5. Valuing public activities through marginal cost pricing

Economic theory says that a consumer will purchase an efficient quantity of a private good if the price charged for the good is its marginal cost. Clarke (1971, 1972) and Groves and Loeb (1975) applied this idea to the evaluation of public activities. What is priced at marginal cost, however, is not access to a public activity but rather influence over the existence or magnitude of the activity. Tullock and I (1976) gave the name "demand-revealing process" to this scheme; it is also known as the pivotal mechanism.

The following example illustrates the demand-revealing process. Suppose that a city is considering the introduction of a system of one-way streets. A little money, which will be raised by an equal assessment on all voters, will be needed for new signs, but the main cost will be convenience or inconvenience, affecting different people in widely different ways. The plan is to be introduced if the aggregate value to the citizens of having one-way streets is positive. All citizens are invited to report their personal valuations of the system.

The first question that arises is, In what units should voters report their valuations? If the demand-revealing process were able to produce Pareto improvements, the units in which benefits are measured would not matter. However, it does not produce Pareto improvements. The system of one-way streets will be regarded as worthwhile if the benefits to those who gain outweigh the costs to those who lose. Thus, the units in which benefits and costs are measured can make a difference.

The unit of measure that comes immediately to the minds of economists is money. The disadvantage of measuring value in money is the implausibility of the idea that money has the same value (marginal utility) to everyone. Since there is no objective measure of the marginal utility of money to individuals, one cannot prove that the marginal utility of money is *not* the same for all persons. Nevertheless, the idea that it is the same for all is hard to sustain.

If there were an accepted way of measuring the marginal utility of money, it would be possible to have people report values in money and then translate them into common utility units (Good 1977). The city could then introduce the plan of one-way streets if the additional utility to those who benefited was greater than the loss of utility to those who were harmed. Even though there is no accepted way of measuring the marginal utility of money, it might be possible to secure agreement on the use of some formula for translating money to utility that would be more attractive than the assumption that money has the same marginal utility to all voters.

If attempts to devise a measure of the marginal utility of money are rejected, then it is relevant to ask whether there is some unit of value (potential sacrifice) for which the marginal utility is likely to be more uniform than the marginal utility of money is. One possibility is time (spent, say, in community service). Everyone starts with the same amount of time. Still, the ability of the rich to free up time by spending money probably makes the marginal utility of time greater for the poor than for the rich.

One could consider a measure of sacrifice measured in pain: How many fifty-volt electrical shocks would you be willing to bear to have the system of one-way streets introduced or rejected? If such sacrifices could be accepted socially, there would still be the problem that there might be masochists for whom such pain would not be a sacrifice.

Among the possibilities that have been mentioned (money and money weighted by a feasible estimate of the marginal utility of money, time, and pain), the one that seems most attractive is time. It is not ideal, but it is arguably more attractive than the alternatives. Thus, to evaluate the proposed system of one-way streets, one would ask each citizen of the city, How many hours of community service would you be willing to provide to have the plan of one-way streets implemented (if that is what you want) or rejected (if that is what you want)?

For people to give meaningful answers to such a question, there would have to be an understanding of the length of time for which the decision would be irrevocable. A person would not be willing to pay very much to reject the plan of one-way streets if a similar amount would be required to reject it again a month later. This is an example of the necessity, discussed in Section 1, of specifying clearly the future consequences of deciding not to act.

When all the responses had been received, the total value (in hours of service) reported by those who wanted the system of one-way streets would be compared with the total value reported by those who wished to retain the system of two-way streets. The system of one-way streets would be introduced if the former was greater than the latter. In the event of a tie, the decision would be made by flipping a coin or by some other random process.

Now comes the part that motivates people to report their preferences honestly, the marginal cost pricing: The "winning margin" is defined as the difference between the total value on the winning side (in hours of service) and the total value on the losing side. Any voter on the winning side who reports a value greater than the winning margin is defined as "pivotal." Of each pivotal voter, one can say that the decision would have gone the other way if that voter had abstained. For exercising such influence, every pivotal voter is required to pay what he or she offered, minus the winning margin. This amount is also what the winning margin would have been, in the other direction, if that voter had abstained. This is therefore the marginal social cost of accommodating the voter's preferences, by the following reasoning: If the voter had abstained, the decision would have gone the other way. By voting, the voter imposed on those who voted the other way a loss of all of the value that they would have received from the opposite decision. But at the same time, the voter provided benefits equal to their reported values to all others who voted for the side that won. The difference between the two amounts, the losses to others minus the gains to others, is what each pivotal voter is required to pay.

That a voter who considers only self-interest cannot do better by reporting a false value is easiest to see by considering all possible cases. If the voter is on the losing side, nothing is paid. Such a voter could change the outcome by increasing his or her reported value, but, since the margin without this voter was greater than his or her value, the payment that would then be required would be more than the activity was worth to the voter. If the voter is on the winning side and is not pivotal, then the voter gets his or her desired outcome and nothing is paid. No improvement is possible. If the voter is on the winning side and is pivotal, then an increase in reported value has no effect on what is paid. Such a voter would be motivated not to report an excessive value, however, because of the possibility that the extra reported value would be decisive, forcing a payment greater than the true value to the voter. A pivotal voter can avoid any payment by reducing the claimed value to an amount less than the winning margin in the other direction with his or her abstention, but in that case the decision goes the other way, and the voter passes up the chance to obtain his or her desired outcome at a cost less than its personal value.

Even though self-interested voters are motivated to report their preferences honestly under the demand-revealing process, for several reasons one cannot guarantee that voters will do so. First there is the possibility of coalitions. If the members of a coalition who want the same outcome all decide to treat a cost to any member of the coalition as a cost to themselves, then each member of the coalition will report as his or her personal value the sum of the value to all members of the coalition. The concerns of the members of the coalition will thus be counted multiply.

There is an important limitation to the distortions that might be caused by coalitions: Whatever a voter has agreed to do, the vote that will promote the voter's personal interest, if the vote is secret, is a vote that reflects the value to the voter alone. Therefore, it is important to have an institution that makes it impossible for a voter to prove how much he or she voted. If votes were counted in dollars, this could be accomplished by requiring voters to vote with money that had been placed in special accounts. The vote would be counted by a computer that would automatically deduct money from the account. A voter would be permitted to see on a computer monitor the amount of money in his or her account, but no paper statement that could be shown to others would be issued. If voting is done in terms of time spent in community service, voters can be limited to voting from time credit previously accumulated in accounts that were similarly not subject to paper reporting.

A variation on the theme of coalitions that might be regarded as troublesome is the possibility of differential sympathy. If a voter has more sympathy for those who want one outcome than those who want the other, this can induce the voter to report a value different from his or her value from personal access to the activity. This should not be regarded as inefficiency, however, The value of a thing as economists understand the term is what a person is prepared to sacrifice, for whatever reason, to have it. The same reasoning applies to the concern expressed by Margolis (1982) that the responses of voters to the demand-revealing process would represent not their personal valuations but rather expressions of willingness to sacrifice for their perceptions of the public good.

Two other variations on this theme are somewhat more troublesome. First, voters may vote extra amounts for the thrill of taking a risk for a good cause. When fraternity members in an experiment used the demand-revealing process to make decisions at their meetings, this seemed to arise (Tideman 1983). Second, voters who expect to be on the winning side might decide independently to vote additional amounts in order to reduce the expected payments for pivotal voters on their side. Similarly, voters who expect to be on the losing side might decide independently to vote additional (or reduced) amounts in order to increase (or decrease) the expected payments for pivotal voters on the other side. These motivations are limited by the possibility that such extra amounts would change the outcome, creating high pivotal payments for all who voted for the side that thereby won. Such an eventuality would not deter additions to votes if the outcome was worth what it cost. However, if voters expected that others on their side would vote out of sympathy for pivotal voters rather than for the value of the public activity itself, then the consequence of their combined decisions would not be worth what it cost them. This possibility would have some deterrent effect.

What makes these variations on coalitions troublesome is that the altered valuations come not from attractions of the public activity itself but from attendant consequences of the valuation process. One might take some consolation from the idea that concern for pivotal voters is relevant only if the election will be so close that one or more voters individually alter the outcome, but the probability of this eventuality diminishes as the number of voters increases. On the other hand, a self-interested reason for anyone to vote at all arises only to the extent that one's vote can be expected to make a difference in the outcome, but the probability of this also diminishes as the number of voters increases.

The division inherent in the idea of winners versus losers under the demand-revealing process is a reflection of the fact that the demand-revealing process is not ideal. It does not generate Pareto improvements. Under the assumption that people respond to the incentive to report their preferences honestly, it generates the information that would be needed to create a Pareto improvement, but any suspicion that the information will be used to try to achieve a Pareto improvement (by charging and compensating people according to the preferences they report) will give people an incentive to provide inaccurate information. Thus, the demand-revealing process does not offer a way to allocate the costs of a public project; it only determines the efficiency of a proposal with a specified allocation of costs.

Still, there is a step that can be taken to cause decisions made by the demand-revealing process to approximate Pareto improvements. After voters have reported their valuations, each voter can be compensated or charged according to an estimate of the impact on him or her derived from a statistical analysis of responses from a set of voters that does not include that particular voter. After all predictable components of individual valuations have been incorporated in the amounts that voters are charged or compensated, all that will remain uncompensated will be the idiosyncratic components of value that cannot be accounted for by personal characteristics that are permissible determinants of taxes and compensation (Tideman 1977).

Well-designed compensation reduces the dispersion of valuations. This reduces the divisiveness of decisions and the average number and average magnitude of pivotal votes. Still, losses cannot be precluded, and this raises questions of fairness. Why is it acceptable that some should lose while others gain?

Any acceptable answer must be couched in terms of constitutions. People are members of collectivities that leave some issues for resolution in on-going processes. Constitutions, traditions, or shared understandings specify ranges of permissible outcomes. Collective decision processes resolve uncertainties within the permitted ranges. Losses within the permitted ranges are possible because constitutions that permit losses are more attractive than alternatives, in terms of the norms of efficiency, fairness, and stability by which constitutions are judged.

As long as close outcomes cannot be precluded, there will be a possibility of pivotal voters. This raises the question of what should be done with the receipts from pivotal payments. If pivotal payments are made in the form of pain endured, then there are no receipts to dispose of, but a complaint can be made that the imposition of a cost not balanced by a benefit is inefficient, as compared to payments in money or useful work. However, if the money or useful work is received by the community, then it is imaginable that people would vote strategically, seeking to increase the total of pivotal payments, in order to increase their shares of benefits derived from public receipt of pivotal payments. When there are more than a few hundred voters, though, the magnitude of the incentive from this source is so small that it deserves to be ignored.

Nevertheless, if one wanted a scheme that was as free as possible of incentives for misstatements, one would specify that any pivotal payments that were collected would be turned over to someone outside the jurisdiction that was making the decision. So that citizens could collectively receive the expected value of their pivotal payments, the right to receive the payments could be auctioned prior to the decision.

When there are three or more options among which a decision must be made, new challenges of valuation arise. First there is the question of how voters should be asked to express their valuations. A value expresses the amount of something (say, time in public service) that a person is willing to sacrifice to have one outcome instead of another. But when there are more than two possibilities, with which alternative should each outcome be compared to establish its value?

Consider the case of three options. Suppose that there are two alternatives to an existing plan of two-way streets – a central-district plan of one-way streets and a citywide plan. Consider a voter who prefers the status quo but believes that if there is going to be a plan of one-way streets it should include the whole city. This voter would be wiling to pay twenty-five hours public service to have the status quo instead of the central-district plan and seven hours to have the citywide plan instead of the central-district plan. How much would the voter be willing to pay to have the status quo instead of the city-wide plan? One might think that the answer would be eighteen hours, the difference between the two previous values. However, that does not take into account the "income effect." If the citywide plan is the starting point from which the value of the status quo is measured, then it could be expected that the voter would be willing to pay more than eighteen hours, say twenty hours, for the status quo. The voter is "richer" and can therefore afford to pay more for the status quo if the payment of seven for the movement from the central-district plan to the citywide plan is not required.

If there are n options under consideration, then there are $n(n-1)/2$ paired comparisons that must be made to express fully the value of the options to a voter. This can be extremely tedious. But if it is not done, a voter can wind up either paying more for an outcome than it is worth or passing up an attractive possibility of achieving a desired outcome. An interesting compromise is to ask a voter to first rank the possible outcomes, then state the value of each one compared to the next lower one, and finally to state the value of the highest compared to the lowest. Only n valuations in all would be required. To assign a valuation to a particular paired comparison, one would then apply a utility function such as

$$U = Q(D) + \ln(T_0 - P) \tag{1}$$

Table 1: *Paired comparisons of three options by 303 voters*

No. of persons	CD	SQ	CW	CD	SQ	CW
100	20	0	30	0	0	45
100	30	0	0	45	20	0
100	0	45	20	0	30	0
1	0	20	60	0	0	45
1	60	0	0	44	0	20
1	0	46	0	20	60	0
Total	5,060	4,566	5,060	4,564	5,060	4,565

where $Q(D)$ is the "quality" of the decision as perceived by the voter, T_0 is the voter's effective initial budget of time, and P is the payment that the voter makes. $Q(n)$ (the quality of the voter's least-favored outcome) is set to 0, while the other Q's and T_0 are solved for from the n willingnesses-to-pay that the voter has reported. It is then possible to calculate the willingness-to-pay for any other paired comparison. To the extent that the utility function is inaccurate, these calculations will be inaccurate, but the expected cost of such inaccuracies may be lower to voters than the expected cost of making all paired comparisons.

Whatever procedure is used to specify valuations, there must then be a procedure for identifying the winning outcome and any payments that must be made by pivotal voters. In normal cases there will be a dominant option, an option that beats all others in paired comparisons. This would be the winner. But it is also possible that the paired comparisons will reveal cycles, and there must be a procedure for specifying the outcome in these unusual cases.

To illustrate the possibility of cycles, suppose that there are 303 voters whose valuations of the three possibilities of the status quo (SQ) the central district plan (CD) and the citywide plan (CW) are shown in Table 1.

By the paired comparisons, CD beats SQ, CW beats CD, and SQ beats CW. To make a decision, one must cut through the cycle. If one uses the rule of cutting a cycle at its weakest link, then SQ is declared the winner since its loss is the smallest of the three losses. When more than three options are under consideration, more complex cycles are possible, and a more general rule for breaking cycles is needed. A rule that is probably as attractive as any reasonably simple rule is that the winner is the option whose worst loss is least bad.

When cycles are possible, it is no longer reasonable to specify that a pivotal voter must pay the net cost of his or her vote. In the example given in Table 1, the winning option without the voter in line 4 is CD, and the comparison of CD with SQ reveals that the cost to all other voters of having SQ instead of CD is 514, which vastly exceeds the value to the voter in line 4.[1]

A rule for pivotal payments that may make sense whether or not there are cycles is as follows. Define w as the winning candidate. Define w_i as the candidate who would have won if i had not voted. Define $L(x)$ as the worst loss of candidate x. Define $V_i(x, y)$ as the value to voter i of having x instead of y. The pivotal payment of voter i is then specified as

$$P_i = \text{Max}\{0, V_i(w, w_i) - [L(w_i) - L(w)]\} \tag{2}$$

In words, the pivotal payment is what the pivotal voter offered for the change induced by his or her vote minus the "generalized winning margin," defined as the difference between the worst loss of the candidate who would have won without the pivotal voter and the worst loss of the actual winner. The pivotal payment is subject to the further constraint that it cannot be negative. For the example, the pivotal payment for the voter in line 4 is $20 - (496 - 494) = 18$. The formula for the pivotal payment is not strategy proof when there are cycles: If the voter in line 4 had reported 65 rather than 60 for the value of CW over CD, then the outcome would have been the same, but the pivotal payment would have been reduced to 13. It might be hoped that cycles would not be so frequent or so predictable as to induce such strategizing. If there were no income effects, then there could be no cycles, and this generalized pivotal payment would be the same as the net cost to all other voters of the pivotal voter's vote.

When options lie in a one-dimensional continuum, preferences are generally conceived as marginal valuation schedules: How much is it worth to a voter to move the decision incrementally along the continuum? When the continuum describes a level of spending, the marginal valuation should be net of any marginal taxes. The point of greatest efficiency is the point where the aggregate value of an incremental increase in position along the continuum is zero and declining. The pivotal payment that is assigned to each voter is the integral of the aggregate marginal valuation schedule of all other voters, from the quantity that would have been chosen if this voter had abstained to the actually chosen quantity. Under the assumption that the aggregate marginal valuation schedule of all voters other than i can be approximated by the linear expression

$$V_i(Q) = b_i (Q^*_i - Q), \tag{3}$$

1. I am indebted to Daniel Richardson for pointing out the possibility of such an example.

where (Q_i^*) is the quantity that is optimal in terms of all preferences other than that of voter i, the pivotal payment assigned to voter i will be

$$P_i = \frac{1}{2}\, b_i (Q_i^* - Q^*)^2, \tag{4}$$

where Q^* is the quantity that is optimal taking account of the preferences of all voters.

With discrete options, pivotal payments tend to be rare because they arise only if an election is close enough to be changed by a single reported preference. With options in a continuum, on the other hand, every voter who reports a nonzero marginal valuation at the chosen outcome is pivotal. But the effect of removing any one voter tends to be so slight that each pivotal payment is extremely small. Nevertheless, the pivotal payments mean that every nonunanimous decision by the demand-revealing process about a continuous parameter will yield a budget surplus.

Seeking to create a mechanism that would not have a budget surplus, Groves and Ledyard (1977) developed a variation on the demand-revealing process in which each voter reports not a marginal valuation schedule but a single number, a quantity of the public activity that will be added to all other reported quantities to determine the quantity of the public activity that will be produced. (With a change in scale, the rule could also be that the quantity produced will be the average of the reported quantities.)

The logical connection between the demand-revealing process and the Groves–Ledyard mechanism is explained in Margolis (1983). Mimicking the fact that, in the standard demand-revealing process, the pivotal charge on a voter is proportional to the square of the difference between what is optimal with and without that voter, in the Groves–Ledyard mechanism each voter is charged an arbitrary standard multiple of the square of the deviation of his or her reported quantity from the mean of all other reported quantities. Then, to eliminate the budget surplus, each voter is credited with a standard multiple of the variance of the reported quantities of all other voters. Since a voter cannot know the financial consequences of his or her vote until all other votes are known, voters are allowed to revise their reported quantities iteratively until they are happy with the consequences of their choices. In addition to achieving budget balance, this mechanism overcomes the concern that, under the demand-revealing process, a voter is subject to uncertainty in the payment that will be required for the initial movement induced by his or her vote, and the resulting income uncertainty induces uncertainty in willingness to pay for subsequent movements. Under the assumption that each voter assumes that others will not respond to any change that he or she makes in reported quantity, the Groves–Ledyard mechanism motivates voters to report quantities that yield an efficient outcome.

The principal difficulty with the Groves–Ledyard mechanism is that its assumption that voters will not expect others to change their reported quantities in response to changes in their own reported quantities is not plausible (Greenberg, MacKay, and Tideman 1977). Furthermore, the problems that it solves (a lack of budget balance and income effects inducing uncertainty in willingness to pay) are not worth worrying about.

6. Conclusion

Revelation of the preferences of voters for public activities can be sought in a number of different ways: by structuring a bargaining process, by offering insurance against uncertainty, by allowing voters to trade influence over one issue for influence over another, or by allowing voters to acquire influence over public activities through individual sacrifice.

Bargaining has the advantage of accommodating every conceivable pattern of preferences and generating Pareto improvements whenever agreement is reached. The general difficulty with bargaining over public activities is the near impossibility of securing agreement as the number of persons who must agree increases. Wicksell sought to overcome this problem by requiring "near-unanimity" but not complete unanimity to pass a spending program. This means that public activities can be imposed on unwilling voters.

Eliminating the element of coercion, Ferejohn, Forsythe, and Noll developed a system that overcomes the bargaining problem by using preset cost shares and allowing the set of persons who will participate in the financing of a public activity to vary. This is workable but less than completely efficient because not all worthwhile activities will secure agreement, and some people will be excluded from the benefits of some activities.

Mechanisms that make use of uncertainty in the direction of movement of a public decision have something in common with schemes of division in which one person divides and the other chooses. Just as a divider divides fairly when he or she does not know which piece will go to whom, one might expect a voter to be truthful if a reported valuation could be used either for charging or compensation. Unfortunately, the parallel is not perfect. A divider who makes one piece clearly larger than the other can expect to receive the smaller piece. A person who asks for excessive compensation, on the other hand, can have some hope of receiving it. Mechanisms that employ uncertainty in the direction of movement motivate truthful responses only if voters are completely risk averse or if they believe that the probabilities of movement in the two possible directions are equal.

In the Hylland and Zeckhauser system of influence points, what motivates restraint in valuations is the rising marginal cost of influence, which results from a voter's "influence" over a parameter being defined as the square root of the number of points that the voter assigns to it. This scheme motivates voters to reveal the relative intensities of their concerns for different continuous parameters of public activity. It does not reveal the intensity of a voter's concern about public activities compared to money or private goods.

The demand-revealing process developed by Clarke motivates people to report the intensities of their feelings about public activities relative to money or private goods, without assuming that the probabilities of different outcomes are known in advance. This is accomplished through marginal cost pricing. The prices can be paid in money, time, or anything else that can be aggregated.

The demand-revealing process does not achieve budget balance, but the departures from budget balance are inconsequentially small. It does not achieve Pareto improvements, but statistical analysis of preferences can be used to compensate for predictable effects that are correlated with any voter characteristics that are permissible determinants of taxes and compensation.

No system for eliciting and aggregating voters' preferences for public activities achieves the ideal of selecting all worthwhile activities, only worthwhile activities, and financing all worthwhile activities as Pareto improvements. Every system needs to be operated within a constitutional framework that protects individual rights.

PART III

Electoral politics

CHAPTER 12

The spatial analysis of elections and committees: Four decades of research

PETER C. ORDESHOOK

It has been more than thirty-five years since the publication of Downs's (1957) seminal volume on elections and spatial theory and more than forty since Black and Newing (1951) offered their analysis of majority rule and committees. Thus, in response to the question "What have we accomplished since then?" it is not unreasonable to suppose that the appropriate answer would be "a great deal." Unfortunately, reality admits of only a more ambiguous response.

It is true that developments in the spatial analysis of committees and elections has covered considerable ground since 1957. Beginning with Davis and Hinich's (1966) introduction of the mathematics of Euclidean preferences, Plott's (1967) treatment of contract curves and symmetry, and Kramer's (1972) adaptation of Farquharson's (1969) analysis of strategic voting in committees with spatial preferences, many of Downs's and Black and Newing's ideas have been made rigorous and general. The idea of spatial preferences – of representing the set of feasible alternatives as a subset of a m-dimensional Euclidean space, of labeling the dimensions "issues," of assuming that people (legislators or voters) have an ideal preference on each issue, and of supposing that each person's preference (utility) decreases as we move away from his or her m-dimensional ideal policy – is now commonplace and broadly accepted as a legitimate basis for modeling electorates and parliaments. Moreover, since Weisbergh and Rusk's (1970) initial application of multidimensional scaling, considerable advances have been made in developing statistical methodologies for measuring those preferences within electorates (see, for example, Aldrich and McKelvey 1977; Enelow and Hinich 1982; Poole and Rosenthal 1984; Chu, Hinich, and Lin 1993) and legislatures (Poole and Rosenthal 1985, 1991; Hoadley 1986).

At the same time, spatial analysis has moved only modestly beyond modeling the simplest possibilities – two-candidate plurality rule elections, exogenously imposed amendment voting agendas, and the formation of majority parliamentary coalitions. Although there are any number of specialized models and empirical case studies, there remains preciously

247

little generalized theory about alternative institutional structures or experience with applying elements of spatial theory to more complex political systems to which we can refer when contemplating the design of political institutions for, say, newly emerging democracies. What, for example, can we say about party-list proportional representation systems employing two or more multimember districts or systems with multiple candidates and runoff provisions that matches the theoretical generality and simplicity of the median voter theorem? What do we know about, say, those political systems, including our own, in which policy cannot be imposed by a single victorious candidate but must instead be approved by multiple branches of government, each of which answers to voters under different rules? Where are the definitive theorems about committee processes that allow for the endogenous determination of such things as voting agendas and subcommittee jurisdictions? Indeed, do we even know whether such results are possible or desirable?

Although we are beginning to address such questions, spatial analysis suffers from some deficiencies that are sufficiently serious so as to make it uncomfortable defending it against the charge of failing to produce the volume of ideas that we could reasonably anticipate in thirty or forty years (for a sense of the rate of progress, the reader can consult my 1976 survey of the literature as it existed in the early seventies and Mueller's 1989 more general survey of public choice). Some of these deficiencies, especially those that pertain to the adequacy of a spatial representation of preferences and the limited institutional structures considered, apply to research on both committees and elections. Other deficiencies are unique to one area or the other. On the other hand, I also want to argue that spatial analysis has altered fundamentally the way we think about voting, elections, and parliaments, and that both implicitly and explicitly it contributes much to those who study democratic politics.

1. Fundamental theoretical achievements

1.1 Social choice

It is tempting to focus on fundamental theorems when surveying a mathematically deductive field with as extensive a literature as spatial analysis (for a comprehensive bibliography, see Coughlin 1992). Surprisingly, though, there are few results that warrant the label "fundamental." There is, of course,

- Black's (1958) theorem about the existence of a Condorcet winner (roughly, if voters have preferences that can be scaled along a single-issue dimension, the median preference is a Condorcet winner – an outcome that defeats every other one in a majority vote);

- the Davis–Hinich–Plott–Sloss (1966, 1967, 1973) generalizations to multidimensional issue spaces (roughly, a Condorcet winner exists if and only if a multidimensional median exists, which requires a very special class of preference distributions; for subsequent refinements see Davis, De Groot, and Hinich 1972; McKelvey and Schofield 1986);
- the McKelvey (1976, 1979) and Schofield (1978) "chaos" results about intransitive social preferences (roughly, if no Condorcet winner exists, the social preference order under majority rule is wholly intransitive with spatial preferences – every outcome can be reached from every other one by some paired sequence of votes over feasible outcomes); and
- Caplin and Nalebuff's (1991) proof that something less that two-thirds rule (64 percent to be precise) can ensure a two-candidate spatial equilibrium for a broad class of electoral preference distributions (see also Greenberg 1979 and Schofield 1985, as well as Enelow's discussion of the literature on majority cycles in this volume).

These theorems, though, have less to do with modeling elections or legislatures than with describing the social preference order as it is defined by majority rule and its variants. Although the labels attached to things convey the impression that these results concern elections or legislatures – candidates choosing platforms, voters choosing between platforms, legislators voting over agendas, and parliamentary bodies negotiating coalitions or governments – those results tell us more about the abstract properties of majority rule applied to Euclidean preferences than anything else. Converting these analyses into models of actual political processes requires greater attention to institutional structure and to the strategic imperatives that alternative structures allow. Indeed, as McKelvey (1979, 1106) himself argues, "any attempt to construct positive descriptive theory of political processes based on majority rule . . . must take account of particular institutional features of these systems, as the social ordering by itself [and by implication, the analyses that focus exclusively on the properties of that ordering] does not give much theoretical leverage."

It is here – supplying institutional detail and giving meaning to an abstract characterization of social preference orders – that the analysis of elections and of committees diverge. Different institutions present us with different restrictions on choice, different relationships between choice and outcomes, different strategic opportunities, and different analytic challenges. The theoretical implication of McKelvey's argument, though, is that the spatial analysis of committees and elections is but a specific application of game theory – of ideas about strategies, extensive and strategic forms, and equilibria – where that application's form is determined by the institution under investigation. Spatial analysis offers a specific characterization of the preferences of some decision makers (voters and committee members) and of the strategies of others (candidates). However, we can say that we possess a model of an election, a parliament, or a legislative committee only after we take into account those features of the situation that define the relationship between choice and outcomes and that structure the interrelationships among different decision makers.

The limitations of spatial analysis we soon describe, then, are of two types. First, there are those things that pertain to the adequacy of the spatial assumption itself – the adequacy of a Euclidean conceptualization of issues and individual preferences and the extent to which relevant decision makers can be said to operate within the same spatial conceptual framework. Second, there is the adequacy of the models we use to describe institutional structure – the adequacy of the game theoretic description of the things that structure choices and dictate the correspondence between choices and outcomes over which spatial preferences are defined.

1.2 Committees

The issue for committees is understanding the nature of cooperative (coalitional) agreements, how those agreements are sustained when they must be self-enforcing, how alternative procedural rules influence final outcomes, and how the messages of voters as expressed in elections are transformed into public policy within a legislature or parliament. We cannot review that literature in detail here except to highlight a few general things.

The usual and simplest approach to the spatial analysis of committees is to suppose that members of the committee are finite in number, have spatial preferences, and must choose a policy in the policy space using some exogenously determined rule such as unconstrained majority rule bargaining, a binary agenda (e.g., an amendment agenda), or issue-by-issue voting. In the case of the first alternative – if the committee is assumed to be unconstrained by any explicit procedural rule aside from the provision that a majority coalition can dictate any outcome – there is an immediate correspondence between that committee's structure and the usual context of social choice theory's analysis of majority rule. The usual cooperative solution hypothesis for a simple majority rule game is the *core* – the set of outcomes that are undominated in a majority vote by any other. Thus, although a Condorcet winner does not correspond identically to the core (a Condorcet winner is the core because it dominates all other alternatives whereas an element of the core need not be a Condorcet winner), the correspondence is close enough to tell us that with spatial preferences, a nonempty core exists, for the most part, only if a Condorcet winner exists (for precise relationships, see Sloss 1973) – only if the distribution of ideal points within the committee satisfies some strong regularity conditions (Davis and Hinich 1966, 1967; Plott 1967; Davis, DeGroot, and Hinich 1972; Kramer 1973; McKelvey and Schofield 1986; again, see Enelow's survey in this volume).

Prior to the focus on Euclidean preferences, judgments about the severity of the likelihood of a nonempty core or a Condorcet winner – of being able to make an unambiguous prediction about final outcomes – were based on two things: (1) since the core is empty for constant-sum cooperative games, an assessment of whether the committee's environment is constant sum; and (2) tabulations of the relative frequency of cyclic social preferences (i.e., for a committee of a given size and for a given number of alternatives, what is the probability, if all preference orders are equally likely, that the social order is transitive?). Neither of these approaches, though, gave much general insight because, first, a nonconstant-sum environment is merely a necessary but not a sufficient condition for a nonempty core, and, second, the assumption of equiprobability is merely a null-model assumption without an empirical referent. But once McKelvey (1976) addressed this problem in a spatial context, we understood more fully the potential for intransitivity and empty cores.

The theoretical pervasiveness of social intransitivities caused considerable consternation and led at least one eminent student of the field to conclude that a science of politics may be a practical impossibility (Riker 1980). However, the fact that a wide class of games possessed empty cores came as little surprise to game theorists, who were armed with a variety of hypotheses – V-sets, bargaining sets, kernels, value theory, and so on – to treat those circumstances in which every outcome can be dominated (defeated in a majority vote) by some other. Unfortunately, all such hypotheses suffer from two inadequacies.

First, these ideas are based on ad hoc assumptions about bargaining and the properties of outcomes, which derives from the practical difficulties of modeling most interesting cooperative processes using extensive- or strategic-form representations. Although it is important to make predictions not only about coalitions and outcomes but also about how agreements are enforced, not all cooperative processes can be reduced to some analytically tractable extensive- or strategic-form game, which is what we require for the study of this subject (for political models that examine enforcement, see Baron and Ferejohn 1987; Bianco and Bates 1990; Niou and Ordeshook 1990, 1994; McKelvey and Reisman 1991). Indeed, the study of parliamentary and legislative coalitions seems resistant to such models owing to the complexity of the processes within these institutions (on the other hand, see Baron 1991 for one such extensive form model of parliamentary government formation). Thus, as a substitute for complexity (and, in all likelihood, as a substitute for equally ad hoc assumptions that would need to be imposed to form a tractable model to study enforcement) the game theorist imposes the ad hoc assumptions upon which cooperative coalition theory rests such as equally probable coalitions, and internal and external stability (for an attempt to bring some axiomatic coherence to this literature, see Schwartz 1990).

The second problem with cooperative solution theory derives from the first. Because that theory does not model the institutional context of bargaining, we cannot judge it as we do an extensive- or strategic-form model – by how well assumptions model institutional structure. Instead, aside from results about existence or uniqueness, we can only judge a particular solution hypothesis by seeing whether its predictions are "reasonable." Unfortunately, the traditional framework of cooperative game theory – games in characteristic function form – provide too abstract a basis for judging reasonableness; fortunately, the spatial analysis of majority voting games gives us what we need. Not only do we learn that the core is almost always empty with spatial preferences but we also learn that the V-set and the several bargaining sets offer predictions that are unsupported by experimental and empirical evidence (see Fiorina and Plott 1978; McKelvey, Ordeshook, and Winer 1979; and for a general survey of the experimental literature employing spatial preferences, McKelvey and Ordeshook 1990b). And although we do not yet have a wholly general and universally accepted hypothesis about coalition formation for even simple majority games, spatial preferences provide an important arena for such explorations (Schofield 1985; Bennet and Zame 1988; Sharkey 1990) since it is there that we can learn also whether a solution hypothesis matches the experimental literature and whether its predictions give us insight into actual parliamentary coalition processes (see, for example, Ordeshook and Winer 1980; Laver and Schofield 1990).

With respect to substantive accomplishments, the spatial analysis of committees, as revealed by Poole and Rosenthal's (1985, 1991) historical study of voting in the U.S. Congress, is that its conceptualization of preferences allows an especially convenient summary of issues, ideology, and legislative party alignments (see also Hoadley 1987). Using all roll calls from all congresses beginning with the first, Poole and Rosenthal portray the emergence and disappearance of issues, the formation and dissolution of parties, and the correspondence between ideology and public policy choices, so as to provide a geometric representation of American political history as that history is reflected in the issues that arise in the Congress and in the legislators' votes on them.

The contributions of a spatial perspective would be slight, though, were those contributions limited to developing an ad hoc solution theory and facilitating the development of methodologies to measure itself. In fact, its primary contribution to our understanding of legislative and parliamentary processes is the framework it provides for studying the various procedures committees can use to reach a decision. In particular, spatial preferences serve as an especially convenient structure for analyzing such things as the manipulation of outcomes by the selection of a voting agenda, presidential vetoes, the influence of bicameralism, and government formation in parliaments. With proofs about an all-encompassing social intransitivity as common starting points, we can better understand, for example,

- the extent to which bicameralism limits outcomes relative to a unicameral legislature (briefly, the greater the spatial separation of preferences in the two legislative chambers, the more likely is a stable outcome to exist and the more likely is the status quo to be preserved; see Hammond and Miller 1987, 1989; Tsebelis 1993; and, extending some of these perspectives to the study of federalism, Weingast 1993),
- how parliamentary procedures such as issue-by-issue voting can yield stability (a stable point – the median on each issue – exists if preferences are separable [Kramer 1972; Shepsle 1979; Shepsle and Weingast 1981] but such a point need not exist if preferences are not separable and committee members are strategic [Kramer 1972 and Denzau and Mackay 1981; for relevant experimental evidence, see McKelvey and Ordeshook 1984; Wilson 1986]),
- how strategic voting might limit the power of an agenda setter (briefly, although McKelvey's 1976 study of global intransitivities implies that agendas can be designed to reach any outcome if all voters vote sincerely, final outcomes are limited to the uncovered set of the alternatives on the agenda if voters are strategic; see Miller 1980; Shepsle and Weingast 1984; McKelvey 1986),
- how a setter's power is increased by expanding the class of agendas at his disposal (normal congressional agendas do not necessarily pit the winner of the previous vote against a new

alternative. Thus, they are not of the amendment agenda type and this increased flexibility enables a dictatorial agenda setter to reach outcomes that lie outside of the uncovered set [Ordeshook and Schwartz 1987]), and

- the circumstances under which strategic voters vote sincerely and, therefore, the circumstances under which it is impossible to ascertain the sophistication of committee members (Austen-Smith 1987).

Although much of what we know about agendas does not presuppose spatial preferences, stripped of the Euclidean topology on outcomes and preferences, our theoretical results would lack geometric intuition and would confront the reader with an even greater array of uninterpreted notations and definitions. More substantively, this literature, taken as a whole, not only reveals the importance of institutional structure but alerts us to the likelihood that many if not most of the interesting battles in a legislature or parliament occur over the selection of rules and procedures. In fact, although an institutional structure, once established, can either induce stability or limit the range of possible outcomes, the power of institutions to manipulate final outcomes implies that group preferences over institutions are subject to the same social intransitivities that we can ascribe to simple majority rule with spatial preferences over policy (Coleman and Ferejohn 1986).

It is here, then, that we begin to see the role of constitutions and social norms. If the alternative rules for selecting a final outcome inherit the intransitivity we ascribe to outcomes, if the rules for selecting those rules inherit the same thing, and so on, then we confront an infinite regress in which it becomes impossible to argue that institutions can so structure political process as to induce stability. Indeed, not only is stability and prediction impossible, but, in more practical terms, it becomes impossible for society to choose (although, to confuse matters further, failing to choose can be conceptualized as a choice). One resolution of such a regress – one way to avert the presumed irrationality or inefficiency of never choosing – is to terminate it through convention (tradition or norms). In the event that such conventions do not exist, society must try to invent them, where among these invented conventions are the things we call political constitutions. Thus, although our route seems indirect, the spatial analysis of committees and social choice takes us to a core question in political theory – how society chooses conventions, and why certain conventions "stick" whereas others do not.

Of course, it is unreasonable to require that spatial analysis alone answer such questions. As we noted earlier, spatial analysis is but a specific application of a more general theoretical structure, game theory, and we must appeal to other elements of that theory (e.g., the properties of alternative equilibria, individual beliefs, and conjectures) to learn why some rules prevail and others do not (Ordeshook 1992; Niou and Ordeshook 1994). Nevertheless, we can offer criticisms of the literature on committees that parallel those we offer later of the spatial analysis of voting and elections. First, with but a few exceptions (see, for instance, the exceptions discussed in Section 3 of this essay), only the simplest institutional forms are examined – simple coalitional processes, simple amendment agendas (despite the fact that legislatures rarely use this procedure except for the simplest circumstances, although see Ordeshook and Schwartz 1987; Banks 1989a), rules that are imposed exogenously (but see Banks and Gasmi 1987 for preliminary analysis of endogenous agenda formation), and legislative subcommittees that abide by rigidly adhered to restrictions on the issues in their domain.

Second, the assumption that legislators or deputies have spatial preferences over policy appears to preclude a full treatment of the relationship between their actions and the actions of those who elect them. The preferences of representatives derive presumably from the preferences of their constituents. Assuming otherwise is to admit the possibility of being inconsistent with the usual assumption that the primary goal of election candidates is to win. That is, it seems inconsistent to suppose that politicians, when acting as legislators or as parliamentary deputies, act in accordance with personally held, well-defined policy preferences, but, when acting as candidates, wholly ignore those preferences and simply adhere to equilibrium strategies defined by the electorate's preferences and the relevant election rule. Specifically, if the electorate's preferences yield an intransitive social order – the essence of McKelvey and Schofield's analysis of majority rule – then what is the basis for supposing that the preferences of a representative are otherwise?

There is, then, a serious theoretical disjuncture between the spatial analysis of legislative and parliamentary committees and that of elections. This disjuncture awaits closure, but even if it can be achieved it is anything but certain that it would sustain a spatial conceptualization of legislative or parliamentary preferences (special assumptions about probabilistic voting are sufficient to ensure a transitive order for the electorate – see, for instance, Ledyard 1981, 1984 and Coughlin 1992 – but rarely does analysis suppose anything but deterministic preferences for legislators). Thus, although the assumption of spatial preferences allows us to structure various questions about, say, the adequacy of cooperative game theoretic solution concepts and to recast our understanding of specific parliamentary procedures, and although Poole and Rosenthal's (1985, 1991) empirical research gives us some confidence that the spatial representation of preferences can be used to summarize important aspects of the issues that the U.S. Congress has confronted in its history, we must remain uncertain as to the full generality of these analyses as models of real legislative and parliamentary institutions and processes.

1.3 Elections

Insofar as the spatial analysis of elections is concerned, that analysis has contributed to our understanding of some fundamental things with respect to two-candidate plurality rule systems. Most fundamentally, we know that there are good reasons for supposing that, for a wide range of circumstances, if two candidates compete in a plurality rule system, they espouse policies near the "center" of the electorate's preference distribution. That is, simple majoritarian processes, even if they do not yield Condorcet winners or some other simple equilibrium of strategies, generate powerful incentives for the approximate convergence of policy by the two candidates or parties that are assumed to be competing.

This centrist tendency of two-candidate winner-take-all elections is established in several ways. All of them begin by formulating an election as a two-player noncooperative game: Typically, citizens are robots who merely choose between voting for a preferred candidate or abstaining; the active players in the election game are candidates whose strategies consist of alternative positions in the policy space. Because Condorcet winners, by definition, cannot be defeated when paired against any other alternative, such a winner is the Nash equilibrium to this game. That is, if both candidates choose the Condorcet winning alternative as their platform, neither candidate has a unilateral incentive to move to some other platform or, equivalently, no party has an incentive to nominate a candidate who advocates a policy other than the Condorcet winner. We can then appeal to those essays, beginning with Black, that assume spatial preferences and that establish sufficient conditions (e.g., unidimensional single-peaked preferences, radially symmetric distributions of preferences) for the existence of such a winner. It is in this literature, then, that we find the median voter theorem, which identifies the electorate's median ideal preference as a Condorcet winner when preferences are unidimensional.

Second, there is the research that substitutes probabilistic voting for the median voter theorem's assumption that voters vote deterministically – for the assumption that small changes in a voter's evaluation of a candidate can effect critically a voter's choice of candidate. Instead, probabilistic voting supposes that the relationship between policy, preference, and choice is continuous. By thus "smoothing" functional relationships and desensitizing outcomes to incremental changes in candidate strategies, the existence of an equilibrium is more readily established (see, for example, Hinich, Ledyard, and Ordeshook 1972; Ledyard 1981, 1984; and, for a general survey of this line of research, Coughlin 1992).

Finally, McKelvey and Ordeshook (1976) and McKelvey (1986), appealing to ideas like Miller's (1980) uncovered set and its derivative concepts, show that even if a Condorcet winner does not exist, but if candidates eliminate dominated strategies, then the candidates continue to adopt centrist policies (see also Feld, Grofman, and Miller 1988; Miller, Grofman and Feld 1989). In fact, we also know that the uncovered set is contained in another set called the Yolk, which generally shrinks as preferences become more dense (Ferejohn, McKelvey, and Packel 1984; Koehler 1990; Tovey 1992a). Thus, although the social preference order might be intransitive, there exist spatial positions that can be judged "better" than others (positions that, as strategies, dominate other strategies), where the adoption of these better positions keeps candidates from wandering "too far" from some center of gravity of preferences, and where "too far" can itself be given precise meaning.

Much of the research that followed Downs, Davis, Hinich, and Plott can be interpreted as ascertaining the robustness of this conclusion about the centrifugal force of winner-take-all elections. After all, there are a great many assumptions that must be satisfied before we can assert that the preceding analyses have much to say about politics. These assumptions include the following:

- only two candidates compete and neither fears the entry of a third;
- candidates are concerned solely with winning rather than with the policy positions they must espouse to win;
- voters are fully informed about the candidate's platforms;
- voters are fully informed about their own preferences;
- candidates are fully informed about the issues that concern voters, voter preferences on these issues, and the relative salience of issues;
- candidates do not deliberately render their platforms ambiguous even if clarity alienates potential support;
- candidates have full spatial mobility and are unconstrained by nomination processes or by the fact that perceptions of candidates change only slowly;
- candidates keep their promises;
- campaign dynamics are irrelevant insofar as we can sustain the assumption that both candidates reveal their platforms simultaneously; and
- all eligible voters vote.

This is a list that is likely to dissuade most people from believing that spatial theory can contribute much to their enterprise. On the other hand:

- Calvert (1987) establishes that even if candidates hold policy preferences, the competitive forces of two-candidate elections compels them nevertheless to converge to policies near the center.

- Shepsle (1972) and McKelvey and Richelson (1974) consider the possibility that candidates might deliberately choose to offer ambiguous platforms; however, if all voters are risk averse, the median preference retains its attraction to candidates.

- Aranson, Hinich, and Ordeshook (1974) establish that if plurality is a random variable whose mean is determined by the candidate's platforms, and if the election is otherwise symmetric, then the maximization of expected plurality and probability of winning are equivalent in the sense that they imply the same election equilibria.

- Austen-Smith and Banks (1989) and Harrington (1991a, 1991b) explore the incentives of candidates to keep campaign promises, and thereby they begin a formalization of the idea of retrospective voting.

- McKelvey and Ordeshook (1985a, 1986) and Bowden (1989) employ the idea of rational expectations to show that even if candidates do not know the precise nature of voter preferences, even if most voters are only imperfectly informed about the candidates' policy positions, and even if all fully informed voters prefer extremist policies, indirect sources of information such as public opinion polls and campaign endorsements are sufficient, in equilibrium, to allow uninformed voters to vote "correctly" and to induce the candidates to centrist policies (see also Ferejohn 1986).

- Lupia (1992) shows how the perspectives developed by McKelvey and Ordeshook (1985a) to treat imperfect information can be extended to analyze voting on referenda in a spatial context.

- Ordeshook (1970), Hinich, Ledyard, and Ordeshook (1972), Ledyard (1981, 1984), and Coughlin (1992) establish that nonvoting, when formulated as a probability of voting, does not necessarily negate the centrist tendency of two-candidate winner-take-all elections, although Hinich (1977) does show that probabilistic voting can lead candidates to converge to the electorate's mean rather than median preference.

- In response to the finding that Condorcet winners and uncovered sets may be difficult to compute and find (Bartholdi, Narasimhan, and Tovey 1990; Tovey 1992b), Kollman, Miller, and Page (1992) show that even if candidates are boundedly rational adaptive decision makers operating in an environment of incomplete information, the median preference exerts a powerful influence on their strategies if those strategies are dictated by some simple search algorithms.

A large experimental literature also demonstrates the robustness of spatial theory's primary results. For example, Collier, McKelvey, Ordeshook, and Williams (1987) demonstrate under a variety of experimental conditions that the median preference exerts a powerful influence on candidate platforms even when voters can vote only retrospectively. Indeed, the median retains its attractiveness even if candidates are rewarded when deviating from it (provided that they realize that reward only if elected) and even if random events perturb their true spatial positions (McKelvey and Ordeshook 1990). Moreover, sophisticated voters, learning that candidates converge, learn also to minimize the cost of voting by choosing to act retrospectively and on the basis of candidate reputations or party labels (McKelvey and Ordeshook 1985b; Collier, Ordeshook and Williams 1989; Williams 1991; Plott 1992).

Admittedly, the attractiveness of centrist policies is weakened by the threat of entry (Palfrey 1984; Greenberg and Shepsle 1987), by the existence of more than two candidates or by voters who can cast preferential ballots (Denzau, Katz, and Slutsky 1985; Cox 1990b), by nonvoting from alienation (Hinich and Ordeshook 1969), by institutional variations that distort the competitive forces generating the alternatives voters confront (Romer and Rosenthal 1978, 1979; Rosenthal 1990), and by the demands of campaign contributors (Aldrich 1983). Nevertheless, despite the caveats and footnotes that must accompany any summary assertion, majoritarian electoral institutions exert a powerful centrifugal force on candidates and parties. If we combine this conclusion with the formal proofs of Duverger's (1959) hypothesis about winner-take-all systems (Palfrey 1989; Fedderson, Sened, and Wright 1990; Fedderson 1992), which assumes that voters vote strategically for viable candidates or outcomes, we find at least one institutional arrangement – winner-take-all elections in which the victorious candidate has a relatively free hand at implementing his or her campaign platform – that yields but a few political parties (two in the abstract equilibrium of the models), all of whom compete with centrist policy platforms.

Of the caveats to this conclusion, though, none is more important than that its validity depends on the assumption that centrist policies exist. The validity of this assumption, in turn, depends on the issues voters use to evaluate candidates. The spatial preference structure assumes, first, that there is a consensus on the criteria (issues) used to evaluate candidates as well as on how public policy and candidate election platforms map into this set of criteria. Second, that structure assumes also that although people's preferences may differ, there is sufficient commonality of interests to allow similar policy preferences as well as agreement about policies that ought to be avoided. Generally, voters are assumed to evaluate candidates and public policy on the basis of some small number (usually one, two, or three) of generalized issues (ideological or otherwise) and ideal points are assumed to cluster sufficiently so that their distribution can be described by standard probability density functions.

There is, though, an alternative to this structure. If voters conceptualize policy in redistributional terms so one person's gain can come only at the expense of someone else, then the usual spatial representation may be inappropriate. Indeed, when the things a government supplies to its citizens are perfectly divisible, transferable, and in constant supply, we can require one dimension for every person or household in society to represent preferences, and ideal points will be widely scattered and located at the vertices of the constraint that defines feasible policy. In this event, there is no reason to suppose that candidates or parties converge (approximately or otherwise) to anything (barring some very specialized assumptions about probabilistic voting, see Coughlin 1992). No proposed coalition is invulnerable to disruption by an appropriately constructed counterproposal, and the only prediction we can offer about final outcomes is that each candidate tries to form some majority coalition and proposes to expropriate all things from those excluded from the coalition.

Thus, the applicability of spatial theory's fundamental theoretical results depends not only on the relevance of a rather special and simple institutional arrangement but also on the types of issues that arise and the structure of preferences over them. Thus, it is essential to understand that the spatial perspective is not intended to be a universal one, but rather a perspective that is only more or less relevant to politics, depending on the nature of the issues that concern society.

2. Fundamental conceptual achievements

If we want to understand better spatial theory's limitations as well as what it contributes to our understanding of politics, we need to consider why it focuses on two-candidate winner-take-all elections. First, there is the fact that the existence of equilibria – at least of pure strategy Nash equilibria – is more difficult to establish when we allow more candidates or more complex institutional arrangements (see, for example, Greenberg and Weber 1985; Greenberg and Shepsle 1987; Cox 1987a, 1990a, 1990b). Suppose we try to model party-list proportional representation systems in which final policy is dictated by a governing parliamentary coalition. If we assume that voters pay some attention to the governing coalitions that form after votes are counted and parliamentary seats allocated, then we are stymied by the fact that we possess only partially satisfactory treatments of coalition formation in committees that allow for the calculation of possibilities in a way that allows unambiguous inferences about the policy consequences of different electoral outcomes, and, thus, that allows an unambiguous definition of best response strategies for voters (for some attempt to grapple empirically with this problem, see Rosenthal and Sen 1973 and 1977, whereas for an initial theoretical excursion, see Baron 1993a).

Second, as political scientists became more adept at game theory, they came to appreciate the necessity for pursuing Farquharson's (1969) agenda of allowing voters as well as candidates to act strategically. But whereas strategic and sincere voting are equivalent in two-candidate plurality elections, the analytic difficulties of allowing strategic voting under nearly any other institutional arrangement at times appear insurmountable, and thus tractable only with heroic assumptions (see, for example, Myerson and Weber 1993). Compounding matters further, of course, is the fact that whenever large numbers of decision makers are allowed to act strategically and when few or none of them possess dominant strategies, then typically there are a multiplicity of equilibria. In this event, it can be a supremely challenging task to characterize all of them, which is what we must oftentimes do before we can begin eliminating certain equilibria as reasonable predictions.

A final explanation for spatial analysis's focus on two-candidate winner-take-all elections is that there does not appear to be any other institutional structure that serves as a convenient focus for research. Moving from the simple winner-take-all format confronts the researcher with a long list of possibilities – the single nontransferable vote (SNTV), approval voting, party-list proportional representation, the single transferable vote (STV), unicameral versus bicameral legislatures, presidential versus parliamentary systems, line-item vetoes – so that every research paper threatens to assume the character of being but a highly specialized (i.e., narrow) creature.

This is not to say that we cannot find valuable contributions to our understanding of alternative or more realistic institutional arrangements.

- Austen-Smith and Banks (1988), for example, establish the strategic complexity inherent in proportional and parliamentary systems as well as the fact that, owing to strategic voting, proportional representation systems need not produce an allocation of seats across parties that matches the distribution of preferences.

- Hinich and Ordeshook (1974) show how the median voter theorem can be adapted to predict the policy biases of an electoral college as compared to a direct vote, and show, in particular, that although the electoral college can be credited with biasing policy in the first half of this century, the increasing homogeneity of the country has virtually eliminated the main sources of bias today.

- Cox (1984a, 1984b, 1987a, 1990a, 1993) makes a concerted effort at modeling alternative voting systems so as to contrast equilibria in them with those found in winner-take-all systems. Of special note is his classification of election systems that yield convergent equilibria and those that yield divergent ones (Cox 1990a, 1990b: briefly, convergence is less likely in systems that allow voters to express second, third, etc. preferences or that give voters few votes relative to the number of seats and candidates), as well as his analyses of strategic voting under SNTV that provides a theoretical explanation for Reed's (1991) finding in Japan of an apparent equilibrium of $s+1$ competitive candidates, where s is the number of seats in an election district (Cox 1993; see also Osborne and Slivinski 1993; and for a survey of earlier research into multicandidate elections, Shepsle 1991).

- Baron (1993) explores the positions of parties in a parliamentary system with proportional representation and offers a sequential bargaining model in which those positions diverge in accordance with our empirical understanding of the consequences of party-list proportional representation, and where the extent of that divergence depends on the process whereby government coalitions are negotiated.

It is true that these analyses rely on specialized assumptions. The models of Austen-Smith and Banks, and Hinich and Ordeshook are one-dimensional and Baron's is two-dimensional; Austen-Smith and Banks assume a transferable good among voters, while they, like Baron, allow only three parties; and Cox's analysis of SNTV assumes that candidate positions are fixed. Each essay, then, is but an incremental advance and none provides a general theoretical result. Nevertheless, we can see in them spatial theory's potential for contributing to our understanding of even these more complex political processes. First, and as I have already noted, it offers a formal conceptualization of individual preferences that links political theory to economic theory (Klevorick and

Kramer 1973; Kramer 1973; Boylan, Ledyard, and McKelvey 1993) and thereby promises a rigorous synthesis of these two disciplines.

Second, because spatial analysis formulates election competition as a game, it brings to the analysis of elections all the tools of game theory as well as an appreciation of the ambiguities inherent in decision contexts in which people's fates are interdependent (e.g., the implications of multiple equilibria, the role of coordination in equilibrium selection, the ambiguities in extensive form representations of social processes). Game theoretic reasoning in the study of elections, moreover, compels us to consider issues that might otherwise be ignored, such as strategic voting in mass electorates. Indeed, it is not unreasonable to argue the profound importance of this contribution as we begin to try to understand not only how political elites might respond to alternative institutional structures but also how "ordinary" citizens respond to them as well.

Third, and somewhat paradoxically, spatial analysis deepens our understanding of politics by its failure to resolve some issues. One of the most pervasive findings of the literature that seeks to identify issues and measure preferences using multidimensional scaling is that, regardless of the electorate under consideration, only one or two issues is required generally to represent preferences (see, for instance, Enelow and Hinich's [1984] and Poole and Rosenthal's [1984] analysis of American voting, Poole and Rosenthal's [1985, 1991] study of issues in the U.S. Congress, and Chu, Hinich, and Lin's [1993] analysis of spatial preferences in Taiwan). On the other hand, more direct evaluations of voter perceptions and of candidate and party platforms suggest that the number of issues greatly exceeds this small number (see, for example, Aldrich and McKelvey 1977, and Hsieh and Niou 1993). Thus, spatial analysis raises important questions about the very meaning of the concept of an issue, about the meaning of public opinion, and about the relationship between public policy and people's evaluations of policy. Enelow and Hinich (1984) and Hinich and Pollard (1981) offer a distinction between "actionable issues" and issues in some basic policy space in which voters somehow imbed actionable issues. The analysis and conceptualization of this idea of multiple layers of issue spaces, though, remains abstract and fails to address such basic matters as how voters connect these layers or even how political elites might try to manipulate the connections. Of course, it may be unreasonable to require that spatial theory alone address such matters. At the very least, then, it is important to appreciate that spatial theory makes evident a research matter that, although fundamental to our understanding of politics, has gone largely unnoticed by researchers who employ different conceptual tools.

Fourth, a spatial conceptualization provides a convenient basis for comparing the performance of alternative institutions. As suggested throughout this essay, the questions we can hope to ask and answer include: Which voting systems satisfy various welfare criteria, such as ensuring the selection of a Condorcet winner when such a winner exists? What are the implications of direct democracy devices such as the town meeting and popular referenda as compared to the indirect mechanisms of representative democracy? What is the influence of such things as bicameralism, presidential vetoes, and legislative subcommittees on final outcomes? Without a spatial topology on preferences, the comparison of outcomes is difficult and an evaluation of the welfare consequences of any difference – a qualitative evaluation of the meaning of "significant difference" – nearly impossible to form (see, for example, Tsebelis's 1993 use of spatial analysis to address the debate over the virtues of presidential versus parliamentary government).

Finally, we should appreciate what even the basic elements of spatial theory tell us about the very foundations of democratic theory. Although the median voter theorem is the best-known result, it is in fact not the most important. That theorem merely establishes a sufficient condition for a rather specialized type of equilibrium. Instead, the most important result appears when we compare the policies likely to prevail in simple plurality rule elections with those likely to prevail in cooperative committees with those likely to prevail in committees using restrictive binary agendas. Specifically, if preferences are Euclidean, then the theoretical prediction is that all three abstract institutional mechanisms yield outcomes that fall within the same subset of the policy space – the uncovered set or some nearly geometrically equivalent subset (although it makes use of a number or results – see, for instance, McKelvey and Ordeshook 1976, and Shepsle and Weingast 1984 – the formal structure of this argument is best summarized in McKelvey 1986).

Among the many things this result accomplishes is that it answers a fundamental question about representation. Specifically, it tells us that, in principle at least, we should be indifferent between having policy determined by a two-candidate election and by the entire electorate debating matters using simple majority rule. Because this latter possibility is impractical, we can view two-candidate elections as a practical solution. Moreover, to the extent that preferences within a legislature mirror those of the electorate, we should also be indifferent between letting the legislature determine outcomes, using whatever agendas it might choose to give coherence to its deliberations, and letting the electorate choose, using agenda procedures of its own design. Once again, then, legislative representation can be viewed as a practical response to the fact that electorates of even a few million persons cannot duplicate the New England town meeting.

Spatial theory, then, provides us with a basic null model of democracy, against which we can compare realistic alternatives and answer such questions as: How great a distortion in the equivalence of these three forms is occasioned by the fact that few voters pay much attention to the policies that legislators enact? What distortions arise owing to alternative schemes of districting and alternative methods of conducting elections? Are there representation schemes that allow a political system to approximate, in terms of final outcomes, a wholly collegial electorate?

3. Science and engineering

Despite spatial theory's accomplishment, we cannot escape the fact that its formal results impose assumptions that depreciate immediate practical application. Anyone trying to use them to convince a constitutional reformer, for example, that he or she ought to prefer one type of political institution rather than another will meet with failure, if not a sense of frustration. Of what interest is it to know that plurality rule induces centrist policies provided that some list of ten or so assumptions are satisfied? Where are the results that assist reformers who must try to establish stable political institutions in the deteriorating economies of the successor states of the former Soviet Union? Can we say whether large or small election districts under SNTV best facilitates the development of political parties? Does spatial theory tell us anything about how to construct a viable federal government with corresponding election rules in an ethnically heterogeneous society? What advice can we offer about alternative methods of electing a president, or even about whether to adopt a presidential or parliamentary system, that students using less analytical methods and perspectives cannot also provide?

In fact, the problem here has less to do with any inherent limitation of spatial theory than it does with the character of political science itself and with an imperfect understanding on the part of formal theorists of their ultimate objective. Once we appreciate this objective and the way it is achieved, then we can better appreciate spatial theory's contribution – actual and potential.

Anyone familiar with electoral systems in even a few randomly selected countries appreciates that such systems come in great variety. Even if we restrict ourselves to the most basic elements of their description, we have at least the following: single-member districts using simple plurality rule; single-member districts using majority rule with a runoff if no one receives a majority on the first ballot; multimember districts using party-list proportional representation; multimember districts using a single nontransferable vote; multimember districts using a single transferable vote; and single or multimember districts using preferential voting such as the alternative vote or approval voting. And our descriptions can be made more complicated by considering thresholds parties must surpass before securing representation, alternative algebraic formulas for allocating parliamentary seats, the possibility of preelection party coalitions and pooling of votes, and the nature of the offices being filled. Not only must we consider whether the voter is voting for a unitary president, a collegial presidency, members of a city council, or deputies to a parliamentary body, we must also consider the ultimate relationship of these offices to policy, since, presumably, it is this relationship that provides the voter's ultimate motivation. Finally, to make matters more complicated still, we must consider that we can easily think of situations in which voters, when entering the voting booth, are asked to participate in two or more of these variations simultaneously.

Clearly, the character of the strategic environments in which candidates and parties compete are nearly endless, and it is unreasonable to suppose that spatial theorists can model every one of them or that a handful of "fundamental" theorems can summarize the differences among them with respect to strategic imperatives of candidates, voters, and political elites. Even a cursory reading of Cox's (1990b) survey of research on multicandidate spatial competition should convince the reader that not only does the variety of election laws allow for a near infinitiy of assumptions about candidate objectives and voter decision rules, but also that simple theoretical generalizations about the structure of competition are unlikely to be forthcoming.

Nevertheless, to see what can be done, consider Romer and Rosenthal's (1978, 1979) study of school board referenda in Oregon. Briefly, the setting for their study is a referendum in which a school board can offer the electorate a take-it-or-leave-it proposal, which if rejected by voters results in the imposition of a generally undesirable reversion outcome – frequently, a school budget of zero (for a general summary of this line of research, see Rosenthal 1990).

Theoretically, their study demonstrates little more than that, by presenting voters with such a proposal those who control the initial proposal have a powerful influence on final outcomes. Specifically, a school board that seeks to increase expenditures can secure passage of a proposal that exceeds the spending increase most preferred by the median voter, which is only logical since voters must choose between a "bad" alternative and a wholly unacceptable one. But if Romer and Rosenthal fail to establish a theorem that establishes a wholly unanticipated consequence, what do they accomplish? We might say that they test their model and find support for its associated hypotheses. But so what, and what hypothesis would we reject if the data failed to support their model? Certainly, we would not be prepared to reject the rational choice paradigm itself. Instead, we (and they) would probably argue that "other factors" mitigated against their model's strategic imperatives, at which point their results might have served primarily as input for doctoral dissertations searching for these factors.

In fact, Romer and Rosenthal's contribution is more fundamental than the proof of some new theorem or falsification of some previously accepted hypothesis. Instead, they give us confidence that spatial theory's perspectives have general relevance and that it provides a way to conceptualize preferences and to model the strategic environment engendered by specific institutional structures. That is, they give us confidence that we can usefully combine a spatial conceptualization of preferences and policy with a game theoretic model of alternative institutional structures when trying to assess the implications of those structures. In addition, they expand our experience with confronting reality with purely abstract tools and with an imaginative recombination of those tools. As such, then, they contribute greatly to what ought to be a fundamental goal of political science as a profession, political engineering – the design and assessment of political institutions.

Romer and Rosenthal's approach does not stand alone. Another innovative demonstration of the applicability of spatial analysis that directly applies the median voter theorem is Klevorick and Kramer's (1973) study of the German regional assemblies used to control pollutants in the Rhine river basin, the *Genossenschaften*. Within each *Genossenschaften*, the voting weights of each industrial and village representative depend on the taxes paid by the relevant entity in the last period, which depend on the tax rate and the amount of pollution each firm and village chooses to produce. The tax rate, in turn, is determined by a majority vote in each *Genossenschaften* and is thereby dependent on the median preference there. But, completing the cycle, this median preference depends on voting weights. So the theoretical question is whether there exists an equilibrium tax – a tax that is a fixed point in the sense that, once all persons adjust their propensity to pollute in accordance with it, the resulting voting weights imply that tax. A characterization of the conditions under which such an equilibrium exists then serves as an important component of any effort to replicate the German experience elsewhere with a similar institutional structure. In the process, moreover, Kramer and Klevorick demonstrate formally how spatial preferences can be derived from preferences of the traditional economic sort – from preferences over consumable goods and profits, combined with constraints on product inputs and production functions (see also Kramer 1973).

Both experimentally and theoretically, this derivation of spatial preferences is developed more fully in Boylan, et al. (1991) and Boylan,

Ledyard, and McKelvey (1993) in a way that allows spatial theory's application to some classic problems of political-economic development. In this model, voters must choose between immediate consumption of a publicly produced good and investing to increase future supply of that good. Marrying the classical economic model of investment and growth to a model of two-candidate competition, where the candidates compete by proposing alternative macroeconomic platforms and voters must weigh future against current consumption, conditions are established for the existence of a two-candidate stationary investment–consumption equilibrium. Moreover, experimental data are offered to suggest that candidates converge to such a policy, at least when voters are fully informed about the relationship between investment and growth.

Like Romer and Rosenthal, this model is important for more than the theorems it offers (which depend critically on fine technical details) or the experimental evidence offered on its behalf (which is subject to the criticism of being little more than a complex IQ test of undergraduate subjects). Because of the model's complexity, theorems describing equilibria impose strong assumptions. It is virtually impossible to derive formally the influence of the model's most interesting parameters (for example, the information voters have, the extent to which the candidates must keep their election promises, or the frequency with which incumbents are allowed to change policy). In this instance, the experimental laboratory seems the only practical device for exploring such matters. What differentiates research here from earlier experimental explorations of election processes (with the possible exception of Plott 1991) is that the stage is now set to use the experimental laboratory as a tool of political institutional design. Since most design problems cannot wait for the development of models and the proof of theorems that apply specifically to them and since such models and theorems are unlikely to be developed in any event, the experimental lab can begin performing the same function in political science as the wind tunnel does in aeronautical engineering.

Each of these studies demonstrates how the spatial analyst's perspective can structure research about political processes and institutions without abandoning scientific rigor. They also demonstrate that we must learn to understand the distinction between and interdependence of engineering and science.

I began this essay by noting that spatial analysis is but a specific application of game theory and that many of its limitations and accomplishments are those of that theory. If the spatial analyst has not fully incorporated features of, say, incomplete information and uncertainty into his models and if he considered only a few of the strategic environments that we think are important, it is largely because the analytic challenges that such circumstances present are severe. Nevertheless, there are inadequacies that derive from an imperfect understanding of our craft and the incorrect incentives that misunderstanding establishes.

Presently, journals are inundated with manuscripts employing the latest faddish techniques and concepts – repeated games, signaling games, sequential rationality, and so on. Although some of this research promises to deepen our understanding of processes that have heretofore been neglected, too often the display of technical skill is merely a substitute for thinking deeply about a problem and for confronting substantive complexity. Too often research consists merely of an adaptation of a particular idea that yields neither a general result nor anything that relates to some specific empirical phenomena or problem. The rewards from lengthening one's vista are too great to ignore, and they often result in "research" that is little more than the repeated application of some newly learned "hammer" to slightly modified "nails."

Of course, fads die and what frequently remains is a residue of new insights, along with an augmentation of the technical skills of the profession. However, it remains true that with attention focused on mere mathematical manipulations and with promotions arriving most quickly to those who can sustain a stream of publications, the type of research cited in this section is often undervalued. Instead, we find manuscripts with a minimal ratio of meaningful results to notation and in which things loftily proclaimed to be "theorems" are based on such restrictive assumptions that they contribute little to our understanding of anything. It would seem that it is often easier to theorize about a planet X than our own.

The application of game theory and spatial analysis will achieve maturity when practitioners suppress the instinct to begin essays with silly sentences like "assume an infinite sequence of candidates" or "we find an equilibrium such that . . ." and to avoid burdening the reader with notation that promises a degree of generality that is lost with the first assumption. We must learn to devalue notation in favor of theoretical insight and to not ape the mathematicians craft but to develop one of our own.

Nevertheless, we are encouraged not only by the essays reviewed in this section but also by the increasing amount of research directed at classes of elections systems other than simple plurality rule and that are motivated by substantive rather than analytic concerns. Of course, there remain any number of issues concerning party formation and fragmentation or of the advantages and disadvantages of presidential versus parliamentary systems that can only be understood with the rigor that spatial analysis and game theory promises. The case studies upon which our current understanding rests are too few in number to permit definitive conclusions. But to pursue these issues, we must learn to value something in addition to nicely arrayed lemmas and theorems. These are valuable things. But too often, "political scientists" prove theorems about things that are of such a degree of complexity that the resulting lemmas, propositions, and theorems require assumptions of such specificity as to preclude generality and even relevance. If the list of assumptions required to establish a particular result exceeds what can be summarized in a single breath, then we have a good indication that the word "theorem" ought to be banned from the corresponding manuscript. At a minimum we must learn to differentiate between those things that can be stated as general principles (e.g., the median voter theorem, the McKelvey–Schofield results about cycling, Duverger's law) and those things that are merely complex combinations of those principles (e.g., manifestations of strategic complexity owing to incomplete information in particular environments).

At the same time, we must learn to value more practical objectives. Natural science does not progress merely because the phenomena natural scientists study are less complex than social processes (which may be true), nor are the engineering efforts that feed off natural science theory successful merely because they rest on a firm theoretical base. Instead, success derives from the interaction of these enterprises. The search for solutions to practical problems uncovers new problems and empirical regularities that are then subject to general theoretical inquiry and explanation, and theoretical results are "tested" when we try to use them to facilitate the discovery of solutions to practical problems.

Unfortunately, this interplay is largely absent from political science. As a consequence, the proponents of formal political analysis too often fail to differentiate between the things that allow pure theoretical investigation and the things that must be studied without resorting to the mass production of lemmas and theorems. Nevertheless, despite the frequent critical tone of this essay, it should by now be evident that spatial analysis – owing to its general structure, to the well-defined problems it poses, and to its self-evident shortcomings – promises to be fertile ground for the synergy of science and engineering. What remains is merely a better developed interest in solving specific practical problems of institutional design and the rewards that come from doing so.

CHAPTER 13

Multiparty electoral politics

NORMAN SCHOFIELD

1. Plurality or proportional representation

Normatively it might be desirable to use *direct democracy* for all social choices. But there are two main difficulties with the principle that all political decisions should be made by calling on the whole electorate to vote by referendum. The first is the gross inefficiency of requiring voting on every decision. The second is the problem of instability. Much theoretical analysis (some reviewed in this volume) suggests that if there is heterogeneity in the electorate, then the *generic voting paradox* exists. Namely, whatever is proposed can always be beaten by some new majority. The only time this will not occur is when the decision can be described in some way as fundamentally one-dimensional. So for example, if all decisions are defined by left or right, then there can exist an equilibrium or "core" political decision that is characterized by having half the voters on one side and half on the other. If there are two or more dimensions, then typically such an equilibrium or core will not exist. I shall return to this question of instability.

If direct democracy is ruled out, then the alternative is representative democracy. This requires "choice" of an electoral system to determine who shall represent the citizens. One system, namely proportional representation (PR), allocates seats to the various parties in something close to direct proportion with the number of votes garnered by those same parties. That is, the entire country can be viewed as a single k-member constituency, where k is the number of seats. It is usually (though not always) the case that when the number of parties is at least three, then no one party obtains a majority of seats. In this case to pass majority legislation, parties must form alliances, or coalitions. Since these may not be predictable before the election, there is no direct

This essay is based on work supported by NSF Grant SBR-9422548. Thanks are due to Jeff Banks, David Austen-Smith, Shaun Bowler, Dan Korn, Michael Laver, Patrick McNutt and David Nixon for advice and suggestions. Annette Milford kindly assisted in the preparation of this manuscript.

271

connection between the voters' desires, their votes, and the outcomes. "Although a pure PR system gives a House of Representatives that, in some sense, mirrors the electorate, PR itself prevents the citizens from expressing a clear choice for a governmental team." (Duverger 1984, 32). Both Duverger (1984) and Popper (1945, 1988) have argued that this choice criterion is a more important normative principle than the one of proportionality.

My view on this matter is that it is more important that arguments for or against a particular electoral system should be based on the empirical political consequences of the system adopted. Most of this chapter will be devoted to an attempt to understand what these consequences might be.

To set the scene it is worth reminding the reader that most of the political systems in the countries of continental western Europe (as well as Ireland, but not Britain) have used some version of PR since World War II. Rose (1984, 75) estimates an index of proportionality between electoral votes and party (seat) strengths that ranges among the PR systems from .84 (Greece) to .99 (Austria). An index of 1.00 means that electoral strength and seat strength in the House are identical.

A PR system can be viewed as a single parliamentary constituency. Any electoral system that is based on many constituencies tends to have a low index of proportionality and should be viewed as a non-PR system. The simplest one to describe is one termed "plurality" by Taagepera and Shugart (1989), also often called first-past-the-post (FPP). Each constituency elects one member by plurality vote. Where this system is used in a situation with highly disciplined parties such as in Britain, I shall term it the "Westminster system" of electoral choice. More complex non-PR systems exist. In Japan, for example, many constituencies return six or seven members. France uses a complex mix of list PR and plurality, while the Russian election of 1993 used a 50 percent PR and 50 percent plurality rule. The United States, of course, uses a plurality system; however, I shall argue below that weak party discipline in the United States means it cannot be identified with the Westminster model.

One of the "empirical" characteristics that has proved useful in discussing the factionalization of a party system is the "effective" number (Laakso and Taagepera 1979). Suppose that n parties are represented in the House, and the proportion of seats controlled by party i is p_i. The Herfindahl concentration index H is defined to be $\sum_{i=1}^{n} p_i^2$. The effective (seat) number N_s is defined to be H_s^{-1}. The same procedure can be used to determine an effective (vote) number $N_v = H_v^{-1}$.

Clearly in a pure PR system N_v and N_s should be identical. In non-PR systems N_s is typically smaller than N_v, since the effect of the electoral system is to increase the concentration among seat ratios. Thus $N_v - N_s$

Table 1. *Vote (p_v) and seat (p_s) proportions in elections in Britain*

Party	1979		1983		1987	
	p_v	p_s	p_v	p_s	p_v	p_s
Ulster Unionists	.013	.016	.014	.023	.012	.020
Conservatives	.439	.534	.424	.611	.420	.578
Liberals	.138	.017	.137	.026	.128	.026
Social Democrats	–	–	.116	.009	.097	.007
Welsh Nationalists	.004	.003	.004	.003	.004	.004
Irish Nationalists	.006	.003	.018	.003	.006	.006
Scottish National Party	.016	.003	.011	.003	.014	.004
Labour	.369	.424	.276	.321	.307	.352
Others	.014	0	.008	0	.011	–
	$N_v = 2.80$		$N_v = 3.38$		$N_v = 3.38$	
	$N_s = 2.15$		$N_s = 2.18$		$N_s = 2.18$	

gives some idea of the degree of distortion (or nonproportionality) between votes and seats created by the use of a particular electoral system (see Rae 1967 and Rae, Hanby, and Loosemoore 1971 for further discussion of distortion resulting from electoral laws).

Comparing the estimates of effective vote and seat numbers obtained by Taagepera and Shugart (1989) for the mid-1980s gives distortion measures ranging from 0.1 (for Sweden) to 1.1 (for Belgium). Belgium, of course, is highly factionalized in the sense that $N_v = 8.1$ while $N_s = 7.0$. In the countries using electoral systems other than PR, the distortion for the U.S. House of Representatives in 1980 is only 0.1 while in France it is 1.2, in Japan 0.4 and in Australia 0.4. In the three countries based on the Westminster system (Canada, New Zealand, and Britain) the distortion measures based on the figures computed by Taagepera and Shugart (1989) generally exceed 1.0. To see the distorting effect of the Westminster system in the British case more clearly consider Table 1.

It is obvious that the two large parties are much favored in the Westminster system. The Conservative party was able to form a majority single-party government after these three elections. To be nonpartisan, note that the same was true of the Labour party after the 1974 election. In that year, with only 39 percent of the electoral vote, Labour gained a bare majority of one seat (that is, 319 out of 636). Clearly the Liberal party (and the Social Democrats in 1983 and 1987) have suffered under the Westminster electoral system and this is reflected in the distortion index ($N_v - N_s$) of 1.2. It is true, however, as both Popper and Duverger observed, that this system does tend to give rise to a majority party after each election, and in some sense it can be argued that the Westminster

Table 2. *Labour/Conservative vote in Britain*

Election	% Votes for Labour/Conservatives	% Seats of Labour/Conservatives
1970	89.5	98.9
1974, October	75.1	93.8
1979	80.8	95.8
1983	70.0	93.2
1987	72.7	93.0

system appears to give the electorate a "binary" choice over the nature of government.

Duverger's argument for the preferability of the plurality, or Westminster, system is made stronger by his hypothesis (usually known as Duverger's law) that a plurality system results in a two-party system (see Riker 1982b). This law is based in turn on an empirical hypothesis that the mechanical distortion induced by the plurality system (clearly seen in Table 1) is coupled with a psychological effect. That is to say, as voters realize the negligible effect of voting for a small party, they switch to voting for one of the two dominant parties. Any effect of this sort in a PR system would be much muted.

Table 1 presents the effective (vote and seat) numbers N_v and N_s in the three elections in Britain. It is evident that the effective vote number increases between 1979 and 1983, and then stays constant. Although concentration across the array of votes falls quite dramatically between these two elections, the seat concentration hardly changes. Another way of seeing this is to compare the total proportion of votes obtained by the Labour and Conservative parties against the combined number of seats they controlled in the elections. Table 2 presents these data for five elections in Britain between 1970 and 1987. It is difficult to argue that the psychological effect is apparent.

Between 1970 and 1974 the popular vote for the Liberals rose from 7.5 percent to 18.6 percent, presumably in response to Heath's handling of the union unrest of the time. In 1979 some of this protest vote returned to the Conservatives (who increased their popular vote from about 36 to 44 percent). Notice however that in 1983 a large group (nearly 12 percent of those voting) chose the Social Democrats, presumably in preference to the Labour party. This split in the opposition vote gave the Conservatives a much enhanced majority in 1983 of 397 seats out of 650. A strong vote for the Liberal–Social Democrat alliance in 1992 probably kept the Conservatives under Major in power.

Notice one feature of the Westminster electoral system in Britain: relatively small swings of the popular electoral vote, principally to or from the centrist parties, tend to give one or the other of the two larger parties a commanding majority. One theme of much of the discussion of Britain's economic troubles in the 1970s (Brittan 1978; Beer 1982; Olson 1982; Schofield 1993a) was the extent to which the British government could be held hostage by particular private interests or groups protecting their ability to obtain "economic rents." It is entirely possible that this effect was made stronger by the way the electoral system magnified voting swings.

However, an argument could be made that the more important effect of the Westminster electoral system is to maintain or exacerbate the degree of economic conflict between the two principal parties. It is a common inference that in two-party Downsian competition (Downs 1957), the two parties converge toward a policy at the "median" voter. Robertson (1976) noticed that this did not occur in the post-war period in Britain. His later work (Robertson 1987) with the manifesto project (Budge, Robertson, and Hearl 1987) indicated, in particular, that Conservative party manifestos seemed to move to the right in the period from 1959 to 1983. In an attempt to understand this phenomenon, the next section considers a simplified one-dimensional spatial model of party competition under general assumptions concerning the motivations of the parties involved.

2. One-dimensional spatial models of government formation

2.1 Two-party competition

In the simplest possible model, voters have preferred policy positions on a one-dimensional interval, W. The distribution of preferred points is given by a density (or distribution) function, f. Clearly there exists some point, x, called the "median voter position," with 50 percent of the voter-preferred points on either side of x. It is usual to suppose that each voter prefers point y to another point z if y is nearer to the voter's preferred (or bliss) point. Now consider a situation where two parties L (for left-wing or Labour) and R (for right-wing or Conservative) present policy positions to the electorate. Suppose further that the electorate believes that each party will implement its declared policy position. If the electoral distribution f is known to both parties (i.e., is common knowledge), then both can compute the electoral response, say $e(L,R)$ $= (e_L, e_R)$. Here (e_L, e_R) are the shares of votes for the two parties under the profile of declarations, (L,R). If there is a single constituency, then popular votes will be transformed directly into seat proportions $S(L,R)$ = (S_L, S_R), where, by definition, $S_L + S_R = 1$. The Nash equilibrium is a pair of policy strategies (L^*, R^*) that gives no party an incentive to change its declarations, L^* or R^*. That is, L^* is the best policy position for Labour to play against R^*, and vice versa.

In general the payoff (u_L or u_R) to each party will be a function of the two parties' declarations (L,R) and the number of seats they obtain. In a model of pure office seeking each party seeks to win a majority of the seats. So for convenience we could choose $u_L(L,R) = 1$, whenever $S_L > S_R$, $u_L = -1$ if $S_L < S_R$, and $u_L = 0$ if $S_L = S_R$. In this situation of binary competition with office-seeking parties and no electoral risk, the Nash equilibrium is that pair of declarations (L^*, R^*) with L^* and R^* both set at the median voter position, x.

Notice, in the pure office-seeking model, that both parties or candidates are assumed to be identical. By symmetry, if there is a Nash equilibrium then the outcome where both parties adopt the same strategy must be an equilibrium. We can elevate this observation to a general principle.

Symmetry principle: *If parties entering into political competition have identical preferences and beliefs and the game form has a Nash equilibrium, then at least one Nash equilibrium is characterized by identical behavior by the parties.*

We could make the above model more complex but realistic, by supposing that there is electoral risk; that is, the parties are uncertain about the precise nature of the electoral response to the declarations (L,R). It is usual to model the situation by supposing that there are "common knowledge" probability functions (say α_L, α_R), which specify the probabilities that party L or R wins the election when the joint declaration is (L,R). The outcome is now a lottery, $g(L,R)$ whose three components are (1) L wins with probability $\alpha_L(L,R)$ (2) R wins with probability $\alpha_R(L,R)$, and (3) $S_L = S_R$ with probability $1 - \alpha_L(L,R) - \alpha_R(L,R)$. Clearly if the "beliefs" α_L, α_R are symmetric in the sense that $\alpha_L(L,R) = \alpha_R(R,L)$ then by the symmetry principle, we would again expect both parties to adopt a centrist position (Ordeshook, this volume, surveys the extensive literature on models of this kind).

Suppose now that there is no electoral risk and that parties are both office and policy seeking. That is, each party desires the perquisites of government (power) and in addition wishes to implement preferred policy points. In this case, any party that chooses a nonmedian policy can be defeated and so lose the "perquisites" of office. Thus, each party strictly prefers to play the median position. The situation is not much changed if there are a number (k) of constituencies. Under the Westminster, plurality system, k also equals the number of parliamentary seats. Let us rank the constituencies in the order $(f_1, \ldots, f_k)$, where $f_i < f_j$ means that the median voter in constituency f_i is to the left of the median in f_j. Then there is a "median" constituency, say f_m. The Nash equilibrium overall will be determined by the Nash equilibrium in the median constituency, and so again we will obtain "convergent" equilibrium policy declarations that coincide with the median voter position in the median constituency, say x_m. (See Austen-Smith 1986, for a model involving constituencies). Note that office-seeking motivations dominate over policy-seeking motivations, since a party must first *win* a majority to control government policy. If we add electoral risk to the model of office- and policy-seeking parties, then the symmetry principle cannot be invoked to assert that parties adopt centrist positions (since the beliefs of the parties concerning electoral risk may vary). In models of this kind it is usually assumed that party L, say, if it wins the election is then committed to the implementation of its declared policy L and receives a policy payoff (inversely proportional to the distance, $L - L_0$, between its declared and preferred policy point). The lottery $g(L,R)$ can then be evaluated using a von Neumann–Morgenstern expected utility function, which weighs the policy payoff and perquisite of office, say, (σ_L) for Labour and (σ_R) for the Conservatives by the appropriate probabilities, say α_L and α_R. Standard assumptions of continuity and convexity are then used to show existence of equilibrium declarations (L^*, R^*) (see Cox 1984a, for example).

Although Downsian convergence need not occur, it is intuitively clear that the more important is the office-seeking component (that is, the greater is the ratio of the perquisite, σ, to the policy payoff) then the greater will be the degree of convergence.

This method of analysis is usually undertaken in the context of a single constituency (that is, essentially under the assumption of PR). However, we can make some comments on the applicability of the model under a plurality (or Westminster) system. It is reasonable that there is some common knowledge of the ranking $(f_1, \ldots, f_k)$ of the distributions. Thus each party, L or R, might plausibly assume that it will always capture a particular set of constituencies. The conflict between the parties is then concentrated in a set of constituencies whose median voters lie in some central domain of W. It is worth considering the nature of political risk within this domain. In the British case it is evident that both the Labour and Conservative parties can assume that they control certain safe seats (namely those with left-wing median voters for Labour, and right-wing median voters for the Conservatives). In the "swing" constituencies it is probably fine political details as much as overall policy declarations that determine which way the constituencies vote.

This suggests, contrary to the one-dimensional model proposed above, that the political game in the swing, or central, constituencies is of high-dimension. In such a situation, political competition can be very complex to analyze. In particular the probability functions, α_L or α_R, may be discontinuous in the policy variables. In fact there may be no "pure" Nash equilibrium. However, work by Miller (1980), McKelvey (1986), Cox (1987), and Calvert (1987) suggests that parties will choose positions inside a domain called the "electoral uncovered set." Since this set is centrally located in the electoral Pareto set and converges to the core (or generalized electoral median position), these results indicate that a form of "weak convergence," rather than strong Downsian convergence should be expected in the two-party model (see also the discussion by Ordeshook in this volume on the two-party model).

Any model involving policy-seeking parties must also face the serious theoretical problem of "credible commitment." In the pure Downsian or office-seeking model, parties choose policy declarations simply as a means of securing votes. As a consequence, there is no intrinsic reason for the voters to view these declarations as noncredible. However, if voters believe that parties have "hidden" policy objectives, why should they also believe that a party would attempt to implement its declared policy if elected, rather than its "true" preferred policy? Consequently, the model of policy declaration should properly incorporate an analysis of the beliefs of the electorate concerning the credibility of declarations. Because of the importance of this observation, it is worth emphasizing it as a theoretical principle.

Credibility principle: *If parties make promises to the electorate, and the voters know that these promises are costly for parties to keep, then the credibility of these promises must be sustained by a system of beliefs and actions.*

In a two-candidate model with myopic behavior, there is nothing in principle to stop the winning candidate from implementing a desired policy, instead of a declared policy. However, with long-lived parties, rather than one-term candidates, it is possible to model electoral punishment strategies that sustain credibility (see Austen-Smith and Banks 1989; Banks 1990).

2.2 Three-party competition

Now consider the effect of including a third party (labeled C for central) which we may identify with the Liberals to accord with the British case. Let us suppose, counterfactually in the British case, that a PR system is utilized. Since there is only one constituency, there are really only two possible outcomes. For fixed declarations (L, C, R), either C

gains a majority or it does not. If it does, then we may suppose that the Liberals implement their declared position C. No matter what the electoral distribution, it is evident that such an outcome can always be destroyed by either L or R moving closer to the center before the election. Thus, it is plausible that "rational parties" (more concerned with the perquisites of office than policy) would move into the center, to reduce the possibility of the Center party gaining a majority. In a pure office-seeking model with PR, it is reasonable, even under electoral risk, to infer that all three parties will declare in Nash equilibrium the same median position x (or their best guess at this position) and share equally in the perquisites of office. This inference is consistent with the symmetry principle (and with theoretical results by Fedderson, Sened, and Wright 1990).

Note, however, that this argument is based on the assumption that parties are office seeking, in the sense of desiring to belong to government. A family of models have been presented in which parties seek to maximize either the number of votes (or in non- PR systems, the number of seats). See Shepsle 1991 for a general review and Cox 1990b for a more recent theoretical model. It should be clear that vote maximizing and office seeking are quite different motivations when there are three parties. (With two parties these two motivations are identical under majority rule.) To see this, note that it is easy to find examples in European countries (such as Denmark, Sweden, and so forth) where the largest party *does not* belong to government (see the discussion below). Although seat or vote maximization would appear to be the political analogue of the Hotelling (1929) concept of spatial economic competition, it does not make obvious political sense. Moreover, pure political competition over seats or votes need have no Nash equilibrium with three or more parties (see Eaton and Lipsey 1975; Shaked 1975).

Austen-Smith and Banks (1988) have proposed an extremely interesting model of three-party competition involving office-seeking parties who compete for seats, not as an end in itself, but to enter government. The policy space is one-dimensional, but parties have no ex ante policy preferences. That is to say, before a party makes its declarations, it has no interest in the policy outcome. However, after the declarations are made, each party has ex post preferences based (as in the previous models) on the difference between declarations and eventual outcomes. However, parties do have ex ante preferences for government perquisites and have substantiated beliefs about the relationship between their declarations, the electoral response, and eventual government policy. Note however that since all parties have identical preferences before their choice of declarations, the symmetry principle suggests that one Nash equilibrium is given by identical party policies.

There is no evidence that multiparty PR systems give rise to identical party declarations. Moreover, the behavior of parties in such systems generally indicates that parties (and party activists in particular) regard policy as important in its own right. On both empirical and theoretical grounds it appears appropriate to model parties as both office *and* policy seeking.

To model this general political "game" it is necessary to make some assumptions about the nature of the policy outcome given policy declarations. Clearly this will depend on the electoral response. To make the notation somewhat more compact, let us suppose the parties preferred policy points are given by the vector $p = (p_L, p_C, p_R)$, that the vector of preelection policy declarations is $z = (z_L, z_C, z_R)$, and that the popular vote (and thus the relative seat strengths at the election) is given by $e(z) = (e_L(z), e_C(z), e_R(z))$. Suppose that no one party obtains a majority but that each of the parties is committed to implementing its declared policy. Then the center position z_C is a core policy. Given their commitment, no coalition can propose a policy that attains a majority over z_C. That is, with no single-party majority, the policy z_C is at the "political median." A conclusion to be drawn from this is that if there is no single majority party, then the policy outcome will be z_C. Moreover, one may predict that party C belongs to any government that forms. (As an example, the centrist Free Democrats in West Germany have belonged to every government but two.) Notice that if the center party adopts a policy position near enough to the electoral median, then neither L nor R can obtain a majority under PR.

Clearly in order to substantiate these inferences it is necessary to be precise about the assumed balance between policy and office preferences. Laver and Schofield (1990) suggested that it is possible to distinguish between models that are essentially office seeking, but incorporate costs of bargaining over policy differences, and models where the primary motivation is to influence policy through coalition government membership. An example of the former type of model is the one proposed by Axelrod (1970), where parties' true positions are known and coalitions involving "large" policy differences do not form. There are empirical difficulties with Axelrod's proposition, to be discussed in the following section. However, the most severe difficulty is theoretical, resulting from a violation of the following incentive principle.

Incentive principle: *If parties have policy-oriented preferences, as well as beliefs concerning the relationship between their declarations and the eventual policy outcome, then each party will optimize its choice of declarations in the light of its beliefs.*

Even though parties have different policy preferences in Axelrod's model, it is evident that the fundamental office-seeking motivation together with the incentive principle will result in policy convergence. That is to say, if parties believe that the coalition whose declarations are closest together will form, then the incentive principle leads to the inference that parties make declarations that are also close together. Since parties differ in their underlying policy motivations, this inference is independent of the symmetry principle.

Schofield and Parks (1993) have recently examined a model based on Axelrod's insight but satisfying the incentive principle. The key notion is that before choosing their declarations, parties face "political" or "coalition risk" in the sense that neither they nor the electorate know with certainty which coalition will form. Instead of supposing (as do Austen-Smith and Banks 1988) that the government coalition is uniquely determined by the party declarations and election results, Schofield and Parks (1993) assume that the declarations and election results define a political lottery. More precisely, given a profile of declarations (z_L, z_C, z_R) and no majority party, it is assumed that the probability that, say, $\{L,C\}$ forms is inversely proportional to $||z_L - z_C||^2$. The three coalition outcomes then have probabilities $\alpha_{LC}, \alpha_{LR}, \alpha_{RC}$, with all three probabilities summing to one. It is also assumed that each two-party coalition "splits the difference" between its declarations in formulating government policy. In this model the outcome is a political lottery $g(z_L, z_C, z_R)$ across three possible coalition events, each one defined by a probability, a policy outcome, and a vector of perquisites. Assuming von Neumann–Morgenstern expected utility, it is shown that a Nash equilibrium exists. As we might expect, the degree of convergence in party declarations at equilibrium becomes more pronounced the more important are perquisites over policy considerations. Moreover, if one of the noncentrist parties attempts to push through a policy that is closer to its preferred position than its declared position, then the probability it will join a majority is reduced. Since the equilibrium declaration (z_L^*, z_C^*, z_R^*) is optimal for each of the three parties, any move by one party away from its equilibrium position results in a loss of expected utility. Thus each party is obliged to implement its equilibrium policy. The credibility principle is satisfied because of the existence of political risk (over the precise form of the coalition government).

The model proposed by Schofield and Parks does not take into account the possible formation of new parties. The "depolarization" of conflict that occurs in the three-party PR model (due to the tendency to convergence) may, in fact, be mitigated by the fear of the creation of new "extreme" parties. (For example, in West Germany, again, centrist policies of the Christian Democrat-Free Democrat coalition and the rise of nationalist sentiments may have contributed to the recent growth of the Republican party.)

No matter how many parties there are, if policy considerations are fundamentally one-dimensional, then there will always be a median party or legislator defined by the election result. That is, after the election, one of the parties will find itself at the political median, with a majority neither on its left nor on its right. It is convenient to call such a party the "core party." In the three-party case considered above, it is possible for the core party to be either one of the two noncentrist parties, L or R, but in this case that party must have a majority. If no party has a majority, or if it is the center party that controls a majority, then the center party must be the core. In the two noncentrist majority cases, there may be no obvious connection between the majority party's policy position and the electoral median. However, in three-party PR situations commonsense (and empirical evidence) suggests that the most likely occurrence is that neither noncentrist party obtains a majority. In this case, it is plausible to infer that the median party declaration, z_C, is near the electoral median, and that the outcome of policy negotiations generally is the political median declared by the centrist core party. Indeed, it is reasonable to expect this center party, on occasion, to form a single-party minority government, arguing that this is legitimated by the election results. (The next section discusses empirical evidence from multiparty governments in Europe that is relevant to this inference.)

In contrast, consider the situation under the plurality, Westminster, electoral system. Suppose (z_L, z_C, z_R) are policy declarations close to the parties' preferred positions (p_L, p_C, p_R). As we saw above, it is reasonable, even under electoral risk, to suppose that both L and R can be sure of capturing certain constituencies. While the electoral strength of the Center party will be concentrated in the "center" constituencies, there is no guarantee that C can win these constituencies. As we saw in Table 1, the British Liberal/Social Democrat parties in 1983 took over 25 percent of the popular vote yet captured only 23 (or 3.5 percent) of the constituencies.

Even with relatively "noncentrist" policy declarations, the Conservative Party has been able to obtain a plurality in most of the "centrist" constituencies in recent elections. Although the Labour party has vigorously attempted to present credible center–left policies to the electorate, it has been unable to undermine the Conservative majority.

While all the above discussion has been relatively nontechnical, it would appear that the principal difference between a PR and a plurality electoral system is that the latter is less likely to produce outcomes close to the electoral median. While a plurality electoral system does give voters a "choice," there are two disagreeable consequences. In any Westminster system, and most obviously in Britain, with a relatively weak center party, there is less motivation for the two main parties to move to the electoral center. Moreover, if there is significant "electoral risk," then parties can miscalculate the electoral consequences of policy declarations. The "unexpected" political results can give rise to a high degree of "political uncertainty." Secondly and more importantly, there is no theoretical reason to suppose that political outcomes closely reflect electoral choice (characterized by the median voter position) in plurality systems. Since PR systems seem superior in the sense of reflecting electoral choice, it is worthwhile reconsidering the evidence as regards their alleged tendency to produce factionalization and instability.

3. Multiparty competition under proportional representation in European polities

The first section of this chapter indicated that PR electoral systems reflected the "distribution" of electoral preferences in a faithful manner but also gave rise to relatively high factionalization, as measured by the effective (seat) number, N_S, of the House of Representatives. An early empirical finding (Taylor and Herman 1971; Herman and Sanders 1977; Warwick 1979) was an apparent inverse correlation between factionalization and government duration (see King et al., 1990; Warwick and Easton 1992 for further discussion). Laver and Schofield (1990) have presented data on average government duration and average effective (seat) numbers in twelve European countries (all of which use some version of proportional representation). They found that the inverse law is quite weak; Luxembourg displays an average duration of forty-five months and Italy only thirteen months, although both have N_s equal, on average, to 3.5. (See Table 4, p. 293 for estimates of duration and effective number.) Taagepera and Shugart (1989) have also pursued this relationship and noted that the countries with plurality electoral systems (where N_s is usually equal to 2) have a much higher average duration of approximately sixty months. If government durability is a proxy for "stability," and this is regarded as a normative criterion, then this empirical relationship can be used as a justification for plurality over PR.

In developing the notion of stability, it is useful to consider the type of government coalitions that occur in these twelve countries. Probably the most influential theory of coalition formation is due to Riker (1962). Suppose that parties are purely office seeking and, in particular, that government perquisites can be identified with control of important ministeries or portfolios. Then the political game is essentially zero sum, and it is reasonable to suppose that governments will be "minimal winning." A minimal winning (MW) government is a coalition of parties that controls a majority of seats, but may lose no member party and still retain a majority. The formal argument to justify the MW concept is quite difficult (see Schofield 1978, 1982). In contrast a winning, but non-MW, coalition is called "surplus." Finally, a coalition (or single-party) government that does not control a majority of seats is termed "minority." Laver and Schofield (1990) have analyzed the type of governing coalition in these twelve European countries in the period 1945–87. Of the 218 governments considered, 22 involved a single-party majority, 77 were MW, 46 were surplus, and 73 were minority. Of the 22 majority-party cases, only 5 (all in Sweden and Norway) can be regarded as noncentrist, since each involved a left-wing Labor or Social Democrat party. These data give some corroboration for the model outlined.

As observed, Axelrod (1970) formulated a model in which parties are principally office-seeking but attempt to form coalition governments that minimize ideological "policy differences" across the known policy preferences of the parties (see also de Swaan 1973 for an alternative but similar model, and Taylor and Laver 1973 for an empirical test of the MW and ideological coalition hypotheses). To be more specific, Axelrod proposed that coalitions will be minimal connected winning (MCW); that is, both winning and comprising adjacent parties on the usual left-right (or other significant) dimension. The data collected by Laver and Schofield (1990) up to 1987 show that although 62 governments were MCW (out of the 196 involving no majority party), very few (indeed only nine of these) were not also MW. The judgment on the relative positions of parties on the left-right scale was based on an overall evaluation of analyses by various authors (see Laver and Schofield 1990, appendix B for details). Moreover, 37 of the coalition governments were surplus but not MCW.

While the MW notion predicts 77 of the 196 nonmajority cases, it gives no account of the occurrence of 73 minority governments (this problem was first noted by Herman and Pope 1973). This suggests that both the MW and MCW ideas are flawed.

As we noted in the previous section, the concept of the "core" would suggest, in a one-dimensional policy space, that the median party typically belongs to the government and indeed could often form a minority government. Laver and Schofield (1990, 113) found that 165 governments included the median, or core, party, out of 196 involving no majority party. Of course, if a party controls a majority of the seats, then by definition it is a core party. (Budge and Laver [1992] obtained a similar estimate for a somewhat different set of countries.) However, this still leaves 31 governments that excluded the median party. Below we shall attempt to explain this phenomenon.

Before leaving this discussion of coalition type, it is useful to mention Dodd's work (1974, 1976) on the relationship between type and duration. Dodd suggested that party systems with moderate fragmentation (N_s) would result in relatively long-lived minimal-winning coalitions, while systems with high fragmentation would give short-lived minority or surplus coalitions, depending on whether conflict of interest (CI) was high or low. To describe CI, Dodd assumed that parties had policy preferences on a one-dimensional scale and measured CI by the "cardinal distance" between these preferred points.

Some countries fit Dodd's model quite precisely. Luxembourg has N_s = 3.2 on average, though nine out of ten governments were minimal winning, with average duration equal to forty-seven months. Germany has N_s = 2.5, on average; ten out of twelve governments were minimal winning with an average duration of thirty-three months. On the other hand, five out of the twelve governments in Ireland were minority (based on the "median" Fianna Fail) and had a moderate average duration of thirty months. Finally, Italy and Finland have had a large number of *both* minority and surplus governments. In Italy, surplus governments have tended to be longer lived than minority governments while the relationship is reversed in Finland. In general, then, empirically focused models of coalition formation and duration are not too successful.

A more significant point is that there appears to be a fundamental incompatibility between these empirical analyses and the result of the one-dimensional models of political competition discussed in the previous section. Models of office-seeking party competition typically give convergence in party positions and this is not observed. The alternative models of seat or vote maximization usually result in an equal (that is, symmetric) distribution of seats, and such an outcome is rare. The empirical work presented in Budge, Robertson, and Hearl (1987) and based on the analysis of party manifestos (declarations) in many countries suggests that the policy space is high dimensional. However, much of the variance can be accounted for in a two-dimensional framework. Generalizing the one-dimensional competitive models to two dimensions is extremely difficult. In particular, a fundamental differences is that a core need not exist in two dimensions. (Remember that a core point is one that is unbeaten by any other policy point supported by a coalition of parties, where again parties are assumed to be committed to particular policy positions.) To see this note that a *necessary* condition for a party to occupy the core position in two dimensions is that it belong to the political median on both dimensions. (It should be clear that while the concept of political core and median coincide in one dimension, that they are distinct in higher dimensions.) Formal analysis (Schofield 1986, 1995a) further shows that a necessary condition for a party to occupy the core in a "stable" fashion in two dimensions is that it be "dominant." Loosely speaking, a party is dominant if it controls more seats than any other party. (This argument will be illustrated in the next section.) Thus, a key distinction between models based on one or two dimensions is that they give different empirical predictions concerning minority governments. If the policy space is one-dimensional, then on some occasions a nondominant party may find itself in the core position. The theory outlined in the previous section suggests that it is possible for this party to form a minority government. In contrast, in two dimensions, if a party is not dominant and attempts to form a minority government, then the resulting outcome will be unstable. Consequently, if minority governments are observed are always based on the dominant party, then this should be seen as a corroboration of the two-dimensional model.

Laver and Schofield (1990) found that the dominant party was included in 162 governments (out of the 196 situations with no majority party). This party was often at the median position in the left-right scale, but not always (see Laver and Schofield [1990, 118] for the country-by-country discussion). More particularly, in the forty-five cases where there was a one-party minority government, only three of these consisted of a nondominant party. One instance was a Liberal caretaker government in Sweden that formed in 1978–9 because the bourgeois party coalition collapsed over policy disagreements regarding nuclear energy. (It is interesting that a similar collapse of the current bourgeois coalition is possible because of the opposition of the Center party to the proposed Oresund bridge connecting Denmark and Sweden.) The two other cases involve the Liberals (Venstre) in Denmark in 1945–7 and 1973–5. In these two Danish cases, although other parties were not included in the cabinet, the bourgeois parties did give implicit support to Venstre.

As we shall see, in the two-dimensional model when the core is empty, then there is no theoretical reason to suppose that the government includes the dominant party. It is plausible therefore that the two-dimensional policy-driven theory can give an explanantion for the thirty-four governments that exclude the dominant party. (For future reference note that twenty-two of these cases are associated with Ireland, Norway, Sweden, and Denmark.)

4. A two-dimensional model of coalition bargaining in the heart

To give an idea of the nature of political bargaining in a two-dimensional policy space, consider the highly factionalized situation in the Israeli Knesset after the elections of 1988 and 1992. Table 3 presents the election results.

It is generally accepted that two dimensions are relevant: (a) national

Table 3. *Parties and seats in the Knesset.*

		1988 Election	1992 Election
Labor bloc	Labor (LAB)	39	44
	Meretz (MRZ)		12
	CRM	5	
	Mapan (MPM)	3	
	Shinu (S)	2	
	PLP	1	
	Hadash (HS)	4	3
	ADL	1	2
	Subtotal	55	61
Likud/Religious bloc	Shas (SH)	6	6
	Likud (LIK)	40	32
	Tzomet (TZ)	2	8
	Aguda (AI)	5	4
	NRP	5	6
	Moledet (MO)	2	3
	Techiya (TY)	3	
	Degel Hatora (DH)	2	
	Subtotal	65	59
	Total	120	120

security, defined by attitudes to the Arab territories, and (b) a secular-religious cleavage. (Estimates of the positions of the parties are given in Figure 1 and 2 and are based on Korn 1993 and Nixon et al. 1995.) On the national security dimension, the policy position of Shas (an orthodox Sephardic party) is at the median after the 1988 election. To see this note that a "national security" policy position to the "right" of Shas can only gain fifty-nine votes (less than the required majority of sixty-one) while the one on the "left" gains only fifty-five votes. On the other hand Shas is not at the median in the secular-religious dimension. In such a factionalized system it is difficult to determine the dominant party, but in fact both Labor and Likud can be identified as dominant in 1988. It can be shown that the definition, given in Section 3, implies that the core in Figure 1 is empty. If we assume that the positions of the parties presented in this figure represent their true policy preferences, there are two quite different modeling routes to take. One, based on McKelvey's results (1976), suggests that in the absence of a core anything (namely, any coalition and any outcome) can happen. For reasons, outlined in Ordeshook (this volume) it is now generally accepted that outcomes of such a spatial committee game will satisfy "second order" equilibrium conditions such as characterize the "top-cycle set" or "uncovered set."

However, the uncovered set is defined in terms of the underlying (majority) social preference relation. As such, the theory is mute on the question of which outcomes are associated with which coalitions. Moroever, because "global" preferences are involved, it is extremely difficult to determine whether a point belongs to the uncovered set. In the case of Euclidean preferences, it is much easier to compute a set known as the "yolk" (see McKelvey 1986), though again the yolk gives no coalition prediction. Work by Schofield (1993b, 1993c, 1996) has defined an alternative equilibrium notion called the "heart." Regarded as a correspondence from preferences to outcomes, the heart satisfies the same Pareto, continuity, and convergence properties as the uncovered set (see Cox 1987b for proofs in the case of the uncovered set and Schofield 1995c for the heart). To compute the "political heart" in the case of the 1988 Knesset, Figure 1 shows three median lines joining the three pairs of policy points {*LAB, SHAS*}, {*LAB, LIK*}, {*LIK, SHAS*}. For example, the line joining the Shas and Likud positions is a median since, with the Shas and Likud parties, there are majorities incorporating all these parties to the upper right as well as to the lower left of the line. (For ease of presentation, it is assumed that parties have preferences based on distance from their preferred policy points. The definition of the heart does not depend on this assumption.) The political heart is the set (the triangle in Figure 1) bounded by these three median lines. The fact that these medians do not intersect implies that the core is empty. The proposed coalition theory associated with the heart is that the governments that form will incorporate the parties on the boundary of the heart. (In the case of Figure 1, these parties are Likud, Labor, and Shas.) In fact in 1988–90 a national government led by Likud, but including Labor, formed. The government during 1990–2 was a coalition of the Likud and the religious parties, including Shas. Note that if national security were the only dimension, then the one-dimensional policy-driven theory discussed in the previous sections would predict Shas membership in the coalition, and this is contradicted by the 1988–90 government. On the other hand, a dominant party (namely Labor) was excluded from the 1990–2 government. A point to be emphasized is that the qualitative properties of the heart in Figure 1 are unchanged if all positions and preferences are modified by a small perturbation. Thus, the qualitative prediction is stable even if there is measurement error.

In 1992, Labor gained five seats. The change in underlying coalition possibilities implies that Labor, alone, was dominant after 1992. (Dominance is defined in terms of numerical strength. The key to Labor's dominance is that Labor, Meretz, and Shas together comprise a majority, yet Likud, Meretz, and Shas do not.) The median lines in Figure 2 now all intersect in the Labor position. Assuming parties are committed to their positions, it follows that no policy position can obtain a majority

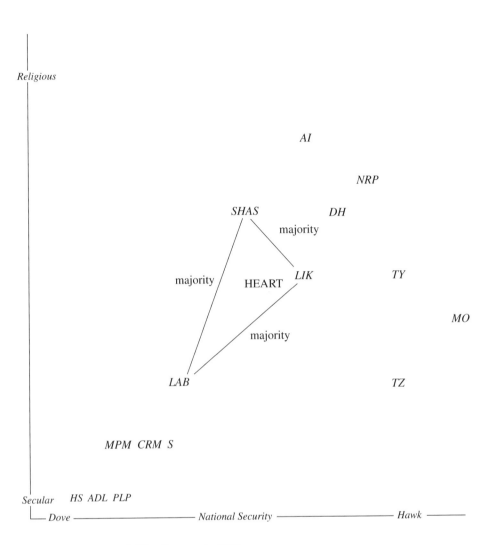

Figure 1. The Knesset in 1988.

over Labor's. Thus, Labor's position is the core point (and, by definition, also the political heart). Thus, the notion of the heart predicts that
Labor would belong to any government forming after the 1992 election.
In fact Labor and Shas (with the support of Meretz, a grouping of
secular parties) formed a coalition government. Shas left the coalition,
and the minority Labor government opened negotiations with the PLO.
As of October 1995 negotiations over Gaza and the WestBank were
close to a successful resolution. See Nixon et al. 1995 for discussion.

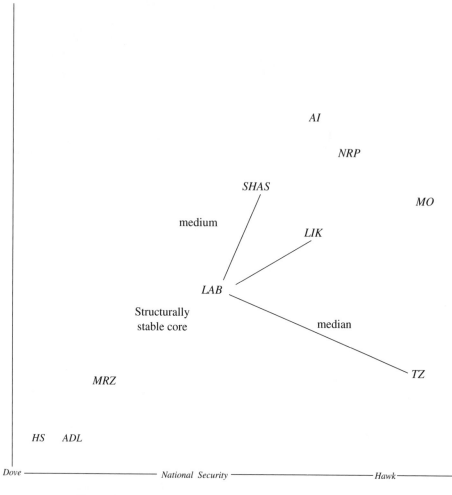

Figure 2. The Knesset in 1992.

It is clear that the outcome after the 1992 election is much preferred by Labor to the 1988 situation; not only does it obtain perquisites of office, but it can have a greater effect on government policy. If there is a significant motivation for parties to seek a core position, then any competitive model that accepts the incentive principle must address the question why convergence does not generally occur. It seems plausible that parties realize that they will be committed to their policy declarations and attempt to choose a position that is optimal with respect to electoral risk and *political* risk (that is, the uncertain outcomes of coalition negotiation). As discussed above, Schofield and Parks (1993) proposed a model where parties assume that the probabilities associated with different coalitions are inversely proportional to the distance between their declarations. Unlike the one-dimensional case, where convergence is a dominant tendency, this two-dimensional model presents parties with mixed motives based on their beliefs whether a situation, such as Figure 1, is more or less likely than Figure 2. In the situation represented by Figure 1, the credibility principle is satisfied, as described above, because of political risk. However, in the situation presented in Figure 2, it was necessary for Labor to appear credible to the electorate, and this it did by its choice of Rabin as leader of the party. It is also plausible that its credibility was enhanced by including the Sephardic party, Shas, in the coalition.

Combining the preelection competitive model of declaration choice (outlined in the previous section) with the postelection cooperative model of coalition bargaining suggests an integrated framework within which to analyze multiparty politics. The research program that can now be conceived starts with fundamental electoral cleavages in the society and models the creation of parties and their choice of policies as an equilibrium process. The last stage of this process would be the implementation of policy through government coalitions. (Baron's [1993a] recent three-party two-dimensional model is a first step in integrating the stages of this process.) The interaction between electoral preferences, party choice, and government formation in PR systems is complex, but no more complicated than actual political behavior in multiparty political systems. It is possible that a fine-grained analysis on a country-by-country basis will give insights into the wide variety in fragmentation and party configurations to be observed in European PR systems.[1]

The typology of political systems offered by Laver and Schofield (1990) is based on a two-dimensional policy-driven model and is compatible with the general focus of this program. As the Israeli example illustrated, the two-dimensional model implicitly emphasizes quite subtle relationships between the positions of the dominant party and the other party positions in the policy space. The implication of the model is a

---

1. Some recent work (Nixon et al. 1995) has attempted to model the most difficult aspect of this program, namely voter behavior. For the 1992 Israeli election, we found that an adaptation of Coughlin's (1992) probabilistic voting model gave a very good prediction of the election returns. However, we found evidence that voters behaved strategically (tending to vote for the two larger parties rather than the smaller parties). Secondly the parties themselves were not pure expected-vote maximizers. A fully developed voter-party model based on the Nash equilibrium concept is currently not available. However see Austen-Smith (1996) and Sened (1996) for recent theoretical work on multiparty elections and coalition formation.

focus on this aspect of the political configuration, and on whether or not the dominant party joins the government coalition. In turn this suggests that we can define a "regime change" when one or other of these features is changed. The typology can then be used to define average duration, in terms of regime changes, as follows (see Table 4).

Each of the "bipolar" systems (Austria or Germany) is characterized by two large, dominant parties and minimal winning coalitions. It is natural to say that a change of regime occurs when a dominant party enters or leaves the coalition. In the "left unipolar" systems (Norway, Sweden, and Denmark) the dominant party is somewhat to the left of center. Typically, when this party is at the two-dimensional core position (perhaps with a majority), then it forms a minority or majority government. Otherwise the bourgeois coalition forms a government. It is natural to characterize a regime in terms of the role of the dominant party in government. In the "center unipolar" systems (Luxembourg and Ireland) the dominant party is also at the median in the usual left-right scale. The second dimension is relevant for explaining coalitions that exclude the dominant party. Most coalitions in Luxembourg involve the dominant party with one of the other two major parties, so we may characterize regime changes in terms of the choice of coalition partner by the dominant party. In Ireland, the regime changes occur when the dominant party (Fianna Fail) enters or leaves government. In Iceland (a "right unipolar" system) the dominant party is on the right (of the left-right scale) and the two-dimensional core is always empty. In this case it is reasonable to identify a regime change with a change in the composition of government.

The other four countries (Belgium, Finland, Italy, and the Netherlands) were labeled "multipolar" by Laver and Schofield (1990). Belgium, the Netherlands, and Finland are somewhat like Luxembourg in that the dominant party is often at the one-dimensional median position, as well as at the two-dimensional core, and typically a member of government. With high fragmentation and two dimensions of policy, the composition of the government coalition is significant, so any "major" change in this can be regarded as a regime change. Finally, in Italy, the Christian Democrats (DCI) have, until recently, dominated the political scene. Regime changes can be identified with the collapse of a DCI-controlled, multiparty coalition to a minority DCI government, or the formation of a new nonminority government involving the DCI.

It is interesting that most coalition governments in the multipolar systems do contain a "center," and dominant party, and may therefore be regarded as more stable than the simple computation based on average duration would indicate. Table 4 lists this new estimate of duration based on change of regime, obtained by ignoring "minor" changes such

Table 4. *Average duration (months) defined by regime change in European politics.*

System	Country	Effective number N_s	Average duration Laver and Schofield (1990)	Average duration between regime changes
Bipolar:	Austria	2.2	38	97
	Germany	2.9	37	74
Left unipolar:	Norway	3.2	32	53
	Sweden	3.2	28	55
	Denmark	4.5	26	39
Center unipolar:	Luxembourg	3.5	45	57
	Ireland	2.6	39	53
Right unipolar:	Iceland	3.7	34	44
Multipolar:	Netherlands	4.5	27	48
	Belgium	4.0	22	38
	Finland	5.0	15	31
	Italy	3.5	13	25
Average		3.7	26	51

as cabinet reshuffles or the appointment of a new prime minister. Also included is the previous estimate of average duration and average effective (seat) number computed by Laver and Schofield (1990). The table is meant only to be suggestive, but it helps to convey the sense that multiparty PR systems are not as unstable as is usually assumed.

However, even with this modified definition of duration, it is clear that Italy, Finland, and Denmark (particularly in the 1970s and 1980s) must be regarded as fairly unstable. It is entirely possible that the extreme political instability in Italy suggested by this table is a direct consequence of the Christian Democrat attempt to control the political game through the distribution of perquisites so as to stay in office. Moreover, this instability is probably a cause of the extraordinary transformation that occurred in Italy in 1993.

5. The "general will"

Rather than criteria of "choice" or "stability" perhaps a more appropriate normative consideration for an electoral system is whether it produces a concordance between electoral preference and political choice. If the policy space is indeed one-dimensional then it is natural to designate the median voter position as the "general will" of the electorate. In a Downsian two-party system under proportional representation, either with office-seeking or policy-seeking motivations and some electoral risk, one would expect to observe "centrist" outcomes close to the electoral median. As we noted in Section 2, however, this conclusion need not be valid for a plurality, Westminster system.

Results by McKelvey and Schofield (1986, 1987) suggest that in two dimensions there is generally no electoral core point. Riker (1982a) inferred from this result that there can be no general will of the electorate. In contrast, however, the electoral uncovered set has been proposed as a social choice set, and it is known to be centrally located with regard to electoral preferences. Indeed, it has recently been shown by Tovey (1992a) under weak symmetry assumptions, that the electoral uncovered set is "small." As we noted above, the uncovered set is generally difficult to compute while the electoral heart can be readily determined if the electoral distribution is known. Just as with the political heart, the electoral heart is bounded by electoral median lines (in the special case that voters have Euclidean preferences). Again, the electoral heart has the continuity and optimality properties of the electoral uncovered set and converges to the electoral core when the latter exists (Schofield 1993a). Schofield (1995b) argues that the electoral heart can be regarded as a representation of the general will of the electorate. Analysis of electoral distributions with many voters suggests in the two-dimensional case that the electoral heart will be small relative to the support of the distribution of voter preferences (Schofield and Tovey 1992; Schofield 1995c).

In all of the PR systems discussed here and in Laver and Schofield (1990) there is some evidence that more than one dimension of policy is relevant (Budge, Robertson, and Hearl 1987; Laver and Budge 1992). The general model of party competition that has underpinned the analysis of this chapter has suggested that Downsian convergence in two dimensions is much weaker than in one dimension. In particular there is a degree of heterogeneity in the range of policy choices offered by the parties. Nonetheless, the outcome of coalition negotiation among parties may result in outcomes near a central domain of the policy space (which we have characterized here as the "political heart"). A general result on the relationship between the political and electoral heart may be interpreted as a "political welfare theorem."

It is interesting to speculate that it is very difficult for a second policy dimension to become relevant in plurality, Westminster electoral systems. (It is possible that the recent election in Canada gives a counterexample to this guess, since issues concerning Quebec[2] and NAFTA

---

2. As of October 1995, the issue of Quebec and secession has become even more significant.

were both relevant.) One further point that should be mentioned is that the tendency of PR systems to find political solutions near the electoral heart in some sense defines their ability to create consensus through compromise. The onset of recession in the 1990s seems to have made it much more difficult for these countries to break out of the tradition of consensus and to make the complex economic decisions that are required.

There is evidence that the electoral system in the United States is very different from a Westminster system. Empirical analysis of voting behavior (Poole and Rosenthal 1991) strongly suggests that party discipline in Congress is generally quite weak. In fact, Alt and Schofield (1972) found that the House seemed to be structured into a dozen voting factions, centered around powerful committee chairs. Moreover, in addition to the usual left–right dimension, a second dimension (which we may call North–South) was found to be significant. The resultant policy heterogeneity would imply (Schofield 1995b) that the congressional heart is quite small with respect to the full electoral domain.[3] Further analysis of the relationship between the electoral and congressional heart would give insight into the political expression of the general will in such a "congressional" electoral system. It is plausible that the balance of power between the president and Congress in the United States accomodates two normative goals: the expression of "choice" by the citizens and the aggregation of preferences into a general will by Congress.

It would seem that the way multiparty PR systems find "the electoral heart" is very different from the process in the U.S. congressional system. The fundamental difference appears not in the degree of stability (or government duration) but in the ability that these different political structures seem to have to respond to rapid, structural change. Though there are formidable theoretical problems to be dealt with in the research program outlined here, it is possible that the rational choice approach will lead to some insights into the fundamental questions of institutional adaptation posed recently by North (1990).

3. It is true however that under the manifesto-like "Contract with America," the Republican party is acting like a disciplined Westminster party in its attempt of fall 1995 to implement the budget and tax cuts.

CHAPTER 14

Interest groups: Money, information, and influence

DAVID AUSTEN-SMITH

Although there are a great many issues concerning interest group formation (Olson 1965; Grier, Munger, and Roberts 1991; Kennelly and Murrell 1991), organization, and activity (Austen-Smith 1981; Moe 1981; Johnson 1988), membership and objectives (Rothenberg 1988, 1992), that are germane to our understanding of the political process, this essay is confined exclusively to (relatively recent) models of interest groups' efforts to influence policy through money and information.

This essay will (1) motivate the need to remove the "black box" characterizing much economic modeling of government by discussing the highly aggregated production function approach to interest group behavior exemplified by Becker (1983), (2) deal (in the second and third sections, respectively) with more micro-oriented models involving money at the electoral and the legislative stages of the political process, and (3) review (in the fourth and fifth sections) the literature on interest groups as strategic providers of policy-relevant information which, though a major concern in the descriptive political science literature, has only recently received attention in the formal literature.

1. The aggregate production function approach

Aggregate level models of interest group influence adopt a production function approach to the political process. The canonic model here is Becker's (1983, 1985)[1], which assumes a given number of interest groups and posits the existence of an *influence function* and a *pressure production function* for each. Although there is a substantive distinction to be made between influence and pressure (Potters 1992), the separation of the two plays no role in Becker's model or any other that uses such a reduced form for the political sector. Consequently, for the remainder of this section I shall combine the two into a *political outcome function*.

1. See also Chamberlain (1978), Coggins et al. (1991), and almost all of the rent-seeking literature reviewed in this volume by Tollison.

The following though a simplified version of Becker's framework captures the central properties of the production function approach. Assume two homogenous groups, $j = 1,2$ of sizes m and n. Group 1 wishes to tax group 2 and use the revenue to subsidize its own members. However, any such policy involves deadweight losses with respect to both tax collection and revenue distribution. Let the cost of providing a subsidy of y_1 to a member of group 1 be $s \cdot y_n$, with $s > 1$; and the revenue from a tax of y_2 on a member of group 2 be $t \cdot y_2$, with $0 < t < 1$. In equilibrium, the budget must balance, that is, $msy_1 \equiv nty_2$.

Each group devotes resources to generating a tax/subsidy program. The technology governing how groups' behavior maps into outcomes is exogenously given and common knowledge. So, define a political outcome function $h(\cdot)$ such that, in equilibrium,

$$h(x_1m, x_2n, m, n) = msy_1 = nty_2. \tag{1}$$

Here, x_j is per capita expenditure devoted by group j to political activities. Since group 1 wishes to see high subsidies and group 2 wishes low taxes, assume h is increasing strictly concave in its first, and decreasing strictly convex in its second, argument. Further assume that

$$\partial h_1/\partial m = h_{11}x_1 + h_{13} \le 0; \; \partial h_2/\partial n = h_{22}x_2 + h_{24} \ge 0 \tag{2}$$

and

$$h_{14} \equiv h_{23} \equiv 0, \tag{3}$$

where subscripts on functions denote partial derivatives as usual. Assumption (2) is a condition on free riding within groups. It states that any efficiencies in political activity gained by a group through increasing size are at least offset by additional costs from free riding within the group. Assumption (3) states that the impact on group j's marginal influence of an incremental change in group k's size, holding k's total outlay constant, is negligible.

Let w_j denote the per capita wealth of group j. Group 1 chooses a per capita level of activity x_1 to maximize group income $m(w_1+y_1-x_1)$, taking group 2's behavior as given; and group 2 chooses x_2 to maximize $n(w_2-y_2-x_2)$, taking group 1's behavior as given. Empirical hypotheses are then derived from the model by examining the comparative static properties of the resulting Nash equilibrium (x_1^*, x_2^*).[2] The central implications of this set up are summarized by

Proposition 1 (Becker 1983): (1) *"An increase in deadweight cost [decrease in* t *or increase in* s*] reduces the equilibrium subsidy"* (381).

---

2. Becker performs the comparative statics on the level of "pressure" each group exerts; a concept that is defined only as a nicely behaved function of group expenditures and size.

(2) *"Politically successful groups tend to be small relative to the size of the groups taxed to pay their subsidies"* (385).

To see the intuition for proposition 1 note that, from the group's maximands, at any Nash equilibrium we must have $dy_1/dx_1 = -dy_2/dx_2 = 1$. Implicitly differentiating through (1) and substituting then yields

$$\left. \begin{array}{l} h_1(x_1^*m, x_2^*n, \cdot) - s = 0 \\ -h_2(x_1^*m, x_2^*n, \cdot) - t = 0 \end{array} \right\}. \tag{4}$$

Since the second order conditions hold by assumption, (4) fully characterizes the equilibrium (x_1^*, x_2^*).

Now consider part (1) of the result and suppose the deadweight cost of subsidizing increases (i.e., $ds > 0$). From (4) and the assumptions on h, $dx_1^*/ds < 0$. Because only group 1 ever attempts to raise subsidies, this inequality and the budget balancing condition yield the result. In equilibrium, group 1 equates the marginal benefits and costs from political activity. Since the effective marginal cost of a subsidy y_1 is given by the (marginal) deadweight cost associated with allocating that subsidy (s), an increase in this cost coupled with diminishing returns to political activity leads to a fall in the resources devoted by group 1 to political outcomes and therefore to a fall in the overall subsidy level. A similar argument applies for group 2 and an increase in the deadweight cost of taxation ($dt < 0$).

Together, (2), (3), and (4) yield $dx_2^*/dn < 0$: an incremental increase in the size of the taxed group (group 2) leads to a fall in the resources that group devotes to political outcomes. With (1), this inequality yields proposition 1(2); in effect, the larger the group bearing a given tax-burden, the less the incentive for its members to devote resources to lowering their taxes. Thus, "groups can more readily obtain subsidies when they are small relative to the number of taxpayers" (Becker 1983, 395).

The substantive conclusions supported by proposition 1 are (1) that economic efficiency and pressure group activity are consistent insofar as any increase in the deadweight cost of a tax/subsidy program leads to group responses that offset such increases; and (2) that small groups need not be disadvantaged in a majoritarian polity simply because they are small. As Becker and others (eg., Mitchell and Munger 1991) have observed, these conclusions are very much in the pluralist tradition of Bentley (1908) and Truman (1952) and point to the importance of the countervailing pressures endogenously generated by any group seeking political favor at the expense of others. Although the second result is familiar from Olson (1965), it is novel to find it coupled with the assertion on efficiency. In the absence of any benchmark against which to judge the influence of interest groups, however, the overall impact of group activity on the political economy remains equivocal: What would the allocation of resources and policy decisions look like in the absence of groups?

Aggregate production function models are not alone in lacking a well-defined benchmark against which to judge the welfare consequences of group activity. They are, however, fairly extreme with respect to their treatment of the polity. This is not an accident. The political outcome function serves as a reduced form characterization of how legislative institutions map the resources and demands of groups into implemented political decisions. Similarly, groups' political activities are characterized by a level of real resource expenditure, normalized in some way by group size. The hope is that such aggregate models can identify general properties of a wide class of political-economic systems. Not surprisingly, the generalities identified are broad aggregate level claims on the consequences and intensity of group activity (deadweight costs matter and attenuate the inefficiencies of any redistributive programs secured by groups; "pressure tends to be greater . . . by groups with intrinsically more influence" [Becker 1983, 391]). Questions about how and when influence is effective in majoritarian legislatures, about why some groups have "intrinsically more influence" than others, about how and why resources devoted by groups should map deterministically into a legislative decision and subsequent bureaucratic execution, about why groups adopt different patterns of activity (campaign contributions, informational lobbying, grass-roots activism, etc.), and so on simply cannot be posed within the aggregate framework. The production function approach is too crude a tool for understanding and explaining the behavior of groups and legislators under various institutional arrangements. Any such explanation must be micro-oriented and amounts to developing a theory of the "political outcome function" itself.

2. Money and electoral influence

Campaign contributions are the most visible electoral activity of interest groups. Thus, it is not surprising to find most formal models of interest group activity focusing on campaign contributions. On the other hand, many other sorts of group expenditures – in particular, those incurred through lobbying elected officials – are not so easily identified, and at least one estimate puts the campaign contribution-to-lobbying expenditure ratio at around 1:10 (Wright 1990). Moreover, the sums involved in campaign contributions are not particularly large: in the 1989–90 U.S. congressional campaign, for example, total candidate expenditures were $147 million, of which 32 percent were given by PACs and 53 percent by individuals, with the residual coming from party committees and personal resources of candidates (Sorauf 1992, 30).

The earliest models of campaign giving essentially made no distinction between electoral policy platforms and subsequent legislative behavior. For example, Ben-Zion and Eytan (1974) assume the existence of a probability-of-winning (equals vote share) function (with the candidate's money and policy platform as arguments) and consider a single group offering money to a single candidate in exchange for adoption of particular policies. In equilibrium, the candidate equates the marginal vote return from policy to that from money, the group maximizes its expected return, and, by assumptions on the vote production function, policy is shifted away from the no-contribution case toward the preferences of the group. The empirical predictions from this model are straightforward: Policy changes most on dimensions of most concern to the donor and least concern to the voters; more money accrues to candidates with higher probability of winning and, in close two candidate races, might be given to both candidates. Similar models with similar conclusions are explored by Welch (1974, 1980). The data support a positive correlation between probability of electoral success and contributions to a candidate (Jacobson 1980; Snyder 1990, 1993) but, although there are some exceptions, do not show that groups typically give to both candidates in a close race (Poole and Romer 1985).

Irrespective of any consistency with the data, these models, in common with the production function approach, are too aggregated to shed much light on how interest groups' campaign contributions influence elections and electoral platforms. In particular, no mechanism for connecting money to votes is postulated and the structure of the (necessarily) implicit contracts between candidates and groups is unspecified. However, as with the production function model, this level of aggregation can be considered a virtue, permitting analysis of empirical regularities independent of any need to specify institutional details. This is Synder's (1990, 1993) position. He finesses specifying vote production functions by focusing exclusively on equilibrium conditions implicit in any model involving purely investor–contributors. Snyder's model is one of a class that takes campaign contributions as independent of policy. It is useful to distinguish between such models and those in which policy plays an explicit role, and I consider them in turn.

2.1 Policy-independent models

Snyder (1990) considers a two-candidate race in which all groups view candidates as potential investments. The groups have no interest in the general policy position of a candidate and treat their behavior as having no effect on the likelihood of any candidate being elected. Instead, they view contributions as part of a contract with the recipient – if elected, the candidate will deliver services of at least a given value to the group. Each candidate i offers services of value s_{ij} to contributor j, payable conditional on election, in exchange for a contribution x_{ij} to i from j. Let p_i denote the probability candidate i wins the election and let ρ be the available return on alternative investment opportunities. Since groups treat p_i as parametric, group j contributes to candidate i only if $p_i s_{ij} \geq \rho x_{ij}$. Assuming candidates maximize contributions and summing over j, (5) must hold in equilibrium

$$p_1 S_1 = \rho X_1; \ (1-p_1)S_2 = \rho X_2, \tag{5}$$

where $S_i = \Sigma_j s_{ij}$ and $X_i = \Sigma_j x_{ij}$. Letting $\xi \equiv X_1/(X_1+X_2)$, (5) implies that in equilibrium,

$$p_1 = \xi S_2/[\xi S_2 + (1-\xi)S_1]. \tag{6}$$

In the special case with $S_1 = S_2$, (6) is simply $p_1 = \xi$. However, it should be emphasized that this is an equilibrium relationship and *not* an *ad hoc* specification of the function mapping contributions into the probability of winning; there is no reason to suppose (6) obtains out of equilibrium.

Let $\bar{S}_i$ be i's capacity constraint on services; if candidate i maximizes her contributions, then she always offers $\bar{S}_i$ in equilibrium. (6) yields the hypotheses

Proposition 2 (Snyder 1990): (1) *If $\bar{S}_1 = \bar{S}_2$, then X_i is an increasing, linear function of p_i; and $p_i = X_i/(X_1+X_2)$. (2), If $\bar{S}_1 > \bar{S}_2$, then X_i is an increasing linear function of p_i; $p_1 < \xi$; and (X_1+X_2) is increasing in p_1.*

Snyder (1990) examines these claims with data for investor contributions (thus excluding contributions from individuals, ideological PACs, and so forth) to candidates for open seats in the U.S. House of Representatives 1980–6 and (Snyder 1993) for (essentially all) seats in the U.S. Senate 1980–6. In both cases the results are strongly supportive of proposition 2(1) but proposition 2(2) is rejected.[3]

Although the empirical success of the model is striking, Snyder is quick to emphasise its limitations. For instance, investor contributions to House open races over the period amounted to only 22 percent of total contributions to these races. More importantly, as it stands the model does not permit us to say *anything* about the influence of group

---

3. It is worth noting that on Snyder's estimate, investor contributions to the open House races over the period averaged around $1,200 (1986 dollars). Assuming $\rho = 1.08$ and $p = 0.5$, this implies average $s_{ij} = \$1,392$.

activity on electoral politics. Not only is policy, generally defined, implicitly treated as fully separable from "services"[4] but, in the absence of any postulated causal connection between contributions and voting, no inferences can be drawn regarding the likely impact of contributions on electoral outcomes.[5] And finally, the model does not offer an explanation of how the presumed "market for contributions" works – for instance, how is s_i determined and how are the contingent claims enforced? Baron (1989a) presents a canonic model that addresses the first question, assuming the existence of a vote production function.[6]

Like Snyder, Baron (1989a) assumes that interest groups and candidates make fully enforceable contingent claims contracts and that groups treat as parametric the probability of candidate i winning (p_i). There are two candidates for a legislative office and a continuum of interest groups. Candidate i offers service s_i to any group that contributes x_i to i's campaign. Interest groups are identified by $\theta \in [0,1]$, reflecting the private returns $R(s_i, \theta)$ they receive from services s_i; $R(\cdot)$ is increasing in both arguments. Consequently, the set of groups that contribute to i's campaign depends on the contingent claims contract (s_i, x_i) offered. Since $R_2 > 0$, θ contributes to i given (s_i, x_i) if and only if $\theta \geq [\hat{\theta}_i| \, p_i R(s_i, \hat{\theta}_i) = x_i]$. $\hat{\theta}_i$ is strictly increasing in x_i and strictly decreasing in s_i and p_i, so the more likely groups believe i will win, the more they contribute to i for any pair (s_i, x_i). An interest group's type, θ, is private information to the group. Letting θ be uniformly distributed on $[0,1]$, total expected contributions to i, X_i, are given by $X_i = (1 - \hat{\theta}_i)x_i$.

Candidate i is assumed to value legislative office at $V_i > 0$ and to provide services at constant marginal cost $c_i \geq 0$. If i loses, i's payoff is

4. Morton and Cameron (1992) provide a critical discussion of the policy separability issue, concluding that services in models such as Snyder's and Baron's (considered momentarily) "are the equivalent of finding lost social security checks for voters; the models do not really analyze services like altering important legislation or intervening in critical regulatory proceedings" (93).

5. This latter remark is qualified by a recent paper by Morton and Myerson (1993). These authors explicitly assume separability between policy and services, and build a model in which they graft exactly Snyder's purely service-induced contribution model onto a two-candidate electoral game. They show that if, in their model, contributors have rational expectations about the probability of electoral success and candidates maximize the probability of winning, then, in equilibrium, *either* one candidate receives all the contributions and wins for sure *or* both candidates receive contributions, locate near the median voter, and have positive probability of winning. But this latter possibility is unstable.

6. Baron (1989b) extends the basic model discussed below to consider the second question. His approach is to use the incumbent's desire for reelection to structure incentives for honoring current contingent claims. Specifically, candidates for office are assumed to commit to a contingent claims contract that includes contributions for the current election *and* for the reelection campaign, with the latter forthcoming only on delivery of the promised services in the intervening legislative period.

normalized to zero. Hence, for any pair of proposals $\{(s_1,x_1),(s_2,x_2)\}$, the candidates' expected payoffs are respectively $p(X_1,X_2)[V_1-c_1s_1(1-\hat{\theta}_1)]$ and $[1-p(X_1,X_2)][V_2-c_2s_2(1-\hat{\theta}_2)]$, where $p(\cdot)$ is the probability that candidate 1 wins conditional on the distribution of campaign contributions elicited under $\{(s_1,x_1),(s_2,x_2)\}$ The function $p(\cdot)$ is essentially a reduced form of the electoral process and amounts to an aggregate vote production function.

The model is solved for Nash equilibria with rational expectations: In equilibrium, (s_i^*,x_i^*) maximizes i's expected payoff given (s_j^*,x_j^*), $i = 1,2$; and $p_i = p(X(s_1^*,x_1^*),X(s_2^*,x_2^*))$. Thus, the contingent claims contracts between donors and candidates are generated as Nash equilibrium proposals by the candidates, with the property that these proposals induce electoral outcome probabilities consistent with groups' beliefs. To derive explicit equilibrium results, Baron assumes

$$p(X_1,X_2) = \beta X_1/[\beta X_1+X_2], \; \beta \geq 1^7 \tag{7}$$

and

$$R(s_i,\theta) = s_i^\alpha \theta, \; \alpha \in (0,1). \tag{8}$$

If $\beta > 1$ in (7), then candidate 1 has an exogenously given electoral advantage, say due to an incumbency effect, and α in (8) is a productivity parameter.

If candidates are symmetric ($\beta = 1$ and $V_i/c_i = V/c$, $i = 1,2$), there is an equilibrium, given (7) and (8), in which $(s_i^*,x_i^*) = (s^*,x^*)$, $p(X^*,X^*) = 1/2$ and both s^* and x^* are strictly increasing in V/c and α. More interesting are the asymmetric cases. Let $v \equiv V_1c_2/V_2c_1$ and assume $v \geq 1$.

Proposition 3 (Baron 1989a): (1) *Suppose $\beta > 1$ and $v = 1$ [$\beta = 1$ and $v > 1$]. Then: p_1 is increasing in β [v], with $p_1 > 1/2$; X_1 is a strictly concave function of p_1 with an interior maximum; X_2 is strictly increasing in $p_2 < 1/2$; and $[X_1+X_2]$ is decreasing in β [v]. (2) If $\beta > 1$ and $v = 1$, then s_1^* (s_2^*) is decreasing (increasing) in β. (3) If $\beta = 1$ and $v > 1$, then $s_1^* = s_2^*$ and $x_1^* > x_2^*$.*

Proposition 3 asserts that if candidate 1 has some exogenously given advantage ($\beta > 1$ or $v > 1$), then in equilibrium that candidate has an electoral advantage despite offering fewer services or requiring higher contribution rates than candidate 2. Somewhat less intuitive are the results on the behavior of candidate 1's equilibrium contributions in the probability of success. Suppose $\beta \geq 1$ and $v = 1$. Then as the equilibrium probability of candidate 1's electoral success increases in β from 1/2, the induced campaign contributions, X_1, at first increase and then decrease

---

7. Unlike Snyder's model, this specification *is* offered as a vote production function.

as p_1 goes to one. The reason for this is that for sufficiently high β, candidate 1 is sufficiently sure of electoral success that her marginal willingness to offer services declines faster than the marginal increase in p_1; hence, the willingness to supply increased contributions falls off. On the other hand, since $p_2 < 1/2$ for all $\beta > 1$, the marginal expected payoff from contributing to candidate 2 continues to increase with p_2 and so campaign contributions do too. In aggregate, these effects lead to the negative correlation between total contributions and p_1.

It is worth noting that Baron and Snyder predict different relationships between total contributions and p_1 for the asymmetric case (see proposition 2[2]); in Snyder's framework, p_1 and total contributions are positively related. The difference between the predictions is entirely due to utility rather than contribution-maximizing candidates in Baron's model. So Snyder's empirical results rejecting a positive relationship between p_1 and total contributions constitute evidence against contribution maximizing behavior.

It follows from the definition of $\hat{\theta}_i$ that a group can contribute to both candidates in a race, and that candidates honor contingent claims from any group that contributes irrespective of whether that group also contributed to her electoral opponent. Indeed, Baron shows that in a symmetric equilibrium both candidates receive contributions from exactly the same set of groups. However, Morton and Cameron (1992) argue that rational office-oriented candidates are more selective in their provision of services. Say that candidate i is *exclusive* if and only if i honors contingent claims with groups that contribute *only* to i and say candidate i is *inclusive* if she honors all contingent claims. In Baron's model, both candidates are inclusive. Suppose there is given capacity constraint on services and suppose candidate 1 (2) is only concerned to maximize (minimize) the probability of winning, $p(X_1, X_2)$. Then if candidate 2 is inclusive, 1 improves her probability of winning by being exclusive. Intuitively, if groups recognize candidate 1 to be exclusive, then they will surely contribute at most to one candidate, irrespective of the other's status. Moreover, if both candidates are exclusive and there is no capacity constraint, the only equilibrium is one in which $x_1^* = x_2^* = 0$. Since the probability-maximizing case approximates the situation when V_i/c_i is large, this argument suggests an explanation of why in any campaign PACs give only to one candidate (Poole and Romer 1985) and give so little (Snyder 1990).

2.2 Policy-dependent models

Policy-independent models inherently involve service-induced contributions and as such are ill suited to understanding interest groups concerned with policy outcomes more generally defined. Moreover, the only connection in such models between group behavior and political outcomes is through the vote function – the higher the proportion of monies a candidate receives, the more likely is a candidate to win. Although empirically true, it is not clear whether money produces winners or whether winners attract money. The models above suggest this identification problem is insoluble without an explicit theory of how money influences votes. Furthermore, until we understand how different candidates lead to different legislative outcomes, the fact that one candidate rather than the other is elected tells us little about the influence of groups on such outcomes. Models that begin to consider these issues explicitly include policy.

Austen-Smith (1987) develops a two-candidate model in which policy is a proportional tax on voter's wealth: There are n voters, each with classical economic preferences over a private good and a public good (proportional to total tax revenue), distinguished only by their respective given wealth levels, w_v, $v = 1, \ldots, n$. Hence, a voter's (v) induced preferences over policies, $u_v(\cdot)$, are single peaked on [0,1]. There are two firms. Given a policy z, firm A produces the private good under CRS and makes a gross return $R_A(z)$, with $R_A(z) > 0$, all $z < 1$, and $R'_A < 0$; and firm B is the contractor supplying the public good with gross return $R_B(z)$, with $R_B(z) > 0$, all $z > 0$, and $R'_B > 0$. These firms are the interest groups. There are two sources of uncertainty in this model. The first is the positions of the candidates. Each candidate i announces a policy $y_i \in [0,1]$, but this announcement is perceived noisily by voters and firms; the policy i implements if elected is given by $\tilde{y}_i = y_i + \tilde{\epsilon}_i$, where $\tilde{\epsilon}_i$ is a random variable with mean zero and variance σ_i^2. The second source of uncertainty is the decision calculus of the voters. Candidates know how the economic consequences of their platforms influence the decisions of voters but do not know how various idiosyncratic nonpolicy issues mitigate these influences (Enelow and Hinich 1984). So given policy platforms (y_1, y_2), the probability that a voter (v) votes for candidate i against k is given by $q_{vi}(Eu_v(\tilde{y}_i) - Eu_v(\tilde{y}_k))$, with q_{vi} increasing in utility difference and $q_{vi} + q_{vk} = 1$. Thus, biased voting is permitted (this is discussed below).

Campaign contributions are derived endogenously from profit-maximizing behavior by firms ($\equiv$ interest groups). Taking candidates' platforms (y) as given, firms A and B play a Nash game between themselves. Let $x_{ji}(y)$ be group (firm) j's contribution to i and write $x_j(y) = (x_{j1}(y), x_{j2}(y))$ and so forth. Equilibrium contributions $x^*(y) \equiv (x_A^*(y), x_B^*(y))$ are given by

$$x_A^* = \text{argmax}. p_1(x_A, x_B^*, y) R_A(y_1) + p_2(x_A, x_B^*, y) R_A(y_2) - x_{A1} - x_{A2} \qquad (9)$$

and

$$x_B^* = \text{argmax}.p_1(x_A^*, x_B, y)R_B(y_1) + p_2(x_A^*, x_B, y)R_B(y_2) - x_{B1} - x_{B2}. \quad (10)$$

The probability that candidate i wins the election is approximated by the normalized expected number of votes i receives; this has some justifications when n is large (Hinich 1977). Thus, $p_i(\cdot) = \sum_v q_{vi}(Eu_v(\tilde{y}_i) - Eu(\tilde{y}_k))/n$ and groups contribute to promote the election of their favored candidate (contributions are *position induced*).

Campaign contributions are entirely used by candidates to reduce the variance with which their respective platforms are perceived. Since voters are risk averse, this leads to an increase in each voter's utility for any platform. Candidates behave as Nash competitors with respect to each other, and Stackelberg leaders with respect to the groups and voters. Specifically, equilibrium platforms y^* are given by

$$y_1^* = \text{argmax}.p_1(x^*(y_1, y_2^*), y_1, y_2^*) \quad (11)$$

and

$$y_2^* = \text{argmax}.p_2(x^*(y_1^*, y_2), y_1^*, y_2). \quad (12)$$

To study the influence of group behavior on policy outcomes, equilibrium electoral platforms when contributions are forbidden (y°) are compared to equilibrium platforms when contributions are permitted say (y^*). Given (9) and (10), it is clear that no group contributes if candidates converge. And given there is a wedge between the platforms, it is clear that groups contribute at most to the candidate offering the closest policy to their respective ideal points. As remarked earlier, this feature is well supported empirically. With these comments in mind, the main result is as follows.

Proposition 4 (Austen-Smith 1987): (1) If $x^*(y^\circ) = 0$, then $y^\circ = y^*$. (2) If $x^*(y^\circ) \neq 0$, then either $[y_1^* < y_1^\circ \ \& \ y_2^* < y_2^\circ]$ or $[y_1^* > y_1^\circ \ \& \ y_2^* > y_2^\circ]$.

If electoral policy platforms are affected at all by interest group campaign contributions, then both platforms move in the *same* direction. And notice that, in contrast to Ben-Zion and Eytan (1974), groups do give money *not* to change candidates' positions but to support their favored policy. Any change is due to strategic candidates trading off gaining votes from policy per se with gaining votes from advertising.

The intuition is that the first-order impact of policy positions on contributions derives from the difference between candidates' platforms and not from their absolute location. With $y_1^\circ < y_2^\circ$ suppose candidate 1, taking y_2° as fixed, moves further to the left. This increases both candidate's 1 contributions and, because the groups perceive the difference between the platforms identically, those to candidate 2. Therefore, if 1 finds it worthwhile to make this move, then it must be that the gain in votes derived from increasing her contributions and expenditures more than offsets any loss in votes from the policy shift per se and from the increase in monies going to her opponent. But then, given no abstention, it cannot be the case that increasing the distance between the platforms "is payoff-improving" for candidate 2. So to attenuate any gains that 1 accrues by opening the gap between their policies, 2 moves to narrow the difference between them; hence, proposition 4.

Biased voting is intended to prevent convergence in candidate platforms, a necessary condition for the antecedent of proposition 4(2) to occur. Unfortunately, given that there is no abstention in the model, it turns out that biased voting is not enough to drive a wedge between candidates' platforms. An additional assumption is required; specifically, that there exists some $\epsilon > 0$ such that $|y_1 - y_2| \geq \epsilon$. Although this kind of assumption can be found elsewhere, it is distinctly ad hoc.

Other policy-dependent models have adopted a similar, purely policy-oriented, perspective on interest group giving. Edelman (1992) derives proposition 4 in a model with an aggregate vote function, two policy-motivated candidates, and a single PAC. Cameron and Enelow (1992) include "firm specific effects," in which $y_1 = y_2$ does not necessarily imply $R_j(y_1) = R_j(y_2)$ for any j, and derive a conflicting result – that money moves both candidates toward their respective donors rather than toward a single donor. Ingberman (1992) explores a model with variance-reducing campaign expenditures that includes an incumbent who chooses her platform first and a challenger who follows. An important feature of Ingberman's model is that the incumbent has a historically given platform and, if she holds to this position, groups and voters perceive her as being less risky than the challenger with respect to her de facto policy if (re)elected – an "incumbency effect." This effect drives the wedge between equilibrium electoral platforms necessary to induce positive contributions. With this setup, Ingberman shows that the incumbent always adjusts her platform "in the direction of increased contributions" (160). Depending on the details of the incumbency effect and the incumbent's historically given position, this incentive is consistent with Austen-Smith's result, with Cameron and Enelow's polarization result, and with a new result in which both candidates are induced to move closer together. In sum, the exact way in which position-induced contributions from policy-oriented groups influence the electoral positions of the candidates seems to be sensitive to details of strategic structure and parametric specification.

Baron (1994) adopts a different approach. As in his earlier work, he assumes (for the most part) that groups are motivated by private benefits, but that the services any candidate might offer depend on the candidate's policy position. If candidate i is elected on platform $y_i \in [0,1]$, then any group j that contributed to i's campaign receives per capita benefits $s_i = s(y_i)$. Such benefits are purely exclusive, and i can refuse to grant benefits to groups who do not contribute. Not every individual in the electorate is a member of a group, and group membership is exogenous.

In the model, two candidates simultaneously choose policy platforms to maximize their respective probabilities of winning. The probability that i wins depends in part on campaign expenditures (equals contributions) and in part on i's platform y_i. Specifically, Baron assumes that a proportion π of the electorate is uninformed about $(y_1, y_2) \in [0,1]^2$ and, given X_i denotes the campaign contributions to candidate i, the expected vote from these voters is simply $\pi X_i/[X_1 + X_2]$. The remainder of the electorate is fully informed and all individuals have quasi-linear preferences over policy and net private benefits, with quadratic policy preferences; informed voters vote sincerely on the basis of which a candidate offers them the highest net payoff. Hence, the probability that candidate 1 wins is $p(X_1, X_2, y) = \pi X_1/[X_1 + X_2] + (1-\pi)G_1(y)$, where $G_1(\cdot)$ depends on the distribution of informed voters across groups and so forth. As in Baron (1989a), groups treat the probability of candidate i's winning parametrically, and equilibria are required to satisfy a rational expectations property. But in contrast to the first paper, the contract (s_i, x_i) is not explicitly derived here.[8] Instead, Baron assumes a structure for the contingent claims contract between groups and candidates that leads to tractable analytic expressions for $G_i(\cdot)$ and X_i in terms of policy platforms (y_1, y_2), the proportion of informed voters in the groups, and so forth. Let γ denote the proportion of informed voters in interest groups and say that campaign expenditures are *informative* if π is decreasing in $[X_1 + X_2]$. Then the principal results are

Proposition 5 (Baron 1994): (1) *If campaign expenditures are uninformative, then as π or γ increases, y_1 and y_2 (weakly) move apart and away from the median voter's ideal point; $p_i = X_i/[X_1 + X_2]$ and $[X_1 + X_2]$ is strictly increasing in π. (2) If campaign expenditures are informative, then y_1 and y_2 move toward the median and*

---

8. In a most ambitious model, Baron and Mo (1993) consider a multistage game in which parties competitively choose policies, following which candidates explicitly bargain with interest groups to determine the contingent claims contracts, and the election is determined by an aggregate vote production function such as (7), above. Bargaining outcomes depend on party policies and the ease with which groups can switch from bargaining with one candidate to bargaining with another. The model generates a tension for parties between adopting convergent policies to win votes and divergent policies to secure contributions; depending on the parameterizations, both effects can be observed.

$[X_1+X_2]$ *is a decreasing in the informativeness of expenditures,*
$|\partial \pi / \partial[X_1+X_2]|$.[9]

The key feature of the model is the distribution of voters between those that are informed and those that are not. Although the decision calculus of the uninformed individuals is not considered (why, for example, don't they treat the behavior of the informed individuals and the groups as signals of candidate locations and vote accordingly?), the model highlights the importance of policy-oriented voting: the more widespread this is among the electorate *not* in any interest group (lower π), the less influence interest groups exert on policy outcomes.

3. Money and legislative influence

A large empirical literature on the influence of campaign contributions on roll-call voting has yielded mixed results (for example, see Chappell 1982; Kau and Rubin 1982; Wright 1985; Wilhite and Theilmann 1987; Keim and Zardkoohi 1988; Langbein and Lotwis 1990). Moreover, most of the money given to legislators comes from interests within the legislators' own districts (Wright 1989). Consequently, there is likely to be a high correlation between how a given legislator would vote based on constituency concerns alone and how she would vote to support donors, suggesting that groups do not give money to influence votes at all. On the other hand, voting is not the only activity subject to financial influence. In particular, Hall and Wayman (1990) find a relationship between campaign contributions and the legislator's behavior in committee. This latter finding is consistent with Denzau and Munger (1986) who explore the relationship with a resource allocation model of legislator behavior.

Denzau and Munger (1986) assume n organized groups and one unorganized group. Each organized group ($j = 1, \ldots, n$) cares only about policy issue y_j, and is supposed to be small relative to the unorganized group. Members of the unorganized group care about the whole vector of legislative outputs $y = (y_0, y_1, \ldots, y_n)$, where y_0 summarizes all the issues of concern only to the unorganized group. Consider a single incumbent legislator who chooses how much legislative effort ($e_j \geq 0$) to devote to each issue y_j; given e_j, the legislative output on issue j is given by the deterministic function, $y_j = y_j(e_j)$. Only organized groups contribute and only members of the unorganized group (hereafter, the electorate) vote.

---

9. Assuming purely policy-oriented groups and position-induced contributions, Baron shows that in this model, both candidates converge to the median and there is no interest group activity in equilibrium. Thus, service-induced contributions are essential here to support equilibrium activity by interest groups.

The legislator chooses current legislative activities to maximize her expected vote total (V) in the coming reelection campaign. Specifically, let $\bar{e}$ denote the legislator's capacity constraint on legislative effort and let $\Delta = \{(e_0, \ldots, e_n) \in \mathbb{R}_+^{n+1} : \Sigma_{j=0}^{j=n} e_j = \bar{e}\}$, then the legislator solves

$$\max_{e \in \Delta} V(y(e), X(y(e))),$$

(13)

where $y(e) = (y_0(e_0), \ldots, y_n(e_n))$; and $X(y) \equiv \Sigma_{j=1}^{j=n} x_j(y_j)$ is the total contribution elicited from the organized groups. V is assumed increasing in X.

The program (13) involves an aggregate vote production function depending on policy outputs and aggregate campaign expenditures. Denzau and Munger interpret the derivative,

$$\partial V/\partial e_j = \partial V/\partial y_j \cdot \partial y_j/\partial e_j + \partial V/\partial X \cdot \partial x_j/\partial e_j,$$

(14)

in terms of the extent to which the electorate (group $j = 0$) is informed about issue $j \in \{1, \ldots, n\}$. Specifically, the greater the extent to which the second term of (14) dominates the first, the less informed is the electorate with respect to issue j, and so the less it is concerned with the legislator's activities on behalf of organized group j. Similarly, Denzau and Munger interpret the derivative $\partial y_j/\partial e_j$ in terms of the incumbent's legislative effectiveness; for example, if the incumbent belongs to the committee under which jurisdiction issue j falls, but not to the committee responsible for issue k, then Denzau and Munger expect $|\partial y_j/\partial e_j| > |\partial y_k/\partial e_k|$.

At the problem's solution, marginal effort (in terms of votes) must be equalized across all issues to which the legislator devotes positive effort, and the marginal value must be negative for any issue that the legislator ignores. Thus, the influence of interest groups' campaign contributions is greatest on issues about which the electorate is ill informed.

Denzau and Munger extend the model to $\ell > 1$ legislators and ask how groups allocate contributions across legislators. Intuitively, group j wishes to give most to the legislator i whose electorate is most ignorant regarding y_j and whose effort-productivity ($\partial y_j/\partial e_j$) is high. They argue that electoral incentives lead to a positive correlation between legislative effectiveness on an issue and the extent to which the legislator's electorate is informed about the issue (e.g., members of the agricultural committee tend to represent farming districts). Consequently, the principal result (that special interests have only limited legislative influence) is reinforced in this broader setting.[10]

---

10. This claim is harder to interpret. With multiple legislators in a majoritarian legislature, we should have legislative output on each issue j depending on all legislators' efforts; $y_j = y_j(e_{1j}, \ldots, e_{\ell j})$. Implicitly, Denzau and Munger assume $y_j(\cdot)$ is additively separa-

The only other model focusing explicitly on money and legislative influence is Snyder's (1991), which studies a pure bribery model of group influence on voting and agenda setting in a majoritarian legislature. Snyder's model is extremely simple (and somewhat cynical): groups either buy votes or (subject to majority approval) policy alternatives directly. Yet even in such an uncluttered environment the relationship between interest group contributions and influence turns out to be relatively complex.

Suppose there is a single group j with quasi-linear preferences, $u_j(y,X) = -(y-z_j)^2-X$; where z_j is j's ideal policy, y is the implemented policy and $X = \Sigma_i x_i$ is j's total contribution to legislators i. There are ℓ (odd) legislators and legislator i's preferences are similarly defined, $u_i(y,x_i) = x_i-\alpha(y-z_i)^2$; where $\alpha > 0$ measures the electoral salience of the issue, assumed common across $i = 1, \ldots ,\ell$. Assume $z_1 < \ldots < z_\ell$ and that the group's ideal point is distinct from the legislative median; say, $z_j > z_{(\ell+1)/2}$. Now suppose that j can perfectly discriminate across legislators (i.e., $x_i \neq x_k$ is possible for any pair of legislators) and, for any agenda $\{y_1,y_2\}$ such that j strictly prefers y_2 to y_1, let $X(y_2;y_1)$ denote the minimal total bribe necessary to insure y_2 wins a majority vote against y_1. Then Snyder proves[11]

Proposition 6 (Snyder 1991): (1) *(voting influence) Assume there is a fixed agenda* $\{y_1,y_2\}$ *such that* $y_1 < y_2$ *and* $z_{(\ell+1)/2} < (y_1+y_2)/2 \leq z_\ell$. *Then* j *"pays the highest bribes to legislators whose ideal points are closest to the median of the legislature, but on the side of the median closer to* $[y_2]$*" (98). (2) (agenda influence) Let* $y_2^*(y_1) =$ argmax.$u_j(y,X(y;y_1))$*. If* y_1 *lies between* $-z_j$ *and* z_j *then there exists a nonempty interval* I *such that* $X(y_2^*(y_1);y_1) > 0$ *if and only if* $y_1 \in$ I*; moreover,* $X(y_2^*(y_1);y_1)$ *is strictly concave in* y_1 *on* I *with an interior maximum.*[12]

Proposition 6(1) is intuitive – all j needs to do is bribe the marginal opponents. But the result runs counter to the specification of many empirical models attempting to correlate campaign contributions with legislative voting behavior; typically, these assume that the relationship

ble in its arguments implying that y_j cannot be determined by any nondictatorial voting process. Nevertheless, their insight that the institutional details of legislative decision-making processes can be critical for understanding the incidence of interest group influence is important.

11. Although, not surprisingly, total bribes are higher without the ability to discriminate across legislators, Snyder proves that the qualitative properties of proposition 6(2) go through in this case also.

12. If the agenda does not satisfy the locational restrictions in proposition 6, then bribes would either be unnecessary or too costly.

between the probability of voting in favor of a donor's position and money received is monotonic increasing (eg., Chappell 1982; Poole, Romer, and Rosenthal, 1987). Proposition 6(2) is less intuitive. What drives the result is that the group's optimal choice of y_2^* to a given status quo y_1 is not a monotonic function of y_1; in effect, it is characterized by the monopoly agenda setting prediction of Romer and Rosenthal (1978). Consequently, a given y_2^* might be best for two different status quo positions y_1, y_1' and the level of bribes required in the two cases might be different. It follows that "the total amount of bribes paid by the [interest group] is not a good indicator of the [group's] influence over policy" (Snyder 1991, 101). If money is given to affect votes, then this result (similar to proposition 3[1] above for electoral campaign contributions) might explain the absence of any clear empirical correlation between money and votes.

Finally, Snyder shows that the more salient an issue is for legislators (high α), the more costly it is for the group to manipulate votes and agendas. This result qualitatively supports Denzau and Munger (1986) – the more germane an issue is to a legislator's constituents, the less readily can an interest group purchase the legislator's decisions.

4. Information and electoral influence

Interest groups do a great deal more than give money (Smith 1984, 1989; Wright 1990; Hansen 1991; Rothenberg 1992). One important activity that has received scant attention in the formal, if not in the descriptive, literature is the informational role played by groups. This is especially true for elections, in which groups provide information directly both to candidates regarding the salience of various issues to the electorate and to the electorate regarding characteristics and behavior of the candidates for office. While there is no formal theoretical work on the first topic, Grofman and Norrander (1990) and Cameron and Jung (1992) consider the impact of interest group endorsements on electoral outcomes.[13]

Grofman and Norrander (1990) consider the voting decision of a typical individual (v) in a simple two-candidate, one-dimensional spatial voting model. The voter (v) has symmetric single-peaked preferences with ideal point (z_v) and knows that candidate 1's policy, $y_1 \in [0,1]$, is to the left of 2's, $y_2 \in [0,1]$. However, the voter does not know the critical value, $\hat{y} = (y_1 + y_2)/2$, that determines v's vote. On the other hand, v does know the respective ideal points of two interest groups z_1 and z_2 (also

---

13. Lupia (1992) also studies a model with endorsements having a similar basic structure to Cameron and Jung (1992). However, the endorser in Lupia's model is neither strategic nor has preferences over the consequences of the endorsement.

with symmetric single-peaked preferences) and the interest groups are presumed to be fully informed about $\{y_1, y_2\}$. Insofar as groups devote more resources than independent voters to investigating the policy stances of candidates for office, this assumption is a natural starting point. An *endorsement* by an interest group is a statement about which candidate that group most prefers; it is not a statement about the exact location of that candidate's position. Assume z_1 is closer than z_2 to the voter's ideal point z_v. Grofman and Norrander's observation in such a case is that if the interest groups' are nonstrategic and if the voter's prior belief is that $\hat{y}$ is distributed uniformly over $[0,1]$, then either v ignores all endorsements or v votes for the candidate endorsed by interest group 1 and the probability that this vote is correct for the voter is $1 - |z_1 - z_v|$.

The assumptions of symmetric preferences, nonstrategic endorsements, and a uniform prior are essential. Given symmetric preferences, the only circumstance under which group 1 and the voter disagree about the preferred candidate is when $\hat{y}$ lies strictly between z_v and z_1. Given nonstrategic endorsements, group 1's preference revelation is honest, and since $|z_v - z_1| \leq |z_v - z_2|$, the uniform prior and Bayes rule now immediately yield that the voter's conditional expected payoff is maximized either by voting with his prior or by voting for the candidate endorsed by group 1.

Cameron and Jung (1992) look at endorsements in a Romer and Rosenthal (1978) agenda-setting model. There is a given status quo $y_1 \in [0,1]$ and a monopolistic agenda setter offers $y_2 \in [0,1]$; y_1 is common knowledge, but a pivotal voter does not know the location of y_2. An electoral interpretation is that y_1 is the incumbent's historically fixed platform, y_2 is the platform adopted by a policy-oriented electoral challenger, and a challenger's position is inherently more uncertain than the incumbent's. Once y_2 is chosen, one or more interest groups with known preferences over $[0,1]$ can offer endorsements. Like Grofman and Norrander, all agents' preferences are symmetric single peaked and interest groups are supposed to be fully informed about y_2, but, unlike Grofman and Norrander, the interest groups here are strategic actors. Endorsements are modeled as cheap-talk messages, and mixed strategies are allowed; so interest groups are free to endorse y_1 or y_2 or to offer no information. Predictions are then derived by analyzing (refined) sequential equilibria to the game; thus, the informational content of any endorsement is determined in equilibrium rather than imposed. Label interest groups so that their respective ideal points are $z_1 < \ldots < z_n$ and assume $z_v < z_n$. The results are

Proposition 7 (Cameron and Jung 1992): (1) *If* $z_v \leq z_1$, *then the voter ignores all endorsements except that offered by interest group* 1;

if $z_v > z_1$ and $n > 1$, then the voter ignores all endorsements except those offered by the closest pair of interest groups such that $z_j < z_v < z_{j+1}$. (2) *Relative to when no endorsements are permissible, the number of alternatives that are offered, accepted, and utility-improving against y_1 for the voter and the challenger increases.*

The first statement of proposition 7(1) is consistent with the Grofman and Norrander analysis, but, assuming strategic endorsements by interest groups, leads to a distinct result with respect to the number of groups whose endorsements can be influential. Moreover, since the challenger's equilibrium platform (y_2) depends both on her preferences and on the likely endorsement decision of the interest groups, the "promise" or "threat" of endorsement effectively induces the challenger to adopt positions more acceptable to the pivotal voter, and this change in incentives relative to the case in which there are no groups leads to proposition 7(2) Although interests group endorsements *given* a pair of platforms can influence voter behavior, the *anticipation* of such influence bears on the challenger's choice of platform per se. Moreover, these effects typically are to the voter's advantage, at least as evaluated ex ante (Cameron and Jung 1992, 29–31).

5. Information and legislative influence

Lobbying is essentially an informational activity (Milbrath 1963; Rothenberg 1989; Smith 1989; Wright 1990; Hansen 1991). Legislators typically make policy decisions under uncertainty, regarding either their political consequences (e.g., how are reelection chances affected?) or their technical consequences (e.g., how will a revised Clean Air Act hurt employment in the auto industry?). Information is thus valuable, and those possessing it are in a position to influence legislative decisions. Interest groups are frequently relatively well informed about the particular issues with which they are concerned. Consequently, legislators have an incentive to listen to the advice of groups and so become better informed. Unfortunately, since the preferences of any given interest group and legislator are not necessarily coincident, there is an incentive for groups to dissemble to elicit legislative actions in their favor. Rational legislators recognize this and are accordingly skeptical of claims that invariably support a group's position. The circumstances under which there can be influential information transmission between (relatively) informed groups and (relatively) uninformed legislators are therefore not clear.

A small but growing formal literature looks at interest group influence with strategic information transmission. Ainsworth (1993), Potters (1992), and Potters and Van Winden (1992) consider lobbying games involving a single interest group and legislator. The legislator takes one of two actions {a,b} uncertain about the state of the world {α,β}. Only the group knows the true state, but the legislator's and the group's preferences over (state, action) pairs are common knowledge. In particular, assume that the legislator wishes to take action a in state α and b in state β. Lobbying is costly. The group can pay a cost $c > 0$ to give an unverifiable message to the legislator about the state of the world or can pay nothing and say nothing.

Depending on the group's preferences and c, a variety of equilibria are possible. Focusing on the most informative equilibria in each case, the key observation is that the closer are the group's and the legislator's preferences, the more readily can information be credibly transmitted. That is, if preferences are perfectly aligned, then the truth is always told and the full information action taken, and if preferences are disparate (i.e., the group prefers action a in state β and action b in state α), then the only equilibrium involves no lobbying and no information transmission. In the interesting case, the group has essentially state independent preferences: whatever the true state, the group prefers action b, but the its payoffs from b under the two states may differ (for example, suppose the group is the Dairy Farmers' Lobby; the actions are decrease (a) or increase (b) milk price support, and the states are whether milk production will be low (α) or high (β).

Specifically, let payoffs be given by

	Action	
	a	b
α	0,A	U,0
State		
β	0,0	V,B

where the first entry in each cell is the group's payoff. Assume A, B, U and V are strictly positive, and $V > U$. Let p denote the legislator's prior belief that the true state is β and suppose p is sufficiently small that the legislator chooses a if choosing on the basis of her priors alone (i.e., $p < p^\circ \equiv A/[A+B]$; let $\sigma(s)$ denote the probability that the group lobbies and says the state is β, $s \in \{\alpha,\beta\}$, and let $v(m)$ be the probability that the legislator chooses b, given the message $m \in$ {group lobbies (m_1), group doesn't lobby (m_2)}.

Proposition 8 (Potters and Van Winden 1992): *Suppose* $p < A/[A+B]$.
(1) *If* $U < c < V$ *then in equilibrium:* $\sigma(\beta) = 1$; $\sigma(\alpha) = 0$; $v(m_2) = 0$; $v(m_1) = 1$. (2) *If* $c < U$ *then in equilibrium:* $\sigma(\beta) = 1$; $\sigma(\alpha) = p(1-p^\circ)/(1-p)p^\circ$; $v(m_2) = 0$; $v(m_1) = c/U$.

Hence, if the cost of lobbying is high relative to the group's gross payoff when the state is "bad" for the group (α), only a group knowing the state is "good" actively lobbies and consequently convinces the legislator to choose $\underline{b}$; and this is the full information decision for the legislator (proposition 8[1]). When the cost of lobbying is sufficiently low, proposition 8(2) says that a group with "bad" information only lobbies sometimes and dissembles; since a group with "good" information always lobbies, not lobbying fully reveals the truth. Therefore, some but not all information is transmitted and, although on average the legislator takes the full information decision, there are occasions in which the group successfully dissembles and the legislator takes action $\underline{b}$ when the true state is β. The incentives for the group knowing α not a lobby all the time are generated by the legislator's occasionally choosing $\underline{a}$ irrespective of any advice to the contrary.

This sort of signaling model casts light on how "influence" might be generated endogenously through lobbying. Furthermore, it makes sense of the commonplace observation in the descriptive literature that legislators are typically lobbied by their "friends" (Bauer, Pool, and Dexter 1963). From a rational choice perspective, this claim is odd since it suggests that groups spend money to "persuade" legislators to do what they were going to do anyway. But as the signaling approach makes clear, in *equilibrium* it appears for the most part that what the lobbying groups and the legislator want coincide, irrespective of whether the group and the legislator were "friends" prior to any lobbying taking place; on average the legislator chooses as the group that lobbies her advises.

In Potters (1992), Potters and Van Winden (1992), and Ainsworth (1993), it is common knowledge that the group is informed. Consequently, saying nothing is also a "lobbying" message; specifically, the situation is isomorphic to one in which lobbying is free but the group can choose to make some expense (say, a campaign contribution) additional to any speech in favor of one action or another as a signal of its true type (i.e., α or β). Thus, these models say little about the decision to lobby per se. Austen-Smith and Wright (1992) develop a two-group/single legislator model in which groups must choose whether or not to become informed and, therefore, in which the decision to lobby per se is explicit.[14]

The possible states of the world, actions, and legislator's preferences are as given above. Two groups, G_a and G_b, have state-independent and strictly opposing preferences; specifically, G_j receives a gross payoff of $R_j > 0$ if action $j \in \{\underline{a},\underline{b}\}$ is taken and receives 0 otherwise. At the start of

14. See also Potters (1992) for an extension of the Potters and Van Winden model to include competing groups.

the process, all agents share a common prior p that the true state is β and assume $p < p°$, so that the legislator chooses $\underline{a}$ in the absence of any further information. G_j can pay price $c_j > 0$ and observe the true state of the world; initially, assume that the legislator is unable to observe the true state directly. The game then begins with the groups simultaneously choosing whether to become informed; though this decision is observable, what they observe if they become informed is not (for example, the group might solicit a private survey to establish the likely electoral consequences for the legislator of choosing $\underline{a}$ over $\underline{b}$).

Having acquired information or not, the groups simultaneously lobby the legislator, giving a speech in private about what the legislator should do. If a group has not acquired any information, then the legislator knows that the group is uninformed and so ignores any lobbying. Thus, the decision to become informed is isomorphic to the decision to lobby, that is, an informed group's decision to "stay home" is equivalent to a lobbying speech (exactly as in Potters and Van Winden's model) but an uninformed groups' decision to stay home" is not – and the legislator's beliefs about the true state are unaffected. Consequently, I shall use "G_j lobbies" equivalently to "G_j acquires information." Having heard the groups' advice, the legislator can choose to verify the information at a cost $c_L > 0$; if she does so and discovers a group to have dissembled, then the group pays a cost (for instance, it is denied access in the future). Finally, the legislator takes an action and payoffs are distributed.

Recalling that the legislator's priors imply choosing $\underline{a}$ in the absence of any lobbying ($p < p°$), the principal results from the model include

Proposition 9 (Austen-Smith and Wright 1992): (1) *There exist* $0 < \underline{p} < p°$, $c_L > 0$ *and a strictly decreasing convex function* $\pi(c_L)$ *such that no group lobbies if* $p < \underline{p}$ *or* $c_L > \underline{c}_L$; *only group* G_b *lobbies if* $p \in (\underline{p}, \pi(c_L))$ *and* $c_L \propto \underline{c}_L$; *both groups lobby if* $p \in [\pi(c_L), p°)$ *and* $c_L^- \leq \underline{c}_L$. (2) *If only* G_b *lobbies, then* G_b *tells the truth only most of the time; the legislator never checks on advice to chose* a *and only checks on advice to choose* b *some of the time; the legislator acts as advised unless she learns otherwise from checking.* (3) *If both groups lobby, then both tell the truth and the legislator always acts under complete information.*

The model thus generates conditions under which there is no lobbying, lobbying by one, and lobbying by two groups. If only G_b lobbies, the situation is similar to that discussed under proposition 8(2). And if both groups lobby, then the legislator surely acts under complete information.

The intuition here is straightforward. Since the legislator chooses $\underline{a}$ absent any additional information, only G_b has an incentive to lobby. However, if p is too low ($p < \underline{p}$), then the chances of the true state being β

are likewise too low to invest in lobbying; and if c_L is sufficiently high to preclude the legislator ever verifying G_b's information ($c_L > \underline{c}_L$), G_b may lie freely so the legislator ignores any message from G_b that the truth is β and therefore it is not worthwhile for G_b to become informed. So assume $p > \underline{p}$ and $c_L < \underline{c}_L$. For $p < \pi(c_L)$ G_b is willing to lobby even though it may discover the true state to be α and (most often) report this to the legislator; the incentive to do this, as in proposition 8(2), is that occasionally G_b dissembles successfully (the legislator does not invariably verify information). But as p increases beyond $\pi(c_L)$, the equilibrium probability of a successful lie by G_b increases, which in turn increases the incentive for G_a to acquire information and engage in *counteractive* lobbying. And when both groups lobby, the legislator can credibly threaten to check on any inconsistent pair of messages, thus inducing truth-telling by both groups.

Proposition 9 yields three testable hypotheses: (1) when a legislator is lobbied by groups from only one side of an issue, these groups are opposed to the legislator's ex ante position; (2) the decision of such groups to lobby an "unfriendly" legislator is independent of the lobbying decisions of opposing groups; and (3) conditional on a "friendly" legislator is purely counteractive. These hypotheses are tested empirically in Austen-Smith and Wright (1994) using data from Senate lobbying on the Bork nomination to the Supreme Court in 1987. None of the three could be rejected.

As in the earlier signaling models, legislators benefit from interest group lobbying; in equilibrium, the truth is told most of the time and so most of the time the legislator takes the full-information action. Further, the more important are the issues to the groups (i.e., the higher is R_j), in general the more likely it becomes that the legislator takes the full-information decision in equilibrium. And proposition 9(3) shows that the presence of competitive interest groups can improve the situation in this respect. Finally, the welfare properties extend to the case in which the legislator can acquire information firsthand; indeed, even if the acquisition cost is smaller than the verification cost (c_L), the legislator can strictly prefer to rely on the advice of interest groups rather than obtain firsthand data. This is because the expected cost of such reliance falls short of any gain in having to invest in data acquisition (see also Rasmusen 1993 on this).

Legislators almost never can ensure a given legislative outcome on their own since legislatures are majoritarian and rarely delegate responsibility for any policy decision to a single agent. Yet virtually all models described so far assume a high degree of monopoly decision-making power. In an effort to relax this assumption, Austen-Smith (1993) presents a model in which there is a given status quo policy ($b_1 \in R$) and a committee has the sole right to propose an alternative (b_2). The committee's proposal is considered in the legislature as a whole (the House) under a closed rule (i.e., the House can choose between the proposal and the status quo but cannot make amendments). Legislators have quadratic preferences over the *consequences* of any bill (b) – given by $y(b,t) = b-t$, where t is the realization of an ex ante unknown parameter lying in $[0,1]$. Assume the (unitary actor) committee has an ideal point ($z_c > 0$), and the ideal point of the median voter in the House (z_h) is normalized to zero; thus, for every $t \in [0,1]$, the committee would like to implement a larger bill than the (median voter in the) House.[15] An interest group can, at a cost, discover the true value of t and lobby either the committee at the agenda-setting stage or the House at the voting stage once the agenda $\{b_1, b_2\}$ has been set, or both. Whether or not the group is informed at all is private information to the group. However, an informed group can prove that it *is* informed if it so chooses, whereas an uninformed group cannot prove that it is uninformed or informed.

The model focuses on identifying when the group lobbies at the agenda-setting stage or at the voting stage and on describing the character and extent of influence on the final policy decision. Unlike previous models, the interest group has state-dependent preferences (specifically, quadratic in the consequences of legislation with ideal point z_g) and all lobbying messages are costless (i.e., cheap-talk signals). Say that lobbying is *informative* if the lobbying message changes an agent's beliefs about t and that lobbying is *influential* only if the action taken by the agent being lobbied consequent on lobbying is distinct from that absent any lobbying. Clearly, influential lobbying is informative but the converse may not be true. Then the main results are summarized by

Proposition 10 (Austen-Smith 1993): (1) *The group does not always become informed; not all informed groups lobby the committee at the agenda-setting stage; there can coexist influential lobbying at both stages of the process; lobbying at the agenda-setting stage is generically influential but lobbying at the voting stage, although typically informative, is not always influential.* (2) *The smaller is* $|z_g - z_i|$, $i \in \{c, h\}$, *the more influential is interest group lobbying of* i.

Ceteris paribus, agenda-stage lobbying in committee is more effective in promoting the group's preferences than vote-stage lobbying – this is consistent with Hall and Wayman (1990) and Wright (1990). And consistent with Potters and Van Winden (1992), the closer together are the group's and any legislator's preferences, the more influence the group

---

15. With quadratic preferences, legislator's i's most preferred bill given any value of t is simply $b_i(t) = z_i + t$.

has with that legislator. But with closely aligned preferences, having more influence is a good thing insofar as the legislator makes decisions with better (objectively more precise) information. Of course, whether or not this is good with respect to a broader normative measure is unclear; for instance, the fact that a legislator's preferences are closely aligned with those of an interest group may in and of itself be cause for concern in a majoritarian system.

6. Conclusion

This review of interest group behavior is necessarily limited. I have not dealt either with the rent-seeking or the endogenous tariff literature, both of which fall within the domain of interest group theory.[16] Nor have I considered interest group influence on the courts (Epstein 1991) or on the bureaucracy (Banks and Weingast 1992), and these omissions reflect more the extent to which formal models of explicit interest group behavior have been applied in these areas than any judgement of relative importance. With such limitations in mind, the formal models of interest group behavior I have discussed are fairly sanguine about the extent of group influence on policy outcomes.

The service-induced contribution models directly assume legislators can "contract" with groups to provide private benefits, but the extent of such benefits must be very small since for anything of policy consequence, legislative decision making is majoritarian and making contracts on such issues for private gain is exceedingly difficult, if not prohibitively costly. Moreover, the empirical work supports this observation. Individual PACs give small sums to candidates (typically less than $2,500, which in turn is less than the legal cap at $5,000), and estimates of the implicit value of services offered are small (Snyder 1990, 1993). On the other hand, money does improve a candidate's chances of election, in which case the composition of a legislature is itself subject to some interest group influence in the aggregate. This is essentially the focus of position-induced models of campaign contributions, in which groups give to promote a favored candidate, taking that candidate's policy positions as given. Although the models here point to the importance of a trade-off between winning votes by policy choice and winning votes by manipulating induced preferences with advertising, they are not entirely satisfactory. In particular, there is as yet no consensus on the appropriate model of how money maps into votes. In the extant models, the issue is either finessed by positing an aggregate vote production function or addressed in a weak fashion by

---

16. See the essays in this volume by Tollison and Magee, respectively. I have discussed several issues in endogenous trade theory elsewhere: Austen-Smith (1991).

assuming some kind of variance-reducing technology with risk-averse voters. Until the issue is better understood, there is little hope of saying anything normative about whether any induced influence over policy is good or bad. Furthermore, the models ignore any signaling aspects of campaign contributions or the incentives of small groups to free ride when giving is position induced. There is virtually no work on these topics in an electoral context.[17]

The other principal policy-related activity of groups is informational, and here the formal literature is even more sparse. However, models of strategic signaling by relatively informed groups, both at the electoral stage (endorsements) and at the legislative stage (lobbying), typically lead to the result that listeners make "better" decisions judged against the complete-information benchmark. The insight from the signaling game literature is that rational listeners (voters or legislators) take account of the incentives for informed speakers (the groups) to provide information strategically to manipulate beliefs in their favor. When it is easiest to lie, the extent of influence is most limited; on the other hand, to provide incentives for informed groups to provide credible information, it is typically essential for, say, legislators to act as the groups advise even though this may be contrary to the interests of the legislators (or of those they represent). So there is a price for being informed in terms of "giving in" to the groups periodically; on balance, the price is small. Having said this, there is no presumption in these models that what legislators wish to do and what is "good," however defined, are the same thing. Furthermore, since legislatures tend to be majoritarian, it is important to generalize the informational approach to multiple groups and multiple legislators to examine the robustness of existing results.

Modeling interest groups in the political economy is hard, but considerable progress has been made. Nevertheless, we cannot say much, on the basis of the current formal literature, about the extent to which interest groups influence policy, and we can say even less about the normative properties of any such influence. The relevant benchmark for a democracy in an uncertain world has yet to be identified.

17. But see McCarty and Rothenberg (1993) for a theoretical and empirical model that admits free riding among groups and integrates position-induced and service-induced motivations for PAC contributions; and see Ball (1995), Austen-Smith (1995) and Lohmann (1993) for signaling models of campaign contributions.

CHAPTER 15

Logrolling

THOMAS STRATMANN

Incentives to engage in the exchange of votes in legislatures, or log-rolling, have existed since the inception of legislatures. Most promi-nently, logrolling is alleged in the United States, where a plurality rule is employed to elect representatives from single-member districts. In legis-latures elected by proportional representation, incentives to exchange votes also exist, however. Often that exchange is more formalized via the formation of a governing coalition (Schofield 1987a).

In the political science literature, early discussions of logrolling go back at least to Bentley (1907). From then until the early 1960s, the exchange of votes in legislatures had been viewed with disdain and thought of as welfare reducing. Beginning with the seminal contribu-tion of Buchanan and Tullock (1962), logrolling was seen as potentially welfare enhancing. Today, no consensus exists in the normative public choice literature as to whether logrolling is on net welfare enhancing or welfare reducing, that is, whether logrolling constitutes a positive- or a negative-sum game. This essay will describe various arguments and avenues via which the exchange of votes can be welfare enhancing or welfare reducing. I will address the following questions: under what conditions logrolling may be welfare enhancing, whether a logrolling mechanism can be designed that has favorable properties, and whether related voting processes may maximize welfare. The public choice lit-erature has wedded logrolling with cyclical majorities by showing that some of the potentially negative impacts of logrolling stem from the possibility of unstable majorities. Instability of coalitions may turn welfare-enhancing arrangements into welfare-reducing ones. Investiga-tions of the apparent stability of coalitions and collective choices in the real world, have explored whether mechanisms exist to induce stability, whether some institutions preserve welfare-enhancing arrangements, and whether chaotic trading, which reduces welfare, can be channeled

Support from a John M. Olin Foundation grant to the Center for the Study of the Econ-omy and the State, University of Chicago, is gratefully acknowledged.

Table 1.

Voter	Issues	
	A	B
1	5	−1
2	−1	5
3	−1	−1

into ordered trading that is welfare enhancing. The role of leaders and parties has been explored as a potentially important mechanism to ensure that vote trading is a positive-sum game. Thus, logrolling potentially can improve welfare in two ways: via the design of a specific voting rule that allows logrolling via additional institutional arrangements.

Recently, logrolling has been studied empirically. The results confirm the prevalence of logrolling in the House of Representatives and support the view that trades are ordered and that a large degree of stability prevails in Congress. The results present evidence for extensive log-rolling among specific agricultural interests, and further evidence exists for logrolling coalitions among legislators representing broader interests such as city, labor, and farm groups.

1. Definition

A logrolling situation is defined as follows: Let (x,y) and (z,w) be pairs of mutually exclusive issues. Let voter preferences with respect to each pair be separable. Let each voter vote sincerely. A logrolling situation exists if

$$xPy \text{ and } zPw, \text{ but } ywPxz$$

where P stands for social preference as defined by the voting rule employed (Bernholz 1974b, 53). For many theorems regarding logrolling, it suffices if the first two social relationships are characterized by R (e.g., x and z do not lose to y and w, respectively).[1]

Logrolling is illustrated in Table 1. Voters 1, 2, and 3 vote on issues A and B using simple majority rule. The payoffs for these three voters on issue A are 5, −1, and −1, and the payoffs for the voters on issue B are

---

1. I will use the terms logrolling and vote trading interchangeably. Alternatively, one can think of logrolling as applying to deals that go into omnibus bills and the term vote trading as applying to deals that are voted on separately.

−1, 5, and −1. If everyone votes sincerely, neither issue A nor issue B passes. However, voters 1 and 2 have an incentive to form a vote-trading, agreement: voter 1 agrees to vote for B and in exchange the second voter agrees to vote for A. In the absence of the vote trade and with sincere voting, both issues fail.[2] In the presence of the vote-trading agreement – which implies sophisticated voting and therefore a misrepresentation of preferences – both issues pass. In this example, total utility is increased by 3 units for each issue and society is better off overall. The trade is welfare enhancing in this case, social choices obtained by simple majority rule are improved by trading votes. If the −1's in Table 1 are replaced by −3's, voters 1 and 2 still have an incentive to trade votes. However, in this case society is worse off overall, by −1 for each issue. Welfare has decreased.

Trading can impose an externality or utility loss on nontraders. If these losses are large, then the community as a whole is worse off. In the first example, logrolling occurs in the context of a positive-sum game; in the second example, a vote trade is arranged in the context of a negative-sum game. The controversy surrounding the optimality of logrolling can be viewed as a discussion over whether logrolling is a positive- or negative-sum game.

2. The normative potential of logrolling

Simple majority rule elicits a simple yes or no vote on a given issue but not the degree to which a voter favors or opposes an issue, that is, it reveals ordinal preferences on binary issues but not cardinal preferences. Thus, majority rule makes no allowances for differences in intensities of preferences among voters. Vote trading occurs because intensities differ. Scholars who look favorably upon logrolling have been intrigued by its potential to reveal intensities of preferences.

The normative logrolling literature asks whether social benefits are maximized if votes are traded in a legislature. Pareto-superior bills are ensured if the unanimity rule is used (Wicksell 1896). In this context, vote trading, combined with the unanimity rule, implies an alteration of bills until every legislator gains from the package. For legislators to come to an agreement to pass an issue under the unanimity rule, the benefits to the voters favoring the issue have to outweigh the losses of those initially opposed to the issue. If this condition holds, logrolling can increase aggregate utility in a committee or legislature that uses majority rule.

2. The distinction between sincere and sophisticated voting was introduced by Farquharson (1969).

Voting under majority rule only allows the voter to register the direction of a preference, not its intensity. This shortcoming of majority rule can in principle be eliminated by vote trading. Individuals exchange votes on issues they do not feel strongly about for votes on issues they do feel strongly about. Buchanan and Tullock (1962) were the first to notice the normative potential of logrolling: that logrolling allows for an expression of different intensities of preferences and that collective choice with vote trading may bring society closer to the provision of a socially optimal level of public goods.

If issues decided upon are local public goods, the logrolling coalition may pass proposals that redistribute income from the minority to the winning coalition, rather than achieve an efficient allocation of resources. However, logrolling can lead to a Pareto-optimal allocation of resources when side payments are allowed (Buchanan and Tullock 1962, 190–2). With money side payments, the redistribution of income accompanying allocative efficiency outcomes is eliminated. The mixing of allocative and distributional issues is one of the forces that drives the instability associated with vote-trading agreements, discussed later in this essay. I will also discuss how the instability caused by mixing allocative and distributive issues points to a definition of jurisdiction that corresponds to the spillover benefits of public goods.

Another positive account of logrolling comes from Coleman (1966), who suggests that the outcomes of vote trades are Pareto efficient. Each member of a committee trades votes with other members on public good issues. Members sell their votes for issues they do not feel intensely about and secure votes on public goods issues that are intensely favored by them. Expected utility is maximized when costs of selling another vote equal benefits from obtaining another vote. At this point, an equilibrium is reached that maximizes a social welfare function. Coleman concludes that majority rule with vote trading is more likely to maximize aggregate welfare than majority rule without vote trading. If by the passage of bills total utility increases, vote trading on public goods is the analog to the Walrasian market for private goods. The socially optimal level of public goods is selected if majority rule is combined with logrolling.

It appears that Coleman's description of the vote-trading process is too optimistic. Vote-trading outcomes may not be stable, implying a lack of equilibrium in the vote-exchange market (Mueller 1967; Park 1967). If trade agreements are broken, instability may arise, and shifting coalitions may lead to a decrease in welfare. The Pareto frontier may not be reached if voters misrepresent their preferences to increase their bargaining power (Mueller 1967). For example, voters have an incentive to announce that they are opposed to issue X even though they favor it, to induce other committee members to vote for another issue Y they favor in exchange for their support on X. In this case, it is not clear how the best trades are chosen to reach a social optimum. An additional complication is introduced if voters cheat. Once the issue X is voted on, some traders have an incentive not to fulfill their part of the bargain. The potential for cheating increases with the number of voters, since the probability that a given vote is decisive decreases with the size of the group. The problem has an analog in private markets, where collusion is impossible if the number of sellers is large. Each seller receives a greater gain from breaking the cartel contract than from abiding by it. Since individuals know about this potential for reneging on trade agreements, they may not enter into them with large groups (Mueller 1967).

Scholars have addressed the question of whether a voting system can be designed that allows the expression of preference intensities as in logrolling thereby resulting in an outcome that maximizes welfare. Reneging on trades occurs because no votes are actually exchanged (Mueller 1973). Thus, part of the problem of achieving Pareto optimality via vote trading can be solved if votes are literally exchanged. Mueller (1973) suggests that a voter be given a certain number of votes and allowed to allocate them to issues he or she feels intensely about. Votes are actually traded and voters cannot form vote-trading coalitions. Physical exchange of votes is not enough to solve the problem of voters' having an incentive to misrepresent their preferences, however, if they are aware of the preference structure of other voters. The literal exchange of votes has desirable properties only if nobody knows about the preferences of other voters, that is, there is no communication between them (Coleman 1967).

A simulation approach has been employed in which voters reveal intensities of preferences for various public goods through the exchange of votes in Walrasian markets (Mueller, Philpotts, and Vanek 1972). Actual vote trading occurs once an equilibrium set of exchange ratios has been established. The results show that, generally, total utility tends to increase if vote trading is allowed.

Were society to decide to use a unanimity rule on allocative efficiency issues, vote trading would lead to an optimal allocation of resources. The concerns surrounding the optimality of logrolling are in part due to an electoral system that does not define jurisdictions according to the spillover of public goods. Further, current voting rules do not distinguish decisions on the redistribution of income from those on allocative efficiency. In Tullock's road example, each access road is a local public good. The problem here is that voters other than the voters affected by the public good decide on the production of the good. A proper definition of the jurisdiction, according to the spillover of the public good, would have reduced the incentive to combine issues of allocative efficiency with issues of income redistribution. To ensure proper definition of the jurisdiction, an appropriate decision has to be made at the constitutional stage. If the constitution were to restrict the legislature to vote only on allocative efficiency issues, vote trading would be more likely to bring society to the Pareto frontier than if votes were traded on issues of redistribution of income.

Nonetheless, there is hope that positive benefits can be achieved even in the current political setup. Congressional leaders have incentives to maximize welfare in the legislature (Koford 1982). In Koford's model, legislators can trade only through the party leader. Party leaders form a kind of clearing house that balances credits and debits, and set prices at which they are willing to defeat or pass a bill. Votes for or against a measure as desired by leaders are paid by the legislators. Leaders who interact frequently with legislators come to know their true preferences. Knowing the legislators' true preferences, and the requirement that all trades are made through the party leaders, ensures that preferences cannot be misrepresented and that leaders can provide efficient vote-trading services. Competition to become a leader ensures that those most skillful at arranging trades become leaders. Leaders from different parties form a collusive duopoly that maximizes joint gains (Koford 1987). Competition between parties occurs over the division of the gains.

Logrolling allows intense minorities to have their way on some issues. This may be desirable, especially in a winner-take-all plurality system such as that in the United States. In an electoral system of proportional representation, minorities are represented according to their relative size within the electorate. In a winner-take-all system, minorities are effectively shut out except when they are clustered within one electoral district. If such clustering exists, this minority can increase its importance and its representation in the political process via vote trading. Logrolling may make the political process more appealing to these minorities.

3. Point voting

Point voting can be thought of as an alternative to logrolling for revealing preference intensities and assuring an efficient allocation of resources. It has been considered as a possible mechanism to elicit preferences for some time (see, for example, Musgrave 1959, 130–1; Mueller 1973). However, it was thought that this process was as vulnerable to strategic manipulation as other voting processes. Voters might not reveal their true preferences and have incentives to allocate all points to the issues they feel most intensely about (Philpotts 1972).

Hylland and Zeckhauser (1979) devise a version of point voting that appears nearly to eliminate the possibility of strategic manipulation. As proposed by Hylland and Zeckhauser, point voting assumes that tax shares have already been assigned and that the only decision left is the level of provision. The goal of the procedure is to reveal intensities of preferences as an alternative to vote trading. An iterative procedure is proposed. First, the government or auctioneer announces quantities of n public goods and voters allocate their vote points to increase or decrease the proposed quantities. Next, the government aggregates vote points and calculates the new quantities of public goods, and the process of allocating vote points continues with the newly proposed quantities. The process stops when the number of all voting points to increase the proposed quantities equals the number of points to decrease the proposed quantities of public goods. Hylland and Zeckhauser's innovation is the way in which vote points are aggregated by the government. They found that voters have an incentive to reveal their preferences honestly if the government aggregates the square roots of the vote points allocated by each voter. Aggregating the square roots provides sufficient penalty for voters who allocate their preferences by placing all of their vote points to their most preferred issue. The procedure ensures that voters allocate to each issue just the sufficient number of vote points to ensure a Pareto-optimal allocation of public goods.

The issue of strategic manipulation of voting procedures is addressed in the work of Gibbard (1973) and Satterthwaite (1975). They show that immunity to strategic manipulation and satisfying the independence axiom are logically equivalent. It follows from their work that voters can improve the outcome of a voting process by misrepresenting their preferences. The point voting procedure overcomes the obvious strategy of misrepresentation of preferences by allocating all vote points to the most preferred issue. The aggregation rule of the square roots of vote points invalidates this strategy. The iterative nature of the procedure allows some scope for strategic manipulation, but such strategies are not apparent.

Point voting is a decentralized way to obtain information on individual preferences for public goods. Intensities of preferences are revealed just as efficiently as private goods markets provide information about consumer preferences. If one thinks of the number of points as the voter's endowment, then the process of deriving the socially optimal level of public goods is similar to the pure vote-exchange model.

4. Negative sides of logrolling: Instability of logrolling equilibria

In Tullock's (1959) early discussion of logrolling, he gave the following example of a situation in which logrolling is expected to occur:[3] voters have to decide on the maintenance of access roads to a main highway, with a few farmers served by each access road. If all voters voted on each road separately, none would be repaired since only a minority of voters benefit from a given road. However, if more than half of the voters form a vote-trading agreement in which they contract to support the repair of each other's roads, then the roads reaching these voters will be repaired. Logrolling can ensure that at least half of the roads are maintained. The road example is a potentially positive-sum game; benefits exceed costs. However, some of the gains from the vote-trading coalition may be lost; members of the coalition repair the roads beyond optimal levels because they do not have to bear the full costs of the repair if costs are shared equally among all farmers. Some of the costs are born by farmers not in the winning coalition. In this case majority rule with trading can lead to too much government spending.[4]

With vote trading voters are better off than if they did not exchange votes on issues of interest to them since bargains among voters are mutually beneficial. An equilibrium is reached when the marginal cost of maintaining the access roads is twice the marginal benefit (Buchanan and Tullock 1962). Buchanan and Tullock's account of the logrolling process is optimistic in that an equilibrium is reached. The road repair example is typical of an entire class of issues decided by majority rule with respect to a mixing of issues of allocative efficiency with issues of redistribution of income. Benefits from building the road exceed costs. Allocative efficiency is improved if the roads are built. However, costs are not born by the beneficiaries alone but by nonbeneficiaries as well, causing an oversupply of the good. Further, resources are transferred from a minority to a majority.

In this early literature on vote exchanges it was hoped that logrolling was the solution to the Arrow paradox. The Arrow paradox can be viewed as resulting from our lack of information on any but ordinal preferences. The Arrow paradox can be avoided if a measure for the intensity of preferences can be found. In this case, given a certain aggregation rule, the outcome that maximizes social welfare could be selected. Intensities of preferences are revealed through vote trades. Thus, it was suggested that logrolling causes cyclical majorities to vanish (Buchanan and Tullock 1962, 333) and that vote trading leads to "free-

---

3. Previous to Tullock (1959), Downs (1957, 55) addressed implicit logrolling, that is, the formation of a platform composed of various proposals. In the political science literature early discussions of logrolling go back to Bentley (1907).

4. Downs (1961) challenged Tullock's argument, noting that there is a tendency for government to undersupply general interest legislation. Mueller also (1989, 333–4) raises doubts regarding the hypothesis that logrolling leads to a larger than optimal size of government.

dom from Arrow's impossibility theorem" (Coleman 1966, 1115). However, it was shown that a social choice process involving logrolling is plagued by cyclical majorities.

Cycling occurs when an alternative proposal beats all other proposals under the voting rule used. Cycling implies the presence of intransitive social preferences. The close relationship between vote trading and cyclical majorities can be illustrated by using Table 1. From this table, four combinations of issue pairs arise: (A,B), $(\sim A,B)$, $(A,\sim B)$, and $(\sim A,\sim B)$. A cycle exists over these issue pairs. After voters 1 and 2 have agreed to form a coalition for the passage of both issues (A,B), voter 3 has an incentive to approach voter 2 for the passage of the $(A,\sim B)$ pair. This combination makes voter 2 better off by 3 units and voter 3 better off by 2 units of utility. Next, voter 1 has an incentive to approach voter 3 with the proposal to pass none of the issues $(\sim A, \sim B)$. Voter 3 will abandon the coalition with 2 to enter a more favorable coalition with 1. From this point, the cycle can start all over again with the combination (A,B).[5] Bernholz (1973) shows formally that preferences that allow for a logroll imply the existence of a voting cycle.[6] Although individual preferences may be transitive, group preferences are intransitive in situations that allow vote trading. The possibility of cycling through logrolling implies that the potential benefits from a logroll may go unrealized if coalitions are not stable.

The sequence of possible trades and outcomes is virtually endless, giving enormous powers to an agenda setter who can stop trades at a point in the sequence that is most advantageous to him or her (McKelvey 1976). If the potential for a cycle exists, an agenda setter can lead the committee through a series of votes to his or her preferred outcome. Shifting coalitions do not only occur when the loser proposes a platform to make a voter abandon a logroll coalition and join the previous loser; shifting coalitions can occur simply because the agenda setter is altering the proposals put before the committee in a particular way. Observationally, shifting coalitions due to agenda setting and those due to seeking better trades are equivalent. The cycling results have severe implications for the normative properties and stability of the political process. Logroll coalitions are predicted to be inherently unstable, and the outcomes of the political process may be far from anything resembling optimality. The

---

5. Caplin and Nalebuff (1988) claim that for reasonable spatial preferences cycles cannot occur for majorities greater than 64 percent.

6. Downs was probably the first to indicate a relationship between vote trading and the voting paradox (1957, 55–60 and 64–9). Other references showing that the existence of logrolling implies the possibility of cycles are Bernholz (1973, 1975), Koehler (1975a, 1975b), Oppenheimer (1975), and Schwartz (1975, 1981).

only way a logroll does not create the potential for a cycle is when a unanimity rule is used (Bernholz 1973).

The theorems of Bernholz and others link the instability of the classical voting paradox with vote trading. They say that, if a majority of voters prefers the passage of some package of minority positions, there exists an alternative bundle of some other minority positions preferred by some other majority. Thus, an agreement is unstable because some voters have the power to overturn it in favor of an alterative outcome. Further, these results are troubling in another dimension. Public choice addresses the issue of how to induce cooperation in collective choices and how to overcome the problems associated with the prisoner's dilemma. Once the cooperation problem is overcome, however, via some vote-trading contracts, the issue of instability of the outcome immediately arises. As in the prisoner's dilemma, players have an incentive to find a more advantageous arrangement: an outcome is potentially unstable if cooperation is an integral part of that outcome. Therefore, it is difficult to induce individuals to cooperate; players know that once cooperation is achieved, some actors have the power to overturn the outcome in favor of another.

Some scholars suggest that the possibility of reneging is unlikely to arise because of credibility issues (Coleman 1967; Mueller 1967). Riker and Brams (1973) stress the possibility that trades may be broken and that this phenomenon causes instability. They emphasize that logrolling is most likely a negative-sum game. The costs imposed on nontraders outweigh the benefits achieved by traders. In this view, logrolling is a negative-sum game and every voter can lose if majorities are cyclical. Rational trades make all members worse off over a cycle, and logrolling is more often a move away from the welfare frontier than a move toward it. The conclusion of this argument is that logrolling is unimportant in legislatures (Riker and Brams 1973, 1240). The Riker and Brams model has been criticized on the grounds that voters do not sell their votes in the best market (Tullock 1974) and that in their model voters are myopic and trade even if it makes them worse off (Bernholz 1974a). Schwartz (1975) responds to Riker and Brams by showing that the outcome in the absence of vote trading can be Pareto inefficient. He shows that when it is, there exists at least one potential vote trade that can make every legislator better off than he or she would have been in the absence of vote trading.

The centralized vote-trading model stands in stark contrast to the previous model in its optimism about the vote-trading process (Koford 1982). In the central vote exchange model reneging is not an issue since vote trades are organized centrally by party leaders. Votes are prices paid for the passage of legislation. Costs of passing the bill are costs incurred by legislators who are opposed to the legislation but vote for it. These costs are minimized: leaders have incentives to select those legislators to help pass a bill for whom it is cheapest to do so. Further, legislators pass only bills for which benefits exceed costs. Thus, vote trading exist within the confines of a positive-sum game.

5. Apparent stability in social choices

It appears that we do not observe endless cycling in the real world. Acts are passed and remain unaltered for a long time. Outcomes from one session to the next do not differ as much as indicated by the cycling theorems. Once Congress has regulated an industry, it takes many years and overwhelming evidence of the inefficiencies of the policy to assure deregulation of the industry. Stability seems dominant. At least some degree of stability is also evidenced by Mayhew's (1966) account of logrolling coalitions between legislators representing city, labor, farm, and western interests. Neither does it appear that reversals and cycles occur in other areas of collective choice. For example, incumbents get reelected and are not defeated by challengers as predicted by cycling theory. No erratic shifts of allocations of resources among government sectors occurs as might be expected if different majorities govern from period to period. Tullock (1981) noted that the theory that predicts cyclical majorities stands in sharp contrast to reality and asks why stability is observed in legislatures, although instability is predicted by innumerable chaos theorems.

Stories about cyclical majorities focus entirely on short-run incentives and assume a degree of myopia. If foresight is added to the story, the results change. If members of the winning coalition have foresight and understand that they will ultimately receive less if coalitions are unstable, cheating on vote trades is less likely. Rational behavior predicts that if one player is breaking a vote-trading agreement to achieve a larger payoff, this player has to expect that subsequently other players will also break vote-trading contracts with him. A degree of myopia is required for the player breaking a vote-trading contract to expect others not to do the same. Cheating is profitable in the short run, but the relevant question is whether cheating is profitable on balance, or in the long run. For an individual player cheating may be profitable if it takes a long time until someone else cheats. The relevant decision rule for cheating is to compare the present value of payoffs under reneging on a vote-trading contract and not reneging. If it pays more to stick to the present agreement, voters will not break the contract. By this line of reasoning, a representative who expects to stay in the legislature for another few sessions is less likely to break vote-trading agreements than a legislator who is serving his or her last term. Misrepresentation of preferences is not profitable if it is not credible. Knowledge of constituency characteristics of committee members serves to decrease the potential of misrepresentation of preferences: committee members have incentives to acquire information about constituency characteristics of fellow members to reduce the potential of preference misrepresentation.

Experimental studies provide hope about the efficiency and stability of logrolling agreements. Experiments with students using the auction method of voting showed that voters did not behave strategically (Smith 1977). Vote-trading situations have a core in many but not all experimental settings (Ordeshook 1986). In this case a core is defined when the sincere outcome is undominated. Experimental results indicate much more stability in outcomes than expected if majority rule is used (Fiorina and Plott 1978; McKelvey and Ordeshook 1980).

The solution concept for zero-sum games proposed by von Neumann and Morgenstern (1953) is stable. They argue for the absence of cyclical majorities, reasoning that if a trader knows a certain trade will be overturned, he may stick to a relatively advantageous trade. In a divide-the-dollar game between three voters, a stable coalition over many periods between two of the voters assures a win of 50 cents for each period. If one of the voters reneges and majorities turn cyclical, the average expected gain is 33 cents. Along similar lines, Oppenheimer (1975) suggests that a bargaining set can be used as a predictor for logrolling. Some experimental evidence suggests the competitive solution will prevail (McKelvey and Ordeshook 1980).

Haefele (1971) and Koford (1982) suggest that party leaders arrange trades, form winning coalitions, and maximize the welfare of party members. Haefele emphasizes the role of parties in legislatures. In his model, parties help the formation of coalitions and induce stability in outcomes. As previously noted, Koford (1982) proposes that party leaders in Congress provide "efficient vote-trading services." Leaders are thought of as passing bills when the total demand for the bill exceeds the total demand against the bill. Leaders maximize expected consumer (representative) surplus. They pass bills for which positive demand exceeds negative demand by forming vote-trading coalitions. If the trading process is organized in this manner, efficiency is enhanced and potential reneging is minimized. Welfare is increased via a centralized process: bills are passed only when total demand for exceeds total demand against. Leaders from both parties cooperate in securing vote trades that maximize welfare of their party members in the legislature. If the majority party would attempt to maximize the surplus of its members only, for example via internal logrolling, the minority party would have incentives to offer vote trades to members of the majority party that designed to break up this coalition. A cooperative duoploy has stronger stability properties than any other equilibrium (Koford 1987). In a later paper Koford (1990) argues that transactions costs (i.e., the costs of informing citizens how their representative voted on a bill) lead to logrolling coalitions that organized along party lines.

One expects the vote-trading coalition to be a minimum winning coalition (Riker 1962). Every unnecessary member included in the winning coalition implies that the net payoff is smaller for the members than needed to secure victory. The largest share for each member is secured when the coalition has the minimum number of members to ensure passage of the bill. However, minimum winning coalitions are potentially unstable (Tullock 1981). Losers always have an incentive to reformulate the platform, so they are included in the winning coalition. Tullock proposes that a form of logrolling that includes nearly every voter in a legislature is a device to form stable coalitions; minorities are not excluded from getting some benefits so that they are not tempted to form alternative coalitions. A formation of larger than necessary coalitions induces stability. In the limit the whole committee is in the coalition.

Instability implies the formulation of new vote-trading contracts. This involves decisions on which issues to trade votes on and decisions on the price of votes. Transaction costs of formulating new vote-trading contracts are assumed to be zero in formal models that produce instability theorems. Once transactions costs of making and breaking a contract are introduced, a degree of stability is introduced (Coleman 1983). An alternative and more formal argument was put forth by Shepsle and Weingast (1981), who argued that institutional structures produce stability. For example, institutions restrict the number of bill reformulations via the congressional committee system and devices such as the closed rule. Institutional arrangements may produce equilibria known as structure-induced equilibria; in these equilibria, committees, viewed as gate keepers, play an important role in arriving at stable outcomes. The committee system admits only certain preferences in the drafting of the bill. The closed rule in Congress prevents amendments from the floor, thereby restricting the number of alternatives. Further, stability may be induced because of constraints on agenda setters. Agenda setters often are not at liberty to pick any pairs of alternatives they wish (Niemi 1983). Constraints on the number of alternatives that are proposed in a legislative body also induce stability (Niemi 1983).

Bernholz (1978) emphasizes that a legislator knows neither the duration of his stay in Congress nor the number of issues that may come up. In this case, a stable prisoner's dilemma supergame emerges since the same types of issues are repeatedly voted on and the same players reappear in successive games. The gains from cooperation are positively related to the stability of the game. In a repeated game, voters cannot do better by violating vote-trading contracts; once a voter breaks a contract, he loses trustworthiness, which is an impediment to future contracting. A shortcoming of this model, as with most models of logrolling, is the impossibility of predicting the types of coalitions formed. All one can say is that once a vote-trading coalition is formed, it should be stable. Assuming repeated games and addressing the consequences of loss of trustworthiness seem appropriate for models of legislatures.

It is useful to view the logrolling literature as belonging either in the category of anarchic trading or in the category of ordered trading. Anarchic trading implies instability, shifting coalitions and negative welfare effects. Ordered trading produces welfare gains and is stable. The theorems that relate logrolling to cyclical majorities, as in the work of Bernholz (1974b), and Riker and Brams (1973), belong in to the anarchic category. The work by Haefele (1971) and Koford (1982) are examples of ordered trading. In this type of categorization, Mueller's (1973) vote-market suggestion is viewed as one mechanism of transforming chaotic trading into ordered trading as occurs in private goods markets. Ordered trading is implied by models that show the importance of legislative structure (Shepsle 1979; Shepsle and Weingast 1981). If instability were widespread in Congress, evidence for reciprocity in vote trades should be virtually nonexistent, supporting the view that trading is anarchic. Evidence presented by Stratmann (1992) does not support the anarchic trading idea. He finds reciprocity among members from agricultural districts voting for their colleague's commodity price supports, quota restrictions, and so forth. In another study, he found nonideological reciprocity between representatives of city, labor, and farm districts on votes for subsidies to these sectors of the economy (Stratmann 1995).

Ordered trading is also predicted by models that view parties as institutions that reduce the transactions costs of organizing logrolling coalitions Koford (1990). By organizing these coalitions, they maximize their members' net benefits. Using party cleavage as a means to organize trades, legislators divide into two groups with similar preferences in each group. The location of the parties is endogenous: their location is such that the issue that divides most legislators divides the party (Koford 1990). One can think of legislators as using party as a device, a marker, along which vote-trading coalitions are organized. The driving factor, however, motivating a legislator to trade votes and motivating his or her choice of trading partners must be the similarities of constituencies between legislators of the same party.

6. Evidence for logrolling

Empirical work on legislatures must face the problem that most theories give little or no guidance on how to proceed in estimating relationships. In the area of logrolling, theory predicts that anything can happen. Paradoxes occur in the literature because everyone is allowed to trade with everyone else. For example, voters mildly opposed to proposition B may trade votes with a minority intensely favoring proposition B in exchange for the minority votes against issue A. If this were true, then no empirical relationships could be found. However, there appear to be some patterns in vote trading and stability in legislatures. For example, the trade among commodity interests within a block of legislators interested in farm subsidies has been reported as ongoing since the inception of government subsidies to the agricultural sector (Black 1928). Caught in this dilemma – the lack of theoretical guidance for empirical work and the appearance of stable empirical relations – empirical work on legislative voting behavior is proceeding on a thin rope in the specification of statistical models. However, progress has been made.

Early studies by political scientists often do not explicitly address the issue of logrolling but report vote trading in the process of their descriptions of legislative behavior.[7] Mayhew (1966) studies the House of Representatives in the United States from 1948 to 1962.[8] He focuses on votes addressing farm, city, labor, and western issues. During that time, most representatives from the Democratic party tended to vote in ways benefiting special interests. Examining the constituency benefiting from various types of legislation, Mayhew argues that legislation benefiting farm, city, labor, and western interests could not have passed if every legislator had voted sincerely. Mayhew observes that Democrats representing various special interests supported each other on four different types of issue. He infers logrolling from statements in the *Congressional Record*, for example, by Alfred Santiano who states "I say to you Members from the farm States whom we have supported time and time again that this policy of Government aid is a two-way street. We want you to support us to the same extent we supported you" (81). Mayhew draws the conclusion that "the Democratic party in 1947–62 was transcendentally a party of 'inclusive' compromise. . . . Some congressmen wanted dams, others wanted mineral subsidies, others wanted area redevelopment funds, others wanted housing projects, still others wanted farm subsidies. As a result, the House Democratic leadership could serve as an instrument for mobilizing support among all Democrats for the programs of Democrats with particular interests. 'Indifferent' Democratic congressmen fre-

---

7. Logrolling can occur either via explicit trades of votes on bills or amendments or via the inclusion of various issues in a single bill voted on as a package. Most studies have focused on the explicit exchange of votes on bills or amendments that are voted on separately.
8. For other early empirical work related to logrolling see Fenno (1973) and Ferejohn (1974).

quently backed such programs 'even against the debatable best interest of the people of their own communities' " (Mayhew 1966, 150). Froman (1967) emphasizes that bargaining between legislators is important for the passage of many types of legislation. Froman describes bargaining as taking the form of simple logrolling (the pork-barrel kind), time logrolling, compromise, and side payments. He provides anecdotal evidence for these types of bargaining. Jackson (1974) hypothesizes that logrolling occurs on those votes that are poorly explained by constituency variables in regression equations. Using this criteria and analyzing roll calls from the 1963 Senate, he comes to the conclusion that vote trading is important for some votes.

More recently, economists have worked on the empirical identification of logrolling and logrolling coalitions in Congress. Kau and Rubin (1979) attempted to identify logrolling and to distinguish between self interest, ideology, and logrolling in congressional voting. In a conditional logit analysis, they used observations on representatives' actual votes on a variety of issues – dichotomous variables – as the explanatory variable for the dependent vote variables. For example, roll-call votes on hijacking and consumer protection were among the votes used to explain a roll-call vote on a highway program. This identification of logrolling coalitions has two shortcomings. First, this analysis may serve to examine what kinds of coalitions form, but no theory underlies the analysis as to what vote variables should be included in the regression equation. Given this lack of guidance from formal logrolling models, this issue is difficult to address. Second, the same unobserved constituency variables or any other set of variables may influence the vote on the left-hand side and right-hand side of the regression equation. In this case the actual vote variable on the right-hand side of the regression equation is correlated with the error term and the estimated coefficient on the vote variable is biased. A solution to this problem is to use the predicted vote index of a probit model that is a function of constituency variables. Voting on bills is an expression of the direction of preferences, not their intensity. However, by using the predicted value of the vote index, a measure of intensity of preferences is found. For example, on votes on increases in wheat subsidies, ceteris paribus, this index is higher the larger the number of wheat farmers among the constituency of the voting representative. Further, the index is a linear combination of observed variables. Thus, no observed variables can potentially cause a correlation between the error and the predicted vote index.[9]

9. Stratmann (1992) uses a three-equation simultaneous probit model to test for the presence of logrolling coalitions. A good first assessment on whether logrolling is important for a particular set of votes can be obtained by simply inserting the predicted vote value into the regression equations.

Empirical work must face the issue of which votes are those where logrolling is expected. Some guidance is provided by theory. Votes that are potentially subject to logrolling are votes where a minority of legislators is intensely in favor (opposed), while the majority of legislators are mildly opposed (in favor) or indifferent. Logrolling gives a specific prediction: xPy and zPw but $ywPxz$. Vote trades are predicted on issues that would not pass if every legislator votes his or her honest preferences but that are passed if logroll coalitions are formed. Likely candidates are votes where the minority interest has won. Among this set of votes, applying Riker's (1962) size principle, likely candidates are votes in which the outcome has been reasonably close. Using this reasoning and the statistical method outlined above, Stratmann (1992) identifies logrolling statistically among agricultural interests on amendments to the 1985 farm bill. Among the findings are that representatives from tobacco districts traded votes with legislators representing other agricultural commodity interests, specifically sugar and peanut farmers. Fairly equal size on the peanut-vote coefficient in the sugar regression and the sugar-vote coefficient in the peanut regression provided evidence for nonideological reciprocity and coalition formation. This finding is consistent with the many anecdotal reports indicating that vote trades have been formed among legislators representing specific farm commodity interests. A recent anecdote comes from former Senator Gore (1992), who writes "As a member of the Southern 'farm block' in Congress, I have followed the general rule that I will vote for the established farm programs of others in farm states . . . in return for their votes on behalf of the ones important to my state."

One expects that legislators marginally opposed to legislation, rather than strongly opposed, are those being sought as members of the logrolling coalitions. The opportunity cost of voting for special interest legislation is lower for a legislator who is marginally opposed than for a legislator who is strongly opposed because of the characteristics of his or her constituency. Thus, if leaders organize logrolling coalitions and vote trades efficiently, they will select legislators as members of the vote-trading coalition who are marginally opposed. Evidence suggests that those legislators who are the cheapest to buy for membership are most likely to be members of the vote-trading coalition. For example, on an amendment on peanut subsidies, it was found that 120 legislators switched their vote due to a vote-trading agreement. These legislators made up a disproportionate share of those who had a probability between 0.3–0.4 and 0.4–0.5 of voting for peanut subsidies: 90 percent of legislators who were in the 0.3–0.4 range switched votes and 65 of 134 legislators who were in the 0.4–0.5 range switched.

In another study, Stratmann (1995) examines some of the votes analyzed by Mayhew. Mayhew (1966) argues that logrolling coalitions were organized in the Democratic party. Stratmann assesses whether vote exchange agreements independent of party pressure determined roll calls in the House of Representatives. Vote trades between interests favoring legislation benefiting city, farm, and labor constituencies were analyzed. It was found that vote-trading agreements were qualitatively and quantitatively important. For one set of estimates, it was found that membership in the vote-trading coalition caused 71 legislators to switch their vote to favor farm subsidies, 135 representatives switched their votes to favor city subsidies, and 58 representatives switched to favor labor legislation.

If logrolling is beset with unstable coalitions, composition of the winning coalitions varies constantly. The net redistribution of benefits will be zero in the long run since every voter is a member of the voting coalition at least sometimes. Using a variance test to examine cyclical majorities in the U.S. Congress, Stratmann (1996) finds no evidence of cycling and finds that federal grants and pork-barrel projects are unevenly distributed among congressional districts. These results point to the importance of institutions in legislative decision making.

Studies that examine the normative properties of logrolling assume that logrolling is an important element of congressional voting. This assumption is validated by casual observation and empirical studies with different levels of sophistication (Mayhew 1966; Kau and Rubin 1979; Stratmann 1992). A question less explored is how logrolling coalitions form. One explanation is that party leaders or presidents organize these coalitions or that logrolling coalitions are formed along party lines (Koford 1987). Observing votes along party lines on redistributive issues (for example, on urban redevelopment programs) does not imply that party leaders are the causal factor that drives the formation of the logrolling coalition. The underlying cause of legislators' trading along party lines may be that it is the lowest cost exchange available. Fiorina (1974) emphasized the difference between reelection constituencies and geographic constituencies. If legislators from the same party have similar reelection constituencies then similarities in election constituencies may lower the opportunity cost of vote trades between party members. Thus, party affiliation is a merely veil behind which legislators with similar constituencies trade votes.

7. Conclusion

In the 1960s and early 1970s, the research on logrolling focused primarily on normative issues. The subsequent literature linked the apparent stability of social choices to institutions that may induce stability and may produce some degree of optimality into the collective choice. Recently, empirical work has reiterated the importance of vote exchanges in legislatures. These studies measure vote trades and point to ways in which logrolling coalitions are formed.

To date, empirical findings appear to point to stable coalitions. For example, the ongoing vote-trading coalitions between farm, city, labor, and western interests has been documented from 1947 to 1962. Further, reciprocity in vote trades has been found, indicating no widespread reneging on vote-trading agreements. Empirical studies on logrolling may help to solve the normative issues surrounding the exchange of votes.

Following the argument by Riker and Brams (1973), one may argue that even if no cycle is observed and coalitions are stable, the fact that a potential for a cycle exists implies that the outcome of the collective decision is arbitrary. However, political institutions may produce incentives that lead to an outcome that is far from arbitrary. Following Koford's (1982) line of reasoning, political leaders calculate utilities and maximize welfare. In this case, the outcome is not determined by an agenda setter who leads a committee to his preferred outcome but by the party leaders' quest to maximize welfare.

So far, the scarce evidence on vote trading appears to be consistent with the hypothesis that leaders efficiently organize vote trades: many of the legislators who voted for a bill because of a logroll agreement were legislators marginally opposed to the passage of the bill. Thus, representatives for whom it was cheapest to vote against constituency interests were solicited as members of the logrolling coalition. These results suggest that these coalitions are not formed as suggested by the cycling theorems. At one step in a cycle, high demanders form a winning coalition with very low demanders, opposing those with moderate intensity. For example, at some point in the cycle wheat farm representatives are expected to trade and form a winning coalition with legislators strongly opposed to peanut subsidies. This implies that legislators with a low probability of voting for peanut subsidies vote for these subsidies due to the vote-trading agreement. The evidence is not consistent with this prediction (Stratmann 1992). Many of the traders are legislators marginally opposed to peanut subsidies. This is consistent with the hypothesis that party leaders arrange low-cost trades that in turn enhance stability. More studies are needed to be more confident that these findings hold for many vote trades.

Evidence for stability in logrolling coalitions and the stable distribution of federal funds among congressional districts point to the importance of congressional institutions. Which institutions specifically induce stability in logrolling agreements or which institutions help to organize coalitions is somewhat ambiguous. Little or no systematic evidence exists that identifies quantitatively the contribution of potentially stability inducing institutions, as, for example, party leaders, the committee system in Congress, or congressional rules. Finding empirical regularities in the voting behavior of legislators and coalition formation in legislatures will indicate which coalitions are stable, give a clue about the causes that lead to the formation of coalitions, and stimulate further research.

CHAPTER 16

Political business cycles

MARTIN PALDAM

1. An overview and the pioneers

The traditional business cycle literature deals with economic fluctuations generated by the uncoordinated actions of private agents. During the century from the Napoleonic Wars to World War I many economies fluctuated systematically around their trend growth. Most researchers agree that these classical business cycles were generated by private agents (see Haberler 1937, 1958; Zarnowitz 1985). A large literature discusses how governments can diminish such fluctuations and stabilize the economy by providing coordination and steering.

However, it has often been shown that attempts to steer the economy have failed, sometimes because of mistakes, but more often because of political pressures and the interests of governments. Policies have been either inconsistent or defeated by other agents or exogenous shocks. Some think that the net result of all attempts to steer the economy is to make it less stable. The political business cycle (PBC) literature takes this view. Here the fluctuations are created by the government or by competition between the parties. *A PBC is thus a business cycle generated by the political system.* We shall cover only PBCs in developed democracies. Section 6.2 discusses the importance of PBCs compared with other business cycles.

1.1 The overview

The cycles are either (α) made deliberately or (β) occur because of the way the political system functions. PBCs of the α-type are made by a

Besides my reading of the literature the survey also includes the results of discussions with many of the authors quoted. I am very grateful to the editor, and as well to Alberto Alesina, Douglas Hibbs, Peter Nannestad, and Peter Skott for comments. The PBC literature is covered in two monographs, Dinkel (1977) and Velthoven (1989), and a conference volume, Willett (1988). An excellent earlier survey of the literature is found in Borooah and Ploeg (1983). Finally, Frey (1996) is a book of readings in the field.

decisive agent who *manipulates* the economy to obtain an advantage. Nearly all PBCs assume the government to be that agent. PBCs of the β-type are the result of the interaction of (many) more agents working under the constraints of democratic *institutions*. Such PBCs are unlikely to be optimal for any agent.

The PBC literature can be divided along two dimensions: time and the nature of the cycle. The idea of the PBC was proposed by a few *pioneers* before 1950. Two waves of research have occurred since then: a *pre RE wave* of 1975–80 using economics from before the Rational Expectations revolution and a *post RE wave* since the late 1980s.

Table 1 classifies PBC theories according to the nature of the cycle and surveys the main ideas in the literature. Note that the various theories since 1975 build upon a small set of economic and political theories. Section 2 covers these building blocks. We then turn to the two main sets of PBCs in Sections 3 and 4. These sections also cover the more general empirical results. Section 5 looks at the many empirical papers dealing with the United States.

A difficult job for any surveyor is to draw the limits of the subject to be covered. I have decided to limit this discussion to the more stylized cycles and write only a short Section (6.1) on the more comprehensive politicoeconomic modeling. I have also excluded literature dealing with budget cycles, which is almost exclusively from the United States and hinges upon much institutional detail (see Pack 1987; Rogoff 1990; and Blais and Nadeau 1993).

1.2 The pioneers: Two strands

The literature before 1975 has two strands. Johan Åkerman started an empiricist one (1946, 1947). Others are Ben-Porath (1975), Hubka and Obermann (1977), MacCracken et al. (1977), and Tufte (1978). They have shown a political element in certain highly visible public payments and prices. For example: Tram tickets in Austria are adjusted more often after elections than before. Social security payments in the United States tend to arrive just before rather than after elections. Governments that want to be reelected surely manipulate the economy. Whether this is a major influence upon the economy is another matter. However, the above authors all give evidence that this is the case, and Tufte provides a great collection of cynical quotations showing that politicians consider their reelection chances when planning economic policies.

The second strand in the old literature takes off from a short article by

Table 1. *Surveying the PBC literature*

	(1) Long PBC, 1.2	(2) Election cycle, 3	(3) Partisan cycle, 4
Duration	Longer run	One election period	Two election periods
Type	β	α, later also β	β, later also α
Main Inventor(s)	M. Kalecki	W. Nordhaus, C. D. MacRae	Pre RE: D. A. Hibbs, 4.1 Post RE: A. Alesina, 4.3
Generating agent	Gov. maximizing popularity	Gov. maximizing reelection chances	Gov. ideological goals (voters interest)
Other actors	Firms and workers	Uniform private agent	Uniform/Post RE: unions
Time horizon of			
Goverment	Shorter than 1/2 PBC	Perfect foresight, 4 years	Shorter than 2 election p.
Workers	Same	Less than an election p.	Same
Voters	Same	Myopic	Does not enter
Economic model	Dynamics of labor mkt.	Dynamic Phillips curve	Phillips curve
Expectations	Unclear	Retrospective RE version later	Pre RE: No expectations Post RE: Rational exp.
Politics			
Politics matter, 2.2	Hardly	No	Yes and governments change
VP function, 2.1	A minimum	Yes	Not necessary
Form	Long/medium run swings	Tightening after election – expansion before	Pre RE:Different trends Post RE: Blips only

Note: Numbers refer to sections of the chapters. "Gov." is government, "RE" is rational expectations and "p." is period.

Kalecki (1943),[1] which is so cryptic as to need interpretation (as Feiwel 1974). One reading is as follows: Public spending makes full employment perfectly attainable. However, it is not easy to maintain since the labor market discipline breaks down when the threat of unemployment vanishes. The result is an overheating of the economy with inflation, strikes, falling productivity, and eventually falling profit shares making a depression (or a dictatorship) necessary. Governments reduce unemployment to get votes. Once discipline returns, the temptation to reduce unemployment will be too big for the government to resist. The cycle then renews. Kalecki does not mention the time dimension, but it seems logical that the duration of the resulting cycle is longer than the seven to nine years of the classical business cycle.

In the 1970s several writers from the new left rediscovered this article and tried to formalize it (see Boddy and Crotty 1975; Sherman 1979). There was a significant wave of strikes and inflation between the late 1960s and the mid-1970s throughout the developed Western world. The overheating crisis led to a large profit squeeze in many countries, a general fiscal tightening, and a major economic crisis. It also led to the flourishing of the Phelps–Friedman theory of the expectations-augmented Phillips curve that was one of the main building blocks in mainstream PBC theories.

2. Political and economic building blocks

PBC theory of the last two decades uses the following building blocks: (1) a VP function (*Vote* and *Popularity*) showing how economic conditions influence the popularity of governments, (2) assumptions about the time horizons in the decisions of the relevant agents, (3) acceptance or rejection of the median voter theorem, (4) a Phillips curve, and (5) assumptions about the political manipulability of the economy.

2.1 The VP function: The Link between the government popularity and the economy

The literature on the VP function was started in the early 1970s by three great papers: Kramer (1971), Mueller (1970), and Goodhart and

---

1. Kalecki's article speaks of PBCs, while a related article by Joan Robinson (1943) is less explicit. A line from that literature leads to a Goodwin–Weintraub business cycle theory. The key mechanism is that too low unemployment causes a profit squeeze and falling investments until unemployment again rises. This causes profits and investments to recuperate and so on. See Skott (1989) for a recent generalization.

Bhansali (1970). Since then almost two hundred papers have appeared. The following is a summary of Nannestad and Paldam (1994) (the references have been omitted). Among the wealth of results obtained, a few appear to generalize. We shall concentrate on five robust results and one dubious one.

> *(VP1)   The responsibility hypothesis* is the theoretical foundation of the VP function. It says that people hold the government responsible for economic conditions. It has been directly confirmed in several microstudies. The implication is that the popularity of the government is positively correlated with economic conditions, as many macrostudies confirm. It further confirms the hypothesis that the VP function fails to appear in countries where it is unreasonable to make the government responsible. That is, countries with many unstable minority governments. The responsibility hypothesis implies a stable two-party (or two-block) system.
>
> *(VP2)   The "big-two" variables* in the VP function have always been unemployment and inflation. Many other variables have been tried; but the big two have generated the most significant coefficients. A government can typically win 0.6 percent of the votes if unemployment falls one percent given that inflation stays constant or vice versa.
>
> *(VP3)   Voters are myopic.* The effect on voter choices of changing economic variables is of a short duration. Most studies find the time horizon to be shorter than one year. A few (notably Hibbs 1982) have found effects extending beyond one year.
>
> *(VP4)   Voters' expectations are retrospective.* Studies have tried to determine whether voters react to expected economic changes or to past experiences but have always found that it makes no difference because voters' expectations are static.
>
> *(VP5)   To rule costs popularity.* The *cost of ruling* is 1.7 percent, with standard deviation of 4.5 percent in the average parliamentarian system. In presidential systems the standard deviation is higher (by a factor of 2). While this result is very robust, there is no generally accepted explanation.[2] It is a troubling result; the average government surely rules exactly

2. The two main explanations are: (1) voters demand political change, (2) oppositions can get away with inconsistent promises to different groups, while ruling enforces consistency. The 1.7 percent is thus a measure of the amount of cheating a political party can get away with in the long run.

as the rational voter expects, so why should the voter punish it by moving his or her vote to the opposition?

(VP6) Voters may have a grievance asymmetry, that is, they punish a government more for a downturn in the economy than they reward it for an upturn. This result has been found in a few data sets, rejected by others, but disregarded by most researchers.

The VP function has an unfortunate instability. The coefficients tend to come and go when, for example, the period analyzed changes. Hence, the VP function is not the most reliable tool.

2.2 Time horizons in politics and the median voter complex

The evidence points to the fact that voters have myopic (VP3), retrospective expectations (VP4). The evidence about the expectations of governments is less clear. There are two views.

The Tinbergen view: A tradition in economics, started by Tinbergen (1956, 1964), has been to develop tools to help governments choose policies to maximize a welfare function over time. This tradition is of a technocratic nature. However, many think that it also has some descriptive power.[3] *The close observer view:* Observers of politics, including many insiders, have often pointed to its short time horizon. (The British Prime Minister Harold Wilson once went as far as to say that "a week is a long time in politics.")

It is not easy to sort out all the evidence and choose between the Tinbergen and the close observer views. One may perhaps say that policy making has several levels depending upon the type of policy, and that each level has a different time horizon. There are certain basic policies, such as school laws and the highway network, that are long run in nature; others are almost fully short run. It is unresolved if the time horizon in economic policy making is longer or shorter than the ones people use when voting. Voters may be myopic simply because they know that policies are. It is clear from Table 1 that the different PBC theories make different assumptions in this respect.

Consider next the following assumptions regarding the median voter complex: *(A) The majority goal:* The goal of all parties is to obtain a

---

3. It is easy to give the tools a normative content, but most writers stress that the tools can be used with any welfare function chosen by the government. When used in the Nordhaus–MacRae theory of the election cycle, the goal of the government is to be reelected.

majority.[4] This is a behavioral assumption that is hard to test directly, even when one can call upon a great deal of evidence. (*B*) *The median voter theorem:* Parties compete to get the vote of the median voter.[5] This is taken to be a logical consequence not only of (A) but of other assumptions as well. (*C*) *Politics does not matter:* Economic outcomes are the same whatever the ideology of the governing party. This assumption seems easy to test.

Arguments using the *shortcut* that (A) $\Leftrightarrow$ (B) $\Leftrightarrow$ (C) are common. Everything appears to hang together nicely: The majority goal (almost) leads to the median voter theorem. Political ideology therefore does not matter (as some evidence shows). This (almost) confirms the median voter theorem, and the majority goal must therefore be true too. However, there are "leaks" in both causal chains. *Neither is a necessary and sufficient condition for any other.* Furthermore, the VP function works well only in two-party systems. The median voter theorem and hence the majority goal demands a two-party system to be valid.

The evidence showing (C) that politics does not matter (see, e.g., Castles 1981) is of two types: (1) comparisons of *average* levels of politically important time series (as unemployment, inflation, and the share of the public sector) under governments of different ideologies, and (2) cross-section comparisons of spending and taxation patterns across local and regional governments. In both studies it is rare to find that variables representing ideology matter (see, however, Sections 6.2 and 2.4).

2.3 The two first Phillips curves: Dead or alive?

A. W. Phillips developed his curve (Phillips 1958) empirically from annual observations for the United Kingdom over a century. The data show that there exists a *negative* relation π between rises in wages (w) and unemployment (u):

$$w = \pi_1(u), \text{ where } \partial\pi_1/\partial u < 0 \tag{1a}$$

and

$$p = w - \sigma, \text{ where } \sigma \text{ is constant} \tag{1b}$$

---

4. Power is necessary to pursue (1) ideological goals, (2) the interests of the party supporters, and (3) the spoils of power. However, (4) power might also be an (addictive) goal in itself. Advocates of the majority goal argue that it is a common operational goal. If the underlying goals are (1) or (2), they are likely to differ from the ones of the median voter. There is then a conflict between the operational goal and the deeper goal. This has led to the idea of the majority goal as a constraint, see Frey and Ramser (1987).
5. The median voter theorem was introduced by Hotelling (1928). See Mueller (1989, chap. 5) or Enelow in this volume.

Equation (1b) makes inflation accounting simple by assuming that the rates of price and wage inflation are parallel.[6] Unemployment is the excess supply of labor. It is therefore difficult to imagine that something like (1) can fail to appear in the data. However, even a casual look at the time series for w and u shows that both series are highly dynamic and their dynamics are different, so (1) is an inadequate model.[7] Two points keep reappearing in the literature:

> *(Ph.1)* The explanatory power of (1) is low. When (1) is esti-
> mated on large data sets like that of Phillips, Grubb, Jackman
> and Layard (1982), Paldam (1983), and McCallum (1986), π
> is always significantly negative, but the R^2s are only about
> 0.25. It is easy to find small data sets where $\pi \approx 0$ or $\pi > 0$.
>
> *(Ph.2)* The dynamics has remained a puzzle. During this cen-
> tury the business cycle has changed to be less regular. This
> has increased the importance of the dynamics. To find a sig-
> nificantly negative π, it has been more and more crucial to
> include something that handles the dynamics.

The neatest dynamization of the Phillips curve available is that of Phelps (1967) and Friedman (1968). They augmented (1) by the expected rate of inflation, p^e, and made p^e an adaptive function, ϕ_a, of past inflation.[8]

$$p_t = \pi_2(u_t - \mu) + p_t^e \text{ where } \pi_2(0) = 0 \text{ and } \partial \pi_2 / \partial u < 0. \tag{2a}$$

$$p_t^e = \phi_a(p_{t-1}, p_{t-2}, \ldots) = \gamma \sum_{i=1}^{\infty} (1-\gamma)^{i-1} p_{t-i}$$
$$\text{where } 0 < \gamma < 1 \Leftrightarrow \gamma \sum_{i=1}^{\infty} (1-\gamma)^{i-1} = 1 \tag{2b}$$

$$p_t = w_t - \sigma \qquad \text{as in (1b)} \tag{2c}$$

The symmetry constant μ is known as the natural rate of unemployment (NAIRU). If $u < \mu$, wages accelerate. If $u > \mu$, they decelerate. Neither situation is sustainable in the longer run. Therefore, $u = \mu$ becomes the steady-state equilibrium condition. Here inflation is constant. Model (2)

---

6. However, σ is the sum of productivity rises and the changes of the wage share. Neither is constant in the short run, and they are not (negatively) correlated.
7. To make a theory explaining why relation (1) should exist has proved easy. One need only show that u is a good proxy for the excess supply/demand on the labor market. This does not explain the dynamics (here many explanations have been tried). Phillips has included a bit of dynamics as systematic movements in the coefficient over the business cycle.
8. Equation (2b) is equal to $p_t^e = \phi_a(p_{t-1}, p_{t-1}^e) = p_{t-1}^e + \gamma(p_{t-1} - p_{t-1}^e)$, so that expectations are adjusted with some fraction of the expectation error made last year, where the fraction, γ, measures the myopia.

is clearly better than model (1), but (2) has rarely performed satisfactorily when used for forecasting. Nevertheless, the *key dynamic assumption* in modern macroeconomics is that p^e can explain *the* missing dynamics.[9] All one has to do is get expectations right.

Model (2) is easy to calibrate to make neat cycles around the equilibrium path with the frequency wanted. This is a useful property of a building block to a PBC theory. It is not even necessary to assume the whole of model (2), only the following:

> *Minimum dynamic Phillips curve:* The slope of the Phillips curve is steeper in the long run than in the short. It is calibrated to make sizable cycles with the desired amplitude.

As it now stands model (2) has no policy variables. We therefore have either to add such variables (as discussed in Section 2.5) or to assume:

> *Manipulability:* The government can steer the economy so that p and u follow a predicted cyclical path.

Manipulability means that policies are efficient. With the advent of RE theory this seemingly innocent assumption quickly turned into a main problem.

2.4 Rational expectations: The problem of policy efficiency

Once most economists got hooked upon the key dynamic assumption, the main thrust of research became developing a theory analyzing how expectations are formed according to standard micro theory. A starting point for the RE theory is to replace equation (2b) with:

$$p^e = \phi_r(I) \qquad \text{where } \partial B(I)/\partial I = \partial C(I)/\partial I \qquad (3)$$

Here I is the information set used in forming expectations, $B(I)$ the benefits of the expectations, and $C(I)$ the costs of collecting and processing the information. The pioneers developing the theory observed that much macroeconomic information is freely available.[10] If the benefits are significant (think of people investing their own money), one reaches the limit where it pays for the agents to collect *all relevant information*. We shall term this High Information Rational Expectations (HIRE) case.

---

9. I have spent some time surveying expectations and think that the p^e-variable is too weak to carry the weight assigned to it in the theory. Actually, most people do not form inflationary expectations (but this is a long story).

10. There is, however, a large initial investment involved in understanding macroeconomic theory and data. Studies show that people are normally poorly informed about these matters.

The other end of the scale is the Low Information RE (LIRE), where agents get only infinitesimal benefits from improving their expectations. They then base their expectations on what they remember about inflation and form myopic, retrospective expectations:[11]

$$\phi_r \rightarrow \phi_a \text{ for } B(I) \rightarrow 0 \tag{4}$$

From polls it appears that when voters form inflationary expectations at all, they are retrospective and myopic, that is, LIRE expectations. Most of the evidence suggests that experts form HIRE expectations.[12] This seems entirely reasonable: All voters together have great influence, but each of the N voters has $1/N \approx 0$ part of that influence. If we measure the benefits as influence, they are therefore zero. An expert derives his whole income from knowing the economy, so his benefits from collecting information are high. This leads to the *policy riddle* of expectations: *Politicians use experts who have high information (HIRE), but have to sell their policies to voters, who have low information (LIRE).* It is thus inherently unclear what expectations the policymakers choose to use as a basis for their policies.

HIRE has dominated the RE literature for several reasons: It was new, and, as the model itself is a piece of relevant information, it was mathematically challenging to calculate the path of the model with RE. This allowed researchers to reap academic laurels by finding interesting equilibrium concepts. The new results were often puzzling and controversial because they showed that manipulability collapsed. *The policy inefficiency result* says that when people and firms make plans optimizing their future actions, they take all predictable policies into consideration. So the path becomes independent of actual policies. Only if the government is unpredictable, can its policies have an effect, and it is transitory. If the model includes an asymmetry, the size and duration of the transitory effects increase. We discuss two asymmetries and thus have three conditions for policy efficiency under RE:

> *(eff1) A policy surprise:* Policies that are surprising (unpredictable) can have a *transitory* effect.
>
> *(eff2) An information asymmetry:* Agents at the central and at

11. The literature often terms HIRE *superrationality* and LIRE *nonrationality*. This is misleading terminology. There is nothing nonrational in forming low-cost expectations if the benefits are low too. It would be irrational if people were superrational when the costs of so being vastly exceed the benefits.
12. The literature is covered in Nannestad and Paldam (1994). Tests for HIRE are made using the antibias result of RE theory. Any known bias can be used to improve the expectation. It therefore enters into the information set. Once it is used, it goes away. HIRE therefore can contain no biases.

the mass level have a large difference in benefits from being informed.

(eff3) A reaction speed asymmetry: Agents are constrained differently – governments by elections and wage setters by contracts uncoordinated with the elections.[13]

2.5 From the manipulability assumption to policy variables

The introduction distinguished between PBCs of the *deliberate* α-type and the involuntarily *occurring* β-type. Models of type α imply that governments can and do manipulate economies. The literature deals with cycles in the main economic aggregates. They are not control variables, but endogenous end-variables. They are the result of all other variables in the economy. If a PBC is observed as predicted by a basic behavioral assumption, one concludes that everything in the theory holds, but this is a big leap of faith. To validate the theory one would like to trace the cycles all the way from the actual policies to the final outcome. The decision variables for the government are tax rates, expenditures, interest rates, and so on. They have three characteristics:

1. The number of instruments is large.
2. Many have closely related macroeffects.
3. Thanks to their microeffects (and for other reasons) they are often politicized.

The politicizing of the instruments induces the government to play them in complex, changing sequences. A complete tracing of a PBC from the decision variables to the aggregate end result is therefore a major job. A first step is to find the cycles in the aggregate policy measures: monetary aggregates, public-expenditure aggregates, taxes, and the public-sector balance. This is, however, only a small part of the way. To cover all the steps, one needs a detailed model. The few attempts that have endeavored to take all the steps will be briefly discussed in Section 6.1.

3. Election cycles

The main election cycle model in the literature was first proposed by Nordhaus (1975) and later developed by MacRae (1977) and others. It is

---

13. The idea of using the existence of wage contracts to generate a reaction speed asymmetry was introduced by Taylor (1979). Empirically, it is clear that wage contracts are uncoordinated with election periods; but *why* this is so is less clear. See for example, Danziger (1992).

a theory of type α – the most Machiavellian of the PBC-theories. We shall term it the "NM cycle." The model considers a democracy with elections every fourth year.

3.1 The Nordhaus–MacRae theory[14]

The NM theory has four components:

> *(NM1):* The policy of the government is determined by the majority goal throughout the election period (2.2).
> *(NM2):* A standard myopic VP function (2.1).
> *(NM3):* A minimum dynamic Phillips curve, with suitable parameters (2.3).
> *(NM4):* The manipulability assumption (2.3).

Combining (NM1) and (NM2) makes the VP function the welfare expression to be maximized. Myopia implies that the government need only consider the VP function in the election year. The government consequently steers the economy during the election period to maximize the VP function in the election year.[15] Together (NM3) and (NM4) imply that the government can manipulate the economy to produce sizable cycles. To get the best possible combination of (u, p) in the election year, the government creates a slump as quickly as it can to reduce expectations (p^e). A boom is created in the election year, with a low u, while p is kept down by the low p^e. The NM cycle looks as drawn on Figure 1.

The original theory uses a minimum dynamic Phillips curve; but the principles used may be applied to any model with the right dynamics. An example is the Stephan (1992) model, which uses the Dornbusch model of exchange rate over/undershooting to model a PBC of the NM-type.

Governments change if the VP function of (NM2) includes a cost of ruling. If governments change, the regularity of the cycle with which they do so comes to depend upon the median voter theorem. However, the model has been amended to allow the two parties to have ideological interests, which they pursue to the extent reelection is likely (Frey and Ramser 1976), and to allow for random timing of elections (Ginsburgh and Michel 1983). Kirchgässner (1983) has shown that by varying agents' time horizons, a whole family of cycles can be generated. The basic form

---

14. The mathematics of the NM model is most thoroughly covered by Kirchgässner (1983), Neck (1991) and Detken and Gärtner (1992).
15. For simplicity, we assume that the government has perfect foresight. Also we disregard a number of technical points. Some math is needed if the myopia is weak, and we have to maximize for more than the election year. Nordhaus also explores VP functions with squared variables, and so on.

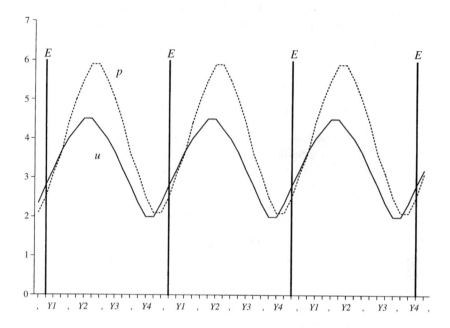

Figure 1. The Nordhaus–MacRae election cycle. *Note:* The years are
*Y*1, *Y*2, *Y*3, and *Y*4. The bold vertical lines show the elections, *E*. Note
further that our sketch includes a reaction lag of about half a year, and
we have made the swings in the rate of price-wage inflation, *p*, larger
than the swings in unemployment, *u*, in accordance with well-known
facts.

of the cycle is very sensitive to the difference among the three time
horizons: (T1) Governments plan four years ahead, (T2) voters are
myopic, and (T3) Price-wage formation implies a time horizon in between. The cycle reduces to nothing if they are just a little different and
turns around if (T1) is shorter than (T2). Our discussion of the information asymmetry (item eff2 in 2.4) argues that there might be a difference
between (T1) and (T2), but three different time adjustment patterns are
difficult to believe.

3.2 Critique and tests of the NM theory
and the NM model

A small puzzle: A Phillips curve is needed to get a NM cycle. Imagine
estimating a Phillips curve in an economy where the NM model is *the*
data-generating process. What would we find? Unemployment and inflation follow the paths drawn on Figure 1. The result will surely be a

Table 2. *The paths of unemployment under different PBCs and
governments*

Year:	Y1	Y2	Y3	Y4
NM election cycle				
All governments	Up	Max	Down	Min
Election promise cycle				
All governments	Down	Min	Up	?
Hibbs partisan cycle				
Left government[a]	Max	Down	Down	Min
Right government[a]	Min	Up	Up	Max
Alesina partisan cycle				
Left government[b]	Down	Up	Natural[c]	Natural
Right government[b]	Up	Down	Natural	Natural

[a] The paths assume that the previous government had the other ideology.
[b] The paths assume that there was an element of surprise in the election.
[c] The natural rate is the sustainable long run unemployment rate.

positive average value of the slope of the Phillips curve: $\partial\pi/\partial u > 0$. If the curve is estimated on these data one would conclude that it breaks down. The NM cycle is thus an explanation that uses a relatively weak version of the expectation mechanism to turn the slope of π. But then there is no Phillips curve and hence no NM cycle.

It is awkward that the three time horizons of the theory must all be different and that the cycle is clearly contrary to the policy inefficiency results in RE theory. This was first pointed out by McCallum (1978), who also ran an empirical test rejecting the model.

The key methodological point when testing a theory is to find *predictions that are so near the theory as to be really robust.* A good test concentrates on these predictions while being insensitive to everything else. The key prediction of the model is that a real tightening is made as early as possible to make the election year as good as possible. So the two first years should be the most contractionary and the election year should be expansionary. Prices should increase most after the election and rise least in the election year. These are the features listed in Table 2. It is therefore not a good test to look for a particular shape in the time path of the variables as McCallum (1978), does in his empirical rejection of the NM cycle (see Section 5).

However, McCallum's finding is not alone. The NM cycle has fared badly in most tests. Nordhaus (1975) found weak support, except for the United States. My tests (Paldam 1979, 1981 and 1982) reached negative results on a large comparative data sample but found a different election cycle in the data. Soh (1986) uses a similarly large data set and finds slightly better results, but the newest large-scale test (Alesina 1991) reaches negative results once more. Most country studies from outside the United States fail to show NM cycles. An exception is Keil's (1988), which uses McCallum's method on United Kingdom data. However, Nordhaus (1990) still claims that there is enough evidence supporting his model.

3.3 An empiricist election cycle: A second-year boom

The path of the economy during the average government is highly variable, so my empirical cycle is weak, but becomes significant with enough data. It has the reverse pattern of the one expected from the NM theory. The most expansionary year in real terms is *the second year,* and inflation goes up in the third year.

The main reason for *the second-year boom* is that the average government – no matter its ideology – makes expensive reforms as soon as possible, that is, the reforms the governing parties promised during the election campaign. These reforms cause the economy to overheat; the government then has to tighten the economy to regain control. Thus, the second-year boom is contrary to the pure reelection strategy of the government. The cycle is the result of the election but is not made to win elections. It is a weak cycle of type β, not a result of manipulations of type α. Alesina and Sachs (1988) and Alesina and Rosenthal (1989) also find a second-year effect, but their findings differ in that they find a partisan effect in the United States: the second-year effect is upward in terms of real GDP growth under the Democrats and downward under the Republicans (4.3).

Election cycle models disregard differences between party ideologies. The NM theory models are the consequence of the majority goal and a VP function, which deals with the *average* voter. The average is not the median, but the NM model falls consistent with the median voter theorem nevertheless. We turn now to the partisan cycle theories that explicitly claim that politics matters, and reject the median voter theorem.

4. Partisan cycles

The theoretical basis of the partisan cycle model has two components:

> *(P1) Governments change.*
> *(P2) The partisanship claim.* Parties successfully pursue different goals, that is,
>> (P2.1) Political parties have *different goals,* even at the operational level,

(P2.2) *Politics matter:* different goals lead to different policies,

(P2.3) *Policies matter:* different policies cause different outcomes.

(P2.1) is a main subject of political science and (P2.2) and (P2.3) are often joined as a generalization of the *manipulability assumption* already discussed.

The partisan cycle model is reached by simplifying (P2) into a two-party model. The *left party* primarily fights unemployment; the *right party* inflation. The advantage the government pursues is ideological. Cycles appear because governments change. We are dealing with cycles of type β, but, by connecting ideologies with the advantages of the parties' core voters, a bridge may be built to the α theories.

(P1) is hardly controversial. The costs of ruling (VP5) cause changes of government. One explanation that fits nicely with the theory uses the (dubious) grievance asymmetry (VP6): if a government pursues one goal successfully, other variables are likely to deteriorate. If it is punished more for the variables that deteriorate than it is rewarded for the variables that improve, governments change.

The consequence of (P1 and 2) was first seen by Hibbs (1975, 1977). He presented more solid evidence for his model than had Nordhaus and MacRae. The NM cycle nevertheless dominated the literature of political business cycles until the late 1980s,[16] when the partisan model reappeared in a RE version pioneered by Alesina.

4.1 Ideologies matter in the long run (Hibbs)

The main content of Hibbs (1975, 1977) is a comparative, empirical study of long-run trends. He finds a strong correlation (with signs as given) between two data sets: (A) a political data set (the share of left parties) and (B) an economic data set (inflation) [+], unemployment [−], and the share of the public sector [+]).[17] The correlations develop

---

16. The Nordhaus–MacRae model used state-of-art economics. Nordhaus's theory was only weakly supported empirically, and MacRae used theory only. Hibbs's model was presented in a paper discussing empirical findings in political science. The story and several others told in this chapter therefore give occasion to consider two facts of life as regards the social sciences: (1) Economics is a larger profession than political science. (2) Economists are more easily convinced by theory than by empirical observation. Furthermore, economists probably have a bias for liking theories that argue that politics do not matter.

17. The idea was to look at the most politically important economic data sets. The data for the size of the public sector are not presented in the paper, but they have played a large role in the discussion.

over time, and Hibbs concludes that (A) causes (B). His finding has remained controversial for the following reasons (the first was discussed by Hibbs himself):

1. In historical processes lasting half a century, complex dynamic interaction occurs between the factors. (A) causes (B), but (B) also causes (A). The personnel in the public sector are voters too, and so on. It becomes hard (perhaps meaningless) to point to a decisive factor.

2. Some writers claim that the key to the complex is a common underlying factor (C), causing both (A) and (B). The possibility most discussed (Cameron 1978) is that small, homogeneous countries tend to have more "solidarity." Hence, they have relatively large public sectors, public employees then support the expansion of the sector, and so forth. This fact takes us to the vast literature dealing with the expansion of the public sector (see Lybeck and Henrekson 1988; Breton et al. 1992; and Borcherding and Holsey in this volume).

3. The facts have sometimes been disputed. If more countries and a larger period are included, the pattern weakens, although it does not disappear.[18]

4. Theories of equilibrium growth predict that economies tend toward one (or a few) steady-state equilibriums, regarding basic sectoral shares, the share of unemployment, and so forth. Perhaps the country-differences observed are of a transitory character, but in that case we are speaking of transitory periods lasting half a century.[19]

4.2 Hibbs's nonexpectation cycle: Partisan trends

From Hibbs's long-run result it follows that politics must matter also in the short run (P2). Hibbs later developed (in Hibbs 1987b; and with Dennis 1988) a class-based theory of party support to explain ideologies by distributional interests. He has also modeled government changes with his complex nonlinear VP function, where government

---

18. If all countries and longer runs are considered, a pattern appears. See Syrquin (1988). The authors of the *patterns of development literature* rarely consider political factors, and there are large residuals in the pattern found, so the two literatures are not necessarily incompatible.

19. The theory of the steady state, as developed in the 1960s and 70s, is at a high level of abstraction. Two results are: (1) The theory points to the existence of few possible steady states. (2) The shift from one steady state to another is likely to take a long time, perhaps as long as half a century.

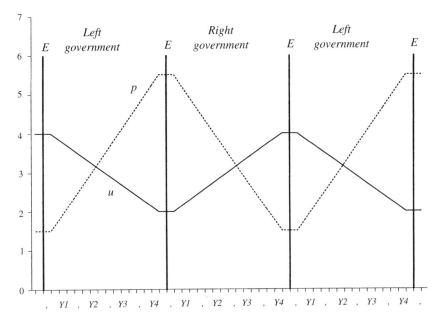

Figure 2. The Hibbs nonexpectation partisan cycle.

popularity is influenced by economic conditions and deteriorates at a constant rate.

The economics of the original Hibbs model is a Phillips curve as (1), in Section 2.3. Party Left prefers one feasible combination (p_L, u_L) and party Right another (p_R, u_R), where $p_L > p_R$ and $u_L < u_R$. When the government changes, the economy follows the same path from the (p_L, u_L)-set to the (p_L, u_R)-set or back. Hibbs estimates these paths for the United Kingdom and the United States where the paths look linear (Figure 2). In later models the paths are more refined, but the key prediction remains the policy-generated trends in the policy-important variables.

This result is significant in the U.S. post–World War II data but has remained less conspicuous in other countries (see Alesina 1989 and Paldam 1991a for large-scale comparative tests). There are trends as predicted by Hibbs in enough cases for the result to be significant, but the phenomenon is not a very important one except in the United States, as discussed in Section 5.

4.3 Alesina's RE cycle: Partisan blips

The first study building REs into the PBC is Minford and Peel (1982). Their model is presented as an election cycle model; but the parties Left and Right have ideologies generated by the interests of their voters. Both parties and the voters have forward-looking RE. Governments can stabilize either real incomes or inflation. The model shows that Right stabilizes inflation and Left stabilizes incomes. A set of complex tests is presented to show that this happens. The Minford and Peel model has remained an island in the literature, as did the attempts to build RE into a PBC by Lächler (1984) and Havrilsky (1987).

The next attempt to construct a RE–PBC model started in 1987 (Alesina was the central figure) and eventually had a major impact.[20] The model still builds upon (P1) and (P2), but all agents have *rational expectations*. The change of governments can therefore matter only transitorily, and only if two conditions (eff1 and eff3 in 2.4) both hold: (1) most elections have an element of *surprise*,[21] (2) agents have asymmetric reaction times, that is, governments can act while wage setters are constrained by wage contracts. This fact gives the average government one to two years to influence things systematically before people build the policies into their behavior. The theory therefore predicts ideologically generated blips in the data in year one and two. After the blip, the variables return to their steady-state growth paths. Left rule thus generates a downward blip in unemployment, and Right a downward blip in inflation. The second variable should presumably blip the other way. In the empirical tests for the United States, the blip appears in the second year.

In the drawing Alesina's main idea (Figure 3), unemployment and inflation blips are shown differently. Alesina finds inflation blips in the second difference to the price level, not in the first difference.[22] Note that these predictions are both sharp and different from the ones of the other two cycles. The differences between the various PBCs are listed in Table 2. Figure 3 also shows that in Alesina's theory there can be blips

---

20. We can only devote a couple of pages to Alesina's work and hence only provide a snapshot of the rapidly growing edifice. It already consists of the listed eleven papers—many with coauthors. There are already new working papers, including his own survey of the literature (August 1993). While Alesina's RE–PBC model came to dominate, it is worth pointing to related ideas that arose at the same time: Cukierman and Meltzer (1986), Havrilsky (1987), Rogoff and Siebert (1988), and Chappell and Keech (1988).

21. There is uncertainty about most elections; the odds quoted by bookmakers are rarely equal to 1. An interesting twist to the idea of a surprise has recently been explored theoretically by Ellis and Thoma (1991). They demonstrate that if the election term is variable, there is a surprise in the election date as well. That allows an economic variable to be permanently different under different governments.

22. The variables of the model should be cointegrated. It is clear that unemployment is $I(0)$, but less clear if the price level is $I(1)$ or $I(2)$, so that inflation is $I(0)$ or $I(1)$. In the long run inflation must be $I(0)$, but the long run seems to consist of pieces that are $I(1)$, and the theory considers four-year periods.

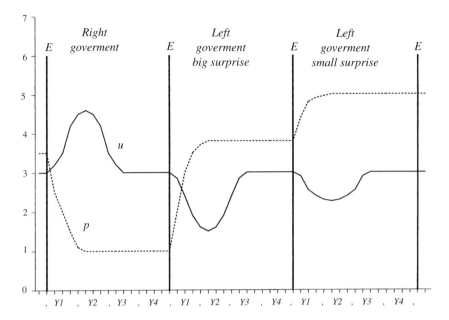

Figure 3. The Alesina rational expectations partisan cycle.

for reelected governments if the reelection has an element of surprise. In Hibbs's theory there is no cycle under reelected governments. The cycle is due to changes in government.

Alesina's partisan cycle model has been tested in large-scale comparative data sets by Alesina (1989), Paldam (1991b), Alesina and Rubini (1992), and Alesina, Cohen and Rubini (1993). The results are almost the same as those as reported for Hibb's model. There are a significant number of cycles, but many exceptions. However, there are more cases of Alesina blips than of Hibbs trends.

4.4 Partisan cycles and the median voter theorem bias

Partisan models explicitly reject the median voter theorem. So it is paradoxical that the model can produce observations deceptively like the median voter theorem, that is, it produces results showing that politics does not matter.

Table 3 shows what happens in Hibbs's model to a variable (x) that has a left and a right target value (x_L and x_R). In case 1 the path between the targets is linear. This makes the *average* exactly the same under the two governments. We thus get a perfect confirmation of the politics-does-

Table 3. *Three examples of a variable under a left and a right government*

Target $x_L=4$ $x_R=1$	Left government		Right government		
	Path	Average	Path	Average	Variance
Case 1	1, 2, 3, 4	2.5	4, 3, 2, 1	2.5	1.67
Case 2	1, 3, 3.5, 4	2.875	4, 2, 1.5, 1	2.125	1.73
Case 3	1, 1.5, 2, 4	2.125	4, 3.5, 3, 1	2.875	1.73

not-matter result. If the government is very efficient in pursuing the goal, we might still get a rejection of the median voter theorem as shown in case 2; but the variance is large, so many observations are necessary for statistical significance. If the government is inefficient as in case 3, we get a perverse result. It is difficult to tell how efficient governments are in pursuing their goals. However, the examples given show that studies based on averages have a strong bias toward accepting the median voter theorem.

If the variable follows Alesina's model, the blips all go in the direction showing that politics matter. However, since they last only one to two years, they are smaller on average than in the data for those particular years. So by comparing government averages, we still have a bias toward accepting the median voter theorem.

4.5 Comparing the shapes of different cycles: Some further evidence

Table 2 shows the shapes of the various PBCs discussed. The patterns are different, and they can be extended into many variants. This poses a problem. Imagine that the true model for unemployment is the natural rate plus white noise and consider a set of observations for one government. In many cases one of the models will surely fit. If one is free to jump between the models, one can make a good running explanation of any data set but, of course, predict nothing. To test the PBC model therefore demands a great deal of rigor in the test.

Another problem is that while a few developed economies are big and closed, most are *small and open*, and are likely to be strongly influenced by fluctuations in the rest of the world economies. If this is the case, it would explain why the strongest partisan cycles have been found in the United States. It would provide a rationale for giving the United States a high weight in comparative studies. However, Høst and Paldam (1990) and Paldam (1991a, 1991b) study the international elements in VP functions and in PBCs. The attempts to purge the data of these elements do not lead to clearer PBCs.

In studies of the effects of government ideology and government changes on the number of *strikes*, two findings have been reported (see Hibbs 1978; Paldam and Pedersen 1982; and Paldam 1983): (1) Hibbs's long-run result applies. In countries where most governments are labor-based, the strike level gradually falls to one-tenth of the old level.[23] (2) When the government changes from right to left, however, there is often a short, sharp strike wave, leading to wage increases. This looks a bit like an Alesina blip but is generated by workers disregarding wage contracts and reacting to expected government policies. So the causality of the blip is the reverse of the Alesina model, even when the logic is the same.

When the biggest blips in the data are investigated, one finds that most are *big-plan blips:* A party has been in opposition for some time and wants to gain power. To that end it develops a big plan to solve the economic problems of the country. The plan contains a magic trick so that it has large benefits and few costs. The party wins and starts to implement the plan. As a result, the economy expands, but the trick fails. The economy deteriorates, and the plan has to be given up.[24] This is hardly what Alesina had in mind. It has to be possible to make voters and parties believe irrationally in the plan to get big-plan blips. Also, they do not demand that the labor market be restrained by contracts, while governments can act.

Finally, it should be mentioned that Hibbs and Alesina keep developing their models (see the newest references to the two authors). The result has been a gradual convergence toward observational equivalence. The beliefs in the profession in quick returns to the steady states under RE are faltering. When Alesina let returns be slow and Hibbs let policies be efficient, the two partisan cycles come to look uncannily alike, even when the theories behind the models keep the differences we have discussed.

5. Mining the data for the United States

A particularly interesting part of the discussion deals with the United States, where the largest PBCs appear. As usual the empirical results for

23. The typical labor-dominated country is relatively *centralized*. The country is often dominated by a social democratic party working closely together with a strong and centralized trade union.
24. The *big left plan* is a packet that increases spending to boost employment. It runs into inflation and b o p difficulties. The *big right plan* decreases taxes and leads to an overheated economy with the same consequences as before.

the United States are unusual. The size and competitive nature of the U.S. academic market cause the exception to dominate research. However, PBCs in the United States are sufficiently irregular and strong to be claimed for all theories as support. Tables 4, 5, and 6 list the main findings. Several of the newest studies nest models to compare their explanatory power. The division in the three separate tables therefore becomes increasingly difficult.

5.1 A note on techniques

The original *binomial* technique used by Nordhaus (1975) divides the election period into a post- and a preelection period. Both unemployment and inflation should be higher in the post- than preelection period. One then counts how often this happens and makes a simple binomial test. The test is sensitive to lags and uses the data inefficiently. Next one would want to study if a *fixed shape* can be made significant, as did McCallum (1978). This study has to be combined with an auto-regressive scheme that explains everything else in the series. As we have discussed this is a debatable technique. Also, the more shapes one includes in the search, the higher is the probability of making a type 2 error.

Hibbs (1977) estimated a joint ARMA partisan model. The time series model is then used to simulate the undisturbed pattern of the cycle. This is termed the *ARMA intervention* technique in the tables. One can also estimate a *politicoeconomic model,* with more or less details, and use it to simulate the undisturbed cycles and calculate the gains from successful manipulations, as do Golen and Poterba (1980). Finally, some newer studies estimate integrated models where there are an ARIMA component, a NM component, and a partisan component. Such integrated approaches demand long data series.

5.2 Election cycles and partisan cycles

It is obvious from Table 4 that support for the NM cycle in the U.S. data has become more dubious the more the data has been scrutinized. The only strong results are the ones using the binomial technique, and it makes the cycle hard to distinguish from the Alesina blip-model. The political cycles in the United States are not easy to explain using election cycle theory. However, there is one special case: The economy did perform a perfect NM cycle under the reign of Richard M. Nixon, 1968–72. Many quotations confirm that Nixon had such manipulations of the economy in mind.

The results from studies of partisan cycles listed in Table 5 are much

Table 4. *Main results of studies of NM cycle on U.S. data*

Reference	Data, period	Technique	Main result
Nordhaus (1975)	u and p ann. 1947/72	Binomial tests – two years after/before election	Strong support for US (little elsewhere)
Tufte (1978)	y, u and transfer payments, 1947/77	Graphs and tables of data	Strong, but nonsystematic support
Lächler (1978)	u ann. 1902/72	Binomial test – changes 1954 examined	Fairly strong support
McCallum (1978)	u quar. 1948/77	Fixed shape tests	Rejection of cycle
Maloney and Smirlock (1981)	u and p quar. 1957/76	Modeling of relations	Some support
Beck (1982a)	u and p month 1961/73	ARMA interventions	Rejection of cycle
Golen and Poterba (1980)	u and p quar. 1953/78	Modeling of relations and simulations	The cycle is not worth the trouble
McGavin (1987)	y and u quar. 1957/81	Fixed shape tests refining McCallum	Mixed results
Pack (1987)	u and p and budget 1957/81	Modeling or relations with political game	Presidents try, but with mixed success
Haynes and Stone (1989, 1990) and Willett (1988)	y, u and p quar. 1951/86	Integrated test for using several techniques	Fairly strong cycle both types[a]
Nordhaus (1989)	u and p, ann. and quar. 1946/88	Several techniques	Mixed results, but support[a]
Davidson, Fratianni, and v Hagen (1990, 1992)	y, u, p, deficit, m ann. 1905/84	Integrated ARIMA and policy variable	Support for both models. Satisfying NM model best[a]

Notes: the variables are y is real GDP, u is unemployment, p is inflation, m is money; "ann." means that the data are annual, "quar." that they are quarterly, and "month" that they are monthly.
[a] Tests both for partisan and election cycles.

Table 5. *Main results of studies of partisan cycles on U.S. data*

Reference	Data, period	Technique	Main result
Hibbs (1975, 1977)	u, qua. 1948/72	ARMA interventions	Strong support
Beck (1982b)	u, qua. 1948/80	Regression model	Almost as strong support
Hibbs (1986, 1987b)	u, p, y, m budget 1953/84	Very rich setup Mixed models in tests	Strong support
Alesina and Sachs (1988)	y & m, ann. 1948/84	Regression model and tables	Strong support, easily seen in data
Alesina and Rosenthal (1989)	y, ann. 1950/84	Regression model	Support
Alesina, Londregan and Rosenthal (1993)	y, ann. 1912/88	Complex regression modeling	Support
Hibbs (1992, 1994)	y, ann. 1952/90	Recursive forecast test with re-gression model	Support

Note: See note to Table 4.

more positive, though it is debated whether they support the nonexpectation or the RE version. The predictions from the two models are converging as discussed. Once both models are provided with realistic lags and it is accepted that the main expansionary year for the left party is the second year, they are hard to distinguish. Further, Alesina confirms that voters have retrospective adaptive expectations (item eff2 in 2.4; see also Alesina, Londregan, and Rosenthal 1992). This opens the door for still more models. Thus, it is no wonder that the literature has not really settled down, even though there appears to be a general agreement about the following stylized facts: (1) there is a significant partisan effect in the U.S. macroeconomic data, (2) most Democrat administrations produce an expansion in the second year whereas Republican administrations produce a slump, and (3) this is clearly a partisan effect.

5.3 The role of money and conclusions on a special case

The political business cycle literature has led to a search for cycles in the monetary variables. This is particularly interesting for two reasons:

1. The independence of the FED in the United States is a much debated issue. How independent is the FED, and how independent should it be?
2. It has often been discussed how much control policymakers have over the money stocks (M1, M2, . . .). PBC models offer an empirical approach to this discussion.

Table 6 show that the results vary a great deal. There are signs of a cyclical path in the money aggregates, but it is not so strong as that in the real growth rate. Also there is no confirmation from any other country that there is a PBC in monetary aggregates.

In 1975 Nordhaus and Hibbs discovered that there was something that looked like a PBC in the U.S. data, and since then some thirty researchers have mined the U.S. data set. Another two decades of observations have been added, and it is still there. Studies from other countries have shown much weaker results. What are we to make of that? One conclusion is the usual one that the United States is a special case. One should never take it for granted that U.S. results generalize. Another is that there is the methodological problem of data mining. Thirty diligent researchers searching one data set are sure to come up with something. Especially, if they begin by observing that there is something looking like. . . .

Table 6. *Main results of studies of monetary cycles on U.S. data*

Reference	Data, period	Technique	Main result
Beck (1982c)	m and r, month 1970/79	policy variables in reaction function	Level shifts follow party, no NM cycle
Richards (1986)	m ann., 1960/84	Cyclicality tests in forecast error	Something before 1975 nothing later
Allen (1986)	various m's, quar. 1954/80	Shape tests on policy part of m	Some NM-like results are significant
Beck (1987)	various m's quar. 1961/84	Reaction functions and shape tests	Puzzle found: NM cycle in outcome not in policy variables
Grier (1987, 1989)	m, quar., 1961/80	Shape tests controlled for other variables	NM cycle confirmed
Havrilesky (1987)	m, ann., 1948/84	Modeling of money shock mechanism	Cycle found, related to the NM cycle
Chappell and Keech (1988)	u and m, ann. 1949/84	Estimation of model and simulations	Partisan effects implied by results
Renford and Trahan (1990)	r, annual 1954/88	Looks at variables	Some evidence of reverse causality

Note: See note to Table 4. Note that several of the papers listed in Tables 4 and 5 include a m variable.

6. Conclusions

At the end we have two items to discuss: (1) The efforts to build more comprehensive politicoeconomic models, and (2) the importance of the PBC relative to other business cycles.

6.1 The future: More comprehensive modeling?

The PBC theories discussed so far have used widely accepted economic models to study precise hypotheses about government behavior. The tests have been joint tests of the economic model and the hypothesis. The development of the PBC theory has therefore hinged on the shifts in the fashion for economic models.

It is arguable that more cumulative results could be reached if government behavior is analyzed directly, by explicitly modeling policy reaction functions. Hereby, it should be possible to test how much governments react to ideologies, and how much they react to changes in their popularities. It should also allow us to study what time horizons they use. The policy reaction functions can then be combined with economic reactions so that a more complete politicoeconomic model is obtained.

The most comprehensible politicoeconomic model is no doubt the simulation system of Frans van Winden (1983) and his collaborators. The system allows the user to includes a wide range of political actors (parties, governments, unions, etc.) and is formulated so that both interests and ideologies can be entered. The simulations show that many combinations of assumptions produce PBCs. The van Winden group has managed to estimate little of the system. The outcome space is therefore huge. Moreover, there is a large threshold effort for the user.

Most of the thrust for a comprehensive modeling of the politico-economic interaction has therefore come from the Zurich group of B. S. Frey, G. Kirchgässner, F. Schneider, and W. Pommerehne. From 1975 to 1985 the group presented about thirty studies of VP functions and policy reaction functions, sometimes integrated into econometric models. The best-known papers are Frey and Schneider (1978a, 1978b). The main finding of the Zurich group was that the pattern is a great deal more complex than the basic ones assumed by the PBC theories. Popularities are always significant in the reaction functions. Ideologies are important to the extent that reelection chances are high, but the total picture from all the studies is far from clear. The models typically refuse to produce neat cyclical patterns. Many other authors have estimated policy reaction functions, but it has proved difficult to reach clear and convincing results. However, it is possible that the future lies in this branch of the literature.

6.2 PBCs and other business cycles

We started this survey by noting that the century between the Napoleonic Wars and World War I was the time of the classical business cycle of seven to twelve years' duration. Even during that period Kitchin (1923) and later Åkerman (1946) presented statistical evidence showing that there was a cycle in the economy lasting about four years. It was a weaker phenomenon than the classical business cycle, but it is significant and can only be explained by PBCs.

There is little doubt that the wild economic fluctuations in the interwar years were exacerbated by political events, bad steering, and a collapse of normal international economic relations. However, the events were of such a character that they are, as of yet, unique. Since World War II economic fluctuations have been smaller in the developed world (the exception being the large shift in the mid-1970s). In most OECD countries the classical business cycle has gone without leaving any traces. In a few (notably the United States) there are still traces. However, most scholars probably agree that the closest thing to a cyclical pattern in the main macroeconomic time series are the PBCs. It should also be clear from our survey that various authors have found different PBCs in the data.

My reading of the evidence is that the Machiavellian-type election cycles in which governments manipulate the economy solely to be re-elected have proved to have little explanatory power. However, an election-promise cycle, with clear partisan influence, appears so often that it can be no accident. It is, however, a problem for the theories that too much of the evidence comes from just one country, the United States, which has an unusual political system.

PART IV

Individual behavior and collective action

CHAPTER 17

When is it rational to vote?

JOHN H. ALDRICH

As for popular suffrage, it may be further remarked that especially in large states, it leads inevitably to electoral indifference, since the casting of a single vote is of no significance where there is a multitude of electors.

Hegel (1984, 202–3)

I'll understand why people vote when I understand why someone, alone in his room, salutes during the national anthem.

Paraphrase of a comment by Gerald Kramer, overheard by author at a conference

The rationality of voting is the Achilles' heel of rational choice theory in political science.[1] Public choice theorists themselves divide over the question of whether turnout can be considered a rational decision. As my paraphrase of Gerald Kramer's comment illustrates, some of the very best theorists think it unlikely, to say the least, though many others have sought for some satisfactory means to conclude the opposite (e.g., Downs 1957; Riker and Ordeshook 1968; McKelvey and Ordeshook 1972; Ferejohn and Fiorina 1974). The stakes are high. Voting is perhaps the most common and the most important action considered by citizens in a democracy. If such a common and important decision faced by ordinary people cannot be understood as "rational," then how can our complex theories of politics, public choice, and even economics stand, if based on such infirm ground?[2] As arcane and complicated as public choice accounts of voting can be, the fundamental problem is really quite simple. Hegel, not often considered a major contributor to public choice theory, put the problem clearly. Akin to classic free riding, the chances of one vote affecting the outcome are so minuscule that the

---

1. The word "voting" is used here as a synonym for turnout, unless noted otherwise.
2. Economics falls under this cloud because all citizens are consumers and the great majority of consumers are citizens. How could they be considered rational in ordinary consumption decisions but not rational in ordinary voting decisions?

instrumental value of turning out is essentially zero and hence a rational actor would never vote. The problem is sufficiently clear that critics of rational choice theory in political science can, and do, use the voting problem as grounds for rejecting the whole of public choice theory.

To put the problem substantively, the basic empirical parameters for which we, as political scientists, must account are sufficiently problematic – and annoyingly regular – to make ordinary equilibrium results about voting hard to conform to them. About half the citizens vote in U.S. presidential general elections, a third in congressional elections, and a more variable fifth in presidential primary elections. The famous declines in the first two turnout rates over the last three decades amount to drop of about 10 percentage points. Since most theories conclude either that it is rational to vote (and, therefore, for virtually all to vote) or that it is not rational to vote (and, therefore, for virtually no one to vote), it is not obvious how to adjust these conclusions to predict such in-between mixes of actual behavior. Granted, the turnout decision can be considered close to a repeated prisoners' dilemma game (Aldrich 1995), so that we can hope that the Folk theorem's infinite equilibria promises the possibility of models whose results are consistent with these empirical regularities (see Fudenberg and Maskin 1986). Still, it is not at all obvious what mechanisms would allow us to deduce these particular regularities (see also the game theoretic models discussed in Section 1.4).

In this chapter, I review the basic arguments that underlie the question of the rationality of voting in the public choice literature and the various strategies that have been taken to devise a theory that implies that it is rational to vote. I suggest that all such attempts, including expected utility maximization, decision theoretic, and game theoretic models, founder essentially over one or another version of Hegel's observation. The problem is, simply, that we will never get anywhere thinking of turnout as a strategic decision to affect election outcomes. In short, Kramer, or at least Fiorina (1976), was right. Voting is, for most citizens, a way to express their preferences. Therefore, a reasonable theory must be based on that realization. Barry (1970) was, nonetheless, wrong when he implicitly consigned such an account to be either outside the domain of rational choice theory or an essentially tautological exercise in which people vote because they want to vote. He was wrong because he, like most theoretists, view elections as a mass of citizens making individual decisions, with at most two candidates as additional actors taking positions to attract voters.[3] In fact, elections are embedded in a highly

---

3. Moreover, the candidates' equilibrium strategies typically have them adopting the same position, leaving everyone indifferent and therefore abstainers.

variegated political system containing a large number of interested actors and groups, besides candidates as mere position takers and citizens as mere vote/abstain automatons. Taking the real political world seriously provides the opportunity both to make interesting choice theoretic models of this ordinary, garden-variety political act and to address otherwise perplexing empirical patterns at the same time.

1. Instrumental models of voting

Rational choice models, in general, make their contribution by assessing how people select among possible actions so as to achieve desired outcomes. The basic presumption is that people are seeking to realize their goals, and theorists are thus seeking to understand how people do (or should best) realize them. Theorists seek to explain which action is chosen out of the full set of possible actions, and these actions (i.e., behaviors) are seen as the investment of scarce time, effort, and resources into goal realization. Rational choice theories are thus designed to be accounts of *instrumental* behavior, connecting means to ends. The basic instrumental theory of voting, therefore, is developed in this section. Three major models complete this basic model of voting, applying the three central decision-making contexts for politics; decision making under risk, leading to the expected utility, or "calculus of voting," model; decision making under (general) uncertainty, leading to the minimax regret formulation; and decision making under (strategic) uncertainty due to the actions of other rational actors, leading to game theoretic models.

1.1 The basic model

Fiorina (this volume) points out that, at least in two-candidate (or two-party) elections, the instrumental prediction of which candidate (or party) will be supported is straightforward. All accounts predict that rational voters will vote for the candidate they think the better choice. There are, in this case, but two actions to choose between, and it never makes sense to vote for the less preferred candidate. While one vote may make no difference, voting for the preferred outcome *might help* and will *never hurt* voters achieve their desired outcome, and voting for the less preferred candidate can *never help* and *might hurt* the chances of voters realizing their goals. All of the wondrous machinery of rational choice theory does not change that prediction, and it is unneeded because the set of available actions are so truncated (as to be two), and their connections to outcomes are so clear. As Fiorina points out, the interesting questions are why and how voters come to prefer one candidate over the other, not how they invest their efforts in the voting booth, once having determined their preferences. It is therefore no surprise that the study of individual voting behavior has drawn extensively from psychology or social psychology. The "action" is in the voters' heads and not in their behaviors.

In many respects, turnout in a two-candidate contest is quite the same as candidate choice. After eliminating the (at least weakly) dominated choice of voting for the less preferred candidate, there are exactly two possible actions; vote for the preferred candidate or abstain. The problem is that it is costly, perhaps not very costly but still costly, to vote while there is little (or, in any event, less) cost in abstaining.[4] With voting more costly than abstaining, the obvious prediction is that the citizen votes if the benefits to voting outweigh the costs and fails to vote when benefits do not outweigh costs. This is, of course, the standard prediction of consumer behavior. Once the consumer has decided which alternative purchase is most preferred, that consumer buys that good if its benefits exceed its costs.

Voting and consumption differ, however, in two critical ways. First, the consumer alone determines the outcome. If he pays for the good, he gets it, if not, he does not. Voting, by contrast, is a *collective action*. If a voter pays the costs of voting, he casts his vote but won't get the desired candidate elected unless that vote and those of all the other voters add up to more than the votes cast for the opposition. Secondly, consumer goods are *private goods*. Once our consumer pays for it, the good is his alone. An election is perhaps the closest real-world example of a pure *public good*. A public good is, among other things, made available to all, if it is made available to one. Thus, the winner of a presidential election is everyone's president, including our examplar voter, whether the voter voted for that candidate, voted against that candidate, or did not vote at all. There is, in elections and in contrast to the market, a radical decoupling of actions and outcomes in two respects. The outcome depends only marginally, at best, on that which our voter did individually, and the result of the election is visited upon our voter no matter what she wants or, more directly relevant, did or did not do to affect that outcome.

This radical decoupling of an individual's actions and the outcome

---

4. Once the voter has determined his or her preferences, there is presumably no difference in the costs of voting for either the more or less preferred candidate. Hence, if you are in the voting booth and have a preference, it is always rational to vote – for the more preferred candidate. Note that abstaining is not cost free, because the rational decision maker must expend effort determining that to be the best choice. Thus, the costs of voting, c (defined below), are really the net costs of voting less abstaining, and these net costs are ordinarily positive.

affects all models of voting that view turnout as an instrumental act designed to affect who wins and who loses elections. It is this radical decoupling that Hegel's remark exemplifies. Three "standard" versions of rational choice models of voting exemplify this point.

1.2 The calculus of voting

Downs (1957) was the first to embed an expected utility model of voting into a general theory of elections. This model was coined the "calculus of voting" in an extension by Riker and Ordeshook (1968), wherein they also provided extensive testing. It is also the basic model Fiorina (this volume) exemplifies as the "pure theory of voter choice in two-candidate elections."

Using his notation (see his figure 1), there are five states of the world (s_1 through s_5) and three actions available to citizens: V_1 (vote for the preferred candidate), V_2 (vote for the opponent) and A (abstain). Ruling out V_2, as he makes clear that all rational choice accounts do, the choice set for citizens reduces to V_1 and A (or, with no confusion any longer, to V and A). If V is chosen and s_1 through s_3 is true, then the citizen gets B in benefits (the utility of candidate 1 holding office, less that of candidate 2 being elected), pays costs of voting (c) and may get noninstrumental rewards from voting per se, d (denoting the oft used example of "citizen duty"). If s_4 is true, the citizen makes a tie and, by fair tie-breaking procedures, can expect to get $B/2$ on average, while under s_5, the voter gets no benefits. In these two cases, the voter still pays costs (c) and gets benefits (d). Choosing A yields no c and no d values but gives the abstainer B under s_1 and s_2, 0 under s_4 and s_5, and $B/2$ under s_3. These considerations form the basic parameters of the decision facing a citizen, regardless of which of the following models is employed.

What makes the calculus of voting an expected utility model is that each citizen estimates (often subjective) probabilities of s_1 through s_5 being true, say p_1 through p_5.[5] As a result, the *expected utility* of a citizen choosing to vote, $EU(V)$, is

$$EU(V) = \frac{p_1(B-c+d) + p_2(B-c+d) + p_3(B-c+d) +}{p_4([B/2]-c+d) + p_5(-c+d),}$$

$$EU(V) = p_1(B) + p_2(B) + p_3(B) + p_4(B/2) - c + d.$$

The expected utility for abstention is

$$EU(A) = p_1(B) + p_2(B) + p_3(B/2).$$

---

5. These are calculated as the probability of the states of the world being true before the citizen chooses.

Voting is the expected utility maximizing choice if $EU(V) - EU(A) > 0$, which by substitution and simplification becomes

$$p_3(B/2) + p_4(B/2) - c + d > 0.$$

If the probability of making (p_4) and breaking (p_3) a tie are set equal (which seems likely to be a fair approximation) and the result is called p, then one votes if

$$pB - c + d > 0.$$

More elegant and more general (and more technically correct) statements are possible, but the calculus of voting boils down to the above, or something very close to it. In a two-candidate contest, a rational, expected utility maximizer calculates the intrinsic costs (c) and the intrinsic benefits (d) of voting, weighs the extrinsic benefits of seeing the preferred candidate in office (B) by the probability that this one vote will materially affect the outcome of the election (p, in this case the probability of making or breaking a tie), and votes if that calculation is net positive.

   The problem, of course, is that any plausible value of p will be incredibly small in any national, state, or local electorate of any size whatsoever. While scholars have provided any number of ways of calculating the probability of casting a tie making/breaking vote, no such technology is really necessary. It is obvious that no one seriously believes that his or her vote would make or break a tie in any modestly sized electorate, let alone a presidential election. As such, with $p \approx 0$, the instrumental, means-to-end portion of the calculus of voting is vanishingly small, no matter how concerned one is about the outcome. Therefore, one should not "rationally" vote to affect the outcome. Vote if it is cheap and if you like to cast ballots (i.e., if $d - c > 0$), but don't vote to affect B.

   Extending this decision context adds nuance. There are many contests on most general election ballots in the United States. By and large, however, these simply add more $pB \approx 0$ terms, and nothing is still nothing, no matter how many times you instrumentally add 0 to 0. Add a long series of elections together and the rational expected utility maximizer time-discounts c and d terms, but time-discounts $pB \approx 0$ terms, as well.

   Add more candidates to choose among and the set of behaviors becomes richer (see McKelvey and Ordeshook 1972). One might want to vote for the second most preferred candidate to avoid "wasting" one's vote on a preferred but hopeless long-shot (for evidence see, for example, Black 1978; Cain 1978; Abramson et al. 1992). But all such calculations involve terms that are based on probabilities of making or breaking ties. The lesson is that *all* votes are *always* wasted, if casting them is done for the purpose of affecting the outcome.

1.3 Minimax regret

If the problem with the calculus of voting is its vanishingly small p-term, perhaps the theory is trying to tell us that voting should not be thought of as a problem of expected utility maximization at all. Ordinary people, psychologists tells us, are not very good with probability calculations (e.g., Kahneman, Slovic, and Tversky 1982). Besides, the p-term is not some external chance event, but a shorthand summary of one's guess about the rational decisions of other citizens. If one takes the strategic decisions of others seriously, one is led toward game theoretic accounts (considered in the next subsection). If one is instead struck by observing people claim that they may have some sense about whether the election is likely to be close or one-sided but really don't have any sense of the probability of *any* state of the world being true, then one is led to an alternative decision theoretic formulation of voting. That is, in this view, voting is still effectively an individual decision, it is just not a problem in expected utility maximization. Instead of seeing the context as what Luce and Raiffa (1957) called "decision making under risk" where p-terms were known or estimated, it is better understood as "decision making under uncertainty," in which probability terms are not meaningful or at least not considered.

The handy feature of the expected utility maximization was that the p-term provided a nice way to "connect" actions and states of the world so that a relatively simple equation for assessing the (expected) consequences of any action was possible. Reducing the consequences of choosing any action to a single number (its expected utility) also made it possible easily to calculate which action was (expected to be) more instrumental in affecting the desired outcomes.[6] Eliminating the p-term and thus the expected utility maximization as the rational choice rule means that no such clear and singular "closed-form" solution to the problem of which action is best flows naturally from decision making under uncertainty. Luce and Raiffa (1957), for example, provide several proposed rules for rational choice in this context, show that some satisfy certain desirable properties in general but not others, and show that, at least among that set, no one such rule stands out.

Ferejohn and Fiorina (1974, 1975) considered one of these rules, the so-called minimax regret rule. This rule has several desirable properties. Compared to all others in Luce and Raiffa's set, it has the nice feature of

---

6. Even more, the simple number incorporates a lot of information, including every logically possible outcome, each of which is discounted by its likelihood of occurrence. As we will see, minimax regret includes considerations of every possible outcome, but the resulting number is derived from a single, particular outcome.

not always predicting that everyone should rationally abstain (or that everyone should vote). Indeed, it predicts that rational, minimax regretters would vote under more circumstances than does the calculus of voting. It also has some intuitive appeal. Imagine, they said, how you would feel if you woke up on the day after the election to find out that, if only you had voted, your preferred candidate would have won. Your having failed to vote caused that candidate to lose. You would, presumably, regret your decision to abstain. Minimax regret simply makes that intuition precise. Suppose s_1 is true. The best choice, if you knew that to be true, would be to abstain, with payoff B. If you abstained, you would have no regrets. If you instead voted your payoff would be $B - c$.[7] Your regret, then, is the difference in the actual payoff and the best you could have gotten, or $(B) - (B - c)$, yielding a regret of c. Of course, you don't know which state of the world is true, and you must choose an action before finding out. What you can do is to calculate the regret you would have for each action and each state of the world. Voting, you have regret c when s_1, s_2, and s_5 are true, and regret 0 when s_3 and s_4 are true. Abstaining, you have regret 0 when s_1, s_2, and s_5 are true, but regret $[(B/2 - c)]$ under s_3 and s_4.[8] Assuming the worst happens, the maximum regret from voting is c and from abstaining is $[(B/2) - c]$. The minimax regret rule is to pick the action that yields the lowest of these maximum regrets. Voting will have this minimum of the maximum regrets when $[(B/2) - c] > c$, or when $(B/4) > c$.[9] Thus, by this rule one votes if $(B/4) > c$ and abstains if $c \geq (B/4)$.[10]

As noted above, minimax regret is not always an optimal choice rule. If there is any circumstance, no matter how unlikely, in which a very bad outcome could occur, one should never choose that action because it would have a large maximum regret. Thus, for example, minimax regret would predict that the rational user of this rule would never cross a street because it is possible she would get hit by a car. Conversely, as

---

7. Ferejohn and Fiorina ignore the d-term, so I will here, but it can be easily added back in. Here, for instance, the payoff would be $B - c + d$.

8. This assumes that $B/2 > c$. It also follows that voting for the less preferred candidate is never the best choice and, as always, can simply be eliminated from consideration.

9. Including the d-term, the result is when $[(B/4) + d] > c$.

10. Minimax regret leads to turnout more often, because the minimax regret account predicts turnout when $B/4 > c - d$, while the calculus of voting predicts turnout when $pB/2 > c - d$. The former will occur more often. Without loss of generality, we can set $B=1$, and, with a little algebra, it turns out that the minimax regret term will be larger whenever $p < 1/2$. That is, the turnout condition for minimax regret will be larger than the calculus unless the probability of making or breaking a tie is .5 or higher. Minimax regret can also be used more often, because it can be used even if p-terms can be formulated, while it can, and the calculus of voting cannot, be used when p-terms cannot, or are not, formulated.

Ferejohn and Fiorina pointed out, voting for anything but the most preferred candidate is never optimal under minimax regret. Tullock wryly noted (1975) that, because it is possible to write in names on ballots, if rational minimax regretters vote, they should always write in their own names (assuming they would like to be president). More importantly, it does follow that there is no minimax regret logic for avoiding casting "wasted" votes. While estimates generally show that only a minority avoid wasting their vote, the minority is a sufficiently robust 10 to 20 percent of mass electorates to be theoretically and empirically consequential.[11]

The wry comment that rational minimax regretters would not cross streets to avoid the (unlikely) event of being run over is actually of some significance. I suspect that many would be either unable or unwilling to calculate the probability of being hit by a car while crossing the street, but most would discount it as unlikely, anyway. And, in answer to the Ferejohn and Fiorina question, when they woke up in the hospital, they would surely say that they regretted their decision to cross the street a great deal. But note that the only times in which abstention is not the best choice are precisely the circumstances in which the vote makes or breaks a tie. People may be unwilling or unable to calculate the probability of making or breaking a tie, but they may be just as willing to discount or ignore such an event as so extremely unlikely as to not bother considering – just as they ignore the probability of being hit when crossing the street. Thus, the positive prediction of turnout in minimax regret swings on the same set of (still just as wildly implausible) circumstances as in the calculus of voting.

1.4 Game theoretic

As noted above, the p-term in the calculus of voting is actually a summary assessment by the actor of the decisions of others. In empirical research, it is often measured either by the individual's belief about how close the election is expected to be (e.g., Riker and Ordeshook 1968; Aldrich 1976) or by the revealed closeness of the actual vote (e.g., Barzel and Silberberg 1973; Silberman and Durden 1975; Settle and Abrams 1976; Cox and Munger 1989). The basic idea behind the use of such measures is that an election expected to be (or actually having been) close made it more likely that the individual's vote would be

---

11. See Black (1978), Cain (1978) and Abramson et al. (1992) for examples of such estimates. Ferejohn and Fiorina argue that real electorates may contain some minimax regretters and some expected utility maximizers, a plausible position to take in general (if of little comfort to those conducting empirical research).

pivotal. The counterargument, of course, is that in an electorate of anything but the smallest of sizes, even a very close election is decided by a very large number of votes. In 1960, for example, John F. Kennedy defeated Richard M. Nixon in one of the closest presidential elections ever, winning 49.72 percent of the popular vote to Nixon's 49.55. That difference of 0.17 percentage points, however, was a difference of 114,673 votes. A realistic citizen's view, therefore, would have been that the election was expected to be extremely close, but that the probability of the state of the world being s_3 or s_4 was extremely small, small enough to be considered effectively zero.

Suppose, then, that a rational expected utility maximizer concludes that it is not rational to vote due to the nearly zero p-term. But our rational citizen would conclude that not only was it is irrational to vote but that everyone else would to. If everyone reasoned that way, then no one would vote. Our rational citizen would therefore conclude that it would be rational to vote because if no one else did, his or her vote would in fact be decisive. But if everyone so reasoned a great many would vote. Knowing this, our rational citizen would conclude that on second (or, more accurately, third) thought, it would again be "irrational" to vote, and this process would continue, on and on, shifting from every rational citizen deciding not to vote, then to vote, then not to vote, and so forth.

The logic of the above paragraph is precisely the logic of strategic interaction, formulated in game theory. Because the decision is a collective one, and because the appropriate action depends upon reasoning about the anticipated actions of others, neither of the above models is an accurate formulation of the problem. Simply put, while expected utility and minimum regret maximization are rules for individual choice, the voting problem is not an *individual* decision-making problem but one of strategic interaction. Minimax regret truncates out strategic interaction entirely, while the calculus of voting abstracts strategic interaction into an exogenous p-term, but that p-term is actually endogenous to the decisions of all actors in this voting game.

Several game theoretic models of the turnout problem have been developed (Ledyard 1981, 1984; Palfrey and Rosenthal 1983, 1985). Palfrey and Rosenthal (1985) believed that the first set of results seemed encouraging because at least some of the Nash equilibria to the voting game yielded substantial turnout.[12] These models had two types of equilibria, one in which no one (or almost no one) voted (similar to the

---

12. A Nash equilibrium strategy is one that is the best choice (or tied for the best choice) for each individual, if all others play their equilibrium strategies. In other words, at a Nash equilibrium, no individual desires to change his or her strategy unilaterally.

calculus of the voting result) or one in which (nearly) everyone voted and did so because there were (nearly) the same number of supporters for each of the two candidates, making everyone's vote "count." The latter, they show, are extremely fragile equilibria, because as the number of supporters of one candidate exceeds the number supporting the opponent, the equilibria with voting disappear. Palfrey and Rosenthal (1985) provide a more realistic assumption of uncertainty among citizens about the preferences of others. They summarize their results as follows:

> In this article, we demonstrate, within the framework of Ledyard's model, that in very large electorates the only voters are citizens with net positive benefits from the act of voting, citizens whose sense of duty outweigh any costs in voting. We have come full circle and are once again beset by the paradox of not voting.
>
> It is important to emphasize, though, that the paradox requires both large electorates and substantial uncertainty. We can in fact have equilibrium with high turnout in large but extremely well informed electorates or in small electorates, even when voting costs are relatively high. (1985, 64)

The latter results for large electorates are the kind described above, in which the two candidates are preferred by an equal numbers of citizens, and are therefore the "knife-edged" equilibria (edges "smoothed" by uncertainty).

In sum, current game theoretic models of turnout are apparently "driven" by the same basic features as the individual decision-making models. They are driven by the intrinsic benefits and costs of voting and by the closeness of the outcome (i.e., whether states s_3 and s_4 apply). They yield either virtually everyone or virtually no one voting, and the real-world situations to which the model corresponds are virtually always those that yield next to no one voting.

Instrumental models of voting, therefore, consistently lead by one route or another to turn on s_2, s_3, and s_4, the states of the world that are (or within a single vote of being) at a tie. Thus, they most often conclude that virtually no one will vote, sometimes predict that nearly everyone will vote, but virtually never predict the in-between levels of turnout observed in American elections. All attempts, whether the calculus of voting, minimax regret, or game theoretic, founder on Hegel's observation: one vote counts for very little. The essential problem can perhaps best be seen in a modified version of Fiorina's decision table (Figure 1, this volume). From that basic table, we can eliminate V_2 as a (weakly dominated) strategy by all rational choice accounts. And, if we treat the implausible states of the world, s_2, s_3, and s_4, as actually impossible, thereby eliminating them as well, we reach the 2x2 decision table in

States	Definition	Description
S_1	$n_1 > n_2 + 1$	Candidate 1 (the preferred alternative) wins by more than one vote without the citizen's vote.
S_5	$n_1 < n_2 + 1$	Candidate 1 loses by more than one vote without the citizen's vote

Payoff Matrix

Acts	S_1	S_5
V	$B - c + d$	$-c + d$
A	B	0

where V is the act of voting for candidate 1
A is not voting
B is the utility of candidate 1 minus
    the utility of candidate 2
c is the cost of voting
d is the noninstrumental reward from voting
modified version of Fiorina, figure 1, this volume,
with:
V_1 renamed V
V_2 eliminated as a (weakly) dominated strategy
S_2 and
S_3 and
S_4 deleted

Figure 1. Voter decision problem for two-candidate simple plurality election with simplifying assumptions. *Source:* Compiled by author, based on Fiorina, figure 1, this volume.

Figure 1.[13] The problem, then, is clear. No matter which of the (now two) states of the world is true, the individual decision maker strictly prefers abstaining over voting unless $d > c$. Since this table applies to everyone, all face the same decision, and all, therefore, should "rationally" abstain. Note that, since all who prefer the same candidate face the same payoffs, each may well find it individually rational to abstain, yet if all who prefer that candidate do in fact abstain, that candidate cannot win. Thus, the decision problem is effectively identical to that of an n-person prisoner's dilemma. It is this collective action problem (what Olson [1965] referred to as the "free-rider problem") that is the

13. While discussion focused on s_3 and s_4, the possibility that the preferred candidate wins by exactly one vote (s_2) is just as implausible as the other two states of the world.

underlying force in all of these models.[14] Perhaps, then, we should consider alternatives to these instrumental models.

2. Voting as an expressive act

Downs, noting that the implication of his original formulation of turnout (as a function of p, B, and c-terms) is universal abstention, proposed adding a new term to the calculus (1957). He argued that people may well reason that, if no one voted, democracy would collapse. He therefore concluded that people might vote to ensure the perpetuation of democracy. Such a value would come from voting, per se, no matter which candidate won or lost and would be obtained by the voter only if he or she actually voted. He argued, in short, that there was a d-term for voting. Riker and Ordeshook (1968) expanded this conception of intrinsic values voters could receive from the act of voting, per se, and it was their version of the d-term that Barry (1970) and others later criticized (although critics generally forgot that Riker and Ordeshook had offered a number of particulars beyond "citizen duty" itself that could be a part of the d-term). Fiorina (1976) expanded Riker and Ordeshook's account by arguing that one intrinsic value in casting a ballot is the expression of support for the voter's preferred party or candidate. Though not a theoretically different concept than the original d-term, it does admit of a simple and direct measure – B. That is, how valuable it is to voters to express their preferences is simply how much more they prefer one candidate to the other. Those with large B-terms care more about expressing their preferences than those who have small B-terms (or are more nearly indifferent). Thus, for example, if we let $d = (d' + B)$, that is, if we let d be composed of the value of expressing support for the favored candidate plus any remaining aspects of the old d-term, the calculus of voting equation becomes

$$pB + d' + B - c,$$

which if that term is positive, the citizen votes (with similar modifications for the other models).

Nothing is theoretically new here. All that is changed is the interpretation of the intrinsic value of turning out, in and of itself. Critics might well point out that this model (whether in calculus, minimax regret, or

14. It is this similarity to an n-person prisoner's dilemma game that, when repeated, leads to the abstract possibility that the Folk theorem can provide a "way out" of the dilemma. As the above-cited game theoretic models indicate, viewing the turnout problem as an instrumental decision has so far left that hope forlorn.

game theoretic form) therefore still indicates that people vote because they want to vote.

Taking that criticism to heart, say by asserting that pB is set to (near) zero for all, means that the turnout decision is not an investment decision. It is an act of consumption, an act of expressing one's preferences. While it doesn't therefore change the theoretical model of an individual's decision problem, it does have significant consequences in other ways. This interpretation now includes in the fixed costs and benefits of voting a term that reflects the particular features of the campaign. If there is little difference between the two candidates, as many found to be the case in the 1976 presidential election between Gerald R. Ford and Jimmy Carter, the B-term will be relatively small, and turnout, even to express one's preferences, will be less likely. If, however, many voters see substantial stakes in the outcome, they will be more likely to turnout because of their evaluation of that outcome, even though they are not doing so to affect that outcome. Thus, turnout is endogenous to the electoral context, even if voters are voting merely to express their preferences.

Fiorina's move of making B a part of the d-term was so clever in part because it made "duty" political in value. While most dismissed Downs's account of the d-term (and while it may or may not be the case that anyone votes because of a fear that if they did not democracy would end), Downs as usual was subtler and deeper than that reading. It may indeed be the case that there is a long-term value for citizens in and of a democracy to vote. Instrumental models of voting base choice on a single contest at a single point in time and are therefore very foreshortened. Not only do American voters chose over numerous contests in each election, but all citizens may place a nonzero time discount on the future. Indeed, the very reason Downs studied parties rather than candidates was so that he could theorize about an essentially infinite stream of elections. In U.S. national elections and in most state and local elections, candidates cannot get on the ballot without being endorsed by a party. Perot's is a very rare case of a candidate whose party in 1992 was merely an expression of his personal candidacy. For virtually all candidates, their party endorsement carries substantial information with it to the electorate. Thus, while Fiorina argues that d includes the political value B of the immediate contest, Downs argued that d (also) includes a long-term utility for citizens. No one has yet modeled that portion of d (which clearly is misstated as a fixed constant). Doing so would not only add a second political component to d, it would also enrich the very simple context so far modeled (and criticized) and integrate voters' choices with those of the larger political system, as will be considered in the next section.

There is, of course, nothing inherently "irrational" in expressing one's preferences (nor, even more obviously, in consuming, if this be voting as consumption). There is nothing irrational in applauding a fine symphony performance or in cheering the success of the home team. It may not be a very "deep" rational choice explanation of voting full of clever strategizing; but the parameters of the act of voting are highly limited, so that complex strategizing is necessarily limited (or illegal). But just as symphonies or home teams that perform well receive greater huzzahs, so, too, should we expect turnout to vary by the characteristics of the election. Indeed, not only is turnout in large electorates made at least partially endogenous to the nature of the electoral choices by Fiorina's reinterpretation of the d-term, but turnout can be (and has been) made at least partially endogenous to the actions and strategies of candidates, parties, PACs, the media, and other actors that dot real-world electoral landscapes, as the next section indicates.

3. Turnout in elections with expressive voters and with candidates and other actors

Descriptions of campaigns in the "golden era" of parties in nineteenth-century America typically use such analogies as "armies" and "religious movements." Parties were primarily local, with ward heelers and precinct captains often known by and knowing their party's supporters personally. Their electoral purpose was to mobilize their supporters on election day, and campaigns were primarily localized shows of strength with torch-light parades, bonfires, and spellbinding speeches. Parties sought, by all means necessary, to get their supporters to the voting booth (or perhaps voting booths, following the machine-adage of getting supporters to vote early and often).

Such partisan efforts at preference expression have waned (possibly one reason that turnout has, on average, declined). Nonetheless, a great number and variety of political actors seek not only to win converts to their preferred side but *also* to mobilize such supporters on election day. Though it may be true that changing one voter from an opponent to a supporter is twice as valuable as mobilizing one more supporter, it may be much easier getting one who already prefers your candidate to vote than trying to change another's preference. Investments in mobilization drives, be they registration drives or turn-out-the-vote campaigns, have been proven effective in increasing turnout (see Kramer 1970; Patterson and Caldiera 1983).

I have proposed a logic for the "strategic politicians hypothesis" (1993 and applied it to "strategic parties" in 1995). Citizens may be purely expressive voters who have no p-term (or assume it zero) in their calculations. They will act the same whether the election is expected to be close or one-sided. As long as the B-, d'-, and c-terms are net positive, they vote, and they abstain if the terms are not. But politicians and those seeking their favors care a great deal about the closeness of elections. A party leader, for example, will want to invest scarce resources in contests that are close, where that investment might make the difference between winning and losing. Why "waste" resources in hopeless contests or sure victories? With victory hanging in the balance, both sides will invest heavily in mobilization drives. Thus, turnout will increase, as the costs of voting are lowered and/or the intrinsic benefits of voting are increased – even though an average citizen may consider his or her vote a mere expression of preference and not an investment in the outcome. With a richer set of possible actions, it is thus strategic political leaders who strategize more "deeply," seeking to manipulate the B-, d'-, and c-terms to enhance turnout among expressive voters.

Several models of electoral processes have sought to develop these insights. For example, spatial models of two-candidate elections, developed from Downs's original work (1957; for a recent statement see Enelow and Hinich 1984), typically conclude that rational candidates will converge to the policy center, in equilibrium. Such models have viewed candidates as position takers appealing to the mass public as voters. Aldrich and McGinnis (1989) note (as did Downs) that with candidates at equilibrium, everyone would abstain from indifference because, in equilibrium, the candidates exactly match each other's strategy, that is, adopt the same policy position. Everyone's B-term would be zero. Campaign expenditures by candidates or parties, such as through turnout drives, can lower the costs of voting and thereby increase turnout. But these strategies will not work if all citizens are indifferent as to who wins. With both candidates at the policy center, the candidate who moves away from the equilibrium position will be preferred by fewer citizens. If, however, that candidate can increase the (smaller) number of citizens who prefer him *and vote*, and thereby get more of his supporters out to the polls than his opponent, he will win, even if the total number of citizens who prefer him is smaller. In this model, we derive equilibrium distributions of party activists and prove that, if turnout increases substantially enough with greater mobilization efforts from partisans, candidates will diverge from the policy center toward their party supporters. Divergence increases the B-term; investment of resources decreases the costs of voting and/or increases other aspects of the d-term. As a result, turnout increases, even for expressive voters.

Uhlaner (1989; see also Morton 1987 and Schwartz 1987) has developed a model with purely expressive voters (organized groups such as

PACs and interest groups) and candidates. In her model, group leaders seek policy promises from candidates that would provide collective goods of value to their group. Such policy positions provide goods of value that she assumes can be transformed into selective incentives. Group leaders can then use those selective incentives to affect the intrinsic costs and benefits of voting among group members, thereby increasing their levels of turnout. Such mobilization efforts can be of genuine value to a candidate and therefore potentially worth adopting group-preferred positions, because they can lead, in principle, to enough increased mobilization among those who prefer that candidate to affect materially the outcome of the election. Thus, mobilization can lead to positive turnout among purely expressive voters, and such a model has the potential to conform to the "in-between" levels of turnout actually observed in American elections (as can the Aldrich–McGinnis model, above). Uhlaner, as she notes, simply assumes that a policy position adopted by a candidate can lead to the creation of selective incentives by some direct or indirect means. Viewing the d-term as composed of B and d' (à la Fiorina 1976) provides an indirect means in both this group and the above party model since the policy position itself provides voters with an expressive value, presumably one that is especially large to members of the group or party.[15] There are, of course, any number of conceivable alternative mechanisms, including that of the group leadership's now investing its own resources in the hope of obtaining some future benefit from the election of the candidate with whom they "bargained."

4. Conclusion

In this chapter, I have argued that there is a genuine voting problem. Investment of costly resources, even if the cost is low, is a poor investment for citizens. Their vote is extraordinarily unlikely to have any discernible impact on the outcome. All rational choice theories that assume a mass electorate undifferentiated except by preferences, whether viewed as an individual decision-making problem under risk, an individual decision-making problem under uncertainty, or a game theoretic decision problem, founder over the unavoidable conclusion that, as Hegel said, "the casting of a single vote is of no significance where there is a multitude of electors."

15. At the same time, such a policy position may be of negative value to others. We might expect in the group context, however, that such policies would be of the intensely concerned minority, weakly concerned majority sort, adding a substantial positive B value to those who support the group's goals, while subtracting only a modest B value from many of those opposed.

While there is a genuine voting problem, it does not follow that turn-out is thereby an "irrational" act. Instead of consigning the actions of a majority of citizens to the mysterious or inexplicable, the obvious tact is to view the voting question as something other than an act of investment in this particular election at this particular time. Here, I argued that turnout should be considered a decision, a perfectly rational decision, to express one's preferences. In general, expressive voting models are based on Hinich's observation (1981) that voting is an act of contribu-tion, but I, as did he, argued that it is a clearly political act of expression and of consumption. As Barry said (1970), it may therefore not be a very rich or deep theory of voter choice. But, at base, the act of voting *is* simple. There are very few strategic options for citizens as voters, per se, especially once they have discerned their preferences over outcomes. Save the complex and valuable machinery of rational choice theory for complicated strategic settings such as maneuvering a bill through Con-gress. But, to say that a simple theory explains a simple decision prob-lem is *not* to say that it is uninteresting, unimportant, or, above all, removed from politics. This simple decision may often be relatively unimportant to citizens, but it is of genuine importance for politics and therefore for political leaders. Embedding this simple decision problem in a genuine and realistic political context (one filled with candidates, parties, interest groups, and others) makes this simple decision political, interesting, and important. While the above-cited examples are still bet-ter understood as indicating potential rather than performance, embed-ding citizens in a political context promises to make a valuable and interesting rational choice theory of voting. In this, voting theory is likely to be similar to consumer theory – a rich, interesting, important, and insightful theory, because it is a part of a fuller theory of politics, just as most of the interesting work in economics embeds consumers in a fuller theory of the economy.

CHAPTER 18

Voting behavior

MORRIS P. FIORINA

The literature on voting behavior may well be the largest literature in all of political science, especially given that it is closely conjoined with the literature on public opinion. From the standpoint of the public choice scholar much of the mainstream voting behavior literature uses arcane language and addresses topics of minimal relevance and importance. Nevertheless, there is much in this literature that should be of interest to the public choice scholar. This essay begins with a general review of the development of the literature and the different intellectual perspectives within it, then proceeds to a more selective review of some specific topics relevant to the study of public choice. Readers interested in more extensive (if less recent) reviews should consult Converse (1975) and Kinder and Sears (1985).

1. Intellectual background

The practical interest in voting behavior undoubtedly dates to the time the first candidates contested the first election. In Britain and the United States political operatives polled constituencies and studied aggregate voting returns in the eighteenth and nineteenth centuries, and elections prior to the secret ballot provide some detailed case studies of individual voting behavior.[1] In the late nineteenth century Frederick Jackson Turner adapted European cartographic techniques to construct electoral maps (Turner 1932). Some impressive pioneering work was carried out at the University of Chicago in the 1920s (Merriam and Gosnell 1924; Gosnell 1927; Rice 1928). Notwithstanding such pioneering early efforts, however, what today is recognized as the modern scientific study of electoral behavior is largely a product of the past half

---

1 For an amusing example see Greenstein (1970, 25, n6) in regard to the 1787 Massachusetts gubernatorial election, wherein the two sides released alternative tallies. Voters classified as "independent gentlemen" and "merchants and traders" by the Bowdoin forces were classified as "usurers," "speculators in public securities," and "stockholders and bank directors" by the Hancock forces.

century.[2] The field was one of the principal fronts in the behavioral revolution of the 1940s and 1950s.[3]

The scientific study of electoral behavior builds on an important intellectual advance – statistical sampling theory – and one of its practical applications – survey research. Before the 1930s political parties and newspapers often conducted "straw" polls of large but nonrandom samples. The best known of these is the infamous *Literary Digest* poll, which forecast a comfortable victory for Alf Landon in 1936. The *Digest* sent a mail ballot to millions of people whose names were drawn from telephone directories and automobile registration lists. Since telephones and cars were not as ubiquitous in the 1930s as they are today, the resulting sample was skewed toward the upper end of the income distribution, with a consequent overrepresentation of Republican sentiment. The *Literary Digest* polling debacle is a textbook example of selection bias.

Selections are not always bad, of course; if the selection principle is not related to the variable of interest, no problem will emerge. Indeed, what is often overlooked is that the *Literary Digest had* provided reasonably accurate forecasts of the 1924–32 elections (Erikson and Tedin 1981). A large part of the explanation is that prior to 1932 the electoral system was not polarized along income lines. Instead, religion, region, and ethnicity were important bases of partisan cleavage (Lichtman 1979). Thus, the class-biased sample the *Digest* normally obtained did not bias its estimate of voting sentiment.

Before the 1930s the only known way to avoid selection bias was to avoid selection – nineteenth-century parties sometimes conducted exhaustive censuses of voters (Formisano 1971). Sampling theory showed that relatively small random samples could provide relatively accurate estimates of population parameters and provided the means to say how small and how accurate. Importantly, national surveys of 1,000–1,500 randomly selected citizens were cost effective and statistically reliable, a fact George Gallup parlayed into a great enterprise.

By the mid-1940s academics joined Gallup, Roper, and a few other

---

2 Converse's (1975) review article in the *Handbook of Political Science* cites only three sources that clearly predate the behavioral revolution, one of which is written in French.

3 Space precludes an extended discussion of the behavioral revolution here. This transformation in political science began in the 1930s at the University of Chicago and was consummated by 1960 (Dahl 1961). Among its principal features were (1) a deemphasis of historical and legalistic varieties of research and a reorientation toward quantitative modes of research (2) a deemphasis of the prevailing normative, reformist tradition of political science and a reorientation toward accurate description and positive theory, and (3) the adoption of concepts and theories from other social sciences, chiefly psychology and sociology.

commercial "pollsters" and the study of public opinion and voting exploded. The old tradition of ecological (aggregate) analysis largely fell by the wayside. But if one research method came to dominate, consensus did not extend to theoretical perspectives. The all-but-forgotten indigeneous tradition of aggregate analysis had looked at voting in common-sensical fashion. How did the Southern vote differ from the Northern? How did the Catholics vote? The cities? The farms? Economic interests, ethnic rivalries, regional traditions, and so forth were the stuff of explanations. With the advent of the sample survey, however, analysts believed that they could get inside the voters' heads, so to speak, and learn more about the mechanisms by which voters reached their decisions.

Thus, the study of electoral behavior proceeded down a path that emphasized individual choice behavior rather than the consequences of those choices for the electoral system as a whole. Competing schools of thought developed. The Columbia school, influenced by emigre scholars and their students, conducted studies of the 1940 and 1948 elections (Lazarsfeld, Berelson, and Gaudet 1944; Berelson, Lazarsfeld, and McPhee 1954). The intellectual motivation for these studies was partly rooted in the experiences that drove some of the investigators from Europe: how had ordinary citizens in highly developed countries been converted to fascism and its associated antisemitism and racism? The Columbia studies began as studies of propaganda and persuasion. Unexpectedly, however, the Columbia school found that presidential campaigns and associated media efforts had little effect on political preferences; the principal effect of the campaign was rather to shore up existing cleavages that had softened since the last election. And the basis of such cleavages lay in the traditional categories of sociology: religion, ethnicity, and occupation – if not class. Since these categories were staple elements of the indigeneous, presurvey research study of elections, the Columbia school was not as much of a departure from the past as much of that which followed. But whereas the indigeneous tradition relied on inferences from aggregate voting returns and shifts, the Columbia studies showed the power of survey research to illuminate the details of individual-level change.[4]

Critics charged that the Columbia school assumed a simplistic "social determinism," a charge given credence by some unqualified statements found in their principal works: "A person thinks politically as he is socially. Social characteristics determine political preference" (Lazars-

---

4. The Columbia studies were "panel studies" – repeated interviews of the *same* cross-section of people over the course of the campaign. Standard cross-sectional surveys (and aggregate analyses) only permit an examination of net change, whereas panel studies permit an analysis of gross change.

feld, Berelson, and Gaudet 1944, 27) How, asked the critics, can social characteristics explain a Democratic presidential vote of 43 percent in 1956 and 61 percent in 1964 (Stokes 1966)? Social characteristics change little between elections. Moreover, how can social determinism explain why Catholics voted 54 percent for Eisenhower in 1956 and 83 percent for Kennedy in 1960? Evidently, the relationship between social characteristics and vote choice varies over time. Whatever the importance of social characteristics, other factors mediate or override such characteristics and determine the outcome of elections.

Chief among the critics was the Michigan school, composed of scholars heavily influenced by social psychology. These energetic scholars built up the edifice now known as the American National Election Studies (ANES). The Michigan school argued that social characteristics certainly were related to political preferences and voting behavior, but the relationship was mediated by partisan "attitudes" – beliefs and feelings about the candidates, issues, and parties (Campbell et al. 1960, chap. 3). Moreover, most voters had a long-standing psychological attachment to one of the two parties that strongly affected their partisan attitudes. This "party identification" resembled a religious affiliation – it was learned in childhood, not based on policy views (more affective than cognitive), almost impervious to change – and it operated as a "perceptual screen" through which other political information was assimilated and interpreted (1960, chap. 6–7).

The Michigan school quickly displaced the Columbia school. Though the Michigan scholars were influenced mostly by social psychology, a public choice scholar cannot help but admire their fine intuitive grasp of marketing. Much of their most persuasive work is based on one or both of two techniques. The first is to offer a seemingly reasonable description of the conventional wisdom about a subject. Upon close examination, however, the data are found to rebut the conventional wisdom. Thus, people who claim to be independents rather than partisans turn out to be less well informed and politically involved, not more (1960, 142–5). And ordinary people appear completely innocent of the kind of ideological thinking assumed by political commentators and elites (1960, chap. 10; Converse 1964). A second technique is to lay down a series of seemingly reasonable conditions that must be satisfied if a particular political fact is to be true. Upon close examination, however, the data show that only a corporal's guard of Americans satisfy the conditions. Thus, issues cannot logically affect the vote choices of many individuals (1960, chap. 8). And the importance of presidential coattails has probably been overestimated (Miller 1955–6).

In general, the hallmark of the Michigan approach was its emphasis on what goes on inside the head of the voter. The Columbia school viewed the voter as a social being. The most important influence on the voter was face-to-face contact in the family, at work, in church, and in other organizations that make up a community. The Columbia scholars examined "cross-pressures" (possession of group affiliations associated with opposing parties, such as a Republican Catholic), selective perception (biased perception/interpretation of data), and other mechanisms that presumably operate psychologically, but these were viewed as the product of sociological forces. For the Michigan scholars, however, voter attitudes were key. These were influenced by social characteristics, to be sure, but the latter occurred far back in the "funnel of causality" (1960, chap. 2). Some scholars worried that the Michigan approach took the analyst so far inside the voter's head that circularity was a threat – was liking "Ike" a cause of voting Republican or just another way of expressing a Republican choice? Others worried that the emphasis on psychological variables took the analyst too far into the subjective world of psychology and too far away from the objective world of politics. But if the theoretical edifice was not worked out to everyone's satisfaction, there was no gainsaying the empirical success of the approach.[5]

A decade of Michigan hegemony began to show cracks in the late 1960s. Speaking from personal experience I can attest that after years of civil rights and antiwar demonstrations, urban riots, the rise of social issues such as drugs and abortion, the campaigns of George Wallace, and the victory of the Nixon–Agnew ticket, it became increasingly difficult to stand before a class of undergraduates and say "issues matter little for most people; rather, voting behavior is based largely on party identification, which is learned in childhood and has little or no political content" (or words to that effect). From a variety of perspectives – a bit ideological, more methodological, and most importantly theoretical – critics began to chip away at the Michigan edifice.

From the beginning, a few traditionalists had criticized the Michigan perspective as a status-quo–preserving outlook that denigrated the ordinary voter's capacity for self-government. Well, even if that were so, what about the empirical evidence? More telling criticisms were made by more empirically minded critics. Some argued that different survey items produced evidence of issue voting much stronger than those relied on in the earlier Michigan work (Repass 1971). Others argued that the relatively more ideological Goldwater campaign, and the generally heightened excitement of the 1960s, demonstrated that voter loyalties and preferences were more subject to environmental influences and less

---

5. It is significant that the abridged version of *The American Voter*, used by thousands of students in the 1960s and 1970s, omitted the chapter titled "Theoretical Orientation" in the original.

internally fixed than previously thought (Field and Anderson 1969; Pierce 1970; Pomper 1972). This revisionist thrust culminated in a massive work, *The Changing American Voter* (Nie, Verba, and Petrocik 1976), that argued that the original Michigan work was carried out during an unusually quiescent period (the 1950s) and that in general voters were more involved, ideological, and issue-oriented than they had been portrayed in the Michigan study.

Some of the methodological revisionists were hoisted on their own petards, as critics showed that methodological artifact – chiefly changes in question wording – underlay some of the more extravagant claims for a new political order (Bishop, Tuchfarber and Oldendick 1978; Sullivan, Piereson, and Marcus 1978). After the dust finally settled, the consensus was that the Michigan school had overstated the political deficiencies of the average voter, but certainly by not as much as the revisionists claimed.

The more serious challenge to the dominance of the Michigan school came from the rational choice movement that was gaining steam during the late 1960s and early 1970s. The first task facing adherents of the rational choice approach was to be taken seriously: most political scientists were dubious about the rationality assumption, and nowhere was the skepticism stronger than among those who studied mass behavior, especially voting. Voting was viewed as an arational, if not irrational activity. Thus, rational choice scholars were happy to make common cause with methodological revisionists, arguing that changing times and different methods revealed voters to be indeed more "rational" than previously supposed. Ultimately, however, the rational choice camp realized that existing empirical evidence did not need to be impeached, only reinterpreted. For much of the portrait constructed by the Michigan school was not directly based in the data, but was a product of inference, indirect evidence, and appeals to psychological theories developed in other contexts.

As usual, there is some historical antecedent here in the classic work of Anthony Downs (1957). Partly anticipating the finding of the uninterested, uninformed voter, Downs (chap. 13) argued that ignorance was rational, given the cost of information and the infinitesimal influence of any single voter.[6] The implication of Downs's arguments was that rather

---

6. In less well known sections of his book, Downs had little trouble rationalizing ideas from the sociological model of the Columbia school. For example, he argued (chap. 12) that rational citizens would reduce information costs by relying on the "opinion leaders" identified by Lazarsfeld, Berelson, and Gaudet (1944), and that information would reach ordinary voters via a "two-step flow" (Katz 1957–8) from elites through an intermediate step of opinion leaders.

than argue that voters were more informed and issue oriented – more "rational" – than they appeared, rational choice scholars should accept the finding that voters are uniformed and consider it evidence *in support of* voter rationality. Indeed, the puzzle political scientists should be pondering was not why voters were uninformed but why so many of them had as much information as they did (Fiorina 1990).

Jackson (1975), Page and Jones (1979), and Franklin and Jackson (1983) criticized the traditional conception of party identification. Rather than something fixed foreover in childhood and relatively lacking in political content, they showed that party identification was simultaneously determined: it affected one's issue positions but was in turn affected by them. Fiorina (1977a) advanced an alternative conceptualization of party identification as a "running tally" of the voter's experiences with the two parties. Party identification could be viewed as an adaptive expectation about the performance of the parties. This formulation was suprisingly consistent with existing findings about party identification but went beyond them as well. For example, if voters and parties held the same positions over time, party identification would be expected to strengthen, an early empirical finding (Converse 1969, 1976). But if the parties and/or significant numbers of voters shifted positions, no strengthening of party identification necessarily could be expected, a proposition consistent with subsequent research (Abramson 1979; Niemi et al. 1985). Another interpretation of party identification congenial to public choice scholars is that party identification is something akin to a prior probability distribution (Zeckman 1979).

At the time of this writing theoretical controversy in the voting behavior field is muted. Researchers oriented toward rational choice ideas work side-by-side with others who hold social-psychological and even psychological orientations. There is a widespread appreciation that most existing data are compatible with a variety of perspectives, and that the perspective of choice is to some extent a matter of personal preference, but to a much greater extent a matter of why one is interested in voting behavior. If the principal interest of the investigator is the comprehension of individual choice behavior, then the psychology implicit in rational choice models looks too crude and undifferentiated. If the principal interest of the investigator is in understanding who won and the kinds of actions they took, then rational choice models look more promising. Both interests are alive and flourishing in the field.

2. A new direction: Back to the macro

In 1964 Philip Converse published an immensely influential article entitled "The Nature of Belief Systems in Mass Publics." Marshaling an impressive array of evidence, Converse left little doubt that ordinary people (the "mass public") did not think ideologically in the same manner as high-level elites. Ordinary people showed almost no evidence of ideological thinking in their responses to open-ended questions about the parties and candidates.[7] They could not explain terms like "liberal" and "conservative" when asked. Their views on specific policy questions were unconnected to each other – a voter would support government intervention in one area but oppose it in another. And, finally, their policy views were quite unstable across time. Converse's article stimulated scores, perhaps hundreds of reactions, critiques, and replications, in a debate that still continues today. Few political scientists of the 1970s would have doubted that Converse's findings had critical implications for the operation of a democratic political system.

Now, imagine that in 1964 an economist had written an article demonstrating that most ordinary consumers did not have preferences that were well approximated by continuous, convex indifference curves, that, indeed, many such consumers did not even have transitive preferences. Assuming, perhaps wrongly, that the author could have gotten the article published in an economics journal, I suspect that few economists would have been much troubled by it. Certainly, it would not have had an impact remotely comparable to Converse's in political science.

Despite their commitment to methodological individualism, economists treat the individual choice behavior of consumers only as a means to the vastly more important task of deriving propositions about the operation of the economy and the outcomes produced. As a non-economist I cannot offer any very precise guess about the reasons for the economist's relative indifference to individual behavior. Some I have known appeal to the law of large numbers and trust in aggregation to smooth out individual perversities. A few regard consumer theory as inherently unverifiable. But for the most part, the belief seems to be simply that aggregates are what is of interest.

A generation ago, V. O. Key, Jr., cautioned the new generation of public opinion specialists that studies of public attitudes ". . . are bootless unless the findings about the preferences, aspirations, and prejudices of the public can be connected with the workings of the governmental system" (1961, 535). Although Key's admonition seems to have had no immediate impact, today there is a growing sentiment within political

---

7. Open-ended questions invite respondents to reply in their own language. Their replies are later coded and tabulated. Close-ended questions invite the respondent to choose from among specified alternatives. A common analogy is essay versus multiple-choice exams.

science that the study of public opinion and voting has burrowed deeply enough into the head of the voter but has not taken a broad enough look at the behavior of electorates. The study of aggregate or macropublic opinion and voting behavior is one of the newer (and to my mind) most exciting areas of work in the field.

In a 1990 article Converse himself notes that the behavior of electorates is much more consistent than the behavior of the individual voters composing them. Specifically, average perceptions of parties and candidates look about right, even if large numbers of individual voters get them wrong. Stimson (1990) pursues this proposition at some length. Not only does the electorate understand that Republicans are to the right of Democrats on nearly all issues, but their understanding is clearer with candidates like Reagan, Goldwater, and McGovern, than with Nixon, Ford, and Kennedy. Aggregation is part of the answer, but Stimson goes further and shows that ordinary voters seem to key off the positions of activists in the two parties. Earlier, Brady and Sniderman (1985) showed that the electorate as a whole is pretty good at estimating the positions of Republicans and Democrats, liberals and conservatives, and blacks and whites on various policy issues. Individual voters possess little information, but Brady and Sniderman offer evidence that voters know whom they like and whom they don't and position groups accordingly.

Continuing in this macro vein, Stimson (1991) argues that the prevailing interpretation of the 1980 election is wrong. Nearly all political science analysts concluded that the election was primarily a retrospective rejection of Carter rather than any ideological turn to the right; Reagan won in spite of his conservatism, not because of it. Applying a modified factor analytic methodology to 139 survey items asked intermittently over a thirty-year period, Stimson makes a provocative case that American public opinion is largely one-dimensional and that in the late 1970s opinion moved sharply to the right on that dimension.[8] Opinion appears to have moved back to the left during the 1980s, though Stimson's methodology cannot differentiate changing opinion from a changing status quo.[9] Looking at Stimson's graphs one can clearly pick out the ebbs and flows of liberal sentiments since 1956.

Such macroresponsiveness of the electoral system is consistent with

8. Stimson's data set is dominated by domestic economic and social welfare issues; some critics argue that had social issue items been asked as early and as often as the former, a one-dimensional solution would not have resulted.
9. For example, between 1980 and 1984 the proportion of voters supporting higher defense spending dropped considerably. Perhaps voters grew less conservative, but more likely they recognized that spending on defense had increased greatly since 1980.

the most recent work of Page and Shapiro (1992). In a massive study of public opinion from the 1930s through the 1980s Page and Shapiro demonstrate conclusively that at the collective level *public* opinion is far more stable than the opinions of the individuals who comprise the public. *Public* opinion is responsive to political events and conditions. *Public* opinion is coherent in that things that should go together seem to go together. And *public* opinion reacts to new developments in ways that appear sensible to the analyst. Page and Shapiro conclude that the collective public is rational, even if the same cannot be said for the individuals who comprise it.

Finally, even party identification, the keystone of the individual, psychological approach has been abducted by the macroanalysts. MacKuen, Erikson, and Stimson (1989) show that movements in the aggregate Gallup-time series on party identification are significantly related to presidential approval ratings and the index of consumer sentiment. Disaggregating national samples by income Fiorina (1991) shows that party identification waxes and wanes with objective economic indicators, with lower strata more sensitive to changes in unemployment and upper strata more sensitive to changes in real GNP.

All in all, individual voters, like individual consumers, may be poorly informed, uninterested, and from a normative standpoint, somewhat irresponsible about their choices. But in inferring that such facts implied an arational or irrational electorate, earlier generations of scholars committed a logical fallacy. The reality seems to be that noisy voters send relatively clear signals.

What should the public choice scholar make of all this? The trend toward analysis and interpretation at the macro level would seem to make the study of voting behavior more useful to the public choice scholar. If a single liberal–conservative dimension dominates public opinion (see also Poole and Rosenthal 1987 regarding congressional voting), median voter models may be better approximations to electoral processes than critics usually concede. If voters extract considerable information from shortcuts such as inferences from the associations of particularly detested or admired leaders or groups and respond as if they have good information about public policy controversies, models that assume well-informed voters may be more firmly grounded than the individual behavior of voters would otherwise suggest. But I would like to go further than suggesting that the study of voting behavior will be more comprehensible and more useful to public choice scholars in the future. Even the microanalytic work that has occupied the field for three decades has contributed to public choice scholarship and will continue to do so. Before proceeding with that argument, however, it will be useful to take a closer look at the logic of voting in two-candidate elections.

States	Definition	Description
S_1	$n_1 > n_2 + 1$	Candidate 1 wins by more than one vote without the citizen's vote
S_2	$n_1 = n_2 + 1$	Candidate 1 wins by exactly one vote without the citizen's vote
S_3	$n_1 = n_2$	The two candidates tie
S_4	$n_1 = n_2 - 1$	Candidate 1 loses by exactly one vote without the citizen's vote
S_5	$n_1 < n_2 + 1$	Candidate 1 loses by more than one vote without the citizen's votes

where candidate 1 is the more preferred candidate, and n_i is the number of votes for candidate i without the citizen's vote.

Decision problem

	S_1	S_2	S_3	S_4	S_5
V_1	$B - C$	$B - C$	$B - C$	$B/2 - C$	$-C$
V_2	$B - C$	$B/2 - C$	$-C$	$-C$	
A	B	B	$B/2$	0	0

where p_i is the citizen's subjective probability of S_i
V_i is the act of voting for Candidate i
A is abstain
B is the utility of candidate 1 minus the
    utility of candidate 2
C is the cost of voting

Figure 1. Vote Decision: Two-candidate simple plurality election.

3. The pure theory of voter choice in two-candidate elections

From an abstract theoretical standpoint, voter choice in two-candidate elections is uninteresting. Figure 1 presents the generic voter's decision problem. Restricting attention to candidate choice, it is clear that voting for the more preferred of the two candidates is a dominant strategy.[10] Not only expected utility maximization but any known voter decision rule identifies the same course of action (Ferejohn and Fiorina 1974). Even if we embed the voter in a strategic context (ignoring the question of whether this makes any sense when 100 million people each have one vote) candidate choice, if not turnout, is uninteresting when the number

---

10. The reason public choice theorists have found this decision problem so fascinating, of course, is the question of why anyone would vote at all rather than abstain. That question is taken up in Aldrich's chapter in this volume.

of candidates equals two. For the mixed strategies identified in such game theoretic formulations give positive probability only to the pure strategies of abstention and voting for one's more preferred candidate (Palfrey and Rosenthal 1985).

Thus, the vast political science literature on voting behavior has no bearing on the pure theory of voting behavior in two-candidate elections; the latter is already complete. Rather, the voting behavior literature is essentially an extensive description of the *preferences* and *beliefs* voters have (the "*B*" term), along with theories and descriptions of how those preferences and beliefs are formed. But that enterprise is something that should be of considerable interest to public choice scholars, for one of the distinguishing characteristics of public choice scholarship is its emphasis on empirical examination of applied theoretical propositions. To the extent that we have accurate, maintained hypotheses about voter preferences, our applied theories of electoral politics, legislative politics, the political business cycle, public policymaking, and so forth will be more accurate. Given that the voting behavior literature contains a wealth of information about the preferences of voters, it is here that the literature can make a contribution to public choice.

4. A fundamental but often ignored consideration

Before proceeding, I reemphasize an important point already noted above – the brute fact that each citizen has one vote to cast and that there are typically large numbers of citizens. Any number of debates over the rationality of the voter and the rationality of electoral processes are misconceived products of forgetting the fundamental irrelevance of the individual voter. Though often ignored this fact has deep roots in public choice.

As noted earlier, Downs (1957) took note of the insignificance of the individual voter for determining the election outcome and of the implications of that fact for the rationality of information gathering. Becker (1958) makes the same point. And if outcomes are the product of thousands, even millions of voters' choices, then as Buchanan observed forty years ago:

> . . . the responsibility for making any particular social or collective decision is necessarily divided. . . . The responsibility for market decision is uniquely concentrated on the chooser. . . . There is a tangible benefit as well as a cost involved in each market chooser's decision, while there is neither an immediately realizable and certain

benefit nor an imputable cost normally involved in the voter's choice. (1954, 337)

In a market where private goods are exchanged, individuals bear the full costs of their choices. They may well find it worthwhile to gather plentiful amounts of information and cogitate at length on their purchases. In a market where public goods are allocated, individuals no longer capture the full benefits or bear the full costs of their choices, but some of them may have a significant enough role in the allocation to give serious consideration to their personal impact. Thus, presidents and governors, legislators, PAC administrators, agency heads, and so forth probably engage in highly instrumental behavior. But citizens voting in mass elections neither bear the full consequences of their decisions nor have much impact on the outcomes. The combination of these two features of large elections means that any conception of voting behavior that is instrumental in nature is highly suspect.[11] Voting is not an investment decision but a consumption decision; it is a way for voters to express a preference. Many citizens take satisfaction in such self-expression, in somewhat the same way that they enjoy rooting for the home team.[12] This may seem like belaboring the obvious, but it is a point that permeates the discussion that follows.

11. Some public choice scholars (eg., Durden and Gaynor 1987) have concluded that there is an instrumental component to voting because ceteris paribus voter turnout increases in close elections – suggesting the effect of a high p term in Figure 1. I am not aware of any persuasive evidence that voter perceptions of the closeness of the election *directly* affect turnout. Rather, as in the Durden and Gaynor analysis, all positive evidence of which I am aware is based on the objective closeness of the election after the fact (see Mueller 1989, table 18-1). The problem with such evidence is that alternative interpretations are equally, if not more, plausible. When a campaign is closely fought, party and candidate organizations increase their efforts, providing more information, mobilizing and transporting voters, and otherwise suggesting to voters that something important is at stake. Such activities may very well raise the B and/or lower the C terms (or raise the D or *duty* term sometimes added to the model). Thus, higher turnout in closely fought elections may reflect the operation of other elements of the voter decision problem, not the p term. Again, see the Aldrich chapter.
12. Brennan and Buchanan (1984) also make this argument, but I think they go too far in suggesting that for all practical purposes the *direction* of the vote should be random. Whether or not behavior is expressive I have no doubt that the aggregate utility of the Public Choice Society was higher in 1984 given the way the members actually voted, than if they had somehow been forced to vote for Walter Mondale. Empirically, voting behavior is highly systematic and quite consistent with the proposition that groups of voters vote their "interests," broadly defined. It is just that there is no individualistic basis for contributing to the group interest. Evidently voters take some psychic satisfaction in expressing their preferences.

5. Some specific topics in voting behavior research

5.1 Ideology, party systems, and other mysterious phenomena

Why are voting specialists so concerned with ideology, party identification, and so forth? After all, if one leafs through randomly selected volumes of *Public Choice*, one finds numerous election analyses, none of which rely on such concepts. Most such public choice analyses concern referenda, which are often "one-shot" decisions on single issues (Biegeleisen and Sjoquist 1988; Fort 1988). Elections so neatly circumscribed in space and time provide a fertile arena in which to analyze voter beliefs and preferences about alternative institutional and economic arrangements. Presidential elections, in contrast, are very complicated in that voters may be moved by all manner of disparate interests, values, and loyalties. And in addition to those complications, congressional elections display important intertemporal relationships of "surge and decline" (Campbell 1993) and moderating voters (Alesina and Rosenthal 1995). While informative and useful, many public choice analyses focus on elections that are unusual precisely in that they are not embedded in a temporal or spatial context.

Concepts like ideology and party identification in no way threaten the public choice approach and should not be viewed as alternatives to or competitors of public choice. Rather, these concepts have been developed and studied precisely because of their relevance to elections embedded in temporal and spatial contexts. Most elections are not de novo choices. Rather, in many locales, much of the time, or for some offices, the candidates of one party or the other win a disproportionate share of the contests. To cite some examples. Between the end of Reconstruction and 1994, the Republicans never won a majority in either chamber of a southern state legislature. Between 1952 and 1994, the Democrats never lost control of the United States House of Representatives. If elections were just a matter of moving closer to the median voter, one would think that losers would eventually learn their lesson and become winners. That such asymmetries persist reflects the operation of concepts like ideology and party identification.

Once again consider the fundamental irrelevance of a single voter. A presidential candidate is a bundle of policy positions – literally scores of them. The voter has no incentive to learn about most of these. It should not be surprising to find that many voters attach labels like "liberal" and "conservative" to candidates as shorthand summaries of their general policy inclinations, the values they espouse, and the groups or interests they favor. Ideology is broader than but not necessarily something distinct from or in conflict with self-interest. Voters do not "consume" ideology in the same sense as they consume the income from lower taxes, but ideology can be an effective shortcut to self-interest. Downs (1957, chap. 7) pointed this out almost four decades ago, but some public choice scholars seem strangely reluctant to accept the argument. We can argue about the extent to which ideology embodies narrow self-interest or a broader social vision (more on this below), but the existence and significance of something commonly labeled ideology is an empirical research opportunity, not an anomoly that should trouble public choice scholarship (Popkin 1991).

Much the same remarks go for party identification, although I think the concept is somewhat broader in that it incorporates judgments of party competence as well as the general direction of party policies.[13] For the past generation the dominant interpretation of American political history has been the realigning elections/party systems approach (Burnham 1970). According to this interpretation, U.S. political history can be viewed as a series of electoral eras, six in number, during which national elections resemble each other and across which they do not. Thus, during the fifth or New Deal party system (1932–64), the Democrats were the majority party losing only to war hero Dwight D. Eisenhower in 1952 and 1956. This system splintered during the 1960s giving rise to a sixth (divided government) system during which the Republicans dominated the Presidency (Aldrich and Niemi 1995). Within each party system, voter preferences, party positions, and election results are in a kind of equilibrium that is destroyed by periodic "critical" or "realigning" elections that separate one party system from another (i.e., such elections alter the structural equations). Thus, the elections of 1932 and 1964 destroyed the old alignments and ushered in the new.[14]

During the stable phases of party systems, party identifications firm up as voters repeatedly find themselves in the same position vis-à-vis the positions of the party candidates. Such identifications become excellent shortcuts to voting behavior across time and offices. But when new issues emerge (for example, racial and social issues in the 1960s) or national calamities occur (for example, the great depression), existing alignments weaken and greater uncertainty and instability reign while the system moves toward a new equilibrium.

13. Voters are quite capable of making the distinction. In 1972 for example, McGovern was not nearly so out of synch with popular sentiment as is commonly assumed. Instead, as Popkin et. al. (1976) note, voters simply viewed McGovern as incompetent.

14. The story is not so neat as these few sentences suggest, of course. For elaboration see Sundquist (1983); and Clubb, Flanigan, and Zingale (1990).

Just as we have expectations and biases about an Indiana product, a Rochester product, or a Virginia product (Mitchell 1988), so voters have expectations and biases about Republicans and Democrats. Such expectations and biases on our part are not considered noteworthy or problematic. The same should hold for the voters.

5.2 Prospective and retrospective voting

When the Michigan studies (Campbell, et al. 1960, chap. 8) found that ordinary voters had low levels of knowledge about government policies currently in effect as well as those advocated by the competing parties, such ignorance was interpreted to mean that issues played a subordinate role in voting behavior and that the policy implications of elections were very muddy. Findings like these contributed to the growing impression of electoral processes as "arational." But clearly, such conclusions presuppose a particular view of elections – elections as choices between alternative policies advocated by the two parties, much like the Euclidean loss formulation in the spatial model (Davis and Hinich 1965). Indeed, findings from the voting behavior literature were the basis of Stokes's (1963) critique of the Downsian spatial model.

Public choice voting behavior scholars, among others, soon offered an alternative view of elections. Given the miniscule impact of any individual voter, why should we expect them to absorb, process, and use information about such esoteric matters as government policies and the competing parties' proposals for change? In an aggregate analysis Kramer (1971) showed that party fortunes in congressional elections varied with fluctuations in the state of the national economy. Thus, elections could be viewed as *retrospective* judgments on party performance, a view rooted in Downs's arguments about informational shortcuts used by voters. Resurrecting arguments of the great mid-century elections scholar V. O. Key, Jr., Fiorina (1981) argued that even at the microlevel, much of the voting behavior literature was interpretable as an electorate engaging in retrospective judgment and more concerned with the outcomes of government actions than the policies that produced them. Barro (1973), Ferejohn (1986), and Austen-Smith and Banks (1989) have incorporated such retrospective views of elections into models of electoral control.

At the same time, the voting behavior literature cautions us not to bounce from one extreme to the other – from elections as informationally demanding prospective choices between two sets of policy proposals to elections as informationally undemanding retrospective judgments of the incumbent's performance. Fiorina (1981) concluded that the ultimate determinant of voter choice was expectations about the two contenders, although such expectations are clearly affected by past experiences. In an extensive analysis of the 1956–88 Senate voting, Lockerbie (1991) shows that expectations have a role at least partly independent of experiences. Working in a Kramer-type framework Chappell and Keech (1985) showed that modeling economic forces as expectations produces statistical results at least as good as modeling them as retrospective judgments. Most recently, MacKuen, Erikson, and Stimson (1992) argue that voter economic forecasts are interpretable in rational expectations terms.

In sum, the picture that is emerging is one in which voters with little personal influence on the election outcome somehow manage to glean information about government performance from observing their environment and utilize such information surprisingly efficiently, at least collectively. Such a process has been simulated in the laboratory (Collier, et al. 1987; McKelvey and Ordeshook 1990). All in all, this line of research indicates the value of comparative analyses such as that of Reed (1994, 1995) who contrasts the effects of prospective versus retrospective voting rules on the type of politicians who win reelection and on their behavior in office.

5.3 Sociotropic versus pocketbook voting

In the years following publication of Kramer's (1971) aggregate analysis, numerous replications, modifications, and critiques reinforced the general point that the American electorate responded to fluctuations in the state of the economy.[15] A controversy erupted in 1979, however, with the publication of Kinder and Kiewiet's analysis of the microlevel basis of economic retrospective voting. Rather than vote on the basis of their personal financial situation ("pocketbook" voting), citizens seemed to vote much more on the basis of their judgments of how the country as a whole had fared under the incumbent administration. In short, voters seemed to have a collective orientation ("sociotropic" voting).

The survey item most often used to estimate pocketbook voting reads:

> We are interested in how people are getting along financially these days. Would you say that you (and your family) are better off or worse off financially than you were a year ago? (responses are coded "better," "same," "worse.")

A supplementary question used by Kinder and Kiewiet reads "Are you making as much money now as you were a year ago, or more, or less?" Sociotropic sentiment is measured by survey items that asked about the

---

15. An exception was Stigler (1973), who managed to wash out the relationships by using a number of nonstandard variable definitions in his specifications. For a survey of this genre of studies see the Paldam chapter in this volume.

voter's perception of changes in business conditions during the past year and questions about the economic capabilities of the parties and the economic performance of the government. Clearly, such capacity and performance questions are invitations for partisan (i.e., biased) voters to reveal their biases. But even if attention is restricted to neutral items like "business conditions," the relationships between collective judgments and the vote far outweigh the ones between personal finances and the vote.

Kramer (1983) offered a strong rebuttal, calling into question the relevance of cross-sectional survey data for any study of interelection change. According to Kramer, in any single election there is a wide range of individual variation around the national average. In economic affairs, the government has some responsibility for the national averages, it has much less to do with most of the individual variation, which arises from nonpolitical personal characteristics and random influences. In short, from a political standpoint, cross-sectional variation in personal finances is largely noise. According to Kramer only aggregate data contain real information, and at that level it is impossible to differentiate sociotropic and pocketbook voting. Rivers (forthcoming) took up the latter challenge. Using pooled time-series cross-sectional estimation, he concluded that personal finances were more important than Kinder and Kiewiet had concluded, but that collective considerations were nevertheless important.

Methodological disputes aside, however, the principal reason for the attention given to the Kinder–Kiewiet finding and the numerous subsequent replications was that the finding tended to be mapped into another broader distinction: self-interest versus altruism. In some sectors of political science there is a tendency to equate the rational choice approach with the claim that people are motivated solely by material self-interest. Thus, those skeptical of or hostile to rational choice approaches seize upon any instance of seemingly nonself-interested behavior as a counterexample to the rational choice approach in general. Such critics naturally read the Kinder–Kiewiet finding as saying that voters ignored their own economic self-interest and instead selflessly voted on the basis of what was good for the country as a whole.

Of course, any such equation is suspect. Though material self-interest is often a maintained hypothesis in public choice research, the rational choice approach admits a much broader range of preferences. As a rational choice partisan whose own empirical analyses (1981) were consistent with those of Kinder and Kiewiet, I did not feel that my identity as a scholar was in any way threatened by their findings. In the first place, Kramer is absolutely correct in pointing out that survey measures of change in personal finances are quite noisy. The birth of a baby, a child entering college, a spouse returning to the labor force – such events may have a far greater impact on one's personal financial situation than the fiscal or monetary policy of the government. In contrast, just by living one picks up information on unemployment, inflation, and the overall state of the economy. And is it not reasonable to believe that a good economy is generally good for me and vote accordingly? Moreover, even if I am faring well under current government policy, that certainly does not mean that I could not expect to fare better under an alternative policy. Holding a large mortgage and enjoying a COLA-protected salary, I may be profiting personally from high inflation; neverthless, I may well feel that over the long run my household will fare better in a low-inflation economy. There is nothing in public choice theory in particular or in rational choice theory in general that requires voters to be as shortsighted and selfish as two-year olds.

In the second place, though public choice scholars are properly skeptical of explanations based on altruism, they do not deny its existence. After all, people do give to charity, sometimes anonymously. Strangers drop coins in the hands of the homeless, give blood, work in soup kitchens, and engage in other selfless behavior. Just because public choice scholars rarely do such things themselves does not mean they deny that others do. All that rational choice demands is that altruism have a price, like anything else. When the price of altruism is high, we observe less of it than when the price is low. In the voting booth the price of altruism is virtually zero: since each individual's vote is insignificant, one can cast it altruistically secure in the knowledge that it will be costless (Tullock 1971; Goodin and Roberts 1975; Brennan and Buchanan 1984). Seen from this standpoint, a voter who insisted on casting her presidential vote solely on the basis of her personal material self-interest would not be rational so much as mean.

Whatever the interpretation one favors, when studying electoral processes public choice scholars should bear in mind that voter utility functions have multiple arguments. Clearly they care about their property values and their tax rates, but just as clearly they care about some public goods and may vote to compel themselves and others to provide them at certain levels. There should be nothing puzzling about such behavior, let alone anything threatening to the public choice research program.

5.4 The media and voting behavior

According to a study cited by Ladd (1993) content analysis of the network evening news telecasts found that in the third quarter of 1992, when most economists felt that economic recovery had begun, the tone of TV news about the economy was 96 [sic] percent negative. Republicans will use such studies to support their long-standing claim of media bias, while the media will respond that they just reported the facts. But even less partisan observers like Ladd feel at least somewhat uncomfortable about such apparently one-sided media coverage. Fortunately for Republicans and citizens alike, most voting specialists believe that media influence, while not insignificant, is at least exaggerated.

Recall the earlier discussion of the Columbia school. Although their studies began as research on propaganda – how candidates, like products, could be sold by modern mass communications techniques – their findings soon led them to alter their focus. Exposure to the campaign with its accompanying heightened media attention seemed to reinforce existing preferences but not to change them. Succeeding research both in the field and in the laboratory came to similar conclusions. By 1960 the thesis of minimal media effects (Klapper 1960) was widely accepted.

One of the major reasons for minimal media effects lies in the topics discussed earlier in this paper. Many people have predispositions like party identification and ideology that affect how news is absorbed and interpreted or, indeed, whether it is absorbed at all. Rather than reject Bush, committed Republicans discount the news, having decided that television announcers are just a bunch of left-wingers; six months later committed Democrats decide that television announcers are just a bunch of cynical yuppies out to get Clinton. Adults learn to discount the media in general – just as very young children learn to discount commercials – and they are more likely to discount the media when messages contradict what they believe on other grounds.

None of this is to claim, of course, that the media has no influence. Since voters often have little information, whatever the media provides, even if it is discounted, can have an effect. This is especially true of voters without strong predispositions – the young and those who are especially uninterested, although such people are less likely to vote at all. In recent years sophisticated field studies (MacKuen 1981) and well-designed experiments (Iyengar and Kinder 1987) have found evidence of two forms of media effect.

The first is traditionally termed agenda setting: the media may not be able to determine what we think, but they can determine what we think *about*. Thus, the media's unrelenting focus on the economy may have made it easier for the Clinton campaign to hold to its motto ("It's the Economy, Stupid!"). A methodological problem that undercuts many agenda-setting studies, however, is that lacking a model of media behavior, it is certainly possible that other causal processes are operating. The media could be setting its agenda by anticipating what voters would be interested in hearing or both media and voter agendas may be set by other factors such as real world developments. Experimental studies avoid such problems, but it is likely that their findings constitute "best case" scenarios for media effects.

A second media effect examined by recent research is called "priming." Laboratory studies in particular (Iyengar and Kinder 1987; Iyengar 1991) indicate that the media can affect the standards of judgment used by voters. Thus, in early 1991 President Bush's approval ratings were higher than would have been expected based on the state of the economy, quite possibly because the media were fixated on his successful prosecution of the Gulf War. Conversely, in late 1992 Bush's approval ratings were lower than might have been expected based on the state of the economy, quite possibly because the media were fixated on the economy. It was not that the media changed voters' minds about how Bush had done on either foreign affairs or the economy, but that the media affected how voters weighed those separate evaluations in arriving at an overall evaluation of Bush (Ansolabehere, Behr, and Iyengar 1993, 147–50).

Finally, it is clear that some contexts provide a more favorable context for media effects than others. For example, there is strong evidence that the media are quite important in presidential primaries (Bartels 1988). And why not? Voters face laundry lists of candidates, many of whom are relative unknowns. Moreover, the usual shortcuts are less applicable than in general elections, if they are applicable at all. Because all the candidates one must choose among belong to the same party, party identification is not helpful. Because all the candidates one must choose among occupy a relatively small part of the ideological dimension (from Bob Dole to George Bush), ideology is of only marginal use. Because the candidates one must choose among either are all associated or all not associated with the performance of the incumbent administration, all of them attack it or all claim credit. In sum, the usual predispositions do not apply.

All in all, media effects are real, but not nearly so important across the board as often suggested in the more popular literature. The reason is that the media is ahistorical and focused on gaffes, scandals, campaign tactics, and so forth (Patterson and McClure 1976), whereas much of voting behavior is a function of longer-term influences such as party identification, ideology, and performance judgments. In a close election, of course, the media can make the difference. But the fear of an omnipotent, irresponsible media is exaggerated. Irresponsible, yes (Sabato 1991); omnipotent, no.

5.5 One policy space or N? Incumbency and the nature of political outcomes

In the early 1970s political scientists noticed that the advantage of incumbency in elections to the U.S. House of Representatives had increased sharply during the decade of the 1960s (Erikson 1972; Mayhew 1974). This observation stimulated a vast outpouring of research on congressional elections, which until then had been viewed as relatively uninteresting contests dominated by party loyalties (Stokes and Miller 1962). It is neither possible nor appropriate to review that far-flung literature here, but one finding from it deserves emphasis.[16]

Whether voters are retrospective or prospective, self-interested or sociotropic, their choices determine the policies that governments implement. As discussed above, however, such choices may determine public policies without being based on the slightest consideration of such policies. Now we make the further observation that such choices may not be based even on consideration of policy *outcomes*. The reason is that public officials provide individual favors as well as general policies, and the former may well be more important to many voters.

One of the explanations offered for the increased advantage of incumbency was that House elections had become less partisan and less ideological and more concerned with the distribution of particularized benefits (Fiorina 1977b). Models that treat the decision between two candidates as tantamount to a decision about public policies may not be a bad approximation when it comes to voting for presidents, governors, and other singly occupied offices. But when it comes to voting for a member of the U.S. House or other plural body, the election determines only one official among many who will collectively determine policy. Thus, in legislative elections, the value of the individual vote is doubly discounted: as always its importance is miniscule given tens of thousands of other voters, but in addition the legislator elected is only one of hundreds who make policy. In such a situation, the instrumental basis of voting is even less plausible than in executive elections.

Nevertheless, it would probably be a mistake to consign all voting for collective offices to the realm of consumption. Public officials often can provide various "services," by intervening in the implementation of public policies (ombudsman activities) and by trading their support for broad public policies in exchange for particularized benefits of little value to executives and legislative leaders but of great value to local groups and individuals.[17] Upon close examination one can interpret legislative committee systems as institutional means for dividing authority so that individual legislators can be pivotal on decisions of particular

16. For a general survey of the congressional elections literature see Jacobson (1992).
17. The passage of Clinton's economic plan in the summer of 1993 was widely described as conditioned on a large number of vote trades in which senators and representatives received constituency benefits in exchange for votes. Similarly, the bargaining associated with passage of NAFTA was likened to that in an "oriental bazaar."

interest and concern to their constituents (Weingast and Marshall 1988). All in all, legislators today can behave something like machine bosses in earlier times, dispensing private benefits in exchange for political support. Thus, incumbent legislators can disarm opposition based on partisan or ideological bases by entering into service relationships with otherwise hostile local interests.

The implication is that public policies may be to some degree accidental by-products of electoral behavior. From the social choice and related literatures, public choice scholars do not expect elections to have much in the way of optimality properties or even consistency properties (Riker 1982a). We can now add to such general negative results the fact that legislative elections may not even elicit expressions of voter preferences, however imperfectly, for public policies but may instead reflect to a significant degree private deals made between legislators and constituents. A conservative district may repeatedly elect a liberal Democrat who provides quality service to local business interests. Liberal "high-demand" constituents may support a conservative representative who ignores ideology and helps constituents maximize their benefits. Ultimately, constituents – and consequently legislators – may focus less on the size and shape of the national pie, and more on the size and shape of their particular portion.[18] And however dissatisfied voters become with the former, the double discounting of their legislative vote inhibits any tendency to express their dissatisfaction in legislative elections. Thus, voters grow increasingly disenchanted with the legislature as a whole, endorse term limits and other radical proposals, and continue to reelect their own member. The commons is polluted as the position of society in the grand policy space becomes in considerable degree a by-product of games being played in myriad subspaces.

6. Summary

The vast literature on voting behavior contains much of interest to public choice scholars. For the most part the literature is primarily a description of the beliefs and preferences of voters. The major lesson to be learned is that few elections can be treated as free-standing decisions on a single issue, about which voter preferences are relatively straightforward to specify, let alone measure. Such a conception of elections fails on two general counts. First, since the individual voter in a large election

18. As Aranson and Ordeshook (1977) note, goods that are public in consumption are often private in production. Thus, legislators may perversely regard the cost side of public goods production as an electoral benefit (Weingast, Shepsle, and Johnsen 1981).

has little or no incentive to learn very much about the candidates and issues, many voters will make use of informational shortcuts like party identification and ideology. The reasonableness of such behavior is reinforced by a second general point. Since most elections are between candidates who are bundles of issue positions and group allegiances and who are associated with previous candidates who bore the same party label, many voters will make use of summary measures of evaluation like party identification and ideology. Such behavior is predicted by the rational choice perspective that underlies public choice research and is not a counterexample.

CHAPTER 19

Public choice experiments

ELIZABETH HOFFMAN

A number of important issues in public choice have been addressed in experimental research.[1] This chapter summarizes experimental research on the role of allocation mechanisms and agent behavior in the ability of groups of agents to achieve optimal allocations of public goods and externalities when there are gains from cooperation and coordination. This line of research includes studies of the free-rider problem with voluntary contributions; studies of the ability of small and large bargaining groups to achieve Pareto-optimal allocations of externalities or public goods; and studies of the design and behavioral implementation of synthetic allocation mechanisms for the allocation of public goods, externalities, and complex commodities.

1. The free-rider problem with voluntary contribution mechanisms

The free-rider problem is a central focus of experimental research in public choice.[2] Economists, psychologists, and sociologists have joined the debate, answers to which are central to a number of larger issues in public choice. The basic premise of economists is that individuals, acting in their own self-interest, will underprovide public goods and positive externalities and overprovide negative externalities, relative to those quantities that would maximize social welfare. In the limit, with pure public goods and no appropriability, no public goods will be provided. Psychologists and sociologists counter both with arguments criticizing the basic assumptions of economic models and with the observation that societies do provide public goods for themselves, sometimes without governmental intervention. Economists, themselves, subscribe to two different "remedies" to the free-rider problem. One group suggests that the only solution is for government to provide public goods and tax

---

1. Interested readers should also consult Davis and Holt (1993), Hoffman and Plott (1994), and Ledyard (1994).
2. Ostrom and Walker (this volume) also address voluntary contribution mechanisms.

citizens to pay for them. The problem then becomes determining the optimal quantity of public goods and the optimal tax structure. The other group, drawing on the seminal work of Ronald Coase (1960) suggests that individuals will realize the benefits from collective action and form private organizations to provide public goods and collect funds to support them. This section outlines the basic voluntary contribution experiments and reviews some results. These experiments address two important problems with voluntary contribution. First, how serious is the free-rider problem under conditions similar to those prevailing in naturally occurring public goods allocation systems? Second, what policies tend to increase or decrease voluntary contributions to public goods provision? The next section outlines and discusses experiments designed to test the Coasian proposition that groups will privately provide public goods for themselves.

The current literature on voluntary contribution begins with a series of articles by Marwell and Ames (1979, 1980, 1981), two sociologists at the University of Wisconsin. Observing that public goods do seem to get provided, they asked the question whether free riding was a characteristic more of economists than of society as a whole. They designed their experiment as follows. They recruited high school students by telephone. Each student was given a set of paper tokens that could be redeemed for money. Each student was asked to make one decision, allocating tokens to two accounts. The private account provided a return of one cent per token invested. The group account (the public good) returned to individuals as a function of the total number of tokens invested in the group account by all members of the group. At low investment levels, each individual token contributed to the group account earned less than one cent to the individual contributing, but larger investments by all participants led to higher payoffs for all participants. Subjects were told they were assigned to groups of either four or eighty participants. In reality, all groups had four participants. A companion experiment (Marwell and Ames 1981) substitutes graduate students in economics for high school students. Marwell and Ames found that, in general, subjects in their experiments contributed about half their tokens to the group account. The only exception was the economics graduate students who contributed very little. They concluded that the free-rider problem was not as serious for noneconomists as economists were suggesting.

These results prompted economists to initiate experimental research on the free-rider problem. Three papers directly motivated by Marwell and Ames' results (Isaac, Walker, and Thomas 1984; Kim and Walker 1984; Isaac, McCue, and Plott 1985) led to an extensive research agenda on voluntary contributions mechanisms (e.g., Isaac and Walker 1988a,

1988b, 1991; Isaac, Schmidtz, and Walker 1989; Isaac, Walker, and Williams 1994; Laury, Walker, and Williams 1995). Economists had several criticisms of the Marwell and Ames experiments. First, the use of telephone surveys and deception about group size called into question the experimentalists' control of the experimental incentives. Second, the one-shot nature of the experiment did not allow subjects to learn about the possible free-riding behavior of other subjects and adjust their behavior accordingly. This applies both to learning within an experimental session and to learning across different experimental sessions. Third, the subject payoff tables did not generate a single Nash equilibrium strategy. Thus, the results could not provide conclusive evidence about free riding. In fact, contributing half one's tokens to the group account was a clear focal point in the payoff structure.

Isaac, Walker, and Thomas (1984) defined the experimental design that has become the standard for this research agenda. In their experiment, students at the University of Arizona were recruited to come to a PLATO computer laboratory at a certain time. Each subject sat at a private terminal and read through a set of instructions explaining a task quite similar to that in the Marwell and Ames experiments. Each subject was given a set number of experimental tokens and could invest those tokens in either an individual or group account. The individual account returned one cent for each token invested by the individual. The group account returned less than one cent for each token contributed by the group. These initial incentives were designed so that contributing zero tokens to the group account was a Nash equilibrium, but contributing 100 percent was Pareto optimal. Subjects knew how many other subjects were in the group because they could see them in the room. Consistency was maintained because they all read the same instructions. Each group of subjects participated in ten consecutive decisions; experienced subjects were brought back to participate with other experienced subjects in new sequences of decisions.

Isaac, Walker, and Thomas (1984) considered group sizes of four and ten subjects, individual returns to the group account of .3 or .75 of a cent, and subject experience. The results do not settle the debate. First, subjects in their experiments continued to contribute well in excess of the Nash equilibrium prediction of zero to the group account. Averaging over replications of the same treatment, contributions ranged from 40 percent to 60 percent of tokens in period 1 to 20 percent to 40 percent of tokens in period 10. Occasionally a group contributed zero tokens in one or more periods, but this was not a predictable or consistent outcome. Certain treatments did encourage or discourage contribution to the group account. Subjects tended to contribute less with repetition or experience, and with a lower individual return from contribution to the group account. Holding individual payoffs constant, group size did not have a significant effect.

These results have led to a significant change in the focus of research on voluntary contribution among economists. The initial thrust was to test the economic model and to show sociologists and psychologists that free riding really was a serious problem. Now the emphasis is on determining what factors contribute to more or less free riding. From a policy perspective, this research has led to a renewed emphasis on the possibility of private solutions to the public goods allocation problem.

For example, Isaac and Walker (1988a) study the effect of communication on free riding in an experiment essentially identical to that reported in Isaac, Walker, and Thomas (1984). They consider two experimental treatments. In one subjects begin each of the first ten decisions with a group discussion of how much each subject should contribute. Each decision is made privately. After ten decisions with communication they make ten decisions without communication. In the other the subjects begin with ten decisions with no communication and end with ten communication decisions. They find that communication unequivocally reduces free riding (increases contributions to the group account), even though all decisions are made in private. Groups that begin with communication typically achieve nearly 100 percent contributions to the group account. Contributions diminish once the group ceases communication each period. Groups that begin with no communication take longer to achieve high levels of contribution with communication, but contributions do increase.

Isaac, Schmidtz, and Walker (1989) consider the effect of having a threshold level of the public good, a provision point. Any contributions below the provision point are lost. Contributions equal to or above the provision point go to the group account as in the previously described experiments. The idea is that provision of a public good generally involves raising enough funds to pay for purchase or construction. If insufficient funds are raised the public good is not provided. Isaac, Schmitz, and Walker (1989) find that higher provision points are associated with greater contributions to the group account, thus suggesting that provision points improve provision. However, they also find that higher provision points also reduce the probability the provision point will be achieved.

Isaac, Walker, and Williams (1994) study the effect of group size with very large groups. Using a clever experimental design, in which they substitute extra credit points for money in large introductory economics classes, they find that very large groups generally achieve higher levels of contributions than groups of size four or ten. Contributions still decline with repetition and with lower private returns to group contributions. Laury, Walker, and Williams (1995) find that subject anonymity, from one another and from the experimenter, do not change average contributions by treatments.

We are now at a crossroads in understanding the role of the free-rider problem in public choice. On the one hand, in the experiments described above, subjects chose the Pareto-optimal allocation of 100 percent of the tokens invested in the group account in few experimental sessions. Generally, subjects contributed 50 percent of their tokens or less. However, it is also true that subjects chose the Nash equilibrium allocation of zero contributions on fewer occasions. Communication prior to each decision round and greater personal benefit from investment in the group account improved provision. Repetition, without communication, tended to reduce group investment, but the effect was not consistent. Changes in group size were ambiguous. Some groups were more cooperative (invested more in the group account), others were less so.

In summary, we can say that, without frequent reinforcing communication, voluntary contributions to the provision of public goods result in positive, but suboptimal, levels of provision. Fund drives with specific goals raise more funds but still may not raise sufficient funds to provide the public goods. However, all these experiments have the characteristic that subjects cannot enforce any agreements made during communication. In the next section we consider experiments with both communication and enforcement. These deal with the allocation of externalities (not public goods), but the experiments with large bargaining groups have similar free-rider problems.

2. Coasian bargaining experiments

In the previous section we considered private voluntary contributions to the provision of a public good, where the optimal provision was generally not known to the participants. In this section we outline experiments in which subjects can bargain to the Pareto-optimal provision of a negative externality and enforce compliance on all parties. This research began as an experimental test of the Coase theorem in the simplest possible environment: two parties to a bargain, no transactions costs, no wealth effects, clearly defined interior Pareto-optimal allocation, contracts signed and strictly enforced.[3]

These initial experiments proceeded as follows. Two subjects who did not know one another sat in a room across a table; a monitor was present. The subjects were presented with a payoff table that associated

3. Hoffman and Spitzer (1982).

a payment to each participant with each of a series of numerical outcomes. One subject would be paid nothing for the lowest numerical outcome and twelve dollars for the highest numerical outcome. The other subject would be paid twelve dollars for the lowest numerical outcome and nothing for the highest numerical outcome. One outcome yielded fourteen dollars for the two subjects jointly. All other outcomes yielded twelve dollars or less for the two jointly. By a flip of a coin, one subject was chosen to be the "controller." The controller had the right to make the decision of which number to choose without consulting the other person. This right was clearly explained in the instructions. The other subject could persuade the controller, possibly by monetary transfer, to choose some other number. Any bargain involving monetary transfer was to be signed by both parties and enforced by the monitor.

Analyzing this experiment as a game, we can see that the core of the game is for the two subjects to agree to fourteen dollars and for the controller to get at least twelve dollars. Considering this as an externality/public goods experiment, the controller becomes the individual with the right to do harm to the other person. The outcome that yields fourteen dollars is the predicted outcome, regardless of which subject is selected as controller. That outcome should always be selected and the controller should always earn at least twelve dollars.

In these initial experiments we ran some subjects through a sequence of one-shot decisions with different partners and some through two successive decisions with the same partner. Half the subject pairs had full information about the payoffs of both subjects; the other half knew only his or her own personal payoffs. Almost every subject pair chose the joint-profit maximizing outcome, providing strong support for the Coase theorem and for the ability of pairs of subjects to achieve an optimal allocation of an externality through private bargaining.

We followed this initial experimental study with a thorough examination of bargaining to achieve an optimal allocation of an externality with groups of three, four, ten, and twenty subjects (Hoffman and Spitzer 1985b). Each of these experiments required subjects to agree to the distribution of taxes and benefits as well as the allocation of the externality. For example, the three-person experiments involved either one controller against two other parties or two joint-controllers against one other party. The joint-controllers would have to agree to a distribution of any benefits derived from the other party; the other party would have to agree to divide the payment to the single controller to achieve a Pareto-optimal allocation of the externality. The four-person experiments involved either three subjects against one, or two against two; the ten-person experiments involved either five against five, or nine against one; the twenty-person experiments involved nineteen against one. The four- and ten-person experiments were conducted with both full and private information. The twenty-person experiments were conducted with private information only. The only substantive difference between the experiments reported in Hoffman and Spitzer (1982) and in Hoffman and Spitzer (1985b) is that the right to be the controller or joint-controllers was determined by winning a game of nim, not by the flip of a coin. We effected that change because we discovered that controllers were more likely to demand their individual maxima if the right to be controller was won in a game of skill and then reinforced by the experimenter (see Hoffman and Spitzer 1985a).

The results of these experiments with large bargaining groups reinforce the two-person bargaining results. Almost all the bargaining groups selected the joint-profit maximum. Moreover, even with large numbers of joint-controllers or with groups having to agree to transfer earnings to controllers, subjects succeeded in agreeing to distributions of taxes or benefits. Thus, with communication and enforceable contracts, subjects solved the free-rider problem through negotiation.

In a recent extension, Blake, Guyton, and Leventhal (1992) study Coasian bargaining in a different environment. In their experiments groups of three subjects are presented with a bargaining problem involving selecting from among several specific alternative allocations of subject profits. All sets of allocations contain one selection that is Pareto optimal, but only half the subjects bargain over sets of allocations including a core allocation. In addition, half the subject groups bargain face-to-face and half bargain only through computerized messages. They find that subjects bargaining over sets allocations containing a core are generally able to reach the Paerto-optimal/core allocation as well as subjects in the Hoffman and Spitzer experiments were. However, subjects bargaining over sets of allocations in which there is no core are significantly less likely to agree on a Pareto-optimal allocation. These results are not significantly affected by the technology of bargaining. Thus, these results suggest caution in extending Hoffman and Spitzers results to more general bargaining environments.

3. The development and implementation of new mechanisms for allocating public goods and externalities

William Vickrey (1961) outlined a new auction mechanism, the second-price auction, and showed that participants in such an auction would have a dominant strategy incentive to bid their true values. The reasoning is simple. In a second-price auction the highest bidder wins the auction but only pays the second-highest bid price. Since the winner does not have to pay his or her bid price, the best strategy is to truthfully reveal his or her true value.

Vickrey's result was virtually ignored in the economics literature until it was rediscovered independently by Clarke (1971) and Groves (1976), who were exploring the possibility of designing synthetic mechanisms for achieving Pareto-optimal allocations of public goods and externalities. Clarke and Groves suggested that Vickrey's insight could be applied to the allocation of public goods and externalities by creating a mechanism in which each participant reveals his or her marginal benefit from the public good and is then assessed a personalized tax as a function of the values revealed by the other participants.

To apply the Clarke tax the government asks each consumer for a schedule of his or her marginal willingness to pay for different quantities of the public good. Using those revealed schedules, the government determines the optimal quantity of the public good to provide. Each consumer is then assessed a tax equal to the total cost of providing the public good, minus the sum of the marginal values revealed by the other participants. If consumers have utility functions with no wealth effects on the public good, it can be shown that each consumer has an individual incentive to reveal his or her true marginal willingness to pay schedule.[4]

The only problem with the Clarke tax is that the government runs a deficit. The taxes collected do not cover the cost of providing the public good. The Groves mechanism solves that problem by developing a separate lump-sum tax for each participant that is also calculated independent of the participant's responses.

The work of Clarke and Groves initiated a line of research, which continues today, on the design and implementation of synthetic mechanisms for the optimal allocation of public goods and externalities. At first, the emphasis was on designing mechanisms with the strict incentive properties of the Clarke and Groves mechanisms. For example, the Groves–Ledyard (1977) mechanism requires subjects to submit messages to a dispatch center, indicating a marginal quantity of the public good they wish to contribute and their marginal willingness to pay. The center then adds the marginal proposed quantities to form a total quantity and taxes each participant as a function of the cost of providing that quantity and the responses of the other participants. However, Vernon Smith discovered early, through laboratory experimental research on implementation, that the behavioral properties of synthetic mechanisms do not always correspond to their theoretical incentive properties (Smith 1979).

---

4. General conditions under which such mechanisms create dominant strategy incentives to reveal truthfully one's marginal willingness to pay are summarized in Hurwicz (1979), and Green and Laffont (1980).

Smith (1979) compares the performance of the Groves–Ledyard mechanism with the performance of a new mechanism, the Smith auction mechanism, which formalizes the voluntary contribution mechanism discussed above. In the Smith auction mechanism each subject submits a message to a dispatch center, indicating how many units of the public good the subject wants the group to provide and how much he or she is willing to contribute to that provision. The dispatch center then calculates the average quantity proposed by the members of the group, the sum of the individual contributions, and whether or not the contributions cover the cost of provision. The center reports back to each participant that average quantity and a proposed cost share calculated as the total cost of that provision minus a prorated sum of the other participants' contributions. A subject can either ratify that proposal by sending that message back to dispatch or change his or her proposal. Several different stopping rules have been proposed, including unanimity voting on the final allocation and repetition of the last proposal by all participants.

While this mechanism does not have the strong incentive properties of a Groves mechanism or a Groves–Ledyard mechanism, Smith finds that subjects participating in such a mechanism generally select the Pareto-optimal allocation of a public good and volunteer to contribute a sufficient amount to provide it. Moreover, he finds that the Groves–Ledyard mechanism is difficult to implement, despite its stronger incentive properties. In particular, subjects find it difficult to operationalize the requirement that they submit messages indicating the marginal quantities of the public good they wish to provide and their marginal willingnesses to pay.

Binger, Hoffman, and Williams (1987) study another allocation mechanism with incentive properties similar to the Smith auction mechanism. Their mechanism operationalizes a Lindahl tâtonnement mechanism, without the obvious incentive to underrepresent characteristic of a Lindahl mechanism. In the Binger, Hoffman, and Williams mechanism the dispatch center presents each participant with a proposed personalized lump sum and per-unit tax as a contribution toward provision of the public good. Each participant then sends a message to the center indicating how many units of the public good he or she wants the group to provide, given the proposed taxes. If all participants suggest the same quantity, the center reports back that quantity and the proposed taxes as an allocation, and the participants vote whether to accept that allocation. If the vote is unanimous, the allocation is implemented; if it is not unanimous, the process continues. If all participants do not propose the same quantity, the center adjusts the personalized taxes using an indirect tâtonnement process and then reports back the set of proposed quantities and the new proposed personalized taxes. The process continues until all the participants agree on a quantity and a set of personalized taxes.

Binger, Hoffman, and Williams test the behavioral properties of this mechanism in laboratory experiments using a wide variety of preference profiles and degrees of subject experience. They find the mechanism generally leads subjects to select a quantity of the public good close to the Pareto-optimal quantity, leading to average efficiencies greater than 90 percent.

Recently, research on synthetic mechanisms has focused on designing computer-assisted "smart" markets for the allocation of externalities and complex, networked commodities, requiring coordination similar to that required for the optimal allocation of public goods. These new markets draw upon the insights gained from research on the design and implementation of mechanisms for allocating public goods. For example, the allocation of electric power to end users involves a complex network of generators serving large numbers of customers and interconnected distribution lines. Because of the complexity of the distribution problem, the large capacity of generators required for efficient operation, and the public goods nature of the coordination problem, electric power used to be referred to as a natural monoploy requiring either government provision or, at least, direct government regulation. Similar goods include natural-gas pipeline distribution; airline takeoff, docking, and landing slots at interconnected airports; and the distribution of water through canals in arid lands.

In the mid-1980s, Vernon Smith and his colleagues at the University of Arizona Economic Science Laboratory became interested in the possibility of designing a computer-assisted market to allocate such goods.[5] The idea can be illustrated with reference to electric power distribution on the western United States grid. Electricity is produced in large coal and hydroelectric generating plants, generally located far from major population centers, and then distributed to communities that purchase power for their consumers over high-voltage transmission lines. Once power is sent to the transmission line it is a public good. Any community with access to the line can withdraw power. Moreover, power is lost in transmission as a function of resistence and distance traveled.

Smith and his colleagues suggested that one could design a networked market mechanism with the following characteristics. First, communities that wished to purchase power could submit schedules of bids to buy quantities of power at specified prices. Second, producers of power could submit schedules of offers to sell quantities of power at specified prices. Third, owners of transmission lines could submit offers to transmit power over specified distances. Fourth, a computer model would incorporate all

---

5. See McCabe, Rassenti, and Smith (1991) for a survey of the literature on smart markets up to 1991.

the engineering information regarding transmission losses, distance, and the need for a systemwide power reserve to determine prices at each node and prices for transmission that maximized the gains from exchange in the system. Finally, buyers and sellers that could trade profitably at the prices dispatched from the center would do so.

They proposed using a two-sided extension of the Vickrey auction as their market mechanism: a uniform price, double auction market. In this market, buyers submit limit orders to buy specified quantities of the good at specified prices. Sellers submit limit orders to sell specified quantities at specified prices. The computer algorithm combines the buyer and seller bids and offers with transmission offers and engineering information on transmission losses to suggest prices at each node that maximize the revealed gains from exhange. Buyers and sellers can revise their limit prices for a prescribed length of time until the market closes. Dispatch continuously updates proposed market-clearing prices on the basis of new information. When the market closes all buyers who bid greater than or equal to the market price (including transmission costs) purchase units and all sellers who offer to sell at prices less than or equal to the market price sell units. Excess demand or supply at the market price can be rationed in a variety of ways, including random selection and first into the market.

Smith and his colleagues have designed a market model for an electric grid, a gas pipeline network, an airport-slot allocation problem, and a work-assignment problem. They have also studied the behavioral properties of the uniform price double auction market in a simple induced demand and supply environment and are discussing designing a market for water allocation in arid lands. They find that buyers and sellers generally underreveal the value of inframarginal units in such markets. That is to say, buyers generally bid less than the true value of infra-marginal units and sellers generally offer prices greater than their true cost. However, the market mechanism tends to force buyers and sellers of marginal units to truthfully reveal the value of those units or be forced out of the market. In general, these markets converge to prices and quantities that maximize the true gains from exchange within a few trading periods.

This success in designing and testing laboratory prototypes of smart markets has led to considerable interest in implementing such markets for the sale of real commodities. For example, the Arizona Stock Exchange, established in 1992, is the first fully computerized stock exchange to use a uniform price, double auction market to trade stocks daily after the close of the New York Stock Exchange. Large investors, such as TIAA/CREF, use the market heavily because they can trade for less than one-eighth the commission charged by New York Stock Exchange traders. The owners of the Arizona Stock Exchange maintain a working relationship with the University of Arizona Economic Science Laboratory to test any proposed new trading mechanisms.

There is also considerable interest in the electric power and gas pipeline markets by governments interested in privatazation of public utilities. Vernon Smith has traveled to Eastern Europe, Australia, New Zealand, and China to demonstrate the power and efficiency of these proposed market mechanisms. The state of California is privitizing both electric power and water, and is interested in exploring alternative market mechanisms.

4. Conclusion

Experimental research in public choice has generated important results on the behavioral implications of mechanisms for allocating public goods and externalities. Voluntary contribution mechanisms, which theoretically result in zero contributions, generally result in positive, although suboptimal contributions. If participants can communicate face-to-face prior to making private contributions, however, contributions rise to near optimal levels. On the other hand, the Groves–Ledyard mechanism, which should lead to optimal contributions, is not reliable behaviorally. In addition, Coasian bargaining yields optimal allocations when a core exists, despite the potential for a public goods problem in coordinating large numbers of bargainers.

Experimental research in public choice is also valuable in the design and testing of new allocation mechanisms that might be implemented for public goods, externalities, or complex commodities. Using experimental techniques, a scholar can design a new mechnanism, determine its theoretical incentive properties, and then study its behavioral properties in a controlled laboratory environment. Participants in existing allocation mechanisms for electricity, natural gas, or water are not likely to change to smart markets without large-scale testing of these market mechanisms. The experimental laboratory provides the first test site.

PART V

Public choice in action

CHAPTER 20

Modern bureaucratic theory

RONALD WINTROBE

I begin with three parables.

Parable 1: The daily life of the civil servant (anonymous folk tale). The typical civil servant arrives in Ottawa (Washington, Paris, Rome – it doesn't matter) around 9:30 A.M. From 9:30–10:30 he[1] reads the *Globe and Mail* (*The Washington Post, Le Monde, Corriere della Sera,* etc.). At 10:30 it is time to go for coffee. Around 11:00 A.M., he returns and begins to make a number of phone calls in order to arrange lunch. Lunch begins around 1:00 P.M. with two or three martinis (customs vary elsewhere – check *The Economist Guides* for details in other countries). The civil servant returns around 3:00 P.M., sits down at his desk and immediately begins to doze off. Around 4:30 P.M., the nagging thought of becoming ensnarled in rush-hour traffic awakens him, he stirs into action and rushes out, pausing only to stuff the unread business and current affairs section of the *Globe and Mail* into his briefcase, along with his copy of *Fine Wines of Canada* – a present from a local interest group. By 5:00 P.M. he has arrived home.

Parable 2: The servant as master. In Joseph Losey's film *The Servant*, the central character (played by Edward Fox) hires a manservant (Dirk Bogarde) to cook, clean, and generally take care of his needs. The servant is highly competent and slowly begins to make himself indispensable. At one point he brings in an attractive woman (Sarah Miles) whom he refers to as his "sister" to help with the housekeeping. As they begin to take over the house, the master's will fades. In the film's central scene, the sister lolls seductively around the kitchen counter top and the kitchen sink tap drips slowly, loudly, and meaningfully while she complains of the heat to the master. The phone rings, and the "master" finds himself helpless to either answer the phone or turn off

I am grateful to Albert Breton, Gianluigi Galeotti, Dennis Mueller, Pierre Salmon, and Robert Young for helpful comments, and to the Lynde and Harry Bradley Foundation for financial assistance.
1. The typical civil servant in the folk tale is male.

the dripping tap. By the end of the film, the servants have completely taken over the house, and the master has lapsed into decadence, corruption, and helplessness.

Parable 3: The banality of evil. In her book *Eichmann in Jerusalem*, Hannah Arendt described the career of Adolph Eichmann, chief of Jewish Affairs in the Nazi SS. From 1933 to 1939, he organized the expulsion of Jews from Germany and Austria. After that he had the administrative responsibility for organizing their deportation to the concentration camps. He was the transport "coordinator" of the final solution to the Jewish question. Arendt portrayed him as "the perfect bureaucrat" and, indeed, he presented himself that way at his trial, saying things like "officialese is my only language." His basic defense was that he only acted under superior orders; he argued that he could not be responsible for the deaths of the Jews because his office did not deliver the Zyklon B cyanide gas to the camps. The prosecution tried to paint him as an archfiend. However, as Arendt saw it, he simply did not appear that way – he appeared to be "normal" and was in fact pronounced normal by six psychiatrists (as one of them put it: "he is more normal than I am after examining him"). So Arendt coined the phrase "the banality of evil" to describe a bureaucratic system in which normal people could be induced to perform hideous acts under orders.[2]

Each of the parables provides an answer to the fundamental question about bureaucracy with which this survey is concerned – namely, *How much influence or power does the bureaucracy have over what (and how much) governments do?* More precisely, how much is the allocation of resources in the public sector, and the size of the public sector, a reflection of the preferences of bureaucrats as opposed to those of citizens, politicians, or interest groups? The parables illustrate different extreme, indeed, pathological answers to this question. The second parable implies that bureaucrats completely control their political masters. The third parable says that bureaucrats are automatons who robotically carry out their masters' wishes. And if the first parable were literally true, there would be no public sector output to worry about.

Now, economic or rational choice theories of bureaucracy are also parables. Their strength lies in their analytic rather than metaphorical power, that is, in their capacity to make transparent the processes or mechanisms underlying politico-bureaucratic relationships. Further, by providing a consistent framework from which hypotheses may be drawn and tested, they may be capable of ultimately sorting truth from error.

---

2. The description in parable three is taken largely from Breton and Wintrobe (1986, 906–7).

Thus, unlike artistic or literary parables, economic models provide answers to our fundamental questions by first asking, and then assuming, answers to a set of other questions. The basic ones are: What do bureaucrats want? How do they try to get it? How do their political masters control them?

With respect to the first question *What do bureaucrats want?*, economists being who they are, the most common answer to this question has been simply "Mo' money!" (a bigger budget). However, as a general answer, this appealing but simple idea has been largely discredited and more sophisticated answers have been developed (bigger discretionary budget, influence on public policy, power, or simply utility).

A rich variety of bureaucratic strategies has now been developed in response to our second question, *How do they get it?* That is, what are the sources of bureaucratic power? One simple answer is *asymmetric information* – the bureau has information (e.g., on the costs of its activities) or expertise that its political "masters" do not possess. By itself, however, asymmetric information is a very general notion, and in most of the models discussed, other, more precise mechanisms are developed, such as *agenda control*, in which bureaucrats try to control the outcome of votes by citizens or congressional bodies by specifying the alternatives to be voted upon; or *selective efficiency*, in which bureaucrats control their masters' choices by being efficient at the things they want to do, and inefficient at those they do not.

The final question addressed is *How can bureaucrats be controlled?* At a minimum, any model of bureaucracy must specify at least two sets of actors: the bureaucrats who are subordinates or servants and their superiors (masters) or sponsors. In the early public choice literature, stress was placed on the power of bureaucrats vis-à-vis their superiors due to control of information. However, modeling in the last ten years or so has shifted decisively toward the superior's side, and a rich menu of control instruments has been described and analyzed in the literature. They may be classified under four headings: (1) *Authority*. For example, giving orders or specifyng rules, which are merely generalized orders, in that they apply to a number of subordinates and persist unless explicitly revoked or changed. Other sources of authority include the power of appointment and the power to structure the *sequence* of decisions. (2) *Competition*. The sponsor can utilize competition among bureaus, or among bureaucrats within a particular bureau, or among other groupings of bureaucrats to keep them in check. (3) *Trust or loyalty*. For example, the sponsor can appoint bureaucrats whose careers are tied to theirs and who will therefore make decisions in the sponsor's interest, or the superior can use efficiency wages in order to gain the subordinate's loyalty – by paying the subordinate a wage higher than his marginal productivity the superior increases the cost of job loss to the subordinate, and this promotes loyalty. (4) *Incentives*. Principal-agent models in particular analyze other incentive payment schemes that try to alter a bureaucrat's interests so as to make them consonant with those of their superior.

Of course the same problem – the control of subordinates – repeats itself at every layer in the hierarchy. From this point of view, the earlier literature on bureaucracy was somewhat inconsistent in that it assumed that politicians or sponsors had great difficulty in controlling bureau heads, but, by attributing a single utility function to the organization – that of the bureau head – it implicitly assumed that the bureau head had no difficulty whatsoever in controlling his own subordinates.

Each of the models considered below provides a consistent set of answers to these three questions. In doing so, they also answer our fundamental question – to repeat, how much control or influence do bureaucrats have over what and how much governments do? And they also provide answers to other questions, for example, what are the consequences of bureaucratic maximization and sponsor control for the quality and quantity of public output? A related issue is the *efficiency* of bureaucracy. Are government firms necessarily less efficient than private firms? If so, why? Another issue is the *responsibility* of bureaucrats. Suppose, for example, that an organization engages in immoral or criminal activity. How much responsibility do individual bureaucrats within the organization bear for the actions of the organization?

I group the work that has been done on bureaucracy from the economic or rational choice perspective into three main traditions. Section 1 deals with *budget maximization and other bureaucrat goals,* models that follow Niskanen (1968) in assuming that one can impute a specific utility function to bureaucrats. There have been many variations on this theme – such as assuming that bureaucrats maximize their discretionary or surplus budget rather than the total budget. Other variations involve changes in the nature of the constraint faced by bureaucrats or in the techniques available to bureaucrats to obtain a bigger budget.

Section 2 discusses the relations between bureaucrats and their congressional masters, the focus of much recent formal modeling in the United States. The question here is the issue of political *control* or of agency *discretion* in a U.S. style system.

A third class of models, discussed in Section 3, is *property rights theories*, the distinguishing feature of which is the attempt to ground models of bureaucratic behavior in more general propositions that flow directly from the peculiarities of transacting in the politico-bureaucratic environment. Here I include work on the efficiency of private versus public bureaus, a mostly empirical tradition grounded in the theoretical contributions of De Alessi (1969) and Alchian (1965). A different line of thought was begun by Breton and Wintrobe (1982), who emphasized the importance of the limits of formal contracts within hierarchies and therefore the importance of *trust* or *networks* that substitute for legal contractual enforcement in underpinning bureaucratic exchange. Finally, a third set of papers falling within this tradition deals with the difficult problem of the role of authority in hierarchies and the related problem of bureaucratic responsibility.

1. Budget maximization and other bureaucratic goals

The central problem of much of bureaucratic theory using the constrained utility maximization approach has been the growth of "bureaucratic" organizations, especially governments. It has been fashionable to put responsibility for this growth on bureaucrats, rather than on the demands of citizens or the behavior of politicians. Popular ideas were crystallized by C. Northcoate Parkinson in his famous *Parkinson's law*, in which he suggested that bureaucrats, like rabbits, are bound to multiply. Another version of Parkinson's law is that administrators multiply at the same time as the organization's output and its direct labor force are declining. The basis for either law is Parkinson's observation that between 1914 and 1928 the number of ships in the British Navy declined by 67 percent and the number of officers and men by 31.5 percent; but the admiralty (the Navy administration) increased over this same period by 78 percent, providing, as Parkinson notes, "a magnificent Navy on land" (Parkinson 1957, 7).

William Niskanen formalized the idea of bureaucratic empire building into a systematic economic theory – its counterpart to the servant-as-master parable above. Niskanen's model is based on two assumptions: First, bureau heads desire as large a budget as possible. This is justified on the ground that income, prestige, power, and amenities are a positive monotonic function of budget size; moreover, pressure from subordinates for larger budgets on the one hand and from executive and legislative committees on the other ensures the survival of the budget-maximizing bureaucrat in the same way that competition produces the survival of the profit-maximizing firm.

The second assumption is that bureau heads are monopolists, so they get the budget they desire, subject only to the constraint that this budget cannot exceed the total value to citizens of the bureau's services. Although the relationship (in the United States) between bureau heads and legislative committees is nominally one of bilateral monopoly, Niskanen argued that the bureau head knows the preferences (the demand curve)

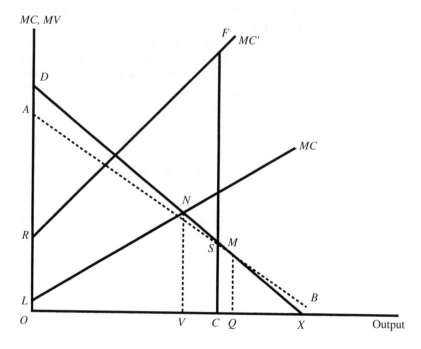

Figure 1. The Niskanen model.

of the legislative committee, while the legislative committee lacks the skill and expertise to obtain accurate information on the bureau's costs of production. This enables the bureau to exploit the legislative committee. The bureau head can fool the politicians either by pretending that public services cost more than they really do or by deliberately seeking out expensive production processes and pretending that these are the only ones available.

To show the implications of Niskanen's model, we need to develop these ideas more rigorously. One version of Niskanen's model is shown in Figure 1. The "demand" for the bureau's services is depicted as *DX*. Assume that *DX* represents the true marginal valuation by citizens, and that politicians translate this demand into funds allocated to the bureau at different possible prices for the service. The true marginal costs of the service are *MC*, and therefore the optimum service level for both citizens and governing politicians is *DX* = *MC*, namely output level *OV*.

OVNL however, is not the optimum output for the bureau head, who desires as large a budget as possible. One way for the bureau head to exploit his position is to use expensive production processes with declining cost curves. Thus, imagine the same service provided by a process with marginal costs like *AB*. The bureau head presents this cost curve to the politicians as the true minimum costs of the service; politicians choose output *OQ* rather than *OV* and provide the bureau with a total budget of *AMQO*.

Assuming the bureau head successfully fools his political master in this way, where will the process end? Only where the bureau's cost curve has been artificially shifted up and twisted so as to lie identically on *DX*. In equilibrium, the output of the bureau equals *OX* and its budget equals the area under the demand curve (*OXD*). At that point, the bureau extracts all of politicians' and consumers' surplus from its provision of the service.[3] The value of additional output to politicians and citizens is zero, and only this prevents the bureau from expanding any further. However, the minimum cost of that output may exceed the maximum budget possible (*OXD*), as would be the case if marginal costs were *MC'* rather than *MC*. In that case, the bureau is said to be "budget-constrained" and equilibrium is at the point where total cost (the area under *MC'*) and total budget (the area under *DX*) are equal, that is, at output level *OC* with budget *FCOR* or *DSCO*.

Thus, all bureaus are too large. Indeed, with linear budget and cost curves, the bureau supplies exactly twice the output that would be produced by a competitive industry facing the same demand and cost conditions (Niskanen 1971, 46).

1.1 Extensions of the basic model

The assumptions of the Niskanen model are very restrictive, and there have been several attempts to generalize the model. J. L. Migué and Gerard Bélanger (1974) pointed out that, *contra* Niskanen, a manager or a bureau head cannot pursue such goals as budget, output, salary, prestige, or status simultaneously. At the margin, a choice must be made among these goals, so that a bureau head who is interested in any other goal besides budget will not behave as Niskanen suggested. Interestingly, Niskanen himself (Niskanen 1975; and again in Blais and Dion 1991, 22) states that he accepts their argument.

To understand their point, note that in the budget-constrained region, production is at minimum cost, and no expenses other than those contributing to productivity are incurred. On the other hand, if the bureau head were to produce a smaller output and ask for a smaller budget he could obtain a budget larger than that required to produce the output, and with the excess or *discretionary budget*, as Migué and Bélanger call it, he

---

3. Note that it is not necessary, as is often alleged, for the bureau to make an all-or-nothing offer to the legislature to obtain this result.

could pursue other goals – for example, hiring staff to make his life easier, redecorating his office, hiring prestigious (but unnecessary) researchers, and so on.

Beyond a certain point, then, the bureau head sacrifices discretionary budget for every increase in output (and total budget). Rather than a general hypothesis about bureaucratic behavior, budget maximization represents a special case – the case of a bureau head who cares *only* about the size of his bureau, to the exclusion of all other goals. Wykoff (1990) provides a nice diagrammatic treatment that demonstrates that budget-maximizing and "slack-maximizing" bureaus are similar in their price elasticities and generation of flypaper effects but differ in their response to lump-sum grants and their relative responses to lump-sum and matching grants.

Chant and Acheson (1972, 1973) and Acheson and Chant (1973) took a different approach to the bureau's utility function. They focused specifically on the behavior of a central bank (the Bank of Canada) and tried to explain the bank's behavior – in particular, its choice of goals and instruments – on the assumption that the bureau had a stable preference function between prestige and self-preservation. The approach explained a number of aspects of central bank behavior, especially their predilection for secrecy (a common feature of bureaucracy, as Max Weber suggested long ago). However, the theory is difficult to operationalize in a way that makes precise predictions possible (it is hard to think of behavior that is inconsistent with *either* prestige or self-preservation).

The models so far are concerned with the utility function of a bureau. Breton and Wintrobe (1975) extended the Niskanen model in a different way – by reexamining the bureau's constraint. They pointed out that the bureau's monopoly power in Niskanen's model rests entirely on its control of information. Suppose, for example, that information on true marginal costs were costlessly available to the sponsor. The bureau would then be forced to produce the optimal output (*OV* in Figure 1). The Niskanen solution only obtains if the sponsor is helpless to counteract the distortions of the bureau. Yet the sponsor has formal authority over the bureau, and, as Downs (1967) had already emphasized, there are a host of techniques or control devices that are routinely used by managers in both private and public organizations to counteract information distortion. These include direct monitoring, external data checks, duplicating or overlapping zones of responsibility, and so on.

The benefit of using these control techniques is that they allow the sponsor to reduce the excess budget of the bureau. The instruments, however, are costly. The sponsor can be expected to use each to the point where marginal benefits equal marginal costs. The equilibrium size of the bureau's budget is therefore equal to the bureau's optimum minus the excess eliminated by the sponsor's use of antidistortion devices. Again, Niskanen's model appears as a limiting case; namely, that where control devices are so costly that it does not pay to use them. On the other hand, one could rationalize the traditional assumption about the neutrality of public servants as an assumption that control devices are costless and therefore the excess budget is always zero!

Both these extensions imply that excess costs of output and not excess output (oversupply) are the major source of inefficiency in bureaucratic production. In the Migué–Bélanger version, the main source of inefficiency is that the economic rent that would be appropriated by inframarginal consumers under competitive conditions is appropriated by the bureau for discretionary uses. The greater their preferences for discretionary budget as opposed to output, the greater the excess costs of output-problem and the smaller the oversupply problem. In the Breton–Wintrobe model, whether excess output or excess costs of output is the major source of inefficiency depends on the relative productivity of devices for controlling these two sources of inefficiency. Now, the sponsor can control excess output if he can simply discover the bureau's true costs. Controlling excess *costs* of output, however, requires this information *plus* information as to the true *minimum* costs of the service. Consequently, bureau heads will realize that they can appropriate more rents for themselves by taking their rents in the form of excess budgets rather than excess outputs. Put simply, it is easier for bureaucrats to fool sponsors by fattening their actual costs than by producing at minimum cost and then falsifying cost information to politicians.

1.2 Bureaucrats as voters

There have been a number of attempts to develop other mechanisms by which expansion-minded bureaucrats can increase the size of the public sector. Borcherding, Bush, and Spann (1977) and other papers in the pioneering volume edited by Borcherding (1977) emphasized the motive for bureaucrats to vote more often than other people and to vote for parties favoring bigger government and provided evidence that voter participation rates were in fact higher for public bureaucrats. Blais, Blake, and Dion (in Blais and Dion 1991) recently examined evidence using forty-three elections in eleven countries over the last thirty-five years to see if there is a systematic preference for the Left (not just increased participation) on the part of public sector employees. They find clear confirmation of this hypothesis in four out of the eleven countries, with a typical coefficient of 5 percent (i.e., when all other socioeconomic variables are controlled for, support for the Left is 5 percent higher in the public than in the private sector). These pure rent-seeking models are the closest economic analogues to our first parable, since they imply that the public sector need achieve no social function to sustain itself. However, they do not necessarily confirm bureaucratic rent seeking; government employees may just be more inclined to participate in elections or more left-wing in their preferences than employees of private firms. To put it differently, the fact that support for the Right is 5 percent higher in the private than in the public sector could be interpreted equally well as confirming the existence of rent seeking (or "influence activities" as Milgrom and Roberts [1988] label private sector rent seeking).

1.3 The role of the agenda

Another extension is the "agenda manipulation" model, originated independently by Mackay and Weaver (1979) and by Romer and Rosenthal (1979). Romer and Rosenthal (1979) apply the model to referenda. On a given ballot, voters have a choice only between a proposal offered by a (monopoly) budget-maximizing bureau and some institutionally defined reversion level of expenditure. The lower the reversion level, the higher the budget the bureaucratic setter is able to extract from voters. The authors find support for the model using data from local school districts in Oregon. They suggest that "direct democracy situations" are more consistent with Niskanen's monopoly assumption than the congressional legislative context to which Niskanen (1971) first applied it (Romer and Rosenthal 1979, 564). Indeed, Niskanen himself suggests that these results are the "strongest evidence" for his general theory of bureaus (Niskanen, in Blais and Dion 1991, 22).

1.4 Some evidence

Finally, we may briefly look at least at some of the more important evidence that bears directly on the Niskanen model. First of all, do bureaucrats maximize the size of their budgets? Johnson and Libecap (1989) analyzed very large samples (15,000 cases, 45 agencies) from the U.S. federal government to determine the effect of agency growth on bureaucratic salaries. All of their tests yielded insignificant and sometimes negative relationships except one case where there was a significant positive relationship, and the coefficient there was very small (.044), implying that "an agency must more than double its size in order for salaries to increase by 4 percent relative to an agency that did not grow."[4]

---

4. Johnson and Libecap (1989), 446. Other studies, reviewed in the chapters by R. Kiewiet and Robert Young in Blais and Dion (1991) similarly provide little evidence for the budget maximization assumption.

Carroll (1989, 1990) develops a competitive model of bureau production. In it, bureaus have a choice between competing via cost reductions ("price competition") or through promotional activity (lobbying, conducting benefit-cost analyses, etc.). Bureaucrats who are primarily interested in output would tend to oversupply such activities. Carroll (1989) estimates indexes of competition (Herfindahl indices) for thirty-four federal sector public service industries comprising nearly 300 federal agencies. Her results show a surprisingly competitive structure. In 1980, for example, 10.2 percent operate in industries with a Herfindahl of .80 or higher – close to pure monopoly, 17 percent are fairly concentrated ($H = .5$ to $.8$) while 72.8 percent – 214 out of 294 bureaus – operated in a competitively structured environment ($H = .1027$ to $.4837$, averaging .2495).

She also tests to see if budget *growth* (16.6 percent on average between 1980 and 1985) is related to bureau monopoly power. The results do not indicate a significant positive relationship between bureau market share and growth (in one case, the coefficient is significantly negative, in the other, insignificantly positive). Of course, it is not obvious that this contradicts Niskanen's basic model, which is static and has nothing to say about bureaucratic growth. Growth could only occur in that model if bureaucratic monopoly power were increasing over time (or if the capacity of bureaus to extract rents from politicians were growing). The simplest explanation of bureaucratic growth is that it results from an increase in the political demand for the services of the bureau; this is indeed Carroll's strongest empirical result.

2. Agency discretion: Bureaucrats vs. Congress

This section considers a number of papers that expand on the interaction between bureau and sponsor in a U.S.-style context where the sponsor consists of a legislative review committee backed by the full legislature. Miller and Moe (1983) developed a model based on Niskanen but which departs from his in two fundamental ways: (1) The bureau is not allowed to price discriminate. Instead, the committee announces its intention to pay a flat "price" per unit of bureau output. (2) Two kinds of legislative oversight are considered: "demand revealing," in which the committee reveals its demand function to the bureau before knowing the bureau's costs of output, and "demand concealing," in which the bureau is forced to submit a supply schedule indicating how much it will produce at different "prices" prior to the committee's revelation of its preferences. In either case bureaucratic output is smaller than Niskanen suggested. Imposing a per unit price on the bureau robs it of its power to trick the supplier by pretending that cost curves are always downward sloping. Indeed, under demand-concealing oversight, output is at the socially efficient level.

One difficulty with this analysis lies in the first departure above – an assumption extensively used in later work by Bendor, Taylor, and Van Gaalen. It is justified on the ground that such prices are often used (e.g., $X per tank, $Y per plane in defense bureaus). However, what the committee really needs to know (in the case of defense, for example) is the price of security from external aggression, not the prices of inputs into that security such as tanks or planes. Otherwise, the bureau could still trick the committee, for example, by insisting that the appropriate choice of inputs requires (expensive) planes to begin with, followed by (cheaper) tanks for subsequent units. For many if not most bureaus (defense, foreign affairs, health, and welfare), it is hard to believe that *output* prices are available to congressional committees.

All the models considered so far exploit information asymmetry to create bureaucratic discretion. Bureaucratic discretion can arise even when information is complete, as Hill (1985) and Hammond, Hill, and Miller (1986) showed. Their models exploit the fact that every alternative is vulnerable under majority rule. Thus, the bureau can implement a policy closer to that preferred by some of the legislators to the one actually passed by a majority vote and have the support of a (different) majority of the legislature. Similarly, a president could appoint a bureau head who will create an "implementation coalition" that the executive prefers to the expressed wishes of the legislature but that would also have the support of a majority of the legislature.

A different line of attack was initiated by Weingast (1984) and Weingast and Moran (1983), who pointed out that congressional monitoring of bureaucratic inputs is only one method of congressional control and probably an inefficient one. Other important techniques include (1) use of *constituency groups* who monitor agency inputs and outputs; (2) *control of appointments* (the most obvious example is that of Alfred Kahn at the CAB, who initiated the deregulation of airlines; presumably, this was no surprise to those who appointed him since his views were well known); (3) *competition for budgets* among agencies; and (4) *ex post sanctions*. The smooth operation of these administrative arrangements involves little direct participation by Congress. Consequently, evidence of infrequent congressional investigations or policy resolutions, congressional inattention, the superficiality of annual appropriations hearings, and so forth, is as consistent with congressional *dominance* of the bureaucracy as it is with the idea that the bureaucracy is completely in charge of decision making in the public sector. Weingast and Moran provided evidence in favor of congressional dominance by showing that the reduction in the Federal Trade Commission's (FTC) "activist" policies in the 1970s was not an instance of Congress's reining in an "out of control" bureaucracy, as had often been argued, but of turnover in the FTC's

Figure 2. Preferences of different agents in the Ferejohn–Shipan model.

congressional control committee, which brought members opposed to FTC activism to power. Similarly, Weingast (1984) explains the deregulation of the New York Stock Exchange by the Securities and Exchange Commission (SEC) as the result of a change in congressional, not bureaucratic, preferences.

Calvert, McCubbins, and Weingast (1989) expanded on the role of the appointment process in limiting agency discretion (see also Banks and Weingast 1992). In their simple, basic model, active monitoring of the agency's decisions plays no role, yet the legislature and executive have complete control over the policy outcome through the process of appointing the agent. Their model leads to a novel definition of agency discretion as "the difference . . . between the agency's choice and the choice the elected officials thought they were getting when they agreed on a nominee. Any other difference from either elected official's wishes is attributable to the appointment process, not the agency" (Calvert, McCubbins, and Weingast 1989, 598–9).

The Ferejohn–Shipan (1990) model allows the agency a greater role in policymaking. One reason for this is that, in contrast to the Weingast–Moran model, they assume an open rather than closed rule for the Congress, that is, Congress is free to amend legislative proposals from congressional committees. This both reduces the power of committees and, less obviously, increases the power of the agency. The reason is that the agency can, in effect, exploit differences between the committee and the full House. Indeed, holding constant the position of the committee, the further away the House's position is from the agency's preferred position, the better the agency does. In Figure 2 A, C, and H stand respectively for the positions of the agency, the median member of the committee, and the House. $C(H)$ is the point to the left of C that C regards as indifferent to H. The agency does not introduce policies to the left of $C(H)$, since, if it did, the committee would introduce legislation that the House would amend and the outcome would be H. So $C(H)$ is the agency's best choice. Note that the committee, though it might be quite dissatisfied with $C(H)$, cannot credibly threaten to overturn it. And note that a shift in H to the right shifts $C(H)$ to the *left*, thus increasing agency influence on policy.

Ferejohn and Shipan demonstrate the effects on agency choice of the presidential veto and judicial review. The most important conclusion of this (complex) analysis is that judicial review shifts the equilibrium in the direction of the median member of Congress. Note, however, that responsiveness is to the will of the current Congress, not that of past Congresses that may have enacted the original legislation.

Another set of models uses formal principal-agent theory to explore the congressional–bureaucratic relationship. Principal-agent theory imposes a particular modeling structure. First, the principal is assumed to know the agent's utility function and to be able to predict how the agent will respond to incentives devised by the principal; secondly, the principal can *precommit* to an incentive scheme; and thirdly, the contract is *self-enforcing* for the agent, that is, he carries out actions that maximize his own utility, given the incentives devised by the principal (Bendor 1988; Radner 1992). Thus, in the U.S. context (the focus of virtually all of these models) the legislature's budgetary and monitoring choices are endogenized by basing them on the anticipated reactions of the bureau. In a series of papers, Bendor, Taylor, and Van Gaalen (1985, 1987a, 1987b – henceforth BTV) developed two kinds of models: in the first, politicians reward or punish the bureaucracy in various ways, but their budgetary, monitoring and other choices are not based on the anticipated reactions of bureaus. In the second, they (i.e., politicians) anticipate the bureau's strategic behavior and are capable of precommitting to incentive schemes designed to control this behavior. The two models have sharply different implications in a number of respects, especially concerning the degree of political control over the bureaucracy. For example, in BTV (1987a), the problem for Congress is how to control bureaucratic *deception*. Several instruments are available, including harsher budget cuts and better monitoring. Two models are developed: in the first, increasing the level of these instruments does not necessarily reduce deception; in the second, where the legislature's choices of those variables are based on the anticipated reactions of the bureau, it does. BTV (1987b, 888) develop specific conditions under which we can "ignore" the bureaucracy's role in policy formation and a unitary actor interpretation of the executive branch is appropriate. So these models are "Taylorite" (Bendor 1988; Breton 1992) in that they demonstrate the possibility of using modern scientific techniques to control the bureaucracy.

3. Property rights theories

The models examined in this section ask how property rights within bureaucracy – or between bureaus and politicians – differ from those in market exchange and investigate the implications of such differences.

One of their virtues is that they are theoretically grounded in a way that the models discussed in the previous two sections are not. To illustrate the difference between the two types of theories, recall that one way to define a bureau is as an organization that does not sell its output in the marketplace (Downs 1967, 25) or does not sell its output at a per-unit rate (Niskanen 1971, 25). If, instead, the bureau exchanges its output for a budget, it is tempting to suggest that the bureau head would maximize the size of its budget. But this doesn't follow unless the size of the budget is a good proxy for the *utility* of the bureau head – hence, the complications discussed in the last section about discretionary budget, slack maximization, and so on.

In contrast, property rights theories try to derive implications more directly from the nature of bureaucratic production. We consider three different theories in this vein: ownership theories, network-based exchange models, and efficiency wage theories.

3.1 Ownership rights

One set of arguments emphasizes a difference in "ownership rights" between private and public firms, and consequent differences in the incentives of owners to monitor management (Alchian 1965; De Alessi 1969). Owners of private firms (shareholders) can sell their rights in the market at relatively low cost, whereas the "owners" of the public sector (the citizenry of a particular political jurisdiction) cannot transfer their voting rights and can dispose of them only by moving to another jurisdiction. The theory suggests that this change in property rights (the costs of ownership transfer) implies that, as owners of public firms, citizens are less motivated to monitor the activities of their agents – the politicians in office – than are shareholders to monitor private managers. Consequently, bureaucrats in government are less efficient than those in private firms.

This argument is flawed in two respects (Wintrobe 1987). First, even if politicians have greater discretion than corporate managers, this does not imply that they monitor bureaucrats in the public sector any less. If politicians have greater freedom to neglect the interests of voters and to pursue their own objectives, why should they cede any of this to the bureaucrats under them? Consider the behavior of politicians who have a great deal of freedom in office, namely political dictators. Do they typically cede this discretion to the bureaucrats under them or do they use it to increase their control over them to pursue their own aims? Was Stalin lax in his "supervision" of the Russian bureaucracy?

Secondly, the benefits of diversification imply that rational shareholders tend to hold stock in a large number of corporations. So the incentive to monitor the activities of each one must be small. Indeed, there is a striking similarity between the arguments that have been made with respect to private versus public production and "managerial discretion" models of the modern corporation originated by Berle and Means and elaborated by Marris (1963, 1964), Williamson (1964), and others. The classic thesis in that literature is that corporate managers do not maximize profits but pursue objectives of their own (in addition to profits) such as sales, growth, and nonpecuniary forms of consumption (for example, excess staff or leisure). Indeed, the Migué–Bélanger model of bureaucracy is in part an adaptation of Williamson's (1964) model of the private firm.

In the literature on corporations, there has developed a substantial counterattack to the Berle and Means thesis, which emphasizes that managerial discretion is limited both by the possibility of a takeover bid and by competition from other managers. However, each of these mechanisms has its counterpart in the public sector. Elections may be regarded as a process by which opposition parties "bid" for control of the public sector. And there is competition among public sector managers as well as private ones.[5]

Other arguments include Alchian and Kessel's (1962) suggestion that profits provide a clear and stronger criterion for evaluating the behavior of subordinates in for-profit corporations than in government agencies or nonprofit enterprise, where there is simply no obvious *measure* of success or failure. Similarly, it is often argued at a popular level that public employees have less incentive to be efficient or a greater incentive to pursue nonpecuniary rewards such as leisure because they cannot "take home" the profits or benefits of greater efficiency (i.e., in private organizations, unlike public bureaus, there is a "bottom line"). However, these arguments are also flawed in that they compare entire organizations or bureaucracies in the private sector to individual government bureaus in the public sector, and this comparison is obviously incorrect. The relevant comparison is either between both organizations as a whole (firms versus governments) or between individual bureaus in each (the financial department of General Motors versus the U.S. Treasury). When we compare firms and governments first, it is clear that in both cases there is an adequate measure of the performance of the whole organization – profits in the case of firms and popularity as measured by election results or opinion polls in the case of governments. On the other

5. Wintrobe (1987) discusses each of these mechanisms in more detail and assesses their relative strengths in the public and private sectors. Vining and Boardman (1992) criticize his arguments in detail. Wittman (1989) develops a general argument for the efficiency of the public sector along these lines.

hand, the output of an individual bureau is typically unmeasurable whether the bureau is part of a private or public organization.

What, then, of the massive amount of evidence that documents the inefficiency of public production? These studies tend to show that costs of production, in general, are higher in public than in private production when both provide similar services. In part, the error here is also due to the simple confusion between bureaus and bureaucracies. Private firms provide services in economic markets, that is, in markets in which there is a (more or less) simple exchange of goods for money. Public firms may do this to some extent, but, being public, they are subunits of and responsible to the government as a whole and therefore to the political marketplace (the market for votes) as well. As Borcherding (1983) has emphasized, since political objectives cannot be realized at zero cost, and since these nonzero costs are included in the measured costs of public firms, these studies reveal nothing about the relative efficiency of public and private firms: one cannot know whether the extra costs incurred are simply the costs of serving these objectives or are a genuine inefficiency.

Many studies try to control for this by pointing out similarities between the public and private firms being compared (the most famous example is Davies 1971; a recent noteworthy attempt is Boardman and Vining 1989). However, one could also list all the ways in which a man resembles a woman and come up with a very long list.

3.2 Bureaucratic networks and exchange

Another approach to understanding bureaucratic behavior focuses on the limits on formal contracts within bureaucracies. Breton and Wintrobe (henceforth BW) took this approach in their 1982 book, *The Logic of Bureaucratic Conduct*, and subsequent publications (Breton and Wintrobe 1986; Wintrobe and Breton 1986; Breton 1988, 1992; Wintrobe 1988; McKee and Wintrobe 1993). Following work on the economics of reputation in markets by Telser (1980), and Klein and Leffler (1981), BW considered a world where there are gains from trade, but formal contracts are limited. More precisely, within bureaucracies there are always numerous ways in which a subordinate (S) could be induced to perform his tasks with greater efficiency, if only he was sure that he would be rewarded for doing so. Thus, S could offer extra effort – more accurate information, more inventiveness at getting the job done, and so on. S's superior, B (for boss), typically also has many things to offer in exchange – more rapid promotion, bigger bonuses, a larger budget, travel privileges, and so on. Such trades between S and B may increase organizational productivity in which case they are called *efficient trades*. Alternatively, subordinates may attempt to collude to obtain resources by deception (information distortion) trickery (e.g., agenda manipulation), sabotage, or through formal collective actions such as strikes or slowdowns. In these latter cases, the agreements or trades are obviously *inefficient* from the organization's point of view.

Whether the agreements are efficient or inefficient, they are not contractually enforceable, so either party faces the prospect that the other cheats or reneges on his or her (possibly implicit) obligations; hence, the demand for some guarantee that they be repaid. *Trust* or organizational *networks* are capital assets accumulated between subordinates, and between subordinates and superiors to fill this gap and allow exchange. BW (1982) suggested that this asset may be accumulated by foregoing opportunities to cheat, hence, making an investment in the future relationship. Salmon (1988) described an alternative process based on conjectures and refutations. Coleman (1990) provides an extensive discussion of the development of trust in a number of social contexts.

The next step is to derive a link between the level of these investments and organizational productivity; BW (see also Wintrobe and Breton 1986) assumed that superior–subordinate ("vertical") trust links tend to enhance productivity while subordinate–subordinate ("horizontal") links tended to diminish it. This permitted the development of a number of comparative static implications; it is difficult to measure trust, but one can derive a theoretical link between various aspects of organizational *structure* (e.g., levels of turnover, monitoring, "perks," supply of promotions, etc.) and productivity if these variables can be shown to affect the incentives to accumulate vertical and horizontal trust in plausible ways. For example, an increase in promotion possibilities increases vertical and decreases horizontal trust. An increase in demand for the organization's output increases the supply of promotions within the organization; hence, the model predicts a positive relationship, ceteris paribus, between demand and productivity. This provides a simple explanation for the well-known procyclical behavior of productivity.

The second pillar of the model is competition. Competition within any bureaucracy takes several forms: among bureaus for resources, among bureaucrats for jobs and for "membership" in bureaucratic networks. There is no a priori reason to believe that the market for managers in the public sector is any less competitive or efficient than the market for corporate managers. Theories of government bureaucracy that attribute monopoly power to heads of bureaus in the public sector, on the ground that no other agency is producing that particular output (defense, foreign affairs, or whatever), miss this simple point: the bureau may be a monopoly, but the bureau *head* is not a monopolist.

A central question is whether bureaucratic competition is necessarily efficient from the superior's point of view. Bureaucrats engage in *selec-*

tive behavior – they use their networks in the interests of superiors when that furthers their own interests, but not otherwise. Essentially, vertical trust substitutes for legally enforceable property rights, so that, when this is plentiful, competition induces efficient behavior from the superior's point of view. Wintrobe (1988) suggested that, over time, vertical trust declines and horizontal trust increases and used this analysis to explain the decline of the Soviet system. Ferrero (1993) suggests that Soviet-style "campaigns" to increase production – puzzling in standard models – can be explained as incentives to increase the supply of vertical trust. Carroll (1990) considers this problem, but from an entirely different point of view. She provides evidence that in the U.S. bureaucracy, bureaucratic growth is the *result* of competition (rather than monopoly, as in Niskanen's model).

Some evidence for the existence of bureaucratic networks was provided by McKee and Wintrobe (1993) in support of Parkinson's law, that is, the observation that the administrative component of an organization (A) expands at the same time as the organization itself and as its direct labor force (L) is declining. According to BW, the law is a simple implication of the existence of vertical networks, combined with the assumption that the organization is sufficiently large that cuts in personnel are made according to formal criteria such as seniority. When the organization declines, subordinates who have vertical networks with their superiors can be protected from dismissal only by promoting them to a rank (e.g., administrators) where they can't be dismissed. So one observes an increase in A at the same time as L declines. McKee and Wintrobe (1993) tested the law and this explanation of it on two rather different organizations – the U.S. Steel industry and the Canadian school system. They found that the law held in both cases, and in one case (the steel industry) they were able to show that the decline in L and the increase in A were *strictly contemporaneous* – an implication of the BW version of Parkinson's law, but not of other possible versions related to budget maximization.

Bagnoli and McKee (1991) tested whether the sponsor controls the "game" among bureaus by structuring incentives so that bureaus always have an incentive to defect on any collusive agreements among each other. They provided evidence that such mechanisms to increase competition among bureaus are used more frequently, the more difficult it is to use authority mechanisms such as direct monitoring. McKee (1988) suggested that the sponsor's incentive to accumulate vertical networks is larger when the bureau does not face external competition for its market and tested this hypothesis in two Canadian provinces, Ontario (where the public school system faces external competition) and British Columbia (where it does not), and found corroborative evidence.

The most frequent criticism of BW is their assumption that horizontal networks among employees reduce productivity (see Acheson 1988; Salmon 1988; Fung 1991). Why, for example, would employers tend to encourage socialization among employees if employee networks reduce productivity? Tirole (1986) and Laffont (1988, 1990) have attempted more rigorous demonstrations of the proposition that horizontal collusions are detrimental to productivity.

Others have analyzed the interaction between trust and supervision. Galeotti (1988) suggests that more detailed rules actually increase the scope for discretionary behavior and informal transactions. Frey (1993) extends the theory by proposing a simple rational choice explanation for the old sociological proposition that supervision tends to destroy trust. The famous Hawthorne experiments in sociology might appear to be inconsistent with this view by implying that supervision – or, at least, increased attention – *increases* productivity. However, Jones (1992) suggests that the "Hawthorne effect" is an artifact of subsequent interpretations of the data, rather than the data themselves, and that there is in fact no evidence that supports it.

It has been suggested that networks are inherently fragile and cannot effectively substitute for law-based property rights (e.g., Acheson 1988). Putnam makes exactly the opposite argument in his celebrated and controversial (1993) explanation of the efficiency of government in contemporary Italy. Here, it is political not bureaucratic networks that are being considered. The effectiveness of government depends on the distribution of networks or trust or social capital within the polity. Putnam argues that government is *effective* when there are strong horizontal networks within the community and ineffective when networks are predominantly "vertical" (patron–client, etc.) He provides evidence that the pattern of effective government in the different regions today is remarkably similar to that *centuries* ago, implying that networks can be astonishingly stable. However controversial the conclusion, this and other recent (see, e.g., Coleman (1990), Steven Cornell and Joe Kalt [1995]) applications of the theory of trust or social capital to politico-bureaucratic behavior are certainly thought provoking.

3.3 Effects of organizational structure[6]

Hammond (1986) and Hammond and Miller (1985) approach this subject using a metaphor from social choice theory in which a group's ultimate

---

6. Modern work on the labor economics of private firms, which is not reviewed here, also derives many important implications about firm structure. See Lazear (1991) for a good survey. Wintrobe (1982), following many sociologists, models structure in terms of the level of *bureaucratization*, that is, degree of adherence to rules and procedures, and derives the effects on this variable of changes in size, technology, and so forth.

Agenda 1	Agenda 2	Agenda 3

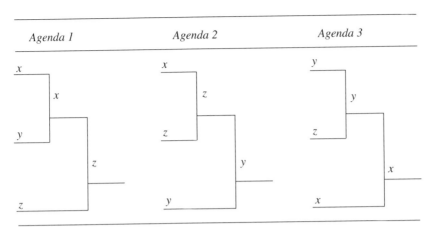

Figure 3. Organizational structures as agendas (Hammond 1986, 382).

decision depends on its *agenda* or the sequence in which binary comparisons among alternatives are made. Thus, as is well known, if three people
compare alternatives *x, y* and *z*, a different outcome may result if *x* is first
compared to *y*, and the winner pitted against *z*, than if, say, *x* is compared
to *z* and the winner compared to *y*. The basic insight in Hammond (1986)
is that the agenda provides a precise way of thinking about the effect of
organizational structure or bureaucratic decision making: a particular
organizational structure is, in effect, the organization's agenda (Hammond 1986, 382). Thus, Figure 3 (taken from Hammond) illustrates three
different agendas, each of which yields a different winner. If the diagrams
are rotated counterclockwise 90 degrees, each looks something like the
traditional pyramidal hierarchy. Hammond uses this framework to show
that structures affect (a) *outcomes* – small changes in the structure
change the options that reach the manager and therefore his decisions; (b)
strategic behavior – different structures induce subordinates to misrepresent their preferences in different ways; and (c) *beliefs* – different organizational structures convert the same raw data into different organizational beliefs.

The analysis is illustrated with a host of examples – the effects of geo-
graphical versus professional structures on U.S. foreign policy decision-
making, of the introduction of PPBS, and so forth. Of course, like most of
social choice theory, the analysis is essentially nihilistic, as is that of
Hammond and Miller (1985), where various nostrums of public administration (e.g., "decisions should be made in the light of all available knowledge," and "decisions should be made on the basis of a clear assignment of
authority and responsibility") are shown to be inconsistent with one an-

other on the basis of axiomatic social choice theory. All of this lies at the opposite pole from the unitary, rational actor model of an organization toward which the principal-agent models examined above are driven.

3.4 The role of authority and the question of bureaucratic responsibility

The issue of the role of authority within hierarchies was most provocatively raised by Alchian and Demsetz (1972), who asserted that the firm "has no power of fiat, no authority, no disciplinary action any different in the slightest degree from ordinary market contracting between any two people . . . telling an employee to type this letter rather than to file that document is like telling my grocer to sell this brand of tuna rather than that brand of bread. . . ." (Alchian and Demsetz 1972, 777). One way out of this odd conclusion follows from the work by Shapiro and Stiglitz (1984), Bowles (1985), and subsequent papers on "efficiency wage" models. In these, employers have authority over workers; they try to get it by raising wages over that obtainable elsewhere. Since all employers have the same incentive to do this, the result is that wages rise to above market-clearing levels, hence inducing unemployment as a "worker discipline device." Bulow and Summers (1986) suggested an alternative version of this model, in which the economy can be divided into two sectors, one with "good" jobs and one with "bad" jobs, and the prospect of falling into the "bad" jobs sector rather than unemployment serves to discipline workers.

One important proposition that has emerged from this work is the "excess supervision" proposition (Shapiro and Stiglitz 1984; Bowles 1985). The employer can deter shirking or other forms of malfeasance by the employee in two ways: (1) by paying higher wages or (2) by supervision or monitoring. To the employer, either method is a real cost but from the social point of view, paying higher wages is simply a transfer while supervision uses up real resources. A Pareto improvement is therefore possible if employers could be induced to shift resources from supervision to wage payments. The implication is that many of the Kafkaesque features of modern bureaucracies (public or private) – red tape, constant monitoring, and accounting for one's actions – are indeed socially inefficient from the standpoint of theoretical welfare economics, even apart from any possible deleterious effects on the psyche of individuals.

Yet another explanation of the authority relationship is provided by Hart and Moore (1990), who extend the work of Grossman and Hart (1986). Grossman and Hart defined ownership as residual control rights, that is, the right to use an asset in any way that has not been voluntarily given or contracted away or that the government or some other party has not taken away by force (694). Hart and Moore suggested that one important right of ownership of an asset is the right to exclude others from the use of that asset. This can give the owner or employer power over an employee if the employee's productivity and hence his earning capacity depends on access to specialized assets controlled by the employer.

It seems clear, then, that there *is* a difference between an order from one's employer and one from a customer at a grocery store. The difference would appear to lie in the cost of disobedience. In the pure exchange model, both the buyer and seller have perfectly good alternatives available to them and the cost of disobedience is nil. In the authority model, the cost of disobedience is larger either because of the prospect of unemployment, falling into the "bad" jobs sector, or losing access to specialized and productivity-enhancing assets. Under any of these circumstances the employer has *power* over the employees. And this power is not at all related to monopoly – it arises under and is perfectly consistent with perfect competition.

The authority model raises the issue of the *responsibility* of subordinates in a bureaucratic system for the actions of the organization of which they are a part. In her famous book (1976) on the trial of Adolf Eichmann, Hannah Arendt, using a command model of bureaucracy (individuals within the hierarchy simply follow orders from the top), found it logically difficult to assign responsibility. Indeed, on the command model, it can even be difficult to distinguish between the perpetrators of a crime and their victims, who almost always "assist" (in the sense of obeying orders) in the commitment of the crime in one way or another. Eichmann consistently claimed innocence on the ground that he was only following orders, a defense subsequently used everywhere by functionaries in dictatorships in Chile, Argentina, and the former Communist countries to excuse themselves from crimes committed by the regime.

BW (1986) addressed this issue with respect to the Nazi regime – the paradigmatic case of authoritarianism. They presented evidence from standard historical sources (including Arendt herself) to show that the command model of the Nazi bureaucracy is false. In fact, "orders" given and lines of command were extremely imprecise, there was considerable entrepreneurship within the bureaucracy and fierce competition among many agencies and bureaus to "solve" the Jewish question. As Arendt herself emphasized, "It must be remembered that all these organs, wielding enormous power, were in fierce competition with one another – which was no help to their victims since their ambition was always the same: to kill as many Jews as possible. . . ." (Arendt 1976, 71). Once the regime is seen in this light, it is not difficult to convict Eichmann and others like him of guilt.

A strikingly different picture of authority relationships (and, implicitly, of bureaucratic responsibility) can be found in Akerlof's (1991) paper "Procrastination and Obedience." Akerlof discusses various forms of individual behavior that are commonly observed but are, to varying degrees, "pathological" – including procrastination, excessive obedience to authority, and membership in cults. In each case the model is that of a "near-rational" individual engaged in making a sequence of decisions over time. At each moment, the individual is close to being rational in his decision making, but the cumulative effect of his decisions is an outcome that he clearly would have liked to avoid. Akerlof applies the model to Stanley Milgram's (1974) famous experiments on obedience. In the typical experiment, the experimenter poses as a scientist conducting a learning experiment. The scientist conducts the subject into a room where there is a large machine for administering shocks and a fake "learner" (actually an actor) visible to the subject through a glass window. The subject is instructed to administer shocks to the learner when he or she gives wrong answers to questions asked by the scientist. (The learner is actually not connected to the shock machine.) As the experiment proceeds, the learner keeps giving wrong answers, and the scientist responds by asking the subject to keep escalating the shock level. The general, and surprising, result is that most subjects obey the scientist to an incredible degree, administering ever larger shocks to the learner, even well beyond the point of supposed "danger" to the victim and in spite of the victim's cries of pain and demands to be set free.

Akerlof explains these results as the consequence of "near-rationality" combined with the key feature that the escalation of the shock level is made in a series of small steps. Presumably, most subjects invited to administer a very large and dangerous shock to the learner right at the beginning of the experiment would not do so. At each step, however, the extra disutility of administering a shock of say 300 volts (compared to 280, which the subject has already committed himself to) is small. So the individual compares the disutility (to him or her) of the *escalation* (from 280 to 300) rather than the disutility of administering a shock of 300 to the disutility of disobedience to the scientist and agrees to escalate. In this way, the near-rational individual is led, in a series of steps on each of which he is close to utility maximizing, to end up performing actions that are totally irrational.

This shows how it is possible for "normal" (near-rational) people to get drawn into a system where they end up behaving in a pathological way – the phenomenon Hannah Arendt called "the banality of evil." Whether that is in fact what happened in Nazi Germany, Stalin's Russia, or elsewhere is not at all clear. And if evil is to be explained this way, why not good as well (e.g., the near-rational individual is led, by a series of small steps, into a career of helping others), thus robbing individuals of all responsibility? But there is no doubt that the analysis is an interesting extension of economic models of behavior.

4. A final stroll through the garden of modern bureaucratic theory

In conclusion, it might be useful to step back from the details of the models examined in this chapter and pause briefly to look at the "state of the art" of analytic research in bureaucracy. To do so, I take the liberty of employing a metaphor, in which contemporary models of bureaucracy comprise a garden. Through this garden, we can discern three paths. The first is relatively easy to follow since it goes in a straight line and once on it the only question is which way one is traveling. The gardens here represent the issue raised in our second parable: whether bureaucrats are really servants or actually the masters in relationship to politicians. The path begins at the hardy Niskanen plant (*bureaucratus dominus* – still flowering! – although it no longer spreads since the terrible acid rain of Libecap and Johnson), leads, through Miller and Moe and Weingast, to the unitary actor plant of Bendor, Taylor, and van Gaalen (oddly enough, although a straight line, the theoretical path never leaves Stanford University), that is, to modern principal-agent theory and the conditions for dominance by the principal. At this point, one of the best new gardeners, gazing at the garden, foresees only a "bewildering thicket" of results (Bendor 1988). However, the dreaded weed *formalis excessivus* has been kept safely in check through liberal application of comparative institutional analysis and solid empirical work, and the garden is healthy and prospering, although it is not obvious if there will ever be much more to see from going up and down this path.

The garden beside the second path is less elegant. The issues here are those raised in our first parable – whether bureaucracies are competitive or monopolistic, and efficient compared with private firms. Some early planting by Alchian and de Alessi has sprouted hundreds of poorly guided empirical tests, which continue to spread despite heavy spraying by Breton and Wintrobe, Borcherding and Weingast. Recently, however, there is at least one nice flower (Carroll's [1989] model and empirical tests), and perhaps more are on the way. Hardly anyone uses the monopoly assumption any more since competitive plants have swept "the field" (Wittman 1989). But the theory here is still relatively underdeveloped, despite its obvious importance.

The third path is the most complex and difficult. And the gardens along it are sometimes hard to see. But they contain some rather strange and exotic plants, compared to the typical flora in economics. This is the garden of bureaucratic relationships, the subject of our third parable above. To really appreciate it, the visitor first has to trespass a bit into an adjacent (private) garden, where he will notice a very old and sturdy bush planted by Coase in 1937. This is *firmus naturus* – the command or pure authority model of the firm. At the other end there is a bristling, thorny bush bought at a reduced price by Alchian and Demsetz in 1972 (which indeed has turned out to be infected; it symbolizes the insistence that exchange within the firm is no different than in the market).

In between these two, there are some new plants. One can see the rather pretty Hart and Moore flower and a whole row of upright efficiency wage plants all representing exchange with costly disobedience. From there, if one gazes back to the public garden, one can see the exotic and possibly poisonous Akerlof orchid more clearly. This is a hybrid from the costs of disobedience seed, norms, and the structure of decision making fertilized with just a touch of irrationality. Beside it is the deadly Breton–Wintrobe bush, planted in 1986, and the intriguing but potentially aimless Hammond plant. If one were to go further in this direction, one would end up in the vast territory tended for years by sociologists and organization theorists. But this part of the garden is so weedy! Still, the enormous Coleman (1990) forest there is a wonder to behold, and economists especially will appreciate the Granovetter (1985) plant embedded in the rocks.

The garden of bureaucratic models has been carefully tended by both economists and political scientists in recent years and this is surely one reason why it looks so healthy. However, especially in this last area, more cuttings from sociology might be necessary if the garden is ever to become really beautiful. But be careful with the Akerlof plant![7]

---

7. It is not quite rational.

CHAPTER 21

The positive theory of public bureaucracy

TERRY M. MOE

Modern government is bureaucratic, so a theory of government worthy of the name must in no small measure be a theory of bureaucracy. Over the years, however, bureaucracy has resisted theoretical progress, and public administration, whose intellectual terrain this is, has gained a reputation for being far less developed than other areas of political science.

Two barriers to theory stand out. The first is that bureaucracy is a complex subject with no natural focus for analysis. Legislators vote, for instance, but what do bureaucrats do? Similarly, the legislature is organized by committees and party leadership, but what aspects of bureaucracy call for comparable attention and analysis? There are no obvious answers, and scholars have responded by studying everything about bureaucratic behavior and organization that somehow appears relevant.

The second is that these efforts have traditionally been guided by organizational theories from sociology and social psychology, which have not pointed a way out of the thicket. Rather than providing focus and analytic power, they revel in the inherent complexity of bureaucracy. And as generic theories of all types of organization, they have no special interest in politics and are not designed to explore the political foundations of government (Moe 1991).

Public choice is in the process of changing all this, in what amounts to a revolution in the theory of bureaucracy. It did not come easily, and major problems remain. But progress has already been substantial. The turning point came during the early 1980s with the rise of the new economics of organization (Moe 1984). In this line of theory – consisting largely of transaction costs economics, agency theory, and the theory of repeated games – economists developed powerful analytic tools for addressing issues of organization (Milgrom and Roberts 1992). And positive political theorists, whose approach to government had long been framed by social choice theories of voting, quickly began putting the two together in moving toward a theory of public bureaucracy. Throughout, their efforts have been aided by a unifying focus on political control, which the new economics is especially well suited to investigate.

455

As in any literature, there is good reason to dispute some of the claims and models that have surfaced along the way. Nonetheless, taken as a whole this work sheds new light not only on how bureaus behave but also on how their basic organizational properties emerge out of politics – thus providing, in nascent form, what public administration has for decades been seeking: a truly political theory of bureaucratic organization.

My purpose here is to put this literature in perspective, and, by looking at the major ideas and approaches orienting the field over time, to give readers some sense of how the positive theory of public bureaucracy has evolved. I will also try to suggest why these developments are so promising and what special problems need to be overcome if bureaucracy is to be well understood.

First, a few caveats. This is a big, diverse literature, and I have had to be selective to make things manageable. I spotlight only a relatively small number of works, which means that many worthy contributions go unrecognized. I have also excluded whole areas that, however important on other grounds, are not central to the core I focus on here. This applies to the extensive research on regulatory agencies, which is rather specialized (Noll 1989), as well as to the Simon–March school of bureaucratic theory, whose methodology puts it at the fringes of public choice (Bendor 1988; Moe 1984). It also applies to work on the internal aspects of bureaucracy, most of which is about organizations in general rather than public bureaucracy per se (Miller 1992; Hammond and Miller 1985; Breton and Wintrobe 1982).

1. Early theories of bureaucracy

Public choice first made its mark on bureaucratic theory during the mid-1960s with the appearance of two innovative books, Gordon Tullock's *The Politics of Bureaucracy* (1965) and Anthony Downs's *Inside Bureaucracy* (1967). Both were attempts to show that bureaucracy can be well understood and a powerful theory someday constructed by assuming bureaucrats are rational actors largely motivated by self-interest.

This was a sharp departure from existing scholarship and a quantum change in the way rational choice was applied to organizations. At that time, the enormously influential work of Herbert Simon and James March offered the only theory of bureaucracy grounded in rational choice (Simon 1947; March and Simon 1957). But its methodology was unconventional, and its emphasis was on the cognitive limitations of problem-solving individuals. Self-interest and its correlates – strategies, conflict, opportunism, coalition formation – were mostly ignored, along with their profound consequences for organization. Tullock and Downs brought all this to center stage and, for the first time, argued for a full-blown rational theory of bureaucracy more in tune with standard neoclassical methods.[1]

Although both were especially interested in government, they cast their nets widely to address a full gamut of topics on organizations generally. Tullock's is a theory of authority relationships. Downs's is a theory of all large organizations whose outputs are not evaluated in external markets. In each case the analysis is informal, but still based on clear assumptions about actors and their contexts, with the focus on motivation. Tullock builds on the assumption that bureaucrats are motivated by career advancement. Downs creates five motivational types – conservers, climbers, zealots, advocates, and statesmen – and shows how the changing mix of these types shapes the growth and operation of bureaucracy. While in content these analyses are very different, their bottom lines turn out to be much the same. Rational bureaucratic behavior promotes inefficiency, excessive growth, capture, weak accountability, and related problems that undermine effective government.

With these two books, public choice made a stunning entree into the world of bureaucratic theory, upsetting the good government vision of public administration and charting a bold new path for analysis. Downs, especially, was widely read by political scientists and cited for what he had to say about agency life cycles, control problems, communication foul-ups, and other central issues. His typology of bureaucratic motivation, which he put to ingenious use, became quite popular.

Future work in public choice, however, did not build explicitly on either of these books. Their sweeping approach to bureaucracy did not provide a clear analytic focus for constructing new theories, nor did it suggest any productive strategies of formal modeling. Many found these books exciting, but no one knew what to do with them.

Before long another pioneer in public choice, Vincent Ostrom, laid down a still more direct challenge to public administration, contending that rational choice should provide a new foundation for the entire field. His book, *The Intellectual Crisis of Public Administration* (1973), generated immediate controversy, was widely read and assigned, and, perhaps more than any other work before or since, ushered rational choice into the intellectual framework of public administration.

While Tullock and Downs want to explain bureaucracy, Ostrom is concerned with institutional design: what administrative arrangements are most compatible with the public interest? Spinning an analysis that is

---

1. Both, especially Downs, interpreted self-interest broadly to include suprapersonal values of various sorts, for example, regarding good policy or the public interest.

part public choice and part normative philosophy, he argues that central-ization, hierarchy, and consolidation – the core prescriptions of classic public administration – are bad, and that fragmentation, decentraliza-tion, and checks and balances are good. Two strands of public choice theory are central to his case. One is the Simon–March school, which justifies decentralized structures on grounds of cognitive limitations. The other is the Tiebout (1955)-inspired literature on public goods, which argues the efficiency of a fragmented, decentralized system of political jurisdictions.

Ostrom's work, unlike Tullock's or Downs's, helped stimulate a new research tradition. Its guiding theory, however, is about how govern-ment ought to be organized, rather than why government is organized as it is. And its substantive focus, as the Tiebout influence suggests, is on municipal government. Throughout the 1970s and 1980s, as a result, this grew into a specialized literature, one that addressed local political is-sues (such as water resource development) and local political structures (like police departments) that, for better or worse, are not of much interest to scholars in either public choice or public administration. The Indiana school, as it is often called, thus became a peripheral part of the public choice movement (Mitchell 1988).

2. The Niskanen tradition

For takeoff, what the movement needed was some sort of catalyst, a clear analytic basis for cumulative work. It came in the form of William Niskanen's *Bureaucracy and Representative Government* (1971), which to this day is surely the most cited and influential theory of bureaucracy to emerge within public choice.

The key to Niskanen's success is that, unlike his predecessors, he restricts his focus and simplifies with a vengeance. While he too defines bureaucracy generically and is interested in grand issues – in his case, the size and efficiency of government – his attention centers on public agencies and their budgets. His model is a simple, cleverly designed vehicle for getting at these things. He assumes bureaucrats are budget maximizers, endowing them for the first time with a simple utility func-tion amenable to formal modeling. And he strips away the complexities of budgetary politics by building his model around just two actors, the bureau and its legislative sponsor.

Their relationship is one of bilateral monopoly, with the bureau hold-ing two pivotal advantages. First, its position as sole supplier gives it a monopoly over information about the true costs of production. Second, the bureau knows how much the legislature values every level of output, and it can use this information to present a take-it-or-leave-it offer (of a given output for a given budget) that it knows the legislature will accept. It has information power, and it has agenda power.[2]

These powers enable the bureau to act as a perfectly discriminating monopolist, forcing the legislature to accept an oversized budget it barely prefers to no budget at all, while any surplus is kept and spent by the bureau. The bottom line is that government is too big and grossly inefficient.

Early critiques of Niskanen centered on his assumption of budget maximization. The most influential of these was by Migue and Bélanger (1975), who argue that bureaucrats maximize the "discretionary budget," namely, the difference between the total budget and the minimum cost of production. This makes sense, for any such slack in agency budgets is available to bureaucrats to spend as they wish – on more staff, travel, or favored programs. Slack is the bureaucratic equivalent of personal income.

When bureaucrats maximize slack, Niskanen's conclusions about budgets and outputs are altered somewhat, but the picture is still gloomy. Government remains horribly inefficient. And in a recent retrospective on his book, Niskanen (1991) himself agrees that slack is a more appropriate maximand than the total budget. Presumably, this shift is also prompted by empirical studies showing that the salaries and careers of bureaucrats are not significantly related to the size of agency budgets after all (Young 1991).

The most telling critiques of Niskanen have centered on issues of bureaucratic power. As I have suggested, bureaus dominate in his model for two reasons: they control information and they control the agenda. Yet Niskanen is not at all clear about this (Bendor 1988). He tends to treat them both as informational, as though it is the agency's control over information that allows it to present the legislature with take-it-or-leave-it budgetary offers. This impression is confusing, for, as we will see, the agenda control Niskanen imputes to bureaus is ultimately rooted in authority, not information. The two sources of power are different, and they need to be treated separately.

When subsequent work sought to clarify matters, agenda control turned out to be the big chink in Niskanen's armor. The first indication came from Romer and Rosenthal (1978), who showed that the power of agenda control depends on the "reversion level," which is what the chooser receives if the agenda setter's offer is rejected. The farther the reversion level is from the chooser's ideal point, the greater the agenda-setter's power to get her most preferred outcome. In budgeting, the most

---

2. Information power can be construed as a type of agenda power (see Bendor 1988), but I think distinguishing the two is helpful here.

reasonable reversion level is the status-quo budget. Yet Niskanen assumes the reversion level is zero, and thus that legislators are forced to choose between the bureau's offered budget and no budget at all. This gives the bureau far more power than if the reversion level were the status quo. A more reasonable assumption thus leads to more moderate – and less gloomy – conclusions about the size and efficiency of government.

The larger question, however, is why bureaus have agenda power at all. This is the subject of an article I coauthored with Gary Miller (Miller and Moe 1983), which points out that Niskanen's model is curiously one-sided: bureaus are strategic actors driven to achieve their own ends, while the legislature is passive – it sits by idly as the treasury is looted. Not only should the legislature be treated as a strategic actor too, but any political model must also recognize that the legislature has authority over the bureau and can structure their bargaining in any way it wants. Their relationship is not simply one of bilateral monopoly. It is an authority relationship in which the legislature has the legal right to tell the bureau what to do. The legislature is the principal, the bureau the agent.

It follows that the legislature need not, and presumably would not, put up with the kind of agenda control Niskanen grants the bureau. It might conceal its own demand, for example, or force the bureau to submit a complete schedule of budget-output combinations for legislative choice. It might engage in monitoring and oversight to gain information. It might impose sanctions when the bureau is caught lying. And so on. The fact is, the bureau has to play the budget game according to rules set by the legislature – and in this crucial sense, it is the legislature that sets the bureau's agenda, not the other way around. As we go on to demonstrate, introducing these new elements into Niskanen's framework yields a much more moderate view of bureaucratic power and the size and scope of government. Niskanen's well-known conclusions turn out to be extreme cases, dependent on a kind of agenda control no strategic legislature would ordinarily allow.

From this point on, Niskanen's original approach began to give way to the new economics of organization. Attention still centered on the bureau and the legislature, but their relationship was now understood in game theoretic or principal-agent terms. Take-it-or-leave-it agenda control was out as a basis of bureaucratic power. The focus was now on asymmetric information – notably the bureau's private information about costs – and the legislature's authority to set the rules and assert control: typical concerns of the new economics.

From a public administration standpoint, there is something especially appropriate about this. Weber (1947) recognized long ago that bureaucratic expertise gives rise to a profound dilemma for government. It is needed if policy is to be carried out effectively, and indeed is the prime reason politicians delegate authority to bureaus in the first place. Yet it is also a powerful weapon that bureaucrats can turn against their political superiors. What public administrationists have been saying for decades, but in different language, is that the information asymmetry inherent in bureaucy produces a serious control problem for politicians, who must use their authority to do something about it.

These issues were raised within the Niskanen tradition well before it was transformed by the new economics. Breton and Wintrobe (1975), for instance, argued early on that the legislature could undercut the bureau's power by investing in monitoring and control. The more recent work, however, has been explicitly grounded in new economics thinking.

Leading the way were Bendor, Taylor, and van Gaalen (1985, 1987a), who expanded on the Miller–Moe critique in a series of articles that take a deeper look at problems of asymmetric information and authority. Their analysis highlights the dependence of legislative control upon bureaucratic attitudes toward risk (since deception, oversight, and sanctions all generate uncertainties) and the legislature's ability to commit to an incentive scheme ex ante: key components of the new economics that had previously gone unappreciated in this stream of work.

They were followed by Banks (1989b), who rejects Bendor et al.'s approach to commitment – which relies on a (quite plausible, but informal) reputational argument – and develops a one-period sequential equilibrium model in which the legislature ignores reputational concerns and can only threaten and credibly commit to sanctions that are in its short-term interests to carry out. He goes on to explore how the legislature can exercise its auditing and sanctioning powers to assert budgetary control over an agency endowed with private information. This analysis was later extended by Banks and Weingast (1992), who allow legislators to take auditing and monitoring into account in their initial design of agencies – thus affecting which types of agencies get created in the first place and how ex post control mechanisms are designed to work.

This is the state of the art in the Niskanen tradition, which, thanks to progress, is losing its identity as a separate line of work. It is now best thought of as an integral part of the larger literature on political control. As such, it remains distinct mainly because of its heritage and its focus on budgets. Meantime, Niskanen's simple claims about big government have emerged as a special case too. The new-wave models have shown that the size and scope of government can vary considerably, depending on a host of complications and contingencies.

Despite these transformations, Niskanen's work has had a profound impact on the path of bureaucratic theory. While the natural inclination in the early days was to see bureaucracy as a complex organization subject to a tangled array of authorities, constituencies, and pressures, theorists in the post-Niskanen world have often been prone to reduce bureaucracy, as he did, to a unitary bureau driven by a single goal – and to shift their attention, as he did, from the bureaucracy to its relationship with the legislature.

3. The Chicago school and interest group capture

About the time Niskanen's book was first published, another pathbreaking work also appeared, George Stigler's "The Theory of Economic Regulation." This signaled the arrival of the Chicago school, known for its free-market approach to economics, as an intellectual force in the study of politics. Stigler sought to show that regulation is not only bad economics but also bad politics, for the rational foundations of politics, he argues, inevitably promote the capture of regulatory agencies by the very groups they are supposed to be regulating.

Stigler's article was both timely and sensational, just as Niskanen's book was. During the decades following the New Deal, when regulation grew like Topsy, evidence mounted that regulatory agencies were vulnerable to group capture. Political scientists offered various explanations – life cycles, iron triangles, interest group liberalism – but Stigler was the first to develop a coherent theory anchored in rational choice.

The theory is simple. Specialized business interests have much to gain from regulation if the rules are designed on their behalf. And they can ensure as much through their control of politics. As Mancur Olson (1965) has shown, their small numbers (by industry) combined with the concentration of benefits gives them much stronger incentives to organize for political action than taxpayers and other large groups, over whom the costs are widely dispersed. Group power is thus grossly unbalanced in favor of small, concentrated interests. Politicians respond by setting up bureaus to do these groups' bidding, and the bureaus, in turn, do what the politicians say. The result is a captured bureaucracy – one that, contrary to political science notions, does not "get" captured over time, but is designed from the outset to promote the regulated interests.

Stigler soon suffered the same fate as Niskanen, however: his simple claims were shot down as his theory was generalized by others. Two lines of elaboration have received widespread attention. One is due to his Chicago colleagues, Sam Peltzman (1976) and Gary Becker (1983), who not only formalized his basic ideas but also complicated and modified them immensely – arguing that large, diffuse groups actually have more power (due to voting, for instance) than Stigler gives them credit for, and that regulatory outcomes are more pluralistic. In the end, the generalized Chicago school theory is more a theory of pluralism than a theory of capture. Capture is a special case.

The second elaboration comes from James Q. Wilson (1980), whose simple revision of Stigler's theory has been highly influential in shaping scholarly thinking. Wilson notes that the costs of regulation can be either concentrated or diffused, as can the benefits, yielding a four-way typology of group environments – each of which gives rise to a different pattern of agency creation and group influence. Stigler assumes that benefits are concentrated and costs diffused, producing capture. But when one of the other group environments obtains, the result is something entirely different – more pluralistic, for example, or more majoritarian. Again, capture is a special case.

Capture aside, all these efforts stand out as pioneering attempts to develop interest group theories of politics that link social interests directly to bureaucracy and public policy. They go about it, moreover, in a distinctive way that sets them apart from the rest of the literature. First, all are grounded in the logic of collective action: they begin with a state of nature lacking organized political groups, and their key actors emerge spontaneously as regulatory issues arise, with relative power determined by Olson's logic. Second, these theories black-box the institutions that convert group inputs into political outputs: bureaucracy and public policy are taken as reflections of the underlying balance of group power, with no theory of how this happens or why. Institutions are left out.

The more recent literature seeks to fill in the institutional details that the Chicago school ignores. But while the temptation is to think that the new work must be "building" on the Chicago foundation, it really does not. As we will see, most of it arose out of social choice theories of voting and agenda control. It was not anchored in Olson's logic of collective action, and indeed, it initially paid no serious attention to interest groups. Even when it later sought to incorporate groups, moreover, it did not go back to Olson's logic and try to derive the group universe from first principles. Typically, it simply took existing groups as the relevant actors and went from there.

This shift away from Olson makes good sense and corrects for a serious flaw in the Chicago theory. In actual battles over structure or policy, the groups that count are those that are already organized, not latent groups that magically spring up in response to a regulatory issue. And many of these organizations represent interests – of environmentalists, consumers, minorities, etc. – that Olson claims should *not* be organized or powerful at all. Going back to Olson's first principles is not just an unnecessary complication for the early phase of institutional theory. It misconstrues reality.

4. Legislative control and congressional dominance

During the early 1980s, political science was swept by the new institutionalism. Until then, despite the provocative work of Niskanen and the Chicago school, most positive theorists were preoccupied with voting and little interested in bureaucracy. The new institutionalism changed all this, but in a way that was heavily shaped by the social choice origins of positive theory.

For positive theorists, the rationale for studying institutions arose out of a voting puzzle. Voting theories predict endless cycling, whereas in reality politics is highly stable. Why so much stability? The answer is that institutions structure voting and bring order out of chaos. From the beginning, then, the theory of political institutions was grounded in social choice, and what was interesting about institutions arose from their connection to voting.

Given this orientation, the natural focus was on legislatures, whose members vote and are elected through the votes of constituents. As a result, the theory of institutions, although it aspired to generality, quickly evolved into a theory of legislatures anchored in social choice. From this point on, the rest of the political world came to be viewed through legislative lenses – and out of this world view sprang empirical claims about legislative superiority and power. Method and substance were merged.

Bureaucracy attracted interest as a topic in legislative theory. Obviously, the policies legislators vote on are empty abstractions until they are implemented, and they can be implemented in various ways depending on who controls the bureaucracy, how well, and toward what ends. The theory of legislatures, then, quickly focused on how legislators could control the bureaucracy to their own advantage. The study of political control thus served as the bridge to the modern theory of bureaucracy.

But how to develop a theory of control? Social choice was well suited to the analysis of voting, but control clearly turned on other issues – of information, authority, rewards and sanctions, and monitoring – that social choice could not readily handle. The new economics of organization, rapidly developing at just this time, was ideally suited to the job (Moe 1984); and positive theorists moved eagerly to graft it onto their social choice base. The effect was dramatic: enhanced analytic power, a burst of interest in political control, and a new hybrid – but still legislative – theory of bureaucracy that meshed social choice and the new economics.

Barry Weingast stands out as the most influential figure in the early theory of legislative control. Of his several articles on the subject, one cowritten with Mark Moran on congressional control of the Federal

Trade Commission is widely cited as seminal (Weingast and Moran 1983; see also Weingast 1981, 1984). Its theme is congressional dominance.

Their theory begins with a social choice model of legislative voting, in which a committee uses its agenda powers to engineer legislative policy on the floor. The committee then becomes a principal, seeking faithful implementation of its policies by the bureaucracy and wielding an array of control mechanisms – oversight, budgets, appointments, threats of new legislation – so formidable that the bureau has overwhelming incentives to comply. Congress dominates. Evidence from the FTC bears this out, they argue, showing that its behavior was highly responsive over time to changes in congressional preferences.

Part of Weingast's argument, here and elsewhere, is that political scientists misconstrue the facts of congressional oversight – low interest, sporadic and poorly attended hearings – to mean that control is ineffective. The same facts, he argues, are observationally equivalent to those associated with strong legislative control: when agencies anticipate sanctions and avoid them through assiduous compliance, there is little need for active oversight, and most of the time nothing much would be happening. What appears to be apathy and inattention would arise from successful control.

This theme was more fully developed by McCubbins and Schwartz (1984). Reelection-minded legislators, they argue, have little incentive to engage in the "police patrol" oversight of bureaus that the literature presumes. Their incentive is to satisfy constituency groups – and have them bear the costs of monitoring – by simply responding to group "fire alarms" when something goes wrong. This approach not only makes electoral sense, they say, but also produces tight control: when fire-alarm oversight is activated, Congress's weapons are so powerful the bureaucracy will shape up. Indeed, bureaus will tend to anticipate sanctions and comply from the outset.

These and related articles (Fiorina 1981b; Barke and Riker 1982; Weingast 1984) stimulated interest in the study of political control. Yet their claims of congressional dominance also provoked controversy, and for good reason. As I pointed out at the time (Moe 1987), they do not really develop a theory of control. They never model the goals, strategies, or resources of the bureaucracy itself and have no basis for understanding its capacity to resist or take autonomous action. The profound importance of private information, which so empowered Niskanen's bureau, is given short shrift here, along with the entire bureaucratic side of the control relationship. Only the legislative principal is a serious subject of theory.

Moreover, their claims about the great efficacy of legislative control are quite out of keeping with the whole thrust of the economic theory of agency – which is that control is costly and often entails substantial slippage. To judge from agency theory, the theme of this literature ought to be that Congress has a difficult time controlling the bureaucracy, and that the latter has much autonomy. This is precisely what mainstream work by political scientists has long maintained. It is also what Weingast and Moran's empirical analysis of the FTC would have shown, I believe, had they not overlooked important aspects of FTC history and behavior (see Moe 1987).

In some sense, the problem here is just the reverse of what we found with Niskanen. Niskanen overstates bureaucratic power by assuming a strategic bureau and a passive legislature. The congressional dominance theorists overstate legislative power by assuming a strategic legislature and a passive bureau.

5. Ex ante control, exchange, and the politics of structure

The early theory of congressional dominance was a theory of ex post control. It asked how legislators could prevent "runaway" bureaucracy by monitoring agency behavior, rewarding compliance, and punishing noncompliance. This was a reasonable place to begin, yet it clearly left a major part of the control story unexplored. For legislators (and presidents) also have the authority to exercise control ex ante: by building in goals, structures, and personnel systems that promote agency compliance from the outset. Through strategic choices about organization, in other words, they can *design* bureaucracy to do their bidding.

Positive theorists quickly recognized this and moved to incorporate ex ante control into their analyses. This simple step, although an obvious one in retrospect, may well represent the most important single development in the modern theory of bureaucracy. While Congress remained the center of attention, and while bureaucratic organization assumed importance mainly as a means to an end – congressional control – the analytical tools were now in hand for explaining how bureaucracy emerges out of politics and why it takes the organizational forms it does.

5.1 Ex ante control

The study of ex ante control is grounded on issues of delegation. Why does Congress delegate authority to an agency, rather than passing detailed laws enforceable in the courts? When it delegates, does it prefer vague mandates that give agencies tremendous discretion or highly specific mandates that severely limit what agencies can do? And when agencies have a measure of discretion, how can Congress use structure to channel their behavior toward legislative ends?

The most influential early work on delegation was by Fiorina (1982a, 1982b, 1986; see also Aranson, Robinson, and Gellhorn 1982), who developed a theory based on the incentives and uncertainties faced by legislators. The best-known product is his shift-the-responsibility model. The idea is that legislators seek to claim credit for the constituency benefits of agency programs and to avoid blame for the costs. Delegation allows them to disguise their responsibility for policies – to fool people – by kicking unresolved issues over to the agency. This enhances their ability to avoid blame (which is good) but reduces their ability to claim credit (which is bad). They delegate when the gains from blame-avoidance outweigh the losses from reduced credit claiming – which, he argues, is often the case, especially when costs are concentrated or benefits diffused.

Subsequent work on ex ante control praises Fiorina's shift-the-responsibility model without really embracing it. The more common assumption is that the contending groups on important political issues are organized and informed about what legislators are doing. In these accounts, legislators design structures to aid some groups and disadvantage others, but little emphasis is placed on strategies of fooling anyone. Much of this work, however, builds on Fiorina's broader efforts to anchor delegation in the calculations of legislators.

Perhaps the most direct link between Fiorina's work on delegation and the more recent work on ex ante control is provided by McCubbins (1985). McCubbins points out that Fiorina does not treat bureaus as strategic actors, and that, when bureaus do behave strategically, delegation creates agency problems that Congress must address. He goes on to frame the relationship in principal-agent terms, and, with the help of social choice, develops a theory of how Congress delegates under conditions of conflict and uncertainty. He argues that both these conditions prompt legislators to favor delegations broad in scope – but also to favor reduced discretion through procedural rules and oversight. The net result is less discretion, despite the broad mandates – and Congress succeeds in gaining tight control. "In general, Congress possesses all the powers it might ever need to ensure agency compliance" (728).

Soon thereafter came two articles by McCubbins, Noll, and Weingast (1987, 1989) that gained widespread attention, generated great controversy, and established ex ante control as a growth industry. Their big splash was due in part to their audience. McNollgast (as they are now, for convenience and amusement, collectively known) addressed themselves to the law-and-economics community, arguing that administrative procedures are explained not by normative concerns for fairness, due process, or equity, but rather by the self-interested strategies of legislative actors. Such an argument grew naturally out of rational choice thinking, but it challenged conventional legal perspectives, and it demanded and got a spirited response (Mashaw 1990).

McNollgast see the relationship between Congress and the bureaucracy as a principal-agent problem in which an enacting coalition within the legislature seeks to minimize bureaucratic drift. They argue that, while the prior literature emphasized ex post control, efforts to monitor, reward, and sanction agencies are costly to employ and, at any rate, do not work very well. This is an implicit way of saying that the earlier work on congressional dominance – their own work – was indeed off base. Their new claim is that, precisely *because* ex post control is highly problematic, Congress places great emphasis on ex ante control, which works much better. Ex ante control emerges as the key to understanding how Congress gets its way – which it continues to do, on their account – and why bureaucracy looks and performs as it does.

McNollgast focus on how the enacting coalition can design administrative procedures to prevent bureaucratic drift. Properly chosen, procedures can mitigate problems of asymmetric information by forcing agencies to take certain kinds of technical or constituency information into account, or to publicize their policy aims well in advance of formal promulgation – creating an early-warning system for politicians and ruling out faits accompli. The Administrative Procedures Act, they argue, is a prime example of how Congress uses procedures to open up agency decision making and guard against insulation.

Procedures also enfranchise favored constituencies by selectively granting them access and participation rights, thus injecting special interests directly into the informational and early-warning system, as well as shaping decisions according to the balance of group power. In these ways, legislators stack the deck in favor of groups within the enacting coalition and ensure that changes over time in the interests and relative powers of groups are mirrored in agency process and policy. If wisely structured, the agency should be on autopilot: programmed to do Congress's bidding.

Two alternative theories soon appeared, one of them my own (Moe 1989, 1990a, 1990b; Moe and Caldwell 1994; Moe and Wilson 1994), the other developed by Horn (1988, 1995). Both share basic themes with McNollgast – regarding the role of procedures in stacking the deck, for instance – and both rely heavily on the new economics. But Horn and I highlight a key foundation of structural choice that McNollgast initially overlooked.

The overlooked factor, which I call political uncertainty, arises from the incomplete property rights inherent in democratic politics. Today's power-holders have only a temporary grip on public authority and do not own the agencies or programs they create. As a result, they cannot commit tomorrow's authorities to protecting them. Tomorrow's authorities will have the right to do what they want, and there is uncertainty about whether they will respect past deals or renege on them. This is especially so if elections or changes in group power threaten to give opposing interests greater access to public authority.

Political uncertainty has a profound effect on strategy and structure. Today's authorities know that, if their creations are to generate benefits for favored constituents over time, they must be protected from future authorities and thus insulated from democratic control. The best way to do this is through ex ante control mechanisms – decision procedures, civil service rules, independent forms of organization, timetables – that not only stack the deck, but lock in the bias to protect it from changes in group power and public authority. Today's enacting coalition, in other words, wants to ensure that tomorrow's legislature *cannot* control the bureaucracy.

This puts a different spin on things. McNollgast's enacting coalition fixes its gaze on the bureau, which threatens to drift away. The coalition relies not only on deck stacking but on procedures that force the bureau to reveal information, open its internal processes, and suffer outside intervention to keep it in check. As Horn and I emphasize, however, the enacting coalition must also cast a wary eye on the legislature itself, indeed on all future authorities and group opponents, and use structure to insulate against their control. Because of political uncertainty, the coalition often does not want openness or intervention and favors structures that shut out most opportunities for external control.

It follows that the shortcomings of ex post control are more severe than McNollgast suggests, and are not just due to the usual slippage in any principal-agent relationship. They are built-in by Congress, which has strong incentives to create an autonomous bureaucracy that pursues the original intent of the law – and resists Congress's own efforts at ex post control. Ex ante control emerges as a two-edged sword: it promotes the "dominance" of today's Congress by rendering tomorrow's Congress increasingly impotent.

5.2 Political exchange and the politics of structure choice

Political uncertainty changes the thrust of McNollgast's initial argument, but its forward-looking logic is readily incorporated into their basic framework. Indeed, some of the most innovative work on legislative intent and its protection through the courts – issues that revolve around considerations of political uncertainty – has been contributed by McNollgast through extensions of their early theory (McCubbins, Noll, and Weingast 1992, 1994; see also Ferejohn and Weingast 1992b).

What most distinguishes the work that Horn and I have done from McNollgast's is the underlying purpose of our theories. McNollgast seek to understand bureaucracy by developing the theory of legislative control, and the analysis is primarily about legislators, not bureaucracy. Horn and I have no special interest in legislative control and see ourselves as building a theory of public administration – much as Downs, Tullock, and Ostrom had been in past years.

Horn's work remains well within the mainstream, but he shifts the spotlight from legislative control of bureaus to the exchange relationship between legislators and their constituents. Its essence is that legislators want political support, constituents want governmental benefits, and both have much to gain from trading with one another – yet their efforts are plagued by transactions costs. Much as Williamson (1985) has done for private organizations, Horn pursues a theory of public bureaucracy by exploring the transaction costs of legislative exchange.

Bureaucratic drift, for instance, generates transaction costs that inhibit political deals. Drift lowers the expected value for constituents, and thus the support they are willing to offer legislators in exchange. The commitment problem induced by political uncertainty is another source of transaction costs. If today's legislators cannot commit future authorities to honor current political deals, constituents will discount their value and provide less support. To maximize political support, legislators minimize these and other transactions costs (e.g., legislative decision costs, uncertainty costs) by making strategic choices about bureaucratic structure. The basic properties of bureaucracy thus emerge from legislative efforts to minimize transactions costs.

Whether Horn's transaction costs approach is more powerful than McNollgast's principal-agent approach remains to be seen. They are different ways of talking about the same issues. Nonetheless, Horn's analysis is ambitious, integrating into one framework the various arguments about complexity, uncertainty, expertise, drift, and commitment that positive theorists have made over the years and exploring a range of substantive topics central to public administration: organizational form, internal procedures, civil service, budgets, privatization, and state-owned enterprise. His analysis of civil service, in particular, is a much-needed contribution that is sure to stimulate controversy and research.

The unifying theme in Horn's work is the pervasive importance of the commitment problem, and thus political uncertainty, which he sees as the driving force behind much of structural choice and the reason why so much of bureaucracy is insulated from political control. This is a central theme of my own work as well. But my approach departs from the mainstream.

As may be obvious by now, I am not happy with a theory of bureaucracy that arises from a theory of legislatures. I begin instead with the basics of politics – public authority and the struggle to exercise it – and move toward a systemic view of the "politics of structural choice" in which no type of player or relationship assumes preeminence. The task is to figure out how the system works and who does what within it. Throughout, I highlight an issue long at the heart of both public administration and public choice – the effectiveness of bureaucracy – that, with all the talk about legislative control and exchange, modern theory rarely discusses.

One of the oddest things about McNollgast, Horn, and other mainstream works is their virtual omission of presidents, except as veto threats. My own work brings presidents fully into the analysis and suggests why their inclusion is essential. In part, this is simply because they have powerful impacts on structure. But it is also because their preferences and strategies are so different from those of legislators. Presidents actively pursue strong leadership in the broader interests of society, they seek central control over bureaucracy for themselves, and they have executive powers of unilateral action for imposing their own structures.

A theory-with-presidents points to distinctly presidential components throughout bureaucracy – including the institutional presidency, a defining feature of modern American government that positive theorists largely ignore. It also emphasizes that many bureaucratic structures are designed by groups and legislators to insulate parochial interests from presidential influence, and that presidents counter by adding on structures of their own. These structures and dynamics are fundamental to American bureaucracy, and they are missed when presidents are simply lumped into the enacting coalition.

McNollgast and Horn also have little to say about interest groups. They frame politics in terms of legislators and voters, while submerging groups (along with presidents) in the enacting coalition. My own approach, essentially an institutional version of the Chicago theory of group influence, treats interest groups as strategic actors and shows how their calculations and demands find translation in governmental structure.

This clarifies the distinctive role of interest groups – and suggests why, in a world of political uncertainty and compromise, group politics leads to bizarre, grossly ineffective forms of organization. It also clarifies the distinctive role of politicians, whose interests are only partially aligned with the groups', and spotlights a key issue the mainstream glosses over: the extent to which politicians have autonomy from groups, and what structures they pursue when they have it. Some of the bureaucracy arises from politicians responding to groups, some from politicians building structures for themselves. None of this can be understood, nor can bureaucracy be explained, when groups and politicians are merged in the enacting coalition.

I will offer one final point of contrast. Both Horn and McNollgast develop theories that are peculiar to American politics. Horn sometimes applies his theory to other nations, but the logic remains American. A basic theme of my own work is that different institutional systems generate different politics of structure and thus different bureaucracies.

The American separation of powers system fragments power and makes new laws exceedingly hard to enact. Anything that is formalized, therefore, tends to endure – which prompts all actors to rely heavily on formal structure in protecting their interests and solving their commitment problems. The result is a bureaucracy that is vastly overformalized and disabled by its own organization. In a Westminster parliamentary system, this does not happen. Power is concentrated, passing and overturning laws is relatively easy, and formal structure therefore has little strategic value as a protector of interests or solution to commitment problems. This yields a bureaucracy that is *not* buried in excessive formalism and far better suited to effective performance. The logic of politics is very different in the two systems, and so as a result are their bureaucracies. This sort of attention to institutional context, in my view, should be central to any theory of bureaucracy. But it is impeded by the mainstream's fixation on Congress.

The problems I associate with the mainstream are likely to be overcome with time. For now, the diversity represented by these three lines of theory (McNollgast's, Horn's, and my own) represents a state of transition and progress. They are the first attempts to show, in fairly comprehensive fashion, how the internal structure of bureaucracy arises out of politics and, as such, are concrete steps toward the kind of bureaucratic theory envisioned years ago by the pioneers of public choice.

6. Spatial models of political control

Theories of ex ante control, political exchange, and the politics of structural choice are now at the heart of the modern theory of bureaucracy. They try to explain what bureaucracy *is*. Over the last decade or so, however, most of the work by positive theorists has taken the bureaucracy as given and has explored how it *behaves* in response to the control efforts of other actors, especially Congress. For the most part, these theories center on ex post control as the earlier literature did. And, while growing attuned to basic themes from the new economics (like commitment), they are framed by the familiar spatial models of social choice theory – again, a reflection of the earlier literature.

Because these models usually take as exogenous what a theory of bureaucracy must ultimately explain – the nature of bureaucracy itself – they are best viewed as important supplements to the core of the modern theory.

6.1 Multiple principals

Their most obvious contribution is in moving from dyadic models of congressional control to broader models in which multiple principals – legislators, presidents, the courts – jointly exercise control. John Ferejohn has been a leader in this modeling effort, and his work is illustrative.

Ferejohn and Shipan (1990) provides a nice baseline. Here, the authors cite Weingast and Moran (1983) as seminal and proceed with a more general model in which presidents may veto legislation, the courts may return wayward agencies to the status quo, and Congress, stylized as a one-house voting body with a gatekeeping committee, may pass laws. All actors have ideal points along a one-dimensional policy space.

Their game theoretic analysis is very much a reflection of its heritage. Attention centers less on bureaucracy than on congressional influence and how it is qualified by presidents and courts. Two themes stand out. The first is that presidents can use the veto to reduce Congress's control and enhance their own. The second is that the courts operate to bolster congressional influence.

This second theme is telling; for under different distributions of ideal points, the courts can also undermine congressional influence. Here and elsewhere, however, positive theorists have emphasized the courts' role as backstoppers of Congress, and this has clearly given impetus (and spin) to the recent integration of courts into the theory. Presidents, who spell trouble for Congress, have been explored less seriously. And with little sympathy. Often, their control is either downplayed or viewed as unwarranted.[3]

While such imbalance is regrettable, there are also good reasons the courts are figuring so prominently in recent attempts to expand the theory. One is that the very success of positive theory has sparked law-and-economics scholars to become active contributors to the literature – and they emphasize the courts. Another is that the courts are pivotal to

---

3. For an interesting line of work, see Kiewiet and McCubbins (1985, 1988). The question of whether to discuss their models here raised another judgment call; I've chosen not to because their focus is on the Congress, the president, and the appropriations process, and only indirectly on bureaucracy.

one of the theory's most fundamental issues: the protection of "original intent" from the ongoing exercise of political control.

This issue was first highlighted, in fact, in an early law-and-economics article by Landes and Posner (1975). Well before Horn and I sought to integrate the notion of political uncertainty into bureaucratic theory, Landes and Posner applied the same reasoning to the courts. If bargaining among groups and politicians is to succeed, they argued, players must anticipate that the deals they strike – their original intent – will be protected from future exercises of political influence. An independent judiciary solves the problem, they say, because it can be counted upon to protect today's deals from tomorrow's influence.

While the basic insight about original intent is profoundly important, the claim about the courts is tenuous. Independent judges may just as well act on their own preferences to violate original intent. Nonetheless, as spatial modelers target the judiciary, they tend to argue that the courts do indeed protect original intent – or at least that they should. The positive and the normative are intermingled.

The current literature's take on courts and presidents is perhaps best reflected in the innovative work of Eskridge and Ferejohn (1992), who show how rational choice theory can be used to assess Supreme Court decisions in two key cases about bureaucracy – *Chadha*, which eliminated the legislative veto, and *Chevron*, which required greater judicial deference to agency discretion. Using spatial models, they argue that the legislative veto and judicial activism are valuable and worth saving, since both protect original intent and limit "excessive" presidential control.

Although this is a provocative step forward, several things are amiss here. They assume congressional preferences do not change over time, when such change is actually the crux of the commitment problem that threatens original intent. Similarly, they downplay the fact that activist judges can violate original intent rather than protect it. And finally, they make the anomolous assumption (given their heritage) that agencies are pawns of the president and thus that agency discretion translates into "excessive" presidential control. This is handy for making their normative case but otherwise has little to justify it.

Ferejohn and Weingast (1992) help to fill these gaps by offering a similar model (without presidents) that explores changing congressional preferences and alternative judicial motivations. They show that it makes a big difference which goals judges pursue and they argue for a "procedurally based jurisprudence" (which judges, of course, may not embrace) that ties decisions to original intent. They also argue that original intent can be protected from changing congressional preferences by means of gatekeeping committees – whose preferences, they assume, remain closer to original intent than the floor's do.

The movement toward a theory of multiple principles is still in its infancy, and even basic questions remain unanswered. But, as this work by Ferejohn and his colleagues suggests, positive theorists have moved well beyond the early dyadic models of congressional control. The next several years will doubtless see rapid progress toward a more general spatial theory.

6.2 Multidimensionality

For simplicity, most spatial models assume that policies are arrayed along a single dimension. A long-standing theme of social choice, however, is that multidimensionality changes things dramatically, to the point where voting processes can lead to chaos in which virtually anything can happen and players with agenda control can engineer "democratic" outcomes much to their own liking (McKelvey 1976).

A small but fascinating part of the spatial modeling literature has explored the consequences of multidimensionality for political control. This work has been framed by the early insights of Jeffrey Hill (1985), who noted that, because Congress makes decisions by majority rule and because many policies can command the support of some majority, a strategic bureau can shift policy away from the original-intent status quo and toward another majority-supported point closer to its own ideal – thus taking advantage of Congress's collective action problems, engineering its agenda and evading control.

Hill's early work has been generalized by Hammond, Hill, and Miller (1986) and Hammond and Knott (1992). Their spatial models are built around multiple principals – the president and one or more legislative houses and committees – and two policy dimensions. What they show is that presidents and agencies can take advantage of Congress's collective action problems and that, as a result, presidential influence and bureau autonomy are greater than the mainstream suggests and congressional control is less. In the process, they shed light on how the appointment power, rarely considered in spatial analyses, promotes the influence of presidents relative to Congress.[4] They also outline the conditions under which the relative influence of the players varies, indicating when claims of congressional control do and do not hold.

This is an important line of work that, perhaps because of its disruptive conclusions, has not had great influence on the mainstream. The typical spatial analysis continues to use one-dimensional models, with Congress and its committees treated as unitary actors who decide and have ideal points just like the others. In a literature so firmly tied to

4. See also Calvert, McCubbins, and Weingast (1989).

social choice, this is odd indeed. If social choice teaches us anything, it is that majority rule and multidimensionality produce collective action problems of great consequence. This theme is precisely what the mainstream shunts aside.

6.3 Transaction costs

Another oddity is equally, if not more, troubling. Although the larger theory of bureaucracy is increasingly based on the new economics of organization, the new economics does not always fit comfortably into the technology of spatial modeling, and, with some exceptions, its central concerns tend to get squeezed out. The result is a spatial theory that often ignores or contradicts the basic tenets of the new economics.

The new economics points us to the transaction costs of exchange. And these costs can be enormous, especially within Congress. Some are due to the collective action problems arising from multidimensionality, majority rule, and the tremendous burdens these entail for bargaining, coordination, and commitment. They are also due to the forbidding number of veto points embedded in the legislative process. Bills must pass through subcommittees, committees, and floors in each house, they must be endorsed in identical form by both, and they are threatened along the way by rules committees, filibusters, holds, and other obstacles. And all this says nothing about technical complexity, uncertainty, time, opportunity costs, and all the usual sources of decision costs.

Spatial models take a few veto points into account and occasionally recognize certain majority rule problems. But the standard assumption is that transaction costs are zero, and thus that ideal points translate directly into policy outcomes. In a world of high transaction costs, all these theories threaten to be grossly at variance with reality. This, indeed, is the central thrust of the new economics: transaction costs change everything. Most obviously, the transaction costs of congressional action are so high that the likely outcome for most proposals, regardless of the distribution of ideal points, is that *nothing will happen*: Congress will be unable to act even when the ideal points suggest it should. Party leaders, committee chairs, and various norms and rules can reduce transaction costs somewhat (Weingast and Marshall 1988; Cox and McCubbins 1993). But the obstacles to legislation remain formidable.

This has far-reaching implications for political control. Among other things, it means that presidents and bureaus can use their executive powers of unilateral action to shift the status quo, and that Congress will often be incapable of responding, whatever the relevant ideal points might suggest. The executive advantage, moreover, goes well beyond what even Hammond and his colleagues suggest, for executives are not restricted to policies that some majority will support. Transaction costs will often prevent majorities from acting, allow tiny minorities to block, and allow presidents and bureaus to get their way by default (Moe and Wilson 1994). By ignoring transaction costs, then, spatial models tend to understate presidential and bureaucratic power and exaggerate congressional power.

More generally, while spatial models are presented as key components of the broader theory of bureaucracy, they are really not in tune with it. In a sense, they are throwbacks to a bygone era, assuming away much of what the new economics shows to be important and making claims about politics that stand up only in a world the new economics disavows. This is not to downplay the progress made thus far. But the conceptual foundations of control models must change considerably if they are to contribute fully to an institutional theory founded on the new economics.

6.4 From spatial models to the new economics

This is beginning to happen, albeit slowly. In part, it is evident in the way certain concepts from the new economics have found their way into spatial theories. More significantly, however, control models have appeared in recent years that take their orientation almost entirely from the new economics. This work is still rather rare, but it is likely to be the wave of the future.

As I noted earlier, new-economics models grew naturally out of the Niskanen tradition, where the spotlight was on how legislatures could make rational budgetary decisions when information is largely controlled by bureaus (Bendor, Taylor, and van Gaalen 1987; Banks 1989; Banks and Weingast 1992). In the broader literature on political control, which traces its roots less to Niskanen than congressional dominance, the new economics has been influential from the beginning – but social choice has framed most of the analytics. This is changing.

Perhaps the most notable effort to date is by Calvert, McCubbins, and Weingast (1989). These authors develop a game theoretic model in which a president and a legislature, as multiple principals, jointly choose the agency head and can individually veto agency actions. Their analysis spotlights control problems central to the new economics (private information and agency drift) and the mechanisms for countering them (monitoring, budgets, firings, and new legislation). In the end, they argue, as elsewhere, that bureaus are securely under political control.

The nemesis of these new-economics models is complexity. They are inherently complicated and their implications threaten to be so hedged about by qualifications and conditions that they are either trivial or difficult to interpret and apply. The most reasonable strategy for coping with these problems is through radical simplification. But this can create problems of its own. Calvert et al. (1989) for instance, follow this strategy by assuming that the legislature is a single unitary actor and that the president and the legislature can costlessly veto anything the agency does – conditions that not only simplify reality but raise questions of how applicable their theory is to anything we should care about.

Much the same is true for the new-economics models arising from the Niskanen tradition. Their rarified treatments capture but a small part of the relationship between legislatures and bureaus (even as it relates to budgets), ignore presidents and other political authorities, but still generate highly complex and conditional conclusions.

Among the newly emerging crop of political control models, moreover, these problems of complexity seem to be growing. Lupia and McCubbins (1994), for example, use a principal-agent framework to explore the connections between legislative learning and bureaucratic design and control. The resulting theory is at once innovative in its analysis of learning, and yet so monstrously complicated and contingent that it is unclear where the innovation takes us.

Finally, while it may appear that not enough is being simplified away, these efforts to build new-economics models of political control nonetheless have an ironic tendency to simplify too much when it comes to core components of the new economics itself. In effect, they often ignore or reject central lessons of the larger theory, with profound consequences for the way political control is understood. Most notably, they downplay the collective action problems and transaction costs that threaten to disable Congress as an actor and that give presidents and bureaus opportunities for gaining influence at Congress's expense.

As far as complexity is concerned, the task for the future is not to avoid simplification, and certainly not to disavow the new economics. The task is to make the right kinds of simplifications, and to preserve the essence of what the new economics identifies as important.

More generally, assuming complexity problems can ultimately be resolved, the overarching task for the future is to bridge the gap that has separated models of political control from the core work on ex ante control, political exchange, and the politics of structural choice. The new-economics models of control open up exciting opportunities for doing just that, for, unlike spatial models, they deal equally well with issues of ex post control and issues of agency design. They can provide the basis, then, for closing the gap and for putting theories of control to far more productive use in fleshing out the contours of a full-blown theory of bureaucratic organization and behavior.

7. Conclusion

All literatures have their problems. And in this case, it is especially important that criticisms not be allowed to get in the way of the most basic point to be made: that public choice has genuinely revolutionized the theory of bureaucracy. By contrast to the baseline it inherited from public administration, which for decades had struggled without much success, the magnitude of progress has already been astonishing.

From the pioneering work of Downs, Tullock, and Ostrom, to Niskanen's path-breaking theory of the budget-maximizing bureau, to Chicago school theories of capture and pluralism, to the more recent theories of political control, exchange, and the politics of structure, public choice has taken great strides toward showing how the fundamentals of politics find reflection in the organization and performance of bureaucracy. And this is only the beginning. The pace of change has picked up considerably with the arrival of the new economics, and the future will surely yield a proliferation of innovative new work.

How much better will the theory of tomorrow allow us to explain bureaucracy? That depends on how successfully the problems of the current literature are addressed. And the most vexing of these have less to do with technical issues (which my colleagues are good at solving) than with matters of broad perspective, which are rooted in the heritage of public choice and are not so easily changed.

For many years, social choice theory has occupied center stage within the field and, in subtle but pervasive ways, set its intellectual agenda by framing the way issues are approached and understood. Since the new institutionalism, theorists have proceeded in normal-science fashion, moving outward from a legislative core to take in the rest of the system, starting with the bureaucracy. The trajectory makes good sense, of course. And it may eventually prove the most effective path to progress. But for the time being, it has produced a theory that sees the political world through legislative lenses and makes excessive claims about legislative power.

In this view of the world, the bureaucracy is an interesting subject for theory because it is delegated legislative authority and is an object of legislative control. Presidents are relevant because they can veto legislation. Courts come into play because they can backstop legislative deals. All are "understood" in legislative perspective. And all are secondary in importance and power to the legislature.

The kind of progress we most need, it seems to me, is movement toward a more balanced understanding of public bureaucracy and its fit with other political institutions. This, in turn, calls for certain kinds of new work. It calls for serious attention to the presidency and the courts as full-fledged institutions in their own right, with powers, motivations, and organizational properties that are profoundly important to an explanation of bureaucracy and control. Legislatures, too, need to be more fully explored, but especially with reference to the downside of legislative power: the transaction costs and collective action problems that make it difficult for legislatures to take strong action on their own behalf and render them vulnerable to exploitation by others.

And then there is the bureaucracy itself, which, given the legislative bent of mainstream theory, has received less attention than one might think. Too often, bureaucratic theories are really not pursued for what they can tell us about bureaucracy, but rather for what they can tell us about how much power Congress and other authorities have and what mechanisms they employ to get their way. Bureaucracy is treated as little more than a means to these more important ends and not as an institution worthy of intensive explanation in its own right. This has to change. A theory of bureaucracy will never succeed if it is really designed to do something else.

Perspective is what guides research, and research along these lines is likely to come slowly as long as the legislative perspective continues to dominate. But it will surely come, as theorists continue to branch out from their legislative base. And I suspect it will grow considerably with time, as the new economics gains the upper hand in its friendly struggle with social choice and, through its abstract approach to the fundamentals of organization, promotes a more broadly based theory in which voting and legislatures have no inherent methodological attraction.

CHAPTER 22

The political economy of taxation

WALTER HETTICH AND STANLEY L. WINER

1. Introduction

Taxation enables governments to draw resources from the private sector, thus creating the basis for effective political power, a fact pointed out forcefully many years ago by Joseph Schumpeter (1918), who traced the creation of the modern state to the emergence of the power to tax. To understand the functioning of the public economy, it is essential to know how governments make use of this power and how they shape and employ different tax instruments to achieve their political and economic aims.

Statistical information on the public sector reveals that there is much to be explained. Significant differences in the design of revenue systems and in the use of tax instruments exist among developed nations, as well as among states and provinces in countries with decentralized public sectors, such as the United States and Canada. We also find changing characteristics of tax systems over the course of economic development and frequent adjustments in the structure of taxation in response to short-term economic and political shocks.

Although the tax literature is large, most of it does not explain these facts. Traditionally, public finance has focused on normative questions, often within a framework that makes no allowance for political institutions and for choices of public decision makers who pursue their own ends. The role of explaining differences in the use and composition of taxation thus falls to public choice, which acknowledges the importance of utility maximization by private and public agents and provides explicit models designed to investigate collective decisions. Taxation provides an ideal testing ground for public choice theories since significant analytical questions are at stake and excellent quantitative data can be drawn upon.

Financial support of the Social Sciences and Humanities Research Council of Canada is gratefully acknowledged. We would like to thank the editor, Tim Besley, and Joel Slemrod for helpful comments.

This article analyzes tax structure, where taxation is defined to include borrowing. The discussion pays particular attention to the explanation of broad characteristics of tax systems, of the equilibrium mix of tax instruments and of overall patterns of public revenues. One may object to the limited scope since policymakers have other tools available, some of which, such as regulation, may at times serve as substitutes for taxation. Furthermore, taxation is related to expenditures and to the determination of budget size. While these links are acknowledged, we restrict the subject matter as much as possible to tax or revenue structure to keep it within manageable bounds. This narrower focus is also desirable in the service of constructing a more effective theoretical framework and of tying it to empirical research.

2. Models of political economy

Explaining tax structure requires a theoretical framework that specifies how political choices are made and shows their interaction with the private economy. There are several characteristics that make a model of political economy attractive for the task. It is desirable that the analysis be able to accommodate multidimensional choices. Decisions on tax structure, such as the simultaneous determination of tax rates on income and consumption, or on capital and labor, involve competing issues of collective choice and cannot be analyzed in a single dimension. The model should also have a well-defined and stable equilibrium making it possible to employ comparative static analysis, the most widely used and successful approach in economic theory.

Most political models of taxation assume the existence of certain democratic institutions, such as the right of citizens to participate in competitive elections. This is similar to the treatment of property rights in the analysis of the private sector, where such rights are generally taken as given. Among available models, expected vote maximization appears most suited to deal with tax structure in a democratic setting (Coughlin 1992, 224). It satisfies the desirable characteristics mentioned above and can be adapted to deal with various problems of agent control and representative government. The model differs from other approaches by treating voting choices as probabilistic and by assuming that candidates maximize expected plurality or expected votes, while being uncertain of how voters will respond to their platforms. Competition for office continually pressures political actors to search for policies that ensure electoral success. This competitive process also determines the behavior of the governing party or government, which formulates tax and other policies so as to maximize the number of votes expected in the next election.[1] Tax structure can thus be viewed as representing an equilibrium strategy adopted as part of a competitive political process.

A second approach frequently used is the median or decisive voter model (e.g., Romer 1975; Roberts 1977). The analysis assumes that voters are presented with competing alternatives and that they support the one yielding the highest utility. Existence of equilibrium and stability can be established only if choice falls into a single dimension and if voter preferences concerning the issue are single peaked. As long as behavior is nonstrategic, the alternative preferred by the median voter must win. Median voter analysis can be combined with agenda setting by giving bureaucratic decision makers the power to choose the alternatives faced by voters, although the source of such power is not explained within the model. While the median voter framework can be used to examine certain selected issues of tax policy, it is not designed to deal with the broader aspects of tax structure that are inherently multidimensional.

The problem of potential instability of outcomes or cycling arises in all multidimensional models of majority choice that treat voting decisions as discrete rather than probabilistic. This has led some political economists to ask why actual policy outcomes are so rarely reversed in practice and why cycling seems an infrequent occurrence in the real world. A possible answer concerns the role of institutions. Some analysts argue that equilibria are enforced by the political rules of the game or by the accepted context within which alternatives can be offered for collective choice (Shepsle and Weingast 1981). Those who adopt this view analyze the working of particular institutions, such as the U.S. Congress, and relate parliamentary rules, committee structures, and other aspects of institutional design to the nature and stability of policy outcomes. The difficulty lies in linking institutional characteristics to specific aspects of tax structure and in generating hypotheses that can encompass a variety of institutional arrangements, a challenge that has been met so far only with partial success.

A quite different approach to the modeling of government disregards voting procedures as effective constraints on political action and pictures the state as Leviathan, with taxes used by those in power to maximize total revenue from the private sector (Brennan and Buchanan 1980). Since taxpayers have no political control, rate–revenue relationships or Laffer curves, representing the adjustment of private economic activity to taxation and attempts to evade it, are the only force restraining tax

---

1. See, for example, Mayhew (1974) and Denzau and Munger (1986). Since plurality maximization and vote maximization lead to the same policy choices in the absence of abstention, we shall refer only to vote maximization.

design and budget size. The model does not specify how agents join the group wielding power and what determines the stability and existence of the dictatorial political equilibrium. However, the simple objective function that is postulated allows the explicit derivation of a detailed tax structure consistent with the goals of a monopoly government and makes possible comparisons with predictions derived from models based on electoral choice.

3. Tax structure in expected vote maximization

3.1 Policy equilibrium

Explaining the creation of tax systems is part of the broader question of how governments choose policy instruments and policy outcomes. There are four essential elements in this process: the goals pursued by the government, or governing party; the reactions by the voters to the impact of the policies; the framework of political competition within which the government's strategies are determined; and the constraints imposed by the general equilibrium structure of the private economy.

All of these elements are present in the model of expected vote maximization.[2] Competition for office forces each party to choose a vector of policies (s) so as to continually maximize expected political support S, which depends on the effects of these policies on voter utility. Total support can be expressed as $S = S(s,x)$, where x represents exogenous factors affecting S, including the given policies favored by opposing parties, and where a budget constraint and a relationship representing the resources and behavioral responses in the private economy are part of the model's structure and have been substituted into the support function.

Existence of a Nash equilibrium in the electoral game requires that $S(s,x)$ be continuous in the space of all policies. This condition may be satisfied if we interpret S as the party's expected vote in the next election and treat voting as probabilistic.[3] Assume that the probability π_i of a voter's support depends on utility obtained, which in turn depends on s and x. Then, if π_i is continuous in s and x, support (consisting of the sum of voter probabilities) must also be continuous. Uniqueness of the Nash equilibrium requires that $S(s, x)$ be strictly concave in s and strictly convex in the policies of the opposition.

---

2. The original formulation is in Downs (1957). For a modern formalization, see Enelow and Hinich (1984), Ledyard (1984), and Coughlin (1992).

3. For a further discussion of the assumptions required for the existence of an equilibrium in a probabilistic voting model, see Coughlin (1992) and Enelow and Hinich (1989). A clear exposition is also given in chapter 11 of Mueller (1989).

In the development of the theory of tax structure, the aim has been to characterize the nature of fiscal policy choices made by participants in a competitive electoral system, where voters have heterogeneous tastes and interests, rather than to find the solution to a particular electoral game. This can be achieved by examining how the government or governing party creates tax instruments and shapes the revenue system to maximize expected support as part of its continuous effort to remain in power. One should note that opposition parties pursue an analogous process in designing their competing fiscal platforms. However, to simplify exposition, we refer only to the government or governing party in the following discussion.

3.2 The formation of tax structure

Imagine a fiscal system where the government provides one public good G and imposes N proportional tax rates t_i, one for each voter, applied to the activity representing that voter's tax base B_i. Assume that the probability of support from any voter π_i can be written as a function of the difference I_i between component b_i, reflecting the voter's valuation of public services, and a second component c_i, representing the loss in full income from taxation, including excess burden. Hence

$$\pi_i = f_i(I_i); \; i = 1, 2, \ldots, N \tag{1}$$

where $I_i = b_i - c_i$ and $c_i = T_i + d_i$, with T_i ($T_i = t_i \cdot B_i$) being the ith voter's tax payment and d_i the dollar equivalent of his welfare loss from taxation.[4] Assume also that b_i depends only on G, and that c_i is independent of G. The expected total vote or support is

$$S = \sum_{i=1}^{N} \pi_i = \sum_{i=1}^{N} f_i(I_i). \tag{2}$$

The structure of the private economy enters through B_i and d_i. Assuming that activities of different taxpayers are independent and G does not affect any tax base, we can write for each i:

$$B_i = B_i(t_i, x_i); \; \partial B_i/\partial t_i < 0 \tag{3a}$$

$$d_i = d_i(t_i, x_i); \; \partial d_i/\partial t_i > 0 \tag{3b}$$

---

4. The model is a modification of Hettich and Winer (1988). In the present formulation, $f_i(I_i) = f_i(b_i - c_i)$ equals the probability of voting and is explicitly incorporated into the model. Note that f_i now translates the net fiscal surplus I_i into a probability of voting.

where x_i represents exogenous factors such as the voter's taste for leisure and the costs of tax avoidance and evasion activities.

In the absence of administration costs, the government's problem is to choose tax rates $t_1, t_2, \ldots, t_N$ and the level of the public good G to maximize expected total support (2) subject to the budget constraint

$$G = \sum_{i=1}^{N} t_i \cdot B_i. \tag{4}$$

Assuming that all available fiscal instruments are used, the first order conditions include

$$\frac{\partial f_i / \partial I_i \cdot \partial c_i / \partial t_i}{B_i(1 + \epsilon_i)} = \lambda; \quad i = 1, 2, \ldots, N \tag{5a}$$

where $\epsilon_i = \partial B_i / \partial t_i \cdot t_i / B_i$ is the elasticity of base B_i with respect to t_i and λ is the Lagrange multiplier associated with the government budget constraint, and

$$\sum_{i=1}^{N} \frac{\partial f_i}{\partial I_i} \cdot \frac{\partial b_i}{\partial G} = \lambda. \tag{5b}$$

Condition (5a) indicates that whatever the level of public services may be, the government adjusts tax rates among voters until the reduction in expected votes or marginal political cost (MPC) of raising an additional dollar, that is, the left side of (5a), is equalized across taxpayers. In other words, the politically optimal tax structure minimizes total political costs for any given level of revenues collected. The second condition shows that the governing party adjusts the aggregate size of government until the marginal political benefit of spending another dollar on public services is equal to the common MPC.

The solution is presented in Figure 1 for the case with two taxpayers, where it is assumed that the political cost of, or opposition to, taxation is independent of the level of the public good. We imagine that the taxable activity for both is gainful employment and that they differ in their tastes for leisure and in the ease with which they can trade off leisure for work. As a result, they have different Laffer curves or rate-revenue relationships, shown in the lower part of panels 1a and 1b. They also vary in political tastes, that is, in the intensity with which they react to the loss of a dollar in full income by reducing expected support (depicted by differently shaped marginal political cost functions). The government is assumed to have full knowledge of all functions.

Panel 1c shows the determination of budget size. The MPC curve is

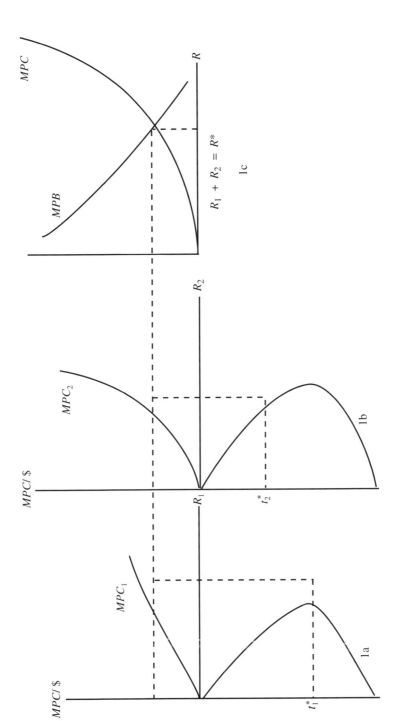

Figure 1. Tax structure in political equilibrium.

the horizontal addition of marginal political cost functions, while
marginal political benefits (MPB) equal the vertical sum of individual
marginal political benefit functions, being expressed per dollar of expenditure. The desired budget is R^* and must be raised jointly from
the two individuals.[5]

The analysis indicates that the resulting tax structure is complex, with
as many different tax rates as there are individuals. Complexity is increased further if we allow each taxpayer to conduct J taxable activities,
with $j = 1, 2, \ldots, J$ and $B_{ij} = B_{ij}(t_{i1}, t_{i2}, \ldots, t_{iJ}, x_i)$. Equations (4) and
(5a) now become:

$$G = \sum_{i=1}^{N} \sum_{j=1}^{J} t_{ij} \cdot B_{ij} \qquad (4')$$

$$\frac{\partial f_i / \partial I_i \cdot \partial c_i / \partial t_{ij}}{B_{ij}(1 + \epsilon_{ij}) + \Sigma_{k \neq j} t_{ik} \cdot \partial B_{ik} / \partial t_{ij}} = \lambda; \; i = 1, 2, \ldots, N; \qquad (5a')$$
$$j = 1, 2, \ldots, J.$$

The new solution involves $N \times J$ tax rates, one for each separate activity
conducted by every different taxpayer. We can use Figure 1 to illustrate
the differentiated treatment of activities by reinterpreting the diagrams
as referring to a single taxpayer and two of his taxable activities, each of
which has a different rate-revenue relationship and marginal political
cost function associated with it. To raise any fixed amount of revenue at
minimum political costs, the government equalizes MPC per dollar of
revenue, imposing two different tax rates that reflect the factors shaping
the curves in each of the two panels.

3.3 Tax structure and administration costs

A tax system that treats every taxpayer and each of his activities differently would be very difficult and costly to implement. The government
may reduce complexity in order to economize on administration and
enforcement costs, since such spending reduces its ability to provide the
public good valued positively by voters.

It seems reasonable that the costs of tax administration increase with
the number of tax rates (see also Yitzhaki 1979). Cost savings can be
achieved by sorting individuals into tax brackets within which all individuals face the same rate. However, there is also a drawback to grouping. Marginal political costs per dollar of revenue will now vary among

---

5. Drawing the MPB and MPC curves independently implies that G does not enter into
   (5a).

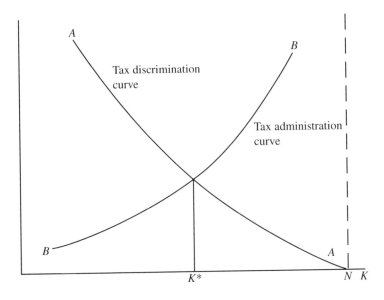

Figure 2. The politically optimal number of rate brackets.

individuals within each group (and also among groups), implying increased total political costs for any given budget.

Sorting requires the government to perform a balancing act: it must create the optimal number of groups while correctly allocating taxpayers among them. This is illustrated in Figure 2, showing a tax discrimination curve, relating the marginal loss in support from optimally grouping individuals to the number of groups K (Hettich and Winer 1988). The tax administration curve links K to the marginal gain in support from increased output of the public good made possible by savings in administration costs. Movement to the right along the horizontal axis implies a rising number of groups and, therefore, a lower degree of sorting. As K increases, the total loss in support is reduced through more differentiated treatment of taxpayers. The marginal reduction in loss is larger where K is small, resulting in a negative slope for the tax discrimination curve. On the other hand, a more differentiated tax structure leads to greater administration costs, with incremental costs increasing as K and the degree of complexity of the system grow, suggesting a positive slope for the tax administration curve. The equilibrium number of groups K^* is determined by the intersection of the two curves.

We have illustrated the sorting analysis with regard to the formation of rate brackets. The methodology can also be used to understand the creation of tax bases. Grouping taxable activities into bases economizes on administration costs, while at the same time increasing the political costs of raising a given amount of revenues. Thus, the optimal number and size of tax bases can be understood as an endogenous outcome, determined by the equilibrium of the sorting process.

An extension of the grouping argument can explain special tax provisions, such as exemptions, deductions, and credits. We have discussed the sorting of taxpayers and activities as separate processes, implying that tax bases can be defined differently for each taxpayer. A further reduction in administration costs can be achieved by standardizing bases across individuals. As before, this leads to a loss in support from those individuals who are now treated less favorably. We can restore some of the lost variation by giving them a deduction or exemption. The use of special provisions thus allows the government to achieve a higher degree of politically desirable differentiation among taxpayers, while standardizing the definition of tax bases across individuals.[6]

3.4 The relation between tax and expenditure structure

In the discussion of Figure 1 and in Section 3, the tax and expenditure sides are linked only through the budget constraint and the endogenous determination of budget size, while opposition to taxation does not depend on the level of the public good. A further link is created if we make tax bases and welfare losses from taxation dependent on public expenditures by including G in equations (3a) and (3b) (Kiesling 1990). In this case, the first order conditions for support maximization (5a) and (5a′) depend on G, and the amended condition corresponding to (5b) implies that the political costs of raising tax rates to finance another dollar of G are now less in the case of a public good that is complementary to the private activities on which the additional taxes are imposed.

It can be argued that the original formulation of the probability of voting, when accepted in its full generality, already implies an explicit connection between the size of the public sector and the choice of tax structure. Since voters' net evaluations of the public sector I_i depend on G, the numerator of the left side of (5a) will in general be a function of G. The formal implications of this for the sorting process and the resulting tax structure have not yet been established.

One can imagine how the link between expenditures and taxes may

---

6. Unlike the explanations for special provisions that are offered in the normative literature, this reasoning does not depend on consideration of such provisions as a hidden substitute for public expenditures or as a means of subsidizing favored private activities.

operate in practice. Assume two groups of individuals having low and high evaluations of the public good. Holding other things constant, the low demanders pay a lower tax rate than the high demanders, whereas in the simpler case shown in Figures 1 and 2, differences in such evaluations do not influence tax rates since only the sum of marginal evaluations is of importance. In the more complex world, the government trades off the gain in support from discriminating according to net evaluations against the loss in support resulting from lower public goods output caused by higher administration costs. As before, unlike individuals are grouped together and discrimination is imperfect in equilibrium.

While the formal analysis assumes that the government knows the characteristics relevant for sorting, considerable cost differences in discriminating effectively among heterogeneous individuals on the two sides of the budget may exist in practice. Information on individual characteristics on the tax side is easier to acquire than knowledge of benefit evaluations. One can therefore imagine a government initially creating a tax structure on the assumption that support is independent of the level of G and subsequently amending it for certain broad classes of individuals having similar evaluations of public output. For example, persons over sixty-five may be given a special exemption to acknowledge a lower evaluation of expenditures on physical and human capital. We expect the cost of reformulating tax bases to exceed the cost of creating new special provisions. As a result, the direct link between expenditures and taxes via the influence of net evaluations of the fiscal system on voting behavior may appear primarily through the introduction of special provisions.

4. Tax structure in alternatives to expected vote maximization

In a world where vote-maximizing political parties compete for office, tax structure will be complex, consisting of a system of interdependent elements similar to those observed in actual tax systems including multiple bases, rates, and special provisions, with the structure and level of taxation being determined endogenously. The median voter model does not deal with such complexity, being restricted to policy choices in one dimension. In analyzing taxation with this model, a partial approach must be chosen where only one parameter is allowed to vary, with the rest assumed to be given from outside the model, or where sufficient restrictions are imposed to generate single-peaked preferences with respect to a feasible set of multidimensional tax schedules.

In seminal contributions, Romer (1975) and Roberts (1977) assume the existence of a linear progressive income tax on a given base, together with a predetermined level of public goods, and investigate the choice of the marginal tax rate when voters are differentiated by ability. Choice of the rate together with the government budget constraint determines the level of transfers received by voters who do not make positive tax payments. If average income exceeds median income, and given conditions under which preferences are single peaked with respect to tax rates, the voter with the median ability demands and receives a positive marginal tax rate. The exact rate chosen, and thus the degree of redistribution, depends on assumptions about the size of government and the elasticity of labor supply. As government size increases, the higher marginal rate needed to balance the budget generates larger deadweight losses, while larger elasticities of labor result in greater excess burdens. The rising losses in full income dampen the median voter's desire for redistribution.

Meltzer and Richard (1981) endogenize the size of government in this framework by assuming that all expenditures are for redistributive purposes. Once the single tax rate is determined by the median voter, the level of redistributive transfers is given by the government budget constraint. In the aggregate, the extent of redistribution is limited by work disincentives.

Some authors have attempted to extend the median voter result to the explanation of nonlinear marginal tax schedules that cannot be characterized by one tax rate (Snyder and Kramer 1988; Cukierman and Meltzer 1991; Berliant and Gouveia 1993). The problem in making such an extension is that the set of feasible tax schedules is very large, both in number and dimension, implying a multidimensional issue space over which voting occurs. In such situations, and in the absence of probabilistic voting, majority rule equilibrium is unlikely to exist. Authors who attempt to solve these problems in a median voter context specify conditions under which preferences are single peaked over the set of individually optimal nonlinear tax schedules.[7]

Research based on the framework of structure-induced equilibria starts with the existence of particular political institutions (Shepsle and Weingast 1981). An example is the work by Inman and Fitts (1990), who focus on universalism as a norm to overcome political instability, with each legislator agreeing to support the allocations preferred by every

---

7. The work surveyed so far assumes the existence of redistributive fiscal institutions. There is some research, initiated by Aumann and Kurz (1977), that explores the birth of redistributive fiscal systems using cooperative game theory. Fear of ruin in the redistributive game is an important determinant of marginal tax rates. Gardner (1981) examines the effects of changing the rule defining the characteristics of a winning coalition. Peck (1986) introduces work disincentives and shows that marginal tax rates may fall below 50 percent.

other member of the legislative body (see also Weingast 1979 and Snyder 1993). As long as benefits are concentrated within particular districts, while taxes are spread over a wider constituency, the norm leads to larger budgets and more extensive use of special tax provisions (or tax expenditures) than would occur with no decision externalities. Although the approach shows promise, it has not yet been extended to deal with the general nature of tax structure or with the specific influence of institutional features such as congressional committees on actual tax design.

Unlike the other approaches, the Leviathan model assumes that the state is unconstrained by majority rule and has unlimited power to tax private activity (Brennan and Buchanan 1980). The logic underlying the choice of tax structure is that of price discrimination, limited only by the existence of Laffer curves. Leviathan prefers broad tax bases because they minimize the possibility for tax avoidance and levies higher rates on less elastic bases to maximize revenues. Special provisions can expand discrimination. Although administration costs and the endogenous formation of bases and special provisions have generally not been discussed in the literature,[8] it appears that a tax structure chosen by Leviathan would be multidimensional, containing all the basic elements observed in actual tax systems. As mentioned earlier, the source of Leviathan's power and the stability of the dictatorial equilibrium have not been explained.

5. Taxing the future

So far the discussion has ignored the time profile of taxes. Generalizing the analysis to deal with intertemporal issues adds substantial complexity: intertemporal preferences of voters and of politicians become relevant, and the consistency over time of tax policies by successive governments becomes important.

While the time profiles of *all* revenue sources are of concern to voters and to politicians, the treatment of intertemporal issues can be simplified by separating revenue sources into public debt, having an explicit intertemporal character, and taxation of current activity, connected to debt finance primarily through the government budget constraint (which now includes the deficit as a source of funds, and interest payments on outstanding debt as a use of funds).

The extensive literature on debt finance cannot readily be classified according to modeling tradition. For this reason, this section is orga-

---

8. An exception is Wilson (1989) who explicitly incorporates administration costs into a Leviathan model following Yitzhaki (1979).

nized by major issues. None of the models introduced so far have been extended to encompass all the relevant factors underlying debt finance. A fully comprehensive model will deal with the following issues.[9]

The relationship between debt finance and the excess burden of taxation. Any government concerned with the welfare of its citizens issues debt to smooth current tax rates over the business cycle (Barro 1979, 1986). Since the excess burden of current taxation rises with the square of tax rates, issuing debt when current tax revenues temporarily decline, and retiring debt when revenues are high, results in lower overall excess burden than a policy of adjusting rates to balance the budget in every period.[10]

The same government increases reliance on deficit financing over the business cycle, if growth is expected to increase in the long run. Shifting the composition of revenues toward a more rapidly growing tax base – in this example, future economic activity – permits the government to raise the same total revenue with a lower overall excess burden (Hettich and Winer 1984).

Heterogeneity of preferences for public goods and the commitment problem. Voters cannot be sure that future majorities share their preferences for public goods. This, coupled with the difficulty of committing future governments to a policy chosen in the present, provides a complementary explanation for debt finance (Persson and Svenson 1989; Persson and Tabellini 1990; Tabellini and Alesina 1990).[11] For example, voters in a presently dominant coalition who favor a small public sector, and who anticipate that more liberal governments will be elected in the near future, may vote for more public borrowing today to constrain the size of the public sector in the future.[12]

This motivation for debt finance introduces another link between the revenue and expenditure sides of the budget. Incorporating this ratio-

---

9. For more extensive discussion of these issues and additional references to the literature, see Ingberman and Inman (1988), Persson and Tabellini (1990), and Alesina and Tabellini (1992).

10. Consideration of the time profile of consumption may also explain the use of debt finance. Politicians may issue debt when undertaking public investment to smooth current tax payments and hence the disposable income of taxpayers. A government may also find it politically profitable to use its greater borrowing power in bad economic times to help the liquidity-constrained voter smooth his or her consumption over time.

11. For further discussion of the commitment problem and the time-consistency of revenue structure, see for example, Fischer (1980) and Lucas and Stokey (1983).

12. Tabellini and Alesina (1990) suggest that reliance on debt finance will increase with the likelihood of disagreement between current and future voters.

nale requires the introduction of heterogeneity in preferences for public goods. In addition, a more sophisticated definition of equilibrium is required, where all agents behave rationally given current *and* expected future policies, and where in each period the equilibrium policy satisfies the government's objective in that period.[13]

The role of intergenerational conflict. Conflict between generations reflects another aspect of heterogeneity among voters to be recognized in any comprehensive vote maximization model. Voters who do not plan to leave any positively valued bequests may support deficit financing (Buchanan and Roback 1987; Cukierman and Meltzer 1989). Assuming that debt obligations are honored, such voters can use debt finance to increase their own consumption while reducing their bequests below zero by the present value of the future tax liabilities.[14] Even in the absence of bequest-constraints, a coalition of current voters may appropriate resources from future generations in a similar fashion (see, for example, Tabellini 1991 and the references cited therein). The conditions under which governments do or do not honor debt obligations inherited from the past is a central issue in this framework.

Debt finance and the nature of political institutions. An important relationship between debt finance and the degree to which political power is fragmented has been suggested (Alesina and Drazen 1991; Roubini and Sachs 1989).[15] When fragmented systems are subjected to unfavorable economic shocks, politicians may find it difficult to agree on the increases in current taxation required to prevent large deficits.

A quite different argument centers on the consequences of voter myopia for the choice among revenue sources (Buchanan and Wagner 1977). Since a balanced budget policy of cutting taxes and issuing debt involves immediate benefits for taxpayers, while raising taxes to retire debt involves short-run costs, democratic systems may contain an inherent bias towards deficit financing when voters are myopic about the longer-term consequences of public financing decisions. Incorporating this explanation for debt finance requires that the working of political institutions be explicitly modeled, a challenging task in any tradition.

---

13. For further discussion of the definition of an equilibrium, see Persson and Tabellini (1990, 155).
14. Cukierman and Meltzer (1989) argue that reliance on debt finance is greater the larger the fraction of individuals with a relatively small part of total wealth, since in this case the fraction of the population that wishes to leave negative bequests is larger.
15. Fragmentation may involve dispersion of power across branches of government as in the United States or across members of the governing coalitions that typically exist in countries that use proportional representation.

6. Empirical research on the political economy of tax structure[16]

The different branches of the empirical literature on tax structure can be distinguished by the underlying theoretical models. A substantial body of work is based on vote maximization.[17] In addition, there is empirical work relying on the median voter model, the Leviathan model, and the structure-induced equilibrium tradition. Finally, there is a branch that does not use collective choice models, but views tax structure as chosen to maximize the welfare of a representative citizen or to minimize the aggregate welfare cost of taxation.

To investigate the empirical literature, it is helpful to consider a stylized vote maximization model and the associated estimating equations. Assume that competition for office forces the government to choose a revenue structure $s = \{s_1, s_2, \ldots, s_K\}$ and the level of a public good G to maximize expected support or votes S continually. The vector s, defined to contain only nonnegative elements, includes all aspects of revenue structure such as tax bases and rates, special provisions, and the stock of public debt. The expected vote function $S = \Sigma_i \, n_i \cdot \pi_i$ is defined over N groups of voters, each consisting of an exogenously determined number (n_i) of relatively homogeneous members.[18] The probability that a representative taxpayer in group i votes for the government, π_i, depends on the way his indirect utility v_i is affected by fiscal structure, by a vector of endogenous variables $z(s,G)$ that are partly determined by the choice of s and G (including aspects of intergovernmental fiscal relations)[19], and by a vector of exogenous variables x.

The government's optimization is subject to a budget constraint, $G = R - A$, where R is total revenues from all sources and A is total administration costs.[20] Optimization is also subject to the general equilibrium structure of the economy and fiscal relationships with other governments, written schematically as $F(s,G,z,x) = 0$.

---

16. Due to space constraints, the review of empirical research in this section is selective and references to the literature are intended to be only illustrative.
17. Empirical work based on van Winden's (1983) interest function, which is a weighted sum of voter utilities with weights reflecting effective political influence, is similar to that based on vote maximization.
18. The appearance of interest groups in this formulation follows Coughlin, Mueller, and Murrell (1990a, 1990b).
19. Suppose that we are modeling the choice of tax structure by a province or state in a federal system. Then the vector z will include the tax-price of public goods provided by the central government. As a result of the relationship between the tax systems of the two levels of government, this tax-price may be affected by the revenue structure chosen by the state government. See, for example, Feldstein and Metcalf (1987).
20. Total revenues R may be interpreted to include borrowing net of interest payments.

In summary, the government's problem is:

$$\max_{\{s, G\}} S = \sum_{i=1}^{N} n_i \cdot \pi_i(v_i) \; ; \; v_i = v_i(s, G, z, x) \tag{6a}$$

subject to

$$G = R\,(s,\, z,\, x) - A\,(s,\, z,\, x), \tag{6b}$$

$$F\,(s,\, G,\, z,\, x) = 0 \tag{6c}$$

$$s_j \geq 0, j = 1, 2, \ldots, K \; ; G > 0. \tag{6d}$$

The first order conditions include

$$-\frac{\partial}{\partial s_j}(S - \mu F) \,/\, \frac{\partial}{\partial s_j}(R - A) \geq \lambda \; ; \; s_j \geq 0; j = 1, 2, \ldots, K \tag{7a}$$

$$\frac{\partial}{\partial G}(S - \mu F) = \lambda; \; G > 0 \tag{7b}$$

where λ is the Lagrange multiplier associated with the budget constraint and μ is the multiplier associated with the general equilibrium structure. Implementing the politically optimal tax structure requires that fiscal instruments be adjusted until the marginal effect on expected votes per dollar of net revenue (net of administration costs) is equalized across all fiscal instruments in use. The inequalities in (7a) acknowledge that because of high fixed political costs or for other reasons, some feasible instruments may not be used, a fact that may complicate empirical applications of the model.

One way of representing the solution to the first order conditions, assuming that it exists, is by a set of simultaneous semireduced form equations of the following kind:

$$s_j = s_j(s_1, s_2, \ldots, s_{j-1}, s_{j+1}, \ldots, s_K, G, z, n_1, n_2, \ldots, n_N, x)$$
$$s_j \geq 0; j = 1, 2, \ldots, K \tag{8a}$$

$$G = G(s_1, s_2, \ldots, s_K, z, n_1, n_2, \ldots, n_N, x) \; ; G > 0. \tag{8b}$$

While these equations may seem very general, they are far from the most general representation possible. In particular, the model has been simplified by suppressing expenditure structure and the link between the tax and expenditure sides of the budget. Moreover, the instruments s_j are assumed to be already formed and do not emerge from the sorting process described in the previous section.

Existing empirical research on tax structure in the vote maximization tradition can be surveyed according to how estimating equations (8) have been operationalized. Some authors have estimated a system of equations, where the dependent variables are different revenue sources or the corresponding revenue shares. Examples include Pommerehne and Schneider (1983) where the revenue structure of Australian national governments is explained; Inman's (1989) model of fiscal structure in U.S. cities; the analyses by Chernick (1992) and Hunter and Nelson (1989) of U.S. state revenues; and Winer and Hettich's (1991) model of revenue composition in nineteenth-century Canada.

Other studies in the vote-maximizing tradition analyze particular parts of a larger revenue system. Examples include Moomau and Morton (1992) on property taxation and Winer and Hettich (1992), who consider the relationship between reliance on income taxation by U.S. states and the existence of a state income tax deduction for the payment of local property tax. Kenny and Toma (1992b) examine the choice between income taxation and the inflation tax in the United States.

Empirical research based on the median voter framework results in estimating equations that are quite similar to those found in vote-maximization studies (Sjoquist 1981; Gade and Adkins 1990; Goodspeed 1992). This should not be surprising since the model has the same basic structure as equations (7) except that the objective function is replaced by the utility function of the median voter. The same holds for representative agent models not based on a collective choice mechanism where the objective function is replaced by the utility function of a representative citizen. Most of this work (Feldstein and Metcalf 1987; Metcalf 1993) investigates the tax structure of U.S. states. Finally, the similarity extends to estimating equations reflecting the view that governments minimize the aggregate welfare cost of taxation. Research based on this assumption includes Barro's (1979, 1986) investigations of debt and tax smoothing, as well as papers by Mankiw (1987), Poterba and Rotemberg (1990), and Trehan and Walsh (1990) on the choice between seigniorage and current taxation.

Vote maximization, median voter, and representative agent models are not observationally equivalent, however, when differences among voters are acknowledged. Heterogeneity plays a significant role only in the vote maximization approach. Distinguishing between models thus hinges on consideration of how differences in preferences or political influence among voters affect tax structure. Investigating this issue fully requires that more structure be placed on the underlying models and thereby on the estimating equations than has typically been the case.

One way of investigating the importance of heterogeneity in political influence is to include as regressors the size (n_i) of various interest groups and proxies for the potential gains or losses from the policy process. Econometric studies adopting this approach include Renaud and van Winden (1987) and Inman (1993) as well as many of the vote maximization studies cited earlier. Although this work is partially successful, empirical results concerning the role of interest groups are not very strong.

The problem may be partly attributable to the difficulties of appropriately representing interest groups in an estimating equation (Winer and Hettich 1991). Interest group size, which appears in the stylized model, may not be an adequate proxy for interest group influence since effective influence may depend on additional factors such as wealth. Measures of the potential gains or losses of various groups are not necessarily correlated with effective influence either and are often difficult to use because of correlation with aggregate economic factors that also appear as regressors.

Qualitative and historical, as opposed to econometric, evidence concerning the role of special interest groups seems to be more definitive. Studies by Witte (1985), Martin (1991), and Mueller (1990) on the evolution of tax structure in the United States, by Gillespie (1991) on the evolution of tax structure in Canada, and by Webber and Wildavsky (1986) on world tax history suggest strongly that some groups are more influential than others. It is a matter for concern for both sides when the applied econometricians have such a hard time capturing what astute students of tax history regard as obvious.

The role of interest groups aside, investigations using the vote maximization and representative agent frameworks have identified three types of variables that often play a statistically significant role in the determination of revenue composition in democratic states. First, revenue composition in any political jurisdiction depends on the relative size of alternative potential tax bases, with relatively larger or faster growing bases being relied upon more extensively.[21] Second, revenue composition depends on the extent to which tax burdens can be shifted to other jurisdictions, with sources of revenue that permit shifting being favored.[22] A third significant factor in the determination of tax structure is interjurisdictional tax competition. A debate is emerging over the modeling of such competition

21. This result is consistent with the view that increasing reliance on relatively faster growing or larger bases keeps tax rates and excess burdens to a minimum. It may also be consistent with the view that spreading the tax on a large base minimizes political opposition to taxation by reducing the burden any single taxpayer bears relative to the costs of organizing opposition.

22. Shifting can be accomplished through the taxation of interjurisdictional trade or by strategically adjusting revenue structure to make use of interjurisdictional fiscal arrangements. For example, deductibility of state income taxes against federal tax liabilities leads U.S. states to rely more heavily on income taxation. See Winer and Hettich (1992) for references.

since it is not clear how to identify the jurisdictions that any state may compete with (Case, Hines, and Rosen 1993). There is also a dispute over whether the data indicate that competition forces tax rates of competitor states to move together, or whether and to what extent interstate variation in tax systems can persist. Some authors conclude that a state's geographic neighbors follow suit when it raises its tax rates (Besley and Case 1995a; Case 1995). Others (Chernick 1991) argue that there may be tax haven effects in the face of interstate commuting, with residential states maintaining lower rates and adjacent states where employment is centered having higher ones.[23]

The number of empirical papers that are based either on a Leviathan or structure-induced equilibrium model is still quite limited. As noted previously, Leviathan would impose a multidimensional tax structure similar to that used by a democratic regime, although with higher average tax rates. It is not surprising, therefore, that empirical research based on the assumption that governments maximize the size of the budget by Kau and Rubin (1980) or Breeden and Hunter (1985) utilizes estimating equations that are also consistent with vote maximization.[24] Figure 3 illustrates the difficulty of distinguishing between the two models. The figure shows that as the Laffer curve for any particular taxable activity shifts outward due to economic growth or other factors, the change in tax structure under Leviathan (who tries to be at the point of inflection of the relevant curve) will be highly correlated with the evolution of tax structure in a competitive democratic regime.

One way to distinguish between Leviathan and a democratic regime is by investigating the role of democratic institutions in the evolution of tax structure. Such institutions do not appear in the stylized model (7) since vote maximization usually treats them as implicit constraints on political optimization. But if they could be represented in estimating equations and shown to be significant determinants of tax structure, the Leviathan model would be contradicted, since democratic institutions would be established as binding constraints on political agents. Similarly, evidence that interest group pressures had significantly influenced tax structure would refute the assumption of the Leviathan model that the government cares only about economic factors and is oblivious to interest group politics.

---

23. The two views are not necessarily inconsistent (Winer and Hettich 1992). Low tax jurisdictions may be able to coexist with high tax jurisdictions at a point in time as long as interstate tax differentials stay within a certain band.
24. While the model of Kau and Rubin (1981) focuses on the size of government, it is a seminal contribution to the empirical Leviathan literature that contains many interesting suggestions concerning the relationship between tax structure and the size of government.

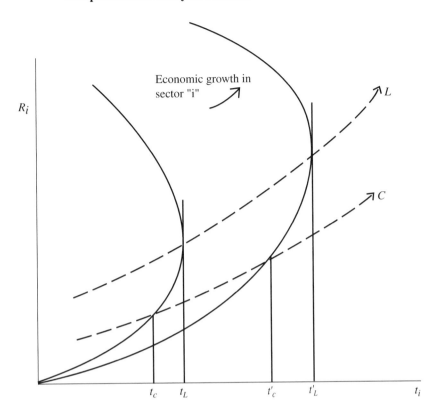

Figure 3. Tax rates and revenues under Leviathan (L) and political competition (C) as economic activity expands.

Schneider and Pommerehne (1980) provide evidence on the effect of electoral constraints on tax structure in Australia. Holcombe and Mills (1995) show that the probability of the reelection of incumbents is positively associated with the size of the U.S. government deficit, and Berry and Berry (1990) argue that adoption of lotteries by U.S. states is related to electoral considerations, while Besley and Case (1995b) relate tax structure to term limits for U.S. governors. As yet, much of the evidence is qualitative and historical, including work by Steinmo (1989) and Winer and Hettich (1990) on the effects of parliamentary versus congressional government and Hansen (1983) on the relationship between institutional features of U.S. state politics and tax structure.

Formal integration of institutional factors into empirical research on tax structure is most advanced in the structure-induced equilibrium approach, although work here is just beginning. In a significant contribution, Inman and Fitts (1990) construct a model of decision making under the norm of universalism in a system with single-member constituencies. The aggregate budget and the structure of taxation are determined not by optimizing a support function for a national political party, as in (7) above, but rather by aggregating politically optimal fiscal policies across constituencies. Since individual legislators do not take into account the full social cost of the programs delivered on behalf of their constituents, the overall budget is inefficiently large, as are the number and size of tax-expenditures.

Estimation results by Inman and Fitts for a long time period in the United States suggest that institutional features, such as the decline of centralized authority in the House of Representatives following reforms of Congress in the mid-1970s, have had a significant effect in increasing total expenditures but appear to have left tax policy, as measured by the aggregate size of tax-expenditures, unaffected. Their explanation for differing results on the two sides of the budget relies on the unchanged power of the House Ways and Means Committee over the tax reform agenda and on the power of strong, independent presidents to block tax changes.[25]

7. Efficiency, equity, and the structure of taxation

Our main focus has been on the essential features of tax structure in a political equilibrium, without judging observed results in relation to preset normative standards. Given the rather extensive normative literature on public finance and public economics, one may ask whether an equilibrium tax structure can also be evaluated with reference to the major concepts of that literature.

A primary concern of normative analysis is economic efficiency. Application of the concept in the present context suggests the following question: Is tax policy in a competitive political equilibrium consistent with location of the private and public economy on the Pareto frontier? While much of the literature on optimal taxation is concerned with Pareto efficiency, it cannot answer this question since it makes no allowance for political institutions.[26] An analysis of the efficiency of tax structure in a competitive political equilibrium must take account of

---

25. In addition, there are several interesting nonquantitative explanations of the 1986 U.S. tax reform in the structure-induced equilibrium tradition, including Fitts and Inman (1992), Stewart (1992), and McCubbins (1992).

26. The classic reference work for the theory of optimal taxation is Atkinson and Stiglitz (1980).

the endogenous aggregation of heterogeneous voter preferences and of the use of resources required to achieve collective outcomes. This differs from the approach used in optimal taxation, where efficiency is investigated in relation to a norm defined by maximizing an exogenously specified welfare function subject to the structure of the private economy.

The recent literature on probabilistic voting models includes a discussion of the efficiency properties of political equilibrium. It is argued that under certain conditions, political competition between parties that maximize expected votes leads to public policies consistent with attainment of the Pareto frontier (Coughlin and Nitzan 1981; Ledyard 1984).[27] The essential idea is that when voter–taxpayers care only about how policies affect their welfare, any political party that ignores policy changes that can make some voters better off without making any other voters worse off is likely to do more poorly at the polls than the opposition. Political competition ensures that in equilibrium, no such Pareto-improving policies remain to be implemented.[28]

This result suggests that a different normative analysis may be possible. While traditional welfare economics focuses on the conditions under which markets produce optimal outcomes and on the circumstances under which they fail, the new type of analysis would be devoted to the success and failure of competitive political institutions and to the corresponding effects on public policies. While the implications of the approach for the study of taxation remain to be developed, the argument suggests a shift in emphasis away from the analysis of welfare functions and their implications for specific tax rules to the study of information flows in the tax policy process and to the operation of bureaucratic and political procedures used in shaping actual tax systems (Winer and Hettich 1993).

The second concept central to the normative literature on taxation is equity. Traditionally, a distinction is made between vertical equity, referring to the influence of taxation on the distribution of income, and horizontal equity, relating to the question of how similar taxpayers should be treated by public policy.

If we rely on the notion of political equilibrium, vertical equity becomes an endogenous outcome of the analysis, resulting from decisions by voters in a competitive political setting. In such a framework, normative judgments become one step removed from particular distributional

27. See Coughlin (1992) for an extensive discussion of this point. For implementation of the idea in the framework of an computable general equilibrium model, see Winer and Rutherford (1992).
28. A vigorous defense of the efficiency of political markets is given by Wittman (1989).

policy effects, relating instead to the nature and acceptability of the underlying collective institutions.

Similar reasoning also implies that horizontal equity has no independent justification in the analysis. The theory of tax structure suggests that treatment of individual taxpayers depends on their Laffer curves, on how they translate losses in full income into voting decisions, and on administration costs. There is no reason to believe that a vote-maximizing government in a competitive political system would rely primarily, or exclusively, on the income tax as a source of revenues, as advocated by Henry Simons, the main proponent of the principle of horizontal equity in tax design.[29] Nor would we expect such a government to use comprehensive income, the index most often proposed as a measure of economic position, as a guide to the sorting of activities and taxpayers in the creation of actual tax structure.[30]

A final normative approach to taxation focuses on constitutional limitations of government power. Proponents of this view often start from the Leviathan model reviewed earlier, using it as a justification to advocate extensive constitutional restrictions on the power to tax (Brennan and Buchanan 1980). When we relate the constitutional perspective to a world with competitive political equilibrium, the question arises how constitutional reforms differ from other policies adopted as part of the ongoing political process. While such reforms can be viewed as contracts that are more difficult to revise and that are made for longer periods than regular agreements, they nevertheless must be accepted and implemented within the existing political framework, thus becoming an endogenous outcome like other policies concerned with fiscal matters.

One may, of course, argue that existing political institutions are inadequate if judged by normative principles, such as liberty and justice, and propose different collective arrangements governing fiscal choices, a line of inquiry going back to the influential work by Wicksell (1896). Nevertheless, the question remains under what circumstances self-motivated, rational decision makers will adopt particular constitutional rules. Appeals to choices made behind a veil of ignorance, although helpful in clarifying philosophical principles, cannot resolve the problem of adoption and implementation.[31]

---

29. The classic work is Simons (1936). For an examination of Simons's writings concerning taxation, see Hettich (1979).
30. The most extensive attempt to implement the comprehensive income measure as a tax base is found in the *Report of the Canadian Royal Commission on Taxation* (1966), but the notion has had an important influence on more recent reform attempts, including the Tax Reform Act passed by the U.S. Congress in 1986. For a critical review of the concept of horizontal equity and of attempts to measure it, see Kaplow (1989).
31. Choice behind a veil of ignorance was proposed by Rawls (1971). See Brennan and Buchanan (1985) for an examination of rules and of the reasons for their adoption.

8. Conclusion

Explaining observed differences in the use of taxation and in the structure of fiscal systems is an important task for public choice. Taxation lies at the heart of political power and is crucial to the operation of the public sector, thus providing a test case for judging the relevance of collective decision models. At the same time, empirical testing is facilitated by the existence of excellent quantitative information on government revenues, including data of both a cross-sectional and a historical nature.

The growing literature concerned with the analysis of tax structure can claim some success in dealing with the most significant issues, but there is room for improvement. Several directions for further research are possible. Examples of theoretical issues requiring more attention are the integrated treatment of the tax and expenditure sides of the budget and the relation of borrowing or debt to other revenue sources. Unresolved empirical questions include how to impose interesting restrictions on the parameters of estimating equations, how to take appropriate account of the equilibrium nature of fiscal systems, and how to reflect interest group power and institutional factors more fully in empirical work. Finally, work on ways to distinguish more clearly among the fiscal predictions of competing collective choice models would make a significant addition to the literature.

Analysis based on collective choice models contributes a new perspective to the understanding of tax systems. It shows that their essential characteristics can be seen as the outcome of optimizing economic and political behavior and that tax structure can be interpreted as a set of related components in equilibrium. As a consequence, policies must pass a political as well as an economic test and changes in one part of the system may lead to unexpected repercussions elsewhere as the government attempts to reestablish political equilibrium. Future theoretical and empirical research on taxation should take account of the nature and implications of such linkages.

CHAPTER 23

Rent seeking

ROBERT D. TOLLISON

Rent seeking is the socially costly pursuit of wealth transfers. The concept of rent seeking was introduced to the economics profession by Tullock (1967). In his original presentation the basic idea that transfer seeking could lead to social costs was so simple that it has been automatically assumed that the idea had to have clear precursors in the literature. Nonetheless, even though one can find vague resemblances to the idea in many earlier writings, no one has uncovered a forerunner to Tullock's idea. His 1967 paper represents an original and important development in economic theory.

The early doctrinal development of the theory of rent seeking proceeded as follows. Krueger (1974) gave the field a name in her paper "The Political Economy of the Rent-Seeking Society." For better or worse this terminology has stuck. Bhagwati (1980, 1982) has persisted in an attempt to rename the field Directly Unproductive Profit Seeking (DUP), but the term "rent seeking" seems to have carried the day. Although she presented some empirical estimates of the costs of rent seeking, Krueger's paper was primarily theoretical in nature, showing how rent seeking can lead to social costs in the adoption of policies to restrict international trade. Krueger was unaware of Tullock's paper. Posner (1975), who was aware of Tullock's paper, wrote the first empirical paper about rent seeking. His estimates suggested that the social costs of rent seeking in the regulated sector of the U.S. economy could be substantial. Cowling and Mueller (1978) presented estimates of the welfare loss from monopoly power in the United States and United Kingdom, which included calculations of costs associated with rent seeking. They found high social costs of monopoly in both economies, emphasizing that their social cost estimates were, in contrast to Posner, for private monopoly power. As I will discuss later, the empirical magnitude of rent-seeking costs is now a matter of some controversy in the literature. As noted above, Bhagwati became interested in the theory of rent seeking in the early 1980s, basing his original works on his earlier contributions to the theory of economic growth. Finally, in an effort to solidify the earlier contributions and to stimulate work in the field, Buchanan, Tullock, and Tollison (1980) published a collection of papers on rent seeking that has been both widely cited and influential in the subsequent development of the field.

The remainder of this essay will detail the various aspects of the theory of rent seeking as it has evolved since Tullock's seminal paper.[1]

1. Definitions and semantics

Tullock originally framed his theory of rent seeking in contrast to the prevailing wisdom in the late 1950s and early 1960s, which held that the deadweight costs of monopoly and tariffs were empirically quite small. Harberger's (1954) famous calculations on the extent of monopoly power in the United States, and the discussions of how little British economic welfare would be increased if the United Kingdom joined the Common Market are good examples of this type of thinking (Mundell 1962). Microeconomics was on the verge of being trivialized. Tullock advanced an argument that rectangles as well as triangles matter in the calculation of the social costs of such policies as tariffs and monopolies, that is, Tullock introduced the concept of a trapezoidal society.

Tullock's point was simple though full of potential pitfalls. He argued that expenditures made to capture a transfer were a form of social cost. The social cost arises because the resources used for transfer seeking have a positive opportunity cost somewhere else in the economy with respect to engaging in positive-sum activities. Transfer seeking is at best a zero-sum activity in that it simply shuffles dollars among people and groups and is probably negative-sum if traditional deadweight costs result as a by-product of such activities (Tullock 1980b). Social costs clearly arise in the process by which resources are shifted from positive- to zero- and negative-sum activities. Rent seeking thus embodies a social cost in terms of the foregone product of the resources employed in rent seeking.[2]

Several points should be kept in mind. The theory of rent seeking does not condemn all types of profit seeking. As Buchanan (1980b) articulated clearly, traditional competitive profit seeking or entrepreneurship in the competitive model (seeking quasi-rents) does not qualify as rent seeking. Such profit seeking is productive; it creates value such as

---

1. See Tollison (1982, 1987) for earlier surveys of the theory of rent seeking.
2. This result assumes a labor market equilibrium in which, for example, a lawyer's wage is an accurate proxy for his opportunity cost as an engineer and in which the lawyer is indifferent at the margin with respect to choice of profession.

new products. Rent seeking is unproductive; it destroys value by wasting valuable resources.

Normally, the concept of rent seeking is applied to cases where governmental intervention in the economy leads to the creation of artificial or contrived rents. Seeking such returns leads to social costs because output is fixed by definition in, for example, a government regulation. Entrepreneurship in this setting can only be said to be negative; it will simply dissipate rents and lead to no increase in output. Nonetheless, it is quite possible to conceive of rent seeking as taking place in a nongovernmental setting. Buchanan (1983), for example, argued that the rivalry of siblings for an inheritance can lead to rent-seeking activities within families, and Frank (1986) has shown how certain labor markets involving competition for position (the rat race and tournaments for example) generate costly rent-seeking activities by participants.

Another point to keep in mind is that to the degree that the process of rent seeking involves the provision of utility or real income to participants in the process, these benefits should be netted out against the cost of rent seeking. As Congleton (1988) has argued, if the rent seeker takes the regulator out to dinner, the value that the regulator places on the dinner must be subtracted from the social costs of rent seeking.

A final definitional point to bear in mind is that bribes are technically not a rent-seeking cost. A bribe is a transfer, and as such, it represents a method of influencing governmental behavior that does not involve explicit rent-seeking costs since rent seeking involves the expenditure of costly resources to procure a transfer. Hiring a lawyer or a lobbyist to obtain a favorable law is rent seeking; bribing a legislator for the same law is not. This is not intended as a moral defense of bribery; it is simply an analytical distinction that will be useful later.

Moving beyond bribes, however, once artificial rents have been created, it is hard to avoid the implication that rent seeking will occur along some margin. If a tax deduction is offered, tax shelters will be created and used. If civil servants are paid a wage in excess of their marginal revenue products, queues will develop for government jobs. All of these processes involve the use of scarce resources to seek transfers; the process is relentless.

2. Theory

Any pool of rents will do for analytical purposes. Normally, the exposition of rent seeking stresses rents arising from regulation, monopoly, or tariffs. Standard economic analysis treats such rents as pure transfers, with no effect on the economy. Tullock's insight converted such transfers into potential social costs.

Posner (1975) stated the first version of a rent-seeking game, describing a constant-cost game in which the probability of winning is proportional to investment and the available rents are exactly dissipated. He posited risk-neutral bidders, a fixed prize, and a given number of bidders. Where, for example, the pool of rents equals $100,000 and there are ten rent seekers, each bidder will offer or expend resources of $10,000 to capture the rents. In Posner's model rent seeking is analogous to buying a lottery ticket with a one in ten chance of being successful. Under such conditions rents are exactly dissipated; $100,000 is spent to capture $100,000.[3]

Posner's exact dissipation hypothesis is popular in the literature because it makes empirical work easier. A rectangle is a definite area whose value can be reasonably estimated. Moreover, Posner's model is robust with respect to the free entry and exit of bidders (Corcoran 1984; Higgins, Shughart, and Tollison 1985). That is, it naturally generalizes to a concept of a long-run equilibrium of bids and bidders. Rents are perfectly competed away with an endogenous number of bidders, and the prize to the winning rent seeker represents only a normal rate of return on his rent-seeking investment.

Two points about this exact dissipation result should be kept in mind. First, it is important to understand that this is an equilibrium result under the postulated conditions. Government cannot simply put the regulatory favor or monopoly right up for rebidding and expect that bidders will not adjust their bids for such unexpected takings. If takings are expected, the original bids will reflect the relevant probabilities. Either way, instability in government policy comes to be reflected in a rent-seeking equilibrium outcome. Government cannot simply endlessly bid off regulatory favors.[4] Second, the concept of an equilibrium in a rent-seeking contest does not mean that an incumbent possessor of a monopoly right will not make expenditures to defend and protect his monopoly. These investments will most likely show up as business expenses, which means that the observed rectangle for the monopolist is net of his rent-protection costs. This point goes to the symmetry of rent-seeking and rent-protecting expenditures and to the durability of monopoly rights (these two points are discussed below). It does not defeat the concept of an equilibrium in the original rent-seeking game; initial bids will be deflated to reflect the expected costs of defending the monopoly right.

The constant-cost rent-seeking game represents a popular equilibrium

---

3. Keep in mind the above point that rents are not transfers or bribes but must be expended in real resources devoted to regulatory favor seeking.
4. This is the problem with Crew and Rowley (1988).

hypothesis. The exact dissipation model is like the model of perfect competition; it is a useful, though not necessarily descriptive, analytical construct for increasing understanding of how the world works.

This does not mean, however, that all or even most rent-seeking contests are perfectly competitive in nature. Tullock (1980a) presented classes of models where rent seeking is imperfectly competitive in the sense that the competitive process for rents leads to over- or under-dissipation of the available rents. That is, more or less than the value of the rents is expended to capture them. Rent seeking in these models does not take place under constant-cost conditions. These cases are interesting, and they are generated by assumptions about risk aversion, limitations on the number of bidders, imperfect information, and so on. They are not very popular, however, because imperfect dissipation makes the problem of deriving reduced-form equations with which to estimate rent-seeking costs much more difficult and case specific (Fisher 1985). One can no longer simply estimate the area of a trapezoid; the task is now to estimate the area of something more or less than a trapezoid that is a function of behavior in the economy. This is clearly a harder modeling problem.

As between Tullock's analysis of over- and underdissipation possibilities,the overdissipation possibility does not seem to be very plausible. In this case, rent seekers are somehow led to bid more than the value of the prize. That is, they would be better off by not playing the game in the first place. While this is perhaps possible once, through the distortion of information to rent seekers about their expected chances of winning, such behavior should not persist for long. The regulator/bureaucrat should be able to mislead only once. In the next round of rent seeking, bids will be adjusted to reflect "true" probabilities of winning; bureaucratic prospects properly will be discounted.[5]

The best known version of a maximalist hypothesis about rent seeking is the black-hole tariff result of Magee, Brock, and Young (1989). They devise circumstances under which the rate of return to lobbying switches in a fashion so as to lead to huge (proportionately) amounts of the resources in an economy being devoted to lobbying. Indeed, in the black-hole case, almost 100 percent of the economy is devoted to lobbying. This result is driven by assumptions under which the returns to

---

5. Casual evidence can be gathered by playing a simple game with your class. Offer five dollars as the prize. Ask the students to write down their bids for the five dollars and seal them without communicating with their fellow students. All bids must be paid to the professor; the professor funds any losses and pockets any profits from the contest. Collusion among bidders may be allowed. Results vary, but the contest illustrates in a practical way the complex nature of rent-seeking contests.

capital from lobbying (versus production) became magnified or arbitrarily large, so that it becomes rational for capital to invest nearly all its resources in redistributive competition. By symmetry, labor follows suit. The returns from lobbying are magnified because of the assumption that changes in product price have very large effects on factor prices. Lobbying almost consumes all productive activity in this stylized economy. This is an important result that deserves further study. A central issue in this regard will be the empirical relevance of the black-hole model. Economic historians may be able to find examples of such cases; the only one that comes immediately to mind is the case of certain hyperinflations. In general, however, overdissipation results would seem to be rare, given the theoretical preconditions on which they are based.

Underbidding, where rent seekers in the aggregate spend less than the value of the prize, is another matter. There are several plausible bases for underbidding equilibria, including risk aversion (Hillman and Katz 1984), comparative advantage among monopolizing inputs (Rogerson 1982), and game theoretic considerations (Tullock 1980a, 1985). As stressed above, such considerations make the problem of analyzing the costs of rent seeking more difficult and case specific, but be this as it may, underdissipation seems an intuitively more plausible description of the real world. Even given that rent-seeking costs are submerged into normal business costs, it is hard to think of many examples where rent-seeking expenditures bulk very large in relation to the expected rewards.

The minimalist hypothesis is that rent-seeking costs are approximately zero. Dougan and Snyder (1993) have argued that there are powerful and plausible incentives to convert rent-seeking costs into transfers. Something close to this result seems to underlie Becker's (1983) work on pressure groups, though it is not explicit in his theory. The problem is complex. Obviously, recipients of transfers would prefer to receive them as money transfers. If they did not, rent seekers would find out what the recipients prefer and give it to them (fishing trips, for example). Dougan and Snyder argue this point well. They stress that transfers are endogenously determined, and so the social costs of transfers are minimized by successful interest groups. It will also be generally more efficient for rent seekers to deal in money transfers (bribes). Nonetheless, there is no competitive mechanism that guarantees such a result. If monopolizing inputs are able, by acting as an interest group themselves, to control the processes of rent assignment, then bribes and auctions for regulatory and other governmental favors will be illegal, and the use of monopolizing inputs to compete for such favors will be pervasive. These inputs become, through their own influence, a necessary cost of doing business with the government, and the interest of the monopolizing inputs resides in maximizing the costs associated with transfers.

The minimalist approach basically implies that the world is efficient. Indeed, the pleas of economists to the contrary are simply part of whatever rent-seeking equilibrium exists. But how do you test this hypothesis? This is the key. Perhaps the effects of a dramatic exogenous shift in a relative price could be traced out, showing how rents are either captured as transfers or dissipated through rent seeking. But the point is to show how a theory that suggests that rent-seeking and deadweight costs are minimized by political competition can be stated in a testable form. Thus far in the literature this has not been done.

All this is to say that exact dissipation appears to be a useful general conjecture about equilibrium in rent-seeking contests, but this theory must be adapted to the circumstances of any particular case of rent-seeking. Like the model of perfect competition, the model of exactly dissipated rents is a vehicle and starting point for helping us to understand actual rent-seeking processes.

3. Measurement of rent-seeking costs

There are numerous empirical results on the social costs of rent seeking, depending on the methodology, coverage, and economy analyzed by the author. Krueger (1974) suggested that 7 percent of Indian GNP was wasted in rent seeking and 15 percent of Turkish GNP was lost due to rent seeking for import licenses. Posner (1975) estimated that as much as 3 percent of U.S. GNP was lost due to the social costs of monopolization through regulation. These are obviously substantial sums of money in any economy. Cowling and Mueller (1978) derived an estimate that the rent-seeking and deadweight costs of private monopoly in the United States was 13 percent of gross corporate product.[6]

Subsequent empirical work in this area has proceeded along several lines. A reasonable amount of work has followed the lead of Krueger in seeking to examine the rent-seeking costs of trade intervention in various economies. In general, these works come up with higher numbers than Krueger. Magee, Brock, and Young (1989, chap. 15) provide a survey of this research. Ross (1984), for example, estimated that trade-related rent seeking accounted for 38 percent of GDP in Kenya.

Other work has attempted to estimate the costs of rent seeking for economies as a whole. This analysis has taken two general forms. First, there are the lawyer regressions. Various authors, including Laband and

---

6. Cowling and Mueller (1978) also make the important point that since many rent-seeking costs are buried in business expenses, there is a bias toward underestimation in the way most studies calculate rents. That is, observed rents will understate the true costs of rent seeking.

Sophocleus (1988), Magee, Brock, and Young (1989), and Murphy, Shleifer, and Vishny (1991), have added lawyers in various regression formats set up to explain GNP or rates of growth in GNP, both in the United States and across countries. The robust conclusion of this work is more lawyers, lower growth, lower GNP.[7] Some of these admittedly simplistic regression estimates suggest that lawyers reduce aggregate income by as much as 45 percent.

Eschewing a regression-based approach, Laband and Sophocleus (1992) attempted an aggregate, sector-by-sector accounting of rent-seeking costs in the U.S. economy. They counted expenditures on such items as locks, insurance, police, and the military as being driven by rent-seeking or rent-protecting incentives. On this basis they estimated that almost one-half of the U.S. GNP in 1985 was consumed by such costs.[8] Their approach will surely be controversial. A small sample of the categories that they treated as rent-seeking costs include crime prevention (FBI), police (corrections), restraint of trade (FTC), residential investments (locks), commercial investments (guards), educational investments (library theft), property-rights disputes (tort litigation), and government (defense, lobbyists, PACS). Following an accounting-like procedure, these authors go sector-by-sector to obtain their estimates of rent-seeking costs.

The results of the various studies are summarized in Table 1. In one sense, the table shows the importance of the rent-seeking insight. No longer can the costs of tariffs, monopolies, and theft be called a trivial issue in virtually any economy. These are generally not small numbers.

As with all empirical work, these various approaches are only as good as the theories and models upon which they are based. Several points are worth making here. One is that lawyers per se may not be the problem; the problem may be the nature of legal processes. The vast expansion of tort and plaintiff-driven litigation is not necessarily due to the fact that lawyers lobby successfully for such changes in the law. Indeed, the use of the legal process to resolve conflicts may simply have expanded in recent years because other forums for conflict resolution (the church, the family) have become less effective. Moreover, there is a quotient of trust in any economy. Buying a lock is a response to the security of property rights in a society. This security can be produced in a variety of ways (including moral exhortation), but in the face of the

---

7. Magee carries the analysis a step further by looking at the rent-seeking costs of having an additional lawyer in the legislature. He estimates that each additional lawyer in the U.S. Congress costs more than $1 billion. See Rauch (1992, 984).

8. For a similar exercise, see Joseph Phillips in an appendix to Baran and Sweezy (1966), who estimated the "cost" of monopoly capitalism at 56 percent of U.S. GNP.

Table 1. *Estimates of the costs of rent seeking*

Study	Economy	Year	Rent-seeking costs
Krueger	India	1964	7% GNP
Krueger	Turkey	1968	15% GNP (trade sector)
Posner	United States	Various years	3% GNP (regulation)
Cowling & Mueller	United States	1963–6	13% GCP[a] (private monopoly)
Cowling & Mueller	United Kingdom	1968–9	7% GCP[a] (private monopoly)
Ross	Kenya	1980	38% GDP (trade sector)
Mohammand & Whalley	India	1980–1	25–40% GNP
Laband & Sophocleus	United States	1985	50% GNP
Regression-based studies	Various Countries	Various years	Up to 45% GNP

[a]Cowling and Mueller (1978) use gross corporate product as the basis of their calculation.

relevant probabilities, buying a lock can hardly be seen as an unproductive investment. Given the prevailing ethos, a lock protects property rights, and the protection of property rights enhances the productivity of resources over what they could produce without the lock. To argue that one can be wealthier without locks and lawyers implies that there are feasible reforms in behavior that will reduce such costs. This is certainly believable, but this is exactly the burden that estimators of the costs of rent seeking face. The lock and the lawyer are only wasteful to the extent that these resources can be feasibly reallocated to more productive uses. Alternatively, contributions to churches should be regarded as substitutes for locks.

This discussion presages a later discussion in the conclusion of this paper, but the point is directly germane to the problem of how to measure rent-seeking costs. In principle, the cost of rent seeking is simply the increase in GNP that would result if a feasible way to reallocate resources from locks and lawyers to more productive uses could be found by a political entrepreneur. This figure could be high or low, but it is probably low given the ability of rent-seeking inputs to resist such reallocations. And the mere resistance of the inputs is yet another reason not to waste resources attempting such a reallocation (Tollison and Wagner 1991).

The bias of this argument is apparent – the range and extent of feasible reform in the rent-seeking society is not large, and the logic of this argument is inherent in the theory of rent seeking. Reform will be resisted, and this resistance is, one-for-one, a social cost of reform. This issue is covered in more detail in the conclusion, but it suggests that when one says that rent seeking costs an economy X percent of GNP, this is tantamount to saying nothing of particular importance. Perhaps more fairly, one is reminded of Fisher, Griliches, and Kaysen's (1962) estimates of the costs of automobile styling charges. These authors did not present their estimates as social costs, but simply as a type of "bill" that the consumer had to pay. As with all such bills, the question was simply, is it worth it? This is the spirit in which estimates of the costs of rent seeking should be understood.

4. Sunk costs and rent seeking

Consider the following case (McCormick, Shughart, and Tollison 1984). A monopoly right is granted forever, and all rent-seeking expenditures to capture the right are made *ex ante* by rent seekers. In this situation, the rent-seeking costs are sunk. The economy is poorer by the amount of the rent seeking plus the deadweight costs of the monopoly; abolishing the monopoly right cannot get the rent-seeking costs back. Indeed, abolishing the monopoly right in such a case amounts to a contradiction in terms; it was granted forever.

Now consider the case where the rent-seeking costs have not been completely capitalized, that is, where the holders of the monopoly right must engage in rent-protecting expenditures each period because there are threats to the political status of the monopoly. In this situation, if the monopoly is deregulated, the ongoing rent-seeking expenditures, in addition to the deadweight costs of the monopoly, can be returned to the economy.

The moral of this story about sunk costs and rent seeking is clear. The gains from deregulation are greater where rent-seeking costs have not yet been capitalized. Other things being equal, the most cost-effective program of deregulation is to concentrate on industries that fight back, for here the social gains from deregulation are the largest. This result suggests a test for the overall rationality of government efforts to promote deregulation.

This is a point about social gains. Consumers could not care less whether monopoly rents have been capitalized. But the logic of the argument is to point out that the gains from deregulation are potentially the highest, paradoxically, where deregulation is fought the hardest.

5. Rent protection

Not only do individuals use real resources to seek transfers, but, as noted previously, they also sometimes use real resources to protect their

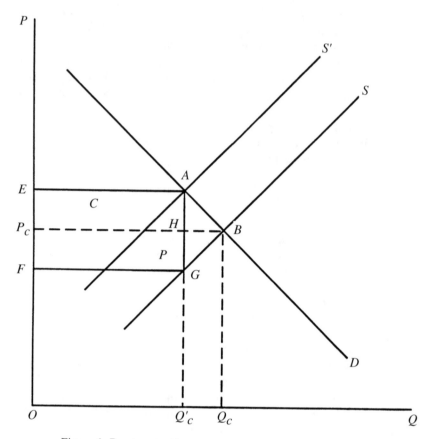

Figure 1. Rent protection.

rents from encroachment by other rent seekers. In contrast to rent seeking, this behavior is called rent protection. The basis for such behavior is clear. Not all "suppliers" of wealth transfers find it economically rational to allow their wealth to be taken away (why spend a dollar to save a dime?). Some will find it worthwhile to fight back (spend a dollar to save two dollars).

The simple example of an excise tax on a competitive industry will illustrate the concept of rent protection. In Figure 1, as a result of an excise tax on the industry's product, the industry supply curve shifts from S to S'. The traditional analysis of this case stresses three basic results: (1) ABG is the deadweight cost of the tax; (2) $EAGF$ is the tax revenue that is transferred to the government; and (3) the incidence of the tax is split between consumers (C) and producers (P) as a function of the elasticities of demand and supply.

Assume that consumers (*C*) are unorganized and have no rational incentive to organize to resist the loss of consumer surplus that the tax imposes on them. However, let producers be organized and prepared to lobby against the tax. In the case at hand, producers may rationally spend up to their loss of producer surplus (P_cBGF) to resist the tax or to keep it from being higher than it is. These expenditures are a rent-seeking (rent-protecting) cost in Tullock's terms, and so they must be added to the traditional cost of the excise tax (*ABG*) to obtain the total social cost of excise taxation in this case, P_cBGF plus *ABG*.[9] Obviously, if consumers organize to resist the tax, the social costs of tax resistance rise even further.

It is a mainstay of optimal taxation theory that the excess burden imposed by selective excise taxation (*ABG*) is minimized for a given amount of revenue raised, when such taxes are placed on commodities with relatively inelastic demand curves. Unfortunately, this rule cannot stand up to the above analysis. It is quite easy to show that when P_cBGF is counted as part of the social cost of excise taxation, taxing an industry with a more elastic demand curve, but with no organized, rent-protecting opposition to the tax, is socially preferable. Moreover, considerations of monopoly only strengthen the analysis (Lee and Tollison 1985).

Virtually all welfare analyses of monopoly and regulation ignore rent-protecting activities of organized opponents of such governmental programs. A more general welfare analytics will include traditional dead-weight costs, rent-seeking costs, and rent-protecting costs (see Baysinger and Tollison 1980; Wenders 1987). An important contribution to this literature in recent years has been McChesney's (1987) concept of rent extraction. He has generated results on rent seeking in which regulation or legislation is threatened and then withdrawn as a way to stimulate the formation of interest groups from which politicians can exact tribute.

6. Rent seeking and the distribution of income

Before Tullock, the effect of monopoly on the distribution of income was clear – the monopolist got richer and consumers got poorer (Comanor and Smiley 1975); monopoly rents were simple transfers. In the rent-seeking approach, the impact of monopoly on income distribution is a more complicated issue. Of the original formulators of the theory, only Posner relates his analysis to the distribution of income. He states: "There is no reason to think that monopoly has a significant distributive effect. Consumers' wealth is not transferred to the share-

---

9. Note that there is no double-counting involved in this calculation; the triangle, *HBG*, enters twice.

holders of monopoly firms; it is dissipated in the purchase of inputs into the activity of becoming a monopolist" (1975, 821).

Posner's argument seems logical. Rent seeking dissipates monopoly rents, translating potential transfers into social costs. The effect of monopoly on the distribution of income in the rent-seeking society would thus appear to be nil. However, the argument needs to be scrutinized carefully.

Using the simple example employed by Posner, suppose that there are $1 million in rents to be captured and ten risk-neutral bidders for a monopoly right. Each bidder bids $100,000 for the franchise; $1 million is spent to capture $1 million; at a social level the monopoly rents are exactly wasted. The example, however, embodies a distributional consequence. Clearly, one of the ten bidders wins the competition and receives a net return on his efforts of $900,000. Without more information, one cannot clearly say in this stylized example whether rent seeking increases or decreases the degree of inequality in the distribution of income. The most logical presumption, given that rent seekers earn normal rates of return on their investments in rent seeking, is that consumers (poor?) are worse off and rent seekers (rich?) are no better off than before. A type of low-level, wasteful inequality is thereby generated. It seems a little farfetched, however, to think that rent seeking generally promotes a leveling or only a mild inequality in the income distribution. Set in a world of tradition, class, privilege, power, and differential organization costs, rent seeking most likely promotes more significant inequalities in the distribution of income.

Perhaps more realistically, there will not be an equal distribution of rent-seeking ability in a society. Thus, the mechanism by which rents are assigned is likely to affect the distribution of wealth to the extent that Ricardian rents are earned in rent seeking. Consider a regulatory-hearing mechanism for assigning rents and suppose that some lawyers or economists earn inframarginal rents in rent seeking. On average, these individuals will be wealthier than their marginal competitors and wealthier than they would be without a rent-seeking mechanism of the particular type that rewards their skills. The choice of such a transfer mechanism increases the demand for lawyers (and possibly economists) above that which would hold with (say) an auction mechanism for assigning monopoly rents. So, first of all, the mechanism will alter the distribution of wealth by occupation. Moreover, if the requisite talents of the favored occupation cannot be reproduced at constant costs, the inequality of wealth in society may be further affected. For example, suppose the qualities of a good businessman/speculator are more fungible among the population than the qualities of a good lawyer, then inframarginal rents will accrue to the best of the legal profession in regulatory hearing cases.

With an auction no Ricardian rents would be earned. The distribution of wealth would differ between these two societies as a consequence.

The main point, then, is that rent seeking will affect the distribution of income. Estimating the actual impact of rent seeking on income distribution has not been done and would amount to a formidable task.[10]

7. Rent seeking and the political order

What is the relationship between the political order and the amount of rent seeking that it begets? There are no easy answers here.

Rent seeking can be seen as a two-stage game. First, there is competition to control the political apparatus that creates, enforces, and assigns rent flows. This is related to issues such as who controls the legislature or how monarchs are selected. Second, there is the rent-seeking behavior that has been discussed thus far, namely, the competition to capture the rents that inhere in particular instances of monopoly and regulation. These two stages are linked in the discussion that follows, presenting a problem of some importance for rent-seeking theory.

The problem is easy to exposit. At base, in a world where rent-seeking waste is exact and complete, there is no marginal incentive to create monopolies. Investments in monopoly creation lead only to a normal rate of return. Political entrepreneurs will seek a higher margin of return for investment. As discussed earlier, there exist incentives to convert rent-seeking waste into transfers, which make the creators of monopoly rents better off. Better to receive a transfer than to see transfers wasted.

In this context, consider two types of models. In one, rent-seeking waste is exact and complete. Here, the incentive to create monopoly will be low because there are no excess returns from doing so, but the social cost per instance of realized monopoly will be high. In the other model politicians have succeeded in converting rent-seeking costs into transfers. There are thus significant excess returns to monopoly creation; hence, there will be more monopolies in such a society. Returns to politicians are only transfers in this society, but this society will have more monopolies and more Harberger losses than the first society – the social cost per instance of realized monopoly will be low.

The dilemma is now clear – which society will be wealthier? There does not appear to be an a priori way to say that one society has less monopoly and more waste per monopoly and the other has more monopoly and less waste per monopoly.

Indeed, the issue becomes murkier when one returns to the first stage of rent seeking discussed above. If there is a lot to be gained from

---

10. For more discussion along these lines, see Higgins and Tollison (1985).

controlling the government (as in the second case above where rents are converted to transfers by political actors), perhaps a lot is spent at the first stage of the contest to control the government. Alternatively, where there is not much to be made through monopoly creation, little effort may be expended to capture control of the state. Of course, this is all quite ad hoc. For example, the divine right of monarchs with clearly defined rules of royal succession was a fairly low-cost means of transferring control of the state, even though the early nation-states were fairly effective at using monopolies as a source of revenue (Ekelund and Tollison 1981).

One can thus find odd combinations of first- and second-stage incentives. Majoritarian democracy, for example, appears to give away regulatory rents through in-kind auctions, which maximize the incentive to create monopolies at the second stage while allowing maximal dissipation to acquire legislative majorities at the first stage. One, almost perversely, gets lots of Tullock and Harberger waste in such a case. The point is that rent seeking takes place within a given political order and that this order impacts on the character and amount of rent seeking that is subsequently observed. Of course, the control of rent seeking is not the only objective in designing or evaluating a state, but the issue clearly deserves to be on the list of relevant considerations.[11]

8. Positive economics

The theory of rent seeking has been advanced as an evaluatory theory. It is a procedure to evaluate reforms that can lead to potentially lower social costs in the economy. In this sense the theory of rent seeking is a normative theory. The idea that political behavior is motivated by wealth transfers also has a long tradition as a positive economic theory of regulation and government.[12] A thumbnail sketch of this theory will round out this essay on rent seeking.

One way to think about legislation is in terms of the interest group theory of government. Individual citizens can want or demand laws for any reason – for example, the law makes the world a better place, the law promotes the production of a public good, the law makes them wealthier, and so forth – but will generally act in some group context to obtain the passage of a desired law or the defeat of an undesired law.

A basic principle as well as a basic conundrum underlies the demand for legislation. The principle is that groups who can organize for less

11. See Higgins and Tollison (1985).
12. See Stigler (1971) and the references cited there. Also, see Peltzman (1976), McCormick and Tollison (1981), and Becker (1983).

than one dollar in order to obtain one dollar of benefits from legislation will be the effective demanders of laws. The conundrum is that economists have little idea about how successful interest groups are formed. That is, how do groups overcome free-rider problems and organize for collective action so as to be able to seek one dollar for less than one dollar? The plain truth is that economists know very little about the dynamics of group formation and action. Olson (1971) offered a by-product theory of interest group formation in which a private good was provided to members at a monopoly price, with the monopoly profit being used to finance interest group activities. Stigler (1974) later criticized this theory on the grounds that there was no reason to assume that the interest group had any monopoly power over the sales of the by-product. What has not been generally recognized is that this is a testable proposition. The Sierra Club, for example, may very well face a downward sloping and inelastic demand curve for its calendars. Some empirical research would be quite useful to test the importance of Olson's by-product theory of interest group formation.

Indeed, for whatever reason that organization is undertaken, lobbying for special interest legislation becomes a relatively low-cost by-product of being organized. Lawyers may agree collectively to a code of ethics to address such matters as attorney–client privilege and then proceed to adopt provisions in their code that restrict competition among lawyers. A firm is an example of an organization that can be used for lobbying purposes at very low marginal cost, and so is a labor union.

In the interest group theory, the supply of legislation is an inverse demand curve. Those who "supply" wealth transfers are individuals who do not find it cost effective to resist having their wealth taken away. In other words, it costs them more than one dollar to resist having one dollar taken away.[13] This concept of a supply curve of legislation or regulation suggests that the costs of political activity to some individuals exceed the potential gains (or avoided losses). The supply of legislation is, therefore, grounded in the unorganized or relatively less-organized members of society.

The individuals who monitor the supply–demand process are politicians, bureaucrats, and other political actors. These individuals may be conceived of as brokers of legislation, and they essentially act like brokers in a private context – they pair demanders and suppliers of legislation. That is, they seek to pair those who want a law or a transfer the

13. "Supply" as used in this context is not the ordinary concept of voluntary supply at higher prices. It is voluntary in the sense that giving up one dollar is cheaper than spending ten dollars to resist giving up one dollar. It is not voluntary in the sense that the state is a coercive mechanism.

most with those who object to it the least. In the usual logic of the interest group theory, brokers will concentrate on legal arrangements that benefit well-organized and concentrated groups for whom the pro rata benefits are high at the expense of diffuse interests, each of whom is taxed a little bit to fund the transfer or legislation. By efficiently pairing demanders and suppliers of legislation, the political brokers establish an equilibrium in the market for legislation, and this equilibrium is disciplined by periodic elections.

Perhaps the most basic issue related to the demand for legislation is how to explain why laws persist over time. That is, why is the work of one legislature not overturned by the next legislature? Landes and Posner (1975) sought to answer this question by addressing the role of the independent judiciary in promoting durable legislation. Their analysis was framed in terms of the interest group theory of government. Obviously, an interest group would not bid very much for a protective statute if it lasted only for the current legislative session and was repealed by the next. To be worth anything to the interest group, a law must be durable – that is, it must have a present value of benefits that exceeds the costs of obtaining it.

Landes and Posner focused on the role of the independent judiciary in this regard. They posited that the institutional arrangements surrounding judgeships lead judges to behave so as to resolve legal disputes in terms of what the propounding legislature actually intended. Given that independent judges actually behave in this manner, the present value demand curve for legislation rotates to the right, and laws become more valuable because they last longer. The enacting legislature's intent is upheld in this theory of the independent judiciary, making each legislature's actions more durable and worth more to interest groups. Where the judicial branch acts to increase and sustain the durability of legislation, its budget and judicial salaries increase.[14]

Other margins of the political process can be extended to increase the durability of legislation. The institutions of the legislature can make it costly to repeal a law once it is passed, and interest groups can seek their rents through constitutional (hence, more durable) rather than ordinary legislation. Bicameralism, constitutional amendments, the committee system, and majority size are just a few of the ways in which the durability of legislation can be increased. The point is that the independent judiciary is not the only institutional margin by which the value of the legislative system as an "exchange process" can be maximized. And, indeed, one can argue that the system was designed and has evolved

---

14. Note that the judiciary is not really "independent" in this theory.

through time to solidify an exchange process between interest groups and political brokers.

The Landes–Posner theory of durable legislation is an important contribution to the economic theory of legislation. It explains why laws persist over time and how legal environments differ across jurisdictions. Although originally addressed to issues of an independent judiciary, it is also a general theory of the demand for legislation.[15]

There are various ways to approach the issues surrounding the production and supply of legislation. As such, the public choice literature has mingled considerations of production with considerations of supply in what might loosely be called a "reduced-form" approach. This means that aspects of the legislature's productive process, such as the size of the legislatures, are comingled with aspects of the political and economic environment, such as population and income, to reflect factors underlying the supply of legislation, transfers, and regulation.

Without going into the details, the basic idea is to let an interest group have a budget constraint and then face the problem of buying influence (votes is a special case) from a bicameral legislature in a given political and demographic environment (McCormick and Tollison 1980). In this setting, what factors will inform interest group success and what factors will be related to a fertile breeding ground for interest groups? The following stylized model has proven useful in this respect:

$$L = f(POP, INC, ASSOC, SIZE, RATIO, MAJ),$$

where L is legislation passed per session as a proxy for influence; POP is population; INC is real income; $ASSOC$ is the number of trade associations; $SIZE$ is legislative size; $RATIO$ is the ratio of the size of the House to the size of the Senate; and MAJ is the size of the legislative majority. Most of the expectations of such a model are obvious and not worth going into here. But the point is to measure interest group influence and then to explain this influence as a function of the costs and benefits facing interest groups in their lobbying activities.

This "reduced-form" supply of legislation function is only for purposes of illustration. Several studies have used this general approach and illustrated its explanatory power.[16] The basic point is that the supply–demand model of legislation is useful and relevant. The model works empirically, and it offers insights into the processes by which legislation is produced across legislatures and over time. It has also been employed to explain specific episodes of legislative change (Shughart and Tollison

---

15. There have been a number of confirming empirical tests of the Landes–Posner theory. See Tollison (1988, 1991) for a review of these results.

16. See Tollison (1988, 1991) and the references cited there.

1985) and to explain the number of interest groups across U.S. states (Crain and Tollison 1991). Moreover, this positive theory of government simply applies the elementary principles of the theory of rent seeking. If the social costs of government action are analyzed in terms of rent seeking, it is a natural extension of this logic to suggest that a positive theory of government will be based upon similar principles.

9. Reform

Once the Pandora's box of rent seeking has been opened, great difficulties confront any theory of economic reform. The reason is simple – the objects of reform (monopolists and transfer recipients in general) will spend resources to resist reform and to protect their transfers. These rent-protecting expenditures are the simple analogues of rent-seeking expenditures – they are one-for-one social costs just as rent-seeking expenditures are. And the point is not just that such expenditures will defeat reform initiatives in a political setting, it is that such expenditures defeat the utilitarian rationale for such deregulatory effects. An incumbent monopolist will easily find it worthwhile to defeat a utilitarian reformer by spending enough of its monopoly rents to make deregulation socially unprofitable (Tollison and Wagner 1991). This is the difficulty in achieving any analytical rationale for reform in a rent-seeking society.

The presumption of a passive monopoly underlies typical discussions of the social value of economic reform. But such passivity is surely implausible in most circumstances. For an intentional monopolist who sought actively to secure a monopoly position, sudden passivity when confronted by a reformer is inexplicable. But it is surely the same for an accidental monopolist. To come into a position of receiving T per period without having had to expend anything to get the transfer does nothing to make the recipient more eager to relinquish the transfer. A monopolist will resist the reformer's efforts in any event.

To assess the gain from economic reform in the presence of an active monopoly, the gain in the case of a passive monopoly (H [Harberger costs] must be reduced by the cost of bringing about and maintaining the reform. The reformer must expend resources in trying to secure the reform. But the reformer's efforts to do so will induce the monopolist to resist. A utilitarian reformer will count both his costs in trying to secure reform and the monopolist's costs in resisting reform as subtractions from the potential gain from that reform (H).

There are several ways of showing that a utilitarian reformer would not try to reform an active monopolist. One way is simply to ask how much the monopolist would be willing to spend to avoid being reformed into a competitive industry. The answer here is "up to T," which exceeds H. Any expenditure less than T will leave the monopolist better off than she would be if she were reformed into a competitive industry. And any expenditure in excess of H by the monopolist will render the value of the reform negative to the utilitarian reformer.

To be sure, this simple formulation of the matter begs some pertinent questions. The monopolist would spend up to T if he were assured of success, but would spend less if the reformer had some likelihood of success. But how much would the reformer spend in trying to secure reform? It would normally be expected that both the reformer and the monopolist would make some expenditure in securing and resisting reform, the result being that each side has a chance of winning. One simple way to model this process is to assume that both the monopolist and the reformer are risk neutral, each side's chance of success being equal to its spending as a share of total spending. In this setting the monopolist can induce the reformer to choose alternative employment by spending H in defending his monopoly. Thus, for an expenditure of H, the monopolist can be certain of retaining $T - H$.[17]

There are, of course, alternative ways to model this process. Moreover, reform may still proceed under a distributional rationale about monopoly, regulation, and transfers; but this is a different story. The moral of this story is not completely nihilistic. The important point is to prevent the emergence of socially unproductive transfers in the first place. This falls into the realm of constitutional economics and the prevention of certain types of transfers (tariffs) from arising through the operation of ordinary politics (Buchanan 1980a).

17. This is for the case of the accidental monopolist. An active monopolist will have originally spent T to secure his monopoly right. In the forced exchange with the reformer, he must now spend an epsilon greater than H to avoid losing the entire capital value of the monopoly right. The fact that present losses of defending a monopoly right can duplicate earlier losses of monopolization is not a surprising result. Given that one side or the other is going to prevail and have influence on regulatory outcomes, the struggle is a forced exchange in which losses reflecting a multiple of original losses are possible (overdissipation).

CHAPTER 24

Endogenous protection: The empirical evidence

STEPHEN P. MAGEE

Endogenous: Developing from within; originating internally. In physiology, the process in a plant or animal by which food is changed into living tissue.

Endogenous protection: A description of the internal process by which the level of protection is explained by all individuals and groups in an economy and the political system acting in their self-interest.[1]

1. Introduction[2]

There are two ways to accumulate wealth: produce it or take it away from someone else. The former is production, which increases wealth. The latter is predation, which transfers wealth. Production is a cooperative effort in which both parties gain. Predation is a noncooperative effort in which the predators gain but the prey lose. Endogenous protection is a consequence of political predation.[3]

Political power can create wealth and economic wealth can create political power. It is this mutual attraction between power and money that motivates redistributive activity. Individuals and groups devote resources to redistribution as long as the expected gains exceed the costs.

The author is indebted to Greg Hallman and Casey Hamilton for assistance in the preparation of this paper and to Bill Hornung, Chet Hornung, Chris Magee, Frances Magee, and especially Dennis Mueller for helpful comments on earlier drafts. They are not responsible for remaining errors.

1. Webster's New Universal Unabridged Dictionary, 1983, Dorset and Baber.
2. For a more extended discussion of endogenous protection, see Young and Magee (1986) and Magee, Brock, and Young (1989). For other reviews of the literature in this area, see Sandler (1981), Baldwin (1986), Deardoff and Stern (1987), Nelson (1988), Hillman (1989), and Vousden (1990). For a bioeconomic approach to this subject and public choice, see Magee (1993).
3. Protection discourages imports into a country either by taxing them (a tax on imports is called a "tariff") or by limiting the quantity of imports to a certain number every year (a quantitative restriction is called a "quota"). If the foreign country agrees to limit the quantity of exports to this market, this is called a "voluntary export restraint," or a VER. For a nontechnical introduction to protection generally, see Bhagwati (1988).

They invest in both production and predation until the marginal returns from each are identical. Lobbies are predatory groups. Protectionist lobbies contribute funds to a protectionist party to maximize their economic gain from the political system. When the protectionist party sponsors a tariff, say, it gains votes using the campaign contributions from the protectionist lobby but it loses votes because voters are upset over higher-priced imports. Endogenous protection is the equilibrium level of the tariff (or other form of protection) that maximizes the difference between the votes gained and the votes lost. This theory of endogenous policy is a general one that can explain any government policy.

There are two theoretical branches. One is Mayer's (1984) median voter model of endogenous protection. There are no lobbies or campaign contributions in Mayer's model. The second approach is a special-interest model in which pro- and antiprotectionist lobby contributions are channeled to the political parties. Contributors to this approach include Brock and Magee (1974, 1975, 1978), Baldwin (1976, 1982, 1984, 1986, 1988), Findlay and Wellisz (1982), Hillman (1982, 1989), Young and Magee (1986), Magee, Brock, and Young (1989), Grossman and Helpman (1994) and Mayer and Li (1994).This survey contains only a sample of the existing work and focuses on the special interest approach because the preponderance of the empirical work is in that area.

Five major ideas emerge from the theory of endogenous protection. First, endogenous policies are economically inefficient. Second, endogenous policies are politically efficient. Third, government policies are interest group based.[4] Fourth, government policies are just like prices in economic markets. Fifth, politicans are largely powerless, so that endogenous protection has no policy implications.

First, government policies are economically inefficient. Democracies overinvest in the predatory political activity because (1) there is an absence of well-defined property rights in the public purse; (2) there is loss of output from the resources wasted in lobbying (which economists call "rent seeking"); (3) there is collateral damage from political predation, which parallels pollution in private markets; and (4) lobby competition leads to prisoners' dilemma outcomes, in which the equilibrium is inferior to a more cooperative outcome. Predatory overgrazing of the public purse is nothing new. Cro-Magnon man overkilled megafauna by driving large herds of bison and reindeer into pit traps. Washington, D.C., a relic of the last Ice Age, has long been a focus of inefficient animal harvest (Weatherford 1985). Today's Washington is located where the Potomac River hits the Atlantic seaboard. This was a junction

---

4. To quote John Stuart Mill, " a good cause seldom triumphs unless someone's interest is bound up in it " (Bhagwati 1988, 18).

of north–south and east–west routes traveled by prehistoric mastodons. About 20,000 years ago, prehistoric man sat on that site and slaughtered the migrating mastodons. There are no mastodons today. This view that predatory political activity is economically wasteful leads economists to a mistaken conclusion that political markets are not efficient and that government policies should be economically efficient. This view is wrong, since successful politicians, by definition, provide exactly what their constituencies want.

This leads to a second idea, that political markets are efficient – they are politically efficient. Rational politicians maximize votes, not economic efficiency. We have economically inefficient policies, such as protection, because they maximize the votes for the protectionist party. There is little that economists can do to eliminate protection because any change from the current level would generate more opposition than support. When politicians maximize votes, they promote political efficiency. Political efficiency delivers to voters and interest groups what they want. The current debate over the quality of public education in America clarifies this point. Three-fourths of adults in the United States do not have a college education and neither want nor need a prep school–Ivy League education for their children. Our democratic system provides what parents and children want: football, band, and inflated grades. Democracy is quite efficient.

The idea of political efficiency also applies to nondemocracies. Consider Bolivia. Bolivia has had more than 190 coups in the last 160 years. Such low barriers to political entry and exit make Bolivia a highly competitive political system. Illiteracy is not even a barrier to politics. (Enrique Penaranda's mother said: "If I had known he was going to be the president of Bolivia, I would have taught him to read and write.")

There is a trade-off between economic efficiency and political efficiency. Just as investors cannot have both high returns and low risk, efficient political systems are usually not efficient economies. Bolivia is politically efficient; Japan is not. Only one political party has dominated politics in Japan since the late 1940s. Though Japan has an inefficient democracy, it has a more efficient economy. Because of this trade-off, policies become less efficient economically as democracies become more efficient politically. U.S. protection is an example of the simultaneous growth of politically efficient though economically inefficient policies. Since 1970, the United States has become more politically competitive but the economic efficiency of protection has declined. Protection has shifted from tariffs to voluntary export restraints, which are economically wasteful but deliver a lot of votes.

A third idea is that policy is driven by groups. Interest groups can deliver large numbers of voters and funds. There are economies of scale in politics because it is more effective to pursue groups than individual voters. Politicians are brokers between groups and individual voters. The policies that result, such as protection, represent the price that particularized (lobby) groups can exact from generalized (voters) groups. The greater the economies of scale in fund raising, the higher will be the price (tariff) exacted by organized groups. Group behavior in endogenous protection builds on a bioeconomic theory of the pyramid of nature (Magee 1993) where carnivores eat herbivores, the herbivores eat herbs, and so on. The game theoretic structure of the $2 \times 2 \times 2 \times 2$ model of endogenous protection is a biological dominance hierarchy applied to the modern democracy – parties dominate lobbies and lobbies dominate voters and firms, and so on. (Magee, Brock and Young 1989).

A fourth idea is that government policies play the same role in politics that prices play in an economy. Both are equilibrating variables that adjust until opposing redistributive forces balance. Suppose the textile industry has a 20 percent tariff but the leather industry has only a 5 percent tariff. If any attempt to change either tariff generates more opposition than support, then these are the equilibrium prices in political markets for textile and leather protection. Political or economic shocks that alter the supply or demand for protection will change the tariff rates.

A fifth is that politicians are largely powerless to control the level of protection. They have no more control over tariffs than an auctioneer has over the price of pork bellies. Politicians are just market makers who adjust prices in political markets until the supply of protection equals the demand. The resulting price is the endogenous level of protection. Politicians can indulge their own preferences only when political markets are less than competitive. This means there can be no policy implications of endogenous protection. In an efficient political market, policies such as protection maximize votes. Any deviation from vote maximization opens a politician up to potential defeat. For example, all of the reasons one might contemplate for changing the level of protection have already been considered. Only political entrepreneurs who are more skillful than incumbents will come up with innovations. If they are sufficiently skillful, they will replace the incumbents. Competitive political markets are like efficient economic markets for stocks, bonds, foreign exchange, and commodities. Only unforeseen economic and political shocks cause prices and protection to change. The "shoulds" of normative economic welfare analysis are empty exercises when policies are endogenous.[5] Welfare

---

5. Politicians from opposing parties in Congress invite economists to testify on both sides of an issue. A White House staffer told me that after the economists have canceled each other out, Congress proceeds to give the lobbies what they want, subject to a voter constraint.

economists bemoan this point. They lament the unfairness of lobby groups preying on unsuspecting voters. The response of an endogenous protection theorist is that people like sheep but also eat sheep. The rose colored glasses of Pareto optimality do not fit the reality of power politics. As Justice Frankfurter said: "There are two things you do not want to observe – the creation of laws and of sausage." Perhaps the only solution to the unfairness of endogenous politics is Zen meditation.

How does endogenous protection differ from exogenous protection? Almost all older economic studies of protection are about "exogenous" protection because they do not explain why protection is high or low. They simply take protection as given and study the impact of protection on other parts of the economy. Endogenous protection explains both how protection affects the economy and how the economy affects the level of protection.[6] The general equilibrium theory of endogenous protection is a mathematical description of political predation. It explains the tariff-equivalent level of protection, lobbying expenditures, product prices, factor prices, the distribution of income, and the probabilities of election of political parties when each group in a democracy pursues its own self-interest.

Endogenous protection explains why national tariff rates decline with the level of economic development and why national tariff rates have declined through time. Figure 1 shows how national tariff rates decline

6. The first papers on endogenous protection were written by Brock and Magee (1974, 1975, 1978, 1980). They simultaneously solved the problem of optimal contributions by protectionist lobbies and the vote-maximizing tariff that the political parties would set. However, they did so in a partial equilibrium framework. Findlay and Wellisz (1982) provided the first special interest model of endogenous lobbying in general equilibrium, but with the level of protection being exogenous.

Mayer (1984) followed with the first model of tariffs with endogenous voters, but with no special interests or lobbies. He assumed that all parties would choose the policy favored by the median voter. Young and Magee (1986) followed with the first $2\times2\times2\times2$ model with two goods, two factors, two lobbies, and two political parties in general equilibrium. Magee (1990) showed how the amounts of national rent seeking could be measured from a general equilibrium model of endogenous protection using actual tariffs, factor intensities of production, and consumption.

Important work on endogenous policy generally has been provided by Lindbeck (1975, 1976, 1977, 1985, 1986, 1989).

Early and important empirical work on endogenous protection was done by Pincus (1975), Baldwin (1976, 1982, 1984, 1986, 1988), Caves (1976), and Anderson (1980). See also the later papers Helpman and Krugman (1985), Krugman (1986), and the computable general equilibrium models of Whalley (1985).

The theory of endogenous protection grew out of the pioneering work done by Downs (1957), who showed that it is rational for voters to remain uninformed, and Olson (1965), who observed the exploitation of organizers by the apathetic (i.e., those who lobby for protection generate benefits to nonmember free riders in the industry who gain from the protection but did not help obtain it). For related work see Magee (1972, 1980, 1990).

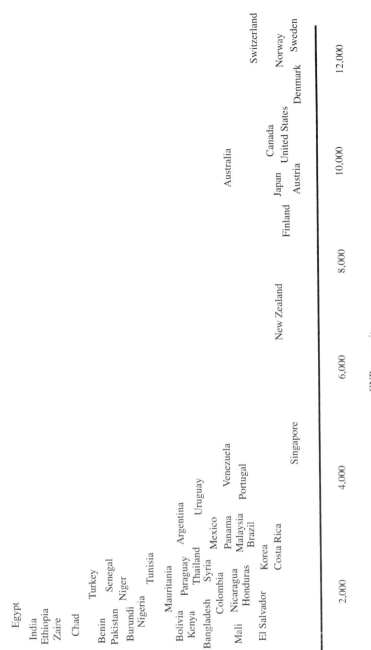

Figure 1. National average tariff rates (c. 1975) and GNP per capita in 1980. National tariff averages were calculated as total tariff revenue divided by the value of imports. More recent tariff data were not used because the data sources for this figure did not report European Community tariff revenue by country after the mid-1970s. *Source*: Magee, Brock, and Young (1989, chap. 17).

as economies develop. Endogenous protection predicts that an exogenous increase in the capital stock of an advanced economy leads to reduced protection (because protection helps labor) and higher export subsidies on capital-intensive goods (since the economy has more capital, capital has more political clout) and a higher probability of the election of the procapital party (because it receives more lobbying funds from capital). Both of these political developments offset diminishing returns and cause the return on capital to increase. This explains why endogenous protection predicts increasing returns to politics in general equilibrium.

Traditional economic assumptions about exogenous protection predict that small countries should have free trade while large countries use protection to exploit foreigners by lowering the world price for the large country's imported goods. This prediction is rejected by the data. Larger countries have lower tariff rates because massive land areas impose higher transport costs. This natural protection against the encroachment of foreign goods reduces the need for man-made protection. In addition, for the last fifty years, the United States, a large country, has pressured for freer world trade. Surveys of economists reveal a similar pattern. Economists in larger countries (the United States and Germany) favor freer trade while economists in smaller countries do not. Frey et al. (1984) found that though 79 percent of American economists and 70 percent of German economists favored free trade, the proportion was only 47 percent in Switzerland, 44 percent in Austria, and 27 percent in France.

Endogenous protection explains both anomalies in the previous paragraph. First, large U.S. multinational firms, embodying physical and human capital, flourish most in large countries and favor not only free trade overseas but also export promotion from the United States. Second, industrial concentration rises in import-competing industries as countries get smaller. Public choice theory predicts that as the benefits of protection are concentrated on fewer firms, protection will be higher in smaller countries.

The equilibrium approach to endogenous policies challenges a frequent political science finding that no equilibrium exists or that there are many equilibria.[7] Endogenous protection is also unsettling to economists because it suggests their influence over policymakers is marginal to nil. In an endogenous political equilibrium, there is little that well-

---

7. Economic factors also dominate political explanations of protection. Industry factors explain 53 percent of the variability of pre-EC tariff rates in the advanced countries while country effects (presumably political) explain only 20 percent (Magee, Brock, and Young 1989, 254).

meaning economists can do to eradicate inefficient policies such as tariffs. For example, in May of 1930, over one thousand members of the American Economic Association signed a petition opposing passage of the pending Smoot–Hawley tariff which raised the average U.S. tariff rate on dutiable imports to 59 percent (Lake 1986). One month later, Herbert Hoover signed the Smoot–Hawley tariff into law. U.S. imports fell by nearly two-thirds between 1929 and 1933, thus transmitting the Great Depression overseas (Magee 1972, 651). The special interest orgy that led to the Smoot–Hawley tariff so completely ignored economists that Congress raised the tariff on U.S. cashew nut imports by 1,000 percent. Cashew nuts were not even produced in the United States at that time (Bhagwati 1988, 21). Even when economists are right, they are largely ignored.[8]

Most work on endogenous protection focuses on redistributive motivations for trade policies. Lindbeck's (1985) work on endogenous policy divides redistributive policies into four useful groups: broad horizontal redistribution (labor to capital), life cycle redistribution (social security), vertical redistribution (rich to poor), and fragmented horizontal redistribution (from general interests to special interests). He makes the important point that protection provides nonbudget methods of redistribution, which explains why it is politically superior to production subsidies and consumption taxes.

2. The $2\times2\times2\times2$ theory of endogenous protection: Compensation, endowments, magnification, obfuscation, and increasing returns

There are four ways in which humans can interact: they can be cooperative, selfish, altruistic, or spiteful (Magee 1993). My behavior is cooperative if I help myself and help others; it is selfish if I help myself but hurt others; it is altruistic if I hurt myself but help others; and it is spiteful if I hurt both myself and others. Figure 2 illustrates these interactions. Cooperative behavior is the dominant form analyzed in economics because

---

8. Economists frequently quote Keynes's statement that practical men are "usually the slaves of some defunct economist." Bhagwati suggests that the ideas of economists are important. Bhagwati lauds Carlyle's admonition to a dinner companion who was challenging Carlyle's ideas. Carlyle said "There was once a man called Rousseau who wrote a book containing nothing but ideas. The second edition was bound in the skins of those who laughed at the first" (Bhagwati 1988, 17).

Marx took a different view, namely that ideas are endogenous. An illustration is the explosion of academic papers on the virtues of protection in the 1980s in the United States. This was a time when U.S. politicians were looking for justifications to keep Japanese goods out of the U.S. market.

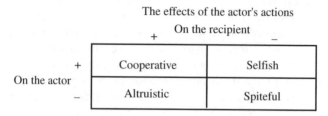

Figure 2. The four forms of human interaction. *Source:* Magee (1993).

of the assumption that voluntary transactions necessarily involve mutual gain. Selfish behavior is the dominant form of Darwinian animal behavior and of political interaction. Groups form to gain at the expense of others and to protect themselves from other groups. One can think of cooperative economic relationships as horizontal because both parties gain. Political relationships can be thought of as primarily vertical because they are about rights, redistribution, domination, and power. Neoclassical economists write about the cooperative box while Marx emphasized the selfish box.

The 2×2×2×2 model of endogenous protection by Magee, Brock, and Young (1989) merges neoclassical cooperation and Marxian domination into a single model. The result is that capital has more influence in the political systems of capital-abundant countries while labor has more influence in labor-abundant countries. The mathematical framework of the 2×2×2×2 model is a small, open, advanced country that has two factors of production (capital and labor), two goods (one exportable and one importable), two lobbies (one for capital and one for labor) and two parties (one procapital and the other prolabor). The emphasis is on long-run effects, so the country follows the Heckscher–Ohlin international trade model. It exports the capital-intensive good, which receives an export subsidy from the procapital party in exchange for campaign contributions from the capital lobby. The country imports the labor-intensive good, which receives protection from the prolabor party in exchange for campaign contributions from the labor lobby. Goods markets and factor (capital and labor) markets are perfectly competitive, but the tariff and export subsidy influence domestic prices. Lobbies channel resources to the parties to maximize the incomes of their memberships. Parties choose levels of their policies to maximize their probabilities of election. Individual voters are rationally ignorant, meaning that they underinvest in information about political races.[9]

9. The game theoretic setup is that the political parties "Stackelberg lead" all players, while the lobbies "Stackelberg lead" everyone except the parties. Reversal of this

There are five important results in the $2\times2\times2\times2$ theory of endogenous protection:

1. the compensation effect
2. the endowment effect
3. the magnification paradox
4. the principle of optimal obfuscation
5. increasing returns to politics

The first three help explain why protection has declined in the advanced countries for most of the post-World War II period and the fourth explains why quantitative restrictions on trade increased in the 1980s. The $2\times2\times2\times2$ theory is interest group based. In the advanced countries, organized labor typically pushes for protection while skilled labor and large, capital-intensive and/or technology-intensive multinationals pressure for freer trade and export subsidies. Protection has always been interest group driven. It exists in every single country of the world because more votes are gained from campaign contributions from protectionists than are lost from the protection itself. Export subsidies are less visible and may be economically more important. For example, the Europeans expended \$25 in export subsidies for every \$100 in agricultural exports in 1990 (Sosland 1993).[10] Twenty-five percent export subsidies are much higher than the prevailing rates of advanced country protection.

Two hundred years ago, the landed aristocracy in England received protection against agricultural imports while the bourgeois manufacturing class on the Continent obtained protection from imports of manufactures (Kindleberger 1951, 1975). The spread of democracy reduced trade restrictions as the vote gave consumers a more direct voice. How-

pattern is unreasonable because it implies free trade, zero distortions, and Pareto-optimal policies.

The exogenous variables that drive the $2\times2\times2\times2$ model are the country's capital–labor endowment ratio, the world price of exportables relative to importables, the coefficients in the utility functions for capital and labor, the parameters in the production functions for the two goods, and the parameters for the importance of policies relative to money in the probability of election election. The endogenous variables are the tariff and export subsidies, the probabilities of election of the parties, wages and rental rates, the amount of capital and labor given to each party in campaign contributions, total factor incomes, the domestic price ratios of the goods (inclusive of policy effects and probabilities of election), and total output, consumption, and trade of both goods.

10. Export subsidies and promotion are much bigger than is popularly imagined in the advanced countries. Implicit export promotion occurs in the United States through all manner of programs, including subsidies to public education. In 1980, \$96 billion was spent in the United States on public elementary and secondary schools, and \$64 billion was spent on higher education. This equaled 40 percent of U.S. exports that year, which were \$342 billion (*Statistical Abstract of the US* 1986, 142, 150, 794). While only a fraction of U.S. education results in greater exports, there is an unmeasured stimulus.

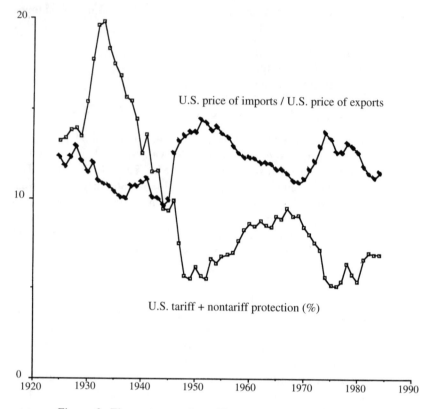

Figure 3. The compensation effect: protection compensates for low-priced imports. The components of U.S. tariff and nontariff protection are shown in Figure 7. Before 1950, only nontariff protection is shown in the figure here. *Source:* Magee, Brock and Young (1989, table A.13.1).

ever, narrow interests are still a driving force behind protection. (Notice in Figure 7 below that an index of the ad valorem equivalent of nontariff U.S. protection increased almost 50 percent between 1976 and 1984. This increase was almost exclusively driven by powerful protectionists in only three product areas: steel, autos, and textiles/apparel.) Today, the United States protects American manufacturing from imported manufactures from East Asia and American agriculture from a variety of cheap foreign food imports.

2.1 The compensation effect

It is rational for special interest protectionist groups to expend lobbying funds until the marginal benefits equal the marginal costs. Starting from an endogenous political equilibrium, what should the protectionist lobby do if the economic fortune of its economic clientele declines? The answer is that a protectionist lobby should channel more funds to the protectionist party, because the lowered rate of return from economic activity makes political activity a more attractive investment. The equilibrium response of the protectionist party is to provide increased protection.[11] The compensation effect suggests that the increased protection will partially (though not fully) compensate the group for its initial setback. The tendency for politics to partially compensate for unexpected negative shocks makes endogenous protection insurance after the fact. An unexplored question is the welfare benefit by which compensation effects make economic markets more complete.

The three components of the compensation effect can be summarized as follows: in the face of economic setbacks, there is increased lobbying pressure, the political system delivers more favorable policies, and the policies provide partial compensation to the injured group.

A recent example of the compensation principle is the effect of the decline in the world price of U.S. manufactured imports in the last decade. Advances by the Japanese and other countries in autos, steel, and textiles reduced world prices of U.S. importables. Following the compensation principle, labor in importables increased lobbying and received more protection, particularly in older industries, through voluntary export restraints, primarily with the Japanese. The compensation principle predicts two effects on the prolabor party (e.g., the Democrats in Congress): they gain votes from increased campaign contributions but lose votes because of their higher protection. The reverse pattern holds for procapital Republicans. The net effect is negative for Democrats in the short run but positive in the long run. Wages fall because of the initial decline in the price of imports, but partial compensation is provided for labor by the political system's increase in protection.[12]

Figure 3 illustrates the compensation effect. Decreases in the prices of U.S. imports are generally matched by increases in the average U.S. tariff rate.[13] Notice that since 1976, total U.S. protection has been rising in response to declining U.S. import prices.

11. The effect of the economic shock on the protectionist party is to reduce its probability of election in the short run (i.e., with Leontief production), to have no effect on its probability of election in the medium run (with Cobb–Douglas production), and to increase its probability of election in the long run (when the elasticities of substitution between the factors of production become greater than one).

12. Hillman (1982) finds that a decline in the world price of a product does not unambiguously yield a compensation effect. The decline in the world price may cause the domestic industry to become weaker rather than stronger politically.

13. Choi (1991) determines from vector auto-regression techniques applied to annual data from 1900–84 that the price series leads the tariff series. This rules out U.S. tariffs driving the price series through a large country terms-of-trade effect.

Historical examples of the principle are agricultural protection and rent controls, which have increased following sudden drops in the income of affected groups (Lindbeck 1985). In both the nineteenth and twentieth centuries, protection increased during periods of worldwide depression but decreased during periods of world prosperity (McKeown 1983).

2.2 The endowment effect

Country factor endowments (e.g., the ratio of capital to labor) directly affect the national level of protection. The larger any factor in an economy, the more favors it receives from the political system. Simply stated, the endowment effect reflects political clout. Since protection helps the scarce factor in an economy, national levels of protection should increase with the quantitative importance of the scarce factor.

In the United States, labor is the scarce factor. The endowment effect predicts that U.S. protection moves directly with the ratio of U.S. labor to the other factors of production.[14] Protection has fallen since World War II in the United States and other developed countries because of capital deepening. As capital has grown more rapidly than labor, unskilled labor has become a less important factor of production in the United States, and its political influence has waned. Up until 1976, U.S. protection declined. As shown in Figure 4, the number of U.S. workers per unit of real capital today is about half what it was at the turn of the century. After adjusting for other factors, both time series and cross-country data indicate that country factor endowments are statistically significant in explaining national tariff rates. The endowment effect is also consistent with the phenomenon of declining success of the prolabor party in U.S. elections. Democratic presidential candidates have lost five out of the last seven presidential elections, and in 1994, the Democrats lost control of the Congress.

Majorities can tyrannize minorities through voting (Riker 1980). Witness the progressive income tax that imposes heavier taxes on richer taxpayers. The endowment effect suggests a similar result with endogenous protection: economic power dominates economic weakness. Support for the endowment effect is that procapital parties hold power for larger fractions of the time in capital-abundant countries, while prolabor

---

14. We do not have a time series available on U.S. human capital. Ideally, we would want the ratio of unskilled labor to human and physical capital. In the absence of data on human capital, I use the total labor to physical capital ratio in Figure 3. For an early version of the endowment effect, see Magee and Young (1983).

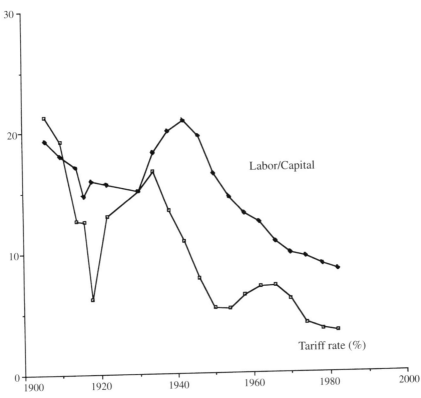

Figure 4. U.S. tariffs (%) and the number of U.S. laborers per $100,000 in real capital. *Source:* Magee, Brock, and Young (1989, chap. 13).

parties hold power for larger fractions of the time in labor-abundant countries (Balash 1992).

2.3 The magnification paradox

If production technologies change such that capital–labor ratios in exportables and importables move closer together, factor prices (wages and returns to capital) become more responsive to product prices. This is the magnification effect of international trade theory (Jones 1965). If the price of textiles rises, wages rise by an even larger percentage. Increased magnification makes a labor lobby contribute more for textile protection because each dollar increases wages by more than before.

U.S. factor intensities have become more similar in the United States in the last forty years (Choi and Magee 1991), so that magnification has increased. Increased magnification of factor prices with respect to product prices causes protectionist forces to devote more economic resources to politics but to come away with a lower equilibrium level of protection. Since the protection is more potent, protectionists receive more redistribution than before, despite the lower tariff. The paradox is that increased magnification increases protectionist lobbying but reduces tariff rates. This appears to be the case for most of the post-World War II period in the United States.

2.4 Optimal obfuscation

Redistribution, like theft, is most successful if undetected. Protectionist parties are sensitive to the criticism that they sell out to special interests. This causes parties to complicate protection to reduce this negative impact. A rational party moves to more indirect and obscure forms of protection as long as the vote gain from the reduced negative voter effect exceeds the votes lost, because the less potent form of protection generates less campaign funds from the protectionists. In a subsequent section, we use this principle to explain the recent growth of obscure forms of protection such as voluntary export restraints.

2.5 Increasing returns to politics: An endogenous political theory of economic development

There are increasing returns to factor endowments: the more capital an economy has, the higher are its returns to capital. If capital is already powerful, politics makes it even more powerful. Endogenous politics reinforces economic power. Countries such as the United States, Germany, and Japan provide greater political protection to capital and this attracts even more capital. As advanced countries acquire more capital, their political systems increase the legal protection of property rights. International capital gravitates to countries where it is most protected.

Conversely, in poor countries, labor dominates capital politically. Capitalists will be more heavily taxed and some will leave the country. The remaining capital is less effective politically. A bimodal distribution of world capital endowments is implied by the endowment effect. It predicts an observable gap between countries with high and low capital endowments. This means that endogenous politics reinforces existing patterns of economic development and contributes negatively to developing countries converging on advanced countries (Magee and Magee 1994). Notice in Figure 1 that there is a bimodal distribution of GNP per capita. In that figure, New Zealand is the only country in the gap between the high- and low-income countries.

Increasing returns to politics is supported by two pieces of evidence. First, cross-national studies indicate that procapital parties hold power longer in capital-abundant countries, while prolabor parties hold power longer in labor-abundant countries (Balash 1992). Second, anecdotal evidence is provided by the recent political collapse of some of the Soviet-bloc economies. Ideologically, these governments were prolabor and the low values of their postcollapse capital stocks per capita are evidence of capital implosion.

The standard economic view is that protection harms developing countries. Michaely, Papageorgiou, and Choksi (1991) provide the following evidence on the economics of protection and growth in developing countries from 1950–85:

1. The introduction of severe trade restrictions significantly retards the subsequent growth of gross domestic product.
2. Slow growth countries that adopt trade liberalization grow faster.
3. The stronger the liberalization of trade, the faster the subsequent gross domestic product growth.
4. Large countries are less likely to pursue sustained trade liberalization.
5. Sustained liberalization is associated with political stability.
6. Sustained liberalization is associated with improved trade balances.

The results are an economic endorsement of free trade. Developing countries started moving to freer trade in the 1980s. That process continued into the 1990s, as illustrated by Mexico's embracing the North American Free Trade Agreement (NAFTA).

3. Implications of the 2×2×2×2 theory

There are five implications of the 2×2×2×2 theory of endogenous protection:

1. Endogenous protection is politically efficient.
2. Rent seeking (resources expended on political predation) is a transaction cost of democracy but can lead to economic black holes.
3. U.S. Republican administrations generate more protection than do Democratic ones.
4. Inefficient forms of protection raise questions about the economic efficiency of democracy.
5. The evolution of increasingly inefficient protection (from tariffs

to quotas to voluntary export restraints) is explained by optimal obfuscation.

3.1 Endogenous protection is politically efficient

Classical trade theory emphasizes that protection is bad for the economy and free trade is better. Protection lowers the welfare of small countries, because protectionists gain less than proexport and consumer groups lose. But not a single one of the over 150 countries in the world displays free trade. As John Kenneth Galbraith would say, classical trade theory blooms in the ivory tower but wilts in the real world. Even Hong Kong, the lone historic example of free trade, has adopted protection as its local production has increased in the last decade. The empirical poverty of classical trade theory obliges us to explain protection in other ways.

At least three theories have been advanced to explain protection. The first uses the prisoners' dilemma model (Messerlin 1981). The best strategy for protectionists (who want tariffs) and proexport interests (who want export subsidies) would be to cooperate, not lobby, and agree to free trade. However, under such an agreement, the best strategy for each lobby is to cheat and seek policy intervention under the table. Consequently, the equilibrium outcome is for both players to cheat and lobby, so that protectionists get protection while proexport interests get export subsidies. The prisoners' dilemma game is the only 2×2 game in which the payoffs are such that the equilibrium outcome (protection) differs from the economically efficient outcome (free trade).

The second came from strategic trade policy, which is a partial equilibrium model based on oligopoly theory (Brander and Spencer 1985). Oligopoly theory explains economic behavior when a few large firms are present. Protection expands the size of the domestic market for home producers. If this allows firms to exploit economies of scale, their costs fall and protection would give them a competitive edge in export markets, provided that foreign governments do not retaliate. Thus, industry protection should be positively correlated with industry export success. This implication was rejected in a study of over 200 four-digit traded U.S. products. High U.S. import protection was associated with lower shares of that product in world export markets (Dick 1993).

A third explanation of protection is provided by 2×2×2×2 endogenous policy theory, which has already been discussed. A protectionist party in a free-trade economy can increase its votes with the campaign funds it raises from protectionists. Parties introduce both welfare-increasing and welfare-reducing policies so long as the votes gained from the associated special interest contributions exceed votes lost

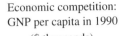

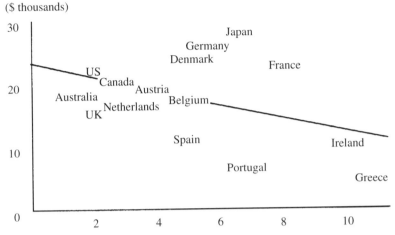

Figure 5. The trade-off between economic competition and political competition. *Source:* Guilli, Masciandaro, and Tabellini (1991).

from the economic inefficiencies of the policies (Magee, Brock, and Young 1989).

An endogenous policy equilibrium displays political efficiency but not economic efficiency. When parties choose vote-maximizing policies, non-zero protection is optimal for the prolabor party in an advanced country. Recall that economic efficiency occurs when there is no change that would increase one person's welfare without lowering someone else's by even more. The same idea applies to politics. An endogenous equilibrium is, by definition, politically efficient because there is no other value for each party's policy that would increase the party's probability of election.

Figure 5 illustrates the trade-off between economic and political efficiency. Notice that countries like the United States, which are most competitive economically (have the highest incomes per capita), are the least competitive politically (have the fewest turnovers of the government every decade) and vice versa. Since the mid-1970s, the trade-off has also been demonstrated by the replacement of tariffs with voluntary export restraints (VERs). VERs are politically efficient since they are easy to impose and maintain, but they are very harmful economically. At the country level, the trade-off is also present for small countries in classical theory because protection always lowers their aggregate welfare. The distribution of the gainers and losers from protection in small countries is interesting. Simulations of endogenous protection revealed the standard result that 60 percent of the time, protection helped the protectionists, but by less than the harm done to everyone else. Forty percent of the time, everyone in the economy, including the protectionists themselves, was worse off with protection and lobbying. The latter were prisoners' dilemma outcomes.[15]

In contrast to Marx, endogenous protection suggests symmetric exploitation. Capital exploits labor through the political system in advanced countries where capital is abundant while labor exploits capital in developing countries where labor is abundant. This happens because endogenous politics reinforces economic strength. Evidence noted earlier supports this view. Procapital parties have been in office longer during the post-World War II period in capital-abundant countries, while the reverse has been true in labor-abundant countries (Balash 1992).

3.2 Rent seeking as a transaction cost of democracy and economic black holes

Redistributive conflict over the level of protection generates lobbying and economic waste. Tullock(1967) spawned the work on rent seeking by observing that all the producer's surplus caused by tariffs might be wasted by protectionist lobbying. Krueger(1974) defined "rent seeking" as economic resources wasted in generating artificial scarcity through the political system. Endogenous protection builds on this literature.[16]

Rent seeking increases with country age (Olson 1982). Economic sclerosis spreads through time as lobbies learn to exploit the political system. As the U.S. and other Western economies age, protection should increase. Are there any theoretical limits on how high the protection can go or on the resources that can be consumed in lobbying for protection?

Maximalists point to economic black holes, in which all of an economy could disappear in redistributive fights over shares of the pie (Magee, Brock, and Young 1989, chap. 15). One would not expect a black hole, even theoretically, because of diminishing returns in production, consumption, and even voter responses to policies and money. However, 100 per cent of an economy can disappear into lobbying in equilibrium,

---

15. The prisoners' dilemma outcomes usually occurred when a country's capital–labor endowment ratio was about average, meaning that neither capital nor labor had a marked advantage in its economy relative to its trading partners. The other 60 percent of the cases occurred when a country had an extreme endowment ratio, so that the dominant factor could exploit the weak factor with endogenous politics.
16. See Tollison's chapter in this volume for a survey of rent seeking.

under some technical conditions.[17] (Examples include wars, ghettoes, coups, and the period just before hotly contested elections.)[18]

Empirical work indicates that capital–labor ratios are more similar for exportables and importables in advanced countries, so that advanced countries have higher magnification – a greater responsiveness of wages, for example, with respect to relative import prices (Magee 1990). This means that advanced countries should devote more resources to lobbying over trade policy and, because of the magnification paradox, have lower equilibrium tariffs. A mnemonic device is to think of advanced country tariffs as Tylenol and developing country tariffs as Aspirin. Advanced country tariffs are more potent, so lower doses provide more protection.

The one part of this puzzle that appears inconsistent with the facts is that there is more total rent seeking in developing countries. This may be explained by other factors such as greater political competition, less informed voters, younger governments, and weaker institutions.[19] The Tylenol tariff also provides an intuitive explanation of black holes. As the black hole is approached, magnification increases and the endogenous tariff gets smaller and smaller.

Minimalists on the rent-seeking question include Bhagwati (1982), who suggests that lobbying over trade policy can increase welfare. Minimalists cite two examples. First, a higher tariff for a large country can allow it to push down the world price of its imported good and increase its welfare at the expense of its foreign trading partners. Second, the theory of the second best implies that greater protection might offset the welfare distortions caused by these other taxes if there were high domestic taxes on all goods except the importable. Third, exporters lobbying in their foreign markets (e.g., the Japanese lobbying in the United States) can reduce world protection and increase welfare.

Tullock (1988) has posed an underdissipation puzzle on the question of rent seeking: Why is so little expended, relative to the benefits, on everything from protectionist lobbying to police protection? For exam-

---

17. High magnification and degrees of relative risk aversion approaching one.
18. What can cause an economic black hole? As noted above, when production technologies change such that capital–labor ratios in exportables and importables get closer together, international trade theory predicts that a general equilibrium magnification parameter increases (the elasticity of factor rewards with respect to product prices). When factor prices become more responsive to product prices, protection and other government policies become more important to lobbies. As a result, a protectionist lobby contributes more for protection because it has a higher payoff.
19. Another reason for higher tariffs in developing countries is that their governments are more reliant on tariff revenue because tariffs are easier to collect. In 1990, international trade taxes were 3 percent of total government revenue in the advanced industrial countries while they were 30 percent in Africa (International Monetary Fund 1992, 42).

ple, in the United States less than one-thousandth of the value of the U.S. budget is spent annually on lobbying. On the tariff question, complete dissipation would involve lobbying expenditures equal to the entire area of producer's surplus created by the tariff. This area might equal $50 to $100 billion per year whereas the total amount of lobbying annually in the United States for the entire federal budget cannot be over a few billion. There are many explanations of this phenomenon but none appear capable of explaining the degree of underdissipation we observe. We discuss below how collateral damage caused by inefficient redistributive policies can be large.[20]

While rent seeking may be wasteful, it is simply a transaction cost of running a democracy (Magee 1990). Viewed in this way, rent seeking is not an evil to be eliminated, but a cost to be minimized. Countries that provide conflict resolution and public goods at lower costs have a competitive edge. The implied research agenda is the cross-national study of constitutions, redistribution and political prisoners' dilemmas.

3.3 Republican protectionism and isoprotection curves

U.S. protection has gone up more under Republican administrations in the United States than under Democratic administrations. Democratic administrations favor prolabor policies such as low unemployment and high inflation. Both of these reduce the pressure on Congress for protection. Conversely, Republican presidents display macroeconomic policies that generate more protection (high unemployment and low inflation). This pattern has definitely held in the postwar period for Republican presidents Eisenhower and Reagan with somewhat weaker results for Nixon and Ford. The reverse has been true for the macroeconomic and trade policies of Democratic presidents Roosevelt, Kennedy, Johnson, and Carter.

Isoprotection curves have the same axes as the Phillips curve. These curves show combinations of unemployment and inflation for which the level of protection is constant. Figure 6 shows two isoprotection

20. Olson (1965) suggested that protectionist underdissipation is explained by free riding by members of the protectionist lobby. Hillman and Riley (1989) show that asymmetric valuations of the object of the rent seeking can lead to underdissipation. Ursprung (1990) finds that if the sought-after prize is a public good, total rent seeking will not exceed the average stake of an individual rent seeker. Hillman (1989) gives the following sufficient conditions for complete dissipation: constant returns, symmetric information, risk-neutral contenders, and identical valuation of the prize. Becker (1983) also argues that small groups will be successful in taxing larger groups for their subsidies. For detailed information on contributions to a specific political campaign, see Ferguson (1989).

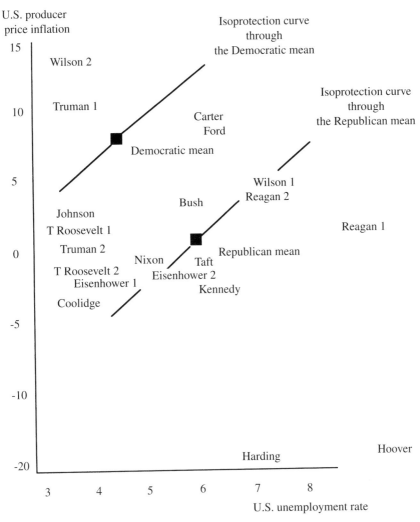

Figure 6. Isoprotection curves for the U.S., 1900–92. *Source:* Magee, Brock, and Young (1989, chap. 13).

curves.[21] Notice that the Republican isoprotection curve (with higher unemployment and lower inflation) is consistent with the higher average

21. Only two isoprotection curves are shown. Imagine, however, that the figure is filled with curves parallel to those shown. Curves in the lower right are associated with high-tariff rates while those in the top left are associated with low-tariff rates. Movement along a curve is associated with constant tariffs. Franklin Roosevelt was excluded from this analysis because his terms included both the Great Depression and World War II.

level of tariffs under Republicans compared to Democrats. The two largest U.S. tariff increases in this century occurred under Warren Harding in 1922 (the Fordney–McCumber tariff) and Herbert Hoover in 1930 (the Smoot–Hawley tariff).[22] Empirical estimates of the slopes of these curves indicate that every 1 percentage point increase in the U.S. unemployment rate requires a 2 percentage point increase in the U.S. inflation rate to keep the U.S. tariff rate constant.

3.4 Inefficient policy choice, VERs, and optimal obfuscation

Why are tariffs, voluntary export restraint agreements (VERs), quotas, and other relatively inefficient policies used for redistribution rather than more efficient ones? Since a tariff equals an equivalent consumption tax and production subsidy, the same redistribution benefits to producers of import-competing goods or scarce factors could be obtained by a production subsidy alone. This would avoid the social cost of the consumption deadweight loss and all of the voter antagonism to tariffs.

There are two reasons why tariffs rather than production subsidies are used: (1) Tariffs are a major source of revenue for young countries; they are easier to collect. (2) In a progressive tax system, a person's tax share is higher than his income share. Tariffs reduce the individual's direct tax burden while subsidies raise it. The tax burden of the subsidy is borne by higher-income people while the cost of the tariff, in terms of lost consumer surplus, is spread across the whole population. Thus, individuals with above-average incomes favor tariffs over the more efficient production subsidy (Mayer and Reizman 1990).[23]

---

22. Harding and Hoover would be on the highest isoprotection curves in the figure: namely, the ones in the bottom right corner with high unemployment and deflation.
     Reagan's first term had the third highest predicted increase in protection this century, partially due to a rise in the U.S. unemployment rate from 6.4 to 8.5 percent and a drop in the U.S. inflation rate (for producer prices) from 9.7 to 4.2 percent per annum – compared to the Carter administration. Historically, Congress has been more protectionist than the executive branch. In the last two decades, however, the executive branch has become increasingly protective of older industries in its negotiation of voluntary export restraint agreements and in administrative protection (antidumping, etc.).
23. Wilson (1990) argues that constitutional limitations may force polities into inefficient forms of taxation. But there can be welfare gains if politicians are also induced to reduce their provision of transfers. Thus, a switch from production subsidies to tariffs as the form of protection may reduce the level of excess burden and make both parties better off. Hillman (1989) and the optimal obfuscation argument above suggest that governments prefer tariffs to subsidies because the welfare-reducing effects of tariffs are less transparent to voters.

Voluntary export restraints (VERs) are the biggest innovation in protectionist policy since World War II (Ethier 1991b). They are quantitative restrictions levied by the exporting country that allows the exporters to capture the tariff-equivalent revenue from higher export prices, which are a form of monopoly profits. Over one-third of Japan's exports of manufactures to other industrial countries is subject to VERs (Ethier 1991b). Because of this, the Europeans had to rethink the gains from trade in their dealings with the Japanese in their preparation for EC-1992.[24] The United States discovered that trade with the Japanese brought the usual trade gains but a loss of billions in tariff-equivalent revenue.[25] Over one hundred VERs now manage almost 10 percent of world trade, including much of the world's trade in textiles and apparel. VERs are the most prominent means by which importing countries aid their aging industries suffering from low-wage imports.[26]

Figure 7 shows that by the early 1980s, VERs and other quantitative restrictions on U.S. imports were as economically restrictive as all U.S. tariffs.[27] VERs are an ingenious form of protection. In the 1970s and 1980s, the Japanese produced government policies as efficiently as they produced cars. This is related to their probusiness government and the recruitment of the best and the brightest college graduates into the government ministries. Compared to tariffs, a VER achieves higher levels of protection, transfers tariff-equivalent revenue to Japanese exporters, and reduces pressure on protectionist U.S. politicians from free traders. Japanese exporters use the VER to freeze out smaller rival firms and potential entrants; wages fall in the short run because fewer automo-

---

24. One could predict that the national compromises required for European unification would involve substantial increases in protection against outsiders.
25. For a good theoretical analysis of this process, see Hillman and Ursprung (1988). Das (1990) found that variables that increase the likelihood of protection due to increased lobbying by domestic firms may also increase foreign lobbying against protection. It is possible that total protection may in fact fall. VERs have also expanded both because of increased foreign lobbying and because they are opaque to voters. For steel and autos, it is hard to imagine that these American industries would have come up with such ingenious VERs without help from the Japanese.
26. Until the 1970s, international trade provided a constraint on market power by domestic labor unions and oligopolistic industries. However, the VER is reversing that result. The VER pulls foreign exporters into the lobbying process and they assist import-competing interests in getting protection. As Godek (1989) notes, VERs subsidize both foreign producers and domestic producers. Since both domestic and foreign lobbying resources are brought to bear for the VER, it has a higher tariff equivalent than the domestic lobby could obtain by itself.
27. The tariff rate was measured by dividing U.S. tariff revenue by value of U.S. imports. This yielded a tarif rate of about 3.5 percent. VERs and other quantitative U.S. import restrictions were equivalent to a tariff of another 3.5 percent on all U.S. imports. All U.S. import restrictions combined are like a tariff of 7 percent on all U.S. imports.

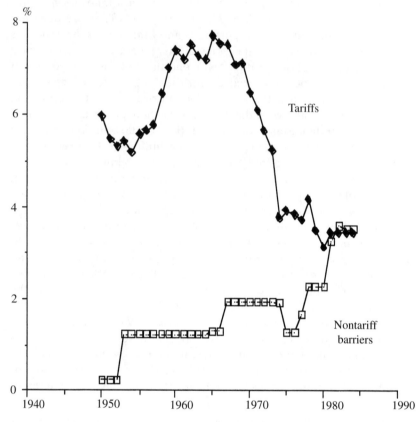

Figure 7. Tariff equivalents of U.S. tariffs and nontariff barriers, 1950–84. *Source:* Magee, Brock, and Young (1989, chap. 13).

biles are built; and profits increase because prices are higher and wages are lower (Ethier 1991b).[28] VERs are dramatic examples of the evolution toward politically efficient (easy to impose and highly redistributive) rather than more economically efficient policies, such as tariffs and subsidies.

The welfare costs of these quantitative restrictions are high. Table 1 shows computable general equilibrium model (CGE) estimates of the tariff equivalents in the United States of the three most important VERs (Tarr 1989).

---

28. The Japanese civil service may have been half-again too smart in constructing their VERs. If a trade war ever develops between the United States and Japan in the 1990s, it will be partially caused by the billions of dollars of tariff-equivalent revenue that VERs transferred from the U.S. Treasury to Japanese exporters.

Table 1.

Textiles and apparel	40%
Automobiles	23%
Steel	7%

Figure 7 indicates that U.S. VERs keep foreign goods out of the United States at the same rate as America's 3.5 percent tariff. But VERs impose a welfare loss on the United States equal to that of a 25 percent tariff on all U.S. imports. The U.S. tariff rate has not averaged 25 percent since 1909. The maximum U.S. tariff equivalent following the 1930 passage of the infamous Smoot–Hawley tariff was only 20 per cent in 1933 (Magee, Brock, and Young 1989, 327). The dollar loss to consumers of U.S. VERs has been estimated to equal $21 billion, $14 billion of which is a direct transfer of U.S. government tariff-equivalent revenue to foreign exporters (Tarr 1989).

3.5 The efficiency of democracy

The previous discussion suggests that Western democracies are not economically efficient in setting protection. A number of writers disagree. Becker (1983), for example, argues that competition in political markets drives the actors to minimize economic deadweight losses because policies that harm other groups induce opposition. Legislators or special interest groups have an incentive to find policies that help a large majority of the citizenry. Democracy is partially efficient because U.S. political parties, candidate reputations, and government structure adapt to solve maladaptive relationships between the governing and the governed (Wittman 1989). Democracy is not so much a way of reconciling conflicting preferences as of properly aggregating information. Majority rule uniquely minimizes the sum of errors that neglect a deserving agent and errors that reward an undeserving agent (O'Flaherty 1990).

Does economic inefficiency stem from indirect democracy (i.e., having elected representatives make decisions rather than voters directly)? A study of two referenda in Switzerland examined what happens when the electorate votes directly on the question of protection. One of the measures passed, the other did not (Weck-Hannemann 1990). Bureaucrats managed to get protection passed by combining a popular issue with protection. On the other vote, the voters showed more sophistication in rejecting agricultural protection in 1986. Protectionists wanted to raise the prices of oversupplied agricultural products, but voters wanted to perpetuate low prices.

Thus, the apparent economic inefficiency of democracies (in allowing inefficient protection) cannot be explained just by the fact that indirect democracies have elected representatives bought off by special interests. There is the additional problem that voters are underinformed.

4. Endogenous protection and the theory of lobbying

Tariffs escalate as a product moves through the cycle of production from a raw material to the final product. In the advanced countries in 1970, the average tariff rate was 3 percent on primary goods, 6 percent on semifinished goods and 13 percent on final goods. This phenomenon is easily explained by the theory of public choice. There are relatively few importers of raw materials (usually large multinational corporations), there are more importers of semifinished goods, and there are thousands of importers of finished products. The large size and high concentration of importers raw materials mean that importers can more easily overcome free-rider problems and fight for low tariffs. Concentration drops and free-rider problems increase as we move to semifinished and finished goods. Importers of finished products are the most fragmented and hence, less effective in fighting protectionist producer lobbies. Thus, protection is highest on finished goods.

Should a protectionist lobby contribute to the party most likely to get elected or the one providing the highest protection? The simplest models of endogenous protection suggest it should only give to the high-tariff party. If parties are smarter than lobbies, they will set their vote-maximizing policies in advance of elections, anticipating how much money will flow in. Since the protectionist lobby cannot increase the tariff level set by either party, the best thing it can do is to get the protectionist party elected. The illogic of giving to both parties can be demonstrated by, say, the Sierra Club's contributing to both an environmental candidate and a propolluter candidate. The money given to one candidate cancels the effectiveness of the money given to the other. There is casual empirical support for specialized contributing even in complex multi-issue races. In the 1964, 1968, and 1972 presidential races, 93, 86, and 92 percent, respectively, of large contributors gave to only one party.

The Hotelling or median voter result is one in which both political parties quote identical positions. In the $2\times2\times2\times2$ model, the result usually does not hold with lobbies present. If parties are Stackelberg leaders, neither lobby should contribute any funds in the Hotelling case since the policy after the election will be the same regardless of which party is elected.[29] For this reason, the Hotelling case cannot be an equi-

---

29. In game theory, a Stackelberg leader is a player who has better information. The reader might wonder whether lobbies might try to alter policies of both parties with

librium. Do candidates for office take identical positions on the issue of protection? In the 1992 U.S. presidential race, Bush and to a lesser extent Clinton were for the North American Free Trade Agreement (NAFTA) while Perot was strongly against it.

The Stolper–Samuelson theorem in international trade theory says that the abundant factor in an economy gains from freer trade while the scarce factor wants protection. Applied to the United States, the theory suggests that physical and human capital want free trade while (especially un-skilled) labor wants protection. The theory predicts that capital and labor from every industry will lobby on opposite sides of the free trade–protection issue. In contrast, the Ricardo–Viner–Cairnes specific factor model predicts that both capital and labor in the export industries should lobby for free trade while capital and labor in the import-competing industries should lobby for protection (Neary 1978).

These theories were tested on U.S. industry lobbying over the Trade Reform Act of 1973. In nineteen out of twenty-one industries, capital and labor lobbied on the same side (i.e., both either favored protection or favored free trade [Magee 1980]). This supports a specific factor approach and rejects Stolper–Samuelson. However, these results are biased in favor of the specific factor model, because U.S. trade acts require renewal every five years. In cross-section estimates of national tariff rates, a long-run Stolper–Samuelson model does very well, explain-ing about 75 percent of the variation in cross-national tariff rates (Magee, Brock, and Young 1989).

The reconciliation of these results is that specific factor models are better at explaining short-run lobbying behavior while long-run models are better at explaining long-run and cross-national levels of protection. Early work on lobbying by Olson (1965) and Stigler (1971) indicated that we should expect greater resources devoted to lobbying by concen-trated industries. A monopolist should spend the most since the benefits of the lobbying would not have to be shared with other firms in the industry. In the endogenous tariff literature, the evidence on this issue is very mixed. To illustrate, Marvel and Ray (1985) found that U.S. protec-tion in manufacturing is higher in concentrated industries while Ray (1990) found the reverse.[30]

funds. But this suggests a game theory setup in which the lobbies "Stackelberg lead" the parties. In this setup, free trade always emerges as the equilibrium. The empirical irrelevance of such a result rules it out.

30. Bauer, et al. (1963) conducted a survey in the 1950s that throws light on the profiles of individuals who were active in free trade and protectionist lobbies. They found that free traders are better educated, wealthier, more politically active, and members of the Republican party while ultra-protectionists are more likely to be found in the Democratic party.

How can we measure power in a lobbying context? H. P. Young (1978) shows that in

Standard public choice theory explains why agriculture is politically weak in developing countries but strong in the advanced countries (Balisacan and Roumasset 1987). In the United States and other advanced countries, agricultural lobbies are very powerful and obtain high levels of protection against imported food. In poor countries, producers are typically small subsistence farmers who, because of high transportation and communication costs, are thus disadvantaged in forming political coalitions. Poor urban consumers are geographically concentrated and want cheap food, because it constitutes a high proportion of their budgets. Industrialists want also cheap food because this holds down urban wages. The balance of political power in low-income countries favors urban consumers and industrialists over farmers. Many poor countries have government policies that lower the price of food.

When countries become more advanced, however, manufacturing becomes capital intensive and profits become less sensitive to wages and the price of food. The share of food in the total consumer expenditures drop so there is less political pressure from urban consumers. With fewer and larger farmers, industry concentration increases and transportation and communication costs fall. All of these factors explain why farmers have greater political power relative to consumer groups and high levels of protection in advanced countries.

5. A median voter theory of protection

An alternative to the 2×2×2×2 model of endogenous protection focuses almost exclusively on voters. This is an approach emphasized by Mayer (1984). He employs a Heckscher–Ohlin international trade model with no lobbies or political parties; he assumes that both parties will pick a tariff favored by the median voter. Because the distribution of wealth is skewed, the median voter in all countries has a higher ratio of labor to capital than the economy as a whole. Parties will thus choose a positive tariff if imports are labor intensive, because this transfers wealth from capital to labor.

This approach has the elegance of simplicity, but also some problems. A voter approach to a redistributive issue such as protection is flawed by cycling. With endogenous voter preferences, Arrow paradoxes and

the United States the president is eighty-eight times more powerful than a representative or senator since that is the number of representatives and senators it would take to go from a simple majority to the two-thirds vote required in both chambers to override a presidential veto. A rational lobby would be therefore indifferent between paying $88 million dollars to the president for a measure versus paying $1 million to each of 88 representatives and senators to override a presidential veto.

voter cycling always emerge on redistributive issues (Magee, Brock, and Young 1989, chap. 5). This means that no clear winner will emerge with majority voting or any other form of voting. Cycling may be a problem for Mayer with positive voting costs. In many voting models, there are also no equilibria. This has unsatisfactory empirical implications. The relative stability of protection both through time and across industries suggests that the equilibrium approach taken in the 2×2×2×2 model may be richer empirically. Although campaign contributions generally have been incorporated into spatial voting models, political scientists are behind economists in incorporating and testing them in general equilibrium. Finally, Mayer's model implies positive tariffs in advanced countries but negative tariffs in developing countries.

The lobbying approach of Magree, Brock, and Young (1989) in the 2×2×2×2 model of endogenous protection explains rational party and lobby behavior but avoids the aforementioned negatives. It also has flaws. Austen-Smith (1991) points out that it has no rational microfoundations for individual voter behavior. But, if it is irrational for individuals to vote, it is difficult to provide rational microfoundations for voting. The 2×2×2×2 modelers sidestep this conundrum by using probabilistic voting based on voter rationality in the aggregate. In this setup, voters are more likely to vote for parties with more money (because they convey more information) and less likely to vote for parties with more distorted policies (because of the economic costs these policies impose). There is evidence both ways, but the evidence against voter rationality is the more amusing. Warren G. Harding, president of the United States in the early 1920s, told an amazed reporter that the United States should adopt a tariff to help the struggling industries of Europe get back on their feet (Boller 1981, 231). In fact, the tariff would have had the opposite effect. More than half the voters in the average congressional district do not know the name of their congressman. Neither voters nor American presidents can master the issues in a complex democracy.

Mayer and Li (1994), in response to Austen-Smith (1991), provide microfoundations for the political actions of voters. They find that Magee, Brock, and Young's results generally hold, with the following important exceptions. The MBY tendency for a protectionist lobby to contribute only to the protectionist party holds with risk neutrality but will not hold if the protectionist lobby is sufficiently risk averse. In fact, the protectionist lobby might give only to the least protectionist party if its nonpolicy preferences for that party were sufficiently strong. Finally, the MBY result of interest groups not lobbying when both parties propose the same tariff holds if only policies matter, but need not hold when lobbies have nonpolicy preferences.

6. Trade-related rent seeking, the collateral damage theory, and lawyers

What empirical evidence do we have about the proportion of a country, GNP devoted to rent seeking (i.e., the expenditure of resources on predatory political activity)? Krueger (1974) estimated that 7 percent of the GNP of India and 15 percent of the GNP of Turkey was lost to rent seeking over import licenses alone. She indicated that, with competitive rent seeking, the entire value of the economic gains to producers may be wasted in lobbying expenditures. For example, if a 10 percent tariff will create $5 billion in additional wealth for protectionists, protectionists might then waste as much as $5 billion on lobbying to capture it. Others have criticized the term "rent seeking" as not technically accurate in describing the process (Bhagwati 1980, 1982). But our academic system is stuck with the term and any change would be like changing gauges on a railroad after it has been standardized.

The low levels of observed lobbying expenditures indicate that free riding may reduce lobbying significantly. Simulations indicate that between 5 and 15 percent of an average economy's capital and labor in tradeable goods would be expended on lobbying for protection if there were no free riding within lobbies (Magee, Brock, and Young 1989).[31] The actual amounts spent are much lower.

The traditional belief is that expenditures on rent seeking was the biggest social form of predatory political activity. However, a collateral damage theory has emerged, with evidence that the side effects of political predation can be much larger than the rent-seeking expenditures themselves (Magee 1992). This study incorporated lawyers into a Barro (1991) endogenous growth equation for fifty-four countries and found that lawyers have both positive and negative effects. After accounting for five other determinants, economic growth displayed an inverted-U shape when plotted against normalized lawyers. This means that there is an optimal density of lawyers. Countries can have too many and too few lawyers, indicating that legal systems provide both positive and negative externalities. Germany and Japan were at the top of the inverted-U curve, with the optimum lawyer ratio, while the United States was far to the right of the optimum ratio with 40 percent too many. Rent-seeking lawyers create negative externalities just like pollution. The negative economic impact of the excess lawyers is over five to ten times the rent-seeking expenditures themselves. There is an annual GDP loss of about

31. A study of simulated rent seeking over trade policy in the United States between 1958 and 1987 found no change in the fraction of capital devoted to rent seeking but a doubling of the fraction of labor devoted to rent seeking (Choi and Magee 1991).

$1 million for every lawyer added to the American labor force and a $1 billion loss for every lawyer added to the U.S. Congress.

Does trade expansion increase or decrease income inequality within countries? The Heckscher–Ohlin theory suggests that protection in advanced countries makes incomes more equal, because protection transfers income from capitalists to labor, while the reverse is true in developing countries. An indirect test yielded mixed results: trade expansion reduces equality in Latin America but does the reverse in Southeast Asia (Fischer 1991).

Kurth (1979) presents an interesting case study relating industry interests and political alliances. He provides evidence that protectionist forces helped Hitler come to power and pushed his militarism. Kurth starts with the question, How does a major power market its steel? He notes that the German steel industry was at a disadvantage relative to that of Britain after World War I because Germany did not have as strong a consumer goods sector as did Britain or a domestic automobile industry (Britain was number two in the world) or an overseas empire that consumed steel in the construction of railroads. The best uses of steel production in Germany in the 1920s were in the export market (to Eastern Europe) and in the production of armaments. Thus, the steel industry in Germany in the 1920s supported the National People's Party, which favored rearmament, revision of the Treaty of Versailles, and tariff barriers against steel imports from western Europe.

Two other sectors emerged in Germany in the 1920s: chemicals and electricity. The chemical industry had a very strong interest in free trade because I. G. Farben was not only the world's largest chemical corporation but also the largest corporation in all of Europe. Both the chemical and electrical industries wished to promote mass consumption and therefore supported parties favoring social welfare, democratic politics, and free trade. These industries joined with labor in opposition to the coalitions of the steel industry and the agriculturists. I. G. Farben made a strategic mistake when, based on widespread forecasts (reminiscent of the 1970s) that world petroleum supplies would soon be exhausted, it diverted most of its new capital investment in the 1920s into building enormous plants to produce gasoline from coal using a process known as hydrogenation.

The Smoot–Hawley tariff and the rise in world tariff barriers following the stock market crash in the United States and the beginning of the Great Depression, however, dealt a serious blow to the free-trade policy of the German chemical and electrical industries. Suddenly, a coercive trade option (Ostpolitik) of the German steel industry became more attractive to chemicals and electricity. Furthermore, the depression-induced declines in world oil prices in 1930–1 and the opening up of the vast east

Texas oil fields in 1931 meant that Farben would face massive imports of cheap American oil. The only solution for Farben now was a strong protectionist government that would guarantee a market for its coal-based gasoline or a government that would buy the gasoline itself and consume it in large quantities for armaments and military expansion.

In 1932 these developments caused the German chemical and electrical industries to switch from opposition to cooperation with the nationalistic and protectionist German steel and grain producers. Since the National People's Party was not popular enough to win the elections of 1932, the protectionist steel industry and later the newly protectionist chemical and electrical industries shifted their financial lobbying support to a National Socialists Party under Hitler. In 1933 when the Nazis came to power, the foreign policy goals of the steel industry (rearmament), the revision of the Versailles Treaty, high protection, and the domination of eastern Europe became the foreign policy of Germany under Hitler.[32]

7. Other empirical estimates

Baldwin (1976, 1982, 1984, 1986, 1988) has done the most empirical work in the area of endogenous protection.[33] His analysis of the 1973 U.S. Trade Bill showed that Democrats in both the House and the Senate were significantly more protectionist than were Republicans (Baldwin 1986). Protectionist labor union contributions were given primarily to representatives who eventually voted against the act. Both the president and Congress were also more likely to adopt protectionist legislation just before an election.

A historical comparison of tariffs in the late nineteenth century for the United States, Germany, France, and Britain found the following

32. Another interesting implication of Kurth's study is that Keynes's emphasis on government spending was taken up as a political marketing gimmick by consumer goods industries who wished to expand the purchasing power of the middle class. They wished to expand the role of government to promote broad-based spending power. Thus, many consumer industries who gave lip service to conservative ideologies may have lobbied for progressive taxation and economic stabilzation. In this sense, Keynes, like most economists, was a handmaiden of economic interests. Ideas, too, are endogenous.

33. Baldwin (1986) has a good survey of theories and empirical work on trade policies in developed countries. His survey includes Caves's (1976) adding machine model, Cheh's (1974) adjustment assistance model, Ball's (1967) equity concern model, Constantopolous (1974), Feenstra and Bhagwati's (1982) efficient tariff, Fieleke (1976) and Baldwin's (1982) government concern for low-income workers model, Helleiner's (1977) international bargaining model, Lavergne's (1983) status-quo model, and Ray (1981) and Lavergne's (1983) comparative cost model. See also Krasner's (1976) and Keohane's (1984) hegemonic theory of protection.

pattern of winners over losers across all the countries: producers over consumers, heavy industrialists over finished manufacturers, big farmers over small farmers, and property owners over laborers. Substantial land-owners and large-scale basic industry were the most consistent winners (Gourevitch 1977). A cross-national study of tariffs in thirty-five coun-tries in 1971 found that tariff rates were positively correlated with indi-rect taxes (e.g., sales taxes) as a percentage of government revenue, the size of the central government relative to total government, and the instability of exports (Conybeare 1983). Tariffs were negatively corre-lated with the commodity diversification of international trade, gross national product, GNP per capita, manufacturing as a percentage of GNP, and government as a percentage of GNP. Refinements indicate that tariffs decrease with the share of government in GNP while quotas increase. This implies that government activities are a substitute for tariffs but not for quotas (Godek 1986).

Several recent papers have performed time-series tests. Bohara and Kaempfer (1991) find that U.S. tariffs are endogenous with respect to inflation, real GNP and unemployment while tariffs "Granger cause" both inflation and the trade balance over the period 1890–1970. Crucini (1994) finds significant increases in tariff rates caused by U.S. price deflation over the period 1900–40, a result strengthening the Friedman–Schwartz deflationary-monetary theory of the Great Depression. En-dogenous tariff increases caused by monetary deflation in the Smoot–Hawley period helped internationalize the depression. Das and Das (1994) found that U.S. unemployment has been an increasingly impor-tant contributor to tariff imposition from 1949–88 while the trade bal-ance has been decreasingly important.

8. Bioeconomics: Rent seeking is a rule not an exception

Magee (1993) proposes a new bioeconomics field in which political econ-omy is viewed as a pyramid of nature. In modern economies, economics describes win–win interactions while politics and law describe win–lose interactions. In advanced societies, politics is just a dominance hierarchy of competing groups. In the animal kingdom, politics and economics are not separate compartments. For animals, the pecking order determines all: the strongest chickens in a flock get the best food, mates, roosts, and respect while the weaker chickens take what is left. And so it is in advanced democracies. Nearly all animal species display either territori-ality, dominance hierarchies, or both. Animal territoriality is nature's equivalent of private property.

The insights provided by bioeconomics are (1) that rational choice is a subset of a larger Darwinian survival model (psychologists have discovered that over half of human decision making is noncognitive), (2) that 60 percent of human personality traits are genetic rather than environmentally driven, (3) that animals prey on others in groups just as humans prey on each other in lobbies (lions must hunt in prides to prevent even larger bands of hyenas from driving them off of their kills), (4) that the colonizing of birds and the group grazing by bovines parallels the city behavior of humans, (5) that success by both animal and human dominants is related to testosterone (the chemical equivalent is steroids for athletes), and (6) that opportunistic specie strategies are the rational approach in high-variance economic environments of the developing economies while sedentary specie strategies are optimal for lower-variance advanced countries.

In addition, protection, the focus of this survey, may foster product mutations by increasing variance in national economic environments. Biologists have discovered that favorable mutations are more likely to survive if populations are separated. The isolation of the Galapagos Islands provided a sanctuary in which exotic life forms could evolve. Protection may have the same benefit for the innovation of national products. The infant industry argument parallels the protection that mammals and birds give their young until they are strong. Older industry protection parallels the economic support that democracies afford senior citizens and is equally reduction resistant. Protection increases bioeconomic fitness.

9. Summary

The economic cost of lobbying and rent seeking is just a transaction cost of democracy. Alternative national constitutional setups explain the variability in these transactions costs. The theory of endogenous protection offers the following insights: (1) tariffs and other policies are equilibrating variables like prices in economic markets; (2) political equilibria are not economically efficient; (3) there are trade-offs between political efficiency and economic efficiency; rent seeking can be estimated, even though it cannot be observed; (4) in many cases Hotelling equilibria are ruled out (both parties will not choose the same policy with endogenous politics); (5) prisoners' dilemma lobbying equilibria emerge about 40 percent of the time; (6) the worldwide drop in advanced country protection since World War II and low tariffs in advanced countries is explained by the increase in physical and human capital relative to labor; (7) endogenous protection compensates for economic setbacks (protection is like implicit insurance against negative economic shocks); (8) the magnification paradox explains why tariffs are more potent forms of redistribution in advanced countries; (9) Republican presidencies in the United States have displayed greater increases in protection than Democratic ones because they generate more protectionist pressure on the Congress (i.e., higher unemployment and lower inflation); (10) isoprotection curves (loci of inflation and unemployment rates along which equilibrium tariffs are constant) can be drawn in the Phillips curve diagram that illustrate this phenomenon; (11) the welfare effects of endogenous protection range from welfare improvement to economic black holes (in which virtually 100 percent of resources are devoted to redistributive battles – e.g., high-crime ghettoes); and (12) endogenous policy suggests optimal obfuscation and a theory of the second-worst (i.e., since redistribution must be disguised from the voters, the equilibrium policies chosen are usually inefficient).

Mark Twain once said that Wagner's music is not nearly as bad as it sounds. Testing endogenous protection is similar – it is simple but not as simple as it sounds.

CHAPTER 25

Why does government's share of national income grow? An assessment of the recent literature on the U.S. experience

CHERYL M. HOLSEY AND THOMAS E. BORCHERDING

> Taxes are what we pay for civilized society.
> Oliver Wendell Holmes, *Compania de Tobaco v. Collector* (1904)

> In general, the art of government consists in taking as much money as possible from one part of the citizens to give to the other.
> Voltaire, "Money," *Philosophical Dictionary* (1764)

> . . . read my lips: No New Taxes!
> George H. W. Bush, Acceptance Speech,
> *Republican National Convention* (1988)

The twentieth century has witnessed a fundamental and systemic change in politicoeconomic systems. Turn of the century mature, market-based economies with government spending to national income ratios of one-twelfth to one-sixth have been transformed into mixed economies that place greater and greater emphasis on collective decision making. Nowhere is this phenomenon more obvious than in the case of the richest of the industrialized economies where government expenditures now frequently comprise 40 percent and more of current gross national product.

It is not surprising that a change of this magnitude has attracted enormous attention in the literature. Predictably, much of the focus of this research has been on modeling and explaining government growth. Since such growth implies a dramatic shift from private to public allocation, additional concerns have arisen: (1) Is increased government size simply a

The authors wish to thank the Claremont Institute for Economic Policy Studies, which provided research support through a grant from the Lincoln Foundation, and to Maria Khader and Gokce Soydemir for research assistance, Pamela Martin and Mary Vingerelli for typing assistance, and Dennis Mueller for helpful editorial suggestions.

natural consequence of modern industrial society, or does it indicate instead that rent-seeking groups have become increasingly powerful and more capable of manipulating government expenditures toward their own ends? (2) Does increased government expenditure represent investment in capital and social infrastructure, or does it hamper economic development, leading to slower GNP growth rates? The answers to these questions have important implications for the economic future of the postindustrial world.

Concern over these issues has driven research on the causes and implications of government growth. Unfortunately, our survey is necessarily selective and touches only on the important topics. We begin by acquainting the reader with the scope of U.S. government growth.

1. Patterns of U.S. government expenditure

The growth in government is illustrated by the U.S. government expenditure patterns presented in Table 1. Over the last nine decades, U.S. government expenditures as a percentage of GNP increased by approximately 500 percent. Although increases in government expenditures in the first half of the century evidenced wide variations in growth, more recent increases have occurred at fairly constant rates. With the exception of the 1970s, government's share of GNP has increased by approximately 4 percent per decade in the post–World War II era. There has also been a striking change in the fiscal structure of the federal government: While state government has not quite trebled, federal government expenditure is more than nine times its 1910 level.[1]

Table 1 reveals an across-the-board increase in government's share of GNP. While insurance trust (Social Security) growth is the most dramatic, large increases have also occurred in public welfare, interest on the debt, and national defense. In considering post–World War II growth, we find that only national defense remains at its 1950 level. By 1988 police and fire protection as well as "other" expenditures are one-third greater than their 1950 levels, while education has grown by half. There has been more than a two-fold increase in both interest on the debt and welfare payments, but insurance trust/social security exhibits the largest growth rate, more than trebling its size in this thirty-eight-year period.[2]

1. These statistics are slightly different if one attributes the expenditure of federal grants to subnational governments. For 1988 this accounting method implies a nonfederal expenditure share of 17.0 percent and a federal expenditure share of 22.4 percent.
2. Western European and OECD data (Lybeck 1988) show differing absolute shares, but similar accelerations, indicating a growth of the "welfare state" and concomitant rises in education and debt servicing. In all mature post–World War II economies, government has risen dramatically in both absolute and relative terms.

Table 1. *U.S. public sector expenditure patterns, 1902–88*

	Expenditure by level as a percentage of GNP			Expenditure by category as a precentage of GNP[a]							
	Total	Federal	State & local	National defense[b]	Insurance trust[c]	Interest on debt	Welfare	Education	Police & fire	Health & hospital	Other[d]
1902	7.7	2.7	5.0	.8	.0	.5	.2	1.2	.4	.3	4.4
1913	8.1	2.4	5.7	.6	.02	.4	.1	1.5	.4	.3	4.7
1922	12.6	5.1	7.5	1.2	.1	1.9	.2	2.3	.5	.5	6.0
1932	21.4	7.3	14.1	1.2	.3	2.3	.8	4.0	1.0	1.0	10.9
1940	20.5	10.1	10.4	1.6	1.0	1.6	1.3	2.8	.6	.7	10.9
1950	24.6	15.7	8.9	6.4	2.4	1.7	1.0	3.4	.5	1.0	8.3
1960	29.9	19.2	10.7	9.7	3.5	1.9	.9	3.9	.6	1.0	8.6
1970	33.9	21.2	12.7	8.6	5.0	1.9	1.8	5.7	.7	1.4	9.0
1980	35.1	22.6	12.5	5.5	7.3	2.8	2.4	5.3	.8	1.6	9.6
1988	39.4	24.9	14.5	6.2	8.0	4.2	2.4	5.3	.9	1.6	11.0

[a] Due to rounding, percentages by category may not sum to total.

[b] National defense also includes international relations expenditure.

[c] Insurance trust includes employee retirement, unemployment compensation as well as old-age and survivors insurance.

[d] Other includes local sanitation, natural resources, local parks and recreation, housing and urban renewal, some veteran's services as well as general administrative expenditures.

Sources: Government expenditure, by level of government and category of expenditure, and GNP for 1902–70 from U.S. Bureau of the Census, *Historical Statistics of the United States: Colonial Times to 1970* (Washington D.C.: U.S. Government Printing Office, 1975), series Y 533–566 and F 1–5, respectively. Government expenditure by category for 1980 from U.S. Bureau of the Census, *Statistical Abstract of the United States, 1981*, table 468. Government expenditure by level for 1980 and 1988, by category for 1988, and GNP for 1988 from *Statistical Abstract, 1991*, table 465, tables 466 and 509, and table 702, respectively.

2. Modeling government expenditure

Research advances on causality of government growth have been limited by the absence of a generally accepted theory of collective decision making. Two basic paradigms are employed in the literature, what we term here the "apolitical" and "political." Each assumes fundamentally different motives for public provision of services. The apolitical paradigm assumes that government provision arises because private markets fail to provide desired levels of particular services.[3] The political paradigm, on the other hand, assumes that public provision is due not to private market failure but to the rent seeking of agents who wish government to redistribute income in their favor.[4] A third, eclectic but underdeveloped paradigm assumes that collective decisions are determined by both apolitical and political motives.

Since the apolitical paradigm stresses the productive, community service aspect of government provision, it views collective decision making as a compromise between individuals desiring various levels of the service. These compromises are most frequently modeled within the context of the Bowen (1943) median voter model in which collective decisions are determined by majority rule, where the median voter plays the pivotal or marginal role in determining government expenditure levels.[5] The median voter model explains government expenditure growth by changes in factors affecting the median voter's demand curve. Borcherding and Deacon (1972) and Bergstrom and Goodman (1973) were among the first to model the median voter and apply it empirically. Since the subjects of their respective analyses were nonfederal governments, they argued political (redistributive) considerations were neutralized by a more fundamental competitive force, taxpayer mobility (Tiebout 1956). Recent empirical applications of the Bowen model are surveyed in Inman (1979, 1987).

The political paradigm, in contrast, views public services as selfishly redistributive (i.e., transfers of purely private goods to politically fa-

---

3. According to this paradigm, dissatisfaction with desired expenditure levels is the result of market failure due either to the presence of externalities or pure public goods, or the "community's" desire to redistribute income, another sort of public good motivation. Bator's (1960) well-known study takes exactly this apolitical position and its title is most illustrative.

4. Stubblebine (1963) is the earliest detailed challenge to Bator (1960) and others espousing this "social imbalance" approach.

5. Bowen's model yields Paretian results when the median voter faces the average marginal tax-price, leading to much speculation about the latter in real-world fiscal systems (Borcherding 1985). Lindahl (1919) offered a model similar to Bowen's over two decades earlier.

vored groups), hence government expenditures are determined by the most influential agents. Meltzer and Richard (1978, 1981) and Meltzer, Cukierman, and Richard (1991) adapt the median voter model to account for rent-seeking behavior, while Peltzman (1980), Becker (1983, 1985) and Coughlin, Mueller, and Murrell (1990a, 1990b) develop sophisticated models in which interest groups lobby for political favors. Political models derive demand for government by analyzing the costs and benefits incurred by various agents as they seek redistributive rents. Thus, increases in the size of government occur when the costs of rent seeking decrease, the benefits increase, or when rent-seeking groups gain differential political influence.[6]

The third and eclectic line of research assumes an admixture of apolitical and political motives. Denzau and Munger (1986) and Congleton (1991) model public expenditures decisions as a (rivalrous) function of both the general voting populace and organized, narrow-interest group preferences. In Kristov, Lindert, and McClelland (1992), individuals join interest groups to enhance not only their own interests but those of others, where concern for others may be founded on either altruistic (apolitical/spillover values) or self-serving (political/coalition enhancing) motives. Niskanen's (1971) bureaucratic monopoly model fits this latter category, since high-demand (extra-median) voters coalesce with bureaucrats to maximize the budget.

Distinguishing between the paradigms is crucial not only in understanding government growth but also in evaluating the implications of such growth. If the apolitical model fully explains collective decision making, then growth in government is a natural consequence of changing market and social conditions.[7] Political models, on the other hand, provide an equally extremist conclusion: the growth in government is fully explained by increased rent-seeking activity. Of course, either implication is possible within the context of existing apolitical and political

---

6. Coughlin, Mueller, and Murrell (1990a) argue, however, that increasing interest group power does not necessarily lead to greater government expenditure levels. It could, instead, produce other fiscally induced benefits such as lower tax rates for influential groups. Regulatory advantage is another possibility that does not necessarily have budgetary effects (Posner 1971).

7. This also assumes that government produces services in a least-cost manner. Since government may not face the same competitive forces as private firms, this is a questionable assumption. While there is a literature that addresses this cost minimization issue, to date it has not been applied to government growth, except indirectly by Borcherding, Bush, and Spann (1977) and Borcherding (1983), who look at deviations from least-cost allocations as politically induced transfers. Such transfers increase, for example, as public employee interest groups grow in political power or as the fraction of politically privileged suppliers increases.

models. The challenge is to test between paradigms to establish which provides the best explanation of government growth.

A thorough review would reveal a staggering number of hypotheses that explain government's growing share of GNP. Each employs one of the paradigms adumbrated in this section. Key hypotheses concerning apolitical sources of government growth are presented in the next section, while Section 4 addresses salient political growth theories. Thoughts on the eclectic approach combining the apolitical and political paradigms are found in the concluding section.

3. Public expenditure growth within an apolitical context

As noted, the apolitical model bases demand for government expenditure on the median voter's demand curve ignoring the political institutions in which choices are made. Derivation of this demand curve must account for a joint-supply production function, since voters gain utility from publicly provided services, while governments are only partial providers of inputs necessary to produce these services (e.g., educational services depends on parental education and involvement).

Among the first to formally recognize this discrepancy between government inputs and final citizen–consumer valued outputs, Buchanan (1965) posits a positive relationship between final service levels and input levels for shared consumption goods and a negative relationship between service and population levels.[8] Bradford, Malt, and Oates (1969) and Oates (1977, 1981) extend this analysis by modeling publicly provided service levels as a joint-supply function of both publicly provided inputs and community environmental factors. Their research suggests, for example, that societies of law-abiding citizens will receive higher levels of public safety from a given level of police inputs than more lawless communities.

The general procedure for deriving the demand for expenditure on publicly provided inputs is to first solve the median voter's maximization problem in terms of final service outputs, where demand is a function of that voter's income, general preferences, tax-price per unit of services, and the price of related private goods and services. While this yields a demand curve that implies all the usual assumptions, it is important to recognize that both desired service levels and tax-price are a function of publicly provided inputs as well as population and community environmental inputs. Since service levels are a function of input levels, straight-

---

8. Although Buchanan's model addressed club services that could be provided by private markets, his analysis can (and has been) extended to the publicly provided services.

forward manipulation of the demand for publicly provided services yields the median voter's, hence the government's, *derived* demand for expenditure on publicly provided inputs.[9] This derived demand curve is a function of the median voter's income, preferences, the price of publicly provided inputs, population, and community inputs as well as the price of private goods and services.

To explain increases in the size of government within the context of the median voter model, it is, of course, insufficient to identify only time-trended changes in exogenous variables that have increased the median voter's demand for expenditure on publicly provided inputs. Since government's share of GNP has expanded at the expense of private consumption, adequate theories must also explain why government expenditure has grown *relative* to private expenditure. As the following subsections illustrate, changes in each variable in the voters' demand function, as well as several variables not usually considered in neoclassical analysis, serve as potential explanators of public sector growth.

3.1 Input prices

Baumol (1967) hypothesized that because the government sector is largely a service industry with relatively low capital–labor intensities, productivity rises therein are likely to be small compared to those in "progressive" manufacturing and other private-sector, capital-intensive industries.[10] Increasing (real) wage rates causes the marginal and unit costs of government services to increase. This increase in the relative price of government services, in turn, implies an increase in government expenditures, if demand is own-price inelastic.

Spann's surveys (1977a, 1977b) support Baumol's rising price of government services contention. Spann estimates a 1.5 percent annual price rise, which also confirms the Bradford, Malt, and Oates (1969) finding. It is nearly identical to the 1.4 percent of Peltzman (1980), who notes the differences between the 1929–74 rise in the private goods and services price deflator and that of government's implicit price index. More recent evidence continues to support the Baumol hypothesis (Lybeck and

---

9. Put in simple Marshallian (perfect) joint-supply terms, the demand for public expenditures (public inputs) equals the demand for final public services less the supply of community environmental inputs. For more detailed derivations of the demand for expenditure on publicly provided inputs without these limiting Marshallian fixed coefficients, see Inman (1979) and Hamilton (1982).

10. Baumol, Blackman, and Wolff (1985) present a refined version of this model in which industries may be classified as asymptotically stagnant in addition to the stagnant and progressive categories offered by the original model. The modified model, however, does not affect conclusions concerning public sector growth.

Henrekson 1988a; Ferris and West 1993). The earliest studies of price elasticities (Borcherding and Deacon 1972; Bergstrom and Goodman 1973) estimated price inelastic demand curves for virtually all government services, which subsequent studies by Perkins (1977) and Gramlich (1985) have replicated. Thus, there exists strong support for identifying increased input prices in the face of price inelastic demand as one of the determinants of government's increased share of GNP.

3.2 Income

An hypothesis put forth by Adolph Wagner (1893) holds that as society progresses, government involvement in fiscal–budgetary matters rises even faster. Thus, the implications of Wagner's law require estimates of income elasticities for publicly provided goods greater than one.[11]

Tests of Wagner's hypothesis have yielded mixed results at best, and accumulated evidence is unsupportive of the law. Mueller (1989) concludes that the majority of studies produce income elasticity estimates less than unity. Although both Peltzman (1980) and Hamilton (1982) have argued that these standard estimating techniques have produced downward biased estimates, corrected estimates have failed to produce elasticities exceeding unity.[12] Recent studies by Ram (1987), Gemmell (1990), and Henrekson (1990) have refined the estimating techniques that found income elasticities exceeding one, while applying them to fresh data. Their results have failed to support Wagner's law.[13]

3.3 Preferences

While an increase in household preferences for publicly provided services relative to private market services would certainly imply an in-

---

11. An income elasticity greater than one implies that at some point public spending exceeds national income. A close reading of Wagner reveals, however, that at some later stage an equilibrium level of government expenditure comes about with a constant share of national income. This implies a long-run income elasticity of unity.

12. Peltzman argues that past estimates have been biased downward since they employ "transitory" rather than "permanent" income, a point Friedman (1957) noted for savings in his study of aggregate consumption. Hamilton theorizes that income levels are positively correlated with community environmental factors and that omission of these variables from the estimating equation biases income elasticities toward zero. However, neither Peltzman's inclusion of permanent income nor studies such as that of Schwab and Zampelli (1987) that include measures of community environmental factors have produced income elasticities exceeding one.

13. These refinements include the employment of real rather than nominal exchange rates in cross-country studies, and the use of cointegration econometric techniques on time-series data.

crease in government's share of GNP, changing tastes rarely are cited as an explanator of government growth. Both North (1985a) and Lindbeck (1985), however, do mention taste changes. Lindbeck notes that altruism may initially and partially determine which groups receive transfers. He hypothesizes that transfers such as price supports for farmers originally may have gained popular support because the recipients consisted of poorer segments of the population whose living standards had been dramatically reduced as a result of the industrial revolution. North cites two periods in which changing preferences or ideological convictions may have caused government expansions: (1) the movement away from the Madisonian system of government in the late nineteenth century and the early part of this century due, in part, to a growing conviction that (then current) political and economic outcomes were deemed unjust, and (2) the movement away from purely market-based economies in the 1930s due to the increased demand for economic stability created by the Great Depression. These discussions suggest that citizen–consumers set higher priorities on certain government services than they did a century ago. It is possible, therefore, that changing preferences played a role in increasing the size of government. To date, little research has explored this hypothesis.

Preference differences between communities have long been suspected of contributing to differences in nonfederal U.S. public spending. Bergstrom and Goodman (1973), for example, employed socioeconomic variables to control for the effects of differing preferences. The inclusion of such variables has since become standard in cross-sectional studies on government expenditure patterns. However, the effects of preferences on public expenditure levels are difficult to determine, since socioeconomic variables may reflect supply–cost differentials for producing government services as well as variance in consumer preferences.

3.4 Population

In assessing the impact of population growth on government expenditure growth, Borcherding (1985), using a median voter demand, shows that population increases have both positive and negative influences on relative government size. On the one hand, holding production costs at the margin constant, increased population levels imply decreased government size since publicly provided inputs can be shared. This same change also implies increased public expenditure levels, however, since the tax-price per unit of providing these shared inputs has fallen encouraging a larger quantity demanded. As such, the overall effect of population growth on public spending is an empirical issue.[14]

Borcherding finds that the two effects tend to cancel out: In the first eight decades of this century, population growth produced between a negative 5.0 percent and a positive 1.3 percent growth in government's relative size. While it is difficult to ascertain significance levels with this technique, Borcherding's findings are confirmed by other studies (e.g., Peltzman 1980). These and others surveyed by Borcherding (1985) yield population elasticity coefficients on per capita government spending not significantly different from zero.

3.5 Community inputs

Hamilton (1982) has developed the Bradford, Malt, and Oates (1969) theory concerning community environmental factors into a formal model where the median voter's service level depends upon community environmental inputs as well as government purchased inputs. He shows that lower levels of community resources increase the median voter's tax-price per unit of service. Since demand curves for virtually all publicly provided goods appear to be own-price inelastic, reduced community contributions systematically increase government expenditure levels.

Testing this model has proved difficult because community resource levels are usually measured by the same socioeconomic variables that indicate community preferences (see Subsection 3.3). Schwab and Zampelli (1987), however, attempted to overcome this "identification problem" by separating community taste from community cost effects. Their empirics support the supposition that differences in community resource levels lead to cross-community variations in both the unit costs of producing publicly provided services and government expenditure levels.

While the community input model has yet to be applied to government expenditure growth, there is reason to believe that changing community environments may positively affect government expenditure levels. This century has seen dramatic socioeconomic changes, such as women entering the labor market and the advent of single-parent households. If such events create a populace more difficult to serve (i.e., the community provides fewer resources to the production of publicly provided services), these increase the full cost of the service at the margin and, given price-

---

14. Borcherding (1985) shows that the net effect of population on government size is sensitive to the estimates of "publicness" and price elasticity that combine to measure the population elasticity coefficient.

inelastic demands, cause a larger government sector. The recent writings decrying the "lack of community" reflect this diminished supply of socially complementary inputs to the publicly provided ones (e.g., Etzioni 1993; Whitehead 1993; Wilson 1993). This is a promising, underresearched explanator of a growing share of government in GNP.

3.6 Household production prices

Both North (1985a) and Breton (1989) examine government growth within the context of industrialization and its effects on household production. As Breton (1989, 725) notes, a "typical [traditional] extended family system or kinship network provides shelter, food, protection, security and insurance to its members," but increased geographic mobility and the participation of women in the labor force has greatly increased familial costs of providing these services.[15] As a result, traditional family functions have been increasingly replaced by lower-cost government and private market provisions. Although neither North nor Breton empirically test these propositions, both provide arguments supporting their contentions that much of the increase in social security and welfare programs is due to sharply changed patterns of household production.[16]

3.7 Transaction costs and exchange

In a series of studies, North (1984, 1985a, and 1985b) and North and Wallis (1982, 1986) hypothesize that the industrialized world's drive toward ever greater specialization and division of labor has much increased the transaction costs of market exchange, causing the government sector to grow. Unlike neoclassical theory, which assumes away transaction costs, these studies emphasize that the bargaining, measurement, insurance, and enforcement costs of private exchange constrain an economy's ability to specialize, causing agents to seek transaction cost-reducing services from both the private and public sectors to realize more fully the gains from trade. The increased specialization of the past one-and-a-half centuries has raised transaction costs of ex-

---

15. North and Breton promote the notion of government as the comparative advantage provider of certain services because government is more successful at internalizing the organizational problems associated with free riding and adverse selection than are autonomous and fracturing private households.
16. Smolensky, Pommerehne, and Dalrymple (1979) find the effect of the retired fraction of the labor force, as well as female-headed households, is positive. Wilensky (1976) finds evidence for the former as well.

change because trade volume has risen enormously and is much more impersonal in nature. As a result, agents have increased demands for transaction cost-reducing services. North and Wallis cite (1986)[17] the substantial growth in the transaction sector to substantiate their claim that

> the transaction sector grew from roughly one-quarter of GNP in 1870 to more than one-half of GNP in 1970. Government share of providing transaction services grew from 3.7 percent of GNP in 1902 to 13.9 percent of GNP in 1970. (North and Wallis 1986, 389)

Unfortunately, why government's share of the transactions sector rose *relative* to the private sector's is not well explained.[18] Attempts to speak to this organizational change in comparative advantage follow.

3.8 Taxation and collection costs

Kau and Rubin (1981) argue that changes such as improved record keeping, fewer self-employed individuals, and the shift of women from the household to the workplace have increased the costs of both legal tax avoidance and illegal tax evasion, thus reducing the deadweight losses associated with taxation and producing higher public expenditure levels.[19] Since larger government expenditures are generated by an *increase* in the quantity of services supplied, this hypothesis would seem, on the surface, to conflict with Baumol's (1967) theory that increased government expenditures are caused by a *decrease* in supply. West (1991) resolves this apparent paradox by showing that Kau and Rubin's supply curve of public activity reflects the sum of the marginal costs of taxation *and* the marginal production costs of the service. A decrease in the former must, other things equal, increase supply causing voters to increase their quantity demanded of the public services. Since the marginal production costs of the service are unchanged, public expenditures necessarily increase. As West's analysis illustrates, Kau and Rubin's

---

17. Their figures are problematic since they admit that it is quite difficult to determine which government services should be designated as transactions cost reducing and which are intermediate producer or final consumer goods.
18. Borcherding (1965 [rev. 1977]) shows that the growth of employment in the private service sector is only *half* that of government for the period 1900–60.
19. Interestingly, North and Thomas (1973) argue that the rise of the nation-state at the end of the Middle Ages was predicated upon tax collection costs falling. Thus, the growth of money-driven exchange over in-kind barter made state fiscal interventions economically viable, encouraging the relative increase in the fraction of state action in the economy.

findings that government expenditure increases because quantity demanded *increases* differ fundamentally from Baumol's findings that government expenditure increases because quantity demanded *decreases* in the face of price-inelastic taxpayer demand.

In their empirical analysis, Kau and Rubin employ various socioeconomic variables as proxies for the decreasing deadweight losses of tax collection over time. In particular, empirical results identify increased female labor force participation as an important determinant of increased tax revenue/expenditure levels. Henrekson (1990) and Ferris and West (1993) undertake similar analyses and find additional support for Kau and Rubin's hypothesis.

A difficulty with the empirical tests of Kau and Rubin's potentially important hypothesis, however, is that empirical specifications of this theory are likely to be observationally equivalent to the empirical specifications of several other theories of the apolitical *genre* (Henrekson 1990). While, for example, the finding that government expenditure levels are positively related to increased female labor force participation support Kau and Rubin's hypothesis, their result provides support for the theory that increased household production costs cause government growth and the equally plausible theory that decreased community input levels is an explanator. In fact, increased female labor force participation could just as well reflect a fundamental change in social preference structures, implying that changing attitudes of the citizenry have been at the root of expenditure increases. More sophisticated theories that identify the unique, and necessarily rival, empirical implications of each model must be developed before these competing hypotheses can be appropriately tested against one another.

3.9 Concluding remarks on the apolitical approach

As this section illustrates, there is no dearth of hypotheses to explain government growth using the apolitical paradigm. Interestingly, only the Baumol hypothesis that increased input prices have led to a *relatively* larger government sector receives uniformly strong empirical support. Rising per capita incomes and increased population as explanators of relative public sector growth (Wagner's law) are not supported by empirical evidence, while theories concerning preference changes, decreased levels of community inputs, increased home production prices, and increased transaction costs are interesting conjectures but have yet to be convincingly established. Empirical findings supporting the decreasing deadweight loss of tax collections as a determinant of government revenue/expenditure growth are also fascinating but require a great deal more study.

4. Public spending growth in a political context

In the 1950s economists began questioning the naive view that government is the benevolent servant of the people. Largely because of the development of the new public choice approach, the focus turned to the darker side of collective decision making, the rent-seeking motive.[20] Rather than assume that certain services naturally lie within the government's domain, these researchers began to consider the implications of the political decision process by which rational agents, citizens, and government officials choose government allocation of particular services while leaving others to the private market. Such *realpolitik* reasoning, ascribing self-interest to all involved in collective decisions, produced a variety of political models in which *all* the various agents – politicians, bureaucrats, special interests, and the general voting public – are assumed to exploit government allocation for their own narrow ends. Not surprisingly, government growth within the context of these models reflects "polity" failures caused by rent seeking not considered in the apolitical approach.

Aside from the obvious contrast in paradigms, political theories of government growth differ from apolitical hypotheses in that explanations are not couched within the context of a single model. While apolitical hypotheses focus solely on the median voter model, political theories incorporate a wide array of political and combined apolitical/political models. Subsections 4.1 and 4.2 present two purely political, but independent, models of government growth motivated by rent seeking. Although subsequent subsections employ combined apolitical/political models, they also theorize that greater government expenditure levels are due to increased rent-seeking activity.

4.1 Rent seeking within the median voter model

Meltzer and Richard (1981) assume that (1) public services are purely private goods that serve selfishly redistributive ends, and (2) the mean income of the community exceeds the median income in such a way as to encourage a growth dynamic. Since the median voter, by hypothesis, is the median-income earner, and since he or she also determines the tax-rate, it necessarily follows that redistribution takes place favoring the

---

20. The term "rent seeking," of course, did not come into currency until the 1970s, but the concept is much older. Adam Smith, for example, is concerned with rent seeking throughout the *Wealth of Nations* (1776). Neoclassical modeling from the mid-nineteenth century through the immediate post–World War II period managed to suppress this analysis of motivation, using what Borcherding (1983) refers to as the tacit assumption of Victorian welfare economics: Public action is always productive.

lower half of the income distribution via "subsidized" tax prices.[21] Exploitation is constrained, however, because voters weigh the marginal benefit of higher tax rates (more income redistributed) against the marginal cost (decreased work incentives by the top-half of income earners implying less income is available for redistribution) in determining the final levels of redistribution. The importance of this model for explaining the growth of government is that increases in mean voter income relative to median voter income (increasing inequality) cause greater redistribution, hence greater government expenditure. In applying their model, Meltzer and Richard cite two examples of such changes: the extension of suffrage to low-income citizens in the nineteenth and twentieth centuries and, more recently, increases in the number of retired persons due to the advent of the social security system.

In testing their theory, Meltzer and Richard (1983) employ U.S. time-series data and find that government expenditure levels are positively related to the ratio of mean to median income as well as to median-income levels. Unfortunately, their results have not proven robust in subsequent studies by others who include the mean/median income variable in more general specifications. For example, while Aubin et al. (1988) use French time-series data and find support for the supposition, results for Sweden are mixed. Lybeck (1986) and Henrekson (1988) reject the hypothesis, but Henrekson (1990) later offers some weak support, and Henrekson and Lybeck (1988) conclude that changes in income distribution are an important determinant of Swedish government growth. In cross-country comparisons, Mueller and Murrell (1985, 1986) provide weak support with their cross-sectional data set;[22] however, the Kristov, Lindert, and McClelland (1992) test on pooled, cross-sectional, time-series data produced a negative coefficient estimate for the mean/median income variable.

4.2 Rent seeking and income-based coalitions

Peltzman (1980) recognizes the force of Meltzer and Richard's model, but probes more deeply into the vote-gathering and coalition-forming

---

21. Liang and Meltzer (1993) develop a dynamic version of the model that allows for intergenerational as well as intragenerational transfers. Interestingly, Peacock (1992) attributes the origins of the Meltzer–Richard model to Alexis de Tocqueville's *Democracy in America* (1835–9).

22. Mueller and Murrell replace the mean/median variable with a measure of the skewness of the pretransfer income distribution. They find a positive relationship between government expenditure and the percentage of the adult population who vote, providing support for Meltzer and Richard's hypothesis that government growth is, in part, due to extensions of the franchise.

processes. He agrees that differences between groups are a source of redistributive rent seeking, but the intensities of their rent-seeking activities (hence, their successes and failures) turn on the transaction costs and returns of forming effective coalitions and preventing the formation of blocking ones. Peltzman first establishes that the richest group will be forced to redistribute to the poorest one via the actions of self-interested, vote-maximizing politicians. He then models the maximization problem from the perspective of the poor, concluding that the poor provide greater political support for redistribution (1) as the gap between high-income and low-income groups increases, and (2) as incomes are more equally distributed among individuals in the low-income group. In the first case, a larger income differential between the two groups increases the benefits of redistribution; in the second case, the political transaction costs are lower since there is greater solidarity of interests within the low-income group. Government growth within this model is explained by increases in between-group inequality, decreases in within-group inequality, or the simultaneous occurrence of both.

While the theoretical model is framed in terms of rich and poor, Peltzman's empirical analysis recognizes that ability to affect political outcomes also plays a role in redistribution. Thus, the analysis focuses on redistribution to the more politically effective middle-income group.[23] Peltzman conducts an (impressive) array of tests on an (equally impressive) array of data sets[24] and concludes that government growth in the post–World War II developed economies is due largely to decreases in within-group inequality. More specifically, it is due to "the *leveling* of income differences across a large part of the population – the growth of the 'middle class' " (emphasis his; Peltzman 1980, 285).

As with Meltzer and Richard's model, subsequent studies based on more general expenditure specifications have employed Peltzman-type variables. Mueller and Murrell (1985, 1986) include, for example, a measure of pretransfer income skewness in their specification, but their empirical results do not support Peltzman's arguments. It is questionable, however, how well their choice of variable reflects the original Peltzman hypotheses, since it is not clear whether the Mueller–Murrell variable measures inequality between groups or inequality within the

---

23. Peltzman reminds the reader of Stigler's formulation of [Aaron] Director's law: "Public expenditures are made for the benefit of the middle classes, and financed by taxes which are borne in considerable part by the poor and the rich" (Stigler 1970, 1).

24. He estimates separate regressions for 135 years of U.S. aggregate data, 165 years of British data, 95 years of Canadian data, and 95 years of Japanese data. In addition, Peltzman undertakes cross-sectional analysis of sixteen developed countries over several time periods, as well as analysis of U.S. state and local data over several time periods.

beneficiary group. Kristov, Lindert, and McClelland (1992), on the other hand, formally incorporate Peltzman's arguments into their model and conclude that his hypotheses, though consistent with growth in other types of transfer payments, are inconsistent with increases in social insurance (Social Security) expenditure.

4.3 Economic development, political stability, and minority coalitions

The previous two main models (Subsections 4.1 and 4.2) employ an income class approach to redistribution, one where democratic processes are exploited by the majority to extract rents from the minority. As Downs (1957) suggested, however, causality may be reversed: Smaller groups organized along special interest consumer or producer lines have lower costs of coalescing politically than do less cohesive, larger groups of citizens.[25] Thus, well-organized minority groups are the effective rent seekers and unorganized, politically inert majority groups are the exploited. Demsetz (1982), North and Wallis (1982, 1986), North (1985a) and Olson (1982) have applied this special interest group framework to the issue of government growth, hypothesizing that the expanding public sector is due largely to greater minority-group pressure and enhanced lobbying efforts.[26]

Demsetz (1982) and North and Wallis (1982, 1986) argue that economic development lies at the heart of redistribution. Since specialization and the division of labor that accompanies development place workers with similar concerns in close proximity, it lowers the political transaction costs of rent seeking, creating a multitude of new interest groups. Simultaneously, as communities expand and become more heterogeneous and markets become more impersonal, the general interest is less easily articulated and hence, its representation is less vigorously pursued. Greater numbers of interest groups are also implied as within-industry entrepreneurs react to expanding markets and increased competition by joining forces to lobby for regulatory protections that diminish competition as well as for direct state financial support to members of their groups.

---

25. Stubblebine (1963), Olson (1965, 1971, 1982), Stigler (1970), and Niskanen (1971) also provide detailed discussions of this phenomenon. It is, however, an ancient proposition found in Adam Smith's *Wealth of Nations* (1776).

26. Denzau and Munger (1986) provide one particularly well-modeled scenario explaining the slippage between politicians' behavior and constituents' general interests that allows this to happen. Positive transactions costs play an important role in allowing this. Interestingly, Denzau and Munger show that this slippage or shirking – currently known as the "principal-agent" problem – allows otherwise unrepresented interests differential political power under certain circumstances.

In a somewhat indirect test of the interest group hypothesis, Demsetz analyzes the relationship between income inequality and government expenditure levels. Although his study produces mixed results, his empirical evidence is consistent with the conclusion that much of the post–World War II growth in U.S. government expenditure (1950–72) is due to the increasing pressure applied by minority-based coalitions.[27]

Far from competing with the preceding theory, Olson's model provides the missing link in the event chain where economic development is followed by the growth in numbers and strength of interest groups and, subsequently, by higher levels of government expenditure. Olson recognizes that even in fertile political grounds powerful interest groups do not appear overnight, rather development of these coalitions takes time and a stable environment for such associations to gain strength and become entrenched. He surmises, therefore, that greater numbers of interest groups and larger government expenditures are found in countries that (ironically) have enjoyed extended periods of political stability.[28]

Interest group theories of government growth imply two related, but distinct, hypotheses: (1) economic development and/or political stability produce ever larger numbers of powerful interest groups, and (2) these larger numbers of more powerful interest groups positively impact government expenditure levels. Murrell (1984), Mueller and Murrell (1985, 1986), and Kennelly and Murrell (1991) provide corroborating evidence for the first hypothesis by finding a positive relationship between the number of interest groups in OECD countries and the number of years since each country began its political and economic modernization process. Although the second hypothesis has undergone extensive empirical testing[29] at both individual and across-country levels, results are not yet

27. Results for earlier expenditure growth (1920–42) are not supportive. Demsetz theorizes that lower-income groups were unable to exercise their vote in a particularly self-interested manner until after World War II when the lower cost of mass communication between political entrepreneurs and interest groups came into effect. Interestingly, Demsetz hazards the prediction that low-cost communication to the broad class of voters may in the future choke off some special interest spending, or at least its relative growth rate. New cable news sources, radio talk shows, and electronic bulletin boards may have such an influence on future fiscal choice, though to date no research informs us as to how important these new informational sources are likely to be.

28. A second important implication of Olson's model is that inefficiencies created by high levels of rent seeking in politically stable environments inhibit economic growth rates. It is this second conclusion, in fact, which Olson (and Choi 1983) employ in empirical tests – a point we shall return to in our conclusions (Section 5).

29. Such studies include those by Mueller and Murrell (1985, 1986), Henrekson and Lybeck (1988), contributors to the volume by Lybeck and Henrekson (1988), Wyckoff (1988), Congleton and Shughart (1990), Naert (1990), Henrekson (1990), Nelson (1992), and Ferris and West (1993).

conclusive. This literature is limited since there is little agreement on how to measure interest group influences. Instead, proxy variables have been constructed using a wide variety of, and in some cases extremely diverse, data such as the number of consumer and business interest groups, union membership, number of trade unions, number of political parties, farm population, number of government employees,[30] and even the import/export ratio (Cameron 1978). It is not surprising that results are often conflicting, making the accumulated evidence difficult to evaluate.

4.4 Social affinity and economic development

In an extension of basic interest group models, Kristov, Lindert, and McClelland (1992) develop their concept of "social affinity" to explain public sector growth. Using the Becker (1983, 1985) framework, Kristov, Lindert, and McClelland assume that public redistribution levels are determined by the relative efforts of two interest groups – one in favor of greater redistribution, the other against. They then develop the concept of social affinity, which assumes that individuals care about others' income levels as well as their own. Although this concern may be purely altruistic or a reciprocal one of providing social insurance in case of dire financial situations, it is limited by the fact that individuals care more about themselves than others. The authors use this expanded framework to develop a model of political activity where interest group activities are not based solely on monetary gains or losses as in the Becker model[31] but on each individual's concern about others' monetary well-being as well. Thus, two "mixed" interest groups arise, each composed of gainers and losers from the transfer payment process. A second interesting feature of the model is that it formally allows for free riding, since some individuals will not care enough about outcomes to expend the effort to join either interest group.

Kristov, Lindert, and McClelland use their framework to explain the role of economic development in the growth of government expenditure. Since economic development increases incomes beyond subsistence, it frees lower-income individuals to expend effort on political activity. As incomes rise, however, individuals in the taxed group are

---

30. Government employees are often included in interest group models due to the Borcherding, Bush, and Spann (1977) argument that bureaucrats are an especially effective interest group.

31. The Kristov, Lindert, and McClelland social affinity idea is an ancient theme in political economy. Adam Smith's earlier book, *The Theory of Moral Sentiments* (1759), allows social sentiments to enter as arguments in an individual's utility function, but rival to own-income variables. To Smith, manifestations of social affinity are present in collective action but are dominated by narrower self-interest factors.

less sympathetic toward lower-income groups and are thus more likely to resist redistributional efforts. In early stages of development, they hypothesize, greater efforts by the poor dominate political activity, which leads to greater transfers and government growth; in the later stages of development, however, counterdistributional groups play the dominant role and public sector expansion tapers off.[32]

Although Kristov, Lindert, and McClelland do not directly test their government growth hypothesis, they do test a related prediction of their social affinity model. Social affinity is assumed to be a form of social insurance so that middle-income individuals, the politically pivotal agents, lobby for redistribution if they believe there is a greater possibility that they may at some future time join the poorer rather than the richer group. Thus, Kristov, Lindert, and McClelland predict that growth in transfer payments are positively related to the high-income to middle-income ratio and negatively related to the middle-income to low-income ratio. Estimation conducted on pooled cross-section, time-series data for OECD countries generally supports these income ratio tests.

4.5 The Leviathan theory

In developing the Leviathan theory of government growth, Brennan and Buchanan (1977, 1978, 1980) emphasize that aggregate expansion has not been the only fundamental change in government expenditure patterns. In addition, there has been a critical shift in the federal fiscal structure. Whereas state and local spending dominated total U.S. government expenditure in 1902 by a ratio of two to one, budgets evolved such that current federal expenditure is now nearly twice that of state and local governments. Within a general public choice framework in which the government seeks to maximize its budget, constrained by citizen mobility and interjurisdictional competition, Brennan and Buchanan show that public sector expansion and the centralization of government functions are not unrelated. Greater centralization, they suggest, reduces voters' fiscal locational choices, thereby increasing government's monopoly power. With less competition, the government is able to exploit more fully its citizenry and generate substantial increases in tax/expenditure levels.

As Nelson (1987) and Zax (1989) have separately illustrated, the Leviathan theory, within the context of a two-tiered federalist structure,

---

32. As mentioned in footnote 21, this acceleration of political activity by the poor to seek redistributional relief as things improve for them and the increased tensions it creates in societies that are more equal was early noted by de Tocqueville in *Democracy in America*.

entails two empirically testable hypotheses: (1) government expenditure is positively related to the degree of centralism (the size of the central government relative to the noncentral government), and (2) government expenditure is negatively related to the degree of fragmentation (the number of lower-tier governments).[33] Though a number of studies have attempted to test the Leviathan theory, the empirical results are mixed. Oates (1972, 1985) and Forbes and Zampelli (1989) do not provide empirical support, but Giertz (1981), Nelson (1987), Wallis and Oates (1988), and Zax (1989) do for one or both hypotheses.[34] In reviewing the empirical literature on Leviathan, Oates (1989) resolves most of these discrepancies and concludes that, at least at the local level where citizens are assumed to have the greatest mobility, the evidence is generally supportive of both the centralism and the fragmentation hypotheses.[35]

4.6 Fiscal illusion

The topic of fiscal illusion has become a literature in itself, and only the briefest summary is possible here. Oates presents an overview of these illusion theories and defines fiscal illusion as "a *systematic misperception* of fiscal parameters" (emphasis his; Oates 1988, 67). Research, thus far, has emphasized revenue sources of illusion, and Oates (1988, 60) categorizes the various forms as "(1) complexity of the tax structure, (2) renter illusion with respect to property taxation, (3) income elasticity of the tax structure, (4) debt illusion, and (5) the flypaper effect." These theories argue that citizens underestimate the tax price for publicly provided services because complex revenue structures "disguise" some taxes; renters make only indirect payments on property taxes; taxes tied closely to income levels "automatically" increase with economic growth; voters underestimate future tax liabilities due to public debt; and voter ignorance causes them to erroneously perceive lump-sum grants as lowering tax prices on the margin. While, in general, these theories imply public spending levels greater than that preferred by the fully informed median voter, they indicate expenditure growth only if voters underestimate tax prices still further. Greater complexity in tax structure, such as that

---

33. We use the terminology of centralism and fragmentation developed by Zax to distinguish the two hypotheses. Borcherding (1985) cites a great deal more pre-1985 literature that supports the centralization effect as a force raising public spending.
34. Related empirical works include Marlow (1988), Zax (1988), Grossman (1989, 1992), Eberts and Gronberg (1990), Joulfaian and Marlow (1990, 1991), and Kneebone (1992).
35. Oates (1989) implies, however, that other theories may also be consistent with these empirical results. He therefore refrains from concluding that the empirical evidence fully supports the Leviathan theory.

experienced over the past century, increases the differential between perceived and actual tax rates, thus tax complexity could be one of the determinants of public sector expansion.[36]

While Oates's review of the fiscal illusion literature indicates that empirical tests have produced mixed results, the tax complexity and the automatic income-elastic tax-base hypotheses have received some support,[37] and virtually all empirical studies are consistent with renters' illusion (landlords pay property taxes) and flypaper effects (lump-sum grants are misconstrued as marginal reductions).[38] Despite this apparent support, Oates expresses reservations about accepting these results as strong evidence of fiscal illusion. One empirical estimation problem is that the illusion measures employed as independent regressors are often endogenous rather than exogenous variables, biasing parameter estimates in favor of the illusion hypotheses. In addition, specifications that test for illusion often are observationally equivalent to other equally plausible theories of expenditure variations. For example, while a positive relationship between the number of rental homes and government expenditure may be attributed to renters' illusion, these results may indicate that renters, on the whole, experience lower (implicit) tax rates than do homeowners. Oates concludes, therefore, that a more rigorous theoretical development of illusion theories is necessary before sharply distinguishing tests of illusion hypotheses can be undertaken.

Recent studies have begun to address Oates's concerns. Marshall (1991) develops a test that employs an exogenous illusion variable by regressing state public expenditure levels on the tax "windfalls" produced by the U.S. Tax Reform Act of 1986. She rejects the illusion hypotheses. Turnbull (1992) develops a more rigorous model of the flypaper effect. He introduces uncertainty into the voter decision-making process and derives the conditions necessary for fiscal illusion to generate a flypaper effect. In addition, his analysis reveals that underestimation of marginal tax prices widens the distribution of possible prices,

36. As Mueller (1989) observes, the fiscal illusion literature does not explain who manipulates and reaps the benefits of voter misperceptions. Augmentation of these theories to include bureaucratic or interest group influences would provide a more complete insight into the mechanisms of fiscal illusion. The pre-1985 illusion literature is surveyed by Borcherding (1985).

37. As Oates (1988) indicates, evidence is least persuasive for the automatic income tax elasticity hypothesis. This evidence is weaker still when one considers an empirical test not considered by his survey in which Feenberg and Rosen (1987) use particularly carefully constructed measures of income elasticities to reject the automatic income tax elasticity theory.

38. However, Wyckoff's (1991) empirical results reject several well-known explanations of the flypaper effect, including the fiscal illusion version.

and that this increase in the risk associated with public spending partially offsets the effects of lower expected tax prices in determining public expenditure levels.

4.7 Taxation and deadweight losses in political models

Kau and Rubin's (1981) theory that increasing public sector size is due to decreasing deadweight losses from tax collection (see Subsection 3.8) is equally adept at analyzing government expansion within the political paradigm of rent-seeking models. Also, Browning's (1978) and Becker's (1983, 1985) interest group models predict that larger dead weight losses will discourage rent seeking and encourage taxpayer efforts to resist transfers. Conversely, the decreasing deadweight losses theorized by Kau and Rubin produce larger government expenditure levels (Becker 1983, 1985). Unfortunately, empirical studies of deadweights from rent seeking are notably lacking.

As mentioned in Subsection 3.8, Kau and Rubin argue that the increased cost of both legal tax avoidance and illegal tax evasion has decreased the deadweight losses of taxation, but there is another equally interesting potential source of lower deadweight taxation losses in the United States. The federal tax system has expanded beyond the excises and tariffs employed at the beginning of this century to increasingly focus on personal and corporate income taxes. While the a priori expected deadweights of a more diverse tax structure are uncertain (Atkinson and Stiglitz 1980), the fact that these are much broader tax bases may imply a decrease in the classic deadweight loss for any given level of public activity (Harberger 1974). If it could be shown empirically that the current more pluralistic and encompassing set of taxes has lowered deadweights on the margin, then the overall cost curve of public activities would have shifted down (vis-à-vis the Kau and Rubin model), encouraging larger purchases of public services. To date, the literature has not explored this potential source of government expansion, but future research may very well identify it as a significant determinant of increased expenditure patterns.

4.8 Concluding remarks on political models

In one key respect the political literature contrasts sharply with the apolitical literature. While apolitical theories of government growth generally employ the median voter model, political growth theories encompass a wide range of frameworks from the income coalition models of Meltzer and Richard (1981) and Peltzman (1980) to various forms of interest group models conceived by Becker (1983, 1985), Niskanen

(1971), and Kristov, Lindert, and McClelland (1992). It is likely that several or all of these theories provide the pieces of a "grand" political economy model. In fact, the empirical literature, especially since the 1980s, treats them as if this was the case. The empirical studies cited in Section 4 generally incorporate variables suggested by several different theories in an attempt to discover which frameworks and growth theories best explain public sector expansion.

It is questionable, however, whether these empirical specifications are appropriate for distinguishing between models. Such tests are, by definition, ad hoc and probably mask rivalries and complementarities between models. It is possible, for example, that the Meltzer and Richard hypothesis does not compete with the Peltzman theory but, instead, that both capture different aspects of rent-seeking behavior. In addition, empirical tests of the interest group hypotheses promoted by Demsetz, North and Wallis, and Olson can be accused of ad hoc theorizations behind their estimating methods. As noted in Subsection 4.3, no single set of variables has been identified as uniquely measuring interest group power and influence, a limitation that has confounded interpretation of empirical results.

Recently, the literature has begun to develop more rigorous theoretical underpinnings. Research such as that of Henrekson (1990) and Ferris and West (1993) attempts to separate various growth theories into those affecting supply functions and those affecting demands. Further theoretical focus is necessary before the unique aspects as well as interrelationships between various theories can be fully understood.

5. Remaining difficulties, integrating the paradigm, and conclusions

5.1 Unfinished thoughts on public supply instruments, endogenous growth, and ideology

To this point our survey has treated government as synonymous with public spending. This is too parochial an association, since two other instruments of public supply exist that extend the reach of the state, one of which has little, if any, public budgetary effects. Regulation and "tax preferences" (loopholes) also are effective means of carrying out public policy (Borcherding 1983), yet only the latter has much budgetary consequence. Few have explored this "calculus of instrument choice" (Prichard 1980) to ascertain (1) the actual pattern of public spending, regulations, and tax preferences over time; (2) if these three instruments can be aggregated into a public sector composite that indicates the relative size of government over time; and (3) the interaction between the three instruments causing public spending over time to under- or overestimate the role of government as a share of economic activity. Although pursuing such a research agenda is difficult at this time, further study of public spending as if the two other instruments were supplied in fixed coefficients is not useful.[39]

We have also neglected, except for a brief mention in Subsection 4.3, the very interesting and important literature treating GNP growth as an outcome of institutional choice, particularly the choice of government spending (and the other two aforementioned instruments). Since the 1940s, beginning with Colin Clark (1945), economists have debated how government activity affects national income and its growth.[40] Since government's share of national income depends on the denominator of the government spending to aggregate income ratio as much as on the numerator, fuller explanations of government growth in relative share terms will likely focus on government's effect on overall economic activity. Of course, devotees of "supply-side" fiscal arguments realize that this dialogue has been long underway.

Olson's (1982) "rise and decline of nations" contribution has already been discussed (see Subsection 4.3). Beyond this, several studies present conflicting findings as to whether government actions enhance or retard growth. Barro (1981, 1990, 1991), Grier and Tullock (1989), and Scully (1992) believe that government actions in developed economies tend to slow overall growth, which implies that, on the margin, public activity unambiguously raises the ratio of public spending to total income ratio; Aschauer (1989) asserts, however, that the opposite is true, especially for "infrastructural" expenditures; North (1990) is ambivalent. In a recent paper Keefer and Knack (1993) look at several aspects of political and social institutions that determine the net social utility of public actions. They find that broad Olsonian statements about the productiv-

---

39. Interestingly, the link of debt instruments to public spending has barely been explored by scholars of fiscal behavior. Buchanan and Wagner (1977) argued that acceptance of the Keynesian paradigm encouraged the rapid post–World War II expansion of public sector spending, but their explanations were severely criticized in a symposium devoted to their book and published the following year. In this latter volume Barro (1978), Niskanen (1978), and Tobin (1978) were hostile to the Keynesian explanation on the grounds that is was a special case of tax illusion and rested upon long-term voter ignorance. Beyond the usual explanation of inflationary revenues from seignorage and bracket creep (surveyed in Borcherding 1985), the effects of public-debt financing on the growth of government has not been explored since Buchanan and Wagner, Barro, et al.

40. Clark claimed that government spending shares in excess of 25 percent of GNP would cause per capita income growth to stagnate. Current supply-siders such as Barro and Scully would argue that growth would be quite rapid at 25 percent, possibly revising the "Clark point" up to 30 to 35 percent.

ity (or lack of same) of government need to be couched in careful discussions of other factors that enhance "encompassing" (Olson's term) decision making that discourages rent seeking. Future studies on the relative rise of government will surely consider more closely the endogenous growth question in this institutional/constitutional setting.

This brings us to the last lacuna of this subsection – the role of ideology in affecting the relative expansion of government's share of national income. Few deny that ideology matters in the size and composition of public spending, and Nelson and Silberberg (1987) offer persuasive evidence that it does. Unfortunately, disagreement over what ideology really means clouds the interpretation of the evidence. Kalt and Zupan (1984) argue that legislators, and possibly nonelected elites, never are perfectly disciplined by the constituents who put them in office. These officials take advantage of this principal-agent "slack" and vote their own ideological tastes, as opposed to citizens' ideological preferences. Peltzman (1984) counters, however, that one cannot disentangle the ideological preferences of the legislators from the voters, a position on which Dougan and Munger (1989) concur. Peltzman, and Dougan and Munger hold to the Downsian view that ideology is a social and political shorthand reflecting in self-serving ways narrower constituent interests. Dougan and Munger point out that politicians with well-defined ideologies have an advantage over their more pragmatic competitors, since the ideologically committed politician is less inclined to postelection "chiseling" whereby "brand name" losses are risked. Still, the existence of monitoring or bonding costs acts as an impediment to disciplining elected officials. This friction manifests itself in a variance between the preferences of voters and their elected officials, since the former are interested more in the "package" of promised policies than in any one of the items. Perfect sorting of packages and preferences is no more likely here in the polity than in the private sector market for goods and services. In other words, in a positive transactions cost world slack is inevitable. We should be astonished, therefore, if one of the purchases politicians make with their slack income is not an idiosyncratically ideological one.

In fact, there is much resistance to the denigration of ideology to a mere political signal that masks narrow self-interest. According to North (1990) global changes in voter ideology with associated sharp alterations in membership in the dominant coalition, in their ideology, and in their policies are rare, since such changes require high risk-inclusive returns for members of the new group relative to those offered by established interests. Such changes happen episodically, however, and when they do they require that the new coalitional grouping maintain itself, since the old group will attempt to lure away individual members of the new group. These new coalitions also suffer start-up and organizational diseconomies and are especially prone to free-ridership costs, so only a strong ideology will cement its members together in the face of temptations for its members to defect to the established one. Thus, ideological change is often the dominate force when marked alterations take place in a nation's political life. North believes such changes have taken place over the last two hundred years in the United States as well as elsewhere in the developed world.

Unfortunately, measures of ideology are notoriously difficult to develop and their effects on government spending and other instruments of policy production are controversial. Little conclusively can be said at this time beyond the usual admonitory call for more research.

5.2 Integrating the two paradigms, and some brief conclusions

Buchanan (1978) has observed that complete explanations of government growth will likely contain elements of both apolitical and political models:

> Any plausibly adequate explanation of the expansion of the governmental sector in the modern American economy requires both models, or some mixture of the two. Without doubt, some considerable part of the observed growth in the public sector, at all levels, is directly traceable to the demands of the citizenry, genuine demands for more services accompanied by an increased willingness to shoulder the tax burdens required for financing. But, once this is acknowledged, there can also be little doubt that a significant and remaining part of the observed growth in the public sector can be explained only by looking at the motivations of those who secure direct personal gains from government expansion, gains that are unrelated to the benefits filtered down to ordinary citizens. (6)

One method of assigning weights between apolitical and political explanations of government expansion is to analyze how well a particular paradigm explains public sector growth. Working within the apolitical paradigm, Borcherding (1985) collected estimates of median voter demand parameters and applied them to changes in exogenous variables in the United States from 1902 to 1978. Using the median voter analysis, he explains only 40 percent of the growth rate in U.S. budgets over this period.[41] Henrekson (1990) undertook a similar analysis using Swedish data and found considerably more explanatory power in the median voter model. Taking a slightly different tact, Congleton and Shughart (1990) tested the median voter model against the rent-seeking interest

---

41. This fraction is attributed to rises in the relative price of public services, real per capita incomes, and population.

group model to see which best explained increases in U.S. social security expenditure. They found more support for the median voter model.[42]

A second method of assigning explanatory weights incorporates both the apolitical and political models within the context of a single specification. In fact, the majority of the recent empirical literature includes variables suggested by both paradigms. For example, studies frequently incorporate tests of the Wagner or Baumol hypothesis in the same specification that tests for interest group effects (e.g., Ferris and West 1993).

As we have previously discussed, however, such specifications tend to be ad hoc rather than derived from a "grand" paradigm and are unlikely to reveal fully the mysteries of government expansion. Combining paradigms implies the conception of a more complex political decision-making process. This, in turn, requires a much deeper theoretical investigation than has been offered to date. In particular, difficulties arise in disentangling interest group effects from those implied by shifts in ordinary citizen demands. For example, increased female labor force participation might imply the development of a powerful new interest group or it could suggest a change in any one of the demand variables discussed in Subsection 3.9. As this example illustrates, isolating rent-seeking influences on government expenditure from those of demands arising in the general public will require careful theoretical analysis.[43]

One thing is abundantly clear. Researchers have come a long way from the crude government consumption functions studies, as Coase (1953) contemptuously described them, four or five decades ago. That current researchers self-consciously discipline themselves to offer richer models of choice with more complex institutional constraints is an improvement; that the last twenty years of such efforts have raised as many questions as they have shed light upon is an epistemological fact. Future research will, no doubt, yield high returns, but the exploration costs will be high and the results will be slow in coming. This discovery will, however, be very interesting and link divergent fields and approaches more coherently.

---

42. Congleton and Shughart also test a third mixed apolitical/political model and concluded that its explanatory power was inferior to that of the median voter model.

43. West (1991) undertakes just such an analysis through his careful integration of the Baumol (1967) and Kau and Rubin (1981) models into a single framework. His work produces testable hypotheses that distinguish between the two effects, which Ferris and West (1993) then use in empirical tests.

References

Abramson, Paul R. 1979. "Developing Party Identification: A Further Examination of Life-Cycle, Generational and Period Effects." *American Journal of Political Science* 23: 78–96.

Abramson, Paul R., John H. Aldrich, Phil Paolino, and David W. Rohde. 1992. " 'Sophisticated' Voting in the 1988 Presidential Primaries." *American Political Science Review* 86: 55–69.

Acheson, Keith. 1988. "Bureaucratic Theory: Retrospect and Prospect." In Albert Breton, Gianluigi Galeotti, Pierre Salmon, and Ronald Wintrobe, eds., Villa Colombella Papers on Bureaucracy. *European Journal of Political Economy* 4 (Special issue).

Acheson, Keith, and John F. Chant. 1973. "Bureaucratic Theory and the Choice of Central Bank Goals." *Journal of Money, Credit and Banking* 5: 637–55.

Advisory Commission on Intergovernmental Relations. 1979. *Citizen Participation in the American Federal System*. Washington, D.C.: U.S. Government Printing Office.

Ainsworth, S. 1993. "Regulating Lobbyists and Interest Group Influence." *Journal of Politics* 55: 41–56.

Akerlof, George A. 1991. "Procrastination and Obedience." *American Economic Review* 81: 1–19.

Åkerman, Johan. 1946. *Ekonomisk skeende och Politiska förändringer*. Lund.

——— 1947. "Political Economic Cycles." *Kyklos* 1: 107–17. (Short version of Akerman [1946].)

Alchian, Armen A. 1950. "Uncertainty, Evolution, and Economic Theory." *Journal of Political Economy* 58: 211–21.

——— 1965. "Some Economics of Property Rights." *Il Politico* 30: 816–29.

Alchian, Armen A., and Harold Demsetz. 1972. "Production, Information Costs, and Economic Organization." *American Economic Review* 62: 777–95.

Alchian, Armen A., and Reuben A. Kessel. 1962. "Competition, Monopoly, and the Pursuit of Money." In NBER, *Aspects of Labor Economics*. Princeton: Princeton University Press.

Aldrich, John H. 1976. "Some Problems in Testing Two Rational Models of Participation." *American Journal of Political Science* 20: 713–34.

——— 1983. "A Downsian Spatial Model with Party Activism." *American Political Science Review* 77: 974–90.

——— 1993. "Rational Choice and Turnout." *American Journal of Political Science* 37: 246–78.

——— 1995. *Why Parties? The Origin and Transformation of Party Politics in America*. Chicago: University of Chicago Press.

Aldrich, John H., and Michael M. McGinnis. 1989. "A Model of Party Constraints on Optimal Candidate Positions." *Mathematical and Computer Modelling* 12: 437–50.

Aldrich, John H., and Richard D. McKelvey. 1977. "A Method of Scaling with Applications to the 1968 and 1972 Presidential Elections." *American Political Science Review* 71: 111–30.

Aldrich, John H., and Richard G. Niemi. 1995. "The Sixth American Party System: Electoral Change, 1952–1988." In Stephen Craig, ed., *Broken Contract: Changing Relationships between Citizens and Their Government in the United States*. Boulder, CO: Westview Press.

Alesina, Alberto. 1987. "Macroeconomic Policy in a Two-Party System as a Repeated Game." *Quarterly Journal of Economics* 102: 651–78.

———. 1988a. "Macroeconomics and Politics." In Stanley Fischer, ed., *NBER Macroeconomic Annual 1988*.

———. 1988b. "Credibility and Policy Convergence in a Two-Party System with Rational Voters." *American Economic Review* 78: 796–806.

———. 1989. "Politics and Business Cycles in Industrial Democracies." *Economic Policy* 8 (April): 57–98.

Alesina, Alberto, Gerald D. Cohen, and Nouriel Roubini. 1992. "Macroeconomic Policy and Elections in OECD Democracies." *Economics and Politics* 4: 1–31.

———. 1993. "Electoral Business Cycles in Industrial Democracies." *European Journal of Political Economy* 9: 1–23.

Alesina, Alberto, and Alex Cukierman. 1990. "The Politics of Ambiguity." *The Quarterly Journal of Economics* 55: 829–50.

Alesina, Alberto, and Allan Drazen. 1991. "Why are Stabilizations Delayed?" *American Economic Review* 81: 1170–88.

Alesina, Alberto, J. Londregan, and Howard Rosenthal. 1993. "A Model of the Political Economy of the United States." *American Political Science Review* 87: 12–35.

Alesina, Alberto, and Howard Rosenthal. 1989. "Partisan Cycles in Congressional Elections and the Macroeconomy." *American Political Science Review* 83: 373–98.

———. 1995. *Partisan Politics, Divided Government, and the Economy*. Cambridge University Press.

Alesina, Alberto, and Nouriel Roubini. 1992. "Political Cycles in OECD Economies." *Review of Economic Studies* 59: 663–88.

Alesina, Alberto, and Jeffrey Sachs. 1988. "Political Parties and the Business Cycle in the US, 1948–1984." *Journal of Money, Credit and Banking* 20: 63–82.

Alesina, Alberto, and Guido Tabellini. 1992. "Positive and Normative Theories of Public Debt and Inflation in Historical Perspective." *European Economic Review* 36: 337–44.

Alexander, Paul. 1982. *Sri Lankan Fishermen: Rural Capitalism and Peasant Society*. Canberra: Australian National University.

Allen, Franklin. 1990. "The Market for Information and the Origin of Financial Intermediation." *Journal of Financial Intermediation* 1: 3–30.

Allen, Stuart D. 1986. "The Federal Reserve and the Electoral Cycle." *Journal of Money, Credit and Banking* 18: 88–94.

Alt, James E., and Norman Schofield. 1972. "Complexity in Voting Bodies: The Example of the U.S. Senate." University of Essex. Typescript.

Amar, A. 1987. "Of Sovereignty and Federalism." *Yale Law Journal* 96: 1425–520.

Anderson, Gary M., Delores T. Martin, William F. Shughart II, and Robert D. Tollison. 1990. "Behind the Veil: The Political Economy of Constitutional Change." In W. M. Crain and Robert D. Tollison, eds., *Predicting Politics*. Ann Arbor: University of Michigan Press, 89–100.

Anderson, Kym. 1980. "The Political Market for Government Assistance to Australian Manufacturing Industries." *Economic Record* 56: 132–44.

Anderson, Lee G. 1977. *The Economics of Fisheries Management*. Baltimore: Johns Hopkins University Press.

Anderson, Svein S., and Kjell A. Eliassen. 1991. "European Community Lobbying." *European Journal of Political Research* 20: 173–87.

Andreoni, James. 1988. "Why Free Ride? Strategies and Learning in Public Goods Experiments." *Journal of Public Economics* 37: 291–304.

1989. "Giving with Impure Altruism: Applications to Charity and Ricardian Equivalence." *Journal of Political Economy* 97: 447–58.

1993. "An Experimental Test of the Public-Goods Crowding-Out Hypothesis." *American Economic Review* 83: 1317–27.

Ansolabehere, Steven, Roy Behr, and Shanto Iyengar. 1983. *The Media Game.* New York: Macmillan.

Aranson, Peter H., George Robinson, and Ernest Gelhorn. 1982. "A Theory of Legislative Delegation." *Cornell Law Review* 68: 777–95.

Aranson, Peter H., Melvin J. Hinich, and Peter C. Ordeshook. 1974. "Election Goals and Strategies: Equivalent and Non-equivalent Candidate Objectives." *American Political Science Review* 68: 135–52.

Aranson, Peter H., and Peter C. Ordeshook. 1977. "A Prolegomenon to a Theory of the Failure of Representative Democracy." In Peter H. Aranson and Peter C. Ordeshook, eds., *American Re-Evolution Papers and Proceedings*, 23–46.

1981. "Regulation, Redistribution and Public Choice." *Public Choice* 37: 69–100.

Arendt, Hannah. 1976. *Eichmann in Jerusalem: A Report on the Banality of Evil.* New York: Penguin.

Arrow, Kenneth J. 1950. "A Difficulty in the Concept of Social Welfare." *Journal of Political Economy* 58: 328–46.

1951. *Social Choice and Individual Values.* New York: John Wiley and Sons. Rev. ed. 1963.

1967. "Values and Collective Decision Making." In Peter Laslett and W. G. Runciman, eds., *Philosophy, Politics and Society.* Vol.3. Oxford: Basil Backwell, 215–32.

1977. "Extended Sympathy and the Possibility of Social Choice." *American Economic Review* 67: 219–25.

1983. *Collected Papers*, vol.1, *Social Choice and Justice.* Cambridge, Mass.: Harvard University Press.

Asch, Peter, Gary A. Gigliotti, and James A. Polito. 1993. "Free Riding with Discrete and Continuous Public Goods: Some Experimental Evidence." *Public Choice* 77: 293–305.

Aschauer, David A. 1989. "Is Public Expenditure Productive?" *Journal of Monetary Economics* 23: 177–200.

Atkinson, Anthony B., and Joseph E. Stiglitz. 1980. *Lectures on Public Economics.* New York: McGraw-Hill.

Aubin, C., J. Berdot, D. Goyeau, and J. Lafay. 1988. "The Growth of Public Expenditure in France." In Johan A. Lybeck and Magnus Henrekson, eds., *Explaining the Growth of Government.* Amsterdam: North-Holland.

Aumann, Robert J., and Mordecai Kurz. 1977. "Power and Taxes." *Econometrica* 45: 1137–61.

Austen-Smith, David. 1981. "Voluntary Pressure Groups." *Economica* 48: 143–53.

1984. "Two-Party Competition with Many Constituencies." *Mathematical Social Sciences* 7: 177–98.

1986. "Legislative Coalitions and Electoral Equilibrium." *Public Choice* 50: 185–210.

1987a. "Interest Groups, Campaign Contributions and Probabilistic Voting." *Public Choice* 54: 123–39.

1987b. "Sophisticated Sincerity: Voting Over Endogeneous Agendas." *American Political Science Review* 81: 1323–30.

1991. "Rational Consumers and Irrational Voters. A Review Essay on *Black Hole*

Tariffs and Endogenous Policy Theory by Stephen Magee, William Brock, and Leslie Young, Cambridge University Press 1989." *Economics and Politics* 3: 73–92.

1993. "Information and Influence: Lobbying for Agendas and Votes." *American Journal of Political Science* 37: 799–833.

1995. "Campaign Contributions and Access." *American Political Science Review* 89: 566–81.

1996. "Electing Legislatures." In Norman Schofield, ed., *Collective Decision Making: Social Choice and Political Economy*, Boston: Kluwer, 113–48.

Austen-Smith, David, and Jeffrey S. Banks. 1988. "Elections, Coalitions and Legislative Outcomes." *American Political Science Review* 82: 405–22.

1989. "Electoral Accountability and Incumbency." In Peter C. Ordeshook, ed., *Models of Strategic Choice in Politics*. Ann Arbor: University of Michigan Press.

Austen-Smith, David, and John R. Wright. 1992. "Competitive Lobbying for a Legislator's Vote." *Social Choice and Welfare* 9: 229–57.

1994. "Counteractive Lobbying." *American Journal of Political Science* 38: 25–44.

Austin, A. 1994a. "Coordinated Action in Local Public Goods Models: The Case of Secession without Exclusion." Department of Economics, University of Houston. Mimeo.

1994b. "The Price of Nationalism: The Evidence From the Soviet Union." Department of Economics, University of Houston. Mimeo.

Axelrod, Robert. 1970. *Conflict of Interest*. Chicago: Markham.

1984. *The Evolution of Cooperation*. New York: Basic Books.

Bagnoli, Mark, and Michael McKee. 1991. "Voluntary Contribution Games: Efficient Private Provision of Public Goods." *Economic Inquiry* 29: 351–66.

Bagnoli, Mark, Ben-David Shaul, and Michael McKee. 1992. "Voluntary Provision of Public Goods, the Multiple Unit Case." *Journal of Public Economics* 47: 85–106.

Bailey, Martin J. 1992. "Approximate Optimality of Aboriginal Property Rights." *Journal of Law and Economics* 35: 183–98.

Balash, Peter C. 1992. "The Effects of Relative Factor Endowments upon Economic Voting and Tariffs." Ph.D. diss., Department of Economics, University of Texas at Austin.

Baldwin, Robert E. 1976. *The Political Economy of U.S. Postwar Trade Policy*. Bulletin No.4. CSFI, Graduate School of Business, New York University.

1982. "The Political Economy of Protectionism." In Jagdish N. Bhagwati, ed., *Import Competition and Response*. Chicago: University of Chicago Press, 263–86.

1984. "Trade Policies in Developed Countries." In Ronald W. Jones and Peter B. Kenen, eds., *Handbook of International Economics*. Amsterdam: North-Holland, 571–619.

1986. *The Political Economy of U.S. Import Policy*. Cambridge: MIT Press.

ed. 1988. *Trade Policy Issues and Empirical Analysis*. Chicago: University of Chicago Press.

Balinsky, M. L., and H. Peyton Young. 1982. *Fair Representation*. New Haven: Yale University Press.

Balisacan, Arsenio M., and James A. Roumasset. 1987. "Public Choice of Economic Policy: The Growth of Agricultural Protection." *Weltwirtschaftliches Archiv, Review of World Economics* 123: 232–48.

Ball, David S. 1967. "United States Effective Tariffs and Labor's Share." *Journal of Political Economy* 75: 183–7.

Ball, R. 1995. "Interest Groups, Influence and Welfare." *Economics and Politics* 7: 119–46.

Banks, Jeffrey S. 1984. "Sophisticated Voting Outcomes and Agenda Control." *Social Choice and Welfare* 1: 295–306.

1989a. "Equilibrium Outcomes in Two-Stage Amendment Procedures." *American Journal of Political Science* 33: 25–43.

1989b. "Agency Budgets, Cost Information, and Auditing." *American Journal of Political Science* 33: 670–99.

1990. "A Model of Electoral Competition with Incomplete Information." *Journal of Economic Theory* 50: 309–25.

Banks, Jeffrey S., and Randall L. Calvert. 1992a. "A Battle-of-the-Sexes Game with Incomplete Information." *Games and Economic Behavior* 4: 1–26.

1992b. *Communication and Efficiency in Coordination Games.* Working paper, Department of Economics and Department of Political Science, University of Rochester.

Banks, Jeffrey S., and Farid Gasmi. 1987. "Endogenous Agenda Formation in Three-Person Committees." *Social Choice and Welfare* 4: 133–52.

Banks, Jeffrey S., Charles R. Plott, and, David P. Porter. 1988. "An Experimental Analysis of Unanimity in Public Goods Provision Mechanisms." *Review of Economic Studies* 55: 301–22.

Banks, Jeffrey S., and Barry R. Weingast. 1992. "The Political Control of Bureaus under Asymmetric Information." *American Journal of Political Science* 36: 509–24.

Baran, Paul, and Paul Sweezy. 1966. *Monopoly Capital.* New York: Monthly Review Press.

Barberá, Salvador, and Hugo F. Sonnenschein. 1978. "Preference Aggregation with Randomized Social Orderings." *Journal of Economic Theory* 18: 244–54.

Barke, Richard P., and William H. Riker. 1982. "A Political Theory of Regulation with Some Observations on Railway Abandonments." *Public Choice* 39: 73–106.

Barlow, Robin. 1970. "Efficiency Aspects of Local School Finance." *Journal of Political Economy* 78: 1028–40.

Baron, David P. 1989a. "Service-Induced Campaign Contributions and the Electoral Equilibrium." *Quarterly Journal of Economics* 104: 45–72.

1989b. "Service-Induced Campaign Contributions, Incumbent Shirking and Reelection Opportunities." In Peter C. Ordeshook, ed., *Models of Strategic Choice in Politics.* Ann Arbor: University of Michigan Press.

1991. "A Spatial Bargaining Theory of Government Formation in a Parliamentary System." *American Political Science Review* 85: 137–64.

1993a. "Government Formation and Endogeneous Parties." *American Political Science Review* 87: 34–48.

1993b. *A Theory of Collective Choice for Government Programs.* Research paper no.1240, Graduate School of Business, Stanford University.

1994. "Electoral Competition with Informed and Uninformed Voters." *American Political Science Review* 88: 33–47.

Baron, David P., and John Ferejohn. 1987. "Bargaining and Agenda Formation in Legislatures." *American Economic Review*, Papers and Proceedings 77: 303–9.

1989. "Bargaining in Legislatures." *American Political Science Review* 83: 1181–206.

Baron, David, and J. Mo. 1993. "Campaign Contributions and Party-Candidate Competition in Services and Policies." In William Barnett, Melvin J. Hinich, and Norman Schofield, eds., *Political Economy: Institutions, Information, Competition and Representation.* Cambridge University Press.

Barro, Robert J. 1973. "The Control of Politicians: An Economic Model." *Public Choice* 14: 19–42.

1978. "Comments from an Unreconstructed Ricardian." *Journal of Monetary Economics* 4: 569–81.

1979. "On the Determination of the Public Debt." *Journal of Political Economy* 87: 940–71.

1981. "Output Effects of Government Purchases." *Journal of Political Economy* 89: 1086–121.

1986. "U.S. Deficits Since World War I." *Scandinavian Journal of Economics* 88: 195–222.

1990. "Government Spending in a Simple Model of Endogenous Growth." *Journal of Political Economy* Supplement 98: 103–25.

1991. "Economic Growth in a Cross Section of Countries." *Quarterly Journal of Economics* 106: 407–44.

Barry, Brian. 1970. *Sociologists, Economists, and Democracy.* London: Collier-Macmillan.

1986. "Lady Chatterley's Lover and Dr. Fisher's Bomb Party: Liberalism, Pareto Optimality, and the Problem of Objectionable Preferences." In Jon Elster and Aanund Hylland, eds., *Foundations of Social Choice Theory.* Cambridge University Press, 11–43.

Bartels, Larry. 1988. *Presidential Primaries and the Dynamics of Public Choice.* Princeton: Princeton University Press.

Bartholdi, J., L. Narasimhan, and Craig Tovey. 1990. "Recognizing Majority-Rule Equilibrium in Spatial Voting Games." Georgia Institute of Technology. Mimeo.

Barzel, Yoram. 1993. "Parliament as a Wealth Maximizing Institution: The Right to the Residual and the Right to Vote." University of Washington. Mimeo.

Barzel, Yoram, and Tim R. Sass. 1990. "The Allocation of Resources by Voting." *Quarterly Journal of Economics* 105: 745–71.

Barzel, Yoram, and Eugene Silberberg. 1973. "Is the Act of Voting Rational?" *Public Choice* 16: 51–8.

Bates, Robert H. 1981. *Markets and States in Tropical Africa: The Political Basis of Agricultural Policies.* Berkeley and Los Angeles: University of California Press.

1989. *Beyond the Miracle of the Market.* Cambridge University Press.

Bator, F. M. 1960. *The Question of Government Spending: Public Needs and Private Wants.* New York: Harper and Row.

Bauer, R. A., Ithiel de Sola Pool, and Lewis A. Dexter. 1963. *American Business and Public Policy: The Politics of Foreign Trade.* New York: Atherton Press.

Baumol, William J. 1952. *Welfare Economics and the Theory of the State.* Cambridge, Mass.: Harvard University Press.

1967. "The Macroeconomics of Unbalanced Growth: The Anatomy of Urban Crisis." *American Economic Review* 57: 415–26.

Baumol, William J., Sue A. B. Blackman, and Edward N. Wolff. 1985. "Unbalanced Growth Revisited: Asymptotic Stagnancy and New Evidence." *American Economic Review* 75: 806–17.

Baysinger, Barry, and Robert D. Tollison. 1980. "Evaluating the Social Costs of Monopoly and Regulation." *Atlantic Economic Journal* 8(4): 22–6.

Beard, Charles A. [1913] 1941. *An Economic Interpretation of the Constitution.* New York: Macmillan.

Beck, Nathaniel. 1982a. "Does There Exist a Political Business Cycle: A Box-Tiao Analysis." *Public Choice* 38: 205–9.

1982b. "Parties, Administrations, and American Macroeconomic Outcomes." *American Political Science Review* 76: 82–93.

1982c. "Presidential Influence on the Federal Reserve in the 1970s." *American Journal of Political Science* 26: 415–45.

1987. "Elections and the FED: Is There a Political Monetary Cycle?" *American Journal of Political Science* 31: 194–216.

Becker, Gary S. 1958. "Competition and Democracy." *Journal of Law and Economics* 1: 105–9.

1976. *The Economic Approach to Human Behavior*. Chicago: Chicago University Press.

1983. "A Theory of Competition among Pressure Groups for Political Influence." *Quarterly Journal of Economics* 98: 371–400.

1985. "Public Policies, Pressure Groups and Deadweight Costs." *Journal of Public Economics* 28: 330–47.

Beer, Samuel. 1982. *Britain against Itself*. London: Faber and Faber.

1993. *To Make A Nation: The Rediscovery of American Federalism*. Cambridge. Mass.: Harvard University Press.

Bell, Christopher R. 1989. "Between Anarchy and Leviathan: A Note on the Design of Federal States." *Journal of Public Economics* 39: 207–21.

Bénabou, Roland. 1993. "Workings of a City: Location, Education, and Production." *Quarterly Journal of Economics* 108: 619–52.

Bendor, Jonathan. 1988. "Formal Models of Bureaucracy. A Review." *British Journal of Political Science* 18: 353–95.

Bendor, Jonathan, and Dilip Mookherjee. 1987. "Institutional Structure and the Logic of Ongoing Collective Action." *American Political Science Review* 81: 129–54.

Bendor, Jonathan, Serge Taylor, and Roland van Gaalen. 1985. "Bureaucratic Expertise vs. Legislative Authority: A Model of Deception and Monitoring in Budgeting." *American Political Science Review* 79: 1041–60.

1987a. "Politicians, Bureaucrats, and Asymmetric Information." *American Journal of Political Science* 31: 796–828.

1987b. "Stacking the Deck: Bureaucratic Missions and Policy Design." *American Political Science Review* 81: 873–96.

Bennett, Elaine, and William E. Zame. 1988. "Bargaining in Cooperative Games." *International Journal of Game Theory* 17: 279–300.

Ben-Porath, Yoram. 1975. "The Years of Plenty and the Years of Famine – A Political Business Cycle?" *Kyklos* 28: 400–3.

Bentley, A. F. 1907. *The Process of Government*. Chicago: University of Chicago Press.

Ben-Zion, Uri, and Zeev Eytan. 1974. "On Money, Votes and Policy in a Democratic Society." *Public Choice* 17: 1–10.

Berelson, Bernard, Paul Lazarsfeld, and William McPhee. 1954. *Voting: A Study of Opinion Formation in a Presidential Campaign*. Chicago: University of Chicago Press.

Berglas, Eitan. 1976. "On the Theory of Clubs." *American Economic Review* 66: 116–21.

1981. "The Market Provision of Club Goods Once Again." *Journal of Public Economics* 15: 389–93.

Bergson, Abraham. 1938. "A Reformulation of Certain Aspects of Welfare Economics." *Quarterly Journal of Economics* 52: 233–52.

Bergstrom, Theodore C., and Robert P. Goodman. 1973. "Private Demands for Public Goods." *American Economic Review* 63: 280–96.

Bergstrom, Theodore C., Judith A. Roberts, Daniel L. Rubinfeld, and Perry Shapiro. 1988. "A Test for Efficiency in the Supply of Public Education." *Journal of Public Economics* 35: 289–307.

Berkes, Fikret, ed. 1989. *Common Property Resources: Ecology and Community-Based Sustainable Development*. London: Belhaven.

Berkowitz, D. 1994. "Regional Income and Secession." Department of Economics, University of Pittsburgh. Mimeo.

Berliant, Marcus, and Miguel Gouveia. 1993. "On the Political Economy of Income Taxation." Working paper, University of Rochester.

Bernholz, Peter. 1973. "Logrolling, Arrow Paradox and Cyclical Majorities." *Public Choice* 15: 87–95.

1974a. "Communication." *American Political Science Review* 68: 961–2.

1974b. "Logrolling, Arrow Paradox and Decision Rules – A Generalization." *Kyklos* 27: 49–61.

1975. "Logrolling and the Paradox of Voting: Are They Logically Equivalent?" *American Political Science Review* 69: 961–2.

1978. "On the Stability of Logrolling Outcomes in Stochastic Games." *Public Choice* 33(3): 65–82.

1985. *The International Game of Power.* Berlin: Mouton Publishers.

1992a. "Constitutional Aspects of the European Integration." In Silvio Borner and Herbert Grubel, eds., *The European Community after 1992 – Perspectives from the Outside.* Houndsmill: Macmillan, 45–60.

1992b. "The Economic Approach to International Relations." In Gerard Radnitzky, ed., *Universal Economics.* New York: Paragon, 339–400.

Berry, Francis S., and William D. Berry. 1990. "State Lottery Adoptions as Policy Innovations: An Event History Analysis." *American Political Science Review* 84: 395–415.

Besley, Timothy, and Anne Case. 1995a. "Incumbent Behaviour: Vote Seeking, Tax Setting and Yardstick Competition." *American Economic Review* 85: 25–45.

1995b. "Does Electoral Accountability Affect Economic Policy Choices: Evidence from Gubernatioral Term Limits?" *Quarterly Jouurnal of Economics* 110: 769–98.

Bhagwati, Jagdish N. 1980. "Lobbying and Welfare." *Journal of Public Economics* 14: 355–63.

1982. "Directly Unproductive, Profit-Seeking DUP Activities." *Journal of Political Economy* 90: 988–1002.

1988. *Protectionism.* Cambridge, Mass.: MIT Press.

Bianco, William T., and Robert H. Bates. 1990. "Cooperation by Design: Leadership, Structure, and Collective Dilemmas." *American Political Science Review* 84: 133–47.

Biegeleisen, J. Alab, and David L. Sjoquist. 1988. "Rational Voting Applied to Choice of Taxes." *Public Choice* 57: 39–48.

Binger, B. R., Elizabeth Hoffman, and A. W. Williams. 1987. *Implementing a Lindahl Mechanism with a Modified Tatonnement Procedure.* Economic Science Association.

Binmore, Ken. 1990. "Evolution and Contractarianism." *Constitutional Political Economy* 1: 1–26.

Bishop, George F., Alfred J. Tuchfarber, and Robert W. Oldendick. 1978. "Change in the Structure of American Political Attitudes: The Nagging Question of Question Wording." *American Journal of Political Science* 22: 250–69.

Black, Duncan. 1948a. "On the Rationale of Group Decision Making." *Journal of Political Economy* 56: 23–34.

1948b. "The Decisions of a Committee Using a Special Majority." *Econometrica* 16: 245–61.

1958. *The Theory of Committees and Elections.* Cambridge University Press.

Black, Duncan, and R. A. Newing. 1951. *Committee Decisions with Complementary Valuation.* London: William Hodge.

Black, Jerome H. 1978. "The Multicandidate Calculus of Voting: Application to Canadian Federal Elections." *American Journal of Political Science* 22: 609–38.

Black, John D. 1928. "The McNary–Haugen Movement." *American Economic Review* 18: 405–27.

Blackorby, Charles, and David Donaldson. 1982. "Ratio-Scale and Translation-Scale Full Interpersonal Comparability without Domain Restrictions: Admissible Social-Evaluation Functions." *International Economic Review* 23: 249–68.

Blackorby, Charles, David Donaldson, and John A. Weymark. 1984. "Social Choice with

Interpersonal Utility Comparisons: A Diagrammatic Introduction." *International Economic Review* 25: 345–56.

Blair, Douglas H., Georges Bordes, Jerry S. Kelly, and Kotaro Suzumura. 1976. "Impossibility Theorems without Collective Rationality." *Journal of Economic Theory* 13: 361–79.

Blais, André, E.L. Blake, and Stéphen Dion. 1991. "The Voting Behavior of Bureaucrats." In André Blais and Stéphan Dion, eds., *The Budget Maximizing Bureacrat: Appraisals and Evidence,* Pittsburgh: University of Pittsburgh Press: 205–30.

Blais, André, and Stéphen Dion, eds. 1991. *The Budget-Maximizing Bureaucrat: Appraisals and Evidence.* Pittsburgh: University of Pittsburgh Press.

Blais, André, and Richard Nadeau. 1992. "The Electoral Budget Cycle." *Public Choice* 74: 389–403.

Blake, E. L., J. L. Guyton, and S. Leventhal. 1992. "Limits of Coasean Bargaining in the Face of Empty Cores." *Publice Choice* /ESA Meetings.

Blau, Julian H., and Rajat Deb. 1977. "Social Decision Functions and Veto." *Econometrica* 45: 871–9.

Blomquist, William. 1992. *Dividing the Waters: Governing Groundwater in Southern California.* San Francisco. Institute for Contemporary Studies Press.

Blomquist, William, and Elinor Ostrom. 1985. "Institutional Capacity and the Resolution of a Commons Dilemma. *Policy Studies Review* 5: 383–93.

Boadway, Robin, and Frank Flatters. 1982. "Efficiency and Equalization Payments in a Federal System of Governments. A Synthesis and Extension of Recent Result." *Canadian Journal of Economics* 15: 613–33.

Boardman, Anthony, and Aidan Vining. 1989. "Ownership and Performance in Competitive Environments: A Comparison of the Performance of Private, Mixed, and State-Owned Enterprises." *Journal of Law and Economics* 32: 1–34.

Boddy, R., and J. Crotty. 1975. "Class Conflict and Macro-Policy: The Political Business Cycle." *Review of Radical Political Economy* 7: 1–19.

Bohara, Alok K., and William H. Kaempfer. 1991, "A Test of Tariff Endogeneity in the United States." *American Economic Review* 81: 952–60.

Boller, Paul F. 1981. *Presidential Anecdotes.* New York: Penguin.

Bookman, M. 1992. *The Economics of Secession.* New York: St. Martin's Press.

Borcherding, Thomas E. 1965. "The Growth of Non-Federal Public Employment in the United States, 1900–1963." Ph.D. diss., Duke University. Revised as "One Hundred Years of Public Spending, 1870–1970." In Thomas E. Borcherding, ed., *Budgets and Bureaucrats: The Sources of Government Growth.* Durham: Duke University Press, 45–70.

   ed. 1977. *Budgets and Bureaucrats: The Sources of Government Growth.* Durham: Duke University Press.

   1983. "Toward a Positive Theory of Public Sector Supply Arrangements." In J. R. S. Prichard, ed., *Crown Corporations in Canada.* Toronto: Butterworths, 99–184.

   1985. "The Causes of Government Expenditure Growth: A Survey of the U.S. Evidence." *Journal of Public Economics* 28: 359–82.

Borcherding, Thomas E., Winston C. Bush, and Robert M. Spann. 1977. "The Effects on Public Spending of the Divisibility of Public Outputs in Consumption, Bureaucratic Power and the Size of the Tax-Sharing Group." In Thomas E. Borcherding, ed., *Budgets and Bureaucrats: The Sources of Government Growth.* Durham: Duke University Press, 211–28.

Borcherding, Thomas E., and Robert T. Deacon. 1972. "The Demand for the Services of Non-Federal Governments." *American Economic Review* 62: 891–901.

Borcherding, Thomas E., Werner W. Pommerehne, and Friedrich Schneider. 1983a.

"Comparing the Efficiency of Private and Public Production: The Evidence from Five Countries." *Zeitschrift für Nationalökonomie* Supplement 2, 127–56.

1983b. "Towards a Positive Theory of Public Sector Supply." In R. Prichard, ed., *Crown Corporations in Canada*. Toronto: Butterworths.

Borda, Jean-Charles de. 1781. "Memoire sur les elections au scrutin." *Histoire de l'Academie Royale des Sciences*. Paris.

Border, Kim C. 1983. "Social Welfare Functions for Economic Environment with or without the Pareto Principle." *Journal of Economic Theory* 29: 205–16.

Bordes, Georges. 1976. "Consistency, Rationality, and Collective Choice." *Review of Economic Studies* 43: 451–57.

Bordes, Georges, and Michel Le Breton. 1989. "Arrovian Theorems with Private Alternatives Domains and Selfish Individuals." *Journal of Economic Theory* 47: 257–81.

Bornstein, Gary, and Amnon Rapoport. 1988. "Intergroup Competition for the Provision of Step-Level Public Goods: Effects of Preplay Communication." *European Journal of Social Psychology* 18: 125–42.

Bornstein, Gary, Amnon Rapoport, Lucia Kerpel, and Tani Katz. 1989. "Within- and Between-Group Communication in Intergroup Competition for Public Goods." *Journal of Experimental Social Psychology* 25: 422–36.

Borooah, V. K., and R. van der Ploeg. 1983. *Political Aspects of the Economy*. Cambridge University Press.

Bowden, R. 1989. *Statistical Games and Human Affairs*. Cambridge University Press.

Bowen, Howard R. 1943. "The Interpretation of Voting in the Allocation of Economic Resources." *Quarterly Journal of Economics* 58: 27–48.

Bowles, Samuel. 1985. "The Production Process in a Competitive Economy: Walrasian, Neo-Hobbesian, and Marxian Models." *American Economic Review* 75: 16–36.

Boylan, Richard, John O. Ledyard, Arthur Lupia, Richard D. McKelvey, and Peter C. Ordeshook. 1991. "Political Competition and a Model of Economic Growth: Some Experimental Results." In Thomas Palfrey, ed., *Contemporary Laboratory Research in Political Economy*. Ann Arbor: University of Michigan Press.

Boylan, Richard, John O. Ledyard, and Richard D. McKelvey. Forthcoming. "Political Competition in a Model of Economic Growth: Some Theoretical Results." *American Economic Review*.

Bradford, D. F., R. A. Malt, and Wallace E. Oates. 1969. "The Rising Cost of Local Government Services: Some Evidence and Reflections." *National Tax Journal* 22: 185–202.

Brady, Henry E., and Paul M. Sniderman. 1985. "Attitude Attribution: A Group Basis for Political Reasoning." *American Political Science Review* 79: 1061–78.

Brams, Steven J. 1992. *Rational Politics, Decisions, Games and Strategy*. Washington: Congressional Quarterly Press.

Brams, Steven J., and Paul J. Affuso. 1985. "New Paradoxes of Voting Power on the EC Council of Ministers." *Electoral Studies* 4: 135–9.

Brams, Steven J., and Peter Fishburn. 1978. "Approval Voting." *American Political Science Review* 72: 831–47.

Brander, James A., and Barbara J. Spencer. 1985. "Export Subsidies and International Market Share Rivalry." *Journal of International Economics* 18: 83–100.

Braver, Sanford L., and L. A. Wilson. 1984. "A Laboratory Study of Social Contracts as a Solution to Public Goods Problems: Surviving on the Lifeboat." Paper presented at the Western Social Science Association meeting, San Diego.

1986. "Choices in Social Dilemmas: Effects of Communication within Subgroups." *Journal of Conflict Resolution* 30: 51–62.

Breeden, Charles, and William J. Hunter. 1985. "Tax Revenue and Tax Structure." *Public Finance Quarterly* 13: 216–24.

Brennan, Geoffrey, and James M. Buchanan. 1977. "Towards a Tax Constitution for Leviathan." *Journal of Public Economics* 8: 255–73.

1978. "Tax Instruments as Constraints on the Disposition of Public Revenues." *Journal of Public Economics* 9: 301–18.

1980. *The Power to Tax: Analytical Foundations of a Fiscal Constitution.* Cambridge University Press.

1984. "Voter Choice: Evaluating Political Alternatives." *American Behavioral Scientist* 28: 185–201.

1985. *The Reason of Rules: Constitutional Political Economy.* Cambridge University Press.

Brennan, Geoffrey, and Alan Hamlin. 1992. "Bicameralism and Majoritarian Equilibrium." *Public Choice* 74: 169–79.

Breton, Albert. 1989. "The Growth of Competitive Governments." *Canadian Journal of Economics* 22: 717–50.

1992. *Organizational Hierarchies and Bureaucracies: An Interpretive Essay.* Manuscript.

Breton, Albert, Gianluigi Galeotti, Pierre Salmon, and Ronald Wintrobe, eds. 1988. Villa Colombella Papers on Bureaucracy. *European Journal of Political Economy* 4: Special issue.

eds. 1992. *Preferences and Democracy.* Villa Colombella Papers. Boston and Dordrecht: Kluwer.

Breton, Albert, and Anthony Scott. 1978. *The Economic Constitution of Federal States.* Toronto: University of Toronto Press.

Breton, Albert, and Ronald Wintrobe. 1975. "The Equilibrium Size of a Budget-Maximizing Bureau: A Note on Niskanen's Theory of Bureaucracy." *Journal of Political Economy* 82: 195–207.

1982. *The Logic of Bureaucratic Conduct.* Cambridge University Press.

1986. "The Bureaucracy of Murder Revisited." *Journal of Political Economy* 94: 905–26.

Brinkmann, Matthias. 1978. *Majoritätsprinzip und Einstimmigkeit in den Vereinten Nationen. Konsequenzen und Grenzen staatlicher Gleichberechtigung in der Generalversammlung.* Frankfurt am Main: Haag and Herchen.

Brittan, Samuel. 1978. "Inflation and Democracy." In F. Hirsch, and J. H. Goldthorpe, eds., *The Political Economy of Inflation.* London: Martin Robertson.

Brock, William A., and Stephen P. Magee. 1974. "The Economics of Politics." Paper presented at the Workshop on Industrialization Organization, University of Chicago.

1975. "The Economics of Pork-Barrel Politics." Report 7511, Center for Mathematical Studies in Business and Economics, University of Chicago.

1978. "The Economics of Special-Interest Politics: The Case of the Tariff." *American Economic Review* 68: 246–50.

1980. "Tariff Formation in a Democracy." In John Black and Brian Hindley, eds., *Current Issues in Commercial Policy and Diplomacy.* New York: St. Martin's Press.

Bromley, Daniel W. 1991. *Environment and Economy: Property Rights and Public Policy.* Oxford: Basil Blackwell.

Bromley, Daniel W., et al., eds. 1992. *Making the Commons Work: Theory, Practice, and Policy.* San Francisco: Institute for Contemporary Studies Press.

Brookshire, David, Don Coursey, and Douglas Redington. 1989. "Special Interests and the Voluntary Provision of Public Goods." Typescript.

Browning, Edgar K. 1978. "The Marginal Welfare Cost of Income Distribution." *Southern Economic Journal* 45: 1–17.

Brueckner, Jan K. 1979. "Property Values, Local Public Expenditure and Economic Efficiency." *Journal of Public Economics* 11: 223–45.

1982. "A Test for Allocative Efficiency in the Local Public Sector." *Journal of Public Economics* 19: 311–31.

1983. "Property Value Maximization and Public Sector Efficiency." *Journal of Urban Economics* 14: 1–15.

Buchanan, James M. 1954. "Individual Choice in Voting and the Market." *Journal of Political Economy* 62: 334–43.

1965a. "An Economic Theory of Clubs." *Economica* 32: 1–14.

1965b. "Ethical Rules, Expected Values, and Large Numbers." *Ethics* 76: 1–13.

1973. "The Coase Theorem and the Theory of the State." *Natural Resources Journal* 13: 579–94.

1975. *The Limits of Liberty: Between Anarchy and Leviathan.* Chicago: University of Chicago Press.

1977. "Why does Government Grow?" In Thomas E. Borcherding, ed., *Budgets and Bureaucrats: The Sources of Government Growth.* Durham: Duke University Press, 3–18.

1980a. "Rent Seeking and Profit Seeking." In James M. Buchanan, Robert D. Tollison, and Gordon Tullock, eds., *Toward a Theory of the Rent-Seeking Society.* College Station: Texas A&M University Press, 3–15.

1980b. "Reform in the Rent-Seeking Society." In James M. Buchanan, Robert D. Tollison, and Gordon Tullock, eds., *Toward a Theory of the Rent-Seeking Society.* College Station: Texas A&M University Press, 359–67.

1983. "Rent-Seeking, Noncompensated Transfers, and Laws of Succession." *Journal of Law and Economics* 26: 71–86.

1990. "Europe's Constitutional Economic Opportunity." In *Europe's Constitutional Future.* IEA Readings no.33. Institute of Economic Affairs, London.

Buchanan, James M., and Roger L. Faith. 1987. "Secession and the Limits of Taxation: Toward a Theory of Internal Exit." *American Economic Review* 77: 1023–31.

Buchanan, James M., and Charles J. Goetz. 1972. "Efficiency Limits of Fiscal Mobility: An Assessment of the Tiebout Hypothesis." *Journal of Public Economics* 1: 25–43.

Buchanan, James M., and Dwight R. Lee. 1991. "Cartels, Coalitions, and Constitutional Politics." *Constitutional Political Economy* 2: 139–61.

Buchanan, James M., and Jenifer Roback. 1987. "The Incidence and Effects of Public Debt in the Absence of Fiscal Illusion." *Public Finance Quarterly* 15: 5–25.

Buchanan, James M., and Gordon Tullock. 1962. *The Calculus of Consent. Logical Foundations of Constitutional Democracy.* Ann Arbor: University of Michigan Press.

Buchanan, James M., and Richard E. Wagner. 1977. *Democracy in Deficit: The Political Legacy of Lord Keynes.* New York: Academic Press.

Budge, Ian, and M. Laver, eds. 1992. "The Relationship between Party and Coalition Policy in Europe: An Empirical Synthesis." In M. Laver and I. Budge, eds., *Party Policy and Government Coalitions.* New York: St. Martin's Press; London: Macmillan, 409–30.

Budge, Ian, D. Robertson, and D. Hearl, eds. 1987. *Democracy, Strategy and Party Change.* Cambridge University Press.

Bulow, Jeremy, and Lawrence Summers. 1986. "A Theory of Dual Labor Markets with Applications to Industrial Policy, Discrimination, and Keynesian Unemployment. *Journal of Labor Economics* 4: 376–414.

Burnham, Walter D. 1970. *Critical Elections and the Mainsprings of American Politics.* New York: Norton.

Bush, Winston C. 1972. "Individual Welfare in Anarchy." In Gordon Tullock, ed., *Explorations in the Theory of Anarchy.* Blacksburg: Center for the Study of Public Choice, 5–18.

Cain, Bruce E. 1978. "Strategic Voting in Britain." *American Journal of Political Science* 22: 639–55.

Caldwell, Michael D. 1976. "Communication and Sex Effects in a Five-Person Prisoners' Dilemma Game." *Journal of Personality and Social Psychology* 33: 273–80.

Calvert, Randy. 1986. *Models of Imperfect Information in Politics.* Chur: Harwood Academic Publishers.

———. 1987. "Robustness of the Multidimensional Voting Model: Candidate Motivations, Uncertainty, and Convergence." *American Journal of Political Science* 29: 69–95.

Calvert, Randy, Mathew D. McCubbins, and Barry R. Weingast. 1989: "A Theory of Political Control and Agency Discretion." *American Journal of Political Science* 33: 588–611.

Cameron, Charles, and James Enelow. 1993. "Asymmetric Policy Effects, Campaign Contributions and the Spatial Theory of Elections." *Mathematical and Computer Modelling* 16: 117–32.

Cameron, Charles, and J. Jung. 1992. "Strategic Endorsements." Working paper, Department of Political Science, Columbia University.

Cameron, D. R. 1978. "The Expansion of the Public Economy: A Comparative Analysis." *American Political Science Review* 72: 1243–61.

Campbell, Angus, Philip Converse, Warren Miller, and Donald Stokes. 1960. *The American Voter.* New York: John Wiley and Sons.

Campbell, Donald E. 1992. "Quasitransitive Intergenerational Choice for Economic Environments." *Journal of Mathematical Economics* 21: 229–47.

Campbell, James. 1993. *The Presidential Pulse of Congressional Elections.* Lexington: University Press of Kentucky.

Canadian Royal Commission on Taxation. 1966. Chaired by Kenneth LeM. Carter. *Report.* Ottawa: Queen's Printer.

Caplin, Andrew, and Barry Nalebuff. 1988. "On 64%-Majority Rule." *Econometrica* 56: 787–814.

Carroll, Kathleen A. 1989. "Industrial Structure and Monopoly Power in the Federal Bureaucracy: An Empirical Analysis." *Economic Inquiry* 27: 683–703.

———. 1990. "Bureaucratic Competition and Inefficiency: A Review of the Evidence." *Journal of Economic Behavior and Organization* 13: 21–40.

Carstairs, Andrew McLaren. 1980. *A Short History of Electoral Systems in Western Europe.* London: Allen and Unwin.

Case, Anne. 1993. "Interstate Tax Competition after TRA86." *Journal of Policy Analysis and Management* 12: 136–48.

Case, Anne, James R. Hines Jr., and Harvey S. Rosen. 1989. "Budget Spillovers and Fiscal Policy Interdependence: Evidence from the States." *Journal of Public Economics* 52: 285–307.

Castles, F. C. 1981. "How Does Politics Matter?: Structure of Agency in the Determination of Public Policy Outcomes." *European Journal of Political Research* 9: 119–32.

Caves, Richard E. 1976. "Economic Models of Political Choice: Canada's Tariff Structure." *Canadian Journal of Economics* 9: 278–300.

Chamberlain, John R. 1978. "A Collective Goods Model of Pluralist Political Systems." *Public Choice* 33: 97–113.

Chamberlin, J., J. Cohen, and C. Coombs. 1984. "Social Choice Observed: Five Presidential Elections of the American Psychological Association." *Journal of Politics* 46: 479–502.

Chan, Kenneth, Stuart Mestelman, Rob Moir, and Andrew Muller. 1993. "The Voluntary Provision of Public Goods under Varying Endowment Distributions." Working paper, Department of Economics, McMaster University. Hamilton, Ontario.

Chant, John F., and Keith Acheson. 1972. "The Choice of Monetary Instruments and the Theory of Bureaucracy." *Public Choice* 12: 13–33.

1973. "Mythology and Central Banking." *Kyklos* 26: 362–79.

Chappell, Henry W., Jr. 1982. "Campaign Contributions and Congressional Voting: A Simultaneous Probit-Tobit Model." *Review of Economics and Statistics* 61: 77–83.

Chappell, Henry W., Jr., and William R. Keech. 1985. "Welfare Consequences of the Six-Year Presidential Term Evaluated in the Context of a Model of the U.S. Economy." *American Political Science Review* 77: 75–91.

1986. "Party Differences in Macroeconomic Policies and Outcomes." *American Economic Review* papers and proceedings 71: 71–4.

1988. "The Unemployment Rate Consequences of Partisan Monetary Policies." *Southern Economic Review* 55: 107–22.

Chari, V. V., and H. Cole. 1993. "A Contribution to the Theory of Pork Barrel Spending." Research Department Staff Report no. 156, Federal Reserve Bank of Minneapolis.

Cheh, John H. 1974. "United States Concessions in the Kennedy Round and Short-Run Labor Adjustment Costs." *Journal of International Economics* 4: 323–40.

Chernick, Howard. 1991. "The Effect of Distributional Constraints and Interstate Tax Competition on State Decisions to Tax: An Econometric Model." Paper presented to the NBER Summer Institute on State and Local Finance.

1992. "A Model of the Distributional Incidence of State and Local Taxes." *Public Finance Quarterly* 20: 572–85.

Choi, Kwang. 1983. "A Statistical Test of Olsen's Model." In Dennis C. Mueller, ed., *The Political Economy of Growth*. New Haven: Yale University Press, 57–78.

Choi, Nakgyoon. 1991. "Essays in International Trade: Endogenous Tariff Theory." Ph.D. diss., Department of Economics, University of Texas at Austin.

Choi, Nakgyoon, and Stephen P. Magee. 1991. "Estimates of U.S. Trade Lobbying from an Endogenous Tariff Model, 1958–1987." University of Texas at Austin. Mimeo.

Christy, Francis T., Jr., and Anthony D. Scott. 1965. *The Common Wealth in Ocean Fisheries*. Baltimore: Johns Hopkins University Press.

Chu, Yun-han, Melvin J. Hinich, and Tse-min Lin. 1993. "A Spatial Analysis of Political Competition in Taiwan." Paper presented at the Annual APSA Meeting, Washington D.C.

Clark, Colin. 1945. *The Conditions of Economic Progress*. London: Macmillan.

Clarke, Edward H. 1971. "Multipart Pricing of Public Goods." *Public Choice* 11: 17–33.

1972. "Multipart Pricing of Public Goods: An Example." In Selma Mushkin, ed., *Public Prices for Public Products*. Washington: The Urban Institute, 125–30.

Clubb, Jerome, William Flanigan, and Nancy Zingale. 1990. *Partisan Realignment: Voters, Parties, and Government in American History*. Boulder: Westview Press.

Coase, Ronald H. 1937. "The Nature of the Firm." *Economica* 4: 233–61.

1953. "Government Economic Activities: Discussion." *American Economic Review* 43: 234–42.

1960. "The Problem of Social Cost." *Journal of Law and Economics* 3: 1–44.

Coggins, Jay, Theodore Graham-Tomasi, and Terry L. Roe. 1991. "Existence of Equilibrium in a Lobbying Economy." *International Economic Review* 32: 533–50.

Coleman, James S. 1966. "The Possibility of a Social Welfare Function." *American Economic Review* 56: 1105–22.

1967. "The Possibility of a Social Welfare Function: Reply." *American Economic Review* 57: 1311–17.

1983. "Recontracting, Trustworthiness, and the Stability of Vote Exchanges." *Public Choice* 40: 89–94.

1990. *Foundations of Social Theory.* Cambridge, Mass.: Harvard University Press.

Coleman, Jules, and John Ferejohn. 1986. "Democracy and Social Choice." *Ethics* 97: 6–25.

Collie, Mellissa P. 1988. "The Legislature and Distributive Policy Making in Formal Perspective." *Legislative Studies Quarterly* 13: 427–58.

Collier, Kenneth E., Richard McKelvey, Peter C. Ordeshook, and Kenneth C. Williams. 1987. "Retrospective Voting: An Experimental Study." *Public Choice* 53: 101–30.

Collier, Kenneth E., Peter C. Ordeshook, and Kenneth C. Williams. 1989. "The Rationally Uninformed Electorate: Some Experimental Evidence." *Public Choice* 60: 3–29.

Comanor, William S., and Robert H. Smiley. 1975. "Monopoly and the Distribution of Wealth." *Quarterly Journal of Economics* 89: 177–94.

Condorcet, Marquis de. 1785. "Essai sur l'application de l'analyse à la probabilité des décisions rendues à la probabilité des voix. Paris: De l'imprimerie royale." Translated as "Essay on the Application of Mathematics to the Theory of Decision Making." In K. Baker, ed., *Condorcet, Selected Writings.* Indianapolis: Bobbs-Merrill, 1976.

1788. "On the Constitution and the Functions of Provincial Assemblies." In A. Condorcet O'Connor and M. F. Arago, eds., *Oeuvres de Condorcet.* Paris, 1847–9.

Congleton, Roger D. 1988. "Evaluating Rent-Seeking Losses: Do the Welfare Gains of Lobbyists Count?" *Public Choice* 56: 181–4.

1991. "Ideological Conviction and Persuasion in the Rent-Seeking Society." *Journal of Public Economics* 44: 65–86.

Congleton, Roger D., and William F. Shughart II. 1990. "The Growth of Social Security: Electoral Push or Political Pull?" *Economic Inquiry* 28: 109–32.

Congleton, Roger D., and Wendell Sweetser. 1992. "Political Deadlocks and Distributional Information: The Value of the Veil." *Public Choice* 73: 1–19.

Constantopoulos, Maria. 1974. "Labour Protection in Western Europe." *European Economic Review* 5: 313–18.

Converse, Philip E. 1964. "The Nature of Belief Systems in Mass Publics." In David E. Apter, ed., *Ideology and Discontent.* New York: Free Press.

1969. "Of Time and Partisan Stability." *Comparative Political Studies* 2: 139–71.

1975. "Public Opinion and Voting Behavior." In Fred I. Greenstein and Nelson W. Polsby, eds., *Handbook of Political Science* 4: 206–61.

1990. "Popular Representation and the Distribution of Information." *Information and Democratic Processes.* Chicago: University of Illinois Press.

Conybeare, John A. C. 1983. "Tariff Protection in Developed and Developing Countries: A Cross-Sectional and Longitudinal Analysis." *International Organization* 37: 441–67.

Cooter, Robert D. 1982. "The Cost of Coase." *Journal of Legal Studies* 11: 1–33.

1987a. "Coase Theorem." In John Eatwell, Murray Milgate, and Peter Newman, eds., *New Palgrave Dictionary of Economics.* New York: Stockton Press.

1987b. "Liberty, Efficiency, and Law." *Law and Contemporary Problems* 50: 141–63.

1991. "Inventing Property: The Land Courts of Papua New Guinea." *Law and Society Review* 25: 759–801.

Copes, Parzival. 1986. "A Critical Review of the Individual Quota as a Device in Fisheries Management." *Land Economics* 62: 278–91.

Corcoran, William J. 1984. "Long-Run Equilibrium and Total Expenditures in Rent-Seeking." *Public Choice* 43: 89–94.

Cordell, John C., and Margaret A. McKean. 1992. "Sea Tenure in Bahia, Brazil." In Daniel W. Bromley et al., eds., *Making the Commons Work: Theory, Practice, and Policy.* San Francisco: Institute for Contemporary Studies Press, 183–205.

Cornell, Stephen, and Joseph P. Kalt. 1990. "Pathways from Poverty: Economic Development and Institution-Building on American Indian Reservations." *American Indian Culture and Research Journal* 14: 89–125.

  1991. "Where's the Glue? Institutional Bases of American Indian Economic Development." Harvard University. Mimeo.

  1995. "Where Does Economic Development Really Come From? Constitutional Rule among the Modern Sioux and Apache." *Economic Inquiry* 33: 402–46.

Cornes, Richard, and Todd Sandler. 1986. *The Theory of Externalities, Public Goods, and Club Goods.* Cambridge University Press.

Coughlin, Peter. 1986. "Elections and Income Redistribution." *Public Choice* 50: 27–99.

  1992. *Probabilistic Voting Theory.* Cambridge University Press.

Coughlin, Peter, Dennis C. Mueller, and Peter Murrell. 1990a. "Electoral Politics, Interest Groups, and the Size of Government." *Economic Inquiry* 28: 682–705.

  1990b: "A Model of Electoral Competition with Interest Groups." *Economic Letters* 32: 307–11.

Coughlin, Peter, and Shmuel Nitzan. 1981. "Electoral Outcomes with Probabilistic Voting and Nash Social Welfare Maxima." *Journal of Public Economics* 15: 113–21.

Coward, E. Walter, Jr. 1979. "Principles of Social Organization in an Indigenous Irrigation System." *Human Organization* 38: 28–36.

Cowling, Keith, and Dennis C. Mueller. 1978. "The Social Costs of Monopoly Power." *Economic Journal* 88: 727–48.

Cox, Gary W. 1984a. "Electoral Equilibrium in Double Member Districts." *Public Choice* 44: 443–51.

  1984b. "Strategic Electoral Choice in Multi-Member Districts." *American Journal of Political Science* 28: 722–38.

  1984c. "An Expected-Utility Model of Electoral Competition." *Quality and Quantity* 18: 337–49.

  1987a. "Electoral Equilibrium under Alternative Voting Institutions." *American Journal of Political Science* 31: 82–108.

  1987b. "The Uncovered Set and the Core." *American Journal of Political Science* 31: 408–22.

  1990a. "Centripetal and Centrifugal Incentives in Electoral Systems." *American Journal of Political Science* 34: 903–35.

  1990b. "Multicandidate Spatial Competition." In James Enelow and Melvin J. Hinich, eds., *Advances in the Spatial Theory of Voting.* Cambridge University Press.

  1993. *Strategic Voting Equilibria under the Single Non-Transferable Vote.* Paper presented at the Annual APSA Meeting, Washington D.C.

Cox, Gary W., and Mathew D. McCubbins. 1993. *Legislative Leviathan: Party Government in the House.* Berkeley and Los Angeles: University of California Press.

Cox, Gary W., and Michael C. Munger. 1989. "Closeness, Expenditures, and Turnout in the 1988 U.S. House Elections." *American Political Science Review* 83: 217–31.

Crain, W. M., and Robert D. Tollison. 1991. "The Price of Influence in an Interest-Group Economy." *Rationality and Society* 3: 437–49.

Crane, George T., and Abla M. Amawi, eds. 1991. *The Theoretical Evolution of International Political Economy.* Oxford: Oxford University Press.

Crepel, P. 1990. *Le dernier mot de Condorcet sur les elections.* Paris: Centre d'Analyse et de Mathematique Sociales.

Crew, Michael A., and Charles K. Rowley. 1988. "Dispelling the Disinterest in Deregulation." In Charles K. Rowley, Robert D. Tollison, and Gordon Tullock, eds., *The Political Economy of Rent Seeking.* Boston: Kluwer, 163–78.

Crucini, Mario. 1994. "Sources of Variation in Real Tariff Rates: The United States, 1900–1940." *American Economic Review* 84: 732–43.

Cukierman, Alex, and Allan H. Meltzer. 1986. "A Positive Theory of Discretionary Policy, the Cost of Democratic Government, and the Benefits of a Constitution." *Economic Inquiry* 24: 367–88.

1989. "A Political Theory of Government Debt and Deficits in a Neo-Ricardian Framework." *American Economic Review* 79: 713–32.

1991. "A Political Theory of Progressive Income Taxation." In Allan H. Meltzer, Alex Cukierman, and S. Richard, eds., *Political Economy.* Oxford: Oxford University Press.

Curtis, Richard B. 1972. "Decision Rules and Collective Values in Constitutional Choice." In Richard G. Niemi and Herbert F. Weisberg, eds., *Probability Models of Collective Decision Making.* Columbus, OH: Merrill.

Dahl, Robert A. 1961. "The Behavioral Approach in Political Science: An Epitaph for a Monument to a Successful Protest." *American Political Science Review* 55: 763–72.

Dahl, Robert A., and Charles E. Lindblom. 1953. *Politics, Economics, and Welfare.* New York: Harper.

Dahl, Robert A., and E. R. Tufte. 1973. *Size and Democracy.* Stanford: Stanford University Press.

Danziger, Leif. 1992. "On the Prevalence of Labor Contracts with Fixed Duration." *American Economic Review* 82: 195–206.

Das, Sanghamitra, and Satye P. Das. 1994. "Quantitative Assessment of Tariff Endogeneity." *Economic Letters* 44: 139–46.

Das, Satya P. 1990. "Foreign Lobbying and the Political Economy of Protection." *Japan and the World Economy Journal,* May–June.

Dasgupta, Partha, and Karl Göran Mäler. 1992. *The Economics of Transnational Commons.* Oxford: Clarendon Press.

d'Aspremont, Claude. 1985. "Axioms for Social Welfare Orderings." In Leonid Hurwicz, David Schmeidler, and Hugo Sonnenschein, eds., *Social Goals and Social Organization.* Cambridge University Press, 19–76.

d'Aspremont, Claude, and Louis Gevers. 1977. "Equity and the Informational Basis of Collective Choice." *Review of Economic Studies* 44: 199–209.

Davidson, Lawrence S., Michele Fratianni, and Jürgen von Hagen. 1990. "Testing for Political Business Cycles." *Journal of Policy Modelling* 12: 35–59.

1992. "Testing the Satisficing Version of the Political Business Cycle 1905–1984." *Public Choice* 73: 21–35.

Davies, David. 1971. "The Efficiency of Public vs. Private Firms: The Case of Australia's Two Airlines." *Journal of Law and Economics* 14: 149–65.

Davis, Anthony. 1984. "Property Rights and Access Management in the Small Boat Fishery: A Case Study From Southwest Nova Scotia." In Cynthia Lamson and Arthur J. Hanson, eds., *Atlantic Fisheries and Coastal Communities: Fisheries Decision-Making Case Studies.* Halifax: Dalhousie Ocean Studies Programme, 133–64.

Davis, Douglas D., and Charles A. Holt. 1993. *Experimental Economics*. Princeton: Princeton University Press.

Davis, Otto A., Maurey DeGroot, and Melvin J. Hinich. 1972. "Social Preference Orderings and Majority Rule." *Econometrica* 40: 147–57.

Davis, Otto A., and Melvin J. Hinich. 1966. "A Mathematical Model of Policy Formation in a Democratic Society." In J. Bernd, ed., *Mathematical Applications in Political Science II*. Dallas: Southern Methodist University Press.

1968. "On the Power and Importance of the Mean Preference in a Mathematical Model of Democratic Choice." *Public Choice* 5: 59–72.

Dawes, Robyn M. 1980. "Social Dilemmas." *Annual Review of Psychology* 31: 169–93.

Dawes, Robyn M., Jeanne McTavish, and Harriet Shaklee. 1977. "Behavior, Communication, and Assumptions about Other People's Behavior in a Commons Dilemma Situation." *Journal of Personality and Social Psychology* 35: 1–11.

Dawes, Robyn M., John M. Orbell, and Alphons van de Kragt. 1984. "Normative Constraint and Incentive Compatible Design." Department of Psychology, University of Oregon. Typescript.

De Alessi, Louis. 1969. "Implications of Property Rights for Government Investment Choices." *American Economic Review* 59: 13–24.

Deardorff, Alan V., and Robert M. Stern, eds. 1987. "Current Issues in Trade Policy: An Overview." *U.S. Trade Policies in a Changing World Economy*. Cambridge: MIT Press, 15–68.

Demsetz, Harold. 1967. "Toward a Theory of Property Rights." *American Economic Review* 57: 347–73.

1982. "The Growth of Government." In deVries Lectures, no.4. *Economic, Legal and Political Dimensions of Competition*. Amsterdam: North–Holland.

Denzau, Arthur T., Amos Katz, and Steven Slutsky. 1985. "Multi-Agent Equilibria with Market Share and Ranking Objectives." *Social Choice and Welfare* 2: 95–117.

Denzau, Arthur T., and Robert Mackay. 1981. "Structure Induced Equilibrium and Perfect Foresight Expectations." *American Journal of Political Science* 25: 762–79.

Denzau, Arthur T., and Michael C. Munger. 1986. "Legislators and Interest Groups: How Unorganized Interests Get Represented." *American Political Science Review* 80: 89–106.

Denzau, Arthur T., William H. Riker, and Kenneth A. Shepsle. 1985. "Farquharson and Fenno: Sophisticated Voting and Home Style." *American Political Science Review* 79: 1117–34.

de Swaan, A. 1973. *Coalition Theories and Cabinet Formations*. Amsterdam: Elsevier.

Detken, Carsten, and Manfred Gärtner. 1992. "Governments, Trade Unions and the Macroeconomy: An Expository Analysis of the Political Business Cycle." *Public Choice* 73: 37–53.

Diamond, Peter A., and Jerry A. Hausman. 1994. "Contingent Valuation: Is Some Number Better than no Number?" *Journal of Economic Perspectives* 8: 45–64.

Dick, Andrew. 1993. "Does Import Protection Act as Export Promotion?: Evidence from the United States." *Oxford Economic Papers* 46: 83–101.

Dillon, Patricia, Thomas L. Ilgen, and Thomas D. Willett. 1991. "Approaches to the Study of International Organizations: Major Paradigms in Economics and Political Science." In Roland Vaubel and Thomas D. Willett, eds., *The Political Economy of International Organizations: A Public Choice Approach*. Boulder: Westview Press, 79–99.

Dinkel, R. 1977. *Der Zusammenhang zwischen der ökonomischen und politischen Entwicklung in einer Demokratie*. Berlin.

Dodd, L. C. 1974. "Party Coalitions in Multiparty Parliaments: A Game Theoretic Analysis." *American Political Science Review* 68: 1093–117.

1976. *Coalitions in Parliamentary Governments: A Game Theoretic Analysis.* Princeton: Princeton University Press.

Dodgson, Charles. 1876. "A Method of Taking Votes on More than Two Issues." Reprinted in Duncan Black, ed. 1958. *The Theory of Committees and Elections.* Cambridge University Press, 224–34.

Dorsey, Robert E. 1992. "The Voluntary Contributions Mechanism with Real Time Revisions." *Public Choice* 73: 261–82.

Dougan, William R., and Michael C. Munger. 1989. "The Rationality of Ideology." *Journal of Law and Economics* 32: 119–42.

Dougan, William R., and James M. Snyder. 1993. "Are Rents Fully Dissipated?" *Public Choice* 77: 793–813.

Downs, Anthony. 1957. *An Economic Theory of Democracy.* New York: Harper and Row.

1961. "In Defense of Majority Voting." *Journal of Political Economy* 69: 192–9.

1967. *Inside Bureaucracy.* Boston: Little, Brown and Company.

Dreyer, Jacob S., and Andrew Schotter. 1980. "Power Relationships in the International Monetary Fund. The Consequences of Quota Changes." *Review of Economics and Statistics* 62: 97–106.

Drèze, Jacques H., and D. de la Vallée Poussin. 1971. "A Tâtonnement Process for Public Goods." *Review of Economic Studies* 38: 133–50.

Durden, Garey C., and Patricia Gaynor. 1987. "The Rational Behavior Theory of Voting Participation: Evidence from the 1970 and 1982 Elections." *Public Choice* 53: 231–42.

Duverger, Maurice. 1946. *Les Partis Politique.* Bordeaux: University of Bordeaux.

1954. *Political Parties: Their Organization and Activity in the Modern State.* New York: John Wiley and Sons.

[1954] 1959. *Political Parties: Their Organization and Activity in the Modern State.* Translated by B. North and R. North. London: Methuen.

1984. "Which is the Best Electoral System?" In Arend Lijphart and Bernard Grofman, eds., *Choosing an Electoral System.* New York: Praeger, 31–9.

Eaton, B. Curtis, and Richard G. Lipsey. 1975. "The Principle of Minimum Differentiation Reconsidered: Some New Developments in the Theory of Spatial Competition." *Review of Economic Studies* 42: 27–49.

Eavey, Cheryl L., and Gary M. Miller. 1989. "Constitutional Conflict in State and Nation." In Bernard Grofman and Donald Wittman, eds., *The Federalist Papers and the New Institutionalism.* New York: Agathon Press, 205–19.

Eberts, Randall W., and Timothy J. Gronberg. 1981. "Jurisdictional Homogeneity and the Tiebout Hypothesis." *Journal of Urban Economics* 10: 227–39.

1990. "Structure, Conduct and Performance in the Local Public Sector." *National Tax Journal* 43: 165–73.

Eckert, Ross D. 1991. "U.S. Policy and the Law of the Sea Conference, 1969–1982: A Case Study of Multilateral Negotiations." In Roland Vaubel and Thomas D. Willett, eds., *The Political Economy of International Organizations: A Public Choice Approach.* Boulder: Westview Press, 181–203.

Edelman, Susan A. 1992. "Two Politicians, a PAC and How They Interact: Two Extensive Form Games." *Economics and Politics* 4: 289–305.

Edney, Julian J., and Christopher S. Harper. 1978. "The Commons Dilemma: A Review of Contributions from Psychology." *Environmental Management* 2: 491–507.

Eggertsson, Thráinn. 1990. *Economic Behavior and Institutions.* Cambridge University Press.

Ekelund, R. B., and Robert D. Tollison. 1981. *Mercantilism as a Rent-Seeking Society.* College Station: Texas A&M University Press.

Elazar, D. 1993. "International and Comparative Federalism." *PS: Political Science and Politics* 26: 190–5.

Ellis, Christopher J., and Mark A. Thoma. 1991. "Partisan Effects in Economies with Variable Electoral Terms." *Journal of Money, Credit, and Banking* 23: 728–41.

Elster, Jon. 1979. *Ulysses and the Sirens*. Cambridge University Press.

    1988. "Introduction." In Jon Elster and Rune Slagstad, eds., *Constitutionalism and Democracy*. Cambridge University Press, 1–17.

    1991. "Born to be Immortal: The Constitution-Making Process." Cooley Lectures, University of Michigan Law School. Mimeo.

Enelow, James M., and Melvin J. Hinich. 1982. "Ideology, Issues and the Spatial Theory of Elections." *American Political Science Review* 76: 493–501.

    1983a. "On Plott's Pairwise Symmetry Condition for Majority Rule Equilibrium." *Public Choice* 40: 317–21.

    1983b. "Voting One Issue at a Time: The Question of Voter Forecasts." *American Political Science Review* 77: 435–45.

    1984. *The Spatial Theory of Voting: An Introduction*. Cambridge University Press.

    1989. "A General Probabilistic Spatial Theory of Elections." *Public Choice* 61: 101–14.

    1990. "The Theory of Predictive Mappings." In James Enelow and Melvin J. Hinich, eds., *Advances in the Spatial Theory of Voting*. Cambridge University Press, 167–78.

Epple, Dennis, and Allan Zelenitz. 1981. "The Implications of Competition among Jurisdictions: Does Tiebout Need Politics?" *Journal of Political Economy* 89: 1197–217.

Epstein, L. 1991. "Courts and Interest Groups." In J. Gates and C. Johnson, eds., *American Courts: A Critical Analysis*. Washington, D.C.: Congressional Quarterly Press.

Erikson, Robert S. 1972. "Malapportionment, Gerrymandering, and Party Fortunes in Congressional Elections." *American Political Science Review* 66: 1234–45.

Erikson, Robert S., and Kent L. Tedin. 1981. "The 1928–1936 Partisan Realignment: The Case for the Conversion Hypothesis." *American Political Science Review* 75: 951–62.

Eskridge, William N., and John Ferejohn. 1992. "Making the Deal Stick: Enforcing the Original Constitutional Structure of Lawmaking in the Modern Regulatory State." *Journal of Law, Economics, and Organization* 8: 165–89.

Ethier, Wilfred J. 1991a. "The Economics and Political Economy of Managed Trade." In Hillman, ed. *Markets and Politicians*. Boston: Kluwer Academic Press, 283–306.

    1991b. "Voluntary Export Restraints." In Takayama, Ohyama, and Ohta, eds., *Trade, Policy and International Adjustments*. San Diego: Academic Press, 3–18.

Etzioni, Amitai. 1993. *The Spirit of Community*. New York: Crown.

Faber, Malte, and Friedrich Breyer. 1980. "Eine ökonomische Analyse konstitutioneller Aspekte der europäischen Integration." *Jahrbuch für Sozialwissenschaft* 31: 213–27.

Faiña, J. Andrés, and Pedro Puy-Fraga. 1988. "A Framework for a Public Choice Analysis of the European Community." *Economia delle scelte pubbliche* 2: 141–58.

Farquharson, Robin. 1969. *The Theory of Voting*. New Haven: Yale University Press.

Fedderson, Timothy J. 1992. "A Voting Model Implying Duverger's Law and Positive Turnout." *American Journal of Political Science* 36: 938–62.

Feddersen, Timothy J., Itai Sened, and Stephen G. Wright. 1990. "Rational Voting and Candidate Entry under Plurality Rule." *American Journal of Political Science* 34: 1005–16.

Feenberg, Daniel R., and Harvey S. Rosen. 1987. "Tax Structure and Public Sector Growth." *Journal of Public Economics* 32: 185–201.

Feenstra, Robert C., and Jagdish N. Bhagwati. 1982. "Tariff Seeking and the Efficient Tariff." In Jagdish N. Bhagwati, ed., *Import Competition and Response*. Chicago: University of Chicago Press, 245–58.

Feeny, David. 1988a. "Agricultural Expansion and Forest Depletion in Thailand, 1900–

1975." In John F. Richards and Richard P. Tucker, eds., *World Deforestation in the Twentieth Century.* Durham: Duke University Press, 112–43.

1988b. "The Demand for and Supply of Institutional Arrangements." In Vincent Ostrom, David Feeny, and Hartmut Picht, eds., *Rethinking Institutional Analysis and Development: Issues, Alternatives, and Choices.* San Francisco: Institute for Contemporary Studies Press.

Feeny, David, Fikret Berkes, Bonnie J. McCay, and James M. Acheson. 1990. "The Tragedy of the Commons: Twenty-two Years Later." *Human Ecology* 18: 1–19.

Feiwel, G. R. 1974. "Reflections on Kalecki's Theory of Political Business Cycles." *Kyklos* 27: 21–48.

Feld, Scott F., Bernard Grofman, and Nicholas Miller. 1988. "Centripetal Forces in Spatial Voting: On the Size of the Yolk." *Public Choice* 59: 37–50.

Feldstein, Martin S. 1988a. "Distinguished Lecture on Economics in Governments: Thinking about International Economic Coordination." *Journal of Economic Perspectives* 2(2): 3–13.

1988b. *International Economic Cooperation.* Chicago: University of Chicago Press.

Feldstein, Martin, and Gilbert Metcalf. 1987. "The Effect of Federal Deductibility on State and Local Taxes and Spending." *Journal of Political Economy* 95: 710–36.

Fenno, R. F. 1973. *Congressmen in Committees.* Boston: Little, Brown and Company.

Ferejohn, John A. 1974. *Pork Barrel Politics: Rivers and Harbors Legislation 1947–1968.* Stanford: Stanford University Press.

1986. "Incumbent Performance and Electoral Control." *Public Choice* 50: 5–25.

Ferejohn, John A., and Morris P. Fiorina. 1974. "The Paradox of Not Voting: A Decision Theoretic Analysis." *American Political Science Review* 68: 525–36.

1975. "Closeness Counts Only in Horseshoes and Dancing." *American Political Science Review* 69: 920–5.

Ferejohn, John A., Robert Forsythe, and Roger Noll. 1979. "Implementing Planning Procedures for the Provision of Discrete Public Goods: A Case Study of a Problem in Institutional Design." In Vernon L. Smith, ed., *Research in Experimental Economics,* vol. 1. Greenwich, Conn.: JAI Press, 1–58.

Ferejohn, John A., Richard D. McKelvey, and Edward W. Packel. 1984. "Limiting Distributions for Continuous State Markov Processes." *Social Choice and Welfare* 1: 45–67.

Ferejohn, John A., and Charles Shipan. 1990. "Congressional Influence on Bureaucracy." *Journal of Law, Economics and Organization* special issue 6: 1–20.

Ferejohn, John A., and Barry R. Weingast. 1992a. "Limitation of Statutes: Strategic Statutory Interpretation." *The Georgetown Law Journal* 80: 565–82.

1992b. "A Positive Theory of Statutory Interpretation." *International Review of Law and Economics* 12: 263–79.

Ferguson, Thomas. 1989. "By Invitation Only: Party Competition and Industrial Structure in the 1988 Election." *Socialist Review* 19: 73–103.

Ferrero, Mario. 1993. *Bureaucrats vs. Red Guards: A Theoretical Model of the Stability of Communist Regimes.* Paper presented at the European Public Choice Society Annual Meeting, Portrush, N. Ireland.

Ferris, J. S., and E. G. West. 1993. "Changes in the Real Size of Government: US Experience 1948–1989." Unpublished manuscript, Department of Economics, Carleton University.

Field, J. O., and R. E. Anderson. 1969. "Ideology in the Public's Conceptualization of the 1964 Election." *Public Opinion Quarterly* 33: 380–98.

Fieleke, Norman S. 1976. "The Tariff Structure for Manufacturing Industries in the United States: A Test of Some Traditional Explanations." *Columbia Journal of World Business* 11: 98–104.

Findlay, Ronald J., and Stanislaw Wellisz. 1982. "Endogenous Tariffs, the Political Economy of Trade Restrictions and Welfare." In Jagdish N. Bhagwati, ed., *Import Competition and Response*. Chicago: University of Chicago Press.

Finger, J. Michael. 1991. "The GATT as an International Discipline over Trade Restrictions: A Public Choice Approach." In Roland Vaubel and Thomas D. Willett, eds., *The Political Economy of International Organizations: A Public Choice Approach*. Boulder: Westview Press, 125–41.

Fiorina, Morris P. 1976. "The Voting Decision: Instrumental and Expressive Aspects." *Journal of Politics* 38: 390–415.

1977a. "An Outline for a Model of Party Choice." *American Journal of Political Science* 21: 601–25.

1977b. *Congress: Keystone of the Washington Establishment*. New Haven: Yale University Press.

1981a. *Retrospective Voting in American National Elections*. New Haven: Yale University Press.

1981b. "Congressional Control of the Bureaucracy: A Mismatch of Capabilities and Incentives." In Lawrence Dodd and Bruce Oppenheimer, eds., *Congress Reconsidered*. 2nd ed., Washington, D.C.: Congressional Quarterly Press, 332–48.

1982a: "Legislative Choice of Regulatory Forms: Legal Process or Administrative Process?" *Public Choice* 39: 33–66.

1982b: "Group Concentration and the Delegation of Legislative Authority." In Roger G. Noll, ed., *Regulatory Policy and the Social Sciences*. Berkeley and Los Angeles: University of California Press.

1986: "Legislative Uncertainty, Legislative Control, and the Delegation of Legislative Power." *Journal of Law, Economics, and Organization* 2: 33–50.

1990. "Information and Rationality in Elections." In *Information and Democratic Processes*. Chicago: University of Illinois Press.

1991. "Elections and the Economy in the 1980's: Short-and Long-Term Effects." In Alberto Alesina and Geoffrey Carliner, eds., *Politics and Economics in the Eighties*. Chicago: University of Chicago Press.

Fiorina, Morris P., and Charles R. Plott. 1978. "Committee Decisions under Majority Rule: An Experimental Study." *American Political Science Review* 72: 575–98.

Fischer, Ronald. 1991. "Income Distribution and the Dynamics Fixed Factors Model: Theory and Evidence." University of Virginia. Mimeo.

Fischer, Stanley. 1980. "Dynamic Inconsistency, Cooperation, and the Benevolent Dissembling Government." *Journal of Economic Dynamics and Control* 2: 93–107.

Fishburn, Peter C. 1973. *The Theory of Social Choice*. Princeton: Princeton University Press.

Fishburn, Peter C., and William V. Gehrlein 1977. "Towards a Theory of Elections with Probabilistic Preferences." *Econometrica* 45: 1907–24.

Fisher, Franklin M. 1985. "The Social Costs of Monopoly and Regulation: Posner Reconsidered." *Journal of Political Economy* 93: 410–16.

Fisher, Franklin M., Zvi Griliches, and Carl Kaysen. 1962. "The Costs of Automobile Model Changes Since 1949." *Journal of Political Economy* 70: 433–51.

Fisher, Joseph, R. Mark Isaac, Jeffrey W. Schatzberg, and James M. Walker. 1993. "Heterogenous Demand for Public Goods: Effects on the Voluntary Contributions Mechanism." Working paper, Department of Economics, University of Arizona and Indiana University.

Fitts, Michael. 1988. "The Vices of Virtue: A Political Party Perspective on Civic Virtue Reforms of the Legislative Process." *University of Pennsylvania Law Review* 136: 1567–645.

Fitts, Michael, and Robert P. Inman. 1992. "Controlling Congress: Presidential Influence in Domestic Fiscal Policy." *Georgetown Law Journal* 80: 1737–85.

Forbes, Kevin F., and Ernest M. Zampelli. 1989. "Is Leviathan a Mythical Beast?" *American Economic Review* 79: 568–77.

Formisano, Ronald. 1971. *The Birth of Mass Political Parties: Michigan, 1827–1861*. Princeton: Princeton University Press.

Fort, Rodney D. 1988. "The Median Voter, Setters, and Non-Repeated Construction Bond Issues." *Public Choice* 56: 213–32.

Forte, Francesco. 1985. "The Theory of Social Contract and the EEC." In D. Greenaway and K. Shaw, eds., *Public Choice, Public Finance, Public Policy*. Oxford: Blackwell, 149–75.

Fortmann, Louise, and John W. Bruce, eds. 1988. *Whose Trees? Proprietary Dimensions of Forestry*. Boulder: Westview Press.

Frank, Robert H. 1986. *Choosing the Right Pond*. Oxford: Oxford University Press.

Franklin, Charles H., and John E. Jackson. 1983. "The Dynamics of Party Identification." *The American Political Science Review* 77: 957–73.

Fratianni, Michele, and John C. Pattison. 1976. "The Economics of the OECD." In Karl Brunner and Allan H. Meltzer, eds., *Institutions, Policies and Economic Performances*. Amsterdam: North–Holland, 75–153.

1982. "The Economics of International Organizations." *Kyklos* 35: 244–62.

1991. "International Institutions and the Market for Information." In Roland Vaubel and Thomas D. Willett, eds., *The Political Economy of International Organizations: A Public Choice Approach*. Boulder: Westview Press, 100–22.

Frey, Bruno S. 1974. "An Insurance System for Peace." *Papers, Peace Science Society, International* 22: 111–28.

1978. "Politico-Economic Models and Cycles." *Journal of Public Economics* 9: 203–20.

1983. *Democratic Economic Policy*. Oxford: Blackwell.

1984. "The Function of Governments and Intergovernmental Organizations in the International Resource Transfer – The Case of the World Bank." *Weltwirtschaftliches Archiv* 120: 702–19.

1985. *Internationale politische Ökonomie*. München: Vahlen.

1986. *International Political Economics*. Oxford: Blackwell.

1992. *Economics as a Science of Human Behaviour*. Boston: Kluwer.

1993. "Does Monitoring Increase Work Effort: The Rivalry with Trust and Loyalty." *Economic Inquiry* 31: 663–70.

1996. *Political Business Cycles*. Aldershot: Edgar Elgar.

Frey, Bruno S., and Beat Gygi. 1990. "The Political Economy of International Organizations." *Außenwirtschaft* 45: 371–94.

1991. "International Organizations from the Constitutional Point of View." In Roland Vaubel and Thomas D. Willett, eds., *The Political Economy of International Organizations: A Public Choice Approach*. Boulder: Westview Press, 58–78.

Frey, Bruno S., Werner W. Pommerehne, Friedrich Schneider, and Guy Gilbert. 1984. "Consensus and Dissension among Economists: An Empirical Inquiry." *American Economic Review* 74: 986–94.

Frey, Bruno S., and Hans-Jürgen Ramser. 1976. "The Political Business Cycle: A Comment." *The Review of Economic Studies* 43: 553–5.

Frey, Bruno S., and Friedrich Schneider. 1978a. "An Empirical Study of Politico-Economic Interaction in the U.S." *Review of Economics and Statistics* 60: 174–83.

1978b. "A Politico-Economic Model of the United Kingdom." *Economic Journal* 88: 243–53.

1979. "An Econometric Model with an Endogenous Government Sector." *Public Choice* 34: 29–43.

1984. "International Political Economy: A Rising Field." *Economia Internazionale* 37: 308–47.

1986. "Competing Models of International Lending Activity." *Journal of Development Economics* 20: 225–45.

Friedman, Milton. 1957. *A Theory of the Consumption Function*. Princeton: Princeton University Press.

1968. "The Role of Monetary Policy." *American Economic Review* 58: 1–18.

Froman, L. A. 1967. *The Congressional Process: Strategies, Rules and Procedures*. Boston: Little, Brown and Company.

Frug, G. 1980. "The City as a Legal Concept." *Harvard Law Review* 93: 1059–154.

1987. "Empowering Cities in a Federal System." *The Urban Lawyer* 19: 553–68.

1993. "Decentering Decentralization." *The University of Chicago Law Review* 60: 253–338.

Fudenberg, Drew, and Eric Maskin. 1986. "The Folk Theorem in Repeated Games with Discounting or with Incomplete Information." *Econometrica* 54: 533–44.

Fukuyama, Francis. 1995. *Trust: The Social Virtues and the Creation of Prosperity*. New York: The Free Press.

Fung, K. K. 1991. "One Good Turn Deserves Another: Exchange of Favors within Organizations." *Social Science Quarterly* 72: 443–63.

Gade, Mary N., and Lee C. Adkins. 1990. "Tax Exporting and State Revenue Structures." *National Tax Journal* 43: 39–52.

Gadgil, Madhav, and Prema Iyer. 1989. "On the Diversification of Common-Property Resource Use by Indian Society." In Fikret Berkes, ed., *Common Property Resources, Ecology and Community-Based Sustainable Development*. London: Belhaven Press, 240–72.

Gaertner, W., Prasanta K. Pattanaik, and Kotaro Suzumura. 1992. "Individual Rights Revisited." *Economica* 59: 161–77.

Galeotti, Gianluigi. 1988. "Rules and Behaviors in Markets and Bureaucracies." *European Journal of Political Economy* 4 (extra issue): 213–28.

Gärdenfors, P. 1981. "Rights, Games and Social Choice." *Noûs* 15: 341–56.

Gardner, Roy. 1981. "Wealth and Power in a Collegial Polity." *Journal of Economic Theory* 25: 353–66.

Gardner, Roy, Elinor Ostrom, and James M. Walker. 1990. "The Nature of Common-Pool Resource Problems." *Rationality and Society* 2: 335–58.

1993. "Crafting Institutions in Common-Pool Resource Situations." Paper presented at the Annual Meetings of the Association for Evolutionary Economics (AFEE), Boston, January 1994.

Geddes, Barbara. 1990. "Democratic Institutions as Bargains among Self-Interested Politicians." University of California, Los Angeles. Mimeo.

1991. "A Game Theoretic Model of Reform in Latin American Democracies." *American Political Science Review* 85: 371–92.

Gemmell, N. 1990. "Wagner's Law, Relative Prices and the Size of the Public Sector." *The Manchester School* 43: 361–77.

Gevers, Louis. 1979. "On Interpersonal Comparability and Social Welfare Orderings." *Econometrica* 47: 75–89.

Gibbard, Allan. 1969. *Social Choice and the Arrow Conditions*. Unpublished manuscript.

1973. "Manipulation of Voting Schemes: A General Result." *Econometrica* 41: 587–601.

1974. "A Pareto Consistent Libertarian Claim." *Journal of Economic Theory* 7: 388–410.

Giertz, J. F. 1981. "Centralization and Government Budget Size." *Publius* 11: 119–28.

Gillespie, W. Irwin. 1991. *Tax, Borrow and Spend: Financing Federal Spending in Canada, 1867–1990.* Ottawa: Carleton University Press.

Ginsburgh, Victor, and Philippe Michel. 1983. "Random Timing of Elections and the Political Business Cycle." *Public Choice* 40: 155–64.

Glazer, Amihai. 1989. "The Electoral Costs of Special Interest Politics When Voters are Ignorant." *Economics and Politics* 1: 225–38.

Glazer, Amihai, and Henry McMillan. 1992. "Amend the Old or Address the New: Broad Based Legislation When Proposing Policies is Costly." *Public Choice* 74: 43–58.

Godek, Paul E. 1985. "Industry Structure and Redistribution through Trade Restrictions." *Journal of Law and Economics* 28: 687–703.

1986. "The Politically Optimal Tariff: Levels of Trade Restrictions across Developed Countries." *Economic Inquiry* 24: 587–93.

1989. "Foreign Firm Profits and the Political Economy of International Trade Quotas." Economist Incorporated. Mimeo.

Golen, D. G., and James M. Poterba. 1980. "The Price of Popularity: The Political Business Cycle Reexamined." *American Journal of Political Science* 24: 696–714.

Good, I. J. 1977. "Justice in Voting by Demand Revelation." *Public Choice* 29 special supplement 2: 65–70.

Goodhart, Charles A. E., and R. J. Bhansali. 1970. "Political Economy." *Political Studies* 18: 43–106.

Goodin, R. E., and K. W. S. Roberts. 1975. "The Ethical Voter." *American Political Science Review* 69: 926–8.

Goodspeed, Timothy J. 1992. "Redistribution and the Structure of Local Government Finance." Unpublished paper, Florida International University.

Gore, A. 1992. *Earth in the Balance.* Boston: Houghton Mifflin Company.

Gosnell, Howard F. 1927. *Machine Politics: Chicago Model.* Chicago: University of Chicago Press.

Gourevitch, Peter A. 1977. "International Trade, Domestic Coalitions and Liberty: Comparative Responses to the Crisis of 1873–1896." *Journal of Interdisciplinary History* 8: 281–313.

Gramlich, E. M. 1985. "Excessive Government Spending in the U.S.: Facts and Theories." In E. M. Gramlich and B. C. Ysander, eds., *Control of Local Government.* Stockholm: Almqvist and Wicksell.

1987. "Subnational Fiscal Policy." *Perspectives on Local Public Finance and Public Policy* 3: 3–27.

Granovetter, M. 1985. "Economic Action, Social Structure, and Embeddedness." *American Journal of Sociology* 91: 481–510.

Green, Donald P., and Ian Shapiro. 1994. *Pathologies of Rational Choice.* New Haven and London: Yale University Press.

Green, Jerry, and Jean-Jacques Laffont. 1980. *Incentives in Public Decision-Making.* Amsterdam: North–Holland.

Greenberg, Joseph. 1979. "Consistent Majority Rule Over Compact Sets of Alternatives." *Econometrica* 47: 627–36.

Greenberg, Joseph, Robert Mackay, and T. Nicolaus Tideman. 1977. "Some Limitations of the Groves–Ledyard Optimal Mechanism." *Public Choice* 29 special supplement 2: 129–38.

Greenberg, Joseph, and Kenneth Shepsle. 1987. "The Effects of Electoral Rewards in Multiparty Competition with Entry." *American Political Science Review* 81: 525–37.

Greenberg, Joseph, and Shlomo Weber. 1985. "Multiparty Equilibria under Proportional Representation." *American Political Science Review* 81: 525–38.

Greenstein, Fred I. 1970. *The American Party System and the American People.* Englewood Cliffs: Prentice-Hall.

Grier, Kevin B. 1987. "Presidential Elections and Federal Reserve Policy: An Empirical Test." *Southern Economic Journal* 54: 475–86.

1989. "On the Existence of a Political Monetary Cycle." *American Journal of Political Science* 33: 376–489.

Grier, Kevin B., Michael C. Munger, and Brian E. Roberts. 1991. "The Industrial Organization of Corporate Political Participation." *Southern Economic Journal* 57: 727–38.

Grier, Kevin B., and Gordon Tullock. 1989. "An Empirical Analysis of Cross-National Economic Growth, 1951–80." *Journal of Monetary Economics* 24: 259–76.

Grilli, Vittorio, Dourato Masciandaro, and Guido Tabellini. 1991. "Political and Monetary Histories and Public Financial Policies in the Industrial Countries." *Economic Policy* (October): 342–92.

Grofman, Bernard. 1981. "Fair and Equal Representation." *Ethics* 91: 477–85.

Grofman, Bernard, and Scott F. Feld. 1988. "Rousseau's General Will: A Condorcetian Perspective." *American Political Science Review* 82: 567–76.

Grofman, Bernard, and Barbara Norrander. 1990. "Efficient Use of Reference Group Cues in a Single Dimension." *Public Choice* 64: 213–28.

Grofman, Bernard, Guillermo Owen, and Scott L. Feld. 1983. "Thirteen Theorems in Search of the Truth." *Theory and Decision* 15: 261–78.

Grossman, Gene N. and Elhanan Helpman. 1994. "Protection for Sale." *American Economic Review* 84: 833–50.

Grossman, Philip J. 1989. "Fiscal Decentralization and Government Size: An Extension." *Public Choice* 62: 63–70.

1992. "Fiscal Decentralization and Public Sector Size in Australia." *The Economic Record* 68: 240–46.

Grossman, Sanford J., and Oliver Hart. 1986. "The Costs and Benefits of Ownership: A Theory of Vertical and Lateral Integration." *Journal of Political Economy* 94: 691–719.

Groves, Theodore. 1973. "Incentives in Teams." *Econometrica* 41: 617–31.

1976. "Information, Incentives, and the Internalization of Production Externalities." In S. A. Y. Lin, ed., *Theory and Measurement of Economic Externalities.* New York: Academic Press, 65–86.

Groves, Theodore, and John O. Ledyard. 1977. "Optimal Allocation of Public Goods: A Solution to the 'Free Rider' Problem." *Econometrica* 45: 783–809.

Groves, Theodore, and Martin Loeb. 1975. "Incentives and Public Inputs." *Journal of Public Economics* 4: 211–26.

Grubb, D., R. Jackman, and Richard Layard. 1982. "Causes of the Current Stagflation." *Review of Economic Studies* 49: 707–30.

Guerrieri, Paulo, and Pier Caerlo Padoan, eds. 1988. *The Political Economy of International Cooperation.* London: Croom Helm.

Guha, A. S. 1972. "Neutralitiy, Monotonicity and the Right of Veto." *Econometrica* 40: 821–6.

Gygi, Beat. 1991. *Internationale Organisationen aus der Sicht der neuen politischen Ökonomie.* Heidelberg: Physika.

Haas, J. 1982. *The Evolution of the Prehistoric State.* New York: Columbia University Press.

Haberler, Gottfried. [1937] 1958. *Prosperity and Depression*. Cambridge, Mass.: Harvard University Press.

Hackett, Steven. 1992. "Heterogeneity and the Provision of Governance for Common-Pool Resources." *Journal of Theoretical Politics* 4: 325–42.

Hackett, Steven, Edella Schlager, and James M. Walker. 1994. "The Role of Communication in Resolving Commons Dilemmas: Experimental Evidence with Heterogeneous Appropriators." *Journal of Environmental Economics and Management* 27: 99–126.

Haefele, Edwin T. 1971. "A Utility Theory of Representative Government." *American Economic Review* 61: 350–67.

Hall, J., and Bernard Grofman. 1990. "The Committee Assignment Process and the Conditional Nature of Committee Bias." *American Political Science Review* 84: 1149–66.

Hall, R., and F. Wayman. 1990. "Buying Time: Moneyed Interests and the Mobilization of Bias in Congressional Committees." *American Political Science Review* 84: 797–820.

Haller, H. 1986. "Noncooperative Bargaining of $N > 3$ Players." *Economic Letters* 22: 11–13.

Hamilton, Bruce W. 1982. "The Flypaper Effect and Other Anomalies." *Journal of Public Economics* 22: 347–61.

Hammond, Peter J. 1991a. "Independence of Irrelevant Interpersonal Comparisons." *Social Choice and Welfare* 8: 1–19.

1991b. "Interpersonal Comparisons of Utility: Why and How They Are and Should Be Made." In J. Elster and J. E. Roemer, eds., *Interpersonal Comparisons of Well-Being*. Cambridge University Press.

Hammond, Thomas H. 1986. "Agenda Control, Organizational Structure, and Bureaucratic Politics." *American Journal of Political Science* 30: 379–420.

Hammond, Thomas H., and Jack Knott. 1992. "Presidential Power, Congressional Dominance, and Bureaucratic Autonomy in a Model of Multi-Institutional Policymaking." Paper presented at the Annual Meeting of the American Political Science Association, Chicago.

Hammond, Thomas H., Jeffrey Hill, and Gary J. Miller. 1986. "Presidents, Congress, and the 'Congressional Control of Administration' Hypothesis." Paper presented at the Annual Meeting of the American Political Science Association, Washington, D.C.

Hammond, Thomas H., and Gary J. Miller. 1985. "A Social Choice Perspective on Expertise and Authority in Bureaucracy." *American Journal of Political Science* 29: 1–28.

1987. "The Core of the Constitution." *American Political Science Review* 81: 1155–74.

1989. "Stability and Efficiency in a Separation of Powers Constitutional System." In Bernard Grofman and Donald Wittman, eds., *The Federalist Papers and the New Institutionalism*. New York: Agathon Press.

Hanneman, W. Michael. 1994. "Valuing the Environment through Contingent Valuation." *Journal of Economic Perspectives*, 8: 19–43.

Hansen, J. 1991. *Gaining Access: Congress and the Farm Lobby, 1919–81*. Chicago: University of Chicago Press.

Hansen, Susan B. 1983. *The Politics of Taxation: Revenue without Representation*. New York: Praeger.

Harberger, Arnold C. 1954. "Monopoly and Resource Allocation." *American Economic Review* 44: 77–87.

1974. *Taxation and Welfare*. Chicago: University of Chicago Press.

Hardin, Garrett. 1968. "The Tragedy of the Commons." *Science* 162: 243–8.

1975. "The Tragedy of the Commons." In B.A. Ackerman, ed., *Economic Foundations of Property Law*. Boston: Little, Brown and Company.

Hardin, Russell. 1982. *Collective Action*. Baltimore: Johns Hopkins University Press.

1988. *Morality within the Limits of Reason*. Chicago: Chicago University Press.

1989. "Why a Constitution?" In Bernard Grofman and Donald Wittman, eds., *The Federalist Papers and the New Institutionalism.* New York: Agathon Press, 100–20.

1990. "Contractarianism: Wistful Thinking." *Constitutional Political Economy* 1: 35–52.

1991. "Hobbesian Political Order." *Political Theory* 19: 156–80.

Harrington, Joseph P. 1991a. "The Role of Party Reputations in the Formation of Policy." Working paper, Department of Economics, University of Maryland.

1991b. "A Simple Dynamic Model of Electoral Competition under Incomplete Information." Department of Economics, University of Maryland.

Harsanyi, John C., and Reinhard Selten. 1988. *A General Theory of Equilibrium Selection in Games.* Cambridge: MIT Press.

Hart, H. L. A. 1961. *The Concept of Law.* Oxford: Clarendon Press.

Hart, Oliver, and John Moore. 1990. "Property Rights and the Theory of the Firm." *Journal of Political Economy* 98: 1119–59.

Hausman, Daniel M., and Michael S. McPherson. 1993. "Taking Ethics Seriously: Economics and Contemporary Moral Philosophy." *Journal of Economic Literature* 31: 671–731.

Havrilesky, T. M. 1987. "A Partisanship Theory of Fiscal and Monetary Regimes." *Journal of Money, Credit and Banking* 19: 308–25.

Haynes, S. A., and J. A. Stone. 1989. "An Integrated Test for Electoral Cycles in the US Economy." *The Review of Economics and Statistics* 71: 426–34.

1990. "Political Models of the Business Cycle Should be Revived." *Economic Inquiry* 28: 442–65.

Hegel, Georg Wilhelm Friedrich. 1984. *Hegel, the Letters.* Translated by Clark Butler and Christiane Seiler with commentary by Clark Butler. Bloomington: Indiana University Press.

Helleiner, Gerald K. 1977. "The Political Economy of Canada's Tariff Structure: An Alternative Model." *Canadian Journal of Economics* 10: 318–36.

Helpman, Elhanan, and Paul R. Krugman. 1985. *Market Structure and Foreign Trade.* Cambridge, Mass.: MIT Press.

Henrekson, Magnus. 1988. "Swedish Government Growth: A Disequilibrium Analysis." In Johan A. Lybeck and Magnus Henrekson, eds., *Explaining the Growth of Government.* Amsterdam: North–Holland, 93–132.

1990. "An Economic Analysis of Swedish Government Expenditure." Ph.D. diss., Gothenburg University.

Henrekson, Magnus, and Johan A. Lybeck. 1988. "Explaining the Growth of Government in Sweden: A Disequilibrium Approach." *Public Choice* 57: 213–32.

Henry, C., ed. 1883. *Correspondance inedite de Condorcet et de Turgot 1770–1779.* Paris: Charavay Frères.

Herman, V., and J. Pope. 1973. "Minority Governments in Western Democracies." *British Journal of Political Science* 3: 191–212.

Herman, V., and D. Sanders. 1977. "The Stability and Survival of Governments in Western Democracies." *Acta Politica* 12: 346–77.

Hettich, Walter. 1979. "Henry Simons on Taxation and the Economic System." *National Tax Journal* 32: 1–9.

Hettich, Walter, and Stanley L. Winer. 1984. "A Positive Model of Tax Structure." *Journal of Public Economics* 24: 67–87.

1988. "Economic and Political Foundations of Tax Structure." *American Economic Review* 78: 701–12.

1993. "Economic Efficiency, Political Institutions and Policy Analysis." *Kyklos* 46: 3–25.

Hibbs, Douglas A., Jr. 1975. *Economic Interest and the Politics of Macroeconomic Policy.* Monograph C/75–14, Center for International Studies, MIT.

———. 1977. "Political Parties and Macroeconomic Policy." *American Political Science Review* 71: 1467–97.

———. 1978. "On the Political Economy of Long-Run Trends in Strike Activity." *British Journal of Political Science* 8: 153–75.

———. 1982. "On the Demand for Economic Outcomes: Macroeconomic Outcomes and Mass Political Support in the United States, Great Britain, and Germany." *Journal of Politics* 44: 426–62.

———. 1986. "Political Parties and Macroeconomic Policies and Outcome in the United States." *American Economic Review* papers and proceedings 71: 66–70.

———. 1987a. *The Political Economy of Industrial Democracies.* Cambridge, Mass.: Harvard University Press.

———. 1987b. *American Political Economy.* Cambridge, Mass.: Harvard University Press.

———. 1992. "Partisan Theory After Fifteen Years." *The European Journal of Political Economy* 8: 361–73.

———. 1994. "The Partisan Model of Macroeconomic Cycles: More Theory and Evidence for the United States." *Economics and Politics.*

Hibbs, Douglas A., Jr., and C. Dennis. 1988. "Income Distribution in the United States." *American Political Science Review* 82: 467–89.

Hicks, John R. 1939. "The Foundations of Welfare Economics." *Economic Journal* 48: 696–712.

Higgins, Richard S., William F. Shughart II, and Robert D. Tollison. 1985. "Free Entry and Efficient Rent-Seeking." *Public Choice* 46: 247–58.

Higgins, Richard, and Robert D. Tollison. 1985. "Life among the Triangles and Trapezoids: Notes on the Theory of Rent Seeking." In Charles K. Rowley, Robert D. Tollison, and Gordon Tullock, eds., *The Political Economy of Rent-Seeking.* Boston: Kluwer, 147–57.

Hill, Jeffrey. 1985. "Why So Much Stability? The Role of Agency Determined Stability." *Public Choice* 46: 275–87.

Hillman, Arye L. 1982. "Declining Industries and Political-Support Protectionist Motives." *American Economic Review* 72: 1180–7.

———. 1989. *The Political Economy of Protection.* New York: Harwood Academic Publishers.

Hillman, Arye L., and Elihu Katz. 1984. "Risk-Averse Rent-Seekers and the Social Cost of Monopoly Power." *Economic Journal* 94: 104–10.

Hillman, Arye L., and John G. Riley. 1989. "Politically Contested Rents and Transfers." *Economics and Politics* 1: 17–39.

Hillman, Arye L., and Heinrich Ursprung. 1988. "Domestic Politics, Foreign Interests and International Trade Policy." *American Economic Review* 78: 729–45.

Hilton, Rita. 1992. "Institutional Incentives for Resource Mobilization: An Analysis of Irrigation Schemes in Nepal." *Journal of Theoretical Politics* 4: 283–308.

Hinich, Melvin J. 1977. "Equilibrium in Spatial Voting: The Median Voter Result Is an Artifact." *Journal of Economic Theory* 16: 208–19.

———. 1981. "Voting as an Act of Contribution." *Public Choice* 36: 135–40.

Hinich, Melvin J., John Ledyard, and Peter C. Ordeshook. 1972. "Nonvoting and the Existence of Equilibrium under Majority Rule." *Journal of Economic Theory* 4: 144–53.

Hinich, Melvin J., and Peter C. Ordeshook. 1969. "Abstentions and Equilibrium under Majority Rule." *Public Choice* 7: 81–106.

———. 1974. "The Electoral College: A Spatial Analysis." *Political Methodology* 1: 1–29.

Hinich, Melvin J., and Walker Pollard. 1981. "A New Approach to the Spatial Theory of Electoral Competition." *American Journal of Political Science* 25: 323–41.

Hirschman, Albert O. 1970. *Exit, Voice and Loyalty.* Cambridge, Mass.: Harvard University Press.

Hoadley, John F. 1986. *Origins of American Political Parties: 1789–1803.* Lexington: University Press of Kentucky.

Hobbes, Thomas. [1651] 1960. *Leviathan or the Matter, Forme and Power of a Commonwealth Ecclesiasticall and Civil.* Ed. Michael Oakeshott. Oxford: Basil Blackwell.

Hobsbawm, E. 1990: *Nations and Nationalism Since 1780.* Cambridge University Press.

Hoffman, Elizabeth, and Charles R. Plott. 1994. *Bibliography of Research in Experimental Economics.* Manuscript.

Hoffman, Elizabeth, and M. L. Spitzer. 1982. "The Coase Theorem: Some Experimental Tests." *Journal of Law and Economics* 25: 73–98.

1985a. "Entitlements, Rights, and Fairness: An Experimental Examination of Subjects' Concepts of Distributive Justice." *Journal of Legal Studies* 14: 259–97.

1985b. "Experimental Tests of the Coase Theorem with Large Bargaining Groups." *Journal of Legal Studies* 15: 149–71.

Holcombe, Randall G., and Jeffrey A. Mills. 1995. "Politics and Deficit Finance." *Public Finance Quarterly* 23: 448–66.

Holmström, Bengt R. 1985. "The Provision of Services in a Market Economy." In Robert P. Inman, ed., *Managing the Service Economy: Prospects and Problems.* Cambridge University Press, 183–213.

Holmström, Bengt R., and Jean Tirole. 1989. "The Theory of the Firm." In Richard Schmalensee and Robert D. Willig, eds., *Handbook of Industrial Organization*, vol.1. New York: North–Holland, 61–133.

Horn, Murray J. 1988. "The Political Economy of Public Administration." Ph.D. diss., Harvard University.

1995. *The Political Economy of Public Administration.* Cambridge University Press.

Hösli, Madeleine O. 1993. "Admission of European Free Trade Association States to the European Community: Effects on Voting Power in the European Community Council of Ministers." *International Organization* 47: 629–43.

Høst, V., and Martin Paldam. 1990. "An International Element in the Vote? A Comparative Study of 17 OECD Countries 1946–85." *European Journal of Political Research* 18: 221–39.

Hotelling, H. 1929. "Stability in Competition." *The Economic Journal* 39: 41–57.

Hsieh, John Fuh-sheng, and Emerson M. S. Niou. 1993. *Issue Voting in the 1992 Parliamentary Election in the Republic of China on Taiwan.* Paper presented at the Annual APSA Meetings, Washington, D.C.

Hubka, B., and Gabriel Obermann. 1977. "Zur Wahlzyklik wirtschaftspolitischer Maßnahmen." *Empirica* 1: 57–83.

Hume, David. [1739–1740] 1979. *A Treatise of Human Nature.* Ed. L. A. Selby-Bigge and P. H. Nidditch. Oxford: Oxford University Press.

[1748] 1985. "Of the Original Contract." In David Hume, *Essays Moral, Political, and Literary.* Indianapolis: Liberty Classics, 465–87.

Hunter, William J., and Michael A. Nelson. 1989. "Interest Group Demand for Taxation." *Public Choice* 62: 41–61.

Hurwicz, Leonid. 1979. "On Allocations Attainable Through Nash Equilibria." In Jean-Jaques Laffont, ed., *Aggregation and Revelation of Preferences.* Amsterdam: North–Holland, 397–419.

Hylland, Aanund, and Richard Zeckhauser. 1979. "A Mechanism for Selecting Public

Goods When Preferences Must be Elicited." KSG discussion paper 70D, Harvard University.

1979. "Selecting Public Goods Bundles with Preferences Unknown and Tax System Given." KSG working paper, Harvard University.

Ingberman, Daniel. 1988. "Reputational Dynamics in Spatial Competition." *Mathematical and Computer Modelling* 12: 479–96.

1992. "Incumbent Reputations and Ideological Campaign Contributions in Spatial Competition." *Mathematical and Computer Modelling* 16: 147–70.

Ingberman, Dan, and Robert P. Inman. 1988. "The Political Economy of Fiscal Policy." In Paul G. Hare, ed., *Surveys in Public Sector Economics*. Oxford: Basil Blackwell, 105–60.

Inman, Robert P. 1979. "Fiscal Performance of Local Governments: An Interpretative Review." In Peter Mieszkowski and M. Straszheim, eds., *Current Issues in Urban Economics*. Baltimore: Johns Hopkins University Press, 270–321.

1982. "Public Employee Pensions and the Local Labor Budget." *Journal of Public Economics* 19: 49–71.

1987. "Markets, Government and the 'New' Political Economy." In Alan J. Auerbach and Martin Feldstein, eds., *Handbook of Public Economics*, vol. 2. Amsterdam: North–Holland, 647–777.

1988. "Federal Assistance and Local Services in the United States: The Evolution of a New Fiscal Order." In H. Rosen, ed., *Fiscal Federalism: Quantitative Studies*. Chicago: University of Chicago Press.

1989. "The Local Decision to Tax: Evidence from Large U.S. Cities." *Regional Science and Urban Economics* 19: 455–91.

1993. "Local Interests, Central Leadership, and the Passage of TRA86." *Journal of Policy Analysis and Management* 12: 156–80.

Inman, Robert P., and Michael A. Fitts. 1990. "Political Institutions and Fiscal Policy: Evidence from the U.S. Historical Record." *Journal of Law, Economics and Organization* special issue 6: 79–132.

Inman, Robert P., and Daniel L. Rubinfeld. 1994. "The Transactions Costs of Government." Department of Finance, University of Pennsylvania. Mimeo.

International Monetary Fund. 1992. *Government Finance Statistics Yearbook*. Washington, D.C.

Intriligator, Michael D. 1973. "A Probabilistic Model of Social Choice." *Review of Economic Studies* 40: 157–66.

Isaac, R. Mark, Kenneth McCue, and Charles R. Plott. 1985. "Public Goods Provision in an Experimental Environment." *Journal of Public Economics* 26: 51–74.

Isaac, R. Mark, David Schmidtz, and James M. Walker. 1989. "The Assurance Problem in a Laboratory Market." *Public Choice* 62: 217–36.

Isaac, R. Mark, and James M. Walker. 1988a. "Communication and Free-Riding Behavior: The Voluntary Contribution Mechanism." *Economic Inquiry* 26: 585–608.

1988b. "Group Size Effects in Public Goods Provision: The Voluntary Contributions Mechanism." *Quarterly Journal of Economics* 103: 179–99.

1991. "Costly Communication: An Experiment in a Nested Public Goods Problem." In Thomas R. Palfrey, ed., *Laboratory Research in Political Economy*. Ann Arbor: University of Michigan Press, 269–86.

1993. "Nash as an Organizing Principle in the Voluntary Provision of Public Goods: Experimental Evidence." Working paper, Indiana University.

Isaac, R. Mark, James M. Walker, and Susan Thomas. 1984. "Divergent Evidence on Free Riding: An Experimental Examination of Some Possible Explanations." *Public Choice* 43: 113–49.

Isaac, R. Mark, James M. Walker, and Arlington W. Williams. 1994. "Group Size and the Voluntary Provision of Public Goods: Experimental Evidence Utilizing Large Groups." *Journal of Public Economics* 54: 1–36.

Iyengar, Shanto. 1991. *Is Anyone Responsible? How Television Frames Political Issues.* Chicago: University of Chicago Press.

Iyengar, Shanto, and Donald Kinder. 1987. *News That Matters.* Chicago: University of Chicago Press.

Jackson, John E. 1974. *Constituencies and Leaders in Congress.* Cambridge, Mass.: Harvard University Press.

1975. "Issues, Party Choices, and Presidential Votes." *American Journal of Political Science* 19: 161–86.

Jacobson, Gary. 1980. *Money in Congressional Elections.* New Haven: Yale University Press.

1992. *The Politics of Congressional Elections.* San Diego: Harper Collins Publishers.

Jerdee, Thomas H., and Benson Rosen. 1974. "Effects of Opportunity to Communicate and Visibility of Individual Decisions on Behavior in the Common Interest." *Journal of Applied Psychology* 59: 712–16.

Jessup, Timothy C., and Nancy Lee Peluso. 1986. "Minor Forest Products as Common Property Resources in East Kalimantan, Indonesia." In National Research Council, *Proceedings of the Conference on Common Property Management.* Washington, D.C.: National Academy Press, 501–31.

Johnson, Paul Edward. 1988. "On the Theory of Political Competition: Comparative Statics From a General Allocative Perspective." *Public Choice* 58: 217–36.

Johnson, Ronald N., and Gary D. Libecap. 1982. "Contracting Problems and Regulation: The Case of the Fishery." *American Economic Review* 72: 1005–22.

1989. "Agency Growth, Salaries, and the Protected Bureaucrat." *Economic Inquiry* 27: 431–51.

Jones, Ronald. 1965. "The Structure of Simple General Equilibrium Models." *Journal of Political Economy* 73: 557–72.

Jones, S. R. G. 1992. "Was There a Hawthorne Effect?" *American Journal of Sociology* 98: 451–68.

Josling, Tim, and H. Wayne Moyer. 1991. "The Common Agricultural Policy of the European Community: A Public Choice Interpretation." In Roland Vaubel and Thomas D. Willett, eds., *The Political Economy of International Organizations: A Public Choice Approach.* Boulder: Westview Press, 286–305.

Joulfaian, David, and Michael L. Marlow. 1990. "Government Size and Decentralization: Evidence from Disaggregated Data." *Southern Economic Journal* 56: 1094–102.

1991. "Centralization and Government Competition." *Applied Economics* 23: 1603–12.

Kahneman, Daniel, Paul Slovic, and Amos Tversky, eds. 1982. *Judgment under Uncertainty: Heuristics and Biases.* Cambridge University Press.

Kalai, Ehud, Eitan Muller, and Mark A. Satterthwaite. 1979. "Social Welfare Functions When Preferences Are Convex, Strictly Monotonic, and Continuous." *Public Choice* 34: 87–97.

Kaldor, Nicholas. 1939. "Welfare Propositions in Economics and Interpersonal Comparisons of Utility." *Economic Journal* 45: 549–52.

Kalecki, Michal. 1943. "Political Aspects of Full Employment." Reprinted in: *Selected Essays on the Dynamics of the Capitalist Economy.* Cambridge University Press, 1971.

Kalt, Joseph P., and Mark A. Zupan. 1984. "Capture and Ideology in the Economic Theory of Politics." *American Economic Review* 74: 279–300.

Kanbur, S. M. Ravi. 1992: "Heterogeneity, Distribution and Cooperation in Common

Property Resource Management." Background paper for the World Development Report, Washington, D.C.

Kaplow, Louis. 1989. "Horizontal Equity: Measures in Search of a Principle." *National Tax Journal* 42: 139–54.

Katz, Elihu. 1957–8. "The Two-Step Flow of Communication: An Up-To-Date Report on an Hypothesis." *Public Opinion Quarterly* 21: 61–78.

Kau, James B., and Paul H. Rubin. 1979. "Self-Interest, Ideology, and Logrolling in Congressional Voting." *Journal of Law and Economics* 22: 365–84.

———. 1981. "The Size of Government." *Public Choice* 37: 261–74.

———. 1982. *Congressmen, Constitutents and Contributors.* Boston: Martinus-Nijhoff.

Kay, David A. 1977. *The Changing United Nations. Options for the United States.* New York: Praeger.

Keefer, P., and Stephen Knack. 1993. "Why Don't Poor Countries Catch Up? A Cross Country Test of an Institutional Explanation." Working paper no. 60, Center for Institutional Reform and the Informal Sector, University of Maryland.

Keil, Manfred W. 1988. "Is the Political Business Cycle Really Dead?" *Southern Economic Journal* 55: 86–99.

Keim, Gerald, and Asghar Zardkoohi. 1988. "Looking for Leverage in PAC Markets: Corporate and Labor Contributions Considered." *Public Choice* 58: 21–34.

Kelly, Jerry S. 1978. *Arrow Impossibility Theorems.* New York: Academic Press.

Kemeny, John. 1959. "Mathematics Without Numbers." *Daedalus* 88: 571–91.

Kennelly, Brendan, and Peter Murrell. 1991. "Industry Characteristics and Interest Group Formation: An Empirical Study." *Public Choice* 70: 21–40.

Kenny, Lawrence W., and Mark Toma. 1993. "The Role of Tax Bases and Collection Costs in the Determination of Income Tax Rates, Seigniorage and Inflation." Working paper 92–93–02, Florida State University.

Keohane, Robert O. 1984. *After Hegemony.* New York: Princeton University Press.

Key, V. O., Jr. 1961. *Public Opinion and American Democracy.* New York: Knopf.

Kiesling, Herbert J. 1990. "Economic and Political Foundations of Tax Structure: Comment." *American Economic Review* 80: 931–4.

Kiewiet, D. Roderick. 1991. "Bureaucrats and Budgetary Outcomes: A Quantitative Analysis." In André Blais and Stéphen Dion, eds., *The Budget Maximizing Bureaucrat: Appraisals and Evidence.* Pittsburgh: University of Pittsburgh Press: 143–74.

Kiewiet, D. Roderick, and Mathew D. McCubbins. 1985. "Appropriations Decisions as a Bilateral Bargaining Game between President and Congress." *Legislative Studies Quarterly* 9: 181–202.

———. 1988. "Presidential Influence on Congressional Appropriations Decisions." *American Journal of Political Science* 32: 713–36.

———. 1991. *The Logic of Delegation.* Chicago: University of Chicago Press.

Kim, Oliver, and Mark Walker. 1984. "The Free Rider Problem: Experimental Evidence." *Public Choice* 43: 3–24.

Kinder, Donald, and D. Roderick Kiewiet. 1979. "Economic Discontent and Political Behavior: The Role of Personal Grievances and Collective Economic Judgments in Congressional Voting." *American Journal of Political Science* 23: 495–527.

Kinder, Donald R., and David O. Sears. 1985. "Public Opinion and Political Action." In Gardner Lindzey and Elliot Aronson, eds., *Handbook of Social Psychology*, vol.2, 3rd ed. New York: Random House, 659–741.

Kindleberger, Charles P. 1951. "Group Behavior and International Trade." *Journal of Political Economy* 59: 30–46.

———. 1975. "The Rise of Free Trade in Western Europe, 1820–1875." *Journal of Economic History* 35: 20–55.

King, G., J. Alt, N. Burns, and M. Laver. 1990. "A Unified Model of Cabinet Dissolution in Parliamentary Democracies." *American Political Science Review* 34: 846–71.

Kirchgässner, Gebhard. 1983. "The Political Business Cycle If the Government Is Not Myopic. A Generalization of the Nordhaus Model." *Mathematical Social Sciences* 4: 243–60.

———. 1991. *Homo Oeconomicus: Das ökonomische Modell individuellen Verhaltens und seine Anwendung in den Wirtschafts- und Sozialwissenschaften.* Tübingen: Mohr (Siebeck).

Kiser, Larry L., and Elinor Ostrom. 1982. "The Three Worlds of Action: A Meta-theoretical Synthesis of Institutional Approaches." In Elinor Ostrom, ed., *Strategies of Political Inquiry.* Beverly Hills: Sage, 179–222.

Kitchin, Joseph. 1923. "Cycles and Trends in Economic Factors." *Review of Economic Statistics* 5: 10–16.

Klapper, Joseph T. 1960. *The Effects of Mass Communication.* New York: Free Press.

Klein, Benjamin, and Keith B. Leffler. 1981. "The Role of Market Forces in Assuring Contractual Performance." *Journal of Political Economy* 89: 615–41.

Klevorick, Alvin, and Gerald Kramer. 1973. "Social Choice on Pollution Management: The Genossenschaften." *Journal of Public Economics* 2: 101–46.

Klibanoff, P., and J. Morduch. 1993. "Decentralization, Externalities, and Efficiency." Department of Economics, Harvard University. Mimeo.

Knapp, Andrew. 1987. "Proportional But Bipolar: France's Electoral System in 1986." *West European Politics* 10: 89–114.

Kneebone, Ronald D. 1992. "Centralization and the Size of Government in Canada." *Applied Economics* 24: 1293–300.

Koehler, David H. 1975. "Vote Trading and the Voting Paradox: A Proof of Logical Equivalence." *American Political Science Review* 69: 954–60.

———. 1990. "The Size of the Yolk: Computations for Odd and Even-Numbered Committees." *Social Choice and Welfare* 7: 231–45.

Koford, Kenneth J. 1982. "Centralized Vote-Trading." *Public Choice* 39: 245–68.

———. 1987. "Scale Economies and Rent-Seeking in Legislative Parties." *Public Choice* 52: 35–55.

———. 1990. "Dimensions, Transaction Costs and Coalitions in Legislative Voting." *Economics and Politics* 2: 59–82.

Kollman, Ken, John H. Miller, and Scott E. Page. 1992. "Adaptive Parties in Spatial Elections." *American Political Science Review* 86: 929–37.

Korn, D. 1993. "National Coalitions in Israel: 1984–1990." Ph.D. diss., London School of Economics.

Kramer, Gerald H. 1970. "The Effects of Precinct-Level Canvassing on Voting Behavior." *Public Opinion Quarterly* 34: 560–72.

———. 1971. "Short-Term Fluctuations in U.S. Voting Behavior, 1896–1964." *American Political Science Review* 65: 131–43.

———. 1972. "Sophisticated Voting over Multidimensional Choice Spaces." *Journal of Mathematical Sociology* 2: 165–80.

———. 1973. "On a Class of Equilibrium Conditions for Majority Rule." *Econometrica* 41: 285–97.

———. 1977. "A Dynamic Model of Political Equilibrium." *Journal of Economic Theory* 16: 310–34.

———. 1983. "The Ecological Fallacy Revisited: Aggregate-Versus Individual-Level Findings on Economics and Elections, and Sociotropic Voting." *American Political Science Review* 77: 92–111.

Kramer, R. M., and Marilyn M. Brewer. 1986. "Social Group Identity and the Emergence of Cooperation in Resource Conservation Dilemmas." In Henk A. Wilke, David M.

Messick, and Christel G. Rutte, eds., *Experimental Social Dilemmas*. Frankfurt am Main: Lang, 205–34.

Krasner, Stephen D. 1976. "State Power and the Structure of International Trade." *World Politics* 283: 317–47.

Krehbiel, Keith. 1992. *Information and Legislative Organization*. Ann Arbor: University of Michigan Press.

Krehbiel, Keith, and Douglas Rivers. 1990. "Sophisticated Voting in Congress. A Reconsideration." *Journal of Politics* 52: 548–78.

Kreps, David M. 1990. *A Course in Microeconomics*. Princeton: Princeton University Press.

Kreps, David M., Paul Milgrom, John Roberts, and Robert Wilson. 1982. "Rational Cooperation in a Finitely Repeated Prisoner's Dilemma." *Journal of Economic Theory* 27: 245–52.

Kristov, Lorenzo, Peter Lindert, and Robert McClelland. 1992. "Pressure Groups and Redistribution." *Journal of Public Economics* 48: 135–63.

Krueger, Anne O. 1974. "The Political Economy of the Rent-Seeking Society." *American Economic Review* 64: 291–303.

Krugman, Paul R., ed. 1986. *Strategic Trade Policy and the New International Economics*. Cambridge, Mass.: MIT Press.

Kuhn, Britta. 1993. *Sozialraum Europa: Zentralisierung oder Dezentralisierung der Sozialpolitik?* Wissenschaftliche Schriften 4, Volkswirtschaftliche Beiträge, Band 141. Idstein: Schulz Kirchner Verlag.

Kurth, James R. 1979. "The Political Consequences of the Product Cycle: Industrial History and Political Outcomes." *International Organizations* 33: 1–34.

Laasko, M., and R. Taagepera. 1979. "Effective Number of Parties: A Measure with Applications to West Europe." *Comparative Political Studies* 12: 3–27.

Laband, David N., and John P. Sophocleus. 1988. "The Social Cost of Rent Seeking: First Estimates." *Public Choice* 58: 269–75.

——— 1992. "An Estimate of Resource Expenditures on Transfer Activity in the United States." *Quarterly Journal of Economics* 107: 959–84.

Lächler, Ulrich. 1978. "The Political Business Cycle: A Complementary Study." *Review of Economic Studies* 45: 369–75.

——— 1983. "On Political Business Cycles with Endogenous Election Dates." *Journal of Public Economics* 17: 111–17.

——— 1984. "The Political Business Cycle under Rational Voting Behavior." *Public Choice* 44: 411–30.

Ladd, Everett C. 1993. "As Much about Continuity as Change. As Much about Restoration as Rejection." *The American Enterprise* January–February: 45–51.

Laffont, Jean-Jacques. 1987. "Incentives and the Allocation of Public Goods." In Alan J. Auerbach and Martin Feldstein, eds., *Handbook of Public Economics*, vol.2. New York: Elsevier Science Publishers; Amsterdam: North–Holland.

——— 1988. "Hidden Gaming in Hierarchies: Facts and Models." *Economic Record* 64: 295–306.

——— 1990. "Analysis of Hidden Gaming in a Three-Level Hierarchy." *Journal of Law, Economics, and Organization* 6: 301–24.

Lam, Wai Fung, Myungsuk Lee, and Elinor Ostrom. Forthcoming. "The Institutional Analysis and Development Framework: Application to Irrigation Policy in Nepal." In Derick W. Brinkerhoff, ed., *Policy Analysis Concepts and Methods: An Institutional and Implementation Focus*. Greenwich: JAI Press.

Landes, William M., and Richard A. Posner. 1975. "The Independent Judiciary in an Interest-Group Perspective." *Journal of Law and Economics* 18: 875–901.

Langbein, L., and M. Lotwis. 1990. "The Political Efficacy of Lobbying and Money: Gun Control in the US House, 1986." *Legislative Studies Quarterly* 15: 413–40.

Laury, Susan K., James M. Walker, and Arlington W. Williams. 1995. "Anonymity and the Voluntary Provision of Public Goods." *Journal of Economic Behavior and Organization* 27: 365–80.

Laver, Michael, and Ian Budge, eds. 1992. *Party Policy and Government Coalitions.* New York: St. Martin's Press; London: Macmillan.

Laver, Michael, and Norman Schofield. 1990. *Multiparty Government.* Oxford: Oxford University Press.

Lavergne, Real P. 1983. *The Political Economy of U.S. Tariffs. An Empirical Analysis.* Toronto: Academic Press.

Lazarsfeld, Paul, Bernard Berelson, and Helen Gaudet. 1944. *The People's Choice: How the Voter Makes Up his Mind in a Presidential Campaign.* New York: Columbia University Press.

Lazear, Edward P. 1991. "Labor Economics and the Psychology of Organization." *Journal of Economic Perspectives* 5: 89–110.

Le Breton, Michael. 1994. "Arrovian Social Choice on Economic Domains." Paper presented in the International Economic Association Round Table on Social Choice, Hernstein, Austria, May 1994.

Le Breton, Michael, and John A. Weymark. 1996. "An Introduction to Arrovian Social Welfare Functions on Economic and Political Domains." In Norman Schofield, ed., *Collective Decision Making: Social Choice and Political Economy.* Dordrecht: Kluwer.

Ledyard, John O. 1981. "The Paradox of Voting and Candidate Competition: A General Equilibrium Analysis." In G. Horwich and J. Quirk, eds., *Essays in Contemporary Fields of Economics.* West Lafayette: Purdue University Press.

  1984. "The Pure Theory of Large Two-Candidate Elections." *Public Choice* 44: 7–41.

  1995a. "Is There a Problem with Public Goods Provision?" In John Kagel and Alvin Roth, eds., *The Handbook of Experimental Economics.* Princeton: Princeton University Press, 777–94.

  1995b. "Public Goods: A Survey of Experimental Research." In A. L. Roth and J. Kagel, eds., *The Handbook of Experimental Economics.* Princeton: Princeton University Press.

Lee, D. R., and Robert D. Tollison. 1988. "Optimal Taxation in a Rent-Seeking Environment." In Charles K. Rowley, Robert D. Tollison, and Gordon Tullock, eds., *The Political Economy of Rent-Seeking.* Boston: Kluwer, 339–50.

Leff, Nathaniel H. 1988. "Policy Research for Improved Organizational Performance." *Journal of Economic Behavior and Organization* 9: 393–403.

Lewis, David K. 1969. *Convention.* Cambridge, Mass.: Harvard University Press.

Leys, C., and P. Robson, eds. 1965. *Federation in East Africa: Opportunities and Problems.* New York: Oxford University Press.

Liang, J., and Alan H. Meltzer. 1993. "A Rational Theory of Income Inequality and the Size of Government in a Dynamic Model of Kuznet's Hypothesis." Unpublished manuscript.

Libecap, Gary D. 1989. "Distributional Issues in Contracting for Property Rights." *Journal of Institutional and Theoretical Economics* 145: 6–24.

Libecap, Gary D., and Steven N. Wiggins. 1984. "Contractual Responses to the Common Pool: Prorationing of Crude Oil Production." *American Economic Review* 74: 87–98.

Lichtman, Alan J. 1979. *Prejudice and the Old Politics: The Presidential Election of 1928.* Chapel Hill: University of North Carolina Press.

Lijphart, Arend. 1984. *Democracies.* New Haven: Yale University Press.

1986. "Degrees of Proportionality of Proportional Representation Formulas." *Electoral Laws and Their Political Consequences.* New York: Spartan Press, 170–9.

1990. "The Political Consequences of Electoral Laws, 1945–85." *American Political Science Review* 84: 481–96.

Lindahl, Erik. [1919] 1958. Excerpt from *Die Gerechtigkeit der Besteuerung.* Lund. Translated as "Just Taxation – A Positive Solution." In Richard A. Musgrave and Alan T. Peacock, eds., *Classics in the Theory of Public Finance.* London: Macmillan, 168–76.

Lindbeck, Assar. 1975. "Business Cycles, Politics and International Economic Dependence." *Skandinaviska Enskilda Banken Quarterly Review,* 53–68.

1976. "Stabilization Policy in Open Economies With Endogenous Politicians." Seminar paper no.54, Institute for International Economic Studies, University of Stockholm.

1977. *The Political Economy of the New Left: An Outsider's View.* New York: Harper and Row.

1985. "Redistribution Policy and Expansion of the Public Sector." *Journal of Public Economics* 28: 309–28.

1986. "Limits to the Welfare State." *Challenge* 28: 31–45.

1989. "Policy Autonomy vs Policy Coordination in the World Economy." In Hans Tson Soderstrom, ed., *One Global Market.* SNS: Center for Business and Policy Studies.

Lindblom, Charles E. 1959. "The Science of Muddling Through." *Public Administration Review* 19:79–88.

Litvack, J. 1994. "Regional Demands and Fiscal Federalism." In C. Wallich, ed., *Russia and the Challenge of Fiscal Federalism.* Washington, D.C.: World Bank, 218–40.

Lockerbie, Brad. 1991. "The Temporal Pattern of Economic Evaluations and Vote Choice in Senate Elections." *Public Choice* 69: 279–94.

Lohmann, S. 1993. "Information, Access and Contributions: A Signaling Model of Lobbying." Working paper, GSB, Stanford University.

Lucas, Robert, and Nancy Stokey. 1983. "Optimal Fiscal and Monetary Policy in an Economy without Capital." *Journal of Monetary Economics* 12: 55–94.

Luce, R. Duncan, and Howard W. Raiffa. 1957. *Games and Decisions.* New York: John Wiley.

Lupia, Arthur. 1992. "Busy Voters, Agenda Control, and the Power of Information." *American Political Science Review* 86: 390–403.

Lupia, Arthur, and Mathew McCubbins. 1994. "Designing Bureaucratic Accountability." *Law and Contemporary Problems* 57 (Winter): 91–126.

Lybeck, Johan A. 1986. *The Growth of Government in Developed Economies.* Aldershot: Gower Press.

Lybeck, Johan A., and Magnus Henrekson. 1988a. *Explaining the Growth of Government.* Amsterdam: Elsevier Science Publishers.

eds. 1988b. *The Expansion of the Public Sectors in the West.* North–Holland: Amsterdam.

MacCraken, P. Report. 1977. *Towards Full Employment and Price Stability.* Paris: OECD.

Mackay, Robert J., and Carolyn L. Weaver. 1979. "On the Mutuality of Interest between Bureaus and High Demand Review Committees: A Perverse Result." *Public Choice* 34: 481–91.

1981. "Agenda Control by Budget Maximizers in a Multi-Bureau Setting." *Public Choice* 37: 447–72.

MacKuen, Michael B. 1981. "Social Communication and the Mass Political Agenda." In Michael B. MacKuen and Steven Coombs, eds., *More Than News: Media Power in Public Affairs.* Beverly Hills: Sage, 19–44.

MacKuen, Michael B., Robert S. Erikson, and James A. Stimson. 1989. "Macropartisanship." *American Political Science Review* 83: 1125–42.

MacRae, C. Duncan. 1977. "A Political Model of the Business Cycle." *Journal of Political Economy* 85: 239–63.

Magee, Stephen P. 1972. "The Welfare Effects of Restrictions on U.S. Trade." *Brookings Papers on Economic Activity*, no.3: 645–701.

——— 1980. "Three Simple Tests of the Stolper–Samuelson Theorem." In Peter Oppenheimer, ed., *Issues in International Economics*. London: Oriel Press, 138–53.

——— 1990. "International Estimates of Rent Seeking as a Transaction Cost of Democracy and the Tylenol Tariff." University of Chicago. Mimeo.

——— 1992. "The Optimum Number of Lawyers: A Reply to Epp." *Law and Social Inquiry* 17: 667–93.

——— 1993. "Bioeconomics and the Survival Model: The Economic Lessons of Evolutionary Biology." *Public Choice* 77: 117–32.

Magee, Stephen P., William A. Brock, and Leslie Young. 1989. *Black Hole Tariffs and Endogenous Policy Theory: Political Economy in General Equilibrium.* Cambridge University Press.

Magee, Stephen P., and Frances T. Magee. Forthcoming. *A Plague of Lawyers.* New York: Warner Books.

Magee, Stephen P., and Leslie Young. 1983. "Multinationals, Tariffs and Capital Flows with Endogenous Politicians." In Charles P. Kindleberger and David Audretsch, eds., *The Multinational Corporation in the 1980s.* Cambridge: MIT Press, 21–37.

Mailath, George J., and Andrew Postlewaite. 1990. "Asymmetric Information Bargaining Problems with Many Agents." *Review of Economic Studies* 57: 351–67.

Malinvaud, E. 1971. "A Planning Approach to the Public Good Problem." *Swedish Journal of Economics* 73: 96–112.

Maloney, Kevin J., and Michael L. Smirlock. 1981. "Business Cycles and the Political Process." *Southern Economic Journal* 48: 377–92.

Mankiw, N. Gregory. 1987. "The Optimal Collection of Seigniorage: Theory and Evidence." *Journal of Monetary Economics* 20: 327–41.

March, James G., and Herbert A. Simon. 1957. *Organizations.* New York: John Wiley and Sons.

Margolis, Howard. 1982. "A Thought Experiment on Demand-Revealing Mechanisms." *Public Choice* 38: 87–92.

——— 1983. "A Note on Demand-Revealing." *Public Choice* 40: 217–26.

Marlow, Michael L. 1988. "Fiscal Decentralization and Government Size." *Public Choice* 56: 259–69.

Marshall, Louise. 1991. "New Evidence on Fiscal Illusion: The 1986 Tax 'Windfalls.' " *American Economic Review* 81: 1336–44.

Martin, Cathie J. 1991. *Shifting the Burden: The Struggle over Growth and Corporate Taxation.* Chicago: University of Chicago Press.

Marvel, Howard P., and Edward J. Ray. 1985. "The Kennedy Round: Evidence of the Regulation of International Trade in the United States." *American Economic Review* 75: 190–7.

Marwell, Gerald, and Ruth E. Ames. 1979. "Experiments on the Provision of Public Goods I: Resources, Interest, Group Size, and the Free Rider Problem." *American Journal of Sociology* 84: 335–60.

——— 1980. "Experiments on the Provision of Public Goods II: Provision Points, Stakes, Experience and the Free Rider Problem." *American Journal of Sociology* 85: 926–37.

——— 1981. "Economists Free Ride: Does Anyone Else?" *Journal of Public Economics* 15: 295–310.

Mas-Colell, Andreu, and Hugo F. Sonnenschein. 1972. "General Possibility Theorems for Group Decisions." *Review of Economic Studies* 39: 185–92.

Mashaw, Jerry. 1990. "Explaining Administrative Process: Normative, Positive, and Critical Studies of Legal Development." *Journal of Law, Economics, and Organization* 6: 267–98.

May, Kenneth O. 1952a. "Note on Complete Independence of the Conditions for Simple Majority Decision." *Econometrica* 21: 172–3.

1952b. "A Set of Independent, Necessary and Sufficient Conditions for Simple Majority Decision." *Econometrica* 20: 680–4.

Mayer, Wolfgang. 1984. "Endogenous Tariff Formation." *American Economic Review* 74: 970–85.

Mayer, Wolfgang, and Jun Li. 1994. "Interest Groups, Electoral Competition, and Probabilistic Voting for Trade Policies." *Economics and Politics* 6: 59–78.

Mayer, Wolfgang, and Raymond Riezman. 1990. "Voter Preferences for Trade Policy Instruments." *Economics and Politics* 2: 259–74.

Mayhew, David R. 1966. *Party Loyalty among Congressmen: The Difference between Democrats and Republicans.* Cambridge, Mass.: Harvard University Press.

1974. *Congress: The Electoral Connection.* New Haven: Yale University Press.

Maynard Smith, John. 1982. *Evolution and the Theory of Games.* Cambridge University Press.

McCabe, K. A., S. J. Rassenti, and V. L. Smith. 1991. "Smart Computer-Assisted Markets." *Science* 254: 534–8.

McCallum, Bennett T. 1978. "The Political Business Cycle: An Empirical Test." *Southern Economic Journal* 44: 504–15.

McCallum, John. 1986. "Unemployment in the OECD Countries in the 1980s." *Economic Journal* 96: 942–60.

McCarty, N., and L. Rothenberg. 1993. "The Strategic Decisions of Political Action Committees." Working paper, Department of Political Science, University of Rochester.

McCay, Bonnie J., and James M. Acheson. 1987. *The Question of the Commons: The Culture and Ecology of Communal Resources.* Tucson: University of Arizona Press.

McChesney, F. S. 1987. "Rent Extraction and Interest-Group Formation in a Coasean Model of Regulation." *Journal of Legal Studies* 20: 73–90.

McConnell, M. 1987. "Federalism: Evaluating the Founders' Design." *The University of Chicago Law Review* 54: 1484–512.

McCormick, Robert E., William F. Shughart II, and Robert D. Tollison. 1984. "The Disinterest in Deregulation." *American Economic Review* 74: 1075–9.

McCormick, Robert E., and Robert D. Tollison. 1981. *Politicians, Legislation and the Economy: An Inquiry into the Interest-Group Theory of Government.* Boston: Martinus Nijhoff.

McCubbins, Mathew D. 1985. "The Legislative Design of Regulatory Structure." *American Journal of Political Science* 29: 721–48.

1991. "Party Politics, Divided Government, and Budget Deficits." In Samuel Kernell, ed., *Parallel Politics: Economic Policy Making in the United States and Japan.* Washington D.C.: The Brookings Institution.

McCubbins, Mathew D., and Thomas Schwartz. 1984. "Congressional Oversight Overlooked: Police Patrols Versus Fire Alarms." *American Journal of Political Science* 28: 165–79.

McCubbins, Mathew D., Roger G. Noll, and Barry R. Weingast. 1987. "Administrative

Procedures as Instruments of Political Control." *Journal of Law, Economics, and Organization* 3: 243–77.

1989. "Structure and Process, Politics and Policy: Administrative Arrangements and the Political Control of Agencies." *Virginia Law Review* 75: 431–82.

1992. "Positive Canons: The Role of Legislative Bargains in Statutory Interpretation." *Georgetown Law Journal* 80: 705–42.

1994. "Legislative Intent: The Use of Positive Political Theory in Statutory Interpretation." *Law and Contemporary Problems* 57 (Winter): 3–38.

McGavin, B. H. 1987. "The Political Business Cycle: A Reexamination of Some Empirical Evidence." *Quarterly Journal of Business and Economics* 26: 36–49.

McGinnis, Michael, and Elinor Ostrom. 1996. "Design Principles for Local and Global Commons." In Oran R. Young, ed., *The International Political Economy and International Institutions,* vol. 2. Cheltenham: Edward Elgar: 465–93.

McGuire, Robert A. 1988. "Constitution Making: A Rational Choice Model of the Federal Convention of 1787." *American Journal of Political Science* 32: 483–522.

McGuire, Robert A., and Robert L. Ohsfeldt. 1986. "An Economic Model of Voting Behavior over Specific Issues at the Constitutional Convention of 1787." *Journal of Economic History* 46: 79–111.

McKean, Margaret A. 1992. "Success on the Commons: A Comparative Examination of Institutions for Common Property Resource Management." *Journal of Theoretical Politics* 4: 247–82.

McKee, Michael. 1988. "Political Competition and the Roman Catholic Schools: Ontario, Canada." *Public Choice* 56: 57–67.

McKee, Michael, and Ronald Wintrobe. 1993. "The Decline of Organizations and the Rise of Administrators: Parkinson's Law in Theory and Practice." *Journal of Public Economics* 51: 287–308.

McKelvey, Richard D. 1976. "Intransitivities in Multidimensional Voting Models and Some Implications for Agenda Control." *Journal of Economic Theory* 12: 472–82.

1979. "General Conditions for Global Intransitivities in Formal Voting Models." *Econometrica* 47: 1085–112.

1986. "Covering, Dominance, and Institution-Free Properties of Social Choice." *American Journal of Political Science* 30: 283–314.

McKelvey, Richard D., and Peter C. Ordeshook. 1972. "A General Theory of the Calculus of Voting." In James F. Herndon and Joseph L. Bernd, eds., *Mathematical Applications in Political Science,* vol. 6. Charlottesville: University of Virginia Press.

1976. "Symmetric Spatial Games without Majority Rule Equilibria." *American Political Science Review* 70: 1172–84.

1980. "Vote Trading: An Experimental Study." *Public Choice* 35: 151–84.

1984. "An Experimental Study of the Effects of Procedural Rules on Committee Behavior." *Journal of Politics* 46: 182–205.

1985a. "Elections with Limited Information: A Fulfilled Expectations Model Using Contemporaneous Poll and Endorsement Data as Information Sources." *Journal of Economic Theory* 36: 55–85.

1985b. "Sequential Elections with Limited Information." *American Journal of Political Science* 29: 480–512.

1986. "Information, Elections, and the Democratic Ideal." *Journal of Politics* 48: 909–37.

1990a. "Information and Elections: Retrospective Voting and Rational Expectations." In John Ferejohn and J. Kuklinski, eds., *Information and Democratic Process.* Urbana-Champaign: University of Illinois Press.

1990b. "A Decade of Experimental Research on Spatial Models of Elections and Committees." In James Enelow and Melvin J. Hinich, eds., *Advances in the Spatial Theory of Voting*. Cambridge University Press.

McKelvey, Richard D., Peter C. Ordeshook, and Mark Winer. 1979. "The Competitive Solution for Cooperative Games without Sidepayments." *American Political Science Review*, 72: 599–615.

McKelvey, Richard D., and Thomas Palfrey. 1992. "An Experimental Study of the Centipede Game." *Econometrica* 60: 803–36.

McKelvey, Richard D., and Jeffrey Richelson. 1974. "Cycles of Risk." *Public Choice* 18: 41–66.

McKelvey, Richard D., and Raymond Riezman. 1991. "Seniority in Legislatures." *American Political Science Review* 86: 951–65.

McKelvey, Richard D., and Norman Schofield. 1986. "Structural Instability of the Core." *Journal of Mathematical Economics* 15: 179–98.

1987. "Generalized Symmetry Conditions at a Core Point." *Econometrica* 55: 923–33.

McKeown, Timothy J. 1983. "Hegemonic Stability Theory and 19th Century Tariff Levels in Europe." *International Organization* 37: 73–91.

Meltzer, Allan H., A. Cukierman, and Scott F. Richard. 1991. *Political Economy*. New York and Oxford: Oxford University Press.

Meltzer, Allan H., and Scott F. Richard. 1978. "Why Government Grows (and Grows) in a Democracy?" *Public Interest* 52: 111–18.

1981. "A Rational Theory of the Size of Government." *Journal of Political Economy* 89: 914–27.

1983. "Tests of a Rational Theory of the Size of Government." *Public Choice* 41: 403–18.

Merriam, Charles E., and Howard F. Gosnell. 1924. *Non-Voting, Causes and Methods of Control*. Chicago: University of Chicago Press.

Merritt, D. J. 1988. "The Guarantee Clause and State Autonomy: Federalism for a Third Century." *Columbia Law Journal* 88: 1–52.

Messerlin, Patrick A. 1981. "The Political Economy of Protectionism: The Bureaucratic Case." *Weltwirtschaftliches Archiv* 117: 469–95.

Metcalf, Gilbert E. 1993. "Tax Exporting, Federal Deductibility and State Tax Structure." *Journal of Policy Analysis and Management* 12: 109–26.

Michaely, Michael, Demetris Papageorgiou, and Armeane M. Choksi, eds. 1991. *Liberalizing Foreign Trade*. Vol.7, Lessons of Experience in the Developing World. Cambridge: Basil Blackwell.

Migué, Jean-Luc, and Gerard Bélanger. 1974. "Toward a General Theory of Managerial Discretion." *Public Choice* 17: 27–43.

Milbrath, L. 1963. *The Washington Lobbyists*. Chicago: Rand McNally.

Milgram, Stanley. 1974. *Obedience to Authority: An Experimental View*. New York: Harper and Row.

Milgrom, Paul R., and John Roberts. 1988. "Employment Contracts, Influence Activities, and Efficient Organization Design." *Journal of Political Economy* 96: 42–60.

1992. *Economics, Organization, and Management*. New York: Prentice-Hall.

Mill, John Stuart. [1848] 1965. *Principles of Politial Economy*. Ed. John M. Robson. Toronto: University of Toronto Press.

Miller, Gary. 1992. *Managerial Dilemmas*. Cambridge University Press.

Miller, Gary J., and Terry M. Moe. 1983. "Bureaucrats, Legislators, and the Size of Government." *American Political Science Review* 77: 297–322.

Miller, John, and James Andreoni. 1991. "A Coevolutionary Model of Free-Riding Behavior: Replicator Dynamics as an Explanation of the Experimental Results." *Economics Letters* 36: 9–15.

632   **References**

Miller, Nicholas R. 1980. "A New Solution Set for Tournaments and Majority Voting." *American Journal of Political Science* 24: 68–96.

1983. "Pluralism and Social Choice." *American Political Science Review* 21: 769–803.

1994. *Committees, Agendas, and Voting.* Chur: Harwood Academic Publishers.

Miller, Nicholas R., Bernard Grofman, and Scott F. Feld. 1989. "The Geometry of Majority Rule." *Journal of Theoretical Politics* 4: 379–406.

Miller, Warren. 1955–6. "Presidential Coattails: A Study in Political Myth and Methodology." *Public Opinion Quarterly* 19: 353–68.

Minford, Patrick, and David Peel. 1982. "The Political Theory of the Business Cycle." *European Economic Review* 17: 253–70.

Mitchell, William C. 1984a. "Schumpeter and Public Choice, Part I: Precursor of Public Choice?" *Public Choice* 42: 73–88.

1984b. "Schumpeter and Public Choice, Part II: Democracy and the Demise of Capitalism: The Missing Chapter in Schumpeter." *Public Choice* 42: 161–74.

1988. "Virginia, Rochester, and Bloomington: Twenty-Five Years of Public Choice and Political Science." *Public Choice* 56: 101–19.

Mitchell, W., and Michael C. Munger. 1991. "Economic Models of Interest Groups: An Introductory Survey." *American Journal of Political Science* 35: 512–46.

Moe, Terry M. 1981. *The Organization of Interests.* Chicago: University of Chicago Press.

1984. "The New Economics of Organization." *American Journal of Political Science* 28: 739–77.

1987. "An Assessment of the Positive Theory of 'Congressional Dominance.' " *Legislative Studies Quarterly* 12: 475–520.

1989. "The Politics of Bureaucratic Structure." In John E. Chubb, and Paul E. Peterson, eds., *Can the Government Govern?* Washington, D.C.: The Brookings Institution.

1990a. "The Politics of Structural Choice: Toward a Theory of Public Bureaucracy." In Oliver E. Williamson, ed., *Organization Theory: From Chester Barnard to the Present and Beyond.* New York: Oxford University Press.

1990b. "Political Institutions: The Neglected Side of the Story." *Journal of Law, Economics, and Organization* 6: 213–53.

1991. "Politics and the Theory of Organization." *Journal of Law, Economics, and Organization* 7: 106–29.

Moe, Terry M., and Michael Caldwell. 1994. "The Institutional Foundations of Democratic Government: A Comparison of Presidential and Parliamentary Systems." *Journal of Institutional and Theoretical Economics* 150: 171–95.

Moe, Terry M., and Scott Wilson. 1994. "Presidents and the Politics of Structure." *Law and Contemporary Problems* 57 (Spring): 1–44.

Mohammed, Sharif, and John Whalley. 1984. "Rent Seeking in India: Its Costs and Policy Significance." *Kyklos* 37: 387–413.

Moomau, Pamela H., and Rebecca B. Morton. 1992. "Revealed Preferences for Property Taxes: An Empirical Study of Perceived Tax Incidence." *Review of Economics and Statistics* 74: 176–9.

Morton, B. 1987. "A Group Majority Voting Model of Public Good Provision." *Social Choice and Welfare* 4(2): 117–31.

Morton, Rebecca, and Charles Cameron. 1992. "Elections and the Theory of Campaign Contributions: A Survey and Critical Analysis." *Economics and Politics* 4: 79–108.

Morton, Rebecca, and Roger B. Myerson. 1993. "Campaign Spending with Impressionable Voters." Working paper, MEDS, Northwestern University.

Moser, Peter. 1990. *The Political Economy of the GATT.* Grüsch: Rüegger.

Mueller, Dennis C. 1967. "The Possibility of a Social Welfare Function: Comment." *American Economic Review* 57: 1304–11.

1973. "Constitutional Democracy and Social Welfare." *Quarterly Journal of Economics* 87: 60–80.

1978. "Voting by Veto." *Journal of Public Economics* 10: 57–75.

1982. "Redistribution, Growth, and Political Stability." *American Economic Review* 72: 155–9.

1984. "Voting by Veto and Majority Rule." In Horst Hanusch, ed., *Public Finance and the Quest for Efficiency.* Detroit: Wayne State University Press, 69–85.

1989. *Public Choice II: A Revised Edition of Public Choice.* Cambridge University Press.

1990. "Public Choice and the Consumption Tax." In Manfred Rose, ed., *Heidelberg Conference on Taxing Consumption.* Heidelberg: Springer, 227–46.

1991. "Constitutional Rights." *Journal of Law, Economics and Organization* 7: 313–33.

1996. *Constitutional Democracy.* New York: Oxford University Press.

Mueller, Dennis C., and Peter Murrell. 1985. "Interest Groups and the Political Economy of Government Size." In Francesco Forte and Alan Peacock, eds., *Public Expenditure and Government Growth.* Oxford: Basil Blackwell, 13–36.

1986. "Interest Groups and the Size of Governments." *Public Choice* 48: 125–45.

Mueller, Dennis C., Geoffrey C. Philpotts, and Jaroslav Vanek. 1972. "The Social Gains from Exchanging Votes: A Simulation Approach." *Public Choice* 13: 55–79.

Mueller, J. E. 1970. "Presidential Popularity from Truman to Johnson." *American Political Science Review* 64: 18–34.

Mundell, Robert A. 1962. "Review of L. H. Janssen: Free Trade, Protection and Customs Unions." *American Economic Review* 52: 622.

Murphy, Kevin M., Andrei Schleifer, and Robert W. Vishny. 1991. "The Allocation of Talent: Implications for Growth." *Quarterly Journal of Economics* 106: 503–31.

Murrell, Peter. 1984. "An Examination of the Factors Affecting the Formation of Interest Groups in OECD Countries." *Public Choice* 43: 151–71.

Musgrave, Richard A. 1959. *The Theory of Public Finance.* New York: McGraw–Hill.

Myerson, Roger, and Shlomo Weber. 1993. "A Theory of Voting Equilibria." *American Political Science Review* 87: 102–14.

Naert, Frank. 1990. "Pressure Politics and Government Spending in Belgium." *Public Choice* 67: 49–63.

Nannestad, Peter, and Martin Paldam. 1994. "The VP-Function. A Survey of the Literature on Vote and Popularity Functions." *Public Choice* 79: 213–45.

National Research Council. 1986. *Proceedings of the Conference on Common Property Resource Management.* Washington, D.C.: National Academy Press.

Neary, J. Peter. 1978. "Short-Run Capital Specificity and the Pure Theory of International Trade." *Economic Journal* 88: 488–510.

Neck, Reinhard. 1991. "The Political Business Cycle under a Quadratic Objective Function." *European Journal of Political Economy* 7: 439–67.

Nelson, Douglas A. 1988. "Endogenous Tariff Theory: A Critical Survey." *American Journal of Political Science* 32: 796–837.

1992. "Municipal Amalgamation and the Growth of the Local Public Sector in Sweden." *Journal of Regional Science* 32: 39–53.

Nelson, Douglas A., and Eugene Silberberg. 1987. "Ideology and Legislator Shirking." *Economic Inquiry* 25: 15–26.

Nelson, Michael A. 1987. "Searching for Leviathan: Comment and Extension." *American Economic Review* 77: 198–204.

Netting, Robert. 1993. *Smallholders, Householders: Farm Families and the Ecology of Intensive, Sustainable Agriculture.* Stanford: Stanford University Press.

Neumann von, John, and Oskar Morgenstern. 1953. *The Theory of Games and Economic Behavior.* 3rd ed. Princeton: Princeton University Press.

Nie, Norman H., Sidney Verba, and John Petrocik. 1976. *The Changing American Voter.* Cambridge, Mass.: Harvard University Press.

Niemi, Richard G. 1983. "Why so Much Stability?: Another Opinion." *Public Choice* 41: 261–70.

Niemi, Richard G., G. Bingham Powell, Jr., Harold W. Stanley, and C. Lawrence Evans. 1985. "Testing the Converse Partisanship Model with New Electorates." *Comparative Political Studies* 18: 300–22.

Niemi, Richard G., and Herbert F. Weisberg. 1968. "A Mathematical Solution for the Probability of the Paradox of Voting." *Behavioral Science* 13: 317–23.

Niou, Emerson M. S., and Peter C. Ordeshook. 1985. "Universalism in Congress." *American Journal of Political Science* 29: 246–60.

1990. "Stability in Anarchic International Systems." *American Political Science Review* 84: 1207–34.

1994. "Alliances in Anarchic Systems." *International Studies Quarterly* 38: 167–91.

Niskanen, William A. 1968. "The Peculiar Economics of Bureaucracy." *American Economic Review Papers and Proceedings* 58: 293–305.

1971. *Bureaucracy and Representative Government.* New York: Aldine–Atherton.

1975. "Bureaucrats and Politicians." *Journal of Law and Economics* 18: 617–44.

1978. "Deficits, Government Spending and Inflation: What is the Evidence?" *Journal of Monetary Economics* 4: 591–602.

1991. "A Reflection on Bureaucracy and Representative Government." In Andre Blais and Stephan Dion, eds., *The Budget-Maximizing Bureaucrat.* Pittsburgh: University of Pittsburgh Press, 13–32.

Nitzan, Shmuel, and Jacob Paroush. 1982. "Optimal Decision Rules in Uncertain Dichotomous Situations." *International Economic Review* 23: 289–97.

Nixon, David, Dgamit Olomoki, Norman Schofield, and Itai Sened. 1995. "Multiparty Probabilistic Voting: An Application to the Knesset." Center in Political Economy, Washington University. Typescript.

Noll, Roger G. 1989. "Economic Perspectives on the Politics of Regulation." In Richard Schmalensee and Robert D. Willig, eds., *Handbook of Industrial Organization,* vol. 2. Amsterdam: North–Holland, 1254–87.

Nordhaus, William D. 1975. "The Political Business Cycle." *Review of Economic Studies* 42: 169–90.

1989. "Alternative Approaches to the Political Business Cycle." *Brookings Papers on Economic Activity,* no. 2: 1–68.

North, Douglass C. 1981. *Structure and Change in Economic History.* New York: Norton.

1984. "Government and the Cost of Exchange." *Journal of Economic History* 44: 255–64.

1985a. "The Growth of Government in the United States: An Economic Historian's Perspective." *Journal of Public Economics* 28: 383–99.

1985b. "Transaction Cost in History." *Journal of European Economic History* 14: 557–76.

1990. *Institutions, Institutional Change and Economic Performance.* Cambridge University Press.

North, Douglass C., and R. P. Thomas. 1973. *The Rise of the Western World: A New Economic History.* Cambridge University Press.

North, Douglass C., and John J. Wallis. 1982. "American Government Expenditures: A Historical Perspective." *American Economic Review* 72: 336–45.

1986. "Measuring the Transaction Sector in the American Economy, 1870–1890." In S. L. Engerman and R. E. Gallman, eds., *Long-Term Factors in American Economic Growth*. Chicago: University of Chicago Press.

Nozick, Robert. 1974. *Anarchy, the State, and Utopia*. New York: Basic Books.

Oates, Wallace E. 1972. *Fiscal Federalism*. New York: Harcourt, Brace and Jovanovich.

1977. "On the Use of Local Zoning Ordinances to Regulate Population Flows and the Quality of Local Services." In Orley Ashenfelter and Wallace Oates, eds., *Essays in Labor Market Analysis*. New York: John Wiley and Sons, 201–19.

1981. "On Local Finance and the Tiebout Model." *American Economic Review* 71: 93–8.

1985. "Searching for Leviathan: An Empirical Study." *American Economic Review* 75: 748–57.

1988. "On the Nature and Measurement of Fiscal Illusion: A Survey." In Geoffrey Brennan, ed., *Taxation and Fiscal Federalism: Essays in Honor of Russell Mathews*. Sydney: Australian National University Press.

1989. "Searching for Leviathan: A Reply and Some Further Reflections." *American Economic Review* 79: 578–83.

Oates, Wallace E., and Robert Schwab. 1988. "Economic Competition among Jurisdictions: Efficiency Enhancing or Distortion Inducing?" *Journal of Public Economics* 35: 333–54.

O'Flaherty, Brendan. 1990. "Why are There Democracies? A Principal Agent Answer." *Economics and Politics* 2: 133–55.

Oliver, Pamela. 1980. "Rewards and Punishments as Selective Incentives for Collective Action: Theoretical Investigations." *American Journal of Sociology* 85: 356–75.

Olson, Mancur, Jr. 1965. *The Logic of Collective Action: Public Goods and the Theory of Groups*. Cambridge, Mass.: Harvard University Press.

1969. "The Principle of Fiscal Equivalence." *American Economic Review* 59: 479–87.

1971. "Increasing the Incentives for International Cooperation." *International Organization* 25: 866–74.

1982. *The Rise and Decline of Nations: Economic Growth, Stagflation and Social Rigidities*. New Haven: Yale University Press.

Olson, Mancur, and Richard Zeckhauser. 1966. "An Economic Theory of Alliances." *Review of Economics and Statistics* 48: 266–79.

Oppenheimer, J. A. 1975. "Some Political Implications of 'Vote Trading and Voting Paradox: A Proof of Logical Equivalence': A Comment." *American Political Science Review* 69: 963–6.

Orbell, John M., Robyn M. Dawes, and Alphons van de Kragt. 1990. "The Limits of Multilateral Promising." *Ethics* 100: 616–27.

Orbell, John M., Alphons van de Kragt, and Robyn M. Dawes. 1988. "Explaining Discussion-Induced Cooperation." *Journal of Personality and Social Psychology* 54: 811–19.

1991. "Covenants without the Sword: The Role of Promises in Social Dilemma Circumstances." In Kenneth J. Koford and Jeffrey B. Miller, eds., *Social Norms and Economic Institutions*. Ann Arbor: University of Michigan Press, 117–34.

Ordeshook, Peter C. 1970. "Extensions to a Mathematical Model of the Electoral Process and Implications for the Theory of Responsible Parties." *Midwest Journal of Political Science* 14: 43–70.

1976. "The Spatial Theory of Elections: A Review and Critique." In Ian Budge, Ivor

Crewe, and Dennis Farlie, eds., *Party Identification and Beyond.* London: John Wiley and Sons.

1986. *Game Theory and Political Theory: An Introduction.* Cambridge University Press.

1992. "Constitutional Stability." *Constitutional Political Economy* 3: 137–75.

Ordeshook, Peter C., and Thomas Schwartz. 1987. "Agendas and the Control of Political Outcomes." *American Political Science Review* 81: 179–99.

Ordeshook, Peter C., and Mark Winer. 1980. "Coalitions and Spatial Policy Outcomes in Parliamentary Systems: Some Experimental Results." *American Journal of Political Science* 24: 730–52.

Osborne, Martin J. 1993. "Spatial Models of Political Competition under Plurality Rule: A Survey of Some Explanations of the Number of Candidates and the Positions They Take." Working paper, Department of Economics, McMaster University.

Osborne, Martin J., and Al Slivinski. 1993. "A Model of Political Competition with Citizen-Candidates." Working paper, Department of Economics, McMaster University.

Ostrom, Elinor. 1990. *Governing the Commons: The Evolution of Institutions for Collective Action.* Cambridge University Press.

1992. *Crafting Institutions for Self-Governing Irrigation Systems.* San Francisco: Institute for Contemporary Studies Press.

Ostrom, Elinor, and Roy Gardner. 1993. "Coping with Asymmetries in the Commons: Self-Governing Irrigation Systems Can Work." *Journal of Economic Perspectives* 7: 93–112.

Ostrom, Elinor, Roy Gardner, and James M. Walker. 1994. *Rules, Games, and Common-Pool Resources.* Ann Arbor: University of Michigan Press.

Ostrom, Elinor, Larry Schroeder, and Susan Wynne. 1993. *Institutional Incentives and Sustainable Development: Infrastructure Policies in Perspective.* Boulder, CO: Westview Press.

Ostrom, Elinor, and James M. Walker. 1991. "Communication in a Commons: Cooperation without External Enforcement." In Thomas R. Palfrey, ed., *Laboratory Research in Political Economy.* Ann Arbor: University of Michigan Press, 287–322.

Ostrom, Elinor, James M. Walker, and Roy Gardner. 1992. "Covenants with and without a Sword: Self-Governance is Possible." *American Political Science Review* 86: 404–17.

Ostrom, Vincent. 1968. "Water Resource Development: Some Problems in Economic and Political Analysis of Public Policy." In Austin Ranney, ed., *Political Science and Public Policy.* Chicago: Markham.

1969. "Operational Federalism: Organization for the Provision of Public Services in the American Federal System." *Public Choice* 6: 1–17.

1973. *The Intellectual Crisis of Public Administration.* Alabama: University of Alabama Press.

1980. "Artisanship and Artifact." *Public Administration Review* 40: 309–17.

1984. "Why Governments Fail: An Inquiry into the Use of Instruments of Evil to do Good." In James M. Buchanan and Robert D. Tollison, eds., *The Theory of Public Choice-II.* Ann Arbor: University of Michigan Press, 422–35.

1991. *The Meaning of American Federalism: Constituting a Self-Governing Society.* San Francisco: Institute for Contemporary Studies Press.

1993. "Cryptoimperialism, Predatory States, and Self-Governance." In Vincent Ostrom, David Feeny, and Hartmut Picht, eds., *Rethinking Institutional Analysis and Development: Issues, Alternatives, and Choices.* San Francisco: Institute for Contemporary Studies Press, 43–68.

Forthcoming. *The Meaning of Democracy: The Vulnerability of Democracies.* Ann Arbor: University of Michigan Press.

Ostrom, Vincent, David Feeny, and Hartmut Picht, eds. 1993. *Rethinking Institutional Analysis and Development: Issues, Alternatives, and Choices.* 2nd ed. San Francisco: Institute for Contemporary Studies Press.

Ostrom, Vincent, and Elinor Ostrom. 1977. "Public Goods and Public Choices." In E. S. Savas, ed., *Alternatives for Delivering Public Services: Toward Improved Performance.* Boulder, CO: Westview Press.

Ostrom, Vincent, Charles Tiebout, and Robert Warren. 1961. "The Organization of Government in Metropolitan Areas: A Theoretical Inquiry." *American Political Science Review* 55: 831–42.

Pack Rothenberg, Janet. 1987. "The Political Policy Cycle: Presidential Effort vs. Presidential Control." *Public Choice* 54: 231–59.

Page, Benjamin I., and Calvin C. Jones. 1979. "Reciprocal Effects of Policy Preference, Party Loyalties, and the Vote." *American Political Science Review* 73: 1071–89.

Page, Benjamin I., and Robert Y. Shapiro. 1992. *The Rational Public: Fifty Years of Trends in Americans' Policy Preferences.* Chicago: University of Chicago Press.

Paldam, Martin. 1979. "Is There an Electional Cycle? A Comparative Study of National Accounts." *Scandinavian Journal of Economics* 81: 323–42.

　1981. "An Essay on the Rationality of Economic Policy – The Test-Case of the Electional Cycle." *Public Choice* 36: 43–60.

　1982. "Political Business Cycles on the Labour Market – Aspects of the Dynamic Wage Relation." In K. R. Monroe, ed., *The Political Process and Economic Change.* New York: Agathon Press.

　1983. "Industrial Conflicts and Economic Conditions – A Comparative Empirical Investigation." *European Economic Review* 20: 231–56.

　1991a. "Macroeconomic Stabilization Policy: Does Politics Matter?" In A. L. Hillman, ed., *Markets and Politicians. Politicized Economic Change.* Boston and Dordrecht: Kluwer.

　1991b. "Politics Matters after All. Testing of Alesina's Theory of Partisan Cycles on Data from 17 Countries." In N. Thygesen, K. Velupillai, and E.M. Zampelli, eds., *Business Cycles: Theories, Evidence and Analysis.* IEA Conference, vol. 97. London: MacMillan; New York: New York University Press.

Paldam, Martin, and Peder J. Pedersen. 1982. "The Macroeconomic Strike Model: A Study of Seventeen Countries, 1948–75." *Industrial and Labor Relations Review* 35: 504–21.

Palfrey, Thomas R. 1984. "Spatial Equilibrium with Entry." *Review of Economic Studies* 51: 139–56.

　1989. "A Mathematical Proof of Duverger's Law." In Peter C. Ordeshook, ed., *Models of Strategic Choice in Politics.* Ann Arbor: University of Michigan Press.

Palfrey, Thomas R., and Jeffrey E. Prisby. 1993. "Anomalous Behavior in Linear Public Goods Experiments: How Much and Why?" Social science working paper, no. 833, California Institute of Technology.

Palfrey, Thomas R., and Howard Rosenthal. 1983. "A Strategic Calculus of Voting." *Public Choice* 44: 7–41.

　1984. "Participation and the Provision of Discrete Public Goods: A Strategic Analysis." *Journal of Public Economics* 24: 171–93.

　1985. "Voter Participation and Strategic Uncertainty." *American Political Science Review* 79: 62–78.

　1988. "Private Incentives in Social Dilemmas." *Journal of Public Economics* 35: 309–32.

Park, R. E. 1967. "The Possibility of a Social Welfare Function: Comment." *American Economic Review* 57: 1300–4.

Parkinson, C. Northcoate. 1957. *Parkinson's Law and Other Studies in Administration.* Boston: Houghton Mifflin.

Parks, Robert P. 1976. "An Impossibility Theorem for Fixed Preferences: A Dictatorial Bergson–Samuelson Welfare Function." *Review of Economic Studies* 43: 447–50.

Pateman, C. 1976. *Participation and Democratic Theory.* Cambridge University Press.

Pattanaik, Prasanta K., and Bezalel Peleg. 1986. "Distribution of Power under Stochastic Social Choice Rules." *Econometrica* 54: 909–21.

Patterson, Samuel C., and Gregory A. Caldiera. 1983. "Getting Out the Vote: Participation in Gubernatorial Elections." *American Political Science Review* 77: 675–89.

Patterson, Thomas E. 1993. *Out of Order.* New York: Alfred A. Knopf.

Patterson, Thomas E., and Robert D. McClure. 1976. *The Unseeing Eye: The Myth of Television Power in National Elections.* New York: Putnam.

Pauly, Mark V. 1970. "Optimality, 'Public Goods,' and Local Governments: A General Theoretical Analysis." *Journal of Political Economy* 78: 572–85.

  "Income Redistribution as a Local Public Good." *Journal of Public Economics* 2: 35–58.

Peacock, Allan. 1992. *Public Choice Analysis in Historical Perspective.* Cambridge University Press.

Peck, Richard M. 1986. "Power and Linear Income Taxes: An Example" *Econometrica* 54: 87–94.

Peltzman, Sam. 1976. "Toward a More General Theory of Regulation." *Journal of Law and Economics* 19: 211–40.

  1980. "The Growth of Government." *Journal of Law and Economics* 23: 209–87.

  1984. "Constituent Interest and Congressional Voting." *Journal of Law and Economics* 27: 181–210.

Perkins, George M. 1977. "The Demand for Local Public Goods: Elasticities of Demand for Own Price, Cross Prices and Income." *National Tax Journal* 30: 411–22.

Persson, Torsten, and Lars E. O. Svenson. 1989. "Why a Stubborn Conservative Would Run a Deficit: Policy with Time-Inconsistent Preferences." *Quarterly Journal of Economics* 104: 325–45.

Persson, Torsten, and Guido Tabellini. 1990. *Macroeconomic Policy, Credibility and Politics.* Harwood Academic Publishers.

Phelps, Edmund S. 1967. "Phillips-Curves, Expectations of Inflation and Optimal Unemployment over Time." *Economica* 34: 254–81.

Phillips, A. W. 1958. "The Relation between Unemployment and the Rate of Change of Money Wage Rates in the United Kingdom, 1861–1957." *Economica* 25: 283–99.

Philpotts, Geoffrey. 1972. "Vote Trading, Welfare, and Uncertainty." *Canadian Journal of Economics* 5: 358–72.

Peirce, William S. 1991a. "After 1992: The European Community and the Redistribution of Rents." *Kyklos* 44: 521–36.

  1991b. "Unanimous Decisions in the Redistributive Context: The Council of Ministry of the European Communities." In Roland Vaubel and Thomas D. Willett, eds., *The Political Economy of International Organizations: A Public Choice Approach.* Boulder, CO: Westview Press, 267–85.

Pierce, John C. 1970. "Party Identification and the Changing Role of Ideology in American Politics." *Midwest Journal of Political Science* 14: 25–42.

Pincus, J. 1975. "Pressure Groups and the Pattern of Tariffs." *Journal of Political Economy* 83: 757–78.

Pinkerton, Evelyn, ed. 1989. *Co-Operative Management of Local Fisheries: New Direc-*

tions for Improved Management and Community Development. Vancouver: University of British Columbia Press.

Plott, Charles R. 1967. "A Notion of Equilibrium and its Possibility under Majority Rule. *American Economic Review* 57: 787–806.

——— 1973. "Path Independence, Rationality and Social Choice Theory." *Econometrica* 41: 1075–91.

——— 1991. "A Comparative Analysis of Direct Democracy, Two-Candidate Elections, and Three-Candidate Elections in an Experimental Environment." In Thomas R. Palfrey, ed., *Contemporary Laboratory Research in Political Economy.* Ann Arbor: University of Michigan Press.

Plott, Charles R., and Robert A. Meyer. 1975. "The Technology of Public Goods, Externalities, and the Exclusion Principle." In Edwin S. Mills, ed., *Economic Analysis of Environmental Problems.* New York: Columbia University Press, 65–94.

Poisson, S.-D. 1837. *Recherches sur la probabilite des jugements en matiere criminale at en matiere civile, precedees des regles generale du calcul des probabilites.* Paris: Bachelier.

Pommerehne, Werner W. 1978. "Institutional Approaches to Public Expenditures: Empirical Evidence from Swiss Municipalities." *Journal of Public Economics* 9: 163–201.

Pommerehne, Werner W., and Friedrich Schneider. 1983. "Does Government in a Representative Democracy Follow a Majority of Voters' Preferences? – An Empirical Examination." In Horst Hannusch, ed., *Anatomy of Government Deficiencies.* Heidelberg: Springer, 61–84.

Pomper, Gerald M. 1972. "From Confusion to Clarity: Issues and American Voters, 1956–1968." *The American Political Science Review* 66: 415–28.

Poole, Keith T., and Thomas Romer. 1985. "Patterns of PAC Contributions to the 1980 Campaigns for the US House of Representatives." *Public Choice* 47: 63–112.

Poole, Keith T., Thomas Romer, and Howard Rosenthal. 1987. "The Revealed Preferences of Political Action Committees." *American Economic Review* 77: 298–302.

Poole, Keith T., and Howard Rosenthal. 1984. "U.S. Presidential Elections 1968–1980: A Spatial Analysis." *American Journal of Political Science* 28: 282–312.

——— 1985. "A Spatial Model for Legislative Roll Call Analysis." *American Journal of Political Science* 29: 357–84.

——— 1991. "Patterns of Congressional Voting." *American Journal of Political Science* 35: 228–78.

Popitz, J. 1927. "Finanzwirtschaft der öffentlichen Körperschaften." *Handbuch der Finanzwissenschaft* 2: 338–75.

Popkin, Samuel L. 1991. *The Reasoning Voter.* Chicago: University of Chicago Press.

Popkin, Samuel L., John W. Gorman, Charles Phillips, and Jeffrey A. Smith. 1976. "Comment: What Have You Done for Me Lately? Toward an Investment Theory of Voting." *American Political Science Review* 70: 779–805.

Popper, Karl. 1945. *The Open Society and Its Enemies.* London: Routledge.

——— 1988. "The Open Society and Its Enemies Revisited." *The Economist* 307: 19–22.

Portney, Paul R. 1994. "The Contingent Valuation Debate: Why Economists Should Care." *Journal of Economic Perspectives* 8: 3–17.

Posner, Richard A. 1971. "Regulation by Taxation." *Bell Journal of Economics* 2: 22–50.

——— 1975. "The Social Costs of Monopoly and Regulation." *Journal of Political Economy* 83: 807–27.

——— 1980. "A Theory of Primitive Society, With Special Reference to Law." *Journal of Law and Economics* 23: 1–53.

Poterba, James M., and Julio J. Rotemberg. 1990. "Inflation and Taxation with Optimizing Governments." *Journal of Money, Credit and Banking* 22: 1–18.

Potters, Jan. 1992. *Lobbying and Pressure: Theory and Experiments.* Amsterdam: Tinbergen Institute Research Monograph, no.36.

Potters, Jan, and Frans van Winden. 1992. "Lobbying and Asymmetric Information." *Public Choice* 74: 269–92.

Prichard, J. Robert S. 1980. *Crown Corporations in Canada: The Calculus of Instrument Choice.* Toronto: Butterworths.

Pufendorf, Samuel. 1672. *On the Law of Nature and Nations in Eight Books.*

Putnam, Robert. 1993. *Making Democracy Work: Civic Traditions in Modern Italy.* Princeton: Princeton University Press.

Radner, Roy. 1992. "Hierarchy: The Economics of Managing." *Journal of Economic Literature* 30: 1382–416.

Rae, Douglas W. 1967. *The Political Consequences of Electoral Laws.* New Haven: Yale University Press.

1969. "Decision Rules and Individual Values in Constitutional Choice." *American Political Science Review* 63: 40–56.

1971. *The Political Consequences of Electoral Laws.* Rev. Ed. New Haven: Yale University Press.

Rae, Douglas W., V. Hanby, and J. Loosemoore. 1971. "Thresholds of Representation and Thresholds of Exclusion: An Analytic Note on Electoral Systems." *Comparative Political Studies* 3: 479–88.

Rae, Douglas W., and Michael Taylor. 1970. *The Analysis of Political Cleavages.* New Haven: Yale University Press.

Rakove, J. 1989. "The First Phases of American Federalism." In M. Tushnet, ed., *Comparative Constitutional Federalism: Europe and America.* New York: Greenwood Press, 1–19.

Ram, R. 1987. "Wagner's Hypothesis in Time-Series and Cross-Section Perspectives: Evidence From 'Real Data' for 115 Countries." *Review of Economics and Statistics* 62: 194–204.

Rapaczynski, A. 1986. "From Sovereignty to Process: The Jurisprudence of Federalism after Garcia." *Supreme Court Review* 8: 341–419.

Rasmusen, E. 1993. "Lobbying When the Decisionmaker Can Acquire Independent Information." *Public Choice* 77: 899–973.

Rauch, J. 1992. "The Parasite Economy." *National Journal* 24: 980–85.

Rawls, John. 1971. *A Theory of Justice.* Cambridge, Mass.: Harvard University Press.

Ray, Edward J. 1981. "The Determinants of Tariff and Nontariff Trade Restrictions in the United States." *Journal of Political Economy* 89: 105–21.

1989. "Protection of Manufacturers in the United States." Ohio State University. Mimeo.

1990. "U.S. Protection and Intra-Industry Trade: The Message to Developing Countries." Ohio State University. Mimeo.

Redekop, James. 1991. "Social Welfare Functions on Restricted Economic Domains." *Journal of Economic Theory* 53: 396–427.

1993. "Arrow-Inconsistent Economic Domain." *Social Choice and Welfare* 10: 107–26.

Reed, Robert W. 1994. "A Retrospective Voting Model with Heterogeneous Politicians." *Economics and Politics* 6: 39–58.

Reed, Robert W., and Joonmo Cho. 1995. *A Comparison of Prospective and Retrospective Voting.* Unpublished.

Reed, Steven R. 1991. "Structure and Behavior: Extending Duverger's Law to the Japanese Case." *British Journal of Political Science* 20: 335–56.

Renaud, Paul S. A., and Frans A. A. M. van Winden. 1987. "Tax Rate and Government Expenditures." *Kyklos* 40: 349–67.

Renford, E., and E. Trahan. 1990. "Presidential Elections and the Federal Reserve's Interest Rate Function." *Journal of Policy Modeling* 12: 29–34.

Repass, David E. 1971. "Issue Salience and Party Choice." *American Political Science Review* 65: 389–400.

Rice, Stuart. 1928. *Quantitative Methods in Politics*. New York: Knopf.

Richards, Daniel J. 1986. "Unanticipated Money and the Political Business Cycle." *Journal of Money, Credit and Banking* 18: 447–57.

Riker, William H. 1962. *The Theory of Political Coalitions*. New Haven and London: Yale University Press.

1964. *Federalism: Origins, Operation, Significance*. Boston: Little, Brown, and Company.

1974. "Communication." *American Political Science Review* 68: 1692.

1980. "Implications from the Disequilibrium of Majority Rule for the Study of Institutions." *American Political Science Review* 74: 432–46.

1982a. *Liberalism against Populism: A Confrontation between the Theory of Democracy and the Theory of Social Choice*. San Francisco: Freeman.

1982b. "The Two-Party System and Duverger's Law: An Essay in the History of Political Science." *American Political Science Review* 76: 753–66.

1986. *The Art of Political Manipulation*. New Haven: Yale University Press.

Riker, William H., and S. J. Brams. 1973. "The Paradox of Vote Trading." *American Political Science Review* 67: 1235–47.

Riker, William H., and Peter C. Ordeshook. 1968. "A Theory of the Calculus of Voting." *American Political Science Review* 62: 25–43.

Riker, William H., and Barry Weingast. 1988. "Constitutional Regulation of Legislative Choice: The Political Consequences of Judical Deference in Legislatures." *Virginia Law Review* 74: 373–401.

Rivers, R. Douglas. Forthcoming. "Microeconomics and Macropolitics: A Solution to the Kramer Problem." *American Political Science Review*.

Rivlin, Alice. 1992. *Reviving the American Dream: The Economy, the States, and the Federal Government*. Washington, D.C.: The Brookings Institution.

Roberts, K. W. S. 1977. "Voting over Income Tax Schedules." *Journal of Public Economics* 8: 329–40.

1980a. "Possibility Theorems with Interpersonally Comparable Welfare Levels." *Review of Economic Studies* 47: 409–20.

1980b. "Interpersonal Welfare Comparability and Social Choice Theory." *Review of Economic Studies* 47: 421–39.

Robertson, D. 1976. *A Theory of Party Competition*. London: John Wiley and Sons.

1987. "Britain, Austrialia, New Zealand and the United States 1946–1987: An Initial Comparative Analysis." In Ian Budge, D. Robertson, and D. Hearl, eds., *Ideology, Strategy, and Party Change*. Cambridge University Press, 39–72.

Robinson, J. 1943. "Planning Full Employment." In *London Times*. 22–23/1, or *Collected Economic Papers*, vol.1. Oxford: Blackwell, 1966.

Rogerson, William P. 1982. "The Social Costs of Monopoly and Regulation: A Game-Theoretic Analysis." *Bell Journal of Economics* 13: 391–401.

Rogoff, Kenneth. 1990. "Equilibrium Political Budget Cycles." *American Economic Review* 80: 21–36.

Rogoff, Kenneth, and Anne Sibert. 1988. "Elections and Macroeconomic Policy Cycles." *Review of Economic Studies* 55: 1–16.

Romer, Thomas. 1975. "Individual Welfare, Majority Voting and the Properties of a Linear Income Tax." *Journal of Public Economics* 4: 163–8.

Romer, Thomas, and Howard Rosenthal. 1978. "Political Resource Allocation, Controlled Agendas and the Status Quo." *Public Choice* 33(4): 27–43.

1979. "Bureaucrats versus Voters: On the Political Economy of Resource Allocation by Direct Democracy." *Quarterly Journal of Economics* 93: 563–87.

Rose, R. 1984. "A Question of Degree or Principle?" In Arend Lijphart and Bernard Grofman, eds., *Choosing an Electoral System: Issues and Alternatives.* New York: Praeger, 73–81.

Rose-Ackerman, Susan. 1980. "Risktaking and Reelection: Does Federalism Promote Innovation?" *Journal of Legal Studies* 9: 593–616.

1981. "Does Federalism Matter? Political Choice in a Federal Republic." *Journal of Political Economy* 89: 152–65.

Rosenthal, Howard. 1990. "The Setter Model." In James Enelow and Melvin J. Hinich, eds., *Advances in the Spatial Theory of Voting.* Cambridge University Press, 199–234.

Rosenthal, Howard, and Subrata Sen. 1973. "Electoral Participation in the French Fifth Republic." *American Political Science Review* 67: 29–54.

1977. "Spatial Voting Models for the French Fifth Republic." *American Political Science Review* 71: 1447–66.

Ross, V. B. 1984. "Rent-Seeking in LDC Import Regimes: The Case of Kenya." Discussion Papers in International Economics, no. 8408, Graduate Institute of International Studies, Geneva.

Rothenberg, L. 1988. "Organizational Maintenance and the Retention Decision in Groups." *American Political Science Review* 82: 1129–52.

1989. "Do Interest Groups Make a Difference? Lobbying, Constituency Influence and Public Policy." Working paper, Department of Political Science, University of Rochester.

1992. *Linking Citizens to Government: Interest Group Politics at Common Cause.* Cambridge University Press.

Roubini, Nuriel, and Jeffrey Sachs. 1989. "Political and Economic Determinants of Budget Deficits in the Industrial Democracies." *European Economic Review* 33: 903–38.

Rousseau, J.-J. [1762] 1962. *Le contrat social.* Translated as *The Social Contract.* Harmondsworth: Penguin.

Rubinfeld, Daniel L. 1987. "The Economics of the Public Sector." In Alan J. Auerbach and Martin Feldstein, eds., *Handbook of Public Economics,* vol. 2. New York: Elsevier Science Publishers: North–Holland.

Rubinstein, Ariel. 1979. "A Note about the 'Nowhere Denseness' of Societies Having an Equilibrium under Majority Rule." *Econometrica* 47: 511–14.

1982. "Perfect Equilibrium in a Bargaining Model." *Econometrica* 50: 97–109.

Ruddle, Kenneth. 1988. "Social Principles Underlying Traditional Inshore Fishery Management Systems in the Pacific Basin." *Marine Resource Economics* 5: 351–63.

Sabato, Larry J. 1991. *Feeding Frenzy: How Attack Journalism Has Transformed American Politics.* New York: Macmillan.

Salmon, Pierre. 1988. "Trust and Trans-Bureau Networks in Organization." *European Journal of Political Economy* 4 (extra issue): 229–52.

Samuelson, Paul A. 1947. *Foundations of Economic Analysis.* Cambridge, Mass.: Harvard University Press.

1948. "Consumption Theory in Terms of Revealed Preferences." *Economica* 15: 243–53.

1954. "The Pure Theory of Public Expenditure." *Review of Economics and Statistics* 36: 387–9.

Sandler, Todd. 1977. "Impurity of Defence: An Application of the Economics of Alliances." *Kyklos* 30: 443–60.

1992. *Collective Action: Theory and Applications.* Ann Arbor: University of Michigan Press.

Sandler, Todd, and James C. Murdoch. 1990. "Nash-Cournot or Lindahl Behavior? An Empirical Test for the NATO Allies." *Quarterly Journal of Economics* 105: 875–94.

Sandler, Todd, and John T. Tschirhart. 1980. "The Economic Theory of Clubs: An Evaluation Survey." *Journal of Economic Literature* 18: 1488–521.

Santerre, Rexford E. 1986. "Representative Versus Direct Democracy: A Tiebout Test of Relative Performance." *Public Choice* 48: 58–63.

1989. "Representative Versus Direct Democracy: Are There Any Expenditure Differences?" *Public Choice* 60: 145–54.

Sass, Tim R. 1992. "Constitutional Choice in Representative Democracies." *Public Choice* 74: 405–24.

Satterthwaite, Mark A. 1975. "Strategy-Proofness and Arrow's Conditions: Existence and Correspondence Theorems for Voting Procedures and Social Welfare Functions." *Journal of Economic Theory* 10: 187–217.

Sawyer, Amos. 1992. *The Emergence of Autocracy in Liberia: Tragedy and Challenge.* San Francisco: Institute for Contemporary Studies Press.

Scharpf, Fritz W. 1988. "The Joint-Decision Trap: Lessons from German Federation and European Integration." *Public Administration* 66, 239–78.

Schattschneider, E. E. 1935. *Politics, Pressures and the Tariff.* Englewood Cliffs, N.J.: Prentice–Hall.

Schelling, Thomas C. 1960. *The Strategy of Conflict.* Cambridge, Mass.: Harvard University Press.

1966. *Arms and Influence.* New Haven: Yale University Press.

Schlager, Edella. 1990. "Model Specification and Policy Analysis: The Governance of Coastal Fisheries." Ph.D. diss., Department of Political Science, Indiana University.

Schlager, Edella, William Bloomqvist, and Shui Yan Tang. 1994. "Mobile Flows, Storage, and Self-Organized Institutions for Governing Common-Pool Resources." *Land Economics* 70: 294–317.

Schlager, Edella, and Elinor Ostrom. 1993. "Property-Rights Regimes and Coastal Fisheries: An Empirical Analysis." In Randy Simmons and Terry Anderson, eds., *The Political Economy of Customs and Culture: Informal Solutions to the Commons Problem.* Lanham: Rowman and Littlefield, 13–41.

Schmidtz, David. 1991. *The Limits of Government: An Essay on the Public Goods Argument.* Boulder, CO: Westview Press.

Schneider, Friedrich. 1992. "The Federal and Fiscal Structures of Representative and Direct Democracies as Models for a European Federal Union: Some Ideas Using the Public Choice Approach." *Journal des economistes et des études humaines* 3: 403–37.

Schneider, Friedrich, and Bruno S. Frey. 1988. "Politico-Economic Models of Macroeconomic Policy: A Review of the Empirical Evidence." *Political Business Cycles.* Durham: Duke University Press, 239–75.

Schneider, Friedrich, and Werner W. Pommerehne. 1980. "Politico-Economic Interactions in Australia: Some Empirical Evidence." *Economic Record* 56: 113–31.

Schneider, Friedrich, Werner W. Pommerehne, and Bruno S. Frey. 1981. "Politico-Economic Interdependence in a Direct Democracy: The Case of Switzerland." *Contemporary Political Economy: Studies on the Interdependence of Politics and Economics.* Amsterdam: North–Holland, 231–48.

Schofield, Norman. 1972. "Is Majority Rule Special?" In Richard G. Niemi, and Herbert F. Weisberg, eds., *Probability Models of Collective Decision-Making.* Columbus: Charles E. Merrill.

1978a. "Instability of Simple Dynamic Games." *Review of Economic Studies* 45: 575–94.

1978b. "Generalized Bargaining Sets for Cooperative Games." *International Journal of Game Theory* 7: 183–99.

1982. "Bargaining Set Theory and Stability in Coalition Governments." *Mathematical Social Science* 3: 9–31.

1983. "General Instability of Majority Rule." *Review of Economic Studies* 45: 575–94.

1985. *Social Choice and Democracy.* Berlin: Springer.

1986. "Existence of a 'Structurally Stable' Equilibrium for a Non-Collegial Voting Rule." *Public Choice* 51: 267–84.

1987a. "Coalitions in West European Democracies: 1945–1986." Washington University. Center in Political Economy. Typescript.

1987b. "Stability of Coalition Governments in Western Europe: 1945–86." *The European Journal of Political Economy* 3: 555–91.

1993a. "Manipulation of the Political Economy." Center in Political Economy, Washington University. Typescript.

1993b. "Party Competition in a Spatial Model of Coalition Formation." In W. Barnett, Melvin J. Hinich, and Norman Schofield, eds., *Political Economy: Institutions, Competition and Representation.* Cambridge University Press, 135–74.

1993c. "Political Competition in Multiparty Coalition Governments." *European Journal of Political Research* 23: 1–33.

1995a. "Coalition Politics: A Formal Model and Empirical Analysis." *Journal of Theoretical Politics* 7: 245–81.

1995b. "Democratic Stability." In Jack Knight and Itai Sened, eds., *Explaining Social Institutions.* Ann Arbor: University of Michigan Press, 189–215.

1995c. "Existence of a Smooth Social Choice Functor." In William Barnett, H. Moulin, M. Salles, and N. Schofield, eds., *Social Choice, Welfare and Ethics.* Cambridge University Press, 213–46.

1996. "The Heart of a Polity." In Norman Schofield, ed., *Collective Decision Making: Social Choice and Political Economy.* Boston: Kluwer, 183–220.

Schofield, Norman, and R. Parks. 1993. "Existence of a Nash Equilibrium in a Spatial Model of *n*-Party Competition." Center in Political Economy, Washington University. Typescript.

Schofield, Norman, and Craig Tovey. 1992. "Probability and Convergence for Supra-Majority Rule with Euclidean Preferences." *Mathematical and Computer Modelling* 16: 41–58.

Schotter, Andrew. 1981. *The Economic Theory of Social Institutions.* Cambridge University Press.

Schuknecht, Ludger. 1992. "The Political Economy of Current European Integration." In Hans-Jürgen Vosgerau, ed., *European Integration in the World Economy.* Heidelberg: Springer, 677–702.

Schumpeter, Joseph A. 1908. *Das Wesen und der Hauptinhalt der theoretischen Nationalökonomie.* Munich and Leipzig: Dunker and Humbolt.

1918. "The Crisis of the Tax State." In R. Swedberg, *Joseph R. Schumpeter, The Economics and Sociology of Capitalism.* Princeton: Princeton University Press, 1991.

Schwab, Robert M., and Ernest M. Zampelli. 1987. "Disentangling the Demand Function from the Production Function for Local Public Services." *Journal of Public Economics* 33: 245–60.

Schwartz, Thomas. 1970. "On the Possibility of Rational Policy Evaluation." *Theory and Decision* 1: 89–106.

1972. "Rationality and the Myth of the Maximum." *Noûs* 6: 97–117.

1975. "Vote Trading and Pareto Efficiency." *Public Choice* 24: 101–9.

1981. "The Universal-Instability Theorem." *Public Choice* 37: 487–501.

1986. *The Logic of Collective Choice.* New York: Columbia University Press.

1987. "Your Vote Counts on Account of the Way it is Counted: An Institutional Solution to the Paradox of Not Voting." *Public Choice* 54: 101–21.

1990. "Cyclic Tournaments and Cooperative Majority Voting." *Social Choice and Welfare* 7: 19–29.

Scoble, Harry M., and Laurie S. Wiseberg. 1976. "Human Rights NGOs: Notes Towards Comparative Analysis." *Human Rights Journal* 9: 611–44.

Scott, James C. 1990. *Domination and the Arts of Resistance: Hidden Transcripts.* New Haven: Yale University Press.

Scully, Gerald W. 1992. *Constitutional Environments and Economic Growth.* Princeton: Princeton University Press.

Sefton, Martin. 1993. "Public Goods and Externalities: An In-Class Experiment." Working paper, Department of Economics, Indiana University–Purdue University at Indianapolis.

Sefton, Martin, and Richard Steinberg. 1993. "Reward Structures in Public Good Experiments." Department of Economics, Indiana University–Purdue University Indianapolis.

Sell, Jane. 1988. "Types of Public Goods and Free Riding." *Advances in Group Process* 5: 119–40.

Sell, Jane, and Rick Wilson. 1991. "Levels of Information and Contributions to Public Goods." *Social Forces* 70: 107–24.

1992. "Liar, Liar, Pants on Fire: Cheap Talk and Signalling in Repeated Public Goods Settings." Working paper, Department of Political Science, Rice University.

Sen, Amartya K. 1970a. *Collective Choice and Social Welfare.* San Francisco: Holden–Day.

1970b. "The Impossibility of a Paretian Liberal." *Journal of Political Economy* 78: 152–7.

1976. "Social Choice Theory: A Re-Examination." *Econometrica* 45: 217–45.

1977a. "Unanimity and Rights." *Economica* 43: 53–89.

1977b. "On Weights and Measures: Informational Constraints in Social Welfare Analysis." *Econometrica* 45: 1539–72.

1979. "Interpersonal Comparisons of Welfare." In Michael J. Boskin, ed., *Economics and Human Welfare.* New York: Academic Press.

1983. "Liberty and Social Choice." *Journal of Philosophy* 80: 5–28.

1992. "Minimal Liberty." *Economica* 59: 139–59.

Sened, I. 1996. "A Model of Coalition Formation: Theory and Evidence." *Journal of Politics* 58: 370–92.

Sengupta, Nirmal. 1991. *Managing Common Property: Irrigation in India and the Philippines.* London and New Delhi: Sage.

Settle, Russell F., and Burton A. Abrams. 1976. "The Determinants of Voter Participation: A More General Model." *Public Choice* 27: 81–9.

Shaked, A. 1975. "Non-Existence of Equilibrium for the Two-Dimensional Three-Firm Location Model." *Review of Economic Studies* 42: 51–6.

Shapiro, Carl. 1983. "Premiums for High-Quality Products as Returns to Reputations." *Quarterly Journal of Economics* 98: 659–79.

Shapiro, Carl, and Joseph E. Stiglitz. 1984. "Equilibrium Unemployment as a Worker Discipline Device." *American Economic Review* 74: 433–44.

Shapiro, Ian. 1990. "Three Fallacies Concerning Majorities, Minorities, and Democratic Politics." In John Chipman and Alan Wertheimer, eds., *Majorities and Minorities,* Nomos 32. New York: New York University Press, 79–125.

1994. "Three Ways to be a Democrat." *Political Theory* 22: 124–51.

Shapley, Lloyd, and Bernard Grofman. 1984. "Optimizing Group Judgmental Accuracy in the Presence of Interdependencies." *Public Choice* 43: 329–43.

Sharkey. W. W. 1990. "A Model of Competition Among Political Interest Groups." Bellcore, Morristown. Mimeo.

Shepsle, Kenneth A. 1972. "The Strategy of Ambiguity: Uncertainty and Electoral Competition." *American Political Science Review* 66: 555–68.

1979. "Institutional Arrangements and Equilibrium in Multidimensional Voting Models." *American Journal of Political Science* 23: 27–59.

1989. "Studying Institutions: Some Lessons from the Rational Choice Approach." *Journal of Theoretical Politics* 1: 131–49.

1991. *Models of Multiparty Electoral Competition.* Chur: Harwood Publishers.

Shepsle, Kenneth A., and Barry R. Weingast. 1981. "Structure-Induced Equilibrium and Legislative Choice." *Public Choice* 37: 503–19.

1984. "Uncovered Sets and Sophisticated Voting Outcomes with Implications for Agenda Control." *American Journal of Political Science* 28: 49–74.

1987. "The Institutional Foundations of Committee Power." *American Political Science Review* 81: 86–108.

Sherman, Howard. 1979. "A Marxist Theory of the Business Cycle." *Review of Radical Political Economy* 11: 1–23.

Shughart II, William F., and Robert D. Tollison. 1985. "Corporate Chartering: An Exploration in the Economics of Legal Change." *Economic Inquiry* 23: 585–99.

Silberman, Jonathan, and Gary Durden. 1975. "The Rational Behavior Theory of Voter Participation: The Evidence from Congressional Elections." *Public Choice* 23: 101–8.

Simon, Herbert A. 1947. *Administrative Behavior.* New York: MacMillan.

Simons, Henry. 1939. *Personal Income Taxation.* Chicago: University of Chicago Press.

Simpson, Paul B. 1969. "On Defining Areas of Voter Choice." *Quarterly Journal of Economics* 83: 478–90.

Siy, Robert Y., Jr. 1982. *Community Resource Management: Lessons from the Zanjera.* Quezon City, Philippines: University of the Philippines Press.

Sjoquist, David L. 1981. "A Median Voter Analysis of Variations in the Use of Property Taxes among Local Governments." *Public Choice* 36: 273–85.

Skott, P. 1989. *Conflict and Effective Demand in Economic Growth.* Cambridge University Press.

Sloss, Judith. 1973. "Stable Outcomes in Majority Voting Games." *Public Choice* 15: 19–48.

Slutsky, Steven. 1979. "Equilibrium under α-Majority Voting." *Econometrica* 47: 1113–25.

Smith, Adam. 1978. *Lectures on Jurisprudence.* Ed. R. L. Meek, D. D. Raphael, and P. G. Stein. Oxford: Oxford University Press (from notes of Smith's lectures in 1762–4).

Smith, John H. 1973. "Aggregation of Preferences with Variable Electorate." *Econometrica* 41: 1027–41.

Smith, Rodney T. 1984. "Advocacy, Interpretation and Influence in the US Congress." *American Political Science Review* 78: 44–63.

1989. "Interpretation, Pressure and the Stability of Interest Group Influence in the US Congress." Working paper, DSS, Carnegie-Mellon University.

1991. "A Public Choice Perspective of the International Energy Program." In Roland Vaubel and Thomas D. Willett, eds., *The Political Economy of International Organizations: A Public Choice Approach.* Boulder, CO: Westview Press, 142–80.

Smith, Vernon L. 1977. "The Principle of Unanimity and Voluntary Consent in Social Choices." *Journal of Political Economy* 85: 1125–39.

1979. "Incentive Compatible Experimental Processes for the Provision of Public Goods." *Research in Experimental Economics* 1: 59.

1982. "Microeconomic Systems as an Experimental Science." *American Economic Review* 72: 923–55.

Smolensky, E., Werner W. Pommerehne, and R. E. Dalrymple. 1979. "Post Fiscal Income Inequality: A Comparison of the United States and West Germany." In J. R. Moroney, ed., *Income Inequality: Trends and International Comparisons*. Lexington: D. C. Heath.

Snyder, James M. 1990. "Campaign Contributions as Investments: The US House of Representatives 1980–86." *Journal of Political Economy* 98: 1195–227.

1991. "On Buying Legislatures." *Economics and Politics* 3: 93–109.

1993a. "Comment on 'Local Interests, Central Leadership and the Passage of TRA86.' " *Journal of Policy Analysis and Management* 12: 181–5.

1993b. "The Market for Campaign Contributions: Evidence for the US Senate 1980–86." *Economics and Politics* 5: 219–40.

Snyder, James M., and Gerald H. Kramer. 1988. "Fairness, Self-Interest and the Politics of the Progressive Income Tax." *Journal of Public Economics* 36: 197–230.

Soh, B. H. 1986. "Political Business Cycles in Industrial Democratic Countries." *Kyklos* 39: 31–46.

Solvasson, Birgir. 1993. "Institutional Evolution in the Icelandic Commonwealth." *Constitutional Political Economy* 4: 97–125.

Sommerlad, F., and I. McLean. 1989. "The Political Theory of Condorcet." Working paper 1/89, Social Studies Faculty Centre, Oxford University.

Sorauf, F. 1992. *Inside Campaign Finance: Myths and Realities*. New Haven: Yale University Press.

Sosland Publishing Co. 1993. *Milling and Baking News*. 72 (December 21): 43.

Spann, R. M. 1977a. "Public Versus Private Provision of Governmental Services." In Thomas E. Borcherding, ed., *Budgets and Bureaucrats: The Sources of Government Growth*. Durham: Duke University Press, 71–89.

Spann, R. M. 1977b. "Rates of Productivity Change and the Growth of State and Local Governments." In Thomas E. Borcherding, ed., *Budgets and Bureaucrats: The Sources of Government Growth*. Durham: Duke University Press, 100–29.

Spiller, Pablo T., and Rafael Gely. 1992. "Congressional Control or Judicial Independence: The Determinants of U.S. Supreme Court Labor-Relations Decisions, 1949–1988." *Rand Journal of Economics* 23: 463–92.

Spindler, Zane A., 1990. "Constitutional Design for a Rent-Seeking Society: Voting Rule Choice." *Constitutional Political Economy* 1: 73–82.

Steinmo, Sven. 1989. "Political Institutions and Tax Policy in the United States, Sweden and Britain." *World Politics* 41: 500–35.

Stephan, J. 1992. "Political Exchange Rate Cycles." In Hans-Jürgen Vosgerau, ed., *European Integration in the World Economy*. Berlin: Springer.

Stewart, Charles H., Jr. 1991. "The Politics of Tax Reform in the 1980s." In Alberto Alesina and Geoffrey Carliner, eds., *Politics and Economics in the Eighties*. University of Chicago Press.

Stigler, George J. 1970. "Director's Law of Public Income Distribution." *Journal of Law and Economics* 13: 1–10.

1971. "The Theory of Economic Regulation." *Bell Journal of Economics and Management Science* 2: 3–21.

1973. "General Economic Conditions and National Elections." *American Economic Review* 63: 160–7.

1974. "Free Riders and Collective Action: An Appendix to Theories of Economic Regulation." *Bell Journal of Economics and Management Science* 5: 359–65.

Still, Jonathan W. 1981. "Political Equality and Election Systems." *Ethics* 91: 375–94.

Stimson, James A. 1990. "A Macro Theory of Information Flow." In John A. Ferejohn and James H. Kuklinski, eds., *Information and Democratic Processes.* Chicago: University of Illinois Press.

1991. *Public Opinion in America: Moods, Cycles, and Swings.* Boulder, CO: Westview Press.

Stokes, Donald. 1963. "Spatial Models of Party Competition." *American Political Science Review* 57: 368–77.

1966. *Elections and the Political Order.* New York: John Wiley and Sons.

Stokes, Donald, and Warren Miller. 1962. "Party Government and the Saliency of Congress." *Public Opinion Quarterly* 26: 531–46.

Stratmann, Thomas. 1992. "The Effects of Logrolling on Congressional Voting." *The American Economic Review* 82: 1162–76.

1995. "Logrolling in the U.S. Congress." *Economic Inquiry* 33: 441–56.

1996. "Instability in Collective Decisions? Testing for Cyclical Majorities." *Public Choice.* Forthcoming.

Stubblebine, W. C. 1963. "The Social Imbalance Hypothesis." Ph.D. diss., University of Virginia.

Sugden, Robert. 1985. "Liberty, Preference and Choice." *Economics and Philosophy* 1: 213–29.

1986. *The Economics of Rights, Co-Operation, and Welfare.* Oxford: Blackwell.

1986. *The Evolution of Rights, Cooperation and Welfare.* New York: Basil Blackwell.

Sullivan, John L., James E. Piereson, and George E. Marcus. 1978. "Ideological Constraint in the Mass Public: A Methodological Critique and Some New Findings." *American Journal of Political Science* 22: 233–49.

Sundquist, James. 1983. *Dynamics of the Party System: Alignment and Realignment of Political Parties in the United States.* Washington D.C.: Brookings Institution.

Sunstein, Cass R. 1985. "Interest Groups in American Public Law." *Stanford Law Review* 38: 29–87.

1988. "Beyond the Republican Revival." *Yale Law Journal* 97: 1539–90.

Suzumura, Kotaro. 1983. *Rational Choice, Collective Decisions, and Social Welfare.* Cambridge University Press.

Swedberg, Richard, ed. 1991. *Joseph A. Schumpeter: The Economics and Sociology of Capitalism.* Princeton: Princeton University Press.

Syrquin, Moshe. 1988. "Patterns of Structural Change." In Hollis Chenery and T. N. Srinivasan, eds., *Handbook of Development Economics.* Vol I. Amsterdam: North–Holland.

Taagepera, Rein, and Matthew S. Shugart. 1989. *Seats and Votes.* New Haven: Yale University Press.

Tabellini, Guido. 1991. "The Politics of Intergenerational Redistribution." *Journal of Political Economy* 99: 335–57.

Tabellini, Guido, and Alberto Alesina. 1990. "Voting on the Budget Deficit." *American Economic Review* 80: 37–49.

Tang, Shui Yan. 1991. "Institutional Arrangements and the Management of Common-Pool Resources." *Public Administration Review* 51: 42–51.

1992. *Institutions and Collective Action: Self-Governance in Irrigation.* San Francisco: Institute for Contemporary Studies Press.

Tarr, David. 1989. *A General Equilibrium Analysis of the Welfare and Employment Effects of U.S. Quotas in Textiles, Autos and Steel.* Washington: Federal Trade Commission.

Taylor, John B. 1979. "Staggered Wage Setting in a Macro Model." *American Economic Review* 69: 108–13.

Taylor, Michael J. 1969. "Proof of a Theorem on Majority Rule." *Behavioral Science* 14: 228–31.

1976. *Anarchy and Cooperation.* London: John Wiley and Sons.

1987. *The Possibility of Cooperation.* Cambridge University Press.

Taylor, Michael J., and V. M. Herman. 1971. "Party Systems and Government Stability." *American Political Science Review* 65: 28–37.

Taylor, Michael J., and M. Laver. 1973. "Government Coalitions in Western Europe: 1945–1986." *The European Journal of Political Research* 3: 555–91.

Taylor, Michael J., and Hugh Ward. 1982. "Chickens, Whales, and Lumpy Goods: Alternative Models of Public-Good Provision." *Political Studies* 30: 350–70.

Telser, Lester G. 1980. "A Theory of Self-Enforcing Agreements." *Journal of Business* 53: 27–44.

Thompson, Earl A. 1966. "A Pareto Optimal Group Decision Process." In Gordon Tullock, ed., *Papers on Non-Market Decision Making.* Charlottesville: University of Virginia, 133–40.

Thomson, James T. 1977. "Ecological Deterioration: Local-Level Rule Making and Enforcement Problems in Niger." In Michael H. Glantz, ed., *Desertification: Environmental Degradation in and around Arid Lands.* Boulder, CO: Westview Press, 57–79.

1992. *A Framework for Analyzing Institutional Incentives in Community Forestry.* Rome: Forestry Department, Food and Agriculture Organization of the United Nations.

Tideman, T. Nicolaus. 1972. "The Efficient Provision of Public Goods." In Selma Mushkin, ed., *Public Prices for Public Products.* Washington: The Urban Institute, 111–23.

1977. "Ethical Foundations of the Demand-Revealing Process." *Public Choice* 29 special supplement 2: 71–8.

1983. "An Experiment in the Demand-Revealing Process." *Public Choice* 41: 387–401.

Tideman, T. Nicolaus, and Gordon Tullock. 1976. "A New and Superior Process for Making Social Choices." *Journal of Political Economy* 84: 1145–9.

Tiebout, Charles M. 1956. "A Pure Theory of Local Expenditures." *Journal of Political Economy* 64: 416–24.

Tinbergen, Jan. [1956] 1964. *Economic Policy: Principles and Design.* Amsterdam: North–Holland.

Tirole, Jean. 1986. "Hierarchies and Bureaucracies: On the Role of Collusion in Organizations." *Journal of Law, Economics and Organization* 2: 181–214.

1994. "The Internal Organization of Government." *Oxford Economic Papers* 46: 1–29.

Tobin, James. 1978. "Comment from an Academic Scribbler." *Journal of Monetary Economics* 4: 617–25.

Tollison, Robert D. 1982. "Rent Seeking: A Survey." *Kyklos* 35: 575–602.

1987. "Is the Theory of Rent Seeking Here to Stay?" In Charles K. Rowley, ed., *Democracy and Public Choice.* London: Blackwell, 143–57.

1988. "Public Choice and Legislation." *Virginia Law Review* 74: 339–71.

1991. "Regulation and Interest Groups." In J. High, ed., *Regulation: Economic Theory and History.* Ann Arbor: University of Michigan Press, 59–76.

Tollison, Robert D., and Richard E. Wagner. 1991. "Romance, Reality, and Economic Reform." *Kyklos* 44: 57–70.

Tollison, Robert D., and Thomas D. Willett. 1976. "Institutional Mechanisms for Dealing with International Externalities. A Public Choice Perspective." In Ryan C. Amacher and Richard J. Sweeney, eds., *The Law of the Sea*. Washington: American Enterprise Institute, 123–46.

Tovey, Craig. 1992a. "The Almost Surely Shrinking Yolk." Working paper no.161, Center in Political Economy, Washington University.

———. 1992b. "The Instability of Instability." Naval Postgraduate School, Monterey, California.

Townsend, Ralph E. 1986. "A Critique of Models of the American Lobster Fishery." *Journal of Environmental Economics and Management* 13: 277–91.

Townsend, Ralph E., and James Wilson. 1987. "An Economic View of the 'Tragedy of the Commons.' " In Bonnie J. McCay and James M. Acheson, eds., *The Question of the Commons: The Culture and Ecology of Communal Resources*. Tucson: University of Arizona Press, 311–26.

Trehan, Bharat, and Carl E. Walsh. 1990. "Seigniorage and Tax Smoothing in the United States 1914–1986." *Journal of Monetary Economics* 25: 97–112.

Truman, D. 1952. *The Governmental Process*. New York: Knopf.

Tsebelis, George. 1993. "Decision Making in Political Systems: Comparison of Presidentialism, Parliamentarism, Multicameralism, and Multipartism." Working paper no.178, Department of Political Science, Duke University.

Tufte, E. R. 1978. *Political Control of the Economy*. Princeton: Princeton University Press.

Tullock, Gordon, 1959. "Some Problems of Majority Voting." *Journal of Political Economy* 67: 571–79; reprinted in Arrow and Scitovsky, 1969, 169–78.

———. 1965. *The Politics of Bureaucracy*. Washington, D.C.: Public Affairs Press.

———. 1967a. "The General Irrelevance of the General Impossibility Theorem." *Quarterly Journal of Economics* 81: 256–70.

———. 1967b. "The Welfare Costs of Tariffs, Monopolies, and Theft." *Western Economic Journal* 5: 224–32.

———. 1969. "Social Cost and Government Action." *American Economic Review* 59: 189–97.

———. 1971. "The Charity of the Uncharitable." *Western Economic Journal* 9: 379–92.

———. 1974. "Communication." *American Political Science Review* 68, 1687–8.

———. 1975. "The Paradox of Not Voting for Oneself." *American Political Science Review* 69: 919.

———. 1976. *The Vote Motive*. Hobart Paper No.9, Institute of Economic Affairs, London.

———. 1980a. "Efficient Rent-Seeking." In James M. Buchanan, Robert D. Tollison and Gordon Tullock, eds., *Toward a Theory of the Rent-Seeking Society*. College Station: Texas A&M University Press, 97–112.

———. 1980b. "Rent-Seeking as a Negative-Sum Game." In James M. Buchanan, Robert D. Tollison, and Gordon Tullock, eds., *Toward a Theory of the Rent-Seeking Society*. College Station: Texas A&M University Press, 16–36.

———. 1981. "Why so Much Stability?" *Public Choice* 37: 189–202.

———. 1985. "Back to the Bog." *Public Choice* 46: 259–64.

———. 1988. "Future Directions for Rent Seeking Research." In Charles K. Rowley, Robert D. Tollison, and Gordon Tullock, eds., *The Political Economy of Rent Seeking*. Boston: Kluwer, 465–80.

Turnbull, Geoffrey K. 1992. "Fiscal Illusion, Uncertainty and the Flypaper Effect." *Journal of Public Economics* 48: 207–23.

Turner, Frederick, J. 1893. *The Significance of Sections in American History*. New York: Holt, 1932.

Uhlaner, Carole. 1989. "Rational Turnout: The Neglected Role of Groups." *American Journal of Political Science* 33: 390–422.

Ullmann-Margalit, Edna. 1977. *The Emergence of Norms*. Oxford: Oxford University Press.

Urken, A. B., and S. Traflet. 1984. "Optimal Jury Design." *Jurimetrics* 24: 218–35.

Ursprung, Heinrich W. 1989. "Public Goods, Rent Dissipation and Candidate Competition." University of Konstanz. Mimeo.

van de Kragt, Alphons, John M. Orbell, and Robyn M. Dawes. 1983. "The Minimal Contributing Set as a Solution to Public Goods Problems." *American Political Science Review* 77: 112–22.

van de Kragt, Alphons, Robyn M. Dawes, John M. Orbell, S. R. Braver, and L. A. Wilson. 1986. "Doing Well and Doing Good as Ways of Resolving Social Dilemmas." In Henk A. M. Wilke, Dave Messick, and Christel Rutte, eds., *Experimental Social Dilemmas*. Frankfurt am Main: Peter Lang, 177–204.

van Winden, Frans A. A. M. 1983. *On the Interaction between State and Private Sector. A Study in Political Economies*. Amsterdam: North–Holland.

Vaubel, Roland. 1983. "The Moral Hazard of IMF Lending." In Allan H. Meltzer, ed., *International Lending and the IMF*. Washington, 65–79.

——— 1986. "A Public Choice View of International Organization." *Public Choice* 51: 39–57. Reprinted in Roland Vaubel and Thomas D. Willett, eds., *The Political Economy of International Organizations: A Public Choice Approach*. Boulder, CO: Westview Press, 1991, 27–45.

——— 1991a. "The Political Economy of the International Monetary Fund: A Public Choice Analysis." In Roland Vaubel and Thomas D. Willett, eds., *The Political Economy of International Organizations: A Public Choice Approach*. Boulder, CO: Westview Press, 204–44.

——— 1991b. "A Public Choice View of the Delors Report." In Roland Vaubel and Thomas D. Willett, eds., *The Political Economy of International Organizations: A Public Choice Approach*. Boulder, CO: Westview Press, 306–10.

——— 1992. "The Political Economy of Centralization and the European Community." *Journal des economistes et des études humaines* 3: 11–48.

——— 1994. "The Public Choice Analysis of European Integration. A Survey." *European Journal of Political Economy* 10: 227–49.

Vaubel, Roland, and Willett, Thomas D., eds. 1991. *The Political Economy of International Organizations: A Public Choice Approach*. Boulder, CO: Westview Press.

Velthoven, B. J. C. 1989. *The Endogenization of Government Behavior in Macroeconomic Models*. Berlin: Springer.

Verba, S., N. Nie, and J. Kim. 1978. *Participation and Political Equality: A Seven Nation Comparison*. Cambridge University Press.

Vickrey, WIlliam. 1961. "Counterspeculation, Auctions, and Competitive Sealed Tenders." *Journal of Finance* 16: 8–37.

Vining, R. Aidan, and Anthony E. Boardman. 1992. "Ownership vs. Competition: Efficiency in Public Enterprise." *Public Choice* 73: 205–39.

von Hayek, Friedrich A. 1967. "Notes on the Evolution of Rules of Conduct." In *Studies in Philosophy, Politics, and Economics*. Chicago: University of Chicago Press.

Vorhies, Frank, and Fred Glahe. 1988. "Political Liberty and Social Development: An Empirical Investigation." *Public Choice* 58: 45–71.

Vousden, Neil, 1990. *The Economics of Trade Protection*. Cambridge University Press.

Wade, Robert. 1988. *Village Republics: Economic Conditions for Collective Action in South India*. Cambridge University Press.

Waerneryd, Karl. 1990. "Conventions: An Evolutionary Approach." *Constitutional Political Economy* 1: 83–107.

Wagner, A. 1893. *Grundlegung der Politischen Oekonomie*. 3rd ed. Leipzig: C. F. Winter.

Wagner, Richard E. 1976. "Revenue Structure, Fiscal Illusion, and Budgetary Choice." *Public Choice* 25: 45–61.

Walker, James M., and Roy Gardner. 1992. "Probabilistic Destruction of Common-Pool Resources: Experimental Evidence." *Economic Journal* 102: 1149–61.

Wallis, John J., and Wallace E. Oates. 1988. "Does Economic Sclerosis Set in with Ages? An Empirical Study of the Olson Hypothesis." *Kyklos* 41: 397–417.

Ward, Hugh. 1987. "The Risks of a Reputation for Toughness: Strategy in Public Goods Provision Problems Modelled by Chicken Supergames." *British Journal of Political Science* 17: 23–52.

Warwick, P. 1979. "The Durability of Coalition Governments in Parliamentary Democracies." *Comparative Political Studies* 11: 464–98.

Warwick, P., and S. T. Easton. 1992. "The Cabinet Stability Controversy: New Perspectives on a Classic Problem." *American Journal of Political Science* 36: 122–36.

Weatherford, J. McIver. 1985. *Tribes on the Hill.* New York: Bergin and Garvey.

Webber, Carolyn, and Aaron B. Wildavsky. 1986. *A History of Taxation and Expenditure in the Western World.* New York: Simon and Schuster.

Weber, Max. 1947. *The Theory of Economic and Social Organization.* Trans. by A. M. Henderson and Talcott Parsons. New York: Oxford University Press.

Weck-Hannemann, Hannelore. 1990. "Protectionism in Direct Democracy." *Journal of Institutional and Theoretical Economics* 146: 389–418.

1992. *Politische Ökonomie des Protektionismus.* Frankfurt and New York: Campus.

Wei, S. J. 1991. "To Divide or to Unite: A Theory of Secession." Department of Economics, University of California, Berkeley. Mimeo.

Weingast, Barry R. 1979. "A Rational Choice Perspective on Congressional Norms." *American Journal of Political Science* 23: 245–62.

1981. "Regulation, Reregulation, and Deregulation: The Political Foundations of Agency Clientele Relationships." *Law and Contemporary Problems* 44: 147–77.

1984. "The Congressional-Bureaucratic System: A Principal Agent Perspective (With Applications to the SEC)." *Public Choice* 44: 147–91.

1993a. *Federalism and the Political Commitment to Sustain Markets.* Stanford: Hoover Institution, Stanford University.

1993b. "The Economics of Political Institutions." Hoover Institution, Stanford University. Mimeo.

Weingast, Barry R., and William Marshall. 1988. "The Industrial Organization of Congress: or, Why Legislatures, Like Firms, Are Not Organized as Markets." *Journal of Political Economy* 96: 132–63.

Weingast, Barry R., and Mark J. Moran. 1983. "Bureaucratic Discretion or Congressional Control? Regulatory Policy-Making by the Federal Trade Commission." *Journal of Political Economy* 91: 765–800.

Weingast, Barry R., Kenneth A. Shepsle, and Christopher Johnsen. 1981. "The Political Economy of Benefits and Costs: A Neoclassical Approach to Distribution Politics." *Journal of Political Economy* 89: 642–64.

Weisberg, Herbert F., and Jerrold G. Rusk. 1970. "Dimensions of Candidate Evaluation." *American Political Science Review* 64: 1167–85.

Weissing, Franz J. and Elinor Ostrom. 1991. "Irrigation Institutions and the Games Irrigators Play: Rule Enforcement without Guards." In Reinhard Selten, ed., *Game Equilibrium Models II: Methods, Morals, and Markets.* Berlin: Springer-Verlag: 188–262.

1993. "Irrigation Institutions and the Games Irrigators Play: Rule Enforcement on Government-and Farmer-Managed Systems." In Fritz W. Scharpf, ed., *Games in Hierarchies and Networks: Analytical and Empirical Approaches to the Study of Governance Institutions.* Frankfurt am Main: Campus Verlag; Boulder, CO: Westview Press, 387–428.

Welch, William P. 1974. "The Economics of Campaign Funds." *Public Choice* 20: 83–97.

1980. "The Allocation of Political Monies: Economic Interest Groups." *Public Choice* 35: 97–120.

Wenders, John T. 1987. "On Perfect Rent Dissipation." *American Economic Review* 77: 456–9.

West, Edwin G. 1991. "Secular Cost Changes and the Size of Government." *Journal of Public Economics* 45: 363–81.

Whalley, John. 1985. *Trade Liberalization among Major World Trading Areas*. Cambridge, Mass.: MIT Press.

Whitehead, Barbara Dafoe. 1993. "Dan Quayle Was Right." *The Atlantic Monthly*, April, 47–84.

Wicksell, Knuth. [1896] 1958. Excerpts from *Finanztheoretische Untersuchungen*. Jena. Translated as "A New Principle of Just Taxation." Reprinted in Richard A. Musgrave, and Alan T. Peacock, eds., *Classics in the Theory of Public Finance*. London: Macmillan, 72–118.

Wiggins, Steven N., and Gary D. Libecap. 1985. "Oil Field Unitization: Contractual Failure in the Presence of Imperfect Information." *American Economic Review*, 75, 368–85.

1987. "Firm Heterogeneities and Cartelization Efforts in Domestic Crude Oil." *Journal of Law, Economics, and Organization* 3: 1–25.

Wildasin, David E. 1986. *Urban Public Finance*. Chicago: Harcourt Press.

Wildavsky, Aaron B., and Carolyn Webber. 1986. *A History of Taxation and Expenditure in the Western World*. New York: Simon and Schuster.

Wilensky, H. L. 1976. *The New "Corporatism," Centralization, and the Welfare State*. Beverly Hills: Sage.

Wilhite, Allen, and John Theilmann. 1987. "Labor PAC Contributions and Labor Legislation: A Simultaneous Logit Approach." *Public Choice* 53: 267–76.

Willett, Thomas D., ed. 1988. *Political Business Cycles: The Political Economy of Money, Inflation, and Unemployment*. Pacific Research Institute for Public Policy Book Series. Durham and London: Duke University Press.

Williams, Kenneth C. 1991. "Candidate Convergence and Information Costs in Spatial Elections: An Experimental Analysis." In Thomas Palfrey, ed., *Laboratory Research in Political Economy*. Ann Arbor: University of Michigan Press.

Williamson, Oliver E. 1964. *The Economics of Discretionary Behaviour: Managerial Objectives in the Theory of the Firm*. New Jersey: Prentice-Hall.

1985. *The Economic Institutions of Capitalism*. New York: Free Press.

Wilson, James A. 1982. "The Economical Management of Multispecies Fisheries." *Land Economics* 58: 417–34.

Wilson, James Q. 1980. "The Politics of Regulation." In James Q. Wilson, ed., *The Politics of Regulation*. New York: Basic Books.

1993. *The Moral Sence*. New York: The Free Press.

Wilson, John D. 1989. "An Optimal Tax Treatment of Leviathan." *Economics and Politics* 1: 97–118.

1990. "Are Efficiency Improvements in Government Transfer Policies Self-Defeating in Political Equilibrium?" *Economics and Politics* 2: 241–58.

Wilson, Rick K. 1986. "Foreward and Backward Agenda Procedures: Committee Experiments on Structurally Induced Equilibrium." *Journal of Politics* 48: 390–409.

Wilson, Robert. 1972. "Social Choice Theory without the Pareto Principle." *Journal of Economic Theory* 5: 478–86.

Winer, Stanley L., and Walter Hettich. 1990. "Political Checks and Balances and the Structure of Taxation in the United States and Canada." In Albert Breton et al., eds., *The Competitive State*. Dordrecht: Kluwer, 39–56.

1991. "Debt and Tariffs: An Empirical Investigation of the Evolution of Revenue Systems." *Journal of Public Economics* 45: 215–42.

1992. "Explaining the Use of Related Tax Instruments." Working paper, Sonderforschungsbereich 178, serie 2, no. 189, Faculty for Economics and Statistics, University of Konstanz.

1993. "Optimal Representative Taxation, Information and Political Institutions." Working paper, School of Public Administration, Carleton University.

Winer, Stanley L., and Thomas Rutherford. 1992. "Coercive Redistribution and the Franchise: A Preliminary Investigation Using Computable General Equilibrium Modelling." In Albert Breton et al., eds., *Preferences and the Demand for Public Goods*. Dordrecht: Kluwer, 351–75.

Wintrobe, Ronald. 1982. "The Optimal Level of Bureaucratization within a Firm." *Canadian Journal of Economics* 15: 649–68.

1987. "The Market for Corporate Control and the Market for Political Control." *Journal of Law, Economics and Organization* 3: 435–48.

1988. "The Efficiency of the Soviet System of Industrial Production." *European Journal of Political Economy* 4 (extra issue): 159–84.

Wintrobe, Ronald, and Albert Breton. 1986. "Organizational Structure and Productivity." *American Economic Review* 76: 530–38.

Witt, Ulrich. 1986. "Evolution and Stability of Cooperation without Enforceable Contracts." *Kyklos* 39: 245–66.

Witte, John F. 1985. *The Politics and Development of the Federal Income Tax*. Madison: University of Wisconsin Press.

Wittman, Donald. 1989. "Why Democracies Produce Efficient Results." *Journal of Political Economy* 97: 1395–424.

Wright, John R. 1985. "PACs, Contributions and Roll Calls: An Organizational Perspective." *American Political Science Review* 79: 400–14.

1989. "PAC Contributions, Lobbying and Representation." *Journal of Politics* 51: 713–29.

1990. "Contributions, Lobbying and Committee Voting in the US House of Representatives." *American Political Science Review* 84: 417–38.

Wriglesworth, J. L. 1985. *Libertarian Conflicts in Social Choice*. Cambridge University Press.

Wunsch, James S., and Dele Olowu, eds. 1990. *The Failure of the Centralized State: Institutions and Self-Governance in Africa*. Boulder, CO: Westview Press.

Wyckoff, Paul G. 1988. "A Bureaucratic Theory of Flypaper Effects." *Journal of Urban Economics* 23: 115–29.

1990. "The Simple Analytics of Slack-Maximizing Bureaucracy." *Public Choice* 67: 35–47.

1991. "The Elusive Flypaper Effect." *Journal of Urban Economics* 30: 310–28.

Xenophon. 4th century B.C. *Education of Cyrus*.

Yamagishi, Toshio. 1986. "The Provision of a Sanctioning System as a Public Good." *Journal of Personality and Social Psychology* 51: 110–16.

1988. "Seriousness of Social Dilemmas and the Provision of a Sanctioning System." *Social Psychology Quarterly* 51: 32–42.

Yitzhaki, Shlomo. 1979. "A Note on Optimal Taxation and Administration Costs." *American Economic Review* 69: 475–80.

Young, H. Peyton. 1974. "An Axiomatization of Borda's Rule." *Journal of Economic Theory* 9: 43–52.

1975. "Social Choice Scoring Functions." *SIAM Journal on Applied Mathematics* 28: 824–38.

1978. "The Allocation of Funds in Lobbying and Campaigning." *Behavioral Science* 23: 21–31.

1986. "Optimal Ranking and Choice from pairwise Comparisons." In Bernard Grofman and G. Owen, eds., *Information Pooling and Group Decision Making.* Greenwich: JAI Press.

1988. "Condorcet's Theory of Voting." *American Political Science Review* 82: 1231–44.

1993. "The Evolution of Conventions." *Econometrica* 61: 57–84.

Young, H. Peyton, and A. Levenglick. 1978. "A Consistent Extension of Condorcet's Election Principle." *SIAM Journal on Applied Mathematics* 35: 285–300.

Young, Leslie, and Stephen P. Magee. 1986. "Endogenous Protection, Factor Returns and Resource Allocation." *Review of Economic Studies* 53: 407–19.

Young, Robert A. 1991. "Budget Size and Bureaucratic Careers." In Andre Blais and Stephane Dion, eds., *The Budget-Maximizing Bureaucrat.* Pittsburgh: University of Pittsburgh Press, 33–58.

Zamora, Stephen. 1980. "Voting in International Economic Organizations." *American Journal of International Law* 74: 566–608.

Zarnowitz, Victor. 1985. "Recent Work on Business Cycles in Historical Perspective: A Review of Theories and Evidence." *Journal of Economic Literature* 23: 523–80.

Zax, Jeffrey S. 1988. "The Effects of Jurisdiction Types and Numbers on Local Public Finance." In H. S. Rosen, ed., *Fiscal Federalism: Quantitative Studies.* Chicago: University of Chicago Press, 79–103.

1989. "Is There a Leviathan in Your Neighborhood?" *American Economic Review* 79: 560–7.

Zeckman, Martin. 1979. "Dynamic Models of the Voter's Decision Calculus: Incorporating Retrospective Considerations into Rational-Choice Models of Individual Voting Behavior." *Public Choice* 34: 297–316.

Name index

Abrams, Burton A., 381
Abramson, Paul R., 378, 381n, 397
Acheson, James M., 45n, 46n
Acheson, Keith, 436, 448
Adkins, Lee C., 498
Affuso, Paul J., 112
Ainsworth, S., 315, 316
Akerlof, George A., 452, 454
Åkerman, Johan, 343, 370
Alchian, Armen A., 433, 443–4, 450, 453, 454
Aldrich, John H., 6, 14–15, 16, 247, 259, 374, 378, 381, 387, 388–9, 405
Alesina, Alberto, 344, 356, 359–61, 363, 364, 366, 367, 404, 494, 495
Alexander, Paul, 46
Allen, Franklin, 83n
Allen, Stuart D., 368
Alt, James E., 283, 295
Amar, A., 74n
Ames, Ruth E., 51n, 416–17
Amawi, Abla M., 107
Anderson, Gary M., 144
Anderson, Kym, 530n
Anderson, Lee G., 46
Anderson, R. O., 396
Anderson, Svein S., 118
Andreoni, James, 51n, 60
Ansolabehere, Steven, 411
Aranson, Peter H., 175, 258, 413n, 467
Arendt, Hannah, 430, 451–2
Arrow, Kenneth J., 3, 4, 5, 6, 30–1, 119, 145, 149–52, 163, 173, 174, 179, 195, 201–2, 205–9, 214–15, 222–4, 329
Asch, Peter, 51n
Aschauer, David A., 586
Atkinson, Anthony B., 502n, 584
Aubin, C., 576
Aumann, Robert J., 492n
Austen-Smith, David, 7, 13n, 254, 258, 261–2, 277, 278, 279, 281, 291n, 296, 305–7, 316–19, 320n, 321n, 406, 555
Austin, A., 101, 102n
Axelrod, Robert, 29, 141, 280–1

Bagnoli, Mark, 68–9, 447
Bailey, Martin J., 142
Balash, Peter C., 539, 541, 544
Baldwin, Robert E., 526n, 527, 530n, 558
Balinsky, M. L., 135n
Balisacan, Arsenio M., 554
Ball, David S., 558n
Ball, R., 321n
Banks, Jeffrey S., 63n, 177, 255, 261–2, 278, 279, 281, 320, 406, 441, 461, 477
Baran, Paul, 513n
Barberá, Salvador, 222–3
Barke, Richard P., 465
Barlow, Robin, 85
Baron, David P., 86–90, 176–7, 252, 261, 262, 291, 302–4, 307–8, 309n
Barro, Robert J., 406, 494, 498, 556, 586
Barry, Brian, 219, 374, 385, 390
Bartels, Larry, 411
Bartholdi, J., 161, 259
Barzel, Yoram, 132, 143, 381
Bates, Robert H., 36, 44, 143, 252
Bator, F. M., 565n
Bauer, R. A., 316, 553n
Baumol, William J., 24, 568, 573, 574, 589
Baysinger, Barry, 517
Beard, Charles A., 143
Beck, Nathaniel, 365, 366, 368
Becker, Gary S., 97n, 108, 296–9, 402, 462, 511, 520n, 546n, 551, 566, 580, 584
Beer, Samuel, 75, 76n, 80n, 275
Behr, Roy, 411
Bélanger, Gerard, 435–7, 459
Bell, Christopher R., 99n
Bénabou, Roland, 95
Bendor, Jonathan, 44, 74n, 440, 442, 453, 456, 459, 461, 477
Bennett, Elaine, 252
Ben-Porath, Yoram, 343
Bentley, A. F., 12, 298, 322, 329n
Ben-Zion, Uri, 300, 306
Berdot, J., 576
Berelson, Bernard, 393–4, 396n
Berglas, Eitan, 40n
Bergson, Abraham, 206

656

Subject index